More Praise for *The Last Investigation*

"Gaeton Fonzi brings to the continuing puzzlement over the JFK murder a Chandleresque hardness and wonderment, a sense of a lonely man walking down a dark street, fighting the demons of official power, a loner who was aborted by Congress at the lip of light."
—Oliver Stone

"Historians and researchers consider Mr. Fonzi's book among the best of the roughly 600 published on the Kennedy assassination, and credit him with raising doubts about the government's willingness to share everything it knew."
—*The New York Times*

"Gaeton was a man of extraordinary courage, integrity and talent. In a significant and unique manner he has contributed to history. His journalistic and historical work will endure as the very finest. As an investigative reporter he had no peer."
—Vincent Salandria, author of *False Mystery*

"Gaeton Fonzi was an American hero. Because of his groundbreaking work as a journalist and congressional investigator, long-closed doors into the deep mysteries of the JFK assassination were finally opened, shedding important new light on the case. His investigative memoir is more gripping than any spy fiction, a fascinating journey into the netherworld of power and official secrecy."
— David Talbot, founder of *Salon* and author of *Brothers: The Hidden History of the Kennedy Years*

"Had *The Last Investigation* received the headline attention it deserved on its first publication 20 years ago, we would live in a more peaceful, more hopeful world. The truth does set us free. Gaeton Fonzi's revelations dispel the propaganda that "we will never know the truth" of the murder that ended JFK's decision with Khrushchev and Castro to turn toward peace.

Thanks to this spellbinding story of Fonzi's investigation for the U.S. House Select Committee on Assassinations, we can indeed know the truth. As he guides us through the woods of treason and treachery around the president's assassination, the sun's rays break through – flickering, slanting, then flooding us with light. Those who follow Fonzi's trailblazing journey into the truth of JFK's death will never be the same again."
—Jim Douglass, author of *JFK and the Unspeakable*

"Amidst the hundreds of conspiracy books published in the last 30 years, this is one of the most believable."
—*Library Journal*

"Gaeton was a true intellectual with a brilliant analytical mind. If we ever ultimately come to learn the truth about the JFK assassination, such an official revelation would in large measure be attributable to the dedication, perseverance, and courage of Gaeton Fonzi."
—Cyril Wecht, former president of the American Academy of Forensic Science and the American College of Legal Medicine

"In the clamor of assassination controversy, Gaeton Fonzi is the Quiet Man, the investigator's investigator. If his story does not outrage Americans who still care about democracy, nothing will."
—Anthony Summers, author of *Not In Your Lifetime*

"A rarity among Kennedy assassination books, *The Last Investigation* does not indulge in sensational speculation or bizarre conspiracy theories. Gaeton Fonzi is an extraordinarily skilled investigator, who serves up facts, carefully researched and compellingly presented. This book is destined to become the benchmark against which other efforts are measured."
—Former Senator Richard S. Schweiker, co-chairman of the U.S. Senate Kennedy Assassination Subcommittee

"I consider this book one of the ten best ever published on the JFK assassination. . . . It is not just well-written. In some places it rises to the level of extraordinarily well-written. Almost every chapter is well-planned and organized. And the book as a whole contains a completed aesthetic arc to it."
—James DiEugenio, author of *Destiny Betrayed*

"Fonzi's style is never sensational or out of focus; he is the epitome of the rational, understated authority whose conclusions the nay-sayers will be hard pressed to fault. As a journalist, he asserts nothing more than his wish to set the record straight, and that record paints a picture that is at once gritty, exciting, deceitful and seamy. In short, *The Last Investigation* is a singular milestone in the understanding of America's odyssey from before Dealey Plaza until today."
—*Spectator Magazine*

THE LAST INVESTIGATION

Gaeton Fonzi

Skyhorse Publishing

Skyhorse Publishing books may be purchased in bulk at special discounts for
sales promotion, corporate gifts, fund-raising, or educational purposes. Special
editions can also be created to specifications. For details, contact the Special Sales
Department, Skyhorse Publishing, 307 West 36th Street, 11th Floor, New York,
NY 10018 or info@skyhorsepublishing.com.

Skyhorse® and Skyhorse Publishing® are registered trademarks of Skyhorse
Publishing, Inc.®, a Delaware corporation.

Visit our website at www.skyhorsepublishing.com.

10 9 8 7 6 5 4 3 2 1

Library of Congress Cataloging-in-Publication Data is available on file.
ISBN: 978-1-62636-078-5

Printed in the United States of America

*"Time is precious, but truth
is more precious than time."*
—DISRAELI

For my grandchildren—
in the hope that their future will be
more precious than our past.

CONTENTS

PART ONE

A PANDORA'S BOX

PART TWO

THE INVESTIGATION

PART THREE

A VERY PECULIAR SERVICE

PREFACE 2013
by MARIE FONZI

MY HUSBAND, Gaeton Fonzi, died on August 30, 2012. His body departed this earth, yet he remains with us in his legacy of impassioned words. Those words have filled the emptiness of the "dark, bottomless hole" which he so poignantly described in the prologue that follows this preface. I felt his presence as I reread *The Last Investigation*, listened to his speeches, and read the letters he wrote through the years.

I heard his voice reveal the motivations which propelled him, along with so many others, to unite in an effort to solve the murder of President Kennedy. Throughout the years his repeated message became more desperate: "The American people should not consider the Kennedy assassination as something that is in the history books." When speaking at a Dealy Plaza candlelight ceremony on November 22, 1993, Gaeton explained his interpretation of the significance of the event. "The murderers of John F. Kennedy killed more than a President. They killed something deep in the very soul of this country—the innocent, untarnished belief—naive, perhaps, but gloriously, constantly self-fulfilling—that we are the free-willed possessors of our own destiny. The assassination of President Kennedy," he said, "produced cracks of historic implications in that bedrock of democracy."

As I read Gaet's passionate delivery, I doubted my ability to write a preface worthy of his book. Then I glanced at the message displayed in a frame above his computer: "All you've got to do is word it in." I realized then that this preface to HIS book will be written by HIM, in the hope that through his words he will once again be a part of the reader's "moving, talking, touching, living world."

Numerous researchers called my husband a "hero" in their messages of condolence. However, if he were able to respond, he would brush aside that title even as he relished their recognition of his contributions. "No," Gaet would counter as he cupped his chin within his thumb and fingers as he was wont to do when thinking, "the real JFK heroes are Vince Salandria, Mary Ferrell, and Antonio Veciana, who gave so much in support of their beliefs."

Gaeton, in contrast, simply considered himself a paranoid cynic. Tongue in cheek, he often explained the roots of his paranoia as coming about as the result of a traumatic teenage experience. In a 1970 speech at the University of Michigan he told the faculty and students the whole story: "My cynicism is not based on my years as an investigative reporter. The first morning I reported to work at the Shiny Bright Christmas Ball factory, they stuck me in a pit in the center of a horseshoe-shaped production line." He explained in great detail how the women "would throw empty boxes into the pit and it was my job to break the boxes up as they came flying down at me, fold them flat, and put them into a pile. And when a woman along the line finished with one large box of Christmas balls, she would call for another one to be brought to her by the stock boys. So all day long the place echoed with the cry of women calling for more Christmas balls. However, when they would yell—and some of those women had pretty good vocal chords—they would yell only one word . . . and it wasn't Christmas!

"And so I went out into my career with the echo of that cry careening through my head. And when you're hooked on that kind of ingrained response to life, you can't help being cynical."

Gaet never lost his impatience with a less-than-cynical mainstream media who blindly accepted the conclusions of the Warren Commission. In a piece entitled, "The JFK Assassination Redux:: The Gold Coast Magazine Connection," he recalled, "I didn't realize then that even the big media boys had screwed up, lured and then trapped into a defensive position on the JFK assassination that would last for years and still exists in some cases. The Commission had cleverly withheld release of its 26 volumes of evidence until more than two months after the release of its Report. A lengthy *New York Times* editorial, for instance, lavishly endorsed the Report's conclusions without having available any supporting or contradicting evidence."

He was no easier on himself for what he considered his inadequate condemnation of Commission findings when he wrote his groundbreaking article, "The Warren Commission, The Truth, and Arlen Specter," which appeared in *Philadelphia* magazine two years after the issuance of the Report.

In a 2001 speech at a Faculty Forum at California State Polytech, he told the audience of his own naivete in failing to identify the motives of the Warren Commission Members. He described his reaction to early meetings with Vince Salandria which led to his three historic 1966 interviews with Arlen Specter (now available at the Mary Ferrell Foundation's website). "I'll never forget the numbing disbelief I came away with after my interviews with Specter. Vince Salandria was right, the Warren Report was wrong, there had to be a conspiracy. In the article I wrote: "It is difficult to believe the Warren Commission Report is the truth. Arlen Specter knows it.'

"I look back on that now and I think: What a cowardly way to put it. Why didn't I myself tell the absolute truth? And the absolute truth is that the Warren Report is a deliberate lie. The truth is that the Warren Commission's own evidence proves there was a conspiracy to murder President Kennedy . . . And wasn't that conspiracy to keep the truth from the American people driven by the motivation to maintain political power for those in the core military, industrial and intelligence groups who possessed it? As such, wasn't that also an act of terrorism? We were young once and not so brave. We wanted to cling to the myth of a mystery."

Over the years I watched him become very brave as he fearlessly spoke out against every person and institution he considered dishonest even as he was developing an uncanny ability to see beyond the facade which most of us accepted. In an op-ed column in the *New York Daily News* in 1994, he disputed a CIA revelation that one of their counter-spies was actually a spy for the Soviet government. "In buying the story," he warned, "Congress and the media are making a couple of assumptions. One is that the CIA, in confessing its security lapses, is now telling the truth. They're also assuming the CIA's real priority conforms to its mandate of providing the President the intelligence necessary to protect this country's national security. History has shown neither assumption valid."

While most Americans were naively accepting the CIA's version of this story, Gaet was warning that, "The mirror images are still blurry, but I bet that if and when they come into focus, the CIA's historic priorities will become crystal clear."

In a letter to a friend written years after the HSCA was disbanded, he vented his frustration at those mirror images which confronted them in the investigation: "In the course of winning, we lost. The truth has emerged but we lost control of its emergence. It has emerged disguised, often wrapped in misinformation, befogged with ambiguity, shunted into dead ends, battered into disfigured shards. The powers that be, including those within the government and the major media, continue to work to prevent it from being sculpted into a recognizable whole."

A decade before writing *The Last Investigation*, Gaet wrote an extensive article which appeared in both the *Washingtonian* and *Gold Coast* magazines. In the article, he berated the HSCA for failing to conduct the "full and complete investigation" it had promised. In interviews following the publication of his article, he described the danger in our country as "a force . . . that consists of a group that really doesn't have a true belief in a democratic system." "I think," he continued, "they consider themselves ultra-patriots who know what is good for the country. To me, it reflects a real lack of confidence in the democratic system."

When a 14-year old boy from Kansas called into a radio show, on which Gaeton appeared, to ask, "So what ever happened to Lee Harvey Oswald?" Gaet paused in disbelief and then sadly stated, "The American people are letting democracy slip through their fingers."

In Gaeton's obituary in *The New York Times*, Robert Blakey admitted, as he had finally done a decade before, to my husband's early realization that the CIA obstructed the HSCA investigation. Blakey recalled Gaet's insistence on pursuing the Oswald/CIA connection by saying, "We called him Ahab, because he was so single-minded about that white whale." (However, as Gaet himself said in this book, "Moby Dick was a helluva lot more than just a fish in the ocean.")

Blakey's use of the plural WE is in question since Gaet's House team members presented him with a parting gift of a five-inch paint-encrusted brush attached to a small note with HSCA letterhead:

> Gaeton, If you ever decide to write the HSCA history of the Anti-Castro Cuban inquiry, this may help you pen the story. We suggest you title it WHITEWASH – BOOK II.
> Fondly,
> The remnants of Team III

Clearly, Gaet didn't need a whitewash brush to write *The Last Investigation*. Nor did he ever need one. During the three decades after the end of the HSCA investigation, he continued to expose the truth in many muckracking articles, including a major one whose impact spread from Miami to Chicago and New York, exposing a con man suspected of at least three murders who was free under the FBI's witness protection program.

As a member of the South Florida Researchers' Group, he attended JFK conferences throughout the world and supported the efforts of fellow researchers, as he increasingly earned the respect and trust of both the good guys and the bad guys.

Throughout this book, Gaeton described his many contacts with Antonio Veciana, a founder of Alpha 66, the largest and most active of the militant anti-Castro groups. They developed a bond of mutual respect and affection as Veciana revealed details about his CIA contact, Maurice Bishop, whom he had once seen with Lee Harvey Oswald. In *The Last Investigation* you will read how very closely Mr. Veciana came to identifying Bishop as David Atlee Phillips, Chief of the Western Hemisphere Division. Despite his eagerness to elicit a positive response, my husband understood and respected his friend's reluctance to definitively identify Phillips.

A few months before Gaeton's death, Mr. Veciana wrote him a personal note in which he said, "Since I met you, I admired your capacity and dedication in finding the truth. You sincerely deserve respect for your honesty . . . I will always remember you with respect and admiration."

I have repeated Mr. Veciana's words with his permission, as Gaet would have done, and leave it to the reader to make conclusions.

At a 1995 conference of Cuban Officials and JFK Historians in Nassau, Gaeton met General Fabian Escalante, former Chief of Castro's Counter-Intelligence, who then invited Gaet to visit him in Cuba to discuss "mutual interests." In a letter written several months after the cordial visit, Gaet wrote to a researcher, "Escalante confirmed without a doubt (not that I had any) that Bishop was Phillips and provided me with additional details of the Veciana plot and Phillips' involvement. I also spoke with a Cuban intelligence officer who penetrated the CIA at the US Embassy and worked with Morales."

Through the years Gaeton never failed to respond to anyone who wrote expressing an interest in the assassination of President Kennedy. Even as his illness progressed, he reached beyond fatigue to offer praise and encouragement and to share whatever information he could. I attribute this responsiveness as a lifetime reaction to William Saroyan, who failed to answer the letter of a college freshman named Gaeton Fonzi, who wrote to give Saroyan the exciting news that he was considering him as the topic of his senior research paper. Perhaps it was the brash kid's approach to the Pulitzer Prize winning author:

"Upon reading your works," he wrote, "I discovered that you write like me. But my work is a little more polished. This I did not hold against you, for I would have a hard time proving that you plagiarized me since you came upon the earth before me. You might very well prove that I plagiarize from you except for the fact that I have had nothing published." Perhaps Saroyan did chuckle as he tossed aside the letter which contained 16 questions, each of which would require an essay to answer.

Although I see this early evasion as helping to mold Gaeton into the courteous and obliging "gentleman" so many described, he later gave another reason why he patiently replied to requests—the Kennedy investigation had become his lifetime obsession for multiple reasons. He responded to a young man who had written complaining of "too much of the time and energy I should be devoting to more constructive pursuits absorbed by my alternating senses of anger, frustration and curiosity" while studying the conspiracy literature.

"I don't know about more constructive pursuits," Gaet wrote in reply, "So now I just think it's time I get the Kennedy assassination out of my life. Will I? I doubt it. Nor, of course, do I really want to, knowing that I can't simply divorce myself from living in our place and time. I mean living a life with some degree of meaning and significance. I also don't want to because I have the feeling it would demean the efforts of a few honest researchers out there who do have time and resources and are coming up with new information that helps strengthen the foundation that the truth will need to survive alive in history."

He thanked the writer for his kind words about *The Last Investigation* and concluded, "Hey, guess what. I did kind of accomplish something. I did help resolve some of the questions surrounding the assassination and I did, in however minuscule a way, help the American people realize the Warren Commission Report is a lie." In his book he also told Americans that their government had let them down once again with the inadequate HSCA investigation.

For this, he was awarded the Mary Ferrell JFK Lancer Pioneer Award in 1998, "In Recognition of Lifetime Contributions In the Search For Truth in The Assassination of President John F. Kennedy." Sunshine bathes these words encased in the solid crystal tribute displayed on Gaet's desk.

In his acceptance speech, Gaet said, "Mary Ferrell has flashed a laser of guidance into the future's dark tunnel when she said, 'We must win this struggle for truth.'" He added " . . . but the truth has long ago rushed into our arms seeking our embrace."

In contrast to his being "immensely honored by the Pioneer award, truly awed and humbled by it," he left no eloquent words of pride in accepting the wooden plaque with the seal of the United States Congress which "Honors Gaeton Fonzi, S.I., for outstanding service in the investigation of the Assassination of President John F. Kennedy." The symbol of recognition is nowhere in sight in his office. Apparently, Gaet just couldn't find a comparable place for it once he removed it from the head when we sold our sailboat.

Our son, Christopher, said it all in his Dad's eulogy. He told the many who gathered to honor Gaeton: "As far as my Dad's career, I couldn't cover his achievements and awards if I stood here all day. He was an elegant writer, a tough editor and a meticulous researcher. He's still respected for the work he did in Philadelphia 40 years ago, and in South Florida after that. He was an investigative reporter in the classic sense. He rooted out corruption and he was a legitimate Champion of Truth.

"My father knew how to tell a story, and, more importantly, how to recognize what the real story was. And by the time you got to the third paragraph, you were going to finish reading that story, because he knew how to make it speak to you, and how to make you feel it on a personal level.

"And my father never stopped believing in heroes. He had very little faith in government, but he believed in Joe DiMaggio."

The words of this final tribute will ring true as you read *The Last Investigation*. However, in the end, Gaeton Fonzi, astute observer of human behavior, a man so adept at peeling through the layers of deception to arrive at the truth, was wrong about one thing—the finality of death. As long as Americans read his words; as long as researchers continue to unravel the mystery of the murder of President Kennedy, my husband will be here. He will be here tomorrow . . . and all the days after tomorrow.

PROLOGUE

At some point in each of our lives, we encounter the reality of death and are struck by its absolute finality. For some it comes traumatically, on the field of battle, in an automobile accident or just being at the bedside of a dying loved one, watching in anguish that terrible, hollow last breath of life drift softly from a body. For others it could arrive with the shock of a friend's unexpected demise. I'm speaking now of the feeling that comes immediately after that shock, when our very soul instantly falls into a dark, bottomless hole. The experience involves a sudden realization that someone who was a part of our moving, talking, touching, living world will simply not be any more. He or she will not be here tomorrow. Or all the days after tomorrow. It is a realization that leaves in its wake a dreadful emptiness, a sense of loss so deep and sad there remains forever an abyss in our own lives.

I REMEMBER NOW a very hot day in Dallas in the summer of 1978. The temperature had climbed to 106 degrees. I could see the city's fever shimmering from the dark macadam, feel its heavy heat on my skin. I waited on the south side of Elm Street for a break in the traffic and then moved out into the middle of the center lane. The street is not as wide as it appears in photographs.

I stopped on the spot. *Right about . . . here. . . .* I had studied it in the films and the still photos. *Right . . . here!*

Above me rose the dark shadows of the trees and the heavy foliage of the grassy knoll. There was a stillness there now, a breezeless serenity. On my right loomed the familiar red brick building—flat, hard-edged, its rows of sooted windows innocuous and dull. My mind dropped back into that microinstant of history. . . .

Right here . . . is where a man died, in an explosively horrible and bloody moment. That simple and overpowering truth had been oddly removed from the whirlwind of activity in which I had been involved. A man was killed here, and what had been going on in Washington— all the officious meetings and the political posturing, all the time and attention devoted to administrative procedures and organizational processes and forms and reports for the record, all the chaotic concern for distorted priorities and all the scurrying about in a thousand directions in the mad rush to produce a final report—all that seemed so detached from the hard reality of a single fact: A man was killed here. Wasn't that supposed to have some relationship to what we were doing?

I had been working as a staff investigator for the House Select Committee on Assassinations for more than a year and a half. We were forewarned it would surely be the *last* investigation and, yet, after less than six months of formal investigation, I was one of the few investigators remaining on the staff. The rest had suddenly been fired—a "budget squeeze," we were told. And there I was standing in Dealey Plaza, on the spot where President John F. Kennedy was killed on November 22nd, 1963, and wondering what the hell had gone wrong. What had smothered my initial optimism, my hope that, after all these years, we might finally find out the truth about the Kennedy assassination? Why had I become so bitter and cynical, so depressed and frustrated about the result of all our time and effort? Standing in Dealey Plaza on that very hot day in Dallas, I could not help thinking that perhaps—just perhaps—the powers that controlled the last investigation would not have gone so far astray had they remembered that instant of time when a man's life ended here. *A man's life ended.* . . .

INTRODUCTION

*D*ESPITE THE CLAMOR of the last few years, all the books, the films and the articles, the assassination of President John F. Kennedy is being allowed to go quietly into history. We must not let that happen—not yet, not ever. I fear that if it does become mere history, our vision of what our democratic system is all about, already waning, will dim dangerously. And the system's most elemental imperative will be forgotten: Our Government governs by the consent of *all* the people, not by a small group with the power and resources to impose its own will. The wolves of oligarchy are waiting for that darkness.

I spent three years working for the Government as an investigator of the Kennedy assassination, and many more before that as a member of the community of private researchers following the case. I have seen it from the inside and from the outside and I am deeply concerned. I know how your Government failed in its investigations, what your Government didn't tell you and why, and what your Government was really doing when it told you it was investigating the assassination. I've seen how history has been shaped for you without your knowing it. I believe, also, that unless we do something about it, history will continue to be shaped by powers responsive only to the priorities of maintaining power. And that is relevant to the way we live, both today and tomorrow.

I'm not the only one who is concerned. I still hear the strong, sweet, soft-edged drawl of Mary Ferrell's voice. I still see that remarkable white-haired woman stand before a microphone and raise herself to heights that belie her aging body. For three decades, Mary Ferrell has been a guiding star for those who have devoted a part of their lives to pursuing the truth about the Kennedy assassination. Mostly ordinary citizens like herself, they have flocked to her modest Dallas abode, a bright yellow house warmed with green plants and gentle rocking chairs on its front porch, and, inspired by her enduring patience and guidance, they have struggled to extract those rare gems of truth buried in the mountains of government documents, investigative reports and private research papers she has accumulated. Mary Ferrell has never attempted to commercialize her efforts, nor has she shown a narrow-minded devotion to any particular conspiracy theory. Her voice has authority; it commands respect.

I can hear Mary Ferrell delivering the opening remarks to a symposium of Kennedy assassination researchers in Dallas in October of 1992. This is what she said:

> As the thirtieth anniversary of the assassination of President John F. Kennedy descends on us, I am much concerned that we are on the threshold of a failure from which there will be no forgiveness.
>
> We must win this struggle for truth . . . and do so very quickly, lest the assassination of President Kennedy flounder on some remote shoulder of highway, in a century whose history is on the way to the printer. In the next century, this case could be relegated to obscure questions on high school history examinations. . . .
>
> Time is our most relentless and uncompromising enemy. But what happens during this conference can make a difference. Of course we will be scoffed at and demeaned by the media and the wagging fingers of Warren Commission survivors, scolding us for refusing to believe the conclusions of these honorable men. . . .
>
> But history teaches us that significant changes are often accomplished by small numbers of people, facing large odds. Many of them have succeeded in defiance of the government.
>
> Thomas Paine, John Adams, Thomas Jefferson, Washington and their followers represented a tiny fraction of this country's population. As it was with that tiny fraction, I have every confidence that you are representative of millions who share your view. . . . That is what keeps us united in our cause. It is a view, according to the polls, which is held by the overwhelming majority of our fellow citizens—that a conspiracy and government-sponsored cover-up blotted out the rights of our citizens and sanctity of the rule of law.
>
> And that is what will forever be paramount among all of the issues which continually dog our deliberations. Issues about autopsy photos, magic bullets, pictures of Oswald which are obviously not Oswald,

numbers and styles of coffins, and all the other issues, cannot eclipse the ultimate violation of the rights of citizens in a democracy *designed for the people.* . . .

 If we are truly living in the land of the free and the home of the brave, we'd better damn well prove it now. . . .

Mary Ferrell's remarks reminded me of reactions I had often gotten from people I met while working as an investigator on the case: "We won't ever know what really happened, will we?" Or: "That's a waste of money, isn't it?" Or: "What difference does it make now anyway?"

It *does* make a difference. A President of the United States was assassinated three decades ago and our Government still tells us it doesn't know what really happened. There is no doubt now that the murder was a conspiracy, it says, but it isn't sure of anything beyond that. And yet, most of us—the polls say and the media reflect this— are not angry that our Government never told us what really happened. We don't like it, but we are no longer very upset about it. Lord knows there's enough to worry about today.

But we should be angry. The assassination of President Kennedy was a blatant affront to each and every one of us who believes that we, as individuals, should have some control over who governs us and how we are governed. That's the bedrock of our democracy. We would have been very angry if someone with a gun had stopped us from going into the voting booth, impeding our freedom of choice. We would have seen that quite clearly as a direct attack against the democratic system—not only a flagrant violation of our rights but an outrageous *personal* affront.

The analogy is obvious: The conspiracy to kill the President of the United States was a conspiracy against the democratic system— and thus a conspiracy against each and every one of us. Our choice was denied. That's why it very much still matters.

Understand this, also: The action that brought about the death of President Kennedy is directly related to where we have gone as a nation since then. It is particularly important to what is happening today. That single event prefaced the disintegration of our solid faith in government, fathering the now pervasive and enervating assumption that we no longer have control over our economic or political destiny. Its residue lies in the ashes of the Sixties—in burned out countries and burned out cities and burned out people—and in the debilitating social disparities and continuing civil conflicts of the last thirty years. The assassination and its aftermath bred rampant distrust and disrespect for all established institutions, and that outlook festers yet.

And now, we hardly give a damn when our own Government violates or ignores its own laws, as it has done with distressing regularity over the last two decades. An enormous public apathy greeted the Iran/Contra scandals; we were hardly stirred by the fact that hidden layers of government had pursued a secret foreign policy agenda, circumventing the law of the land, the Congress and the Constitution itself.

And still, it seems incredible that we're not angry. The fact is, we know an effective democracy *demands* a populace ready, willing and able to get riled enough to pressure its elected officials into doing their duty in spite of themselves. Where is that anger now?

The Government has failed us. It is outrageous that in a democratic society, after two official investigations, our Government still tells us it doesn't know what happened.

I hope this book makes you angry about that. Very angry. If it doesn't, we might as well let slip the grip on our individual freedom. It will be gone soon enough.

PART ONE

A PANDORA'S BOX

ONE

OF TRUTH AND DECEPTION

*A*FTER THE FIRST official Government investigation into the assassination of President Kennedy, Sylvia Meagher, writing in a small magazine called *Minority of One*, had this to say about the Warren Commission: "There are no heroes in this piece, only men who collaborated actively or passively—willfully or self-deludedly—in dirty work that does violence to the elementary concept of justice and affronts normal intelligence."

Incredibly strong words. Yet when they were written in 1967—more than three years after the Warren Commission Report was released—most Americans still had no idea what she was talking about.

The members of the Warren Commission *collaborating in dirty work?* That was simply too preposterous to accept. Consider the stature and reputation of these men: Chairman Earl Warren was the Chief Justice of the Supreme Court, the paradigm of objectivity; John J. McCloy had been president of the World Bank and chairman of the board of Chase Manhattan Bank—prestige personified; Allen W. Dulles, former director of the Central Intelligence Agency, an Ivy League patrician who represented America's dauntless defense against the threat of international Communism's evil aspirations; Senator Richard Russell and Congressmen John Sherman Cooper, Hale Boggs and Gerald Ford all had reputations as being reasonable, politically responsible and honest. President Lyndon Johnson had personally chosen these honorable men to investigate the assassination of John

3

Fitzgerald Kennedy. His Executive Order No. 11130 dated November 29th, 1963, directed the Commission to "evaluate all the facts and circumstances surrounding the assassination and the subsequent killing of the alleged assassin and to report its findings and conclusions to him."

On September 24th, 1964, the President's Commission presented its Report. A weighty 888-page volume, it included 81 pages of footnotes in very small type. The footnotes referred to the 26 volumes of Hearings and Exhibits which, said the Commission, supported the statements and conclusions in its Report. By sheer size alone, the Report certainly appeared to have covered "all the facts and circumstances."

However, those 26 volumes of documentary evidence were not published until two months after the Report was issued. And despite not having the corroborating documentation, the major national news media quickly accepted the Warren Commission's conclusions and praised the job it did. The *New York Times*'s Harrison E. Salisbury called the Report "comprehensive, careful, compendious and competent."

Thus, national media shaped the American public's perception of the Warren Commission Report, since most Americans didn't have the time or opportunity to read the Report. Indeed, most journalists, although they had the time and the opportunity and were getting paid to do so, didn't read it. If they had, the Report would have immediately been the subject of intense questioning and criticism. Yet it wasn't. Neither were the Report's conclusions challenged when, two months later, the Commission's 26 volumes of evidence were released, although much of that evidence made obvious the distortions and contradictions in the Report. The media never told the American people what the Warren Commission did to them, how it did it or why.

Although the nation's top journalists and investigative reporters had donned blinders—not an unusual accessory for the Washington press corps back in that pre-Watergate era—a handful of private individuals, first driven by curiosity and then by a growing skepticism, had begun studying the Report and accompanying evidence. They didn't have to dig deeply to come up with a surprising number of unanswered questions and conflicts in the Report. Still, it was years before the public began hearing their voices. They didn't have access to the major media, so their questions and criticisms appeared in such limited-circulation and esoteric publications as *The National Guardian, Liberation, Commentary, Minority of One, The Progressive* and the unlikely *Computers and Automation.*

Then came a few books which were so incisive in their criticism of the Warren Report they couldn't be ignored: Edward J. Epstein's *Inquest*, Mark Lane's *Rush to Judgment* and Sylvia Meagher's *Accessories After the Fact*.

Although the other books achieved wider distribution, Meagher's was especially significant. It grew out of her monumental *Subject Index to the Warren Report and Hearings and Exhibits*, an awesome accomplishment. The Commission hadn't produced such an index, so her work became a seminal reference for the growing body of independent researchers. Meagher's comprehensive understanding of the evidence led her to declare that the Warren Commission's work exhibited "a high degree of negligence," and that its performance was "inept and undeserving of public confidence."

Then, slowly, the American people began to doubt the Warren Commission's strained conclusion that a lone gunman named Lee Harvey Oswald, driven by "a deep-rooted resentment of all authority," had fired all the shots that hit and killed President Kennedy and wounded Governor John Connally. By 1975, the independent researchers had compiled a conclusive, documented list of shortcomings in the Warren Commission investigation and, despite riding a roller coaster of credibility, had made most Americans aware of it. For an overwhelming majority of the American people, those doubts had turned to disbelief and a few politicians began to hear the call for officially reopening the case.

Sylvia Meagher had early and eloquently expressed her hopes in *Accessories After the Fact*:

> If closed minds continue to open, to receive and evaluate objectively the facts which are on the record, we may yet proceed to pursue the truth to its ultimate reaches—regardless of attendant dangers and doubts—so that history will know with certainty what happened in Dallas, and why.
>
> To that end, investigation into the assassination and the related murders should be reopened, entrusted to an uncompromisingly independent, competent, and impartial body—a body committed to the use of adversary procedure, the rules of evidence, and total respect for justice in both the letter and the spirit. In other words, a body different from the Warren Commission.

That's exactly what the American people thought they were getting when, on September 17th, 1976, the U.S. House of Representatives passed House Resolution 1540 which established a Select Committee to "conduct a full and complete investigation and study of the circumstances surrounding the assassination and death of President John F. Kennedy. . . ."

Finally, there was going to be a *real* investigation. Even if the specific individuals who killed President Kennedy couldn't be brought to justice, at least the forces and the motivation behind the assassination would be determined. The Warren Commission was purposely constrained to ignore or distort any evidence that didn't conform to its predetermined conclusion that the assassin was a lone crackpot firing from the sixth-floor window of the Texas School Book Depository building. This new Select Committee would not be bound by such political motivations and need not be concerned (as the Warren Commission reportedly was), that world peace would be threatened if the trails of the investigation led to foreign involvement. Now every avenue, both in and out of the country, within and without the Government itself, would be independently and honestly explored and we would finally know exactly what was down each of those roads. This investigation would be given such power and resources it would, by its very nature, be conclusive and absolute. Rumors and speculations would finally be laid to rest. There would be no need for future investigation; this would be the last investigation.

It had to be, for history's sake. This new investigation was a commitment to the American people that, this time, their Government would not deceive them. This time, the ultimate priority would be to an uncompromising search for the truth.

On July 17th, 1979, the Chairman of the House Select Committee on Assassinations, Ohio Democrat Louis Stokes, called a press conference to formally release the last investigation's "final report."

This report was long overdue. After consuming more than $5.5 million over a two-year period, the Committee had legally ceased to exist the previous December. However, the Committee's Chief Counsel and Staff Director, G. Robert Blakey, wasn't satisfied with the final report the staff had compiled and so, in a bit of bureaucratic legerdemain, he had himself and a few select aides temporarily attached to the office of the Speaker of the House in order to obtain the additional time and money needed to reconstruct a new final report.

That reconstruction was dictated by testimony which emerged in the very last days of the Committee's investigation. After much controversy, acoustics experts, analyzing a tape recording of the sounds in Dealey Plaza when Kennedy was shot, concluded that more than one weapon had been fired. (Part of Blakey's problem with meeting the deadline was the delay caused by the reanalysis of the tape; at varying times he had to be poised to write either a report declaring there was a conspiracy or one declaring there was no conspiracy.) As the final report put it: "Scientific acoustical evidence established a high probability that two gunmen fired at President John F. Kennedy."

The presence of more than one gunman meant there was a conspiracy, yet the Committee had uncovered no hard evidence to indicate the character of that conspiracy. Blakey realized that would be too obvious a shortcoming in what he was determined to make an impressive document because it was, as he early told the staff, "the absolutely *final* report on the Kennedy assassination." Blakey, aware of the political priorities of the Committee members, knew the report had to have attention-getting impact or, as he called it, "sex appeal." The report could not, however, reflect the actual limitations of the staff's investigation without being an embarrassment. Instead, it had to convey the impression that enough hard digging had been done to provide the Committee with an insight into the nature of the conspiracy it had uncovered. Thus it became necessary to restructure the report. The question then became: Who to blame? The answer was Organized Crime. And, in retrospect, that answer should have been obvious from the beginning.

G. Robert Blakey was a 41-year-old criminal law professor at Cornell University when he was asked to take the reins of the Assassinations Committee following the forced resignation of his predecessor, former Philadelphia prosecutor Richard Sprague. Blakey had been with the Justice Department under Robert Kennedy, and his subsequent career was focused on Organized Crime—that nebulous entity which somehow achieved capitalized status over the years. Then head of Cornell's Organized Crime Institute, Blakey was considered one of the country's top experts in the field. He was a fixture at the numerous Organized Crime seminars held periodically by law enforcement interests and had personal contacts in most Federal agencies and in the Organized Crime sections of almost every major police department in the nation.

As soon as he was appointed, Blakey drew upon his colleagues in that particular fraternity to select his senior counsel for the Committee. Two of these appointments are notable. The lawyer he picked to head the Kennedy investigation task force, a bright, brisk Texan named Gary Cornwell, was chief of the Federal Strike Force in Kansas City. Cornwell had achieved major trial victories against key Midwest Mafia bigwigs. Blakey also hired a former New York cop named Ralph Salerno, who became special consultant to the Committee. A man who carries the Mob's organizational chart in his head, Salerno has for years earned a good living lecturing, writing books and appearing on radio and television shows as the *capo de tutti capi* of Organized Crime experts.

Blakey would later claim that he arrived in Washington without an inclination towards *any* conspiracy theory, least of all Mob involvement. Nevertheless his restaffing of key Committee jobs certainly gave it a new look. And when the time came and he had to pin the conspiracy on someone . . . well, there was Organized Crime. But that had nothing to do, of course, with Blakey's personal feelings, that's just the way it looked.

Chief Counsel Blakey was an experienced Capitol Hill man. He had worked not only at Justice but on previous Congressional committees as well. So he knew exactly what the priorities of his job were by Washington standards, even before he stepped in. The first task, he announced in his inaugural address to the staff, was to produce a report within the time and budget restraints dictated by Congress. The second was to produce a report that looked good, one that appeared to be definitive and substantial. Somewhere along the line there would be an effort at conducting what I saw as a limited investigation into the assassination of President John F. Kennedy.

Bob Blakey himself is quite a literate fellow, but to give the report the required look, he brought in a top professional writer, former *Life* magazine editor Richard Billings, another veteran of Congressional committee operations. Together, Blakey and Billings would insure that the report was expertly constructed.

There is substance and there is the illusion of substance. In Washington, it is often difficult to tell the difference. But there was never any doubt that, regardless of the realities of the actual investigation, the Assassinations Committee's historical legacy would *appear* to have substance.

And it does. An impressively hefty tome—686 pages thick, with twelve volumes of appendixes—the Committee's final report seems substantive. And yet, it actually makes very few definitive statements. Instead, it hedges, relying on phrases such as "on the basis of evidence available to it"; and, "the Committee believes"; and, "available evidence does not preclude the possibility"; and an abundance of such words as "probably," "most likely," "possible" and "may have been."

The point is that the Committee report does *not* come to any definitive conclusions; it does not actually state that Organized Crime was involved in the conspiracy to kill President Kennedy. What the report does say is this: "The Committee believes, on the basis of evidence available to it, that the national syndicate of Organized Crime, as a group, was not involved in the assassination of President Kennedy, but that the available evidence does not preclude the possibility that individual members may have been involved."

That last cryptic statement specifically referred to two key mob bosses, Carlos Marcello of New Orleans and Santos Trafficante of Florida.

However, even that allegation, made in the report's "Summary of Findings and Recommendations," is a mere gesture. Because buried in the body of the report is the conclusion that "it is unlikely that either Marcello or Trafficante was involved in the assassination of the President."

This is only one example of the numerous contradictions inherent in the report, the result of the attempt to leave no base untouched, no area unexplored, however cursory the Committee's actual investigation. What the report does in the most quintessential way is—to use the expression popular among Committee staffers—"cover its ass." Which is ironic, because in doing so, the report exposed its own basic conflicts, as well as the shortcomings of what I can only call the Committee's pseudoinvestigation. That problem became clear when the first attempt was made to bring all the sections of the report together.

The Committee was organized into five major teams. These teams did not have formal titles and each had a series of responsibilities that often crossed into other areas. For example, Team Two handled the Organized Crime and Jack Ruby aspects of the investigation, but one of its members was deeply involved in the analysis of the medical information. Originally, each team consisted of two lawyers, three researchers and two investigators. There were also special project teams—ballistics, autopsy, acoustics, photographic and other areas involving expert consultants. By December, 1978, however, the staff had been drastically depleted through firings and resignations. The Committee was due to expire at the end of the month and each team was frantically writing what it thought would be its portion of the final report. When it became obvious that most teams wouldn't be finished before the Committee's demise, a young lawyer named Jim Wolf was given the job of gathering from each team a summary of its findings and putting them together into what would be a draft of the final report. That, at least, would be something for the Committee to release before it officially folded.

When Wolf's compilation from the teams was completed, it totaled more than 500 pages. Wolf then took that compilation and, after a conference with Blakey, drew up the conclusions. That's when it became obvious that there were some basic problems.

One of the key conflicts was Blakey's insistence that the Committee had to come to some conclusion about Oswald's motive. (Oswald's guilt, ruled Blakey, had already been resolved through scientific analysis of the physical evidence.) Unfortunately, one of the areas that most reflected the Committee's inadequacy was its investigation of Oswald himself. Like the Warren Commission, the Committee never truly defined who Oswald really was, what he believed, the nature of his relationships with an odd and mysterious assortment of people, the reasons for the strange things he did, nor why there are gaps in the record of his actions over certain periods of time. The Committee, mostly because of the tangle of political constraints, had a very limited investigative plan. It did very little original work in this area.

One glaring example of the quality of the Committee's investigation is the fact that a women named Ruth Paine was never called as a witness. She just slipped through the cracks of the investigative plan. Yet Ruth Paine was one of the key individuals in Oswald's life, playing an important role immediately before and after the assassination. It was in Ruth Paine's garage, the Warren Commission said, that Oswald stored and retrieved the rifle used in the assassination. Ruth Paine was instrumental in getting Oswald his job at the Texas School Book Depository. (Interestingly, too, her husband, Michael, worked for a major Defense Department contractor and had a Government security clearance.) A now declassified document revealed that it was on Ruth Paine's telephone that a "confidential informant" overheard, immediately after the assassination, a male voice say he didn't believe Oswald killed Kennedy, and then added, "we both know who is responsible." But Ruth Paine was never even interviewed by the Committee.

Another example of the Committee's failure has to do with a dramatic but little publicized piece of hard evidence pointing to Oswald's intelligence connection—the Minox spy camera. Dallas police found the German-made, three-inch camera that looks like a cigarette lighter among Oswald's possessions in Ruth Paine's home four days after the assassination and listed it in their inventory as item 375. When the FBI produced its inventory for the Warren Commission, item 375 evolved into a "Minox light meter." *Dallas Morning News* reporter Earl Golz found the discrepancy in 1978 when he talked to Detective Gus Rose, who had originally inventoried Oswald's possessions. "I know a camera when I see it," Rose told Golz. "The thing we got at Irving out of Oswald's seabag was a Minox camera. No question about it. [The FBI] tried to get me to change the records because it wasn't a light meter. I don't know why they wanted it changed." Golz also checked with the Minox Corporation and found that it didn't sell light meters in the U.S. in 1963, and that the serial number on Oswald's camera wasn't a valid registered number. In other words, it couldn't be traced if Oswald had lost it or had it taken from him. (In a final twist, in 1979, the FBI released a series of photographs of what appeared to be activity at a military installation and announced they were taken with a Minox camera that had belonged to Oswald.)

So, despite a mass of conflicting evidence and an investigation not adequate enough to resolve the issue, Blakey insisted that the Committee conclude that Oswald killed Kennedy because of a left-wing political agenda. Most of the staff attorneys, including JFK Task Force Chief Gary Cornwell, argued against such a conclusion, but unsuccessfully.

Before the compiled draft of the final report was to be presented to the Committee members themselves, Blakey, sensing an undercurrent of discontent among his staff, announced that all staff members would have the opportunity to read the report and discuss it. "I will be disappointed if there is not vigorous debate on many portions of the volume at our staff meeting Thursday night," he wrote in a memo. There was vigorous debate, but on the issue of Oswald's motive Blakey did not cave in.

On the morning of that staff meeting, copies of the draft report were distributed to the staff. I recall Deputy Chief Counsel Ken Klein, shortly after he read it, wandering into my office shaking his head. Klein was a witty little guy with a mop of red hair and perpetually raised eyebrows.

"You know," Klein said with a wry smile on his face, "when I first got my copy I thought they were putting me on. I mean it was like somebody wrote the report and then somebody else came along and, without reading what the first guy had written, wrote the conclusions. You know, I was gonna go into Gary and say, 'Hey, OK, that's funny. Now com'on, give me the *real* report!' "

What bothered Klein was the fact that each team report had built an excellent argument for involvement in the Kennedy assassination by that team's main subject of interest—whether it was Organized Crime, Castro's Cuban agents, anti-Castro Cubans, right-wing militants or Russian intelligence agents. All the subjects had the means, methods and motivation to be considered prime suspects. Each team had taken many pages to detail its relevant evidence. "And then," Klein pointed out, "after all these pages of evidence, all the arguments get thrown out in the conclusion that says, naah, Oswald couldn't have been involved with these guys because that wasn't his motivation! Very funny. All right now, is somebody gonna tell me where the *real* report is?"

When the Committee's "real" report finally was released, that basic conflict remained. Although the largest number of pages—and one complete 1,169-page appendix volume—was devoted to building a conspiracy case against Organized Crime, Oswald's motivation for (probably) acting as its tool was, perversely, ascribed to his "twisted ideological view."

But a 1,169-page appendix, of course, is substance. And irrelevant. In the end, the final report did what it was carefully structured to do: Create the *impression* that Organized Crime was involved in the conspiracy. That was the one point that Blakey wanted to etch in the national consciousness and leave in history's memory. It was his personal bid to finally lay to rest the question of President Kennedy's assassination.

When the report was released, the theme of the front-page headline in the *Washington Post* was echoed by the media across the country: "MOBSTERS LINKED TO JFK DEATH."

Blakey had wanted to be absolutely certain that the reporters at the press conference would accurately interpret the report's interlinear message. "I am now firmly of the opinion that the Mob did it," he told them. "It is a historical truth." Then backstepping from such a seemingly impetuous declaration—covering his ass—he quickly added: "This Committee report does not say the Mob did it. *I* said it. I think the Mob did it."

I don't think the Mob did it. I worked for two years as a staff investigator and then, briefly, as a team leader, on the Assassinations Committee, and I doubt the Mob did it. I think there was a Mob link to Jack Ruby's killing Oswald, but there were stronger links to others in killing Kennedy. Although the House Select Committee on Assassinations took the investigation one step further in concluding there was a conspiracy, like the Warren Commission before it, it failed to meet its mandate. The Committee failed to "conduct a full and complete investigation" and wrote its final report to conceal that fact.

The truth is, the last investigation was simply not broad enough, deep enough, ambitious enough nor honest enough to yield *any* firm conclusions about the nature of the conspiracy. To give the impression that it was, is a charade.

Yet the answer to the assassination of President Kennedy does lie in understanding what happened during the last investigation. It lies in understanding why the Government again failed to pursue the truth—and why it doesn't want to. It lies in knowing about the last investigation's deformed priorities, the manipulations and the political machinations designed to derail the legitimate efforts to solve the case.

And it lies in knowing that the Assassination Committee's disappointing legacy contains a momentous shortcoming: There was a part of the Committee's investigation which, if vigorously pursued, could have broken through to an area of evidence long concealed. It was an area so loaded with explosive potential that the Committee's final report barely dared to touch on it and distorted the conclusions drawn from it.The forces governing the Committee knew that pursuing leads in this area would have opened doors it did not want opened, doors marked with the names of the operators and assets of the Government's intelligence community.

This is the story of what the Committee might have discovered if it had taken its mandate to heart and pursued the truth to, in Sylvia Meagher's words, "its ultimate reaches—regardless of attendant dangers and doubts."

HAUNTING QUESTIONS

I CAN STILL HEAR the sound of Vincent Salandria's voice. It has an odd quality to it, a low, velvet intensity. He was leaning back in his chair, his hands clasped easily behind his head, speaking slowly and casually but with a building rationality. We were in the paneled basement office of his home on Delancey Street in Philadelphia. It was late in 1964, and what Vincent Salandria was telling me was that the Warren Commission Report was not the truth.

I thought he was crazy. If you do not recall that time, you cannot comprehend what a discordant thing it was then to contend that an official Government report might be wrong—especially one which had been issued by a panel of men with such lofty public reputations. I know it's hard for the post-Watergate generation to understand, but then almost everyone still believed what Government officials said. If someone like Salandria came along and suggested that an official Government report wasn't truthful . . . well, Salandria had to be nuts.

At that time, I was a senior editor of *Philadelphia Magazine*. Considered a forerunner of its type, *Philadelphia Magazine* was the first of the city publications to break away from its Chamber of Commerce roots and delve honestly, and with lively literary style, into issues of importance to the general community. Normally, I wouldn't have a reason to get involved in a national story like the Kennedy assassination. But discovering local lawyer Salandria as one of the first critics of the Warren Commission Report was a good angle for a story and *Philadelphia Magazine* was the perfect place to write with wit and urbane cynicism about this oddball young attorney saying crazy things about our Government. I made an appointment to interview him. A small man, olive-skinned with dark eyes and a thin, serious face, Salandria appeared an easy-mannered fellow. But as we spoke I sensed a deep intellectual intensity within him. Eventually, the things he was saying no longer sounded so crazy.

Salandria was then 38 years old, a Penn Law graduate and an ACLU consultant. Immediately after the Warren Commission Report was released in September, 1964, Salandria had written a critique of it for *The Legal Intelligencer*, Philadelphia's local law daily. His article was a highly detailed analysis of the Report's conclusions about the trajectories and ballistics of the bullets which killed President Kennedy. The first time I read Salandria's article, I didn't understand it. It was complex and technical. But I did grasp the sensational implication of Salandria's contentions: There was a possibility that the Warren Commission Report was wrong.

Salandria said his interest in the Warren Commission had begun long before its report was issued largely because he did not like the fact that it was holding secret hearings. He felt that the rise of dictatorships always corresponded to the abdication of interest in governmental function and that free access to information about its function was necessary to maintain that interest. When leaks about the Warren Commission's findings began emerging, Salandria became more concerned.

"I thought you had to be objective about it," he said. "If this had happened in Smolensk or Minsk or Moscow, no American would have believed the story that was evolving about a single assassin, with all its built-in contradictions. But because it happened in Dallas, too many Americans were accepting it."

Salandria began to watch the Warren Commission's activities. He spent his vacations in Dallas to familiarize himself with the murder scene. He ordered the Commission's Report and its accompanying 26 volumes of evidence as soon as they were issued and plunged into a page-by-page study.

"My initial feeling," Salandria told me, "was that if this were a simple assassination, as the Commission claimed, the facts would come together very neatly. If there were more than one assassin, the details would not fit."

Salandria said the details did not fit. There were, he contended, blatant contradictions between the Commission's conclusions and the evidence in the 26 volumes. I found that hard to believe. But Salandria gave me a copy of the Report as well as the 26 volumes of evidence and suggested I take the time to study them carefully. I did and I, too, discovered that the details did not fit.

* * *

Almost fifteen years after I first spoke with Vince Salandria, the House Select Committee on Assassinations issued its report and announced that President Kennedy was murdered as the result of a conspiracy. By then, the Warren Commission's original conclusion, that a lone, psychotically motivated gunman had killed the President, had been badly battered by thousands of facts and pieces of evidence. Now, most Americans believe there was a conspiracy, but they still can't explain why they believe it. They still assume that the Warren Commission's findings were too detailed and complex to penetrate. They don't suspect that the basic facts of the case aren't all that complicated. That's what shocked me. It was simply a matter of understanding what the Warren Commission said about a very limited area of its investigation—albeit, *the* critical area dealing with the immediate moments of the assassination.

Today, through countless viewings on television and in Oliver Stone's movie of that fortuitous film taken by Abraham Zapruder, the world is well acquainted with the scene that occurred on November 22nd, 1963, at about 12:30 p.m., Central Standard Time, on a complex of streets near what is known as Dealey Plaza in Dallas, Texas. The Presidential motorcade had just passed through downtown Dallas. A large crowd lined the streets and waved an enthusiastic greeting to Kennedy, his wife and Governor and Mrs. Connally, all of whom were riding in the third car of the motorcade, a specially built open-topped Lincoln. At the end of Main Street, downtown's principal east-west artery, the motorcade turned right onto Houston Street, traveled north for one block, then made a sharp left turn to the southwest onto Elm Street, passing on its right the seven-story, red-brick warehouse and office building known as the Texas School Book Depository.

According to the Warren Commission Report, the President's car, was traveling about eleven miles per hour and had just turned onto Elm Street:

> Seconds later shots resounded in rapid succession. The President's hands moved to his neck. He appeared to stiffen momentarily and lurch slightly forward in his seat. A bullet had entered the base of the back of his neck slightly to the right of the spine. It traveled downward and exited from the front of the neck, causing a nick in the left lower portion of the knot in the President's necktie. Before the shooting started, Governor Connally had been facing toward the crowd on the right. He started to turn toward the left and suddenly felt a blow on his back. The Governor had been hit by a bullet which entered at the extreme right side of his back at a point below his right armpit. The bullet traveled through his chest in a downward and forward direction, exited below his right nipple,

passed through his right wrist which had been in his lap, and then caused a wound to his left thigh. The force of the bullet's impact appeared to spin the Governor to his right, and Mrs. Connally pulled him down into her lap. Another bullet then struck President Kennedy in the rear portion of his head, causing a massive and fatal wound.

The President and Governor Connally were rushed to Parkland Memorial Hospital where a team of doctors made a desperate but futile effort to save Kennedy's life. He was pronounced dead at 1 p.m. The body was flown back to Washington and at 8 p.m., Eastern Standard Time, a three-hour autopsy was performed by Commander James J. Humes, senior pathologist, and a team of doctors at the Naval Medical Center in Bethesda, Maryland.

Less than two hours after the first shot was fired on Dealey Plaza, a 24-year-old ex-Marine and employee of the Texas School Depository was arrested for the murder of Dallas policeman J.D. Tippit. Oswald was immediately tied to the Kennedy assassination on the basis of a police radio message broadcast at 12:45 describing the suspected assassin. The description was obtained from a 45-year-old steamfitter named Howard L. Brennan who was sitting on a wall on the southwest corner of Houston and Elm watching the motorcade go by when, he said, he noticed a man in the sixth-floor window of the Depository take aim and fire a rifle in the direction of the President. For two days and through more than twelve hours of questioning, Lee Harvey Oswald maintained that he was completely innocent. Then, on the morning of November 24th, he was shot to death by Jack Ruby, a Dallas nightclub owner.

Those were the basic facts of Kennedy's assassination as reported to the American public by the Warren Commission. When Vince Salandria had given me the Report, he had told me that some of those basic facts didn't square with what was in the 26 volumes of supporting evidence and documents. I still found that difficult to believe, even after I found the inconsistencies myself. Then I thought of Arlen Specter. He would explain it all to me; he would resolve the seeming contradictions; he would set everything straight.

I had known Specter before he went to Washington. A former star of Yale Law's debating team, he was exceptionally bright and articulate. He was in his early thirties then, an aggressive Assistant District Attorney who was eager to help with an article I was writing about a corrupt local Teamster boss he was prosecuting. That conviction got him some national publicity, a factor in his appointment as a junior counsel to the Warren Commission. It wasn't supposed to be a job that would garner him much attention, but he had political ambitions and he figured it would look good on his future campaign literature.

(It did; when he returned from Washington he ran successfully for Philadelphia District Attorney and is now a U.S. Senator.) When he was appointed to the Commission, no one—least of all Specter himself—could know that he would be the one to design the single-bullet theory that became the very foundation of the Commission's Report.

I still have what I believe are historic tape recordings of my three interviews with Arlen Specter about the Warren Report. When the Report was issued and, later, when Salandria's article in *The Legal Intelligencer* was first published, Specter, responding to reporters' questions, was vigorous in his defense of the Commission's conclusions. But then, no reporter had thoroughly read the Report or its volumes of evidence. As it turned out, I was the first one to ask Specter specific questions about the Report's inconsistencies. I couldn't believe the hemmings and hawings, the hesitations and evasions I got from the normally cool, collected and verbally masterful Specter. I had caught him off guard. As time went on, when other journalists became acquainted with the Report's incongruities and began hitting Specter with tougher questions, he was ready. But, by then, my encounter with Specter had already convinced me that President Kennedy was murdered as the result of a conspiracy.

This is what it boiled down to: The Warren Commission started from the premise that there was no conspiracy and it was Arlen Specter's role to handle the fundamentals to support that conclusion.

Specter was assigned as junior counsel to Area I, "the basic facts of the assassination." Senior counsel for Area I was to have been Francis W.H. Adams, a former New York City police commissioner. But because Adams was so wrapped up in a major case with his own law firm, he wound up spending only a few days working on the Commission investigation. Practically the entire workload for the most important area of the assassination fell on Arlen Specter.

The rest of the Commission staff worked on five other areas. Area II was concerned with the identity of the assassin; it handled evidence incriminating Oswald as the triggerman. Area III was devoted to Oswald's background. The fourth area looked into the question of whether Oswald was connected with any conspiracy and investigated his movements outside the country. Area V dealt with Oswald's death, including the possibility of a prior connection with Jack Ruby and a sixth area studied the problem of Presidential protection in general. Thus, before an objective evaluation of the facts concerning the assassination of President Kennedy ever got under way, it was decided that four of the six areas of investigation should concern themselves with Lee Harvey Oswald.

So, from the start, Arlen Specter knew very well what his job would be. He began early in January, 1964 and finished by June 1st, the only staff lawyer to meet the deadline. In his report Specter concluded that all the shots fired on November 22nd came from the sixth-floor window of the Texas School Book Depository.

The crux of Specter's conclusions—and therefore, the Commission's Report—is what has come to be called the "single-bullet theory." That is, one shot, the bullet which went through Kennedy's neck, caused all of Governor Connally's wounds. Here's what the Report said happened: Three shots were fired. One hit Kennedy near the top of his back, came out the front of his neck, went through Connally's back, came out his chest, smashed his right wrist and caused a puncture wound in his left thigh. Another went in the back of Kennedy's head and blew out the right front part of his head. A third missed. (There was evidence of a bullet hitting a far curb and someone being hit on the cheek by a piece of it.) The Commission decided that the order of the hits and the miss was irrelevant and made no determination of the sequence.

Specter told me that one of the principal factors in favor of the single-bullet theory was that there was no other way to explain what happened to the bullet which emerged from the front of the President's neck—unless it also hit Connally. There was no indication that it hit anywhere else in the car. There was a crack on the inside of the front windshield and a mark on the chrome above it, but much more damage would have been done if they had been caused by a whole bullet.

Specter's "single-bullet theory" is the foundation for the Warren Commission's conclusion that a lone gunman killed President Kennedy. If Kennedy and Connally were *not* hit by the same bullet, *ipso facto,* as the lawyers say, there *had* to be a conspiracy.

To understand why, we need to go back to Zapruder's home movie. In the Warren Report—and in all the subsequent literature—references to the specific moments surrounding the assassination are based on the individual frames of the film. (Keep in mind that there was a time lapse of about one-eighteenth of a second between frames; 18.3 frames represent one second of passing time.) The most memorable frame, the terrible shot of Kennedy's head exploding, is frame 313. The Warren Commission Report said "the President was probably shot through the neck between frames 210 and 225." It based that finding on the fact that the President was definitely reacting—both hands were grasping for his throat—by frame 225, and on the evidence of a reenactment which showed that Oswald's aim would have been obstructed by an oak tree before frame 210. The Report also concluded that the point at which Connally could have received his injuries was somewhere "between frames 235 and 240." (Given the time difference represented by those frame numbers, Oswald would not have had time to fire his rifle twice.)

The Commission concluded that three shots were fired: Two were hits, one a complete miss. (The number of shots reportedly heard by witnesses ranged from two to more than eight.) The Commission based its conclusion chiefly on the fact that three empty shells were found on the sixth floor of the Depository. Given this assumption and the timing of the shots—the fatal hit was definitely recorded on frame 313—evidence of more than three shots (or of bullets coming from a direction other than the Depository) would indicate the presence of at least one more assassin.

If a separate shot did hit the Governor between the two that hit the President, the shots would have had to be evenly spaced within less than six seconds. But the Commission conceded that " . . . a substantial majority of the witnesses stated that the shots were not evenly spaced. Most witnesses recalled that the second and third shots were bunched together."

Then there is Governor Connally's testimony, during which Specter himself inadvertently developed one of the strongest contentions *against* the single-bullet theory:

MR. SPECTER: In your view, which bullet caused the injury to your chest, Governor Connally?

GOVERNOR CONNALLY: The second one.

MR. SPECTER: And what is your reason for that conclusion, sir?

GOVERNOR CONNALLY: Well, in my judgment, it just couldn't conceivably have been the first one because I heard the sound of the shot . . . and after I heard that shot, I had the time to turn to my right, and start to turn to my left before I felt anything. It is not conceivable to me that I could have been hit by the first bullet.

The Zapruder film itself supports Connally's assertion. As the Presidential car begins to pass from view behind a road sign, about frame 185, the President is waving with his right hand and smiling. Less than a second and a half later, at frame 207, the car is completely behind the sign but the President's face is still visible above it. On frame 225 it is obvious that Kennedy has begun to clutch at his throat. By frame 235, Connally has begun to turn to his right, against— according to the Commission's version—the force of the bullet which had shattered his right fifth rib, smashed his right wrist and punctured his left thigh. Actually, there is no indication that Connally is hit until frame 292, a little more than three and one half seconds later, when he begins to fall back into his wife's lap.

When I asked Specter about that discrepancy, he couldn't explain it. "You can't tell from the films when Connally was hit. . . . What you have on the Zapruder film is, naturally, two dimensional. The Governor is turning around and at some point he's hit. There's the question of reaction time. But I watched—and the Governor watched those films—which, by the way, was fascinating to see—that is, his response as he watched that film for the first time when he was at the Commission the day he testified —and even he can't tell exactly when he was hit, you know."

But Connally had testified that he had time to turn around twice *after* he heard the first shot fired. Mrs. Connally supported her husband, saying she did not see him get hit when she heard the first shot. In order to reach the single bullet conclusion, that testimony had to be ignored.

Whether they consciously acknowledged it or not, Specter and the Commission had a fixed mission: to prove that a lone gunman committed the assassination.

But the single-bullet theory is perhaps more dependent on the medical evidence than anything else. And it is here, in the final autopsy report submitted by the doctors at the Naval Medical Center in Bethesda, that the gravest doubts about the Warren Commission's findings may be raised.

Every Commission exhibit regarding the location and nature of the wounds suffered by Kennedy and Connally—including the key charts and drawings showing the direction and path of the bullets—was produced by artists solely on the basis of the autopsy report, or verbal directions from Dr. James Humes, a Navy Lieutenant Commander and the senior pathologist at the Medical Center who performed the autopsy. Neither the Commission nor Specter ever saw any of the photographs or x-rays corroborating the autopsy report. The Commission had decided, supposedly out of sensitivity to the Kennedy family, not to use these so they wouldn't become part of the record.

Dr. Humes's final autopsy report was submitted on December 20th, 1963. The Commission deduced from it that all the shots had to come from above and to the rear.

Dr. Humes's autopsy report said there was a small hole in the back of the President's head. So Specter and the Commission concluded that this was the entry hole made by the bullet that blew out the right front part of his skull—the fatal hit of the Zapruder frame 313.

From my study of the evidence, however, what most intrigued me were the wounds caused by the single bullet which supposedly hit both Kennedy and Connally. This is the way the Warren Commission Report handled that point:

Another wound, it noted, "provides further enlightenment as to the source of the shots. A hole near the base of the neck [was located] approximately five-and-a-half inches from the tip of the right shoulder joint and approximately the same distance below the tip of the right mastoid process, the bony point immediately behind the ear."

The Report then explained what happened to the bullet which caused that hole:

> The autopsy examination further disclosed that, after entering the President, the bullet passed between two large muscles, produced a contusion on the upper part of the pleural cavity (without penetrating that cavity), bruised the top portion of the right lung and ripped the windpipe (trachea) in its path through the President's neck. The examining surgeons concluded that the wounds were caused by the bullet rather than the tracheotomy performed at Parkland Hospital. . . . No bone was struck by the bullet which passed through the President's body. By projecting . . . at a slight downward angle through the bruised interior portions, the doctors concluded that the bullet exited from the front portion of the President's neck that had been cut away by the tracheotomy.

The bullet which caused this wound, the Commission decided, was the one that hit Governor Connally. "The clothing worn by President Kennedy," notes the Report, "had holes and tears which showed that a missile entered the back of his clothing in the vicinity of his lower neck and exited through the front of his shirt immediately behind his tie, nicking the knot of his tie in its forward flight."

Again, all these conclusions were drawn from Dr. Humes's autopsy report. But in accepting the accuracy of his autopsy, the Commission had to ignore a good deal of evidence which contradicted it.

On December 9th—eleven days before the Commission received Humes's autopsy report, the FBI had submitted a summary report of its own investigation into the assassination. While the Commission would base most of its own findings on information contained in the volumes of this FBI report, it ignored the part dealing with the autopsy findings, written by two FBI agents, Francis X. O'Neill and James W. Sibert, who were present when the autopsy was performed.

According to O'Neill and Sibert, a bullet hole was found not in the back of Kennedy's neck but below his shoulder and two inches to the right of his spinal column. The agents said:

This opening was probed by Dr. Humes with the finger, at which time it was determined that the trajectory of the missile entering at this point had entered at a downward position of 45 to 60 degrees. Further probing determined that the distance travelled by this missile was a short distance inasmuch as the end of the opening could be felt with the finger.

The fact that the bullet had not exited and yet could not be found on the body initially concerned Dr. Humes. However, as the autopsy continued, the FBI Laboratory notified the agents that a nearly whole copper-jacketed bullet had been found on a stretcher in Parkland Hospital. The agents reported the news to Dr. Humes:

> Immediately following the receipt of this information . . . Dr. Humes advised that in his opinion this accounted for no bullet being located which had entered the back region and that since external cardiac massage had been performed at Parkland Hospital, it was entirely possible that through such movement the bullet had worked its way back out of the point of entry and had fallen on the stretcher.

If that were true, then the bullet found at Parkland could not have emerged from the front of Kennedy's throat. But the Warren Commission Report said, "Further exploration during the autopsy disproved that theory." Actually, there was no "further exploration during the autopsy." It was the morning after the autopsy that Dr. Humes called Dr. Malcolm Perry at Parkland, who said he had used a wound hole in the front of Kennedy's throat as the point to make the tracheotomy incision.

If there was a bullet hole in the front of the neck, Dr. Humes concluded, it was obviously an exit wound caused by the bullet which went in the back. The Commission accepted that and ignored the evidence in the FBI report.

However, not one doctor who worked on Kennedy at Parkland Hospital initially described the hole in the front of Kennedy's neck as an exit wound. That apparently was a problem. When Specter was taking their testimony, he asked them to reconsider the question hypothetically. At that point, most doctors said, well, sure, it *could* have been either an entrance or exit wound. However, one doctor— Ronald Coy Jones—maintained that if it were an exit wound it would have to have been inflicted by a bullet of very low velocity, "to the point that you might think that this bullet barely made it through the soft tissues and just enough to drop out of the skin on the opposite side." Certainly it would not have had enough force left to smash through Connally.

Perhaps the FBI was mistaken about the back wound. (That would mean it simply made a gross error in one of the biggest cases it ever handled.) Yet the FBI submitted a supplement to its summary on January 13th, by which time it had seen the official autopsy report. Nevertheless, it not only stuck to its original finding but repeated a key point:

> Medical examination of the President's body had revealed that the bullet which entered his back had penetrated to a distance of less than a finger length.

But Dr. Humes's final autopsy report makes no mention of a wound in the back, only one at the base of the neck, which it described as being higher than the hole in the front of the neck, which would make it consistent with a shot fired from the sixth floor of the Depository.

The Warren Report does not explain or discuss the discrepancy between the FBI version of the autopsy and the final report submitted and signed by Dr. Humes.

After I had interviewed Specter, I called Dr. Humes, who had by then been promoted to the rank of Navy captain. He refused to discuss the matter. "I'm not concerned with what was in the FBI report," he told me. "We did our job and we signed the report and it was very straightforward and unequivocal. We don't feel we should discuss the matter any more. That is the position we are taking and that is the position we have been instructed to take by our superiors."

The Warren Commission Report decided to support its version of the back wound with an illustration. Commission Exhibit 385 is a profile drawing of Kennedy's head and shoulders showing the path of the bullet through the neck. The entrance of the bullet is placed above the shoulders at the base of the back of the neck at an angle consistent with a shot coming in from above and to the rear. It is obvious from the drawing that such a shot would have struck Connally. The drawing was prepared by a medical illustrator at the Naval Medical School solely on the basis of a verbal description given by Dr. Humes. Yet the FBI report was very specific when it said that a bullet hole was found "below the shoulders."

When I asked about the contradiction, Specter said it was just a matter of semantics. "It's a question of whether you call this point shoulder, base of neck or back. I would say it sure isn't the shoulder, though I can see how somebody might call it the shoulder."

Almost every one else who saw the wound called it a shoulder wound. Secret Service agents Roy Kellerman and William Greer, who were present at the autopsy, said it was in the shoulder.

Secret Service agent Glen Bennett, who was in the follow-up car behind Kennedy, said he "saw that shot hit the President about four inches down from the right shoulder."

Secret Service agent Clinton Hill, who saw the President's body at the morgue, testified: "I saw an opening in the back, about six inches below the neckline to the right-hand side of the spinal column."

As a matter of fact, this was where Humes himself had placed the wound on a diagram that was a face sheet to his autopsy notes. So although Humes was to later testify that the entrance wound in the back was above the throat wound, at the time of the autopsy he marked it *below*.

Perhaps Humes's diagram is inconsistent with his original written notes. But it is a question that was never answered—it couldn't be. Humes burned his original notes. And, according to Specter, without any authorization other than Humes's own.

Yet Specter accepted the final autopsy report as unquestionable—not that Specter had any reason to question the integrity or intentions of Humes, a career Navy officer. "I went to see him at Bethesda," Specter told me, "and you should see his whole demeanor, his whole approach to the problem. You just wouldn't think for a minute that the guy's fudging anything." Specter, in fact, spent a good deal of time with Humes working out the single-bullet theory. "I was very impressed with Specter," Humes had said when I attempted to interview him. "He was a very intelligent young man."

But that very intelligent young man could not explain the absolute contradiction between the final autopsy report's location of that critical back wound and the huge body of testimony and evidence that contradicted it. And I was counting on an explanation from Specter because, without it, the evidence cried out conspiracy.

Even if I accepted the highly unlikely possibility that a single bullet *could* have gone through Kennedy's neck, done major muscle and bone damage, passed through Connally and emerged almost pristine, I thought the overwhelming evidence showed that the bullet hole wasn't at the base of Kennedy's neck but more than five-and-one-half inches below it.

In studying the evidence, I discovered further documentation contradicting Specter's single-bullet theory: photographs of the President's jacket and shirt, which were not published in the Warren Report but which were part of the FBI supplemental report of January 13th, 1964.

The Warren Commission Report said the entrance wound caused by the bullet which came out Kennedy's throat was "approximately five-and-a-half inches" below the back of the right ear, but one photograph clearly indicates that the hole in the back of the jacket is almost five-and-a-half inches below the top of the collar, and one-and-three-quarter inches to the right of the center back seam of the coat.

The photograph of the shirt worn by the President shows a hole in the back consistent with the one in the jacket, about five-and-three-quarter inches below the top of the collar and one-and-one-eighth inches to the right of the middle. The discrepancy is obvious.

The locations of both these holes are inconsistent with the wound below the back of the right ear described in the Commission's autopsy report.

I'll never forget asking Specter about that as I sat in his City Hall office in Philadelphia. (It was about a year after he had returned from his Warren Commission job; he had recently been elected District Attorney.)

"Well," he said, "that difference is accounted for because the President was waving his arm." He got up from his desk and attempted to demonstrate his explanation on me, pulling my arm up high over my head. "Wave your arm a few times," he said, "wave at the crowd." He was standing behind me now, jabbing a finger into the base of my neck. "Well, see, if the bullet goes in here, the jacket gets hunched up. If you take this point right here and then you strip the coat down, it comes out at a lower point."

A lower point?

"Well, not too much lower on your example, but the jacket rides up."

If the jacket were "hunched up," I asked, wouldn't there have been two holes as a result of the doubling over of the cloth?

"No, not necessarily. It . . . it wouldn't be doubled over. When you sit in the car it could be doubled over at most any point, but the probabilities are that . . . aaah . . . that it gets . . . that . . . aaah . . . this . . . this is about the way a jacket rides up. You sit back . . . sit back now . . . all right now . . . if . . . usually, as your jacket lies there, the doubling is right up here, but if . . . but if you have a bullet hit you right about here, which is where I had it, where your jacket sits . . . it's not . . . it's not . . . it ordinarily doesn't crease that far back."

What about the shirt?

"Same thing."

Was Specter saying there is no inconsistency between the Commission's location of the wound and the holes in the clothing?

"No, not at all. That gave us a lot of concern. First time we lined up the shirt . . . after all, we lined up the shirt . . . and the hole in the shirt is right about, right about the knot of the tie, came right about here in a slit in the front . . . "

But where did it go in the back?

"Well, the back hole, when the shirt is laid down, comes . . . aah
. . . well, I forget exactly where it came, but it certainly wasn't higher,
enough higher to . . . aaah . . . understand the . . . aah . . . the angle
of decline which . . ."

Was it lower? Was it lower than the slit in the front?

"Well, I think that . . . that if you took the shirt without allowing
for its being pulled up, that it would either have been in line or
somewhat lower."

Somewhat *lower?*

"Perhaps. I . . . I don't want to say because I don't really
remember. I got to take a look at that shirt."

I found it difficult to believe that Arlen Specter didn't take a very
close look at that shirt—and that jacket—at the time of the investigation and that these factors didn't indelibly stick in his mind: Kennedy
was one of the best-tailored presidents ever to occupy the White
House, and if it is possible—but not probable—that he was wearing a
suit jacket baggy enough to ride up five or six inches in the back when
he waved his arm, it is inconceivable that a tightly buttoned shirt
could have done the same thing.

And the Zapruder film shows Kennedy wasn't waving his hand
higher than the level of his forehead before he was shot.

I had questioned Arlen Specter for hours about so many conflicting
areas of evidence that I remember when I walked out of his office
after the second and last session I felt a strange uneasiness, the
numbness of disbelief. Specter had not eased my concerns about the
Warren Commission Report, he had magnified them. The Report and
its 26 volumes of evidence—pages planted with scores of ripped strips
of note paper marking the suspect conclusions and conflicts I had
hoped Specter would explain—were piled in disarray on my desk,
royal blue covers adorned with the majestic gold seal of the United
States Government.

After those interviews with Arlen Specter, my belief in that
Government would never be the same.

THREE

THE RIGHT PLACE, THE RIGHT TIME

B Y LATE 1975, when I was beginning work as a Government investigator on the Kennedy assassination, I had not seen or spoken with Vince Salandria for a number of years. I had, however, continued my research into the Kennedy assassination, written a few articles about it for *Philadelphia Magazine* and even developed a modest national reputation as a Warren Commission critic. (In a 1969 article about JFK researchers, an *Esquire* magazine chart listed me as one of the "Philadelphia Group.") But then I moved to Florida and, because of other demands, found little time to devote to the assassination. But Vince Salandria had become something of a legend among the growing circle of Warren Commission critics. Almost everyone who planned to write a book about the Kennedy assassination first journeyed to Philadelphia to probe Salandria for insights and perspective. Salandria himself, however, never went commercial, never wrote a book, never capitalized on his knowledge. In fact, he spent a good deal of his time and his modest resources helping others and working to "advance the case." By that he meant trying to get the American people to understand what really happened when Kennedy was assassinated—a job most of the national media had fallen woefully short on. But then, for some reason, Salandria became less involved in the investigation and what was going on among researchers, and faded into the background.

But before starting my new job, I returned to Philadelphia to draw upon Salandria's vast knowledge of the evidence and get his opinion about the most fruitful areas of investigation. Salandria was most cordial, and we spent a long winter Sunday talking. Yet I sensed a certain balking in his attitude, a feeling of disappointment in what I was about to begin. Eventually, he explained why he was no longer actively involved in pursuing an investigation of the assassination. It gave me a surprising insight into how far Salandria's thinking had evolved.

"I'm afraid we were misled," Salandria said sadly. "All the critics, myself included, were misled very early. I see that now. We spent too much time and effort microanalyzing the details of the assassination when all the time it was obvious, it was blatantly obvious that it was a conspiracy. Don't you think that the men who killed Kennedy had the means to do it in the most sophisticated and subtle way? They chose not to. Instead, they picked the shooting gallery that was Dealey Plaza and did it in the most barbarous and openly arrogant manner. The cover story was transparent and designed not to hold, to fall apart at the slightest scrutiny. The forces that killed Kennedy wanted the message clear: 'We are in control and no one— not the President, nor Congress, nor any elected official—no one can do anything about it.' It was a message to the people that their Government was powerless. And the people eventually got the message. Consider what has happened since the Kennedy assassination. People see government today as unresponsive to their needs, yet the budget and power of the military and intelligence establishment have increased tremendously.

"The tyranny of power is here. Current events tell us that those who killed Kennedy can only perpetuate their power by promoting social upheaval both at home and abroad. And that will lead not to revolution but to repression. I suggest to you, my friend, that the interests of those who killed Kennedy now transcend national boundaries and national priorities. No doubt we are dealing now with an international conspiracy. We must face that fact—and not waste any more time microanalyzing the evidence. That's exactly what they want us to do. They have kept us busy for so long. And I will bet, buddy, that is what will happen to you. They'll keep you very, very busy and, eventually, they'll wear you down."

It had been over ten years from the time I first interviewed Salandria to our talk that long winter Sunday. Yet, flying back home to Miami that evening, I sat in the dark plane and had an eerie sense of *déjà vu*. As when I first spoke with him, I didn't quite grasp exactly what he was talking about, but I had the uneasy feeling he was advancing some awesomely frightening theories. Then it crossed my mind that, perhaps this time for sure, Salandria was crazy.

* * *

That was late November. A few weeks earlier, I had received a call from U.S. Senator Richard S. Schweiker. I had never met Schweiker but, while working for *Philadelphia Magazine*, I had spoken with his administrative assistant, Dave Newhall, a few times over the years. Newhall, a former Philadelphia newspaper reporter, was familiar with my early interest in the Kennedy assassination. He called to ask if I would help Schweiker check out some leads on the case related to Miami's Cuban exile community.

I had been an investigative journalist for fifteen years and had finally reached the point where I had the time and opportunity to write the Great American Novel, the Holy Grail of every professional writer.

"How long will the job take?" I asked Newhall.

"Figure a couple of weeks."

"Sure, why not?" I said, unaware that it would turn into three years.

At the time, Schweiker was a member of what was officially named the Senate Select Committee to Study Governmental Operations with Respect to Intelligence Activities, headed by Idaho Senator Frank Church—the Church Committee, as it became known in the press. Formed in January, 1975, it began making headlines almost immediately by revealing how the FBI abused its power by harassing dissident political groups and conducting illegal investigations; how the CIA, Army Intelligence and the National Security Agency were involved in domestic snooping; and how the intelligence agencies had planned assassination attempts on foreign leaders. For Schweiker, despite his long stints in both houses of Congress, these were eye-opening revelations. "I've learned more about the inner workings of Government in the past nine months than in my fifteen previous years in Congress," he later told a reporter.

Schweiker had never before been moved to take a special interest in the details of the Kennedy assassination. A moderate conservative Republican, he had something of a Boy Scout reputation: honest, straightforward and perhaps even a bit politically naive—all assets to his loyal Pennsylvania Dutch constituents. He had assumed, as had most Americans, that the Warren Commission Report reflected a comprehensive, objective investigation. He had never had the inclination to question its findings because to do so would be to assume that, at the very least, certain Government officials and agencies could have been involved in a cover-up. Schweiker did not want to believe that. However, when the Church Committee discovered that U.S. Government officials—specifically, CIA agents—had made alliances with the Mafia and other members of Organized Crime in planning assassinations, Schweiker was shaken. "That was so repugnant and shocking to me that I did a backflip on any number of things," he said.

One of those "backflips" was on his assumption about the Warren Report. He was particularly upset when he discovered that former CIA Director Allen Dulles had been aware of CIA assassination plots against Fidel Castro and yet had withheld that information from his fellow members on the Warren Commission. Schweiker got even angrier when he came across an old Associated Press story which indicated that Castro had told a reporter just several weeks before Kennedy's assassination that if the United States tried to eliminate Cuban leaders, then the U.S. leaders themselves would be in danger. "Nobody paid any attention then because nobody knew we *were* trying to kill Castro," Schweiker later said. "But that statement had to have meaning, particularly to Allen Dulles." Schweiker thought Dulles's failure to tell the Warren Commission of the Castro plots was "a cover-up of sensational proportions."

While the Senate and the Church Committee took their summer vacations, Schweiker spent most of his time sifting through the volumes of evidence and the declassified documents in the National Archives relating to the murder of John F. Kennedy. Then, in September, he issued a public statement calling for a reopening of the Kennedy assassination investigation by the Church Committee.

"Recent disclosures have devastated the credibility of the Warren Commission Report," Schweiker said. He called for a new, "vigorous and meticulous" inquiry, citing Dulles's failure to inform the Warren Commission of U.S. attempts on Castro's life. He also cited testimony claiming that the FBI had destroyed and suppressed evidence about its association with Oswald, adding that a transcript of a previously "Top Secret" Warren Commission session revealed that Allen Dulles bluntly told his fellow members that J. Edgar Hoover would probably lie if called to testify.

Schweiker felt the Church Committee could, in keeping within its mandate, initially focus on the role played by U.S. intelligence agencies in investigating the assassination. "We don't know what happened," Schweiker said, "but we do know Oswald had intelligence connections. Everywhere you look with him, there are the fingerprints of intelligence."

That was an understatement. Schweiker had found so many indications of a possible intelligence link to Oswald he was actually shocked. How could American intelligence agencies fail to have records of Oswald's defection to Russia?—especially since Oswald had worked monitoring U-2 spy flights in Atsugi, Japan, then the largest and most secret CIA base in the world. How did Oswald afford a $1,500 trip to Moscow when he only had $203 in his bank account?

How did he get a visa in two weeks, when it normally took six? While en route to Russia, how did he get to Helsinki, Finland, from London at a time when there were no commercial flights scheduled? And why was a Minox spy camera found among Oswald's possessions? Finally, why did the CIA not question Oswald when he returned from Russia?

Schweiker's contention that this was legitimate fodder for the Church Committee was clearly valid. The question was, would Frank Church himself, a politician with a personal agenda, want to tackle the Kennedy assassination?

The Church Committee was one of the larger select committees formed by the Senate, employing more than a hundred full-time staffers, mostly attorneys. Its mandate, however, was unrealistically broad. It not only was supposed to investigate all illegal domestic intelligence and counterintelligence activities on the part of the CIA, the FBI and all the military intelligence agencies, it was also directed to delve into "the nature of and extent to which [these] Federal agencies cooperate and exchange intelligence information," the need for improved oversight, the adequacy of existing laws governing intelligence activities and "the extent and necessity of overt and covert intelligence activities"—among other things.

The Church Committee's report was originally scheduled for release by September, which meant that it would be, in relation to the Committee's mandate, a predetermined exercise in superficiality. To Chairman Church, that was not as important as having the Committee finish its work quickly. He had already told intimates that he was going to run for the Presidency the following year and, because he didn't want to be accused of using the Committee to garner personal publicity, he said he would not announce his candidacy until it finished its job. However, under pressure from the staff, Church had already been forced to extend the Committee's deadline from September to March 5th, 1976. Then Schweiker came up with his proposal to throw the Kennedy assassination into the investigative pot. That upset Church a bit. He knew that looking into the assassination, even from the narrow focus of the intelligence agencies' investigation of it, could extend the Committee's work for months and months, thereby fouling up his personal plans. Church, however, did not want to take a political risk by publicly opposing the suggestion, so he came up with a clever compromise. He said he would permit Schweiker and a Democratic counterpart, Colorado Senator Gary Hart, to set up a two-man Kennedy assassination Subcommittee provided that it, too, would wrap up its work at the same time the Committee was scheduled to finish in March.

Schweiker wasn't happy with the limitations but decided to take what he got. He figured that if he could develop enough solid information or stumble upon a new revelation, the Committee as a whole could then be pressured into tackling the Kennedy assassination even beyond its deadline. So Schweiker jumped in with both feet. Since Church said he could initially spare only two members of the Committee's staff for Schweiker's Subcommittee—he would get a few more later as the Committee staffers wound up their individual projects—Schweiker geared up his own personal staff for a Kennedy inquiry and assigned his Legislative Counsel David Marston (later the U.S. Attorney in Philadelphia) as his point man. Marston, a Harvard Law grad then in his early thirties, took it upon himself to become an instant expert in the details of the Kennedy assassination. He immersed himself in the National Archives files, guided Schweiker to what appeared to be the most fruitful areas of investigation and served as liaison with the independent researchers and Warren Commission critics who had suddenly deluged Schweiker with offers of help. A few other staffers were also assigned to devote the bulk of their energy to the Kennedy case, including handling the kooks and spooks who had started wandering into the office.

Schweiker had his operation going for about a month before he called me. Although he himself never told me, I later learned that he wanted an outside investigator reporting directly to him, not to the Church Committee, for several reasons. He was, first of all, not getting the kind of concentrated staff support he felt his Subcommittee needed. Even those Committee staffers immediately assigned to the Subcommittee couldn't plunge full time into the case because they were busy wrapping up other projects. Schweiker also discovered that the sheer bulk of material that had built up over the years on the Kennedy case was awesome and no Committee staffer had any background knowledge of it. In fact, the lawyer who was assigned to head Schweiker's Subcommittee staff did not even read the Warren Commission Report until two months after the Subcommittee was formed.

In addition, the Subcommittee staff was approaching the Kennedy assassination in the same way the Committee investigated the intelligence agencies' activities: It was doing a paper investigation of documents provided by the agencies themselves. No one was leaving Washington, no one was doing any original probing. Instead, the staffers spent most of their time working with the CIA and the FBI, the very agencies that were suspected of violating their operating charters and engaging in illegal activities. The CIA was especially cooperative with Church. "They were almost anxious to show us everything they had, just so they could prove they had nothing," one staffer later reported. (An interesting point: Although the CIA admitted withholding information from the Warren Commission, the officer assigned to guide the Senate probers through the Agency's files was the very one who had performed the same chore for the Warren Commission.) At any rate, Schweiker was bothered by the approach and, despite the limited time allowed him, felt that he had to dig more deeply if there was going to be a break in the case.

Another reason Schweiker decided to hire his own investigator was this: Although he was taken with the possibility that Kennedy's murder might have been an act of retaliation by Castro, Schweiker wasn't ready to rule out other possibilities. The Subcommittee staff was obviously concentrating on the retaliation theory because, from the pragmatic viewpoint of its paper investigation, it was the one most easily structured into a report within the time limits. Yet Schweiker was personally struck by what he termed "the fingerprints of intelligence" on Oswald's activities before the assassination, as well as Oswald's associations with anti-Castro Cubans. So while his Subcommittee staff was heading down one road, Schweiker wanted the other one checked, too.

Finally, there was this factor: Kennedy was murdered in Dallas, but within hours of the assassination a rush of leads and tips related to Miami suddenly popped up. And now, as word of Schweiker's interest in the assassination spread, he was flooded with suggestions of a Miami connection. As a result, he decided that *if* there was a relationship between the Kennedy assassination and Castro elements—either pro-Castro or anti-Castro—and one of the intelligence agencies, Miami would be the place to look for the clues. Then, when he began receiving specific tips about such a relationship, Schweiker decided he could use a man on the street in Miami to check them out. And I was in the right place at the right time.

IN MIAMI, THE SEEDS
OF VENDETTA

*K*NOWING SOMETHING ABOUT the Miami area is important to understanding the mystery of John F. Kennedy's murder because it played a key role in the history of the times surrounding the assassination.

Miami isn't Miami Beach. The Beach is now Art Deco chic and roller blade cool, but for years it was a geographical addendum to Miami. It was where peacock-dressed tourists and seasonal visitors flocked, an island strip of beachfront high-rises, kitschy-elegant hotels, pseudo-Vegas nightclubs and overpriced eateries, its permanent population of mostly Jewish retirees rocking their brittling bones away on the foredeck of decaying apartments clustered at the south end. Miami was always something else. The actual city is a 34-square-mile jigsaw puzzle piece of real estate slotted within the 2,054-square-mile entity of Dade County. Although there are 27 other municipalities within Dade, the whole county area is generally just known as "Miami." To the east there is Biscayne Bay and the Atlantic Ocean; to the south are the sultry Florida Keys, linked to civilization by a single road and one water pipeline; to the west is the endless sea of sawgrass called the Everglades, one of the country's largest, most primitive natural preserves.

Although many urban areas have undergone transformations over the last two decades, Miami's was unique. Like most big cities during the Fifties, Miami felt the negative effects as the white middle class abandoned the inner city and took off for the suburbs. And although the population of towns to the north and west was booming, Miami itself was relatively stagnant. Few newcomers to South Florida wanted to move back into a city after leaving one up North—despite the fact that most of Miami then had a small-town feeling. Miami was, in fact, a city of neighborhoods lined with modest old homes of white clapboard, painted cinderblock or coral rock, with screened rear "Florida rooms" and front porches. However, with the middle-class exodus and the deterioration of its neighborhoods, the City of Miami began more and more looking like a neglected waif with no hope of capturing a piece of the prosperity that was coming to the Gold Coast. Its downtown began going to hell and its poor black sections began oozing their blight through the rest of the city. Despite the tropical clime, Miami's future wasn't sunny.

Then the Cubans came.

The first small flock came in the early and mid-Fifties: the anti-*Batistianos*, who opposed the military dictatorship of General Fulgencio Batista. Among them was a young lawyer named Fidel Castro; he stayed only briefly, giving fiery speeches at an old movie theater on Flagler Street. One émigré was the wealthy former president Carlos Prío, who ensconced himself in an elegant home on Miami Beach and dispensed millions setting up arms and supply lines to the rebels while maintaining a close association with the American racketeers running the Havana gambling casinos. Then, when it appeared that the corrupt dictator's end was inevitable, came the *Batistianos* themselves along with the nonpolitical types who got out with their nest eggs. Cuba's monied class began moving into Miami's business and banking worlds, setting up their private clubs and fancy restaurants and surrounding themselves with the luxuries necessary to maintain the style of living to which they were accustomed on the island. That's when Miami first began to feel the early rhythms of Cuban culture and social activity.

Then, beginning on January 1st, 1959, came the deluge. Fidel Castro seized power and that wrought as profound a change in the destiny of Miami as it did in the future of Cuba. At first, the flow of exiles into the city was a slow stream moving through Miami International Airport; then, as it became more and more apparent that the ranting *barbudo* was taking his country toward Communism, the stream became a torrent.

"They were new types of refugees," wrote reporter Haynes Johnson. "Instead of a home, they were seeking temporary asylum. . . . They arrived by the thousands, in small fishing boats, in planes, chartered or stolen, and crowded into Miami. Along the boulevards, under the palms, and in hotel lobbies, they gathered and plotted their counter-revolution. Miami began to take on the air of a Cuban city. . . . Everyone talked of home only one hundred miles away. And everyone talked about the great liberation army being formed in the secret camps somewhere far away.''

And along with the exiles and their passion for a counterrevolution came the Central Intelligence Agency. Well before the U.S. Embassy in Cuba closed down in January, 1960, the CIA had stepped up its activities on the island tremendously. It had not only increased the number of personnel operating out of the Embassy itself, but it began putting covert operatives in place as businessmen, ranchers, engineers, journalists and in other "cover" activities in order to recruit and establish a network of anti-Castro dissidents. As counterrevolutionary groups began forming within Cuba, the Agency began supplying them with arms and communications equipment and, for those subversives threatened with exposure, help in escaping. Among the key defectors the Agency helped were two of Cuba's top Air Force officers, Pedro and Marcos Díaz Lanz. The CIA's liaison in that operation was a former Cuban police official named Bernard Barker, who later gained notoriety as a Watergate burglar. Shortly afterwards, Frank Fiorini, a former Philadelphian who was the Cuban Air Force chief of security, also secretly departed Cuba. Fiorini would later also turn up on the Watergate burglary team. By then, he had changed his name to Frank Sturgis.

Within a year after Castro took power, the face of Miami had a definite Cuban character. More than 100,000 exiles had settled in and others were arriving at a rate of 1,700 a week. As the Cuban exile population of Miami grew, so did the presence of the CIA. Eighteen Government agencies handled exile reception and the CIA had contacts in every one, including the mother agency, the Cuban Refugee Center. The CIA used the Immigration and Naturalization Service to set up and maintain a massive debriefing facility at the Opa-Locka air base in northern Dade County. More important, however, the Agency began assigning case agents to keep tabs on the multitude of anti-Castro groups spreading like mangrove roots. At one point, there were almost 700 such groups, some of which had begun active military operations with CIA support. One veteran recalls that the Cuba-bound boat traffic on Biscayne Bay got so heavy "you needed a traffic cop." It confused the U.S. Coast Guard, which didn't always know whether it was chasing a "sponsored operation" financed by the CIA or just a bunch of "crazy Cubans."

The invasion of Cuba's *Bahía de Cochinos*—Bay of Pigs—occurred in April, 1961. The brainchild not of the Cuban exiles but of the CIA, it was spawned at a meeting of the Agency's top brass in January, 1960. Originally, it was not going to be a massive operation. No more than thirty Cuban exiles were to be trained in Panama to serve as cadre for bands of guerrillas recruited within or infiltrated into Cuba. President Dwight Eisenhower's Executive Order signed in March, 1960, merely approved the idea of recruiting a body of anti-Castro refugees to be armed and trained at American expense. When he signed the order, Eisenhower himself said, almost as an aside: "I'm not sure what we will do with these people after we get them." The CIA then set up a training camp in Guatemala and funneled in recruits from Miami. Still, by the time of the 1960 elections, there were only about 300 Cubans in training. It was after Kennedy became President that the plan grew, largely because he put a great deal of confidence in a former mentor from Harvard, a lanky, stoop-shouldered aristocrat named Richard Bissell, the CIA's covert operations chief. It was Bissell who had conceived and nurtured the invasion plan. Bissell played on his direct relationship with Kennedy to keep the CIA's plan from those who knew the most about military operations. An insider, historian General S.L.A. Marshall later wrote: "The Joint Chiefs were never asked to approve any plan; they were not besought to analyze that final plan that became operative. They were figuratively put in a corner and given to understand they should not interfere or pass judgment." Hell, the CIA had single-handedly pulled off a great military operation in Guatemala when it helped dispose of Socialist Jacobo Arbenz's government in 1954. Why couldn't it do it again in Cuba?

Years later, the Church Committee was to discover, from files voluntarily given to it by the CIA, that a select few of the Agency's top officers—including Richard Bissell—had in the spring of 1960 begun setting in motion, as an adjunct to the Bay of Pigs operation, plans to assassinate Castro. The CIA told the Committee that it was involved in nine Castro assassination plots in all, including those with the Mafia. Castro himself later produced a detailed list of 24 plots against his life involving the CIA. What's significant is that both the CIA and Castro agree on when the plans began.

In Miami, even before plans for a Cuban invasion became common gossip, the Cuban exiles' hopes for Castro's overthrow were constantly buoyed by public pronouncements of support from the U.S. Government. In his State of the Union address, President Kennedy himself spoke of "the Communist base established 90 miles from the United States," and said that "Communist domination in this hemisphere can never be negotiated." As soon as Kennedy had been elected, CIA Director Allen Dulles and covert plans deputy Bissell had flown to the Kennedy estate in Palm Beach and sold their new boss on the efficacy of a Cuban operation. They did not tell him that the Agency's plans had recently been upgraded to include an even larger paramilitary force and air strikes. That decision, Bissell would later admit, was "internal."

The most cogent analysis of the consequences of this operation is Peter Wyden's in *Bay of Pigs—The Untold Story* [Simon & Schuster, 1979]:

> No notable event in recent United States history remains as unexplained and puzzling as the Central Intelligence Agency's adventure that became known as "the Bay of Pigs."
>
> . . . the Bay of Pigs is more than a skeleton in the nation's historical closet; more than the first blemish on the magic of the Kennedy name and reputation; more than the collapse of the largest secret operation in U.S. history. It is a watershed.
>
> If the CIA, acting out of control and independently, had not escalated its plans against Fidel Castro from modest guerrilla operation into a full-fledged invasion, President Kennedy would have suffered no humiliating, almost grotesque defeat.
>
> If Kennedy had not been thoroughly defeated by Castro on the beaches in 1961, Nikita Khrushchev almost certainly would not have dared to precipitate the Cuban Missile Crisis of 1962—the crisis which, in the words of former CIA Director William E. Colby, pushed the world 'as close to Armageddon' as it has ever come.
>
> And if the reasons for the collapse at the Bay of Pigs had not been covered up . . . the CIA might perhaps have been curbed, and the country could have been spared the intelligence scandals of the 1970s, the revelations of a government agency routinely, daily, committing unconstitutional acts against its own citizens in its own country.

Wyden, however, misses one significant observation: What the Bay of Pigs plan provided was the historic opportunity for the CIA to begin domestic field operations on an unprecedented scale. For instance, the CIA's presence in Miami grew to overwhelming dimensions. The Agency's officers, contract agents, informants and contacts reached into almost every area of the community. And as pervasive as that presence was before the Bay of Pigs, it was but a prelude to a later, larger operation. The preparation for the Bay of Pigs invasion gave birth to a special relationship between CIA operatives and the Cuban exiles. That relationship would intensify into a mutuality of interests which transcended even Presidential directives and official United States policy.

One factor that led the Central Intelligence Agency to believe it could topple Castro was its success in Guatemala in 1954. Using a force of only 150 exiles and a handful of World War II P-47 fighters flown by American contract pilots, the CIA brought down the legally elected government of Socialist President Jacobo Arbenz in less than a week, firing hardly a shot, and installed the Agency's handpicked leader, Carlos Castillo Armas.

Because of the success of "the Guatemala scenario," Bissell selected veterans of it for the key slots in the Cuban operation. One such veteran was E. Howard Hunt, whom Bissell appointed as the Agency's political liaison to the Cuban exile groups in Miami. A dapper, pipe-smoking Ivy Leaguer and prolific author of spy thrillers, Hunt had—and still does have—a curious reputation. To some in the Agency he is the caricature of the Hollywood spy, given to overplaying the cloak-and-dagger role; indeed, Hunt did serve a stint as a Hollywood script writer. One of the more earnest of the Agency professionals liked to say that Hunt was consistent in his judgment—always wrong. Yet through the years, right up through the Watergate fiasco, Hunt was inevitably chosen to be on the front lines of dirty tricks operations. Despite the fact that there appeared to be so many failures among those operations, Hunt's star continually rose. He was also strangely close to the one man whose markedly unflamboyant character seemed in such contrast to his, the one deemed the shrewdest and most coldly professional of all Agency bosses: Richard Helms.

It didn't take long for E. Howard Hunt to inject himself into the labyrinthine world of Cuban exile politics in Miami. With his faithful sidekick, Bernard Barker, Hunt set up a series of "safe" houses for clandestine meetings, moved through the shadows of Little Havana and doled out packets of money from dark doorways. (At times Hunt carried as much as $115,000 in his briefcase.) Although Hunt attempted to maintain a secret identity ("Just call me 'Eduardo,' " he told the Cubans) and kept the source of the funds a mystery, the exiles soon began referring to their benefactor as "Uncle Sam."

It was Hunt's job to form the *Frente*, the coalition of Cuban exile groups which would serve as the political umbrella for the military army of the invasion. It was apparent early on, however, that Hunt's own conservative right-wing political view affected his handling of the exile groups—he and Barker, wheeling and dealing among the exile-politicians, started as many squabbles as they mediated. In fact, immediately before the actual invasion, Hunt was removed—he says he quit—as the Agency's political liaison because he wouldn't include in the exile coalition a group headed by a democratic socialist named Manolo Ray. With Ray, it would be *Fidelissimo sin Fidel*, Hunt said, and called him a Communist.

Hunt's principal contribution to the Bay of Pigs invasion was his selection of the military brigade's political leader, a psychiatrist-turned-politician named Manuel Artime.* Flamboyant and effective,

---

*In 1975, an informant called the office of Senator Richard Schweiker and said that a friend of Artime's in Mexico City claimed that Artime had "guilty knowledge" of

Artime helped stop a political insurrection at the exile training camp, and his relationship with Howard Hunt eventually grew into an extremely close friendship. They bought homes across the street from each other in Miami Shores and Artime became godfather to one of Hunt's children.

Another of Hunt's major contributions was his selection of an old friend from the Guatemala scenario for an extremely important Agency role. Pulled from his post as a covert operative in Havana was a tall, articulate, charmingly diffident counterintelligence expert named David Atlee Phillips. As in Guatemala, it was Phillips's enormous and primary task to create the Big Lie. As head of the Agency's "propaganda shop" for the invasion, Phillips had to bend the cacophony of the exile groups into an effective symphony, set up broadcast stations that would rally guerrillas within Cuba to join the invaders and establish communications links to provide the secret codes that would trigger the actual invasion. Most important, it was Phillips's job to create the impression that the invasion was a spontaneous action by anti-Castro forces and that neither the United States nor the CIA had anything to do with it. Phillips obviously had to be ingenious.

Later, in the assortment of military and political reviews of why the Bay of Pigs operation was such a dismal failure, the obvious reason was this: The most ambitious clandestine project ever concocted and supervised by the world's most technically proficient experts in deception and secrecy was, in the end, anything but a secret. Just nine days before the invasion, a *New York Times* reporter in Miami wrote: "Men come and go quietly on their secret missions of sabotage and gun-running into Cuba, while others assemble at staging points here to be flown at night to military camps in Guatemala and Louisiana. Since a mobilization order was issued ten days ago . . . contingents of men have been leaving here nightly for the camps of the new revolutionary army. They will be followed next week by professional men and intellectuals who are to be concentrated at an undisclosed spot in the Caribbean area to prepare to serve as military government officials if the revolutionaries gain a foothold on Cuban soil." Certainly, Castro must have at least glanced at the story before checking the baseball scores in the Grapefruit League the next day.

---

the Kennedy assassination. I was unable to reach Artime, who was moving in and out of the country on business, before Schweiker's mandate expired. (Artime had become a wealthy man as a business partner of former Nicaraguan dictator Anastasio Somoza.) Later, when I was with the House Assassinations Committee, my investigative partner, Al Gonzales, contacted Artime. Gonzales told him we planned to interview him and arranged to take his sworn statement. The next week, Artime went into the hospital and Gonzales visited him there. Artime told Gonzales that some cancer was found but he was feeling fine and would return home shortly. Two weeks later, Artime died. He was 45.

President Kennedy told the world that he assumed "sole responsibility" for the Bay of Pigs but privately, he turned to his special
counsel, Theodore Sorensen, and asked: "How could I have been so
stupid to let them go ahead?" Yet many in the top echelon of CIA
officers involved in planning the invasion felt strongly that Kennedy
was responsible for its failure. There would have been no slaughter of
the exiles, they murmured, no 1,200 brave men captured, if Kennedy
had not at the last moment rejected their proposal for massive air
support. That was the word that filtered down to the field operatives,
the Cuban exile community and the remnants of the invasion army,
2506 Brigade. It produced an incredible bitterness on every level. The
military leader of the Brigade, Pepe San Roman, captured and imprisoned by Castro, later said: "I hated the United States and I felt that I
had been betrayed. Every day it became worse and then I was getting
madder and madder and I wanted to get a rifle and come and fight
against the U.S."

The Agency operatives who had led the exiles expressed the same
deep anger. The ever-eloquent E. Howard Hunt, monitoring the effect
at CIA headquarters until the end, later noted in his memoir *Give Us
This Day* [Popular Library, 1973]: "I was sick of lying and deception,
heartsick over political compromise and military defeat. . . . That
night, laced through my broken sleep, were the words Sir Winston
Churchill had spoken to a British Minister of Defense: 'I am not sure
I should have dared to start; but I am sure I should not have dared to
stop.' . . . I saw in his words a warning for those Americans who had
faltered at the Bay of Pigs."

Hunt's close friend, David Atlee Phillips, also remarked on the
incredible emotional impact of the defeat. Writing in his autobiography, *The Night Watch* [Atheneum, 1977], he said:

> I went home. I peeled off my socks like dirty layers of skin—I
> realized I hadn't changed them for a week. . . . I bathed, then fell into
> bed to sleep for several hours. On awakening I tried to eat again, but
> couldn't. Outside, the day was sheer spring beauty. I carried a portable
> radio to the yard at the rear of the house and listened to the gloomy
> newscasts about Cuba as I sat on the ground, my back against a tree.
> Helen came out from the house and handed me a martini, a large
> one. I was half drunk when I finished. . . . Suddenly my stomach churned.
> I was sick. My body heaved.
> Then I began to cry. . . .
> I wept for two hours. I was sick again, then drunk again . . .
> Oh shit! Shit!

I would later discern a line between the disaster of the Bay of Pigs and
the assassination of President Kennedy, but it was not the one linked

to Kennedy's failure to provide air support. A prolific freelancer named Andrew St. George once touched upon it in an article in *Harper's Magazine*. I got to know the bearded, swashbuckling St. George, a rotund, witty, European-bred charmer, during the early course of the Schweiker investigation. I discovered he was all over Miami in the early Sixties, working mostly for *Life* magazine, slipping around the anti-Castro groups and soldier-of-fortune crowd, conning his way along on infiltration operations into Cuba and, it was rumored, often wheeling and dealing more as an activist than as an objective journalist. ("Andrew was a loveable scoundrel," says one anti-Castro Cuban leader who claims that St. George purloined a boat from his group to give to another exile group.) St. George was also one of the first correspondents to join the rebel Castro in his mountain stronghold and monitor the deployment of his guerrilla command. I once asked St. George if he had ever worked for the CIA. He smiled, puffed on a fine cigar and said, "Only when I worked for *Life*." He meant that, in those days, it was hard to tell where the CIA left off and *Life* began and it is St. George's close contacts with the Agency that lend credibility to his observations.

"Had someone asked me during the early Sixties to explain, in twenty words or fewer, why I called the Bay of Pigs a failure," St. George wrote in *Harper's*, "I would have said something like this: It was a military formula applied to an essentially political problem. It was an *inevitable* failure.

"But what evidence did we have, really, to say that the Cuban invasion was a failure? The discredited approach of applying military solutions to political problems, this failed formula we expected President Kennedy to junk with contempt, was instead polished up and adopted as the . . . essential strategy of the Kennedy Administration . . ."

In fact, noted St. George, the biggest beneficiary of the failed Cuban adventure turned out to be the very agency responsible for it:

Within a year of the Bay of Pigs, the CIA curiously and inexplicably began to grow, to branch out, to gather more and more responsibility for the 'Cuban problem.' The Company was given authority to help monitor Cuba's wireless traffic; to observe its weather; to publish some of its best short stories (by Cuban authors in exile) through its wholly owned CIA printing company; to follow the Castro government's purchases abroad and its currency transactions; to move extraordinary numbers of clandestine field operatives in and out of Cuba; to acquire a support fleet of ships and aircraft in order to facilitate these secret agent movements; to advise, train, and help reorganize the police and security establishments of Latin countries which felt threatened by Castro's guerrilla politics; to pump such vast sums into political operations thought to be helpful in containing Castro that by the time of the 1965 U.S. military intervention in the Dominican Republic both the bad guys and the good guys—i.e., the 'radical' civilian politicos and the 'conservative' generals —turned out to have been financed by *La Compañía*. Owing largely to the Bay of Pigs, the CIA ceased being an invisible government: it became an empire.

Following the Bay of Pigs, word leaked out from the White House that Kennedy was disillusioned with the CIA, that he was upset with his CIA advisers for pushing a scheme on him which had been devised during the Eisenhower Administration, that he had been badly informed and misled and pressured by CIA brass who had an egocentric interest in pushing the ill-conceived plan. The President called for the resignation of CIA Director Allen Dulles and covert plans boss Richard Bissell and, one aide reported, said he was going to "splinter" the Agency into "a thousand pieces and scatter it to the winds."

That was misleading. Kennedy was, indeed, damn angry at the CIA, not for planning the Bay of Pigs but for botching it. And he was mad as hell at Castro who, in endless daily harangues and broadcast reviews of the battle, kept rubbing the young President's nose in the humiliating defeat. Kennedy's initial reaction was almost reflexive: Don't get mad, get even. Appointing his brother Robert to oversee the Agency's covert operations, Kennedy did not splinter the CIA but infused it with new life. That solidifying of policy towards Cuba and the massive infusion of funding to the CIA and its anti-Castro front groups became known to insiders as "the Kennedy vendetta."

FIVE

A 'TRAITOR' IN THE WHITE HOUSE

BETWEEN THE Bay of Pigs debacle in April of 1961 and the Cuban missile crisis in October of 1962, a massive and, this time, truly secret war was launched against the Castro regime. President Kennedy set up, under the guidance of his brother Robert, a multiagency coordinating panel called Special Group Augmented (SGA) to supervise a massive covert program to overthrow Castro's government. A counterinsurgency expert, General Edward Lansdale, was appointed to run the program, called Operation Mongoose after the ferretlike animal known for its ability to kill cobras and other venomous snakes. The CIA's Mongoose unit, designated Task Force W, would supervise the Agency's role. And that role was, of course, the most critical one in the scenario: To actually execute President Kennedy's "secret vendetta."

According to a recently released memo written after the first meeting of the Special Group Augmented by George McManus, the CIA's representative to the Special Group: "No time, money, effort—or manpower is to be spared. Yesterday . . . the President had indicated to him . . . that the final chapter had not been written—it's got to be done and will be done."

What followed made the preparations for the Bay of Pigs seem pale by comparison, and its results slowly began altering the attitudes of the anti-Castro militants and CIA operatives in the field. Although a good measure of bitterness and cynicism still lingered, it soon became apparent that a revised, more positive image of the President was taking shape.

Kennedy did his best to reinforce that image. "Cuba must not be abandoned to the Communists," he declared in a speech shortly after the Bay of Pigs, and spoke of a "new and deeper struggle." That was a euphemism for a U.S.-sponsored anti-Castro campaign, which eventually employed several thousand CIA operatives and cost over $100 million a year. Again Miami was the focus of the effort, and this time the CIA moved in on a truly unprecedented scale. On a large, secluded, heavily wooded tract that encompassed an old Naval Air station (now the site of the Metrozoo) and part of the University of Miami's South Campus, the Agency set up a front corporation called Zenith Technical Enterprises Inc. Its code name was JM/WAVE and it soon became the largest CIA installation anywhere in the world outside of the Agency's Langley, Virginia, headquarters.

At the height of its activities, the JM/WAVE station had a staff of more than 300 Americans, mostly case officers in charge of supervising and monitoring Cuban exile groups. Each case officer employed as many as ten Cuban principal agents and each principal agent, in turn, was responsible for as many as thirty regular agents. In addition, the Agency funded scores of front operations throughout the area— print shops, real estate firms, travel agencies, coffee shops, boat repair yards, detective agencies, gun shops, neighborhood newspapers—to provide ostensible employment for the thousands of case officers and agents operating outside of JM/WAVE headquarters. It was said that if any Cuban exile wanted to open his own business, he had but to ask the CIA for start-up capital. The CIA became one of the largest employers in South Florida.

Internally, the JM/WAVE station was also a logistical giant. It leased more than a hundred staff cars and maintained its own gas depot. It kept warehouses loaded with everything from machine guns to coffins. It had its own airplanes and what one former CIA officer called "the third largest navy in the Western Hemisphere," including hundreds of small boats and huge yachts donated by friendly millionaires. There were also scores of pieces of real estate, from backstreet dives to palatial waterfront mansions, for use as "safe houses" or assembly points for operations. In addition, of course, there were paramilitary training camps throughout the Florida Keys and deep in the Everglades. One of the more active sites, used by a variety of anti-Castro groups, was a small, remote island north of Key West called, appropriately enough, No Name Key. It was home to a group called the International Anti-Communist Brigade (IAB), a collection of soldiers of fortune, mostly Americans, who were recruited by Frank Fiorini Sturgis and a giant ex-Marine named Gerry Patrick Hemming.

Like another ex-Marine named Lee Harvey Oswald, Hemming was trained as a radar operator in California. (Hemming would later claim that Oswald once tried to join his IAB group.)

Those were heady times for the anti-Castro groups in Miami. With the CIA providing financing and lessons in sabotage, explosives, weapons, survival, ambushes, communications and logistics, the missions to Cuba began escalating in both frequency and scale. Initially intent on infiltrating small guerrilla bands onto the island, the Agency was soon supervising major raids aimed at blowing up oil refineries and sugar mills. Although some of the more militant exile groups considered themselves independent of the CIA, no group could function very long without Agency coordination. It needed the Agency to make special arrangements with U.S. Customs, Immigration and the Coast Guard because the missions were technically illegal under the Neutrality Act. Whether the exile leaders acknowledged it or not, the Agency was pulling all the strings.

Those were, of course, equally heady times for the CIA. It ran the whole show in more ways than one, eventually achieving a level of influence and control over a major area of U.S. foreign policy which Kennedy himself hadn't envisioned. The JM/WAVE station in Miami became the coordinating center for the conduct of the secret war around the globe. Every CIA station in the world had at least one case officer assigned to Cuban operations who reported to the Miami station. The JM/WAVE station also controlled an international economic strategy, pressuring U.S. allies to embargo all trade with Cuba and supervising a worldwide sabotage program against goods being shipped to and from Cuba. (For instance, it got a German manufacturer to produce a shipment of off-center ball bearings for a Cuban factory.) The operational level of the Agency was also—without Kennedy's knowledge and, it now appears, without even the knowledge of the Agency's newly appointed Director John McCone—continuing its program of assassination attempts against Castro. In giving the CIA new life, immense funding, and incredible power and influence to conduct effective large-scale secret operations, Kennedy had created a force over which he could not maintain control. He came to that painful discovery just when he faced the greatest challenge of his life.

The world never came closer to self destruction than it did during the Cuban missile crisis in October of 1962. Exactly 25 years later, at a Harvard conference attended by key U.S. and Soviet officials involved in the affair, Sergei Mikoyen, whose father was a top adviser to Nikita Khrushchev, said that the Soviet leader had maneuvered Castro into accepting the nuclear missiles because he truly believed that a U.S. invasion of the island was imminent.

Recently released U.S. Government documents indicate that Khrushchev had a valid reason to think so. By February of 1962, General Lansdale had finalized his action program for Operation Mongoose, which called for guerrilla operations culminating in the overthrow of the Castro regime during the first two weeks of October. In his initial presentation, Lansdale had left uncertain whether U.S. military force would be sent in to help, but a month later he wrote a memo noting that the Special Group Augmented "recognizes that final success will require decisive U.S. military intervention." The Pentagon began drafting contingency plans for the invasion and military occupation of Cuba.

By late summer, there was no doubt that the CIA's JM/WAVE operations were effective. The unrelenting infiltration and sabotage missions were creating economic and political pressures which the CIA hoped might push Castro into doing something rash. Then, as the Cuban missile crisis developed, the more fervent of Miami's Cuban exiles were elated by the possibility that it might provoke a final showdown with Castro. President Kennedy himself boosted such hopes with his hard-line responses to the ever-more-blatant buildup of the Soviet presence in Cuba. In September, Kennedy declared that the United States would use "whatever means may be necessary" to prevent Cuba from exporting "its aggressive purposes." In Miami, both the anti-Castroites and their CIA control bosses delighted in the tough talk and looked forward to some real action.

But the way Kennedy ultimately resolved the crisis destroyed the hopes of the exiles and the men conducting the secret war. Cuba and Castro were relegated to a minor role as Kennedy dealt directly with Khrushchev. The Cuban missile crisis ended on November 29th, 1962, with Kennedy's announcement that all IL-28 bombers were being withdrawn by the Soviets and that progress was being made on the withdrawal of offensive missiles. In return, Kennedy said, he gave the Soviets and the Cubans a "no invasion" pledge.

The secret war activists reacted with tremendous shock. They had been risking their lives in a tough guerrilla war against the menace of Communism in the Caribbean; it was astounding that Kennedy should make a *deal* with Khrushchev. If Kennedy's actions at the Bay of Pigs had raised doubts about his sincerity and determination to bring down Castro, his handling of the missile crisis more than confirmed those doubts. Over *café Cubano* at the back tables in luncheonettes in Miami's Little Havana, in the CIA safe houses set in the lush foliage of Coconut Grove, in training camps in the remote Keys and the deep Everglades, wherever the exiles and their control agents gathered, the word "traitor" could be heard. The late Mario Lazo, a prominent exile attorney and close associate of top CIA officials (he considered

E. Howard Hunt "one of the great men of our time"), called it a "soul-shattering blow."

And yet the depth of anger at Kennedy for making the settlement was shallow compared with how the Cuban exiles and their CIA cohorts reacted when it became apparent what the President's new "no-invasion" policy actually meant.

Suddenly, the U.S. Government began cracking down on the very training camps and guerrilla bases it had established. The regular exile raids into Cuba, which had been automatically getting the Government's "green light," were now promptly disavowed and condemned. The Cuban Revolutionary Council, the united front of exile groups established by the CIA, had its subsidy cut off and the Council's president bitterly declared that Kennedy had become "the victim of a master play by the Russians."

The crackdown continued over the next several months, to the increasing confusion and anger of the exiles. On the one hand, they were still being encouraged and supported by the U.S. Government—after all, wasn't the CIA the U.S. Government?—and, on the other hand, they were being literally handcuffed and arrested. It was crazy.

In March, 1963, for instance, when a group of anti-Castro guerrillas were arrested by British police at a training site in the Bahamas, the U.S. State Department admitted it had tipped off the British about the camp. That same night an exile raiding party was arrested and its boat seized in Miami harbor. The Coast Guard announced it was throwing more planes, ships and men into policing the Florida straits; the Customs Service raided the secret camp at No Name Key and arrested the anti-Castro force in training there; the FBI seized a major cache of explosives at another exile camp outside of New Orleans. Weeks later, the Coast Guard assisted the British Navy in capturing a group of CIA-armed Cuban exiles in the Bahamas. Then the Federal Aviation Administration issued "strong warnings" to six American civilian pilots—including E. Howard Hunt's associate Frank Sturgis—who had been flying CIA-backed raids over Cuba. Shortly afterwards, the Secret Service arrested a prominent exile leader for conspiring to counterfeit Cuban currency destined for rebel forces inside Cuba—a plan that had all the earmarks of a CIA operation. Had President Kennedy gone crazy, or was he, indeed, a *traitor?*

Against the pattern of this Federal crackdown, there emerged a counter pattern made up of incidents which, I later discovered, were related to the Kennedy assassination. These incidents involved a series of major raids by anti-Castro groups which took place—in defiance of U.S. Government policy—between the time of the missile crisis and the assassination of the President. In fact, these began at the very height of the missile crisis. At the most politically inopportune moment for Kennedy, one of the largest and most militant of the Cuban groups, Alpha 66, launched a quick strike at a major port in Cuba, killing at least twenty defenders, including some Russians. A week later, the same group sank a Cuban patrol boat. On October 31st, the day after Kennedy lifted his blockade of Cuba as a sign of his peaceful intentions, Alpha 66 struck again. Then, immediately after the crisis ended in November, a leader and spokesman for the group, a fiery and darkly intense former accountant named Antonio Veciana, pledged further raids.

Other CIA-directed Cuban exile groups also continued to defy Kennedy's edict. In April, the Cuban Freedom Fighters bombed an oil refinery outside Havana. In May, another band of anti-Castro rebels struck a military camp near Havana. Shortly afterwards, a group of exile raiders returned to Miami and announced it had blown up another refinery, sunk a gunboat and killed many soldiers. There were at least a dozen other actions which indicated that certain Cuban exile groups, and their CIA field operatives, were continuing the secret war. Despite the fact that none of the groups had been formed without the help of the CIA and that most lacked the equipment and organizational talent to operate successfully without its supervisory support and funding, the Agency denied it had any association at all with the continuing raids.

Indications are that Kennedy himself was confused and did not know what was happening. At a press conference in May, 1963, the President stumbled when responding to a question about whether or not the United States was still aiding the exiles: "We may well be . . . well, none that I am familiar with. . . . I don't think as of today that we are."

Did that mean the President *thought* his orders to halt aid to the exiles were being obeyed? Didn't he *know?*

There were few who had the foresight or knowledge to understand the significance of what was happening at the time, but one who did was Paul Rodgers, a Democratic representative from Florida. As early as February of that year, Rodgers, citing some "serious kinks in our intelligence system," had called for a Joint Congressional committee to oversee the CIA. "What proof have we," he asked with uncanny prescience, "that this Agency, which in many respects has the power to preempt foreign policy, is not actually exercising this power through practices which are contradictory to the established policy objectives of this Government?"

The same month that Rodgers issued his statement, a socially prominent petroleum engineer and consultant, world traveler and CIA intelligence asset named George de Mohrenschildt decided to give a dinner party at his home in Dallas. He invited a young couple, an ex-Marine who had returned from Russia with his emigrant wife the previous summer. It was at that dinner party that Lee Harvey Oswald was introduced to Ruth Paine.

S I X

SEDUCED BY THE WEB WEAVERS

*I*T WAS THIRTEEN YEARS after the Cuban missile crisis that I received a call from U.S. Senator Richard Schweiker's office, asking me to join his investigation into the assassination of President Kennedy. My initial reaction was elation. It was an incredible opportunity, to be given the time and resources to do something I long wanted to do. Finally, years after the deception foisted on the American people by the Warren Commission, the Government was going to make an effort to pursue the truth. Now I was going to be a part of that Government and that effort, and I'd be damned if I was going to be involved in another betrayal of trust.

Yet my journey to Philadelphia and talk with Vince Salandria had dulled my enthusiasm. He had muttered dire warnings that I was getting involved in a world of intrigue that was beyond any gnatlike efforts I might muster. He ventured that I would get lured into a quagmire of inconsequential details. "They'll keep you very, very busy and eventually wear you down," he had said.

Who are "they"? I wondered. And, after all these years, could "they" still be around and would "they" even care about what one individual in Miami might be doing? I had to admit that a bit of paranoia seemed to have slipped into Salandria's thinking. Nevertheless, his words dimly echoed in my mind when I started my job with Schweiker. I suddenly realized, as I began restudying all the old documents and evidence, and analyzing all the new, that I was journeying into a maze that had, over the years, grown larger and more complicated, plotted with elaborate cul de sacs. And yet, in retrospect, I can see that even then certain similar images were emerging along many of the pathways—indications, often almost imperceptible, of gossamer threads weaving through so many of the areas I investigated. Eventually it dawned on me that those strands of untraceable rumors and misinformation appeared to emanate from a common spool.

For instance, one of the first leads Schweiker asked me to check came from a source he considered impeccable: Clare Boothe Luce. One of the wealthiest women in the world, widow of the founder of the Time, Inc. publishing empire, former member of the U.S. House of Representatives, former Ambassador to Italy, successful Broadway playwright, international socialite and longtime civic activist, Clare Boothe Luce was the last person in the world Schweiker would have suspected of leading him on a wild goose chase.

Yet the chase began almost immediately. Right after Schweiker announced the formation of his Kennedy assassination Subcommittee, he was visited by Vera Glaser, a syndicated Washington columnist. Glaser told him she had just interviewed Clare Boothe Luce and that Luce had given her some information relating to the assassination. Schweiker immediately called Luce and she, quite cooperatively and in detail, confirmed the story she had told Glaser.

Luce said that some time after the Bay of Pigs she received a call from her "great friend" William Pawley, who lived in Miami. A man of immense wealth—he had made his millions in oil—during World War II Pawley had gained fame setting up the Flying Tigers with General Claire Chennault. Pawley had also owned major sugar interests in Cuba, as well as Havana's bus, trolley and gas systems and he was close to both pre-Castro Cuban rulers, President Carlos Prío and General Fulgencio Batista. (Pawley was one of the dispossessed American investors in Cuba who early tried to convince Eisenhower that Castro was a Communist and urged him to arm the exiles in Miami.)

Luce said that Pawley had gotten the idea of putting together a fleet of speedboats—sea-going "Flying Tigers" as it were—which would be used by the exiles to dart in and out of Cuba on "intelligence gathering" missions. He asked her to sponsor one of these boats and she agreed. As a result of her sponsorship, Luce got to know the three-man crew of the boat "fairly well," as she said. She called them "my boys" and said they visited her a few times in her New York townhouse. It was one of these boat crews, Luce said, that originally brought back the news of Russian missiles in Cuba. Because Kennedy didn't react to it, she said she helped feed it to Senator Kenneth Keating, who made it public. She then wrote an article for *Life* magazine predicting the missile crisis. "Well, then came the nuclear showdown and the President made his deal with Khrushchev and I never saw my young Cubans again," she said. The boat operations were stopped, she said, shortly afterwards when Pawley was notified that the U.S. was invoking the Neutrality Act and would prevent any further exile missions into Cuba.

Luce said she hadn't thought about her boat crew until the day that President Kennedy was killed. That evening she received a telephone call from one of the crew members. She told Schweiker his name was "something like" Julio Fernandez, and he said he was calling her from New Orleans. Julio Fernandez told her that he and the other crew members had been forced out of Miami after the Cuban missile crisis and that they had started a "Free Cuba" cell in New Orleans. Luce said that Fernandez told her that Oswald had approached his group and offered his services as a potential Castro assassin. He said his group didn't believe Oswald, suspected he was really a Communist and decided to keep tabs on him. Fernandez said they found that Oswald was, indeed, a Communist, and they eventually penetrated his "cell" and tape-recorded his talks, including his bragging that he could shoot anyone because he was "the greatest shot in the world with a telescopic lens." Fernandez said that Oswald then suddenly came into money and went to Mexico City and then Dallas. According to Luce, Fernandez also told her that his group had photographs of Oswald and copies of handbills Oswald had been distributing on the streets of New Orleans. Fernandez asked Luce what he should do with this information and material.

"I said what you do is call the FBI at once," Luce recalled. "Don't waste a minute. Go right in and call up the FBI."

Luce said she did not think about the story again until Jim Garrison's investigation hit the headlines in 1967. She said she called the New Orleans district attorney and told him of the incident but, after talking to him for ten minutes, she decided he was a "phony" and not serious. Through Pawley, however, she did locate and call her "young Cuban" and she reminded him of his conversation with her the evening Kennedy was killed. By then, Luce recalled, Julio Fernandez no longer wanted to get involved: "He said, 'Mrs. Luce, we did just what you said. We got it all to the FBI. They came, took our tape recordings, took our photographs and told us to keep our mouths shut until the FBI sent for us.' He said, 'Mrs. Luce, I am married, I have two children, I am a lawyer with a very successful practice in Miami. I don't want any part of the Kennedy assassination. You couldn't torture it out of me.' " Luce added that Fernandez also told her about the other two members of her boat crew: One had been deported and the other had been stabbed to death in Miami.

Her impression, Luce told Schweiker, based on what she was told by Fernandez, was that Oswald was hired by Castro to assassinate Kennedy in retaliation for the assassination attempts against him. Luce also said she did not remember the names of the other two crew members, nor did she know how to get in touch with Julio Fernandez now. But, she said, Bill Pawley would know all about it.

Schweiker called Pawley and Pawley said he didn't remember a thing. But Schweiker took it as an indication that Pawley just didn't want to get involved, and he still thought that Luce's story, if confirmed, could lead to a significant break. It had to have some foundation; after all, it had come from Clare Boothe Luce. Schweiker asked me to try to find the Julio Fernandez who had called her.

I discovered that there are a lot of Cubans named Julio Fernandez in Miami. And in New Orleans. I spent weeks talking with scores of Cubans named Julio Fernandez. Schweiker was particularly interested in the Julio Fernandez whose name turned up in an FBI document buried in one of the Warren Commission's volumes of evidence. The document dealt with a rumor reported by a neighbor of a Julio Fernandez, something about finding train tickets to Dallas in his trash. I finally tracked down that Julio Fernandez in upstate New York. He was now a college professor and, when I checked him out, knew he wasn't the Julio Fernandez who had called Clare Boothe Luce.

What is interesting in retrospect about the Luce story is that it had characteristics common to so many of the other leads which would be fed to the Schweiker Subcommittee and, later, to the House Assassinations Committee: They were difficult, time consuming and, ultimately, impossible to confirm but could not be dismissed outright because they always contained at least one hard kernel of truth.

For instance, in the case of Luce's lead, it was known that Oswald did approach an anti-Castro group in New Orleans and say he was interested in helping their cause. The fellow he talked to, Carlos Bringuier, was the chief New Orleans delegate of the *Directorio Revolucionario Estudiantil,* known simply as the DRE or the *Directorio.* The *Directorio* was headquartered in Miami and, I would later learn, under the wing of the CIA's JM/WAVE station. A few days after Oswald had walked into Bringuier's small storefront in New Orleans, Bringuier saw him passing out pro-Castro leaflets on Canal Street. They got in a scuffle and both were arrested. Bringuier later debated Oswald on a local radio program where, led on by the right-wing talk show host, Oswald admitted he had lived in Russia and declared he was a Marxist. A recording of that program was nationally disseminated immediately after the Kennedy assassination.

Independent researchers have been looking into Oswald's encounter with Bringuier for years and have discovered some curious things about it. One was that a newspaper photographer had been alerted to Oswald's leafletting on Canal Street before Bringuier even showed up. Oswald seemed bent on getting publicity as a pro-Castro demonstrator and even encouraged Bringuier to attack him. At one point, Oswald was overheard calmly saying, "Hit me, Carlos."

Another curious discovery: On some of Oswald's leaflets was stamped an address for the New Orleans chapter of the Fair Play for Cuba Committee. That address was certainly strange because the building was a hotbed of anti-Castro activity; at one time the CIA-backed Cuban Revolutionary Front had its New Orleans office there. The House Assassinations Committee later learned that Oswald had been seen in that building with extreme right-wing and anti-Castro activists.*

A year later, in December of 1976, when I was about to start working for the Assassinations Committee, I stumbled across some other fascinating facts related to Clare Boothe Luce's tip to Senator Schweiker. That was when I learned, for instance, that her "great friend" in Miami, William Pawley, was a longtime associate of the CIA. Never an official spook, Pawley was nonetheless a member of the Old Boys network and was especially close to CIA Director Allen Dulles. He had helped transform his *Flying Tigers* into one of the first CIA proprietary airlines, Civil Air Transport, and had set up for the Agency a front called the Pacific Corporation as an offshoot of the *Tigers*. He had been involved in the CIA's overthrow of the Arbenz government in Guatemala and he had backed more than one Castro assassination attempt. Pawley once told a Miami reporter: "Find me one man, just one man who can go it alone and get Castro, I'll pay anything, almost anything." But Pawley was not just a backer of exile groups, he wanted to be a participant, and I came across a bizarre story about one of his secret excursions to Cuba.

Early one morning in the summer of 1963, a 65-foot luxury yacht named the *Flying Tiger II* slid away from its dock behind a mansion on Miami Beach's Sunset Island and headed for Cuba. The yacht belonged to Pawley. Aboard were three CIA paramilitary operatives; a cache of heavy firearms and explosives was locked in its stateroom. The yacht was scheduled to rendezvous off the coast of Cuba with an amphibious aircraft, a Catalina PBY, provided by the CIA. Aboard the aircraft were Pawley; a fellow named John Martino, who had worked

---

*Much has been written about 544 Camp Street and Oswald's mysterious connections there. When New Orleans District Attorney Jim Garrison opened his Kennedy assassination probe in 1967, the focus of his investigation was on the anti-Castro activists in that building, including the ultra-right wingers, Guy Banister and David Ferrie.

for Mob bosses in Havana's casinos and had been imprisoned by Castro; *Life* magazine's Miami bureau chief Richard Billings (the same fellow who would later become the Assassinations Committee's chief writer); Billing's photographer, Terrence Spence; a daring Alpha 66 veteran Cuban infiltrator named Eduardo ("Eddie Bayo") Perez; and a raiding party of eleven CIA-trained Cuban exiles. The aim of the mission was for Eddie Bayo and his exile party, using a small, high-speed boat provided by the CIA, to sneak ashore, capture two Russian military technicians from a Cuban missile site and bring them back to the United States. Then, using the documentation that *Life* magazine's staffers would provide, a major press conference would proclaim that here was living proof that Soviet missiles were still in Cuba. The mission was a tragic failure. Radio contact with Bayo and his raiding party was lost and they were never heard from again. The *Flying Tiger II* and Pawley returned to Miami and *Life* never wrote a story about the mission.

There is here an intriguing link with the goals of the Alpha 66 raiders who were attacking Russian ships in Havana harbor at the height of the missile crisis: To embarrass President Kennedy and rip asunder his traitorous deal with Premier Khrushchev.

The end note to the William Pawley story occurred about the time I was scheduled to begin working for the Assassinations Committee. For weeks I had been reviewing the notes and background files I had collected during my work with Schweiker's Subcommittee and, wanting to hit the ground running, had put together an investigative plan for the Committee's Miami station. On my official first day I sent to Washington a list of witnesses I planned to interview and noted those I thought should testify under oath. William Pawley was near the top of that list. Exactly one week later, William Pawley, in bed in his mansion on Miami Beach with a nervous ailment, put a gun to his chest and committed suicide.

At any rate, as I continued to pursue the Luce story for the Assassinations Committee, I interviewed Carlos Bringuier in New Orleans. He said he had never spoken to Luce and that he had never used the name of Julio Fernandez. I believed him. In Miami, however, I did discover that kernel of truth in Luce's story: A few leaders of the *Directorio* had, in fact, been in touch with her.

The *Directorio* was, along with Alpha 66, the most active of all the Cuban exile groups, on both the military and propaganda fronts. In late August, 1962, the group had received national publicity with a daring raid into Havana harbor, its boats shelling a theater where Castro often spoke. The group's spokesman was a sharp, articulate young fellow named José Antonio Lanusa, who handled the regular reports from DRE delegates in various cities. It was Lanusa who, after the Kennedy assassination, had recalled Bringuier's report from New Orleans about Oswald's visit to the storefront, and it was Lanusa who had originally released the story to the press (after contacting his CIA case officer at the JM/WAVE station). It was also Lanusa who had turned copies of Bringuier's report over to the FBI and a tape recording of the radio debate with Oswald. Oddly enough, the FBI never told him to keep his mouth shut about it, Lanusa said. He also told me he'd never spoken to Clare Boothe Luce about the incident, either at the time or later, and he knew of no DRE member who was deported or murdered. And no, he said, he wasn't Luce's Fernandez.

Lanusa said he had only a single contact with Luce, arranged by a CIA associate. He was introduced to Luce at her New York apartment because, he was told, she wanted to write an article for *Life* magazine about his group's raid into Cuba. She said she would turn her $600 fee for the article over to the DRE as a contribution. That, Lanusa said, was the only money Luce ever contributed to the DRE—she never sponsored a boat. When I told him the story that Luce had given Schweiker, Lanusa shook his head. "I think Clare Boothe Luce shoots from the hip without her brain engaged," he said.

Many times in the course of my experiences investigating the Kennedy assassination, I found it strangely difficult to accept the obvious. It's like getting slapped in the face, feeling the sting, but still finding it hard to believe it really happened: *Did I just get slapped in the face?* It was a question I asked myself often.

Could the famous, sophisticated, respected Clare Boothe Luce have deliberately told Senator Schweiker such an embroidered tale of poppycock simply to mislead him and waste his and his investigator's time? Well, she was an old woman in her seventies and perhaps her mind wasn't as sharp as it once was.

It was a couple of years after her initial story to Schweiker, and after I had checked her leads as far as they would go, that I tried setting up a meeting with Luce. I had a tough time. Far from slowing down, she was very active and agile, moving between her New York apartment, her home in Hawaii and her penthouse at the Watergate in Washington. I couldn't make arrangements to interview her until the last months of the Assassinations Committee's existence, too late to have an executive session hearing or get a sworn deposition.

I finally met her at the Watergate amid her splendid collection of museum-quality Chinese art and artifacts. Mrs. Luce was most pleasant and cooperative. Yes, she said, she had originally told the story to columnist Vera Glaser and confirmed it with Senator Schweiker. She then repeated it, virtually unchanged.

However, she also confirmed something we had only recently discovered. While she was in touch with Senator Schweiker, Luce was also calling CIA Director William Colby and telling him what was happening with Schweiker's Kennedy investigation. According to Colby's notes, she admitted to him that she had concocted the name of Julio Fernandez. Colby apparently was confused by it all. When I asked Luce about it, she simply smiled sweetly.

Then I pointed out to Luce that her story reminded me of the Carlos Bringuier incident with Oswald. She smiled again and said, "Why, yes, that's the same type of thing that happened to my boys."

When I walked out of the Watergate late that afternoon, I knew only one thing for sure: An awful lot of time had been spent checking out Luce's story and, in the end, it led nowhere at all.

Shortly afterwards, I saw Luce for the last time, at a luncheon meeting of the Association of Former Intelligence Officers at a country club in Arlington. It was the second time I got to attend a retired spies luncheon and Luce was the guest speaker that day. Her speech was a vigorous defense of the intelligence establishment and a historical review of its successes. I also discovered that Clare Boothe Luce was on the Board of Directors of the Association of Former Intelligence Officers.

Interestingly, that organization was formed in 1975 as an "independent" voice to defend the CIA against its critics. Its founder was the retired intelligence officer who, as the Agency's top psych-warfare expert, was instrumental in the CIA-backed 1954 coup in Guatemala; was the CIA's propaganda chief for the Bay of Pigs operation; and was eventually promoted to Chief of the Western Hemisphere Division, a post representing the highest rung on the Agency's career chart. With the charges coming out of the Church Committee, the Agency needed experienced talent to deal with the media and give all the newly uncovered information about CIA activity the right spin. And, upon his retirement from the Agency, David Atlee Phillips, long the top man in the field, volunteered to do the job.

SEVEN

SEARCHING FOR GHOSTS IN KEY WEST

TIME AND AGAIN, as I probed the tangle of detail that the Kennedy assassination had become, a thread indicating an association with an intelligence activity would appear; sometimes distinct, often only thin and tenuous. Was there *really* any meaning to it? I was tempted by some far-fetched speculations, but I refused to think about them. I was already confused enough.

I'm still puzzled, for instance, by an episode involving a tip that came into Schweiker's office later in his investigation. Although I was then in the midst of pursuing another matter, the new information seemed much too relevant to shunt aside. And, again, its source seemed too valid to dismiss.

A man from Key West had called Schweiker saying he had some information that might be helpful. This man said he had seen Lee Harvey Oswald and Jack Ruby together at the Key West International Airport in the summer of 1963, and he provided details. Schweiker's office called me and I called the man. What he told me led me to drive to Key West and spend more than a week attempting to confirm his story. I was not totally successful, but I did find out more than I expected.

In the files of the FBI's investigation of the Kennedy assassination, there are hundreds of reports of individuals who claimed they saw Lee Harvey Oswald and Jack Ruby together before the President's murder. Most are baseless, but some, however, remain unresolved, including a few which appeared to have come from legitimate sources. That was one reason I decided to go to Key West. Another was an FBI report connecting Jack Ruby to a gun-smuggling operation in the Florida Keys. While I knew there was good evidence linking Ruby to gun smuggling in Texas, there was little on a Florida Keys connection. Perhaps this fellow who called Schweiker's office had stumbled onto something.

George Faraldo, a thin, swarthy man in his late fifties, was the general manager of the Key West airport until his retirement, when he opened a successful marine diesel business on the island. He is well-known in the community, a generally respected family man whose wife sings in the church choir.

At our first meeting, I spent several hours with Faraldo at his office getting the details of his story. On November 22nd, 1963, Faraldo said, he was in the local hospital recovering from a mild heart attack—that's why he was sure the incident occurred prior to the Kennedy assassination, probably that summer. He remembered arriving at the airport that summer morning and seeing a group of about thirty or forty persons clustered in the lobby. Despite its "international" status, the Key West airport then was not large, its terminal building a cinderblock structure the size of a small city post office. Faraldo said there were not usually many people in the terminal, which had only a few ticket counters and a separate small waiting lounge. Faraldo said he learned from talking with a few in the group that they were part of an organization called the Fair Play for Cuba Committee and that they were going to Cuba to help cut the sugarcane crop. Mostly, Faraldo said, they were young boys and girls, "hippie-looking," casually dressed in dungarees, a few in olive-drab fatigues. They were waiting for an Aerovia Q Airline plane to fly in from Cuba and pick them up. Aerovia Q was a commercial airline that regularly flew chartered and scheduled flights between Key West and Cuba, a ninety-mile hop across the Florida Straits. It maintained a ticket counter at the Key West Airport.

Faraldo said he recalled the group waiting around the airport all day and a good part of the night, getting repeated word that the plane was delayed. The group remained quiet and well-behaved, Faraldo recalled; some were sitting in small circles on the floor, a few playing guitars. The reason that Faraldo specifically remembered Lee Harvey Oswald, he said, was because Oswald was the only one who, during the course of the day, kept circulating among the group, chatting briefly with various clusters, then moving on. He didn't, however, appear to be the leader of the group, the one who kept making the announcements about the plane being delayed. That guy had a beard, Faraldo said. Ruby, he recalled, did not mingle much with the group and spent most of the day standing next to the doorway that led to the plane boarding area. Once, Faraldo said, he saw Oswald approach Ruby and talk to him briefly. The Aerovia Q plane the group had been waiting for arrived late in the evening. Oswald got on the plane with the group. Faraldo said he didn't see Ruby get on and doesn't know if he did.

It was an incredible story, yet Faraldo told it in a very credible way. He said he would have had some doubts about recognizing either Oswald or Ruby after the Kennedy assassination if it had been just one of them, but the fact that he recalled both individuals led him to dispel any thought that it may have been a case of mistaken identity.

Faraldo said he didn't observe the group constantly throughout the day, but worked in his office and just made a few trips out to chat. He didn't speak with either Oswald or Ruby. At one point, though, he filmed the group with a movie camera. He was a regular "stringer," or freelance correspondent, for WTVJ-TV, a Miami television station, and he often sent the news director short takes of newsy events around Key West. Faraldo said he would send the unprocessed film to Miami with a crew member of a National Airlines flight who would then give it to a cab driver at the airport to deliver to the television station. And that's what he did with the film he took of the Fair Play for Cuba group, Faraldo said.

Although Faraldo was very believable, I was a bit bothered by an inconsistency in his recollections. He was, on the one hand, absolutely sure that the number of the plane that finally arrived to pick up the group was CU-T583—it just stuck in his mind, he said. On the other hand, he couldn't recall exactly what month the incident occurred and even had some doubts about the year. Still, I reasoned, undulations in recollected detail would be normal after thirteen years.

In our initial interview, I asked Faraldo a number of questions and he remained very credible. More important, he appeared honest and consistently normal; he wasn't an oddball. He was, in fact, a very intelligent man, a college graduate with a degree in engineering. Together we drove to the airport terminal and Faraldo showed me around. We walked through the lobby and he explained the way the group had been scattered about. He then pointed out *exactly* where he saw Oswald and *exactly* where Ruby was standing most of the time. Faraldo appeared so sure of what he was saying that I could almost see images of the two still standing there.

I spent the next few days attempting to check out Faraldo's story. At the very least, I wanted to find out whether or not a Fair Play for Cuba group flew from Key West to Cuba and, if so, when. Perhaps then I could locate others who saw Oswald and Ruby together. I spoke to at least two dozen individuals—pilots, stewardesses, mechanics, ticket counter workers and employees of the terminal itself, including a former janitor. I could not get substantiation of any point, yet I kept getting a few tantalizingly vague confirmations that drove me to dig deeper.

I spoke, for instance, to a woman who worked the ticket counter for National Airlines at Key West in the early Sixties. She said she did remember a group going to Cuba to cut sugarcane. A retired Immigration Department official said he remembered reading about such a group in the newspapers. A Federal Aviation Administration employee also recalled hearing about a sugarcane-cutting group, but he didn't see them because he worked the late shift at the time. The FAA chief at Key West said he didn't remember that at all and that all FAA records of flights were then kept only fifteen days before being destroyed. No one who worked the control tower at the time remembered an Aerovia Q plane flying in late one night to pick up a group of sugarcane cutters. The retired airport janitor, a very old man, did remember such a group, but thought they were "foreigners." The U.S. Customs Department kept no records that could help.

I tried other angles. I spoke to a number of former employees of Aerovia Q Airlines, but none could remember the incident Faraldo described. Then I discovered that Aerovia Q had stopped its regular flights to Key West late in 1961, but Faraldo said it would have been possible for the airline to fly into Key West as late as 1963 merely by filing a flight plan with the FAA.

I also did a page-by-page check of the old bound volumes of the *Key West Citizen*, the local newspaper. Faraldo said he thought the newspaper's photographer had covered the incident, but, when I spoke with the photographer he didn't remember it. He said all his negatives from that time had been lost in a hurricane. Faraldo himself sent me to a historian at the local public library who, he said, "remembers everything." She didn't recall the incident and could find nothing to confirm it in her files.

A spark of hope flared when Faraldo mentioned that he used to keep the manifests, or passenger lists, of every daily flight out of Key West, including those from Aerovia Q. He said he would staple them together at the end of the day, fold them, put them in a white envelope and put the envelope in a cardboard box. And Faraldo remembered specifically where he had kept those boxes in a storage room at the airport. I rushed him back to the airport to check.

With the help of the current airport manager, we rummaged through every possible storage area, without success. The room where Faraldo was sure the boxes had been, was, just two weeks before, gutted after a rainstorm tore off part of the ceiling and flooded it. Faraldo pointed to where the boxes should have been—on a shelf suspended between the ceiling and the air conditioning ducts. The manager said everything from that room was now in a trash heap on the side of the terminal. I spent hours going through a mountain of soggy trash looking for the discarded boxes. I found nothing that resembled manifests.

Then I contacted Ralph Renick, the news director of WTVJ-TV, where Faraldo said he had sent his film. He confirmed that Faraldo had done some freelancing for the station and also said he was familiar with Faraldo's story about Oswald and Ruby. Faraldo had mentioned it, Renick said, about the time of Jim Garrison's investigation in New Orleans. Renick had subsequently gone through his film files but couldn't find anything. "It would have been a damn good story for us to break, obviously," he said. Nevertheless, Renick said, he would check the film files again. He found nothing.

Meanwhile, I kept returning to Faraldo. I was frustrated. At moments I even found myself vaguely recalling reading something about a group of pacifists going to Cuba to cut sugarcane. Faraldo appeared even more frustrated. He seemed extremely upset that his manifest records, which he had so carefully kept for years, had not been retained. We tried to probe deeper into his memory for additional details. We'd sit around his office or in the coffee shop at the airport; we had lunch together a few times. One night his wife invited me for a home-cooked dinner. Over the course of a week we had talked of many things besides the Kennedy assassination and were beginning to get to know each other a little. He was a soft-spoken, intelligent man and I liked him.

One day we were chatting in his office. Over the course of a long conversation Faraldo mentioned that he was a Navy veteran and an experienced pilot, had an avid interest in electronics and considered himself an expert photographic technician. He then mentioned he had a photo lab behind his machine shop. I noted my own interest in photography and asked to see it, assuming he was an amateur photographer who freelanced occasionally for a few bucks; perhaps he even had a nice array of professional quality equipment. However, I was amazed at the collection of sophisticated electronic and photographic gear stocked in Faraldo's shop. I guessed there was well over $100,000 worth of top-notch equipment. I then noticed what appeared to be the housing of an aerial reconnaissance camera sitting on the floor in a corner.

Hey, what's going on here?

Gently, I began probing Faraldo about his use of such equipment. Well, he said, he had made a number of trips into Cuba after Castro took over in order to find out a few things. He told a story about once being suspected of spying by Castro's police and how he was retained and beaten. He spoke of how he hated Castro and how he thought

Batista, whom he had known personally, was "one of the best friends the United States ever had."

When I asked Faraldo specifically about the reconnaissance camera, he said he had flown a number of aerial photographic missions and proudly went into a detailed explanation of how he had designed a special device enabling him to trigger the camera, installed in the belly of the plane, from the cockpit. He said he had taken shots of the Russian missiles in Cuba long before Kennedy announced they existed.

For whom, I tried to ask casually, was he working? "I was told," he said smiling, "I was working for the United States Information Agency." I asked if he thought it possible that he was really working for the CIA. "Yes," he said, "I would think so." I thought that he should more than just think so and decided to press. I asked him who paid for all the sophisticated photo and electronic equipment he had. He looked at me as if I were playing a game with him and didn't answer directly. Finally he gave me a wide grin and said, "No comment."

It's a beautiful ride from Key West to Miami over a long stretch of the Overseas Highway: the big sky a clear deep blue; on one side the ocean, a vista of white caps; on the other, the bay, a crystal expanse of glistening serenity. But I couldn't appreciate the scenery as I drove, because my mind was a jumble of confusion about what I had experienced over the previous days. I wanted to believe Faraldo because he was intelligent and credible, and I liked him. Besides, why would he be lying? Why would he tell such a story and go out of his way to bring it to Schweiker's attention? I remember the questions racing through my mind as I drove back. I also remember feeling as if I had just been slapped across the face.

EIGHT

BOOZY REVELATIONS IN POWDER SPRINGS

ASIDE FROM SPECIFIC REQUESTS to check out certain leads, Senator Schweiker gave me no investigative ground rules to follow. He wanted an investigator who wasn't bound by the parameters of the Church Committee's mandate or under the pressures of its deadline. Because he had uncovered the facts about the CIA withholding information about Castro assassination plots from the Warren Commission, Schweiker had early leaned toward a Castro retaliation theory of the Kennedy murder. His Subcommittee staff, on a deadline and stuck in Washington with only the file records and testimony to rely on, was structuring its report along the same theory. Yet as I discovered information which took me in another direction, Schweiker encouraged me to pursue the evidence wherever it led.

In Miami, my attention was first drawn to a diverse collection of individuals who once had, or still did have, an association with the CIA and anti-Castro activity. Most had the means, motivation and opportunity to be considered suspects in the Kennedy assassination. They all denied having any connection with the assassination, although a few admitted they would have liked to have killed, to use their remarkably similar phrase, "that fuckin' traitor." Such honesty, however, never allayed my suspicions.

It was amazing how, as soon as word of my new job had gotten around the right circles in Miami, offers of help and sources of information began rushing in. Calling me regularly were independent researchers, journalists, private investigators and individuals whose means of support I could never figure out. There were whispered meetings with anonymous informants in the backs of dark bars in Little Havana. There were meetings in parks along Biscayne Bay. The telephone often rang in the middle of the night and a Spanish-accented voice would tip me off about the strange behavior of a certain individual in November of 1963. My files began to grow with hundreds of names and my mind spun with the attempt to keep track of information involving scores of interlinked Cuban groups. Slowly, too, I began recognizing that some of the names coming to me, some of the sources of information contacting me, were the same as those I had come across in the Warren Commission files and the stacks of FBI reports. They were names which had popped up immediately after the Kennedy assassination. And now, strangely enough, here they were again, after all these years. One of them was a cocky bantam of a man named Mitchell Livingston WerBell III.*

Mitch WerBell was an arms dealer who ran a "farm" outside of Atlanta that was really a training camp for professional killers—including police and military types, terrorists and antiterrorists, soldiers of fortune and mercenaries. WerBell may well have been the last of the true swashbucklers, a braggadocio and delightfully entertaining fellow.

WerBell was born in Philadelphia, the son of a wealthy, former Czarist calvary officer. ("My father dragged me all over the world," he told me. "I was raised in some of the best bars in Europe.") When World War II came, he wound up with the Office of Strategic Services (OSS), the forerunner of the CIA. Trained as a paratrooper and a guerrilla warfare expert, he established himself as a stalwart secret agent and came out of the China-Burma theater of operations a dues-paid life member of the Old Boys network of American secret intelligence—the superspy fraternity that included Allen Dulles, William Casey, Richard Helms and E. Howard Hunt, among others.

They don't come more colorful than Mitch WerBell. Seemingly eccentric, he was in his day a blasphemous, often boozy and always raucous bon vivant with a sly sense of humor. He wore a handlebar mustache from time to time, screwed a monocle in his eye and called himself Prince Eric Straf. He boastfully dubbed himself "Mitch the Fifth" after his multiple invocations of that Constitutional amendment before a Senate investigations subcommittee which was questioning him about his business relationship with Robert Vesco.

What drew my interest to WerBell was neither his color nor his

---

*Mitch WerBell and other figures from the heyday of anti-Castro activity were later profiled in greater detail in Warren Hinckle's and Bill Turner's *Deadly Secrets* [Thunder's Mouth Press, 1992].

wit; it was his business, his background and his associates. It appeared that Jack Ruby was involved in arms dealing and smuggling. So was Mitch WerBell. A passionate anti-Communist, WerBell had run a series of weapons manufacturing and marketing firms—principally Military Armament Corporation and its Washington-based parent, Quantum Ordnance Bankers—which supplied countries and select revolutionary groups around the world with advanced weaponry, including the Ingram M-11, a hand-held, quiet machine gun.

WerBell has been called a creative genius for his designs of noise suppressors for automatic weapons and for other "silent-kill" devices. He has also been termed the "principal supplier of the CIA's most sophisticated weapons."

Early in my investigation for Senator Schweiker, I had a long, all-day, liquor-sippin' session with Mitch WerBell in the gun-filled den on his farm in Powder Springs, Georgia. Between sips, he denied an association with the CIA. "I've always cooperated very closely," he said, "but I've never allowed them to pay me one goddamned dime. I don't need it."

Nevertheless, down through the years WerBell has popped up with uncanny consistency in operations which have had the imprimatur of the CIA, either overtly or covertly. He was all over Miami working with anti-Castro activists at the height of Kennedy's secret war against Cuba. He was in Guatemala when assassination teams swept through that country to bolster the reign of the military. He was in the Dominican Republic when the United States moved in to quash the Communist threat. In Venezuela, Uruguay, Chile, Greece, Cambodia, Thailand and Vietnam, WerBell always seemed to be passing through at the most opportune and exciting moments.

My prolific journalistic colleague, the aforementioned Andrew St. George, had taken a special interest in Mitch WerBell over the years and had cultivated a strange and unique relationship with the chesty little guy. St. George has written a number of magazine articles about WerBell, all very well done, politically insightful and perilously revealing, yet most of them are buried in publications with very little credible impact—pulp adventure or girlie magazines. Risky revelation is the last thing that WerBell should have desired, yet the close relationship between subject and journalist remained intact until WerBell's death in 1983. St. George remained a frequent guest at "the farm." (Once, however, WerBell became extremely upset at a St. George article in *Esquire* which revealed WerBell's plans to foment a coup d'état on the Bahaman island of Abaco in order to establish his own tax-free country. But it wasn't that revelation which most bothered the feisty arms dealer, it was the accompanying photo of WerBell attending to a shapely bikini-clad blonde lolling on a chaise longue. WerBell told me that photo almost wrecked his marriage.)

St. George's fascination with WerBell relates to, among other things, his concept of WerBell's role in history. Sometime in the early Fifties, St. George points out, assassination became an instrument of U.S. national policy: "It also became an important branch of our invisible government, a sizable business, and a separate technology involving weapons and devices the ordinary taxpayer paid billions for but was never permitted to see, except perhaps in the technicolor fantasies of James Bond flicks."

Thanks to the complicated technology of his silent-kill weapons, Mitch WerBell was central to the development of the talent with the capability to employ those weapons. Out of that talent came the "special teams" concept. Special teams are assassination teams.

It was the special team concept that the CIA used within its own bureaucratic structure—select individuals were stitched together into a tight, top-secret network outside their normal chain of command— to plan the Castro assassination attempts. But the first utilization of that concept had come in 1954 when, according to St. George, a deep-cover CIA team went off to Hanoi under Lt. Colonel Lucien Conein, one of WerBell's "closest lifelong friends." The Conein mission, code-named "Blackhawk," was to harass and decimate the new Communist rulers of North Vietnam. Its orders included the "elimination of Vietminh cadres." Subsequently, similar missions multiplied as CIA Clandestine Services sent out special teams with the authority to kill whenever "circumstances warranted." There were, among others, the "White Star Training Mission" in Laos, "Operation Lodestone" in Northern Thailand, and "Study Project Minimax" in certain disaffected ethnic regions of Indonesia. Then, in the early Sixties, with the CIA's employment of the hard-bitten hill tribesmen of North Burma, Laos and Southwestern China as "deep penetration" and "long-range reconnaissance" teams into Red China, came large-scale, top-secret U.S. intelligence operations involving unlimited license to kill. Mitch WerBell's business did very well in those days, and Thai King Phumiphon personally hand carved a tiny rosewood Buddha for him.

Besides his general association with assassination operations, there were other reasons why WerBell would interest an investigator probing the Kennedy murder, including his relationship with a few individuals who had popped up in the FBI's original investigation. There was Gerry Patrick Hemming, for instance, the ex-Marine deeply involved in anti-Castro activity, who later claimed he had contact with Lee Harvey Oswald in both California and Miami. Hemming was among those arrested at a training camp in the Florida Keys after

Kennedy's Cuban missile deal with Khrushchev. He also worked as a weapon salesman for Mitch WerBell.

Then there was WerBell's buddy Lucien Conein, whom he had known in his OSS days. "You've got to start with the premise that Lou Conein is crazy," said one of his former CIA bosses once. Crazy enough to always survive. A beefy, scarred, gnarled old grizzly of a man, Conein left Kansas City when he was seventeen to join the French Foreign Legion. In 1941 in France, he switched to the OSS and lived and fought with the notorious Corsican Brotherhood, which was then part of the Resistance. (Later, the Brotherhood became deeply involved in the drug trade and was considered much more effective and dangerous than its Sicilian counterpart, the Mafia.) Moving on to the Far East, Conein was part of an OSS team parachuted into Vietnam to fight the Japanese alongside the Vietminh. He then fought against the Vietminh with the "Blackhawk" operation, helped Ngo Dinh Diem consolidate his power in South Vietnam and then, in a policy turnaround, was the CIA's liaison with the cabal of generals who murdered Diem.

It was Conein's involvement with this last coup which led another old OSS cohort, E. Howard Hunt, to give him a call several years later. Hunt, by then, was working in the Nixon White House. Besides wanting Conein to release a group of phony telegrams which would have squarely blamed President Kennedy for the Diem assassination (Nixon then considered Edward Kennedy his prime political foe), he wanted Conein to run what was, ostensibly, the White House war against the international drug trade.

Conein got involved in a series of sensitive operations with Hunt, some of which, according to a later report in the *Washington Post*, "appear to have stretched so far over the boundaries of legality that they were undertaken in total secrecy." One of these, part of a program called "Gemstone," was "Operation Diamond," a large, secret organization which Bernard Barker was putting together for Hunt in Miami. Barker reportedly recruited some 200 former CIA Cuban agents and organized them into specialized groups for future operations. Among these were intelligence and counterintelligence units known as "Action Teams," the old CIA term for units with paramilitary skills, including assassination.

Then, in November, 1973, Conein got moved out of the White House—though not out from under White House command—to become chief of Special Operations for the Drug Enforcement Administration. He was to be part of Nixon's highly publicized nationwide police campaign, led by White House enforcers with special powers, to combat drug abuse.

It has been suggested that Nixon's antidrug campaign was, in actuality, a bid to establish his own intelligence network. It has also been suggested that it was exactly that bid which brought the sucker setup that was Watergate and Nixon's political assassination.

Assassination, of course, is the buzz word. It struck me, early on in my investigation of Kennedy's murder, how certain individuals who drew my attention for other reasons, would turn out to have some association with assassination operations in their past. More significantly, many of the individuals were connected with others who also drew my attention. The multiplicity of "coincidences" never failed to surprise me. For instance, my attention was drawn to Lucien Conein when I discovered his relationship with E. Howard Hunt, who had attracted my interest because of his activities with Miami's anti-Castro Cubans. When I first learned of Conein's OSS background, I wondered if he had crossed paths somewhere along the way with Mitch WerBell. Their paths, as it turned out, were interlocked.

When Conein set up his Special Operations branch of the DEA, he recruited at least a dozen field operatives from the CIA and set them up in a safe house, an office suite in the La Salle Building on Connecticut Avenue in Washington. The reason for operating outside of DEA headquarters was because the branch was developing a very special plan, which included assassinating the key drug suppliers in Mexico. The question has been raised by syndicated columnist Jack Anderson, among others, of whether or not the White House Plumbers group was at some point developing an assassination capability—not as a foreign policy weapon but for domestic political reasons. (Anderson claimed that a contract was put out on him at one time.) At any rate, the Connecticut Avenue office was funded not by the DEA but by the CIA. Mitch WerBell has admitted that he was in business there with two former CIA men manufacturing ultrasophisticated assassination devices.

So there was much to discuss (or try to), in my meeting with Mitch WerBell that long Georgia day in his gun-filled den, although it turned out to be a verbal *paso doble* with a drunk—or a man who acted drunk. By the time I got to him, WerBell was coming off a long bout with the booze, the result of being caught between the pressures of a few Congressional investigating committees probing his intelligence, arms and drug connections and the even tougher squeeze by Federal agencies he worked for who wanted him to keep his mouth shut. So although we spent several hours talking, WerBell was determined to dance drunkenly around my key areas of interest.

"There's a helluva lot I ain't said yet," he blathered at one point, "and there's a helluva lot I ain't gonna say yet" At times he claimed loss of memory: "I've been in so many places, so many countries, so many fuckin' revolutions, it's beginning to get all mixed up in my mind.''

Yet the transcript of the tape I made during that session with WerBell reveals, despite the staccato verbal ellipses he drunkenly affected, some interesting responses. He admitted his involvement with some Castro assassination attempts (''I was sittin' in Miami with a goddamned million dollars in cash for the guy who was gonna take Fidel out''), but disclaimed any knowledge of the Kennedy murder. ''Now I didn't like Jack Kennedy,'' he said. ''I thought he was a shit to begin with. But I was certain not to be involved in the assassination of an American president, for Christsakes!''

WerBell also denied any gun smuggling or business dealings with Jack Ruby, but half admitted a contact. First he said he had no connection, then added: ''And the reason we didn't . . . I think we may have had an incoming . . . but we don't play with people like that. I mean, it's as simple as that. This guy Ruby, he called, I didn't know who the hell he was, but that was years ago. . . .'' WerBell then lapsed into a drunken mumble.

Later, when I was with the House Assassinations Committee, I thought it might have been fruitful if the Committee, with its subpoena power and power to grant immunity, had called WerBell for formal questioning. But Mitchell Livingston WerBell III was just another one of the characters who didn't fit into the game plan.

NINE

A FUNNY KIND OF GUY

*A*NOTHER PERSON WHO early on in my investigation popped up as a result of his intelligence connections was Frank Fiorini Sturgis, one of E. Howard Hunt's cohorts in the Watergate burglary. Of all the characters I've met in my reporting and investigating career, Sturgis is one of the most intriguing—and that's saying a lot. Sturgis seems to be an easy guy to get to know—he's outspoken, talkative, bluntly candid, usually quite visible; in fact, he frequently injects himself into the public spotlight. At the latest check, he's still very much involved in anti-Castro activity with the dwindling number of militant Cubans remaining in Miami. I spent a lot of time with Frank Sturgis but I haven't figured him out yet.

The names of both E. Howard Hunt and Frank Sturgis had been prominently in the news in connection with the Kennedy assassination long before I joined Senator Schweiker's investigation. A small group of assassination researchers had contended that two of the three men in certain photographs taken in Dealey Plaza on November 22nd, 1963, bore "striking resemblances" to Hunt and Sturgis. The men were reportedly derelicts, or "tramps," as the press came to call them, and were discovered in a boxcar in the railroad yard behind the grassy knoll above Dealey Plaza. (The House Assassinations Committee would later conduct extensive acoustics tests which indicated that at least four shots had been fired—one from the knoll area.) While being taken to police headquarters, the tramps were escorted across Dealey Plaza, where news photographers took several pictures of them. Police later released the tramps and for years no records of their identities were found.

Because of the publicity generated by the researchers, the contention that two of the tramps were Sturgis and Hunt was examined by the Rockefeller Commission in early 1975. (President Ford had appointed the Commission that January to probe possible illegal CIA activities within the United States.) The Rockefeller Commission relied on comparative photo analysis performed by the same FBI expert who did all the Warren Commission's analysis and then concluded that the men in the photographs were not Sturgis and Hunt.

About the time Schweiker began his investigation, a book was published which raised the contention again. Titled *Coup d'état in America** and written by Michael Canfield and Alan J. Weberman with a foreword by Texas Congressman Henry B. Gonzalez, the book incorporated a novel device: It came with positive transparencies of Sturgis and Hunt designed to be overlaid on photos of the tramps. Superimposed, the images did, indeed, bear striking similarities.

I would later discover, however, from my experience with the House Assassinations Committee, that the science of photo comparison and analysis is an exceptionally inconclusive technique. The Assassinations Committee wound up spending $83,154 on it and came up with results which, in some instances, are totally worthless.

In the Assassinations Committee's investigation, not only were photographs of Sturgis and Hunt submitted to a panel of experts for analysis and comparison, photos of others who might be one of the tramps were examined as well. The panel concluded that Sturgis and Hunt were not the individuals in the photographs. It did say, however, that the tramp who resembled Hunt could very well be a fellow named Fred Lee Chrisman, a right-wing activist implicated in the Kennedy assassination during the Garrison investigation in New Orleans. When those results came in, investigators were frantically sent out to track down Chrisman's whereabouts on November 22nd, 1963. (He had since died.) They came back with official records and eyewitness affidavits saying Chrisman was on the West Coast teaching school the day Kennedy was assassinated. So much for the conclusiveness of photo analysis.

What was particularly interesting, however, was the panel's conclusions in its comparison of photos of Frank Sturgis with those of the tramps. It used two basic comparative techniques. One, "metric traits," was a comparison of the measurements of six facial features and their metric relationships; the other, "morphological differences," was simply whether or not various facial features were shaped

---

*Republished in 1992 by Quick American Archives, San Francisco.

the same. The panel concluded that the average deviation between one tramp's features and Sturgis's was "low enough to make it impossible to rule out Sturgis on the basis of metric traits alone." However, the panel said, the morphological differences indicated that Sturgis was not the tramp. In other words, Sturgis just didn't look like the tramp. (The hair and hairline were different, it said, and so were the nose, the chin and the degree of ear projection.)

The Assassinations Committee staffer in charge of organizing the photo panel's work was an exceptionally competent research attorney named Jane Downey, who was a good detail person. One day she came to me and asked me to help gather some of the photographs which would be sent to the panel. I asked her to find out whether or not the experts would take into consideration the possibility that the tramps might be wearing sophisticated disguises. That, in fact, was likely if they weren't just drifters in the wrong place at the wrong time. (As a member of the White House Plumbers, E. Howard Hunt had obtained disguises from the CIA's Technical Services Bureau and used them on more than one job.) Downey promised she would ask the photo analysts about the use of disguises.

Several days later Downey told me she had checked with the photo analysts. "I'm told that there is no way they can tell if disguises were used," she said.

I was surprised. "In other words," I said, "if the tramps were in disguise there would be no way the analysts could tell who they really are?"

"That's what I'm told," said Downey.

"Then why do a photo comparison at all?" I asked. Downey just shrugged her shoulders. "Well," I said, "I hope that point is mentioned in the final report."

"I'm sure it will be," said Downey.

Nowhere in the House Committee's final report, nor in the appendix volume dealing with the photographic evidence, is that fact mentioned.

In my own mind, I've never resolved the question of whether or not Frank Sturgis looked like one of the tramps in Dealey Plaza. There are a couple of photos which have strong similarities, others with few. The same could be said of the Hunt comparison. (My initial interest in both men, however, was not predicated on whether or not they were the Dealey Plaza tramps.)

When the Rockefeller Commission issued its conclusion that Sturgis and Hunt were not in Dallas on November 22nd, 1963, it raised more questions than it resolved. (At the time, I didn't realize how suspicious I should have been about the Commission's report in general. It was later revealed that then-Vice President Nelson Rockefeller really didn't want the CIA to air all its dirty linen and, at one point, quietly called in Director William Colby and urged him not to tell all. Rockefeller, it turned out, had earlier been a member of the White House's Operations Coordinating Board which had cleared some of the illegal CIA activity the Commission was investigating.)

Although the Rockefeller Commission report claimed that Sturgis and Hunt seemed to have legitimate alibis for their whereabouts on November 22nd, 1963, it ultimately concluded: "It cannot be determined with certainty where Hunt and Sturgis actually were on the day of the assassination."

Frank Sturgis absolutely knows where he was on the day *after* the Kennedy assassination. He says the FBI found him at his home in Miami. "I had FBI agents all over my house," he said. "They told me I was one person they felt had the capabilities to do it. They said, 'Frank, if there's anybody capable of killing the President of the United States, you're the guy that can do it.' "

I spent a lot of time with Frank Sturgis, especially during the Schweiker investigation. He had not been long out of prison from his Watergate sentence when we first met and I spent an evening at his home. Afterwards, we were in contact often. Sometimes he would call and we would chat for hours. Frequently, we met at a snack shop or hotel coffee shop. He was always very direct, very outspoken and, I believe, a lot more polished and sophisticated than the obscenity-prone, rough-hewn and undereducated character he sometimes projects. In talking about people he knows, he often refers to someone as his "close friend," but no one really gets close to Frank Sturgis.

He was then in his early fifties and tending toward obesity, a far cry from the muscular figure he once was. Sturgis has led a thousand lives, maybe more. He was born Frank Angelo Fiorini in Norfolk, Virginia, but his parents separated when he was an infant and he grew up with his mother's family in Philadelphia's Germantown. (He would later change his name to his stepfather's, Frank Anthony Sturgis, when his mother remarried. Howard Hunt gave the name of "Sturgis" to the main character in one of his many pulp novels.) Frank Sturgis turned seventeen two days after Japan bombed Pearl Harbor and he immediately dropped out of high school to join the Marines. He was shipped out to the Pacific jungles where he volunteered for the toughest unit in the Marines, the First Raider Battalion—the legendary Edson's Raiders. He learned how to kill silently with his bare hands. He infiltrated enemy encampments, sloshed through amphibious landings and was air-dropped on commando raids. Guadalcanal, Iwo Jima, Okinawa, three serious combat wounds, malaria, jaundice and, in the end, "exhaustion and possible psychoneurosis" and a stay at the Sun Valley Naval Medical Center before his discharge in 1945.

After the war, Sturgis was a plainclothes cop with the Norfolk Police, a part-time student at William & Mary College, and manager of a few bars. He trained as a radio gunner in the Naval Reserves, crewed as a merchant seaman, and did a two-year stint with the U.S. Army in Germany where he served with the Armed Forces Security Agency, was married, widowed, remarried, divorced and married again.

Sturgis claims he got involved in Cuban activities in the early Fifties when he came to Miami to visit an uncle who was married to a Cuban. That's how he got friendly with exiled former Cuban President Carlos Prío, he says. Prío was a multimillionaire who, at the time, was funding mountain rebel Fidel Castro's guerrilla war against General Batista.**

It was through Prío, Sturgis told me, that he was infiltrated into Cuba to join Castro in the mountains. Soon he was a trusted aide, an emissary for Castro on arms deals all over the United States and Latin America, a daring pilot who flew loads of weapons into dangerous mountain airstrips. He became friendly with another daredevil pilot, Pedro Díaz Lanz, and when, after the revolution, Castro appointed Díaz Lanz chief of the Rebel Air Force, Sturgis was named the Air Force's director of security. Nine months after Castro took power, Díaz Lanz and Sturgis publicly decried Castro's Communism, and fled to Miami. A month later they were dropping propaganda leaflets over Havana.

Frank Sturgis says he was never an official paid agent of the Central Intelligence Agency, and the CIA has confirmed that proclamation. Yet Sturgis, while he could not remember the first name of his first wife in his testimony before the House Assassinations Committee, recalled that it was a Friday in 1958 in Santiago, Cuba, that he made his first contact with a CIA agent, while he was still fighting with Castro. Then during the Bay of Pigs and during the heyday of the CIA's secret war against Castro, Sturgis used equipment, flew planes and directed assault craft which were paid for by the Agency. He has admitted that the B-25 he flew on his first leaflet-drop was later repaired with $10,000 which came from E. Howard Hunt, then one of the CIA's local paymasters.

It was Sturgis's relationship with Hunt that had early drawn my attention during my Kennedy assassination investigation. However, both men testified under oath to the Rockefeller Commission that they

---

**Prío would later be convicted of arms smuggling with a Texan named Robert McKeown. After the Kennedy assassination, McKeown told the FBI that he was approached by Jack Ruby about a deal to sell military equipment to Castro. A week before I had scheduled to call Prío for an interview, he went to the side of his Miami Beach home, sat on a chaise outside the garage and shot himself in the heart. The newspapers reported he had financial problems.

first met just prior to the Watergate caper—Hunt said in 1972; Sturgis said in late '71 or early '72. But that seemed strange in view of their deep involvement in Miami's anti-Castro activities in the early Sixties. Sturgis claimed that although he had known of "Eduardo," all his CIA contacts and funding came through Hunt's assistant, Bernard Barker.

There's a lot of circumstantial evidence which contradicts that contention. Sturgis admitted he worked closely with the CIA's top Cuban leader, Manuel Artime, and I have spoken with witnesses who often saw them together in Little Havana. Artime was very close to and in frequent contact with CIA liaison Hunt. In *Give Us This Day*, Hunt himself claims his attention was drawn to the daring leaflet drop of Pedro Díaz Lanz, and he quickly made arrangements to meet with the counterrevolutionary hero. Hunt however, writes nothing of Díaz Lanz's copilot and constant companion.

A few years before the Rockefeller Commission, in October, 1972, while Sturgis was awaiting his Watergate sentence, Andrew St. George interviewed him in his Miami home. It was before the tramp photos were publicized, before the cries for another Kennedy assassination investigation began to peak, before the Rockefeller Commission was formed. St. George was an old friend from the days with Castro in the mountains and Sturgis was glad to see the gregarious Hungarian. He was still stung by his setup at Watergate and the black headlines which made him appear an inept and bungling burglar, and—according to St. George—he blurted out the real story behind the break-in. A few months later, St. George visited Sturgis in a Washington, D.C., jail. "I will never leave this jail alive," he says Sturgis told him, "if what we discussed about Watergate does not remain between us. If you attempt to publish what I've told you, I am a dead man."

In August, 1974, St. George published his interview with Sturgis in *True* magazine. He quotes Sturgis as saying: "The Bay of Pigs—hey, was one sweet mess. I met Howard Hunt that year; he was the political officer of the exile brigade. Bernard Barker was Hunt's right-hand man, his confidential clerk—his body servant, really; that's how I met Barker."

Sturgis today denies he ever said that and curses St. George vehemently.

As I said, my first interview with Frank Sturgis came not long after he was released from his Watergate sentence and he was keeping things relatively low-key. What particularly struck me about that interview was Sturgis's Archie Bunker-like directness. That night he talked effusively, chain-smoking and drinking Coke. (Sturgis is a heavy smoker, but never touches any kind of alcoholic beverage.) He spoke of his early days with Castro, his appointment by Castro at one point to oversee the gambling casinos before the Mob was thrown out of Cuba, and of his later anti-Castro activities. Nor did he hesitate to admit his disgust with President Kennedy for his Cuban missile deal with the Russians. (Sturgis, you may recall, was one of six pilots given special warnings by the Federal Aviation Administration for making raids over Cuba at the time Kennedy was in the delicate negotiations. Sturgis was also, with Gerry Patrick Hemming, cofounder of the International Anti-Communist Brigade, some of whose members were arrested at their paramilitary training site on No Name Key after the missile crisis.)

Sturgis said he thought the Kennedy assassination was definitely a conspiracy (he spoke of the possible motivations of the anti-Castro groups), that Oswald was a patsy and that the Government agencies— the FBI, the Secret Service and the CIA—were all involved in a cover-up. He said he once refused to join the CIA, even though it gave him an application, because he thought it was infiltrated at its highest ranks with double agents—"possibly the same people who conspired to kill Kennedy." He said his theory was that the assassination itself involved groups of agents in Russia's KGB, Cuban intelligence and the CIA. Actually, as Sturgis rambled on and around in circles, there wasn't a conspiracy theory he didn't espouse. By the end of the evening, my head was reeling.

Several months after that interview, the Schweiker Subcommittee Report was released, with the Castro retaliation theory as its strong theme. Now, apparently, Sturgis knew which way to push.

The evening after the report was issued, Sturgis telephoned. He said he had just run into an old friend, a "guy with the Company," who had "revived" his mind about something he had "completely forgot" to tell me over the months we had been in touch. Sturgis now recalled an inside informant telling him about a meeting in Havana that occurred just about two months before the Kennedy assassination. At the meeting were a number of high-ranking men, including Castro, his brother Raul, Ramiro Valdez, the chief of Cuban intelligence, Che Guevara and his secretary, Tanya, another Cuban officer, an American known as "El Mexicano" and—oh, yeah—Jack Ruby. And the meeting dealt with plotting the assassination of John F. Kennedy.

Oh. That's what Sturgis had "completely forgot" to tell me. Just a bit of incidental information, replete with details of the plotters' names. "Hey, Frank," I said, "I'm glad someone revived your mind about that."

Incredible. Frank Sturgis was out pushing Castro-did-it stories again. And as highly unlikely as the story appeared, it did have a sophisticated edge and, as Sturgis was quick to point out, a hint of documentary evidence to back it up. But in fact, Sturgis's story was a dressed-up version of one that first came up during the Warren Commission investigation.

The original story surfaced via a Miami-based investigator named Al Tarabochia, a strong right-winger who worked for the Senate Internal Security subcommittee. Tarabochia wrote a memo, which somehow wound up with the Warren Commission, that told about a Cuban exile source who said he had received a letter from a relative in Cuba. The letter contained the information that "the assassin of President Kennedy's assassin" had visited Cuba "last year." (Later, I would track down the original writer of the letter in Miami, who would say that her information was given to her by someone she didn't recall.) At any rate, Sturgis's "new" hot tip of Ruby being in Cuba seemed to be based on a report that was untraceable.

In fact, immediately after the Kennedy assassination, Frank Sturgis was involved in other "hot tips" which also proved to be without foundation. One involved a reporter named James Buchanan who wrote an article for the Pompano Beach *Sentinel* quoting Sturgis as saying that Oswald had visited Miami in November, 1962, to contact Miami-based supporters of Fidel Castro. The article also stated that, while in Miami, Oswald was in telephone contact with Cuban intelligence. About that time, another story began circulating which indicated that Oswald had demonstrated in Miami's Bayfront Park with a group from the Fair Play for Cuba Committee and had gotten in a fracas with Jerry Buchanan, the brother of the reporter. The FBI traced both stories, found they were untrue, and eventually contacted Frank Sturgis, who denied he had anything to do with them. The FBI reports wound up as Warren Commission documents. One of those documents reveals that both James and Jerry Buchanan were officers in Sturgis's International Anti-Communist Brigade.

I was intrigued by the question of why Frank Sturgis had so early injected himself into the Kennedy assassination investigation. I was intrigued as well by the character of the information he circulated, imbued as it was with just the right amount of documented detail. (For instance, there really was a fracas in Bayfront Park, although Oswald was nowhere in sight.)

There were, however, other moments which made me think I was taking Frank Sturgis much too seriously. I recall one evening chatting with him on the telephone about someone I was checking into, a fellow who had been described to me as "one of the CIA's best-trained Cuban operatives." When I asked about him, Sturgis talked for a while and then said he had a friend who could tell me a lot more. The friend—I'll call him Paul—was an American who had spent seven years in Castro's prisons, charged with plotting to blow up a building that housed Russian agents whom Castro visited regularly. Paul had operated a small bar in Havana as a front, was married to a Cuban who worked for the CIA, and was deeply involved in Miami's anti-Castro activity. Sturgis said he would like me to meet Paul but, because Paul might refuse, it had to be set up to appear as a chance encounter. Sturgis said he would be having breakfast with Paul the next Saturday morning at the Westward Ho restaurant in Little Havana and that I should just "coincidentally" stroll in. "He don't know you're gonna be there, so when you get there I'll just put him on a little bit," said Sturgis. "We're old friends, I've known him for years. It'll be funny. We kid with each other a lot. He's a funny guy."

I spotted Sturgis and his friend sitting at a back booth as soon as I walked into the Westward Ho. Sturgis had his back to the door. I strolled up beside him and slapped him on the shoulder.

"Hey, Frank!" I greeted him, trying to fake sudden recognition. "Howya been? What've you been doing? Haven't seen you around lately."

Sturgis looked up with a surprised, yet blank expression.

"Hey, I know you," he said.

"Sure you do," I said, sitting down beside him.

Sturgis strained for a puzzled expression. "Where do I know you from?" he pondered aloud.

"Frank, how can you forget?" I said, continuing to play along.

"Now wait a minute, don't tell me," said Sturgis. "I'll think of it." He cupped his chin in his hand and donned a look of deep reflection. He appeared to be a terrible actor and I couldn't keep a silly grin from crossing my face. Paul just stared back and forth at us, obviously wondering what the hell was going on.

I thought Sturgis would keep up the act forever, pounding his forehead and mumbling a variety of concocted names. "Oh, I-know-I-know-I-know," he kept repeating in mock frustration, "but I'm drawing a blank wall!"

I couldn't restrain my laughter, more at his display of dramatics than at Paul's puzzlement. Finally, I reached across the table and introduced myself by name to Paul. He shook my hand and then turned to Sturgis. "Well, *now* do you remember who he is?" he asked. Sturgis feigned a mild convulsion of embarrassed laughter. "Oh, sure, sure," he admitted, "I really know who he is. I was just puttin' you on."

"Oh," Paul said, with a smile on his face but obviously not getting the point of the charade.

"Gaeton here," Sturgis said, still laughing, "is a friend of mine who is with the, uh, whattaya callit, you know, the Government committee that's looking into the assassination of John F. Kennedy."

Paul didn't miss a beat. "Oh," he said, "you mean the guy you killed!"

Sturgis's face suddenly froze for a split-second. The smile was gone. Then he shook his head and smiled again. "Oh, yeah, sure," he said, laughing.

I looked at Sturgis and started laughing also. He was right. Paul was a funny guy.

TEN

HIGH NOON IN
NEW YORK

A CHARACTER LIKE Frank Sturgis illustrates some of the dilemmas in investigating the Kennedy assassination: He can't be ignored. He is, by his own admission, a prime suspect. He had the ability and the motivation and was associated with individuals and groups who considered—and even employed—assassination as a method to achieve their goals. Any investigation would have to devote some time and resources to Sturgis. But there were other, similar characters who injected themselves into the investigation and drained time and resources far beyond any valid justification. In some of those cases, I thought I caught a glimpse of an intelligence connection and, in one, there was something more: A force deliberately manipulating the investigation into turns so weird and wild I sometimes wondered if what I was doing was serious reality or if I had been lured into a carnival and thrown onto the loop-the-loop.

The self-proclaimed former mistress of Fidel Castro, Marita Lorenz was a spin-off of Frank Sturgis, in more ways than one. As a result of my "discovering" her during my investigation for Senator Schweiker, she flashed into national notoriety and periodically reignited that flash for years afterwards. She became front-page news in the New York papers, headlined supermarket tabloids and hit most of the network TV celebrity shows, including *Good Morning America*, *Geraldo* and *A Current Affair*.

Lorenz was a centerpiece of Mark Lane's best-selling book, *Plausible Denial* [Thunder's Mouth Press, 1991] and, almost eighteen years after our first encounter, got herself a feature in, of all places, *Vanity Fair*. She shot to celebrity status on the strength of her revelation that she was unwittingly involved with the assassination team that killed President Kennedy. Strangely enough, in my initial interview with her she never mentioned a word about it. But that interview did kick off a bizarre series of events that would track their way from the Schweiker Subcommittee probe right through to the House Assassinations Committee investigation. There it exploded into a drama that, I now suspect, was as well orchestrated as any success-ful comic opera. It consumed a lot of the Committee's time and resources and achieved its covert goal of discrediting a key witness: Marita Lorenz herself. And that, in the end, is what gives it signifi-cance.

A "curvy, black-haired . . . American Mata Hari" is how New York *Daily News* reporter Paul Meskil described Marita Lorenz in his six-part series called "Secrets of the CIA." Almost a year later, a few months after I began working for Schweiker and was beginning to spend time with Frank Sturgis, I stumbled across Meskil's articles. His series, sparked at the time by the Rockefeller Commission and Church Committee hearings on the CIA, dealt mostly with the Agen-cy's role in anti-Castro activities and the action out of its Miami JM/WAVE station at the height of Kennedy's secret war. But Meskil had devoted an entire article each to Sturgis and Marita Lorenz. (He called Sturgis a "bit player in the Watergate drama" but "a real-life James Bond when he did his big jobs for the CIA.") And, in fact, it was through Sturgis that Meskil first learned of Lorenz. Sturgis had casually mentioned that he helped Castro's former mistress escape from Cuba but, strangely enough, could not remember her name. Later, Meskil recalled an article written in the early Sixties in *Confi-dential,* the defunct forerunner of supermarket sleaze sheets ("I may be the only guy in the world with a collection of old *Confidential* magazines," brags Meskil). "Castro Raped My Teenage Daughter!" had to be about the same girl Sturgis had mentioned, Meskil figured. He tracked Marita down and found her living on New York's Upper East Side.

Flashing his prodigious talent for lively tabloid writing, Meskil portrayed Marita Lorenz as a quixotic seeker of adventure and ro-mance—well, at least an opportunist. She was the vivacious nineteen-year-old daughter of an American mother and a German father who was captain of the luxury liner *MS Berlin* when it cruised into Havana harbor in February, 1959, one month after Fidel Castro came to power. Almost immediately after the *Berlin* dropped its anchor, out came an official Cuban launch carrying the big *barbudo* himself, along with a platoon of little *barbudos*, still in their rumpled victory celebration fatigues, dangling grenades and shoulder-slung machine guns. Bejeweled grande dames in evening gowns, thinking they were being raided, their minds flashing with visions of piratic atrocities, screamed, fainted or ran for cocktails, their dinner-jacketed husbands following suit. (Well, according to Meskil's colorful account, anyway.) "I am a friend," Castro shouted, waving in the manner of a non-hostile native. "I like Americans." (Why Castro should shout that at a boatload of Germans, Meskil doesn't explain.) Meskil then goes on to report Marita's story about how Captain Heinrich Lorenz invites the welcoming party to stay for dinner and how, while seated next to little Marita, the feral-eyed Fidel is smitten by the time the Baked Alaska comes around. He offers her a job if she stays in Havana—ever since he won the Revolution his fan mail has picked up and he is in dire need of a secretary. ("My father and I both laughed," Marita recalled, but he probably didn't think it was funny.) No, Captain Heinrich says, little Marita must go back to Germany and finish her education. Marita smiles like a dutiful daughter but, behind Daddy's back, slips Fidel a note with the address of her brother's apartment in New York where she'll be staying for a while after the ship heads back.

A few weeks later, a couple of Cuban officers knock on her brother's door with a message from their leader. Fidel's backlog of mail is worse than he thought, especially with letters from Germans who need to be answered in their mother tongue. Fidel is desperate, he needs her. A Cubana Airlines plane is waiting to bring her back to Havana. Marita does not suggest that Castro might solve his problem with a Kelly Girl. Instead, she hops on the plane.

"I was very idealistic then," she told Meskil. "I was going on an adventure and to my first job. I was going to help the new government. Instead I became Castro's plaything."

It wasn't quite a life of luxury that she lived with Fidel—in fact, the Bearded One was a bit of a slob. And being permanently confined to Castro's living-and-working quarters on the 24th floor of the Havana Hilton eventually became a drag to the teenager. "All I could do was read books, study Spanish, listen to the radio or go on the balcony and look out over Havana," she told Meskil. She couldn't even go shopping for clothes, she said. Castro outfitted her in fashionable olive-green fatigues and gave her a lieutenant's star. What more did a girl need?

Then one night when she was with Castro and his bodyguards in the lobby of the Riviera Hotel, a rugged, wavy-haired fellow wearing a rebel uniform and the insignia of a captain in the Cuban Air Force sidled up to her when Castro wasn't looking and whispered in English: "I know about you."

"Can you help me get out of here?" Marita asked.

"Yes, I'm with the American Embassy," said the stranger. "I'll get you out."

And this, as Meskil wrote, "was her introduction to Commandante Frank Fiorini (later known as Frank Sturgis), Castro confidant and hired agent for the U.S. Central Intelligence Agency."

Sturgis eventually did get Lorenz out, but not before turning her into a spy. She began systematically scavenging among the papers, documents, files and maps that Castro had strewn about his suite and slipping them to Sturgis. "Frank said, 'Get all the data you can,' and I did. I was a regular Mata Hari," she told Meskil, unaware that she was writing his headline.

According to this story, Lorenz became terribly sick one day and Sturgis arranged for two Cuban officers working with him to slip her out of the Hilton while Castro was away. They put her on a flight to New York. Shortly afterwards, Sturgis himself flew out of Cuba with Air Force Chief Pedro Díaz Lanz and set up a base of anti-Castro operations in Miami.

The story then goes on to tell how in early 1960 when Lorenz, recovered from her illness, joined Sturgis in Florida "and volunteered for a mission that meant certain death if she was caught." She told Meskil the details of flying back to Havana in the guise of a tourist, checking into a fleabag hotel to change into her old rebel uniform and (having known Castro would be out of town) slipping back up to his suite in the Havana Hilton. ("Passing the desk was the main thing that bothered me because the desk clerks knew me. I had changed my hair style . . . nobody seemed to notice me . . . I had a snub-nosed .38 caliber Detective Special clipped to the inside of my waistband.") Once again, she scavenged the suite and fled back to Miami with packs of files, documents and maps, one of which had hand-drawn circles marking areas miles away from any population center. Sturgis was waiting at the airport. She didn't know the worth of what she took but Sturgis later told her that "the United States Government is very happy." Three years later, Lorenz told Meskil, another Government agent told her that the maps were "the original groundwork plans" for Soviet missile sites.

That, Lorenz told Meskil at that time, was her only mission back to Havana. She did talk about other anti-Castro exploits out of Miami, but said she was only on three quick boat trips, delivering guns and supplies to anti-Castro guerrillas.

As dramatically as Meskil portrayed Marita Lorenz's exploits, they weren't especially sensational or relevant; in fact, her story seemed quite plausible. Meskil had included enough documentation to give it legitimacy, including a photograph of Marita with Fidel. It was that aura of credibility that sparked my interest in one periodic Miami occurrence that Lorenz had described. She said that when funds were needed for an anti-Castro operation, it came from a CIA man she knew only as "Eduardo." Sturgis would meet him at a safe house from time to time to get cash.

"Years later," Meskil reported, "while reading about the Watergate break-in, Marita saw a newspaper photo of former CIA man E. Howard Hunt and immediately recognized him as the elusive 'Eduardo.' She also recognized a picture of Sturgis, whom she had known as Frank Fiorini."

Meskil hadn't realized how important that revelation was, but I saw it as possibly confirming my suspicion of perjury by both Hunt and Sturgis before the Rockefeller Commission. It also intensified the question of why both men would want to cover up the fact that they were close associates in the early Sixties. If I could get a confirmation from Lorenz and arrange for her to give sworn testimony before Senator Schweiker's Subcommittee, it might be used to put pressure on Hunt and Sturgis. It might even be the first step toward finding out what they really knew about the Kennedy assassination.

I would later discover that the dominant characteristics in Marita Lorenz's life have been change and turmoil. Despite the fact that she was living in a luxury apartment when I first met her, Lorenz and her fourteen-year-old daughter, the illegitimate child of former Venezuelan President Marcos Pérez Jímenez, were collecting welfare from the State of New York. (Lorenz had met the wealthy ex-dictator in Miami in 1961, two years before he was arrested and deported to Spain. "Marcos said he wanted to meet me because he knew I was Fidel's girl," she told me. "He chased me and I finally gave in." Years later, on the *Geraldo* TV show, she would claim Jímenez was "an assignment" from the CIA.*) In 1970, Lorenz had married the manager of an apartment building near the United Nations. Since many of the units were rented to members of the Soviet and Soviet bloc U.N.

---

*A Miami FBI report dated October, 1962, and labeled as an investigation into the "White Slave Traffic Act," reveals another version of her first encounter with the ex-dictator. According to the report, Lorenz complained that she had been threatened by a Ruben ("Rubenzito") Prats as a result of an incident that had taken place in May, 1961. She had been introduced to Prats by "Pepe" Acosta, a pimp who worked out of Miami Beach's Bel Aire Hotel, one of mobster Santos Trafficante's hangouts. Prats had sent her to a party at a Biscayne Boulevard apartment where she and a "few other Latin girls," as the FBI report described them, were to entertain a "Mr. Diaz." Lorenz claimed she left the party early but, according to the FBI report, "Prats demanded $75 from Lorenz, stating he knew she received $100." Lorenz denied she received any money from "Mr. Diaz," but did admit she later received a message from him asking her to visit him. "Mr. Diaz" turned out to be Pérez Jímenez. "Thereafter," said the FBI report, "Lorenz became sexually involved with Pérez Jímenez."

delegations, the FBI recruited her husband as a paid informant. According to his FBI contact, Marita herself volunteered, going through the nightly trash in search of useful information. She eventually split with her husband, remarried and then took up with a Mob enforcer, who ensconced her in the upper East Side digs. Unfortunately, after setting her up, her paramour was irregular in providing financial support, probably due to the nature of his business. However, Marita had managed to survive over the years by being a paid informant for local and Federal police agencies, including the FBI, U.S. Customs and the DEA. For Marita Lorenz, life was lived on the edge.

When I first approached Lorenz, I never mentioned my interest in the Kennedy assassination. I was simply an investigator for Senator Schweiker of the Church Committee who was interested in the relationship between the anti-Castro Cuban militants and the intelligence community. (At the time, the Church Committee was getting a good deal of media attention with its revelations of the CIA's attempts to kill Castro.)

Lorenz was cooperative and apparently more candid with me than she had been with Meskil. She confirmed what she had told Meskil about her relationship with Castro and showed me enough documentation, including photographs, that I believed her. She said, however, the reason she left Castro was that she had become pregnant and was forced to have an abortion. Originally she blamed Castro for the abortion but later decided it was arranged by his inner circle. Lorenz confirmed her secret mission to Havana to steal the documents and maps from Castro's Hilton suite for Sturgis. But she also said she made a second trip later on, this time to murder Castro. Sturgis was involved but wasn't the instigator. The idea, she said, came from his close associate Alex Rorke.

The story was that when Sturgis got Lorenz out of Cuba, she wound up in New York's Roosevelt Hospital, suffering from the effects of the sloppy abortion. Alex Rorke showed up and befriended her. He was a photographer, journalist, pilot, rabid anti-Communist, former FBI employee and the wealthy son-in-law of Sherman Billingsley, the celebrity owner of New York's famous Stork Club. Rorke also worked closely with Miami millionaire William Pawley, the ultra-right-winger who fronted and funded a number of Agency operations.**

**Rorke would later disappear after a mysterious plane flight that arrived in Mexico City on the same day that Oswald reportedly arrived. According to an FBI report, Rorke and his copilot Geoffrey Sullivan had left Miami in a rented twin-engine Beechcraft on September 24th, 1963, headed for Honduras for a "lobster-hauling business deal." That same day they arrived in Merida, Mexico. On September 27th, Rorke and Sullivan departed Merida and arrived in Mexico City, where they remained

Lorenz said that Rorke made the suggestion to kill Castro about two months after she returned to New York from her Havana trip for Sturgis. They then flew to Miami where Rorke and Sturgis put her up in a safe house and spent the next three weeks talking her into doing it. Lorenz said it was early January, 1960, when she returned to Havana with two poison capsules Sturgis had given her. Afraid she would be searched at the airport, she hid them in a jar of cold cream. Lorenz said Castro, obviously unaware that she had previously purloined his files, welcomed her warmly and asked her why she had run away. She said she had missed her mother and her home. After dinner, when Castro fell asleep on the bed, she went into the bathroom to retrieve the capsules and found they had melted into the cold cream. She said that Sturgis was very upset when she returned to Miami and chastised her for putting the pills into the cold cream. "Stupid, stupid, stupid," he said.

It was an incredible story and Sturgis himself later claimed it was true. But it was really of little importance to me in terms of the Kennedy assassination, so I steered the conversation to her anti-

---

for four days. On October 1st, Rorke and Sullivan flew back to Merida accompanied by "a nervous person who appears eager to resume flight," according to the FBI report. The trio then departed for Cozumel and, upon arriving, immediately took off again. It is unclear whether the third person was still with Rorke and Sullivan when they left Cozumel the last time, but the plane was never seen again. The rented Beechcraft had been due back on September 28th. An FBI report dated November 13th, 1963 notes that two wealthy New York right-wingers financed Rorke's venture, which was meant to be a bombing mission to Havana. (Against President Kennedy's directive banning such raids after the Cuban missile crisis, Rorke had already run one successful bombing mission on Havana on April 25th, 1963.) Later in November, the FAA said the CIA reported that the plane crashed in Cuba during Hurricane Flora. However, that hurricane didn't arrive in Cuba until a week after Rorke and Sullivan left Cozumel. I recently discovered a note to me written by Committee researcher Patricia Orr after an FBI file check. She reported that on October 24th, three weeks after the Beechcraft disappeared, a search party was organized by Frank Sturgis's cohort Gerry Patrick Hemming and fellow members of the International Anti-Communist Brigade. The search party set out in a DC-3 on October 31st and was ultimately unsuccessful. Hemming recently told me that Rorke and Sullivan's flight was part of a Castro assassination plan. The third person on the plane, said Hemming, was a anti-Castro veteran named Molina, who was to be infiltrated into Cuba to monitor Castro's movements for the hit teams that were to come in later. (A report dated January 11th, 1962, reveals that Miami Police's intelligence unit was notified by the Secret Service that a Rafael Anselmo Rodriquez Molins, known as "Rafael Molina," was a suspect in a plan to assassinate John F. Kennedy when he visited the family home in Palm Beach. Molina, said the report, was to contact Armando Lopez Estrada, a Miami Cuban later charged with smuggling guns and drugs while working for the CIA in the illegal Contra-supply network.) According to Hemming, meetings to plan the Castro assassination were held aboard a Guatemalan warship in dry dock at Miami Shipbuilding. The ship was to be used in recovering the hit teams after the assassination. Involvement of the Guatemalan government, claims Hemming, meant the CIA had to have coordinated, or even instigated, the mission.

Castro activities with Sturgis in Miami. Eventually she confirmed the story about seeing Sturgis receive money from "Eduardo." She specifically recalled one incident when she was with a group of Sturgis's pals heading down to the Florida Keys to launch a gunrunning mission to Cuba. She remembered it, she said, because they were all hungry and as they passed the farms and ranches of South Florida the men in the car started kidding her about shooting a horse and eating it. She said she got upset and shouted at them. It was then that Sturgis said he had forgotten something and he immediately headed back to Miami. "We turned all the way around," she said, "and went back to the little house and Eduardo had the money."

Lorenz said she saw Eduardo provide funds to the group at least three times. "Eduardo would come to the door and give Frank the money."

When I asked if she was certain that the man she saw was E. Howard Hunt, she said she was very certain. She had recognized him immediately when she saw his photo—along with Bernard Barker's and Sturgis's—in the newspapers when the Watergate story broke.

The day after I interviewed Lorenz in New York, I called her to reconfirm her statement that she had seen Hunt and Sturgis together in the early Sixties. She did, but as I was going over the details of that mission to the Keys and the backtrack to get money, it struck me that I had neglected to ask her who was with her and Sturgis on that mission.

Her recollection seemed a little fuzzy: "There was me, Frank, Patrick [Gerry Patrick Hemming], Alex [Rorke] and . . . there were two cars . . . I don't remember. Just those I mentioned. Maybe someone else. Could be one of the Cubans . . . Rafael Del Piño or . . . I'm not sure. I think it was Rafael Del Piño or Orlando Bosch. I'm not sure. Why, is it important?"

No, not really, I told her, I was just curious. I didn't realize how very important it would later become.

During our interview, I asked Marita Lorenz when was the last time she had been in contact with Frank Sturgis. She said she had not seen him for more than a dozen years, but she had spoken to him a couple of years before when she had seen his photo in the paper in connection with Watergate. She had been so shocked she had decided to give him a call at the Federal prison in Danbury, and he was surprised and delighted to hear from her. He suggested she come to visit him, she intended to but, she told me, she never did. In fact, she never got around to calling Sturgis again.

Except for *Daily News* reporter Paul Meskil, no one outside of Senator Schweiker's office knew I had interviewed Marita Lorenz, but I would later learn that a few weeks after our interview, Frank Sturgis just happened to get back in touch with her again. Just to say hello, renew an old friendship, he said. Soon he was visiting her in New York and involving her in spy games. He had her dating an important Soviet U.N. delegate and she even scored an espionage coup for the FBI by coming away with a box of papers that included the Albanian intelligence code. It was like old times.

I had thought I could convince the staff at the Church Committee of the importance of Marita Lorenz in its probing of the CIA's off-the-book activities, but it decided that since the CIA had truthfully confessed to *all* the Agency's assassination plots against Castro, it didn't need the Sturgis-Lorenz poison pill attempt to muddy up its report. What most disturbed me, however, was the staff's lack of interest in pursuing the lead indicating that Sturgis and Hunt had possibly committed perjury in their sworn testimony before the Rockefeller Commission. One staff member candidly told me, "I don't think perjury would scare either one of them." Maybe not, but I didn't think that was the point; I thought it had something to do with upholding the law.

In the months that followed our interview, Marita Lorenz called me intermittently, usually to ask what was going on in Washington and whether she was going to be called to testify. I had to be noncommittal because, at the time, I didn't know. But whenever she called she made it a point to bring up her old anti-Castro fighting days in Miami and to drop a few names: "Guns and Trafficante? Are we talking about the Bel Aire Hotel? I used to drive up to the back of the hotel and pick them up. Frank arranged it. And someone else who furnished money for guns was Elliot Roosevelt. He lived on DiLido or Star Island, I forget which. This went through Irwin Charles Cardin, the Cobbs Fruit fortune. I used to live with him. Roosevelt would give the money and Cardin would buy the guns."

In these conversations, Lorenz kept inviting me to return to New York because she had since found boxes of material, old notes and documents she had forgotten to tell me about on my visit. She also always mentioned something about her concerns for her safety and the security of her children. (Besides her teenage daughter, Marita also had a four-year-old son by a man she married after she and the apartment manager divorced.) The last thing she wanted, she said, was publicity.

About a week after one these calls from Lorenz, a huge photograph of a youthful Marita with Fidel Castro graced the front page of the New York *Daily News*'s Sunday edition. The story, by Paul Meskil, was headlined: "CIA Sent Bedmate To Kill Castro in '60."

It was the poison-pill story told in long and deftly melodramatic fashion, mostly in Marita's own words, right up through the finding of the melted capsules: " 'It was like an omen. I couldn't just dump a glob of cold cream in his coffee, so I shut the jar and went back to the bedroom and I watched him sleeping. Finally I lay down on the bed beside him. I thought, "To hell with it. Let history take its course." ' "

The story was picked up by most of the major newspapers around the country, including the *Miami Herald*. That brought the local television reporters to Frank Sturgis's front door, where he obligingly confirmed the episode in modest but colorful narrative. He was damn proud of his attempts to kill Fidel.

When I called Marita she blamed Frank Sturgis for instigating the publicity. "It wasn't my doing," she told me. "The article started because of Frank talking. Meskil called me and said, 'You want me to write it my way or are you going to talk to me?' I had to talk because Frank told everything anyway."

She said she was sorry she cooperated with Meskil. "Now it's getting out of hand," she said. "I don't want any more out because I'm getting all sorts of threats. But I can't stop Frank because he knows too much about me. I don't know why he's doing this. At this point, I'm afraid."

I could understand her concern. I lived in Miami where bombings and assassinations in the Cuban community were sparked by even the slightest rumor of a pro-Castro lean. Marita Lorenz had failed to kill Castro. That would be enough to raise skeptical eyebrows among the old Brigade 2506 members sipping *café Cubano* at the sidewalk counters in Little Havana.

I thought of that when I heard the fear in Marita's voice the next time she called. She was sobbing. She had been beaten and threatened, but it wasn't by a Cuban, it was by her Mafiosi boyfriend.

"He says he wants me to keep my mouth shut about Trafficante if they call me to the [Church] Committee," she said. Now, she said, she suspected that someone had broken into her apartment. "I had a box of Albanian codes that I had gotten when I was working with Frank and the Bureau," she said. "Evidently someone took a few pieces of that code because I got a piece back with the message to keep my mouth shut."

Lorenz asked me if Senator Schweiker could do anything to protect her. "I just want to stay alive," she said.

Whatever the Church Committee's interest in Lorenz, Schweiker was concerned about the welfare of a potential witness whose importance hadn't yet been determined. He sent a letter to the Attorney General asking the Justice Department to "take whatever steps are available . . . to insure Ms. Lorenz's safety." In order to avoid further endangering Lorenz with additional media attention, I suggested to Schweiker that his letter be kept confidential. He agreed.

A few days later, Paul Meskil pulled another big headline in the *Daily News*: "ASKS U.S. GUARD SPY IN CASTRO DEATH PLOT." Wrote Meskil: "A member of the Senate Intelligence Committee has requested Justice Department protection for Marita Lorenz, the shapely spy who told the panel she had been recruited in 1960 by the CIA to kill her former lover, Fidel Castro." Not only did Meskil describe her as "an undercover agent for the CIA in the early 1960s," he also revealed she had "performed similar work for the FBI for about 15 years." In fact, the story noted, in 1971 Lorenz had received a letter of commendation from the Bureau's New York office.

As far as spying goes, I thought keeping secrets wasn't one of Marita Lorenz's strong suits. I was beginning to doubt her claims that she didn't want publicity and that she would be a reluctant witness if called to testify before the Church Committee. Still, whatever her motivations now, I still thought she was credible and, based on what could be checked out, that her claim of being involved in anti-Castro activities in Miami was valid. And she remained a convincing witness to the possibility that perjury was committed by E. Howard Hunt and Frank Sturgis.

Marita Lorenz remained in touch with me down through the months the Church Committee was wrapping up and the end of Schweiker's investigation. "Did I get in the report?" she would ask.

"I don't know yet, but I don't think so," I would tell her.

"That's good," she would say. "I don't need the problems."

Yet, again I was getting the impression she wasn't averse to getting herself into situations that might cause problems. She was still working with Sturgis in developing informant deals with the Bureau, the DEA and, likely, the CIA. She told me she was beginning to travel to Miami regularly, working with the U.S. Customs service in uncovering illegal arms sales. (I assumed she had a backlog of information from former lovers connected with the Mob.) One of the Customs agents she was working with in Miami was a knowledgeable veteran named Steve Czukas, whom I had met while working for Schweiker. Czukas was a tough, streetwise fed who had been helpful to me. Maybe not the most sophisticated guy, but I thought he was dedicated and levelheaded enough to handle Marita.

After I first joined the House Assassinations Committee, the calls from Marita Lorenz came more frequently. She had by then learned that my primary interest was in the Kennedy assassination, not in the CIA's anti-Castro plots; now she would tell about new books and articles on the assassination as they appeared. And, inevitably, she would probe me for information about her possible role in the investigation.

"My lawyer called me yesterday and said I'm going to get subpoenaed," she told me one night.

"Where did he get that?"

"He said he heard it over the UP wires," she said. "That's why I'm calling you. I moved and want to give you my new address."

I couldn't tell her how disorganized those early months of the House Assassinations Committee's investigation were, but I assured Lorenz no subpoena was being prepared for her. Then, as the weeks went by and the Committee's direction became clear, I knew Marita Lorenz wouldn't fit into the game plan. The information she had about Castro assassination plots and possible perjury by CIA agents was relevant to the Kennedy assassination as far as probing the Agency's credibility, but the Committee, even early on, appeared reluctant to press that. I eventually told Lorenz it was highly unlikely she would ever be subpoenaed. Her calls dropped to zilch.

In fact, in the months that went by, the only time her name popped up, it came from an unlikely source. Jim Garrison, whom I had met during the Schweiker investigation, called and said he had just returned from a vacation at a spa in Arizona where he met a lawyer from New York who happened to be a deal packager and film promoter. The conversation, naturally, came around to the Kennedy assassination, and the lawyer mentioned he had a client who could put Frank Sturgis and Lee Harvey Oswald together. His client's name was Marita Lorenz. Garrison said, however, that he subsequently learned the lawyer had a sleazy reputation and wouldn't trust the information the guy gave him. But, nevertheless, he thought I should know about it.

Like Garrison, I dismissed it as a wild tip. I had known Marita Lorenz for almost a year and a half, had spent dozens of hours talking with her and I didn't remember her ever mentioning Oswald.

Then, several weeks later, I was at the Assassinations Committee staff headquarters in Washington when someone came up from behind, slapped me on the back and said, "You're fired!"

It was Jack Moriarty. A former Washington, D.C., homicide detective, Moriarty's handsome Irish countenance could have gotten him the stock part of the precinct cop in any Bing Crosby movie. I thought he was one of the best investigators on the staff; smart, soft-spoken and charming enough to ease a confession from a guilty rock. He was smiling when I turned around.

"Just kidding," he said. But Moriarty had news that wasn't a joke. "Someone *is* trying to get you fired," he said.

"Who besides the dozen people I could name off the top of my head?" I asked.

"Marita Lorenz," he said.

That wasn't one of them. Then Moriarty told me he had been asked to take a report from a Customs agent named Steve Czukas who had come to Washington at the orders of his Miami chief to file a complaint with the Assassinations Committee about a member of its staff who was leaking information to Frank Sturgis. That information, said Czukas, came from a Customs informant named Marita Lorenz. She claimed that Sturgis had shown her a "classified Government document" which he said was given to him by a Committee staff member named Fonzi. As a result, said Czukas, Lorenz now does not trust that Committee staffer and will no longer deal with him. Or, as Moriarty's report would later put it, "her concern is of sufficient magnitude to preclude further contact with Fonzi."

Besides the complaint, however, Czukas brought new information he thought the Assassinations Committee should have directly. He said that the Customs Service had put Lorenz and her two children under protective custody in a Miami hotel for two months after she expressed fears that her life was in danger. While there, she admitted that she had been unwittingly involved in the plans to kill President Kennedy. She said she had driven from Miami to Dallas in two cars with a group of men, including Frank Sturgis and Lee Harvey Oswald, with high-power rifles. Two days before the assassination she was ordered to fly back alone to Miami.

It sounded like an incredible story, said Czukas, but there was some documentation. During the time that Lorenz was voluntarily sequestered in Miami, she filled sixteen pages of a green notebook with the details of her involvement. She subsequently gave him the notebook for safe keeping and he had it under lock and key in Miami.

I was stunned and then infuriated. It would take time and effort to deal with this development. I felt Customs was allowing itself to be manipulated by an informant.

I deliberately dawdled. It was more than three months before I put a response on the record. I had no concern about the reactions of my bosses, Chief Investigator Cliff Fenton and Chief Counsel Bob Blakey, because I had documented all encounters with both Sturgis and Lorenz. But in sending Czukas to the Committee, it seemed to me that Marita wanted attention and wanted to be called to testify at the public hearings. What was she trying to accomplish?

Then there was the matter of the "classified Government document" that Frank Sturgis said I had given him. Actually it was an unclassified memorandum written in 1964 by Al Tarabochia, an investigator with the Senate Security Committee, then headed by Mississippi's notorious Commie hunter, George Eastland. The memorandum concerned a rumored visit to Cuba by Jack Ruby. (As mentioned earlier, Sturgis himself had also given me a story about a Ruby visit to Cuba, this one a detailed account of a meeting to plot Kennedy's assassination.) A copy of Tarabochia's memorandum was in Schweiker's working files and, one night, Sturgis called me and asked if he could have a copy, saying he had Tarabochia's permission. I called Troy Gustavson in Schweiker's office, Troy got the OK from Tarabochia and a copy of the memo was sent to Sturgis directly from Schweiker's office.

So much for the "leak." When I called Marita Lorenz, she admitted that Sturgis had shown her "that Tarabochia thing," but denied she said it had come from me. She also denied that she had ever told Czukas she no longer trusted me or that she didn't want to speak with me. On the contrary, she was delighted to hear from me.

"I was down in Miami for a while and was looking for you," she said. I didn't tell her I knew that Customs had picked up her tab for a couple of months and I didn't mention anything about her reported trip to Dallas with Frank Sturgis and Lee Harvey Oswald. Neither did she.

What I found fascinating, however, was that Sturgis was still in such close contact with her, and how much she knew about his current activities. She said, for instance, that Sturgis had recently called, telling her he was "doing something" in Africa. "He was with some heavy people over there," she told me, "some major and some wealthy people who are sponsoring his thing there, raising an army to fight Castro's army in Angola." Sturgis also said he had been in Paris, Switzerland and London, in addition to Africa, and that he had asked her to go to Europe to work with him. "He sent me a first-class, round-trip plane ticket on TWA," she said. She discovered, however, that she couldn't go because on her last trip to Madrid to see her daughter's father, General Jímenez, she didn't have the return fare. Until she repaid the State Department, she couldn't travel abroad.

After I spoke with Marita, I called Steve Czukas, who confirmed she was behind his trip to Washington. She had pressed him very hard, he said. "I went up there just to get them to talk with her. What I'd like to do is get rid of her story, whether she's got something concocted or not. I'd just like to get rid of it, and I'm sure my Service would too. I don't know what's going on, it's so far out of my field, but the sooner she gets to Washington the happier I'll be, I tell you that—*however* she gets there."

To that end, said Czukas, he would turn over her green notebook. In fact, he was anxious to get rid of it; he just wanted to get back to catching simple, tricky smugglers.

In reviewing her notebook, I discovered that Marita Lorenz has very nice handwriting, very legible and graced with a modest flair. "In case of my death or injury or the death of any of my family," she began, "I, Ilona Marita Lorenz, born 8/18/39 in Bremen, Germany, want Mr. Steve Czukas, of Miami, Fla., to hand this letter over to the proper people or Committee."

She wrote sixteen pages of narrative, only five of which actually dealt with the Kennedy assassination.

> After the extradition of my daughter's father, General Marcos Pérez Jímenez . . . I felt lost and drifted back to my old associates, Frank Fiorini/Sturgis and his followers (The International Anti-Communist Brigade), Miami, Fla. I owe Frank Fiorini and Alex Rorke (N.Y.C.) my life (Cuba, 1959) after my close, personal involvement with Dr. Fidel Castro Ruz. I was active in Miami towards the end of 1959, became a member of the International Anti-Communist Brigade and took a blood oath to join Frank Fiorini's secret Assassination group in early 1960.

Marita briefly mentions the poison-capsule caper with Sturgis, attributing the scheme to higher authorities ("I firmly believed Frank F. to be a member of the CIA"), but admits her heart wasn't in it: "It is not in my makeup to take the life of another human being deliberately."

She uses most of the narrative, however, to vent anger over what she claims was an attorney's scheme to cheat her out of the trust funds set up for her and her daughter by General Jímenez before he was arrested and extradited in August of 1963. She also puts a bit of suspicion on the General himself: "The General often personally said he would like to eliminate (kill) both of the Kennedy brothers."

Although it's segmented because of the General's intermittent role in the narrative, here's what Marita wrote about the Kennedy assassination:

> A month or so prior to November 22nd, 1963, I joined Frank Fiorini, Ozzie (Lee), others, Cubans in our group and drove in two cars to the home of Orlando Bosch. It wasn't unusual for Frank Fiorini to study maps (in the past, often we studied waterways, tides, currents, islands in the Bahamas where I was to navigate stolen crafts laden with arms to a certain destination later to be picked up by others.) . . .
>
> This certain, "highly secret meeting" in Bosch's home was to discuss certain streets in Dallas, Texas. I was under the impression we were to "take another armory." I paid little attention and thought more of how I would start life again with my baby. There was talk of a "highly

powerful rifle" and discussions of "feet," "building," "timings," "contacts," "silence," etc.

Another car with 4 men waited outside—the windows were closed tightly, a fan was put on, Mrs. Bosch served Cuban café and a child was told to leave the room.

I was rather disinterested, bored, worried and disgusted and felt I had "outgrown" the Cuban scene. My thoughts were of Marcos, Venezuela, my baby girl . . . and the extradition.

The word "Kennedy," spoken by Frank to Bosch made me say, "What about him?" All eyes were on me, studying me when Ozzie started a dispute with Frank and Bosch about my presence. I then told Frank, "Who needs this hostile, slimy bastard?" I wanted to leave when Frank spoke to all the men on my behalf. . . .

After a major digression into her legal battle for the trust funds, the narrative flows on:

. . . Going back now to the flare-up in Bosch's home and this secret meeting with a street map of Dallas, Texas on the table. I had my mind on other things and I wanted to talk to Frank Fiorini about starting a search party to look for Alex Rorke who was missing. . . .

In Bosch's house that eve. I called Ozzie a "chivato," to Frank and when Ozzie challenged me, I asked him "How did you know the meaning of that word?" (It was Fidel's favorite word for "informant, traitor.") He said he heard it in Cuba.

This meeting seemed more secretive as Frank and the others spoke in whispers.

Sometime in Nov. 1963, still associating with Frank Fiorini and feeling lost, hiding from the press, I told Frank "sure," I'll go with him and others in two cars to Dallas.

I was under the impression we would "take an armory," as we had done before, and which was the reason for the prior "secret meeting" at Bosch's home.

I left my daughter for a few days with my dear friend and babysitter, Willie May Taylor, who was my maid while I was living with General Marcos Pérez Jímenez.

We left after midnight in two beat-up looking cars, about 8 or 9 of us with Frank's "baby," a high powered rifle, scope and silencer attached, in the trunk of our car. Before we left, we were briefed by Frank, Bosch, Pedro Díaz Lanz. No phone calls, no speaking Spanish in Texas, no leaving for restaurants, complete obedience. Supplies, food, and "kits" were dumped into the trunk. We wore dark street clothes and got into the cars.

We drove all night along the coast and nobody spoke much. Frank drove, I sat in the back seat and slept. It was hot & crowded and I sat next to a Cuban. We drove through the city of Dallas to the outskirts to a drive-in motel. . . .

Frank and Pedro registered. We had two rooms . . . each room had 2 double beds. Ozzie brought in a newspaper and everybody read it.

Dressed, I fell asleep on top of one of the beds. Frank brought in food for sandwiches & soda.

Only Frank and Bosch were to answer the phone if & when it rang. That first night, Frank waited for a "member," Ruby. Frank spoke to him outside in the parking lot. This Ruby seemed surprised at my presence and questioned Frank about me, I'm sure.

I later told Frank, "Where'd you get that Mafia punk?" And, "What's really going on? What the hell are we really here for?" Frank studied me and escorted me outside. He replied by saying "You make me nervous. I made a mistake, this is too big, I want you to go back to Miami, take the baby and go home." I agreed and told him that I didn't like his selection of men—Ozzie, Ruby—who were new and not true members. As I was leaving, "Eduardo" (H.Hunt) drove up and there was a discussion on who would drive me to the airport for Miami. Frank and Bosch did, Eduardo waited at the motel. I flew under the name of Maria Jímenez (I am almost sure). I stayed in Miami about one day, and was very happy to be back with my baby. I decided to cut all ties with Frank and his anti-Castro group. I would get nowhere and I was sick of the whole situation.

I had a feeling, a suspicion, that Frank's group was in Texas to kill somebody, because of the secrecy of the whole thing. Never in a million years did I put 2 and 2 together, or was ever even hinted to what they were up to. All I know is that everything I have written, and am writing is the truth, so help me God.

What struck me about that story were its similarities, at least at the beginning, to the incident Marita Lorenz had told me about almost a year and a half before when I first interviewed her. The details about the two cars and the group members were all the same. In her green book, Lorenz simply turned the cars west and had them head for Dallas.

As I said, at the first interview Marita Lorenz had impressed me as a fairly credible witness. Even her story of attempting to assassinate Castro with poison capsules, told without the dramatic embellishments of a tabloid presentation, had elements of plausibility. Now, for whatever reasons, Marita Lorenz seemed determined to befog her credibility. At any rate, I sent her green-covered notebook to Washington, where I knew it would be given an identification number and put into a file. Since the Assassinations Committee's investigative game plan was already in place, it was unlikely that even this apparent ploy would get Marita the attention she seemed to want.

What I didn't realize, however, was that there were other forces at work. It was a couple of weeks after the green book had gone to Washington and, after being away from Miami for a few days, I returned home late one evening to a call from the *Daily News*'s Paul Meskil.

"I've been trying to get in touch with you," he said, "because I think something really big is going down. Unfortunately, I'm not at liberty to tell you the whole thing yet, but I can give you part of it."

The reason Meskil knew something big was going down was that he was going to help it go down. He was going to break a big story. And although, he said, he couldn't provide me with names and places yet, he did begin telling me, in his cryptic newsman style, what it was about: "What this involves is a statement made, and it's down there. It supposedly involves Sturgis and some other people with Oswald and supposedly Oswald was in a training camp down there in the Everglades with them and they all went to Dallas together right before the Kennedy hit."

I interrupted him. "That's from Marita Lorenz."

"I couldn't say it," he said.

I told Meskil about Jim Garrison having some time ago met the lawyer who claimed his client could put Sturgis and Oswald together. Meskil knew the lawyer as a promoter and, as he put it, "a known crook." Said Meskil: "He had a connection to Bernie Spindel, the greatest wiretapper of all time. There was a link to the CIA. I wonder if that guy put the idea in Marita's head. That's funny, because I thought she first told the story to a Federal guy down by you and then she told it to me.

"I gave the piece to the managing editor on Monday and he says the only way we can run this is if we get some official to say we're investigating. So not being able to reach you for a few days I get desperate, so I call Blakey, the Chief Counsel. I didn't give him any names either. I just said I had someone who has made this statement to a Federal officer and to me and it involves this matter. And, boy, he wanted to move on it right away. He says, 'I'll send a couple of people up to talk to you tomorrow.' I said, 'Wait, not so fast. I don't trust some of your people.' I told him I knew some of them are ex-New York cops and before I know it my exclusive will be blown."

I couldn't figure Blakey's reaction. Either he hadn't been paying attention to the whole Marita Lorenz escapade or he was playing games with Meskil.

"Yeah, he seemed excited," Meskil said. "He was even talking about sending her out to Dallas to try to find the motel she says they were at. But I think she'll balk at that because she told me she doesn't want to testify, she doesn't even want to talk to the Committee.''

Then Meskil thought about that for a moment and added: "But I don't know how she figures she's going to dump it on the *News* and have it splash all over the country and then avoid any follow up, because it's inevitable somebody is going to come around to her and say, 'Hey, what's with all this horse shit?' ''

Whatever the horse shit, Meskil wasn't going to let it stand in the way of a fat front-page story. He worked on it a few more days, called Frank Sturgis to get his reaction ("I have never met Lee Harvey Oswald in my life") and then called me the night before it hit the paper. As Meskil put it: "The shit is in the fan now."

The headline said it all: "Ex-Spy Says She Drove to Dallas with Oswald & Kennedy 'Assassin Squad.' '' The story was almost consistent with the one Lorenz had written in her green notebook. Frank Sturgis, Orlando Bosch and Pedro Díaz Lanz were still the men she claimed went on the trip; however, she added "two Cuban brothers whose names she does not know" and some additional embroidery: "She said Oswald [had earlier] visited an Operation 40 training camp in the Florida Everglades, but . . . she knew him only as 'Ozzie.' ''

At the end of the piece, Meskil noted: "Statements she made to *The News* and to a federal agent were reported to Robert Blakey, chief counsel of the Assassinations Committee. He has assigned one of his top investigators to interview her."

Of course, what Blakey had decided, now the story had hit the papers, was that he had no choice but to put the Lorenz tale into the record—part of his policy to touch every base, no matter what. I didn't exactly rush into the assignment. In fact, I decided to wait until I had to go up to Washington on other matters, and then hop up to New York to get Marita Lorenz into the record. That turned out to be more than a month after Meskil broke his big story.

It was a Friday when I called Marita from Washington to say I planned to visit her the next day. She was even more agitated than usual.

"Frank is coming to kill me."

"Sturgis?"

"Yes. He's been threatening me. He doesn't want me to testify before the Committee."

"When is he coming?"

"I don't know. He may be on his way. My daughter is very upset about it. I think she went out to buy a gun. I need help."

If I hadn't gotten all those distraught calls from Marita over the years, I guess I would have reacted with a greater sense of urgency. But I had planned to join a group from the staff for Chinese food at the Szechuan East that evening and I knew I didn't want to get in the middle of a shoot-out on an empty stomach. I told Marita I'd fly up first thing the next morning.

Since I didn't think it prudent to visit Marita alone now, two other staffers joined me: Al Gonzales, the former New York cop who had become my investigative partner in Miami; and Eddie Lopez, the young researcher whose Puerto Rican parents lived in New York. Lopez happened to be standing in front of the peephole in Lorenz's door when I knocked. The door quickly flew open and Eddie went bug-eyed at the barrel of the shotgun, inches from his nose.

"Marita!" I yelled.

She turned her wild stare from Eddie and, recognizing me, dropped the gun to her side. The tension slid from her face.

"Oh, it's you," she said. "I thought it was a Cuban Frank had sent to kill me."

Suddenly I felt it was all getting too ridiculous. Is this what the official Kennedy assassination investigation was getting down to, the stuff of drama from an *arroz-con-pollo* western?

Marita put the shotgun down beside the door and invited us in. She looked tired and drawn. She hadn't slept, and her teenage daughter was out trying to buy a pistol to head off Sturgis before he arrived. Marita had spoken to him yesterday and he said he was on his way up. What should she do?

I thought of a few things to say but not anything that would look good in the next day's headlines ("ASSASSINATIONS COMMITTEE TELLS MARITA. . . .") All I wanted was to get her statement into the record and get the hell out of there. Not that I thought Sturgis would come slamming through the door with his high-power, sniper-scoped, silencer-equipped "baby." I think Sturgis has made some dumb moves in his life, but he wouldn't be foolish enough to provide a trail via telephone threats and warnings.

Anyhow, with Marita jumping up periodically to peek out the window and check noises at her front door, it took us a few hours to get her to repeat the story of the Dallas trip. Her cast of characters remained the same as in the green book—herself, Sturgis, Bosch, Díaz Lanz and "Ozzie"—but this time with the two unnamed Cuban brothers. And now she also added Miami soldier-of-fortune Gerry Patrick Hemming. The caravan was not only getting crowded, it was getting damn uncomfortable—Hemming was six foot six and weighed about 270 pounds. (Later, Marita would remember the names of the two brothers and identify them as the Novo brothers. Still, the coalition made sense because all the individuals were publicly known as associates: Sturgis and Hemming, you may recall, had made headlines as cofounders of an anti-Castro group; as had the Díaz Lanz flight from Cuba with Sturgis; the Novo brothers were in the news, linked to Bosch in Cuban terrorist activity. "Ozzie" was the odd man out.)

I was glad to get back to Miami, where the only danger was getting shot by an irate motorist on I-95. A call from Frank Sturgis was on my answering machine, but all he said was to call him back when I got the chance. Since I didn't hear from Marita on Sunday or Monday, I assumed the drama had faded to a close. It must only have been a commercial break. I received a call from Paul Meskil late Monday afternoon.

"They arrested the kid," he said.

"What kid?"

"Marita's daughter."

"Did Sturgis show up?"

"No, not yet. But Marita was bugging me all morning so finally I told her to call the cops. So she calls these two cops she knows in the Intelligence Division because she's been working with them on a guns and pornography thing with the Mob and about noon today they go out and pick her up. The kid supposedly had gotten a .22 pistol and was waiting for Sturgis to show up."

"Is Sturgis still supposed to show up?"

"That's what she says. He's been calling her."

"It's been coming up on High Noon now for three days," I said.

"Yeah, I know," Meskil laughed. "Maybe the train broke down."

The train didn't break down. It was about one o'clock in the morning when my telephone rang. The caller said he was Detective James Rothstein from the New York Police Department.

"I just arrested Frank Sturgis and he asked me to call you," he said. "It's on the complaint of what'shername, Marita Lorenz. He threatened her in reference to talking with you. I understand you were up here on Saturday."

I felt as if I were suddenly in the middle of Take Five, Scene Four.

"Sturgis said you wanted him to call you if anything happened," said Detective Rothstein. "I don't know what the hell is going on myself."

That's the last thing I would have told Sturgis, but I figured I'd better talk with him anyway.

"It's so damn confusing," Sturgis said when he got on the line. "No, it's not confusing, there's something behind it."

I was beginning to think that myself. I asked him what had happened.

"Well, I come up here to see my lecture people but I had been in touch with Marita because she had wanted me to come up here to tell me about the pressures she was under to put those articles in the paper about me. So I come up here and I had my appointments and I called Marita and she says, 'No, call me later on in the evening.' So I went out with my friend Frank Nelson and we finished dinner about ten-thirty and I called Marita and said, 'Listen, I'll see you tomorrow because it's getting late.' But she says, 'No, come on over this evening.' So I says, 'All right, I'll be over in a half hour.' So I caught a cab and I walk into her apartment and, Christ, these two detectives have guns on me. They tell me I threatened her and that her kid went out and bought a shotgun to kill me. This whole thing is flabbergasting!''

"And you never said anything to her about her Dallas trip story?" I asked Frank.

"No, no, no," he said. "I never asked her to retract any story. All I asked is why she said those things to Paul Meskil. And her answer was that she was pressured. And I says, 'Well, can you tell me?' And she says, 'No, I can't tell you, I got to see you in person.' There's got to be something behind all this."

Frank Sturgis wound up spending 48 hours in the slammer. His bail was set at $25,000, surprisingly high for harassment charges, until his lawyer went to another judge and had it lowered to $10,000. Sturgis's wife, Jan, had to ship up cash and bonds to post it. When he was arraigned, more than a hundred reporters and photographers descended on the human zoo at 100 Centre Street. A courthouse regular who calls himself "Cochise" and wears a red loincloth and fur anklets, got upset at being ejected by the court officers and, after doing a little dance, made yellow rain on one of the photographers waiting for Sturgis. Cochise get arrested.

Timothy Crouse, then writing for the *Village Voice*, provided a perspective: "There was a full moon. Not just any full moon, but the most potent of them all, the one that signals harvest time—the change of seasons, and the cruel lunar tug on many a soft brain. . . . The most bizarre event of all happened just before midnight on Halloween, when two of the most notoriously unreliable sources in America magically turned into a front-page news story that lasted four days. How else but with the aid of occult powers could Marita Lorenz have convinced the Manhattan district attorney that Frank Sturgis had phoned from Miami to threaten her life? Maybe with a little help from Sturgis himself, the press and even the police."

The day after Sturgis was booked I received a call from his wife. Jan is a dark-haired, attractive, very personable woman and, compared with Frank, rather articulate. "It's my own personal opinion," she said, "that Marita is not intelligent enough to think up all these devious plots, and I'm concerned about who is behind her. As soon as I heard the plan about the fourteen-year-old daughter being set up to kill Frank, the first thing that came to my mind was the Lana Turner scenario. I don't know, but I hope it's only a publicity stunt on her part. But if it's not, and it's somebody trying to get to Frank, then it's frightening. I don't mean to be speaking cryptically, but all these things are going through my mind.''

Jan didn't call just to give me her opinion. She said she had proof that Frank was set up. She had been talking with him and he gave her permission to play for me the recording he had made of his last telephone conversation with Marita.

When I got to the Sturgis home, Jan was still fiddling with the tape recorder, trying to find the place on the tape where the conversation with Marita began. She pressed a button and I heard a familiar voice.

"Ooops," she said, smiling as she quickly hit the stop button. "You won't tell Frank you heard that, will you?"

Frank had also recorded all his conversations with me.

The opening lines of Frank's call to Marita set the tone of their conversation:

"Marita? This is Frank."

"Hi, love! Wait, let me go into the other room, the kids are making noise, hold on. . . . Well, hi! I just came back from Mount Sinai, my mother's in Mount Sinai. How are you, are you gonna come up?"

It's a rambling but revealing conversation that goes on for about a half an hour. Sturgis repeatedly attempts to bring the topic around to the story about the Dallas trip. At one point, he mentions he has been talking with me.

"Fonzi says he's going to try to get up to New York," he says.

"For me? Does he want me? Tell him I have memory lapse, I forgot everything."

"He told me also, he says, 'Tell her not to worry about being subpoenaed. I'm not gonna subpoena her.' "

"No, I don't want to be subpoenaed."

"You won't be subpoenaed. He's just going ahead and checking up on all the things that came out in the paper, the statements and so forth."

"Are you gonna come up? You want me to send you the fee? I can. Can't you come up?"

"Yeah, but I don't have the money."

"I'll send it to you today. I'll send it to you tonight."

"Well, you see, my problem is, I went to the doctor yesterday and had to get an ingrown toenail taken out."

"Oh, Jesus, that hurts!"

"Yeah, it smarts."

I am listening to this conversation and I am trying to remember I am part of a serious investigation into the assassination of President Kennedy. The talk finally rambles away from ingrown toenails to deals about movies and books. Marita mentions the lawyer who first dropped the Sturgis-Oswald connection on Jim Garrison in Arizona.

"He's been pressuring me to sign this thing for seventy-five thousand dollars, with a seventy-five hundred advance, but it stinks, I won't sign it."

Frank suggests she not sign anything until he talks to her about contracts and legalities.

"Well, I'm not doing anything," Marita says. "I'm not saying anything. In fact, I'd like to retract everything. But then I'm gonna get in trouble. I've been warned."

"You've been warned?"

"From a visit with two people. They wanted to know where I was on September twenty-second. . . . I mean, November twenty-second, 'sixty-three."

"Were these Government agents?"

"Yeah."

"FBI or CIA?"

"Yeah. That's why I want to talk with you. I got myself in over my head. . . . "

"What I'm trying to figure out is, who pressured you into making these statements? You said two agents. What are their names?"

"I'm not going to tell you. I'll tell you when you get up here."

"Well, OK, then I'll be up there. Why don't you send that to me and then I'll be up there."

"You want me to send that tonight? I'll send it tonight. Jesus, I don't know where?"

"Eastern Airlines."

"Just leave it at Eastern Airlines?"

"Right, I'll call Eastern and pick it up."

Through the whole conversation Sturgis sounds like an innocent and naive victim being lured into a trap. Perhaps a bit too naive. I began to wonder—and still do wonder—if there wasn't an element of collusion in this scene. Frank Sturgis hasn't survived a life cobwebbed with dangerous clandestine missions by being naive.

At any rate, Sturgis picked up that Eastern Airline ticket that Marita Lorenz had sent him and flew to his destiny in New York. In the end, the entire episode seemed to have about as much significance as "Cochise" pissing on a photographer. But, in retrospect, one result of this whole soap-opera scenario—the factor that still feeds my suspicion of collusion—was a successful diversion, from the Schweiker probe through to the House Assassinations Committee, of our limited investigation resources. And, in the process, it injected a dose of slapstick that would impair any future attempt to conduct a serious investigation into the possible involvement of E. Howard Hunt and Frank Sturgis in the Kennedy assassination.

The *Village Voice*'s Timothy Crouse reflected the tone of the entire affair when, after Sturgis was released and the charges dropped, he reported that the New York Police Commissioner was opening an investigation into the farce:

" . . . Will the cops dig up information linking Marita Lorenz, Frank Sturgis, the *Daily News* and certain members of the New York Police Department? Will a conspiracy be uncovered at last? Or will the police report conclude that the whole brouhaha was the work of a single dingbat acting alone? Where is Mark Lane now that we need him?"

He would come later.

ELEVEN

STRANGERS AT THE DOOR

*A*LTHOUGH IT WAS only about a dozen years after the Kennedy assassination when I began working for Schweiker's Subcommittee, it surprised me to learn how absolutely bemuddling the subject had become. Frank Sturgis and Marita Lorenz represented the muckiest aspects of the investigation. There were, however, a number of witnesses who clearly were worth more attention, and I was also pursuing them. Then one afternoon, early in January, 1976, I received a call about one of our leads from David Marston, Schweiker's legal aide and my main liaison with the Senator's office.

"You can give up on Silvia Odio," he said. "The guys over on Committee staff told me they got word she's in Puerto Rico. They're getting ready to track her down."

The Church Committee staffers played everything very close to the vest. They had early on decided that their final report on Kennedy's assassination could be written from documents they had acquired from the CIA and from CIA testimony admitting involvement with the Mob in Castro murder plots. The Church Committee staffers figured they didn't have the time for much original investigation and, if they did any, it might bring up more than they could handle. But what had become known as the "Odio incident" bothered them, just as it had the Warren Commission. They were now thinking about talking to Silvia Odio, just to cover an important base.

But Silvia Odio was missing. She had lived in Dallas at the time of the Kennedy assassination, but the word was that years ago she had moved to Miami, remarried and dropped out of sight. Odio was one of the few witnesses in the Kennedy probe who had not exploited her role or capitalized on her early notoriety. She refused interviews—despite being offered large sums of money—and had gone into hiding. Now, the Committee staff had apparently tracked her down in Puerto Rico. "I understand she just moved back there recently," said David Marston.

"It must have been *very* recently," I said. "I was talking to Silvia Odio in Miami this morning."

"Sonavagun," David laughed. "Imagine. And those supersleuths over there are going after the CIA!"

I had made a special effort to locate Odio because I considered her testimony to the Warren Commission among the most significant of any witness'. Odio had claimed that Oswald was one of three men who came to the door of her apartment in Dallas one evening during the last week in September, 1963. But the Warren Commission had dismissed her testimony because, it said, it had "considerable evidence" that Oswald was not in Dallas at all that September. That simply wasn't true. In fact, in its Report, the Commission had to resort to a blatant deception in order to discredit Odio's testimony.

However, the Commission made the point that *if* Oswald had gone from New Orleans to Dallas on his way to Mexico City in September, he would have had to have private transportation and he did not have a car and could not drive. (Of course, that meant that others would have been involved with him. In which case, the Warren Commission's final assertion that Oswald was not part of a conspiracy would not stand. The House Assassinations Committee would conclude that Oswald did, in fact, leave New Orleans the last week in September and, from his other known movements, had to have access to a car.)

My discovery of Silvia Odio in Miami was important for two reasons: In investigating her story I incidentally opened a new area of evidence with explosive potential; and, the manner in which she and her testimony were later handled by the House Assassination Committee indicated that it was, in its own way, as deceptive as the Warren Commission.

Silvia Odio's background is important. She was the oldest of ten children who were spirited out of Cuba when their parents entered into anti-Castro activity there. Her father, Amador Odio, was among Cuba's wealthiest men, the owner of the country's largest trucking business; he was once described by *Time* magazine as the "transport tycoon" of Latin America. Yet both he and his wife were idealists who had fought dictators from the time of General Machado in the Thirties. Among Castro's early supporters, they were also among the first to turn against him when "Fidel betrayed the Revolution," as

Amador Odio later told me. With liberal leader Manolo Ray, the Odios helped form one of the first anti-Castro groups within Cuba.

Amador and Sarah Odio were arrested by Castro in October, 1961, at their country estate outside Havana. (Ironically, the Odios had once hosted the wedding of one of Castro's sisters on that very estate. Later, Castro would turn it into a national women's prison and Sarah Odio would spend eight years incarcerated there, while her husband was placed in a cell on Isla de Pinos.) At the time, Silvia Odio was 24 years old, living in Puerto Rico with her husband and four young children. (Before marrying, she had attended private school in Philadelphia and law school in Cuba for a while.) After her parents' arrest, her husband was sent to Germany by his firm and he subsequently deserted her and their children. Destitute and alone, she began having emotional problems.

By then, Silvia's younger sisters, Annie and Sarita, were settled in Dallas. Sarita, a student at the University of Dallas, had become friendly with a socially connected clubwoman named Lucille Connell, who was active in the Cuban Refugee Center and the Mental Health Association. When Sarita told her of Silvia's plight, Connell made arrangements to have Silvia and the children moved to Dallas and for Silvia to receive psychiatric treatment.

Lucille Connell became Silvia's closest confidante. Connell later told me that Silvia's emotional problems—brought on by the shock of suddenly being left alone with four young children, her parents' imprisonment and her abrupt fall from wealth to destitution—resulted in attacks of sudden fainting when, "reality got too painful to bear." Connell said she had personally witnessed Silvia suffer these attacks in her home when Silvia had first arrived in Dallas, but with treatment they eventually ended—until the Kennedy assassination.

Silvia Odio had moved to Dallas in March of 1963. She said she wanted only to lead a quiet life, but her deep personal concerns led her and her sisters to maintain contact with politically active Cuban exiles and to join the anti-Castro group called *JURE*, (*Junta Revolucionaria*) which was founded by Manolo Ray, her father's old friend. (This was the same Manolo Ray whose presence, E. Howard Hunt says, forced him to resign from his position as CIA liaison with the *Frente* before the Bay of Pigs; Hunt contended that Ray was much too liberal and leftist to be permitted to join the invasion's political front coalition.) Silvia and her sisters attended a couple of Cuban exile rallies and gave spiritual support to anti-Castro efforts, but being young and with little money, there was not much else they could do.

By September, 1963, Silvia Odio was well-established in the Dallas Cuban exile community, had a decent job, had her emotional problems under control and was doing well enough to be planning to move on the first of October to a more comfortable apartment than the tiny unit she and her four children squeezed into. For the week before her moving date, her sister Annie, then seventeen, had been staying at the apartment to babysit the children and help her pack. I spoke separately with both sisters about what happened that week; with Annie Odio a few weeks after my initial interview with Silvia. Annie was also living in Miami, but both she and Silvia told me they had not discussed the incident in Dallas for several years prior to my asking them about it.

Annie remembered that evening when three men came to the door of Silvia's apartment in Dallas. It was still early when the doorbell rang and it was Annie who went to answer it. One of the men asked to speak to Sarita. He spoke English but when Annie answered him in Spanish he also spoke Spanish. Annie told him that Sarita didn't live there.

"He then said something," Annie told me. "I don't recall exactly what, something about her being married, which made me think that they really wanted my sister Silvia. I recall putting the chain on the door after I told them to wait while I went to get Silvia."

Annie told me that two of the men were Latin-looking and that the shorter, heavyset one had dark, shiny, hair combed back, and "looked Mexican." She also said, "The one in the middle was American."

Silvia was initially reluctant to talk with the visitors, Annie said, because she was busy getting dressed to go out. But she remembers Silvia coming out of the bedroom in her bathrobe to go to the door.

Silvia Odio had also told me that it was early evening and she was getting dressed to go out when the three men came to the door. They stood in the vestibule just inside the small front porch under the bright overhead lights. Silvia said the men told her they were members of *JURE* and spoke as if they knew both Manolo Ray and her father. All her conversation, she said, was with the taller Latin, the one who identified himself as "Leopoldo," although he admitted he was giving her an alias or a "war name," which was common among anti-Castro activists at the time. She said she is less certain of the other Latin's name, it might have been "Angel." But she described him as her sister did, "looking more Mexican than anything else." The third visitor, the American, was introduced to her as "Leon Oswald." She said Leon Oswald acknowledged the introduction with a very brief reply, perhaps in idiomatic Spanish, but she later decided he could not understand Spanish because of his lack of reaction to her conversation with Leopoldo.

There is no doubt in Silvia Odio's mind that her visitor was, in fact, Lee Harvey Oswald. She said she was talking with the men more than twenty minutes and, although she did not permit them in her apartment, she was less than three feet from them as they stood in the well-lit vestibule. (Later, when I went to Dallas, I confirmed her description of the scene.) She said the three appeared tired, unkempt and unshaven, as if they had just come from a long trip.

Leopoldo told Silvia Odio that the reason they had come to her was to get her help in soliciting funds in the name of *JURE* from local businessmen. "He told me," she recalled, "that he would like for me to write them in English, very nice letters, and perhaps we could get some funds."

Silvia was very suspicious of the strangers and avoided giving them any commitment, but their conversation ended with Leopoldo giving her the impression he would contact her again. After the men left, Silvia locked her door, went to the window and watched them pull away in a red car that had been parked in front of the apartment. She said she could not see who was driving the car but did see Angel on the passenger side.

The following day or the day after, she still isn't certain which, Leopoldo called. In our talk she was relatively certain of the gist of what Leopoldo said in that conversation, and it is consistent with her testimony to the Warren Commission. She said Leopoldo told her that "the gringo" had been a Marine, that he was an expert marksman and that he was "kind of loco." She recalled Leopoldo's saying that the gringo Leon had said that "we Cubans, we did not have any guts because we should have assassinated Kennedy after the Bay of Pigs."

On the day President Kennedy was killed, both Silvia and Annie immediately remembered the visit of the three men. Before she had seen a photograph of Oswald or knew that he was involved, the news of the President's death instantly brought back to Silvia's mind that Leopoldo had told her of Leon's remark about assassinating Kennedy. Silvia had just returned to work from lunch and was told that everyone was being sent home. She began to feel terribly, uncontrollably frightened and, while walking to her car, fainted. She remembers waking up in the hospital.

Across town, Annie Odio was watching television at a friend's house. She and some friends had gone to see the President's motorcade pass by at a spot several miles from Dealey Plaza. "When I first saw Oswald on television," she told me, "my first thought was, 'My God, I know this guy and I don't know from where.' I kept thinking, 'Where have I seen this guy?' Then, I remembered, my sister Sarita called me and told me that Silvia had fainted at work and that she was sending her boyfriend to take me to the hospital. The first thing I remember when I walked into the room was that Silvia started crying and crying. I think I told her, 'You know this guy on TV who shot

President Kennedy? I think I know him.' And she said, 'You don't remember where you know him from?' I said, 'No, I cannot recall, but I know I've seen him before.' And then she told me, 'Do you remember those three guys who came to the house?' '' That's when, Annie said, she suddenly knew where she had seen Lee Harvey Oswald before.

Based on background and character alone, Silvia and Annie Odio were highly credible witnesses. Their story held up through my subsequent heavy checking and I was absolutely convinced they were telling the truth. One major factor in their favor was that Silvia Odio had told more than one person about the incident *before* the Kennedy assassination. She had even written to her father in prison and told him of the visit of the three strangers. The Warren Commission obtained a copy of his reply warning her to be careful because he did not know them. I also spoke to Amador Odio himself about it.

By this time, Amador Odio and his wife had been released from their Cuban prisons and were also living in Miami. No longer wealthy, Odio, a handsome, dignified old gentleman was working nights in a low-level manager's job for an airline. But he was still proud and idealistic. He told me that he had received the letter from Silvia and confirmed his reply.

More significantly, Dr. Burton Einspruch, the psychiatrist who was counseling Silvia at the time, recalled that she had told him—*prior* to the assassination—of two Latins and an American who had visited her. Dr. Einspruch also remembered calling her on the day of the assassination while she was in the hospital. He said she mentioned "Leon" and, in what he called "a sort of histrionic way," connected the visit of Leon to Kennedy's death.

Also relevant, I thought, was the fact that the FBI found out about the visit of the three men inadvertently. Both Silvia and Annie had discussed it that day in the hospital room and decided not to say anything to anyone about it. "We were so frightened, we were absolutely terrified," Silvia remembered. "We were both very young and yet we had so much responsibility, with so many brothers and sisters and our mother and father in prison, we were so afraid and not knowing what was happening. We made a vow to each other not to tell anyone." But their sister Sarita told Lucille Connell and Connell told a trusted friend and soon the FBI was knocking on Silvia Odio's door. She says it was the last thing in the world she wanted, but when they came she felt she had a responsibility to tell the truth.

Before I met Silvia and Annie Odio and had the opportunity to evaluate their credibility, I reviewed all the FBI documents and the

Warren Commission records of the Odio incident. There were, I thought, two pivotal points.

First: If the incident did occur as Odio contended, understanding it was key to grasping the truth about Lee Harvey Oswald and the John F. Kennedy assassination. No theory of the assassination would stand without somehow accounting for it.

Second: That was the very point the Warren Commission itself quickly recognized. Therefore it was forced to pummel the facts about its investigation of the incident into lies that would confirm its lone-nut-assassin conclusion.

The Warren Commission was hampered, of course, by the FBI's initial bungling in investigating the incident. Silvia Odio had provided good physical descriptions of her visitors and details about their car. The FBI simply did not vigorously pursue those leads and instead spent valuable time questioning people about Silvia's credibility and her emotional problems. The Bureau's first interview with Silvia Odio was on December 12th, 1963. On August 23rd, 1964, with the first drafts of the Warren Commission Report being written, Chief Counsel J. Lee Rankin wrote to J. Edgar Hoover: "It is a matter of some importance to the Commission that Mrs. Odio's allegations either be proved or disproved."

One month later, with the Report already in galleys, the Odio incident was still a critical concern for staffers. In a memo to his boss, Staff Counsel Wesley Liebeler wrote: "There are problems. Odio may well be right. The Commission will look bad if it turns out that she is. There is no need to look foolish by grasping at straws to avoid admitting that there is a problem."

The FBI did attempt to alleviate that "problem" when it interviewed a soldier of fortune named Loran Eugene Hall on September 26th, 1964. Hall claimed he had been in Dallas in September, 1963, trying to raise anti-Castro funds with two companions, one of whom might have looked like Oswald. The Warren Commission grasped at that straw and detailed that interview in its final report, giving the impression that Hall and his companions were Odio's visitors. It then definitively concluded: " . . . Lee Harvey Oswald was not at Mrs. Odio's apartment in September, 1963."

The Warren Commission did not mention that Loran Eugene Hall was one of the anti-Castro guerrillas arrested at the No Name Key raid at the time of the Kennedy's Cuban-exile crackdown; or that he was part of the International Anti-Communist Brigade whose members, led by Frank Sturgis and Gerry Patrick Hemming, were notorious for disseminating misinformation. Neither did the Warren Commission note in its final Report—even though it *knew*—that the subsequent FBI interviews revealed that Hall's two companions denied being in Dallas; that neither looked at all like Oswald; that Silvia Odio, shown their photographs, did not recognize them; and that Loran Eugene Hall, when questioned again by the FBI, admitted he had fabricated the story. (Still later, when questioned by the Assassinations Committee, Hall denied he had ever told the FBI he had been to Odio's apartment.)

It is no wonder that the critics early pounced on the Odio incident as being the most flagrant of all the Warren Commission distortions. As Sylvia Meagher wrote in her *Accessories After the Fact*: "If the Commission could leave such business unfinished, we are entitled to ask whether its members were ever determined to uncover the truth."

What I recall most about the first meeting I had with Silvia Odio is her fear. It was still very much with her after all those years. She was working as a legal assistant in the law department of a large firm, but she had remained home that morning so we could talk. Her husband, Mauricio, a handsome chap then involved in Spanish-language publishing, had also remained home until he was sure his wife was comfortable. Silvia, then in her late thirties, still youthful and attractive, was nervous, but she seemed bright and morning fresh when we began talking. Yet, after a few hours of going over the incident and her experiences with the Warren Commission, she had visibly aged. I remember being shocked by that, the way her face sagged and lines appeared under her eyes, how clearly apparent was her emotional stress.

When I first called her, Silvia Odio had been reluctant to talk with me at all. She kept asking, "*Why* are they bringing it all up again? What good will it do? I told them the truth but they did not want to hear it. . . . Do you think they really want to know what the answer to the Kennedy assassination is? I have to admit I've become very cynical."

She also admitted being terribly disillusioned with the Government, and the fact that, in the end, she was officially termed a liar. She had been born into a family of culture and class, she had been taught style and respect. She was upset when Wesley Liebeler, about to take her deposition in the Federal building in Dallas, immediately started joking with her about being teased by other Warren Commission staffers for his luck in interviewing the prettiest witness in the case. He then invited her to dinner on the pretext of having additional questions; afterwards, he invited her to his hotel room. She was shocked. She began wondering how seriously the Warren Commission was taking its investigation.

"Why should I get myself involved again?" she asked when I called. "What good will it do me? What good will it do my family?"

Her children were older now, she said, but she still feared for their safety. She wondered if the men who were with Oswald were still alive.

But Silvia Odio was also very angry, and frustrated. "It gets me so mad that I was just used," she told me. I assured her that this time would be different. I told her what *I* believed: that it's absolutely necessary for the American people to learn the truth about the Kennedy assassination because the issue goes to the heart of the democratic system. I told her I was sure Senator Schweiker was an honorable man and would not be involved in anything but an honest investigation. We spoke on the telephone several times before she finally agreed to meet and talk with me. Eventually, she came to trust me.

That was a mistake. I did not know at the time that I would later become part of an apparatus that would wind up using her just as the Warren Commission did, "handling" her testimony, much more subtly but just as deceptively, making certain that her story was not prominently presented to the American people.

Yet, in the end, the House Assassinations Committee had to conclude that Silvia Odio was telling the truth. And it reluctantly did say that its final report: "The Committee was inclined to believe Silvia Odio."

That was a waffling admission but, undeniably, the House Committee had finally authenticated the fact that Silvia Odio was telling the truth. And in doing so, the Committee had also issued an indictment against itself and against its leaders, who refused to pursue the truth to its ultimate ends. Still, once the truth was acknowledged—a quick curtsy to honesty—truth was put aside so the dance could go on.

Yet that small bow revealed a fatal structural crack in the foundation of the House Committee's conclusion that elements of Organized Crime were the probable conspirators in the assassination. Attempting to cover the Committee's ass, the report crossed the bounds of rationality: "It is possible," it noted, "despite his alleged remark about killing Kennedy, that Oswald had not yet contemplated the President's assassination at the time of the Odio incident, or if he did, that his assassination plan had no relation to his anti-Castro contacts, and that he was associating with anti-Castro activists for some other unrelated reason."

The Committee did not speculate on that "other unrelated reason." That door was marked "CIA," and it had already concluded that the Agency had nothing to do with Oswald.

But all that was to come long after my first talk with Silvia Odio. At the time I sensed her story was important, but I didn't realize how significantly it would figure in my investigation.

TWELVE

WAITING FOR THE MAN IN ATLANTA

ABOUT THE TIME I found Silvia Odio in Miami, a California researcher named Paul Hoch sent Senator Schweiker a pre-publication copy of an article which would be appearing in the *Saturday Evening Post*. Hoch had written it with George O'Toole, a former CIA computer specialist and the author of *The Assassination Tapes* [Zebra Books, 1975], a book which revealed that psychological stress analysis of Oswald's voice indicates he was telling the truth when he denied killing President Kennedy. Hoch himself, a physicist at the University of California at Berkeley, was a respected Warren Commission critic known for his plodding dissections of Government documents.

Hoch and O'Toole's article, "Dallas: The Cuban Connection," dealt with the visit to Silvia Odio: "*The Saturday Evening Post* has learned of a link between the Odio incident and one of the many attempts on the life of Cuban Premier Fidel Castro carried out by the Central Intelligence Agency and Cuban emigres in the early 1960s."

Hoch had discovered that Silvia Odio's parents had been arrested because they had harbored a fugitive named Reynol Gonzalez who was wanted for plotting to assassinate Castro in October, 1961. The plotters had planned to fire a bazooka from an apartment near the Presidential Palace and kill Castro while he was standing on a balcony, making one of his marathon speeches. The plot failed (the triggerman copped out at the last moment), the potential killers were arrested, and Gonzalez was later picked up on the Odio estate. However, Antonio Veciana, the chief organizer of the plot, escaped to Miami.

There he founded Alpha 66, which came to be one of the largest, best-financed and most aggressive of the militant Cuban exile groups.

The article pointed out that Alpha 66 had chapters all over the country, that Veciana made frequent fund-raising trips to these chapters, and that one of the chapters he visited was in Dallas at "3126 Hollandale." Digging in the mounds of Warren Commission files, Hoch had found a report by a Dallas deputy sheriff saying that an informant told him that a person resembling Oswald was seen associating with Cubans at "3128 Harlendale."

The article concluded: "Like the two Cubans who, with 'Leon Oswald,' visited Silvia Odio in September, 1963, Antonio Veciana was: 1) an anti-Castro activist, 2) engaged in raising funds for the commandos, and 3) acquainted with Silvia Odio's father. While this falls short of proving it, a real possibility exists that Veciana was one of the two Cubans who visited Silvia Odio, or that he at least can shed some light on the Odio incident."

I doubted that, but I had the advantage of having spoken to Silvia Odio and her father, Amador. If Veciana had been one of Silvia's visitors, I assumed both she and Amador would have confirmed that by now, since Veciana was a very visible figure in Miami's anti-Castro movement. If he hadn't been involved, I doubted that Veciana would know anything about the visit, but thought he might be worth talking with anyway. I didn't give it any priority, though, because I thought the article was overly speculative.

I was, however, intrigued by another possibility which Paul Hoch had raised in a memo to Schweiker, a long, impressively detailed analysis of one of the early Church Committee reports on assassination plots against foreign leaders. In his memo Hoch wondered why Veciana's 1961 attempt against Castro was not mentioned in the Church report. He pointed out that although the CIA claimed its ventures with the Mafia were suspended at that time, Hoch noted that there was an earlier directive still in effect—NSAM 100—which ordered a contingency plan drawn up for Castro's "removal."

Wrote Hoch: "The hypothesis that NSAM 100 and subsequent events were directly related to the Veciana plot deserves careful consideration. This would be the case even if there were no possible link to the Kennedy assassination through the people involved in the Odio incident. . . . It is possible that Veciana was under the direct control of the CIA."

Hoch's inference was intriguing. He was contending, in effect, that since the Veciana plot did not appear in the Church report, it was one the CIA was trying to hide.

Hoch is soft-spoken and conservative, so his conclusions seemed unusually strong: "I suggest consideration of the hypothesis that the

CIA has managed to draw the attention of the Church Committee away from assassination plots other than the Giancana-Roselli one (specifically, away from the Veciana plot) for some reason; and that the CIA has thus diverted attention from possible links between CIA activities and the Kennedy assassination." Then (characteristically), he cautiously added: "Clearly, such hypothesis is speculative."

About that time, there also appeared in *Esquire* an insightful column by its Washington watcher, Timothy Crouse, the same fellow who would later write for the *Village Voice*. Crouse suggested that the CIA, in revealing such flashy "secrets" as its deadly shellfish toxin and toxic dart gun, was really taking the Church Committee through a primrose maze. Crouse was disturbed that the Committee's majority counsel, F.A.O. Schwarz, Jr. ("he has the innocent look of one of the trolls they sell at the toy store his great-grandfather founded"), was accepting at face value the CIA's own enumeration of its misdeeds. "It's pretty unusual," Schwarz admitted to Crouse, "to find that the defendant has developed large parts of the case. It's very helpful."

That bothered Crouse: "It's a queer thing to hear the chief Senate investigator talking as if he and the CIA were partners in the search for the truth. . . . It does not seem to have occurred to Schwarz that the CIA was, is, and always will be, in the business of deception."

Crouse's conclusion was not irrelevant to that reached by Paul Hoch in his memorandum to Schweiker. "A subtle pattern begins to emerge," Crouse wrote. "One suspects that the agency may be trying to peddle certain crimes of its own choice, trying to guide the Church committee toward certain items and away from . . . God knows what."

There were no limits to the kinds of God-knows-what speculations bouncing around my mind by the time I decided to try to locate Antonio Veciana. I'd been procrastinating, figuring that anyone with his long terrorist reputation would naturally be elusive and difficult to find. I didn't know if he was still living in Miami—or even if he was still alive. I might have to put the word out through my contacts in Little Havana, start the tedious chore of combing through public records, spend days on the line or in the streets sniffing for his trail, pull out all the research sources I could muster.

I found Veciana listed in the Miami telephone directory.

When I first called Veciana's home in February, I spoke to his wife, Sira. She was, I would later find, a pleasantly pretty woman in her early forties, whose life was dedicated to the welfare of her family. She sounded slightly nervous when she said her husband wasn't home. I told her who I was and asked for the best time to reach him. She said I should talk to her son Tony, who told me his father was in Atlanta. (Tony, a college student, was the oldest son of Veciana's five children.) I asked Tony when his father would be home. He hesitated, then had a muffled conversation with his mother. "Well, he's in Atlanta and he won't be home for a while," he said. I asked if there were anyway I could reach him and, after another muffled exchange with his mother, Tony asked why I wanted to talk with his father. I had always made it a point never to specifically mention the Kennedy assassination when I approached any of the Cuban exiles, so I simply said that I was a staff investigator for Senator Schweiker, a member of the Church Committee. My interest, I said, was in learning something about the relationship between the Federal agencies and the anti-Castro Cubans during the early Sixties. There was another side conversation between Tony and his mother. "Well, you see," he said again, "he's in Atlanta." Why the hell did this kid keep telling me his father was in Atlanta? I'd heard that before and I was getting a little annoyed. Then it struck me: The Federal penitentiary is in Atlanta. Was he trying to tell me his father was in prison? That, it turned out, was exactly what he was trying to say. He was being protective of his father but, at the same time, he was thinking that I might be able to help in some way.

Tony's hesitation was understandable. I had approached the Veciana family at a time of extreme stress. It was a very close-knit family, as are many Cuban exile families, the father ruling gently but firmly. For the Veciana family to be without its patriarch, without even the stability of his inevitable presence at the main midday meal, was terribly stressful. Eventually, I would come to know the Vecianas well—his wife and his mother, who still lived with them, Tony and his sisters, Ana, then just finishing college, and Victoria, a high school senior, and the two little ones, Carlos, then five, and Bebe, three. Ana, now a columnist for the *Miami Herald*, would later write: "Despite my father's involvement in the maelstrom of Cuban politics, we have led a very normal life—on Cuban terms. We prayed to Our Lady of Charity (the patron saint of Cuba), we spoke Spanglish at home and fought—successfully—to leave the chaperons at home."

Understanding Veciana and his role as the patriarch, the circumstances of his being in prison and the stress that was causing his family, is, I now believe, crucial to understanding why Veciana provided me with the explosive information he did.

When I first spoke to young Tony Veciana, he would not tell me why his father was in prison, although he said his father had been in there for 26 months. "I think there are some people who want him in there," he said, "but I would rather you get the details from him. I think my father would be in favor of talking to you." Tony said he would write to his father and have him put me on his visitor's list. Of course, Tony added, I would first have to bring him some identification. I said I would and that I'd also try to go directly through the Federal prison authorities for permission to visit Atlanta.

A few days later I stopped by the Veciana home to give Tony my card and show him my official identification. It was a small, modest home with a green stucco facade on a quiet street at the northern edge of Miami's Little Havana. Around the abbreviated front yard was a low chainlink fence with a latch gate; to the right of the walk was a small white statue of the Madonna and Child, a slab bench set in front of it. Close by was a concrete planter in the form of a small ship. Dripping ferns and bromeliad hung from the edges of a white aluminum awning shading the tiled front porch. The house, comfortable and unpretentious, was bereft of the fancy iron scrollwork and rococo trim which adorns the domiciles of many of Miami's wealthy and more socially prominent Cuban exiles. You would not guess this to be home to a man of historical importance.

It was another month before I could talk with Antonio Veciana. Shortly after I had made arrangements to go to Atlanta, Veciana was told he would be getting an early parole. I decided to wait until he came home. I was in no hurry, and I had plenty to keep me very busy.

Meanwhile, I did what background checking I could into Veciana and Alpha 66. There was not much in the newspaper files about his early years: An accounting graduate of the University of Havana, he was considered the boy wonder of Cuban banking while still in his early twenties. He rose to become the right-hand man of Cuba's major banker, Julio Lobo, the millionaire who was also known as the ''Sugar King'' of Cuba. Veciana was 31 when Castro took power in 1959.

Alpha 66 emerged early in 1962, with Veciana its founder and chief spokesman. It received more press coverage than other militant exile groups because it appeared better organized, better equipped and consistently more successful in its guerrilla attacks and sabotage operations.

Alpha 66 was the Cuban exile group which especially seemed to taunt President Kennedy. Not content to limit its assaults to attacks against Cuba and Castro's forces, it also went after foreign ships supplying Castro and conducted assassination raids on Russian troops in Cuba. Long before the missile crisis, when Kennedy's policy was to maintain separate U.S. policies toward Russia and Cuba, Alpha 66 seemed bent on provoking a direct conflict between Russia and the United States.

Later, when Kennedy went to a special conference in Central America to rally support for his Cuba policy, Alpha 66 deliberately created an international incident by attacking a Soviet freighter in the Cuban port of Isabela de Sagua. To exacerbate the situation, Veciana conducted a special news conference for the international press in

Washington, detailing the attack and calling on Kennedy to take further direct action against Russia. The *New York Times* noted: "Hit-and-run attacks by Cuban exiles against Soviet ships in Cuba are causing dismay and embarrassment in the Administration."

At the height of the missile crisis, during the delicate negotiations to keep World War III from erupting, Alpha 66 continued its raids into Cuba and assaults on Castro's patrol boats. "We will attack again and again," announced Veciana. After the crisis, when Kennedy had issued his directive to halt the raids and to shut down the exile training camps, Alpha 66 defied the ban by continuing to operate secretly, even attacking British merchant ships in Cuban waters. A lead editorial in the *Times* warned: "No matter how much we may admire the anti-Castroism that motivates its actions, this group is nevertheless dangerously playing with the laws and the security of the United States."

To have the power to raise such a fuss, I figured Antonio Veciana must have been one helluva exile leader.

THIRTEEN

SOMETHING HAPPENED

*I*T WAS ALL SO INCONGRUOUS. One serene morning, thirteen years later, I was thinking about those anxious, nerve-wracking weeks of the Cuban missile crisis as I approached the cozy house on the quiet street in Little Havana to see the man who was once at the vortex of all that turmoil and terror. It was a beautiful blue-sky Florida winter morning, the sun comfortably warm, a nice breeze blowing from the southeast. I thought I'd like to be sailing.

I had contacted Veciana as soon as I learned he was out on parole, about a month after I had first spoken to his son. The only image I had seen of him was from an old newspaper clipping: the dreaded anti-Castro terrorist, a much younger man, his face contorted in anger, sneering a declaration of defiance.

The man who opened the door to the small green home appeared as little like a terrorist as one can imagine. He was, in fact, a very soft-looking man: fairly tall; a smooth, full face; wavy black hair; warm, dark eyes. Not at all muscular, he had a certain heft, a pearish paunch. He was casually but neatly dressed in pressed dark trousers and a fresh white *guayabera*—actually, nondescript attire in Little Havana. But what struck me most when I first met Veciana—and perhaps this is something one would notice more in Miami—was his pallor. He had been out for several days, yet his face still had very much a prison pallor—which is something that comes less from not being in the sun, than from something that happens to the spirit. The prison was still in Veciana's eyes.

We sat in the small front living room, which could very well have been set in my old North Philly neighborhood: two Spanish Provincial couches, one red and one green, fitted with clear plastic covers; large individual photographic portraits of each child adorning one wall; coffee table bearing a gilt-framed formal family portrait; crocheted doilies on the end tables.

As soon as I saw Veciana I knew that he could not have been directly involved in the Odio incident. He simply did not match the description of any of Silvia's visitors. (Certainly, she would have mentioned the large mole, or birthmark, over the right side of his mouth.) Later, when I asked Veciana about the Odio incident, he said he knew Amador Odio and Silvia, but he knew nothing about the incident. That, I thought, knocked out the theory that Hoch and O'Toole had advanced in their *Post* article.

When I sat down with Veciana, I gave him my "cover" story: I wanted to talk with him about the relationship of the U.S. intelligence agencies with the anti-Castro Cuban groups in general. I said nothing of my interest in the Kennedy assassination. Since Schweiker had gotten relatively little media attention compared to the headlines being made by the Church Committee, there was little reason for Veciana to assume the assassination was my priority.

Although Veciana said he would answer any questions I had, initially he seemed defensive. "I will tell you what you want to know," he said, "but I am worried about certain things that can be used against me." He said there were things that happened that he did not understand and which, he believed, were connected with his going to prison on a drug-conspiracy charge. He would be glad to talk about that, because it wasn't true. But there were other things he was concerned about and he said he would talk with me only if I could assure him that any information he provided would not be used against him.

That puzzled me a bit, but I assumed he was concerned about some U.S. laws he may have broken during the course of his anti-Castro activity. I assured him our talk would be confidential and would not be made public. (I felt I could trust Schweiker to back me up and he did. What I didn't realize then was that once something is thrown into the political hopper that is the Federal bureaucracy, its ultimate use is dictated by political ends.) Veciana accepted my assurances; as I came to understand, Veciana himself was anxious to use me. Just released from prison, uncertain and confused about what had happened to him, he took my arrival as an opportunity to establish a defense against any other actions which might be taken against him. This only became clear to me much later.

First off, I asked Veciana for some general background about how he had gotten involved in anti-Castro activity. He said that, as president of the association of certified public accountants in Cuba, he had always been interested in politics and, in fact, was among the leaders of a group of professional association presidents who had secretly worked on Castro's behalf during General Batista's reign. As a result, when Castro took over, Veciana was asked to join the government as a top finance minister. He turned the offer down, he said, because he had a good position in Cuba's major bank. But he knew and worked closely with Castro's highest-ranking government officials.

It was his inside knowledge of the government which gave Veciana an early indication that Castro was really a Communist. His disillusionment grew, and soon he was talking with a few very close friends about working against Castro. Then, he said, certain people came to him and started talking about eliminating Castro.

For some reason, the way Veciana put it made me think of Paul Hoch's memo to Schweiker, which raised the possibility of CIA involvement in Veciana's failed bazooka plot on Castro's life. So I asked Veciana if any of the people who spoke with him about eliminating Castro were representatives of the United States Government. Well, said Veciana, that was something he had never talked about before, but there was an American he dealt with who had very strong connections with the U.S. Government.

For the next hour and a half, I questioned Veciana about this American, one Maurice Bishop, who was, it turned out, the secret supervisor and director of all Veciana's anti-Castro activities. Bishop was the man who had suggested the founding of Alpha 66 and guided its overall strategy. Bishop not only directed the assassination attempt on Castro in Cuba in October, 1961, he also engineered the plan to kill Castro in Chile in 1971. Bishop had the connections to pull strings with the U.S. Government and get the financial support needed. He involved Veciana not only in anti-Castro activity but in anti-Communist activity in Latin America as well. They worked together for thirteen years.

I was fascinated. I knew I had stumbled upon something important. Bishop was obviously an intelligence agency connection—a direct connection—to an anti-Castro group. The CIA had always denied playing a supervisory role in the activities of anti-Castro groups after the Bay of Pigs, claiming it only "monitored" such activity. Yet, here was Veciana, *the* key leader of the largest and most militant anti-Castro group, revealing much more then just a monitoring interest on the Agency's part—revealing, in fact, likely CIA involvement in two Castro assassination attempts which the Agency had not admitted to the Church Committee. I remember wondering how the guys at the Church Committee would handle this one, that is, if they even gave a damn now that they were frantically trying to wrap up their final report.

It was all fascinating but not especially relevant to the Kennedy assassination. I could see no connection between Veciana's activities in Miami and what had happened in Dallas. Then Veciana said he had met with Bishop over the years in places outside Miami—including Dallas, Las Vegas, Washington, Puerto Rico and Latin America—and started talking about chapters of Alpha 66 he had set up across the country. That gave me the opportunity to casually ask him about the one in Dallas.

Yes, Veciana said, he had gone to Dallas and had spoken at some fund-raising meetings at the home of the Alpha 66 delegate there.

I asked him if he knew Jorge Salazar. That was the name mentioned in Hoch and O'Toole's article, in the part about Cubans gathering at "3126 Hollandale." But I did not mention that to Veciana, nor did I say that Lee Harvey Oswald was reportedly seen there.

"No," said Veciana, "I do not know the Salazar that is mentioned in the magazine article in Dallas. And I never saw Oswald at the home where we met."

I was surprised that Veciana should mention Oswald at all. "Why did you mention Oswald?" I asked.

"Because that is what it said in the article. I just read it yesterday. Wait a moment, I still have it in the bedroom."

Veciana got up, went back into the bedroom and returned with a copy of the *Saturday Evening Post* with Hoch and O'Toole's piece. I hadn't realized it was already published.

"No . . . ," Veciana was saying as he sat back down, "I never saw Oswald at that place where we held the meetings . . ."

I was jotting that down in my notebook, not looking at him, as he continued . . .

" . . . but I remember once meeting Lee Harvey Oswald."

I did not look up. In my mind, I fell off the chair. But I restrained myself and, attempting to sound exceptionally casual, I asked in a forced monotone: "Oh, really. How did you meet him? Where? When?"

Veciana said he met Oswald with Maurice Bishop in Dallas sometime near the beginning of September, 1963.

There, in that modest green house in Little Havana, over a dozen years after the assassination of John F. Kennedy, the reality of what I was involved in suddenly hit. The killing of the President was no longer a series of lingering television images, bold headlines, thick stacks of documents, books and files, it had *actually happened*. There were living people with direct connections through time to that moment. As much as the substance of the information itself, it was the absolutely coincidental and credible way it came up, which so stunned me. First impressions are inherently circumstantial judgments, but I had no doubt then—and have none now—that Veciana was simply and truthfully revealing what he knew.

The details are what make the case.

FOURTEEN

THE SPY MASTER PULLS
THE STRINGS

ONE MORNING, about a year and a half after Castro took power, Antonio Veciana's secretary at the Banco Financiero in Havana handed him a business card from a gentleman, who, she said, was waiting to see him. The name on the card was Maurice Bishop. Veciana does not specifically remember the name of the business imprinted on the card but now believes it may have been a construction firm headquartered in Belgium.

Veciana first thought that his caller was a potential customer for his bank and, initially, Maurice Bishop did not lead Veciana to think otherwise. Although he spoke excellent Spanish, Bishop said he was an American and that he wanted to talk with Veciana about the state of the Cuban economy and where it appeared to be going since Castro took over. They talked for quite a while and then, around noon, Bishop suggested they continue their conversation over lunch. Bishop took Veciana to a fine restaurant called the Floridita, once one of Hemingway's favorite watering holes. As they talked, Bishop began to express concern about the Cuban government leaning towards Communism. He also let it be known that he was aware of Veciana's feelings toward Castro. That surprised Veciana because he had told only a few trusted friends about his disillusionment with Castro's government. As it turned out, among those he told were two who had contact with the CIA: One was his boss, Julio Lobo. (Later, in exile, Lobo set up an "independent" front committee to raise $20 million for the return of the Bay of Pigs prisoners.) Another was Rufo Lopez-

Fresquet, who, for the first fourteen months of the Revolution, was Minister of the Treasury and the CIA's liaison with the Castro government.)

As the lunch continued, it became obvious to Veciana that Bishop knew a good deal about him. It also became obvious that Bishop was not interested in Veciana's banking services but, rather, in recruiting him as an active participant in the growing movement against the government of Fidel Castro and Communism. "He tried to impress on me the seriousness of the situation," Veciana said.

Veciana was ready. He had already come to the conclusion that Castro, by moving toward even tighter control than Batista ever had, was a traitor to the Revolution; Veciana had come to despise Castro. He told Bishop that he was willing to work with him and Bishop offered to pay him for his services. Veciana told him that he did not need to get paid to fight against Castro, but when the job was over, if Bishop insisted, they could settle accounts then. It was the summer of 1960; Veciana did not think it would take very long to topple Castro.

Just because it appeared to be so obvious, Veciana asked Bishop if he worked for the U.S. Government. "He told me at the time," Veciana recalled, "that he was not in a position to let me know for whom he was working or for which agency he was doing this."

There were several meetings after that, and Veciana and Bishop got to know one another better. Finally, Bishop told Veciana that he would like him to take a "training program" in order to prepare for the work ahead. This program was a series of nightly lectures and instruction given in a nondescript office in a building which Veciana recalls as being on El Vedado, a commercial strip. He remembers seeing the name of a mining company in the building directory and, on the ground floor, a branch of the Berlitz School of Languages.

In addition to Bishop, who would attend on some evenings, Veciana's instructor was a man he recalls only as "Mr. Melton." Although he was given some training in sabotage techniques and the use of explosives, Veciana's lessons dealt mainly in propaganda and psychological warfare. "Bishop told me several times," Veciana said, "that psychological warfare could help more than hundreds of soldiers, thousands of soldiers." Veciana was also trained in the various aspects and methods of counterintelligence, surveillance and communications. The thrust of all this, however, was not to make him a proficient guerrilla operative but a higher-echelon planner and supervisor. As Veciana put it: "The main purpose was to train me to be an organizer, so I was supposed to initiate a type of action and other people would be the ones who would really carry it out."

The training sessions lasted only a few weeks. By that time, Bishop and Veciana were concocting various schemes to undermine

Castro's regime. Because of Veciana's contacts, several plots to discredit key Communists and funnel the Cuban government's own money into the hands of anti-Castro guerrillas bore fruit. In one instance, Veciana successfully schemed to get Castro's top aide, Che Guevara, to sign a $200,000 check which was slipped to the underground. Veciana also set in motion a propaganda program which destabilized Cuba's currency by creating public distrust of its value.

At Bishop's direction, Veciana also began taking a more active role in the organized underground movement. "Bishop always wanted to be kept informed about what was going on with the various groups," Veciana told me. With his supervisory training and technical expertise, Veciana soon became chief of sabotage for the *Movimiento Revolucionario del Pueblo*, one of the largest underground groups. Formed by Manolo Ray, the MRP was the predecessor of *JURE*.

Although Maurice Bishop refused to acknowledge any connection with the U.S. Government, he was apparently familiar with certain personnel in the American Embassy in Havana; he recommended that Veciana contact specific individuals there to get direct assistance and supplies for the anti-Castro movement. Bishop, however, asked Veciana not to mention his name or the fact that he was sent by an American. Nor did Bishop indicate whether or not the contacts he suggested were intelligence agents.

One of these Embassy contacts was a "Colonel Kail." Kail, who was in the Army, told Veciana the U.S. Government could not directly support him in any way. Kail did say, however, that he could be of assistance with passports and visas for plotters who wanted to escape. In January, 1961, the American Embassy closed, shortly after Veciana last talked with Kail.

Bishop left Cuba before the Bay of Pigs invasion in April, 1961, and Veciana says they had not met for some months prior to it. After the Bay of Pigs fiasco, Bishop returned to Cuba (probably with a Belgian passport) and Veciana recalls that he and Bishop had long discussions about what had happened. He says Bishop told him that Kennedy's refusal to provide air support was the crucial factor in the failure of the operation. Bishop obviously felt a terrible frustration about that because, according to Veciana, it was then that "Bishop decided that the only thing left to be done was to have an attempt on Castro's life."

The assassination of Fidel Castro was something that Veciana and Bishop had discussed before. Earlier that year, Russia's first spaceman, Yuri Gagarin, had visited Castro, and Veciana had suggested an attempt at that time. Bishop, who always seemed critically aware of the propaganda repercussions of any scheme, rejected the idea. "He said that it would cause too much trouble between the United States and Russia," recalls Veciana.

It was decided that an appropriate opportunity would be when Castro made a public appearance on the balcony of the Presidential Palace at a ceremony scheduled for early October, 1961. Veciana had his mother-in-law rent an apartment on the eighth floor of a building within range of the balcony and then made arrangements for her escape to the United States by boat on the day before the planned attempt. (He had already flown his wife and children to Spain as a precaution.) He then recruited triggermen and obtained the weapons. (Weapons availability was not a major problem; a good supply had been air-dropped by the U.S. prior to the Bay of Pigs.) A massive firepower attack, with automatic rifles, grenade launchers and a bazooka, was planned so that all of the aides appearing with Castro that day would be killed.

Then Veciana learned that Castro's intelligence agency, the DGI, was suspicious of him when his cousin, Guillermo Ruiz, a high-ranking DGI officer, asked him why he had been visiting the American Embassy. Veciana said it was only to see about obtaining passports for some friends but Ruiz pointed out that Veciana had been using the wrong entrance. Veciana took it as a warning that he was being watched. Bishop confirmed his fears and suggested that Veciana consider leaving Cuba.

The night before the assassination attempt, Veciana discovered that the landing site for his mother-in-law's escape boat was under heavy surveillance and the boat could not come into the dock. Because his mother-in-law couldn't swim, Veciana says he pushed her into the water and swam out to the boat with her. At that point, he decided it was too dangerous to return to shore and went with her to Miami.

The planned bazooka attack never came off. Fearing the DGI had learned of the plot, the firing team fled the apartment. (And, indeed, the DGI did know that something was up, but only later did it find the apartment and seize the weapons.)

Veciana was not in Miami very long before Maurice Bishop was back in touch. (Veciana would not have been very difficult to find in the close-knit exile community even if Bishop hadn't had access to official Immigration records.) Soon they were meeting regularly and planning anti-Castro strategies. The result was the founding of Alpha 66 which, according to Veciana, was Bishop's brainchild. (The name was a hybrid: "Alpha" symbolized the beginning of the end of Castro; "66" represented the number of fellow accountants Veciana had recruited at the start of his anti-Castro activities.)

Veciana was Alpha 66's chief executive officer, spokesman and fund-raiser. As the organization's military leader, he recruited former Rebel Army officer Major Eloy Gutierrez Menoyo. A daring soldier, Menoyo had the reputation among Cuban exiles of being a socialist, and Bishop expressed some doubts about his loyalty, but Veciana knew Menoyo and convinced Bishop he could be trusted. (Veciana never told Menoyo about Bishop but believes today that Menoyo may have suspected that his friend had some outside guidance.)

With strong management, clever use of propaganda, organizational and fund-raising skills, and expertise in weaponry and military operations, Alpha 66 soon rose to the forefront of Miami's numerous anti-Castro exile groups.

Veciana was all over the place: buying guns and boats, recruiting members, organizing training sites, making fiery speeches, issuing communiques and announcing successful raids into Cuba. At one point, Veciana proclaimed that he had a war chest of $100,000 and that eleven major exile organizations were backing Alpha 66's efforts. Veciana gave not a hint that there was another person behind the scenes—except for one minor slip which no one paid any attention to at the time. At a press conference recorded in the *New York Times* on September 14th, 1962, Veciana announced a series of forthcoming Alpha 66 raids and, in passing, added that the planning was being done by those "I don't even know."

According to Veciana, the special headaches Alpha 66 created for President Kennedy before and during the Cuban missile crisis and the timing of the raids during the Kennedy-Khrushchev negotiations were all deliberately planned by Maurice Bishop. So was a special press conference held in March, 1963, after the crisis, while Kennedy was in Costa Rica trying to gain Latin American support for his new Cuba policy. At the press conference, Veciana announced Alpha 66's successful attack on a Russian ship docked in a Cuban harbor and described the ensuing firefight with Russian troops. "The purpose was to publicly embarrass Kennedy and force him to move against Castro," Veciana now admits. (Bishop was not present at the press conference, Veciana says. But Bishop arranged for two high-ranking Government officials to attend, one in the Department of Health and one in the Department of Agriculture, to give it more legitimacy.) Certainly the press conference got publicity, as Bishop had planned. The *New York Times* said the Government "was embarrassed by the incident," and noted that Kennedy's party in Costa Rica telephoned several times for reports on the situation.

Although Maurice Bishop often suggested specific tactical moves, his concern was more with the overall strategy of Alpha 66 and Veciana's anti-Castro activity. As such, he was not in constant contact with Veciana; they never saw each other more than a dozen or so times in any one year. Although a trust developed, there was no true personal relationship between them, no private matters were discussed that did not bear upon their mutual anti-Castro mission. (That, however, may say less about Bishop than it does about Veciana. Throughout the years I've known Veciana, the numerous times I've been at his home and among his family, the conversation inevitably returns to his passion—Cuban politics and anti-Castro activity.)

Early on, Veciana and Bishop developed an understanding, and the arrangements they had for meeting were right out of the standard operating procedures manual of a covert operative. Every meeting was instigated by Bishop; he would call Veciana and set the time and the place of the meeting. Usually it was in a public place, on a street corner or in a park, and they would walk and talk. There were meetings in Havana, however, which took place at a country club and, once, in an apartment across the street from the American Embassy. If Veciana was traveling, Bishop would come to his hotel. The majority of their meetings over the years were in Miami and Puerto Rico, where most of Alpha 66's operational planning took place. Veciana assumed that Bishop would fly in for these meetings because Bishop would often come in a rented car.

During Alpha 66's most active period, Veciana was constantly on the move, and, for security reasons, not very visible. At that time, Veciana told me, he made arrangements whereby Bishop could find out where he was at any moment. Someone whom Veciana trusted implicitly was designated as the link, although he did not tell this third party who Bishop was or the nature of their relationship. However, this party always knew Veciana's whereabouts and could give Bishop instructions on how to reach him. Veciana told me this third party was not a member of his family, did not know Bishop and therefore would be of no help in locating or identifying Bishop. Although he refused to reveal the name, I thought the fact that Veciana had volunteered the existence of an intermediary as a strong indication of his credibility.

It took me three years to find out the identity of this third party. I learned that this third party was a woman who had not been active in anti-Castro politics; that she had a husband and family she was concerned about protecting; and that she was a Government employee who, if Bishop still had any connections, might be vulnerable to pressure. Veciana's reasons for wanting to protect her identity were legitimate. Whether or not she could have identified Bishop, she was in a position to confirm Veciana's credibility. What happened when I finally discovered her identity, and how that information was handled, gave me significant insight into the House Assassinations Committee's investigation and those who controlled it.

FIFTEEN

THE SUBPLOTS OF DECEPTION

WRITING ABOUT HIS Cuban operational days in *Give Us This Day*, CIA officer E. Howard Hunt recalled his first meeting with Frank Drecher, the phony "real" name he gave his project chief: "Drecher then told me," Hunt writes, "he had adopted the operational alias of Frank Bender in his dealings with the Cubans, whom he told he was the representative of a private American group made up of wealthy industrialists. . . ." Hunt revealed he also used that same cover story and, from the spate of memoirs that have since poured from former CIA officers, it appears to have been a fairly typical line. It was an effective enough cover, sufficiently credible to account for the huge amount of money the operative usually had available.

It was the same cover story that Maurice Bishop used. "He would tell me," Veciana recalls, "that, you know, there are some other people, some very wealthy businessmen, who would like to get rid of Castro also." Bishop was never any more specific than that. Yet down through the years it became obvious that Maurice Bishop's range of contacts and his ability to get strings pulled went far beyond those of any private individual or independent group.

Shortly after Veciana left Cuba, Bishop called and they met on a downtown Miami street corner. They walked about for a while talking. Bishop spoke about how the fight against Castro might be more difficult and longer than they had first envisioned, how he and Veciana would have to work closely together and how they must develop a mutual trust and loyalty. Veciana agreed. Would Veciana, Bishop asked, be willing to sign a contract to that effect? Of course, said Veciana. Bishop then led Veciana to the Pan American Bank Building, a five-story office structure in the heart of Miami's business district. Veciana recalls that they took an elevator and that Bishop opened an unmarked office door with a key. The office had only a desk and a few chairs, but Veciana does remember an American flag standing in one corner.

There was no one in the office when they arrived. Bishop left through another door in the office and returned with two men and some papers, which he asked Veciana to read and sign. Veciana believes the documents were contracts and loyalty oaths. He was not given copies. He recalls that in the contract was a space for a salary figure and, according to his original agreement with Bishop, that had been left blank. Veciana now describes the incident as a "commitment" ceremony. "It was a pledge of my loyalty, a secret pledge. I think they wanted to impress on me my responsibility and my commitment to the cause." Today Veciana cannot recall exactly what the two men who came in with Bishop looked like or if he was introduced to them. He believes they were just witnesses.

I later checked the directory of the Pan American Bank Building for the period Veciana talked about, but there were so many CIA fronts of all types in Miami at the time it was impossible to pick them out by business activity, although the building had a few import-export firms. It also had, in nine separate offices on four different floors, branches of four Federal agencies, including Treasury, State and Health, Education & Welfare. The temporary use of a Government office could have easily been arranged by Bishop. As an investigator working for Congress, I often made use of Federal agency offices myself.

Veciana was impressed with Bishop's range of knowledge of, and his connections with, covert CIA activities, including those the Agency was using as contacts or, to use the CIA term, "assets." For instance, at one point Bishop asked Veciana to monitor an operation code named "Cellula Fantasma," which was a propaganda operation involving leaflet drops over Cuba. ("Bishop told me it cost the CIA $300,000 for that operation," Veciana says.) Veciana's job was to attend a couple of planning meetings and report back to Bishop. One of those involved in planning the action was Frank Fiorini Sturgis. "At that time," Veciana recalls, "I remember Bishop saying to me about Fiorini that he wasn't just another soldier, he was more than that."

While Veciana was certain that Bishop's "businessman" story was hogwash and he was almost certain Bishop worked for the CIA, he had considered the possibility that Bishop worked for a different intelligence agency. Other than the CIA, among the most active monitors of anti-Castro activity was the Army Intelligence section. Veciana specifically recalls being contacted in 1962 in Puerto Rico by an American who called himself Patrick Harris. From a series of long conversations with Harris, Veciana concluded that Harris was Army Intelligence—especially after he told Veciana that he might be able to provide some support for his anti-Castro activities. But Harris first wanted to make an inspection trip to Alpha 66's operational base in the Bahamas. Veciana eventually came to trust Harris and gave him and a couple of his associates a tour of the base, but Harris never did come through with any aid. "I told Bishop about that," Veciana now says, "and he told me not to bother with them, that they could not help me. He was right."

In 1968, Maurice Bishop helped Veciana get a job with the U.S. Agency for International Development, working as a banking adviser to Bolivia's Central Bank in La Paz. It was a very well-paying job and his checks came directly from the U.S. Treasury Department in Washington. "I was very surprised I was hired because I was a known terrorist," Veciana told me. "The State Department, which hired me, once ordered me confined to Dade County because of my anti-Castro activity. Then in La Paz they put my office in the American Embassy. For sure, Bishop had very good connections."

Veciana worked for AID at the Central Bank in La Paz for four years, receiving more than $31,000 a year. Veciana says, however, he did very little bank advising during that period. Instead, he spent almost all his time working on anti-Castro and anti-Communist activities, directed by Bishop. (It has since been reported that the CIA has often used the AID as a front; the CIA even got one of its proprietary companies a multi-million dollar AID contract to train Thailand's border police.)

The fact that Bishop was interested in more than just knocking off Castro is significant because it further discredits Bishop's disenfranchised-capitalists cover story and precludes an operation funded by Organized Crime gambling czars intent on getting their Cuban holdings back. In addition, the type of anti-Communist scheming which Bishop had Veciana carry out incorporated the sophisticated counterintelligence and psychological warfare techniques which would be employed by someone with a strategic overview. For instance, while working for the AID, Veciana traveled around Latin America—with Bishop paying expenses—involving himself in propaganda ploys aimed at the character assassination of leading Communist politicians or weakening the financial stability of left-leaning governments. (Once, when I questioned Veciana about Bishop's competence in light of his failure to assassinate Castro, Veciana smiled slightly and said,

"No, we did not kill Castro, but there were many other plans, many other plots that did work." He did not want to elaborate.)

One of the more complicated plots to kill Castro was developed early in 1971, when Bishop told Veciana that the Cuban leader would probably make a state visit to Chile some time later that year. He suggested that Veciana begin planning another assassination attempt. "He told me," Veciana says, "that it was an opportunity to make it appear that the anti-Castro Cubans killed Castro without American involvement."

Veciana set up his headquarters in Caracas. It was a natural because the Venezuelan bureaucracy is deeply infiltrated by both anti-Castro Cubans and the CIA. There he was able to recruit an experienced and effective team, including two veteran terrorists willing to do the actual shooting. On the surface, the scheme was relatively simple: Towards the end of his visit to Chile, Castro was scheduled to have a major press conference with as many as 400 journalists, including radio and television reporters. Press credentials for the two designated assassins would be obtained from a Venezuelan television station and, despite the tight security, their weapons would be smuggled into the conference room inside a television camera.

According to Veciana, Maurice Bishop not only suggested the operation, he had a major role in setting it up. Bishop provided the weapons and made arrangements with top leaders in the Chilean military—which would be providing security at the conference—for the assassins to be immediately arrested by Chilean soldiers before Castro's own bodyguards could kill them. Bishop said he would arrange their escape from Chile later on. (Ironically, the president of Chile at the time was the democratically elected socialist Salvador Allende. But this didn't prevent the military from pursuing its own agenda and, two years later, in September, 1973, Allende was overthrown in a military coup d'état.)

But this attempt to assassinate Castro also failed. At the very last moment the two designated shooters decided that they would never get out of the conference room alive; they did not believe that Veciana had made arrangements for their capture. Veciana could not, of course, tell them of Bishop or how the arrangements had been made. To make things worse, other anti-Castro Cubans who Veciana had recruited for the scheme also had not believed that Veciana could arrange for the shooters' escape. So, without Veciana's knowledge, they developed a subplot based on the assumption that the shooters would be immediately caught and killed. When the existence of the subplot later came to light, Veciana told me, it produced the crack that eventually led to the end of his relationship with Maurice Bishop two years later.

Among those Veciana recruited in Caracas for the plot were two veterans of the war against Castro, Lucilo Peña and Luis Posada. Both had backgrounds as action men. Peña is now the general director of a major chemical firm and has excellent social and business contacts. But he was once involved in Alpha 66's "Plan Omega," a plot to invade Cuba from a base in the Dominican Republic.

Luis Posada was even more intriguing. When I interviewed him in 1978, he was in jail in Caracas, having been arrested with Dr. Orlando Bosch (probably the best known of exile terrorists, Bosch, you'll recall, was mentioned in Marita Lorenz's green notebook), for blowing up a Cubana Airlines plane that killed 73 persons. Posada was a veteran of the Bay of Pigs, a member of *JURE*, a former lieutenant in the U.S. Army (where he took intelligence staff officer courses), an agent for the CIA and, until his arrest, the owner of a very successful private detective agency in Caracas. In 1971, when Veciana was working with him, he was chief of security and counterintelligence in the Venezuelan secret police, *DISIP*.

According to Veciana, it was Peña and Posada who provided all the credentials and documents necessary to enable the selected assassins to establish their false identities and get into place in Chile. But, says Veciana, they also planted phony documents so that if the two who were going to assassinate Castro were caught and killed, the trail would lead to two Russian agents in Caracas.

It was an elaborate scheme. False surveillance reports were slipped into the files of the Venezuelan secret police to indicate that the Cuban assassins had been seen meeting with the Russian agents. (One of these agents was a correspondent for *Izvestia*; the other was a professor at the University of Central Venezuela.) Also in the files were fake passports, diaries and notes which would be planted in one of the assassin's hotel rooms to prove his contacts with the agents. But the most damaging evidence they concocted was a photograph showing what appeared to be one of the assassins leaning into a car window talking with one of the agents. The photo was actually of another Cuban who closely resembled the assassin. As instructed, this double stopped the Russian agent's car as he left his home one morning, leaned in and asked him for a match. A telephoto shot was taken of this encounter.

Following the failure of the assassination scheme, Maurice Bishop learned of the existence of this subplot. Veciana told me that Bishop was furious. He accused Veciana of taking part in the planning or, at the very least, knowing about the plot and keeping it a secret from him. Veciana still insists that he was unaware of the secondary scheme. He says Bishop investigated the matter and eventually came to believe him, but told Veciana that in any future operations his suspicions would linger. Bishop said that, considering the type of operations in which they were involved, a relationship of less than total trust would be no good. He suggested that they sever their ties.

I believe there was more to it than that. Veciana may have been getting more aggressive and fanatic in his determination to kill Castro while Bishop wanted to pull back. But Veciana was insisting that they increase their terrorist actions and, indeed, may have already instituted some plans himself, including another Castro assassination attempt. Perhaps Bishop feared that Veciana was getting a bit out of hand and had to be cut off. In fact, Veciana initially believed that Bishop had something to do with his going to prison, that it was both a warning to keep his mouth shut and to desist from independent scheming. That was a key factor in Veciana's decision to tell me about Maurice Bishop.

At any rate, when Bishop told Veciana he would like to stop their relationship, he also said he thought that Veciana deserved compensation for the thirteen years they had worked together. In the past, Veciana had rejected the idea of getting paid to fight Castro; now Bishop insisted that Veciana be paid.

It was July 26, 1972. (Veciana recalls commenting to his wife when he got home that afternoon on the irony of the date and its association with Castro's own movement.) Bishop called, asking Veciana to meet him in the parking lot of the Flagler Dog Track, not far from Veciana's home. The track was in session and the parking lot was crowded. Veciana spotted Bishop waiting in a car at the designated spot and Bishop got out of the car holding a briefcase. With him were two clean-cut young men in dark suits who stood out of earshot while Bishop and Veciana spoke. Bishop said he regretted that their relationship had to end but that it would be best for both of them in the long run. He shook Veciana's hand and wished him luck. Then he handed Veciana the briefcase. In it, he said, was the compensation that was due him. When Veciana got home he opened the briefcase—it was stuffed with cash. Exactly $253,000, says Veciana.

And that, says Veciana, was the last time he saw or spoke with Maurice Bishop.

SIXTEEN

AN OFFER HE COULDN'T REFUSE

*I*T IS NOT GENERALLY KNOWN—and researchers have yet to find a reason for it—but there is a period of Lee Harvey Oswald's stay in New Orleans which is largely undocumented. On August 9th, 1963, Oswald was arrested after distributing pro-Castro leaflets and scuffling with Carlos Bringuier. On August 16th, Oswald was again leafletting in front of the New Orleans Trade Mart and was, in fact, shown that evening on the news doing it. On August 21st, Oswald had his radio debate with Carlos Bringuier, which was arranged by the right-wing New Orleans broadcaster William Stuckey, a self-styled "Latin-American affairs expert." Despite seeming to go out of his way to court public attention as a Castro supporter, as soon as Oswald got it he dropped out of sight. Between August 21st and September 17th, there is no validated indication of Oswald's whereabouts.

Aside from visiting his aunt and uncle on Labor Day, Marina Oswald told the Warren Commission, her husband spent this time at home reading and practicing with his rifle. Down through the years, however, Marina Oswald's testimony has been inconsistent, contradictory and admittedly false. The House Assassinations Committee, for instance, found several very credible witnesses who saw Oswald during this period in Clinton, Louisiana, about 130 miles from New Orleans, at a black voter registration drive. With him were David Ferrie, an anti-Castro activist, and either—eyewitness descriptions could fit one or the other—New Orleans businessman Clay Shaw, a CIA asset, or Guy Banister, a former FBI agent who ran anti-Castro activities out of an office at 544 Camp Street, the address on the pro-Castro leaflets Oswald had been distributing. The Assassinations Committee could not determine what Oswald was doing in Clinton, but there was no doubt he was there.

The Warren Commission found records accounting for some of Oswald's activity during this time, but none could be authenticated and portions were later discovered to be false. He reportedly visited the unemployment office, cashed some unemployment checks and withdrew some library books. The FBI could not, however, authenticate Oswald's signature on the unemployment documents and of the seventeen firms where he said he had applied for work, thirteen denied it and four did not exist. Strange also, considering Oswald's meticulousness about such things, three library books returned at the end of this period were overdue. However, even if all the records were true, there is one span of time, between September 6th and 9th, when Oswald's whereabouts are absolutely unknown.

Initially, Antonio Veciana told me that it was sometime in late August or early September, 1963, when Bishop called and asked him to meet in Dallas. Later, as he gave it more thought, he said it was probably early September, perhaps towards the end of the first week of the month.

It was not the first time that Bishop had asked Veciana to meet him in Dallas; they had met there a number of times. Partly because of that, Veciana suspected that Bishop was from Dallas, or at least had some family there. Moreover, he knew that the Colonel Kail Bishop had sent him to see at the American Embassy in Cuba was from Dallas—Kail had mentioned going home to Dallas for Christmas. And when he reported to Bishop about this meeting with Kail, Veciana got the impression that Bishop knew Kail, or at least knew his background, and that they had something in common. In our very first interview, Veciana said, "I think that maybe Bishop is from Texas."

The Dallas meeting with Bishop that September took place in the busy lobby of a large downtown office building. From Veciana's description of its distinctive blue tiled facade, it was probably the Southland Center, a 42-story office complex built in the late Fifties. Veciana recalls that as soon as he walked in, he saw Bishop standing in a corner of the lobby talking with a pale, slight and soft-featured young man. Veciana does not recall if Bishop introduced him by name, but Bishop ended his conversation with the young man shortly after Veciana arrived. Together, they walked out of the lobby onto the busy sidewalk. Bishop and the young man stopped behind Veciana for a moment, had a few additional words, then the young man gestured farewell and walked away. Bishop immediately turned to Veciana and began a discussion of the current activities of Alpha 66 as they walked to a nearby coffee shop. He never spoke to Veciana about the young man and Veciana didn't ask.

On the day that John F. Kennedy was assassinated, Veciana immediately recognized the news photographs and television images of Lee Harvey Oswald as being of the young man he had seen with Maurice Bishop in Dallas. There was no doubt in his mind. When I asked if it could have been someone who closely resembled Oswald, Veciana said, "Well, you know, Bishop himself taught me how to remember faces, how to remember characteristics. I am sure it was Oswald. If it wasn't Oswald, it was someone who looked exactly like him. *Exacto, exacto.*"

To those unacquainted with the world of intelligence, government security and certain areas of law enforcement, it would seem incredible that Veciana did not ask about Oswald or even mention him to Bishop after the Kennedy assassination. Yet those who are familiar with the way that world works know it would have gone against standard operating procedure if he had. One of the cardinal principles of all security operations is that information is passed on or sought after only on a "need to know" basis. Two individuals who have known each other for years, work in adjoining offices at the CIA headquarters at Langley, Virginia, go to lunch together daily, who are close personal and family friends, might not know what each other actually does at his desk every day, or what he's working on—and would never ask. So Veciana did not ask. He does recall, however, feeling very uneasy at the time. "That was a very difficult situation because I was afraid. We both understood, I could guess that he knew that I was knowledgeable of that and I learned that the best way is not to know, not to get to know things that don't concern you, so I respected the rules and didn't mention that ever."

Veciana's fear of possibly becoming involved in the Kennedy assassination was increased by a visit a few days after the murder from Cesar Diosdato, a Government agent who ostensibly worked for the U.S. Customs Service in Key West. Diosdato was a well-known figure among anti-Castro activists in Miami because, technically, preventing violations of the Neutrality Act—which occurred every time an anti-Castro raiding party took off from Miami or the Florida Keys—was Customs' job. With a radio-equipped patrol car, the pistol-packing Diosdato, a beefy, mustachioed Mexican-American, roamed the Keys like a traffic cop, monitoring the launching sites of the exile raiding groups. But he didn't stop them all and the word among anti-Castro raiders in JM/WAVE's secret war was that no attacks could be launched from the Keys without his permission. "He gave us the green light," one former group leader told me. "Without word from him, we couldn't go." As a result, most of the Cubans thought Diosdato was really working for the CIA. Veciana did.

That's why he became particularly apprehensive when Diosdato came by, asking him if he knew anything about the Kennedy assassination or Lee Harvey Oswald. Diosdato approached him casually—they knew each other because Veciana had frequently gone to Key West to get clearance for Alpha 66's raids. It was not an "official" visit, Diosdato told Veciana. "He said he had been instructed to ask a few of the exiles if they knew anything, that's all," Veciana recalls.

Veciana did not ask himself why a U.S. Customs agent would be investigating the Kennedy assassination among Miami Cubans and be brought up from Key West to do it. It crossed his mind that perhaps he was being tested. He decided immediately that he was not going to tell Diosdato anything.

Several weeks later, Bishop and Veciana met in Miami. At that meeting, while Bishop never mentioned their encounter with Oswald in Dallas, they did speak mostly about the Kennedy assassination and its impact on the world and on their anti-Castro activities. Bishop, says Veciana, appeared saddened, but he had a strange request, suggesting the possibility of his involvement.

At the time, there were newspaper stories about Oswald having met with a Cuban couple in Mexico City. Veciana recalls these stories reported that the wife spoke excellent English. Bishop said he knew that Veciana had a cousin, Guillermo Ruiz, in Castro's intelligence service who then happened to be stationed in Mexico City. Ruiz's wife, coincidentally, spoke excellent English. Bishop asked Veciana to try to get in touch with Ruiz and offer him a large amount of money if Ruiz would say that it was he and his wife who had met with Oswald.

Veciana took it as a ploy that might work because, as he told me, "Ruiz was someone who always liked money." Bishop did not specify how much Ruiz should be offered, only that it should be "a huge amount." Veciana, however, was never able to present the offer to his cousin because Ruiz was soon transferred back to Havana and Veciana could not find a safe way to contact him. When he mentioned his difficulties to Bishop a couple of months later, Veciana says Bishop told him to forget it, that "it was no longer necessary." That was the last time he or Bishop ever referred to the Kennedy assassination.

In May, 1964, John A. McCone, the Director of the Central Intelligence Agency, provided an affidavit to the Warren Commission in which he swore that, based on his personal knowledge and "detailed inquiries he caused to be made," Lee Harvey Oswald was not an agent, employee or informant of the CIA. In addition, McCone also swore that "Lee Harvey Oswald was never associated or connected, directly or indirectly, in any way whatsoever with the Agency."

On March 12th, 1964, Richard Helms, then Deputy Director of Plans of the CIA—the man in charge of all the Agency's covert operations—met with Warren Commission General Counsel J. Lee Rankin. The minutes of that meeting reveal that Helms told Rankin that "the Commission would have to take his word for the fact that Oswald had not been an agent of the CIA."

More than ten years later, in November of 1975, the Church Committee issued a report which concluded that, as deputy director, Helms had deliberately kept secret from his own boss, Director McCone, the existence of certain covert operations.

In that light, what Antonio Veciana revealed for the first time on March 2nd, 1976, had historic significance: An individual apparently associated with the CIA had contact with Lee Harvey Oswald prior to the assassination of President John F. Kennedy. Moreover, this CIA operative was involved in a series of Castro assassination attempts in which, for some reason, the Agency was not admitting its participation.

It was all anchored to Veciana's credibility, which weighed heavily in his favor for these reasons: I did not initially question Veciana about the Kennedy assassination; he was not aware of my specific interest in it until later in the interview. While the story about Oswald came up peripherally, the story of Maurice Bishop came up specifically. Veciana had very valid reasons for revealing his relationship to Maurice Bishop to me when he did. (Later on, for equally valid reasons, he would be less than candid about identifying Bishop.)

Veciana had just spent 26 months in a Federal prison on a charge of conspiracy to import narcotics. He had been convicted in Federal court largely on the testimony of a former partner in a sporting goods business in Puerto Rico. Arrested with ten kilos of cocaine, this ex-partner had implicated Veciana, thereby avoiding a long jail term himself. He was the only witness against Veciana. Veciana says that, although no drugs were found on him, the evidence against him appeared very good and even the Federal narcotics agents believed he was guilty.

There is absolutely no indication from any source, including the confidential records of certain law enforcement agencies, that Veciana had any association with narcotics prior to his arrest. In the bitterly competitive world of Cuban exile politics, Veciana's reputation is curiously unspotted. A former associate, now a top executive with a national insurance firm, told me "Veciana was the straightest, absolutely trustworthy, most honest person I ever met."

At the time of our first interview, Veciana still was prison pale. His parole had not yet been finalized so he had to return each evening to a release center. There was a cautiousness, a defensiveness in his attitude and he was admittedly confused about what had happened to him. He was anxious to talk in detail about the case against him and seemed, at times, almost in grudging admiration of the evidence. "I know because I have done that kind of work myself," he said.

At that time, Veciana strongly expressed the feeling that what had happened to him was directly connected to his previous relationship with Maurice Bishop. He suggested that their final disagreements might have caused Bishop to take steps to put him out of action. He said he was anxious to find Bishop and confront him with that possibility; then he would know.

Over the months following that initial interview I watched Veciana change. Soon, that early tentativeness, that cautious wariness, the shade of prison gray in his eyes began to fade as he got back into living, resumed his patriarchal confidence, began moving in his old circles and, I believe, got deeply but very secretively back into anti-Castro activity. As he did, and thought more about his experience, he began to change his mind about Bishop's involvement in his incarceration. Then, one day, he told me he was sure he had been set up by Castro's agents. He still, however, wanted to find Bishop, although now for a different reason. Maurice Bishop could again be of some help to him.

Nevertheless, I later learned that a lot of Veciana's initial assumption stuck with him. One of his close associates told me that Veciana had said, confidentially, that he believed the CIA framed him because he had been insisting on moving ahead with another plot to kill Castro. Indeed, another assassination attempt that might be linked to the Agency when it was frantically trying to build its defenses against a coming onslaught of Congressional investigations would have been devastating for the CIA. Veciana had to be put out of action for a while.

SEVENTEEN

A VERY FAMILIAR FACE

MY FINDING Antonio Veciana and his story could not have come at a worse time for Senator Church and his Select Committee on Intelligence. Church had told his staff, which had already gone over its deadline more than once, that it was getting its absolutely final extension—another month—to finish up the Schweiker Subcommittee report. Church was chomping at the bit, anxious to get into the Presidential sweepstakes. With its sensational reports on assassination plots against foreign leaders and illegal intelligence agency snooping, the Church Committee had gotten the public attention Senator Church had hoped for; now he had other priorities.

Senator Schweiker had immediately recognized the significance of Veciana's story, not only in relation to the Kennedy assassination but also, as Paul Hoch had suggested, in relation to the question of whether or not the CIA had been totally honest with the Church Committee and revealed all its Castro plots. Schweiker thought the new information was explosive enough to reopen the hearings, but he quickly ran into a stone wall with both Church and the Committee's staff leaders.

Although he never told me about it, Schweiker was obviously upset. He wasn't concerned about his own report. That, he felt, was already strong enough in impugning the Warren Commission's conclusions, but he was interested in getting the new information into the record. In a letter to his Subcommittee cochairman, Gary Hart—but clearly directed at Church and his staff leaders—Schweiker wrote: "I

146

feel strongly Veciana should be called to testify under oath, to evaluate his credibility, create an official record of his allegations and examine them. . . . I recognize that this involves some difficulty at this stage of our proceeding, but in view of Veciana's direct link to intelligence community activities subject to the [Church] Committee's jurisdiction, I do not believe we can responsibly refuse to evaluate his allegations.''

That put the Church Committee on the spot. My concern, however, was less with what the Committee would do than how it would do it. I felt we had stumbled upon what could be a totally new area in the Kennedy assassination investigation and that developing it should be done in a structured and comprehensive way. The Committee staff had the power and resources to do that if it truly wanted, or it could mishandle Veciana's information and possibly cause doors to be locked tight forever.

I called Dave Marston, my Schweiker liaison, to ask him what was going to happen. ''Well, I think they'll do something,'' he said. ''I think what they'll do is screw it up. I think they'll go the most direct way, that is, make an official inquiry. So then there will be an official inquiry and if there is anything there, that will take care of it. It will be gone.''

That's exactly what happened. I was asked to bring Veciana to Washington where he was sworn in at a secret executive session. Schweiker was the only Committee member who showed up. A staff attorney questioned Veciana for less than an hour and only the barest details of his story went on record. The question of whether or not the CIA was involved in Veciana's attempts to assassinate Castro was not confronted. Veciana was not asked. A transcript of the hearing went into restricted security files. Not a word about it was mentioned in any of the Church Committee's reports.

Much to my frustration and that of his other personal staffers, Schweiker was scrupulous about keeping the details of the Church Committee staff's work from us. We did not have security clearance and had not signed nondisclosure agreements, so we did not have access to any of that information. Yet the Committee staff itself wanted to make use of me. Since it was busy compiling its final report and I was the only investigator investigating, it made suggestions, through Schweiker, about what I should check and whom I should speak with. That's how I came to know how little the Committee's unenthusiastic efforts to follow up the Veciana lead had produced.

For instance, the CIA claimed it had no employee named Maurice Bishop and no record of any agent ever using that alias. From a discussion with an Army Intelligence asset I had been sent to interview in New Orleans, I also deduced that the CIA had told the Committee that Veciana and Alpha 66 were monitored not by the

Agency but by Army Intelligence. I thought this was a misdirection. I pointed out that Veciana was aware of his contacts with Army Intelligence, that they covered only a limited period of his anti-Castro activities, and that they were separate and distinct from his relationship with Maurice Bishop. Nevertheless, after the CIA denied an interest in Veciana, the Committee staff pursued the Army Intelligence angle up until the end.

Schweiker could see what was happening. Dave Newhall, Schweiker's administrative assistant and a former investigative reporter himself, called me one day. "We just don't seem to be able to get through to the Committee staff about the significance of this," he said. "They're good Wall Street-type lawyers but they don't have street smarts and they don't have enough background in this case. Besides, most of them are packing their bags and looking around for other jobs by now. I think we'd better start moving on our own."

It was the first indication I had that Schweiker was willing to pursue the Kennedy assassination investigation beyond the life of the Church Committee. He had some leeway because it would be a few months before his Subcommittee report would officially be published, since it had to be cleared by the CIA (this was part of the Church Committee's original agreement with the Agency, a standard that would apply to the House Assassinations Committee as well). But since the Committee itself would no longer exist, Schweiker would be on his own, with no subpoena power or legal clout.

To his credit, and a bit against the grain of "proper" Senatorial parameters, Schweiker pursued the Veciana lead for months beyond his Subcommittee's demise and even beyond the issuance of its final report. In fact, it was not until the Reagan strategists, nipping at President Ford's heels for the Republican nomination, had lured Schweiker into the sacrificial role of Vice Presidential candidate, thus convincing him that the political risks of continuing his private Kennedy assassination investigation would be too great, that he decided to drop it.

Also to Schweiker's credit in his investigation was the fact that Veciana's information directly contradicted the thesis being pushed in Schweiker's Subcommittee's report: the possibility that Castro had killed Kennedy in retaliation for the plots against him. In fact, I considered Veciana's own discounting of that theory a point in favor of his credibility. I had spoken to a number of anti-Castro exile leaders, most still very dedicated and fanatically determined to get rid of the Cuban dictator. Almost to a man these exile leaders touted the same theory about the Kennedy assassination: Castro did it. They knew little of the evidence or the facts, they only knew that Castro did it.

Except Veciana, who was a far more dedicated anti-Castroite than any Cuban I ever met. Down through the years, we have discussed the various theories about the Kennedy assassination and he has consistently said: "I don't think Castro did it. I know Castro. He is crazy. Once, when he was down to his last twelve men in the mountains, he said, 'Now, there is no way we can lose!' He is crazy but he did not kill Kennedy. That would have been much too crazy. I think it was a plan, sure." By "a plan" Veciana means a conspiracy. "Bishop would know," he adds. "I think Bishop would know."

The office of a U.S. Senator carries a certain amount of power, of course, but a Senator does not have the right or legal means to demand answers from anyone. Nevertheless, in pursuing the new evidence that Veciana provided, Schweiker's staff made more significant progress in a few months than the House Assassinations Committee would in two years.

The critical question was, of course, this: Was Veciana telling the truth? There were parts of his story which would obviously be difficult, if not impossible, to corroborate. There were many other details, however, which could be easily checked. Confirmation of those details would, at the very least, be an indication of his overall credibility.

His background checked out, as did his professional standing, his position in the Havana bank and his relationship with its owner, Julio Lobo. An official Cuban government newspaper detailed his role in the 1961 Castro assassination attempt and confirmed that the incident had occurred as Veciana had reported. His founding of Alpha 66 and his anti-Castro activities were part of the historical records from that period. There were, however, a few pieces of special significance.

One of Veciana's points about Maurice Bishop's influence—and his obvious connection with the United States Government—was the fact that Bishop had gotten Veciana his position with the U.S. Agency for International Development in South America despite his documented record as an anti-Castro terrorist. Schweiker asked the U.S. State Department to check its files and it wired its answer from La Paz: Veciana did work as a "commercial banking expert" for Bolivia's Central Bank; his contracts were financed by the U.S. AID; they were for the salary and for the time period Veciana had said they were; during this period Veciana's legal residence was in Caracas. (You may recall that during this time, Veciana's and Bishop's 1971 plan to assassinate Castro was developed in Caracas.)

The State Department's telegram also contained, in passing, an unusual revelation. Veciana's application for Federal employment, it noted, had an unexplainable omission—it was unsigned. Yes, Veciana said, he had received a U.S. Government job without ever signing a job application.

There were numerous other aspects of Veciana's story and, as they checked out, they only added to his general credibility. There were, for instance, a number of CIA-sponsored leaflet drops over Cuba, but only a limited number of people knew of the Cellula Fantasma operation by name. One of them was Frank Fiorini Sturgis, who admitted his role in it.

A confidential source, a veteran of the U.S. Customs office in Miami, told me that Cesar Diosdato, the Customs agent who had questioned Veciana, was indeed working for the CIA in Key West, as Veciana had suspected. (The Agency reimbursed Customs for his salary.) This was confirmed by another source who was close to the former head of the local Customs office. (Diosdato subsequently went to work for the Drug Enforcement Administration in California.)

One of the most incredible parts of Veciana's story is his statement that Bishop gave him $253,000 in cash at the termination of their relationship. Perhaps even more incredible, on the surface, was that he would tell me about it. But he had insisted on the absolute confidentiality of the interview. And again, before telling me about the money, he asked that the information be kept confidential. When I asked if he could prove he had the money, or what he did with it, he said he could show how he disbursed it and where, but Senator Schweiker would first have to guarantee him immunity from action by the Internal Revenue Service. Schweiker could not do that. (As a result, when Veciana's sworn testimony was taken before the Church Committee, at Veciana's request that area of questioning was omitted.)

When Veciana first told me about receiving the money, his wife had been doing chores, occasionally rushing into the living room to retrieve their two youngest, who kept escaping from the kitchen. She happened to be passing through at that moment and Veciana interrupted her to say, "Remember, when I mentioned to you how strange that we should get that on the twenty-sixth of July." Indeed, she said, she did.

Also confirmed, of course, was the fact that the dogs were running at the Flagler track that day.

Another point which I thought could be easily checked was the existence of a Colonel Kail at the American Embassy in Cuba. Nevertheless, I was having difficulty finding him until one day, when I happened to be talking with Paul Bethel in Coconut Grove. Bethel was a strong right-winger, a one-time Congressional candidate, an author and the head of the U.S. Information Agency in Havana when Castro took power. He was married to a Cuban, was still very active in anti-Castro activities and was an excellent source of information about the exile community in Miami. (At the time, I suspected only that he had an association with the CIA.) I asked Bethel if he recalled a fellow named Kail at the American Embassy. "Sure," said Bethel. "I knew Sam well. Military attaché. I believe he's retired now, probably back home in Dallas."

Sam Kail was listed in the Dallas telephone directory. When I told Veciana I had found him, Veciana said, "You know, I would like to call him. Perhaps he remembers Bishop." He suggested I listen in on the call.

"Do you remember me?" Veciana asked Kail after he had introduced himself.

Kail was very hesitant, very cautions. "Well, I'm not sure," he said.

"Remember," coaxed Veciana, "the last time I saw you, in December, 1960, you were going home for Christmas."

Kail remembered. "Yes, I did come home that Christmas," he said.

"Then you remember me?"

"No," Kail said. "Can't say that I do."

"At any rate," Veciana went on, "I am trying to find a friend, the American who sent me to you. He was a big help to me in fighting Castro. Now I need to find him. Do you remember Maurice Bishop?"

Kail was silent for a moment. "Bishop?" he repeated. More silence.

"Bishop," Kail said again, as if thinking about it. "Well, off the top of my head, I don't think I recall that name. I'd like to give it some thought." He would think about if for a day or two, he said, and then he would call Veciana back.

Kail never called back. A couple of weeks later at my suggestion Veciana called Kail again. Kail said he had given some thought to the name but, try as he might, he just couldn't recall ever knowing anyone named Maurice Bishop, nor anyone named Bishop who fitted the description Veciana had given. Sorry, he couldn't be of any help.

I first began talking with Antonio Veciana in late February, 1976. In March Veciana and I began looking at photographs of individuals who came close to fitting his description of Maurice Bishop. I showed Veciana more than a dozen, some sent by the staff of the Church Committee, mostly of, I assumed, Army Intelligence operatives. Most of the ones I dug up were of individuals who, at some point or another—but usually not at more than one point—were in the right place at the right time and had some association with the CIA or Lee

Harvey Oswald or the investigation of the Kennedy assassination. But that one point was never good enough.

At first, one person who struck me as possibly being Maurice Bishop was George de Mohrenschildt. As detailed in the Warren Commission Report, the wealthy globe-trotting de Mohrenschildts and a group of anti-Communist White Russian cohorts had befriended the Oswalds as soon as they had returned to Dallas from the Soviet Union, in the summer of 1962. Over the years, de Mohrenschildt's intelligence ties have been firmly documented and he loosely fitted Veciana's verbal description of Bishop. At that time in the early Sixties de Mohrenschildt was teaching at a small school in Dallas called Bishop College. Checking further, I learned that Bishop College once had the reputation of being a hotbed of leftist activity and a known center of Communist agitators. However, it later became known that the college had received major financial support from a foundation which was funded by the CIA. Bishop College appeared to be an Agency decoy. I became excited by the possibilities.

But, shown a number of photographs of George de Mohrenschildt, Veciana stated flatly that he was not Maurice Bishop. (Later, as I checked further into de Mohrenschildt's background, where he had been and when, it was clear he couldn't have been Maurice Bishop.)

Part of the problem we were having was that it was tough to get a good handle on Bishop's physical characteristics. Veciana had known and been in contact with Bishop over a period of thirteen years; the man had obviously changed and Veciana's mental image was an amalgam of those changes. Depending on when I spoke with him, Veciana's guess at Bishop's age when he first met him in 1960 ranged from "over 35" to "under 45." While in some ways Veciana's description of Bishop was fairly consistent—he was tall, "maybe six foot," or "maybe six foot two"; "close to 200 pounds" or "maybe 210 pounds"—there were enough inconsistencies that it had occurred to me that perhaps Bishop had used a disguise. If he had, it was likely a very subtle and sophisticated disguise which would change his appearance only slightly, but enough to fool anyone who knew him and happened to see him with Veciana. (Perhaps, too, since he had taught Veciana the skill of remembering faces, Bishop had deliberately kept altering his appearance for Veciana's benefit.)

Although Veciana's description of Bishop was a bit wavy, he did provide certain discriminating details which gave Bishop a very specific character. He said, for instance, that Bishop was always a very meticulous dresser, neat and well-groomed. In his later years, he wore glasses more often, but took them off to ruminate with the stem on his lips. He was usually well-tanned, although under his eyes there was a certain blotchiness, a spotty darkness, as if from being in the sun too long. He had brown hair, with some gray later. Generally, he was a good-looking man.

At our initial meeting, Veciana had seemed sincere enough when he expressed a strong desire to find Maurice Bishop. He seemed determined then to find out if he had been in prison as a result of their relationship and its end. Veciana said that as soon he was settled, out from under the restrictions of parole and free to travel again, he was going to have an artist do a sketch of Bishop from his description. That, he said, might help him in looking for Bishop.

I didn't think much of that idea until I had shown Veciana a score of photographs and gotten negative results clearly and consistently. Then I realized that, while each of these "suspects" had at least one characteristic that fit with Veciana's description of Bishop, a comprehensive image would have eliminated them immediately. We agreed: A professionally drawn composite sketch of Maurice Bishop would help narrow the focus.

Security was one of my main concerns right from the beginning. The crazy world of Cuban exile politics in Miami has its share of fanatics as well as professional assassins, as the pattern of bombings and ambushes in Little Havana has clearly shown down through the years. A few months before I first spoke with Veciana, an exile leader named Rolando Masferrer, known as *El Tigre* when he headed Batista's secret police, condoned a recent rash of bombings in a local magazine article. "You do not beg for freedom," he wrote, "you conquer it. . . . In the meantime, dynamite can speak in a uniquely eloquent manner. . . . " One morning a week later, half of Masferrer was found in what remained of his car after he had tried to start it. A uniquely eloquent retort.

Veciana was obviously concerned about the risks involved in talking with me, so we decided it would be prudent to have the sketch of Maurice Bishop done in a police department outside the Miami area. Professional composite artists work only for large law enforcement agencies, but I didn't, of course, want to use the FBI.

Through a police department contact in another city, I arranged for Veciana to spend most of the day with their best artist. I had given the police artist a rough description of Bishop by telephone before we arrived so he was able to do some general preliminary sketches to use as a base. Veciana then spent a few tedious hours going through about 300 mug shots picking out individual features which came closest to resembling Bishop's. "The problem," Veciana sighed as he flipped through the photos, "is all these individuals look like criminals. Bishop, he was a gentleman. He looked like a gentleman."

Veciana's session with the police artist caused him to focus much more intensely on Bishop's specific features: a distinctive lower lip; a straight nose but not sharp, nostrils not too narrow; a face longer than it was round; and, again, perhaps the most noticeable feature, a darkened area under the eyes, almost leathery looking.

It was late in the afternoon when the police artist finished a sketch that Veciana proclaimed "pretty good." The artist had warned that composite sketches aren't meant to be exact resemblances of individuals. They are designed to elicit a chain of recall in witnesses and spark recollections of images which lead to some suspects and eliminate others. Veciana said that the sketch of Bishop was not really what Bishop looked like, but he appeared to be satisfied. It was "close."

Veciana returned to Miami and the next morning I took the sketch and some copies to Schweiker's office in Washington. Dave Marston was gone, house hunting in Philadelphia. (His nomination as U.S. Attorney for the eastern district of Pennsylvania was before Congress and he did not lack for confidence.) Dave Newhall looked at the sketch with fascination. "You know, it looks exactly like I thought it would from the description we were working on," he said. "I think the boss will want to see this right away."

Schweiker, who was also a member of the Senate Health Committee, was attending a hearing in the Rayburn Building. We got word to him and, during a break, we huddled in a corner of the anteroom of the chamber.

Schweiker looked at the sketch intensely. His first reaction was a mumbled, "That's pretty good," as if he were commenting on the quality of the artwork. Then, very seriously, he said, "I've seen that face before."

Newhall and I laughed. For an instant we both thought he was just being glib, but Schweiker was, in fact, being very serious. "That's a *very* familiar face," he said, now staring hard at the sketch. "Perhaps . . . maybe it was someone from State who briefed me on something recently. We've been getting a lot of those." He paused and thought a bit. "No, maybe not." He kept staring at the sketch. "He's *very* familiar," he said again.

"Does it look like Harvey?" asked Newhall. William Harvey, the CIA's coordinator in its Castro assassination plots with the Mafia, had been testifying before the Church Committee.

"No, it's not Harvey," Schweiker said. Finally he sighed. "I've got to get back to the hearing. Why don't you take a copy down to the Committee staff? I'll give it more thought later."

The Church Committee staff worked out of a sprawling arrangement of cubicles on the ground floor of the old Dirksen Office Building. Newhall and I signed in at the security desk and a staff attorney who had been working with Schweiker on his Kennedy

Subcommittee emerged from the inner recesses of the office. We showed him the sketch. He looked at it and nodded his head as if in approval. "Fine," he said. "That's fine." He gave no indication that the sketch reminded him of anyone in particular. He took a copy of it and, I assumed, stuck it securely in the Committee's classified files.

That night I flew back to Miami. It was a Friday early in April, more than a month after my first interview with Veciana. During that interval I had spoken with him more than a dozen times. At that point, we had begun to establish a certain relationship. I could drop in at his home. Frequently I would call him on the telephone just to ask a question or two about a minor detail that had come to mind. We had two especially lengthy interviews during which I tried to extract every possible detail Veciana could recall about Maurice Bishop. We traveled to Washington and around Miami to sites where he recalled meeting Bishop. From our formal interviews and informal discussions, I began to accumulate not only a structured image of Maurice Bishop as an intelligence operative but also a sense of the man himself, as Veciana saw him.

At that point, this is what I knew about Maurice Bishop:

He was in Havana in the summer of 1960 when Veciana first met him. He was working undercover, probably using some business association or firm as a front. There may have been some relationship with some business in the building to which Veciana was sent for instruction, maybe with the American mining company or the Berlitz School. Bishop was obviously familiar with the personnel and their positions at the American Embassy. He appeared to be a specialist in propaganda, psychological warfare and counterintelligence, judging from his primary interests and Veciana's activities.

From the character of his Spanish he was probably schooled in the language, but even before Havana he had most likely spent a good deal of time in a Spanish-speaking country. He was very intelligent, very literate and very articulate. He was, as Veciana put it, a gentleman, perhaps from the South, very likely from Texas.

The Church Committee had uncovered the fact that there had been secret operations and certain ultrasensitive missions conducted outside the CIA's normal chain of command. Given that, Bishop may have been among a select clique within the Agency and, as such, trusted enough to be given an "unofficial" Castro assassination mission. Since Veciana's activities in the late Sixties began to go beyond Cuban affairs and encompass other anti-Communist operations in Latin America, it seemed likely that Bishop had moved up the Agency's executive ladder—another indication he was associated with a key power group within the CIA.

At the time of the Kennedy assassination, however, Bishop appeared to be particularly knowledgeable about intelligence operations in Mexico City, since he was not only aware of Oswald's activities there, he also knew that Veciana's cousin was a Castro intelligence officer stationed in the Cuban Embassy.

By the early Seventies, Bishop had broadened his interests and contacts throughout Latin America. However, Bishop's role in the Castro assassination attempt in Chile, and his ability to reach key military personnel there, indicated that he had special relationships in that country. The week before we had constructed the composite sketch of Bishop, I wrote a memo to Schweiker indicating what I thought would initially be primary areas to investigate. The memo noted: "Veciana strongly believes that Bishop had something to do with the downfall of Allende in Chile."

Finally, another indication of Bishop's advancing career was the large amount of money he paid Veciana at the end of their relationship in 1973. Bishop would have had to be in a high position to have access to such funds and, perhaps, also have the power to cover them. And the size of the final payment strongly indicated the presence of the CIA. As illustrated by its JM/WAVE operations in the early Sixties, the Agency has always been lavish in its disbursement of funds.

So the man we were looking for had to fit each of those factors and characteristics. One or two or a few wouldn't do. The search would have seemed like a very difficult job even if we weren't dealing in the world of spooks. But in that nether universe of mirrors and forged reality, multiple pseudonyms, impersonations and suspect records, it seemed almost impossible that we would find the spy who called himself Maurice Bishop. I didn't think we would, and neither did Veciana.

EIGHTEEN

STRANGE SILENCES IN THE LIBRARY

I RETURNED FROM Washington that weekend after the composite sketch was drawn. On Sunday evening I received a call from Dave Newhall. He said he had just heard from Senator Schweiker in Pennsylvania. "The boss was driving home when he suddenly remembered who the guy in the sketch reminded him of," Newhall said. "He stopped the car and just called me from a phone booth."

The drawing of Maurice Bishop reminded Schweiker of David Atlee Phillips, the former director of CIA propaganda for the Bay of Pigs who had risen to one of the highest ranks in the Agency—Chief of the Western Hemisphere Division. He was now retired.

Phillips had come before the Church Committee on more than one occasion. The Committee was especially interested in two phases of Phillips's career: as head of the CIA's task force to prevent the election of the socialist Salvator Allende as president of Chile; and as chief of the Agency's unit in Mexico City, which was responsible for sending the Warren Commission photographs of a man visiting the Soviet Embassy there and erroneously identifying him as Lee Harvey Oswald.

Phillips had retired in the spring of 1975 after 25 years of service with the CIA. At the time, the nation was being stirred by a barrage of press revelations about the illegal activities of the intelligence agencies. Phillips had made minor headlines when he called a press conference at his retirement and announced he would lead an association of retired intelligence officers in defense of the CIA.

157

According to Phillips, one of the major factors that led to his retirement was "the rash of sensational headlines in the world press that leave the impression the CIA is an organization of unprincipled people who capriciously interfere in the lives of U.S. citizens at home and abroad." He said he wanted to "straighten out the record."

Newhall is usually a laconic guy, but there was an edge in his voice when he called that evening to tell me about Schweiker's honing in on David Phillips. "The boss thinks the resemblance is pretty damn close," he said. Schweiker had asked that I dig up a newspaper clipping of Phillips's press conference and show the photo of Phillips to Veciana.

The next morning I checked the date of the press conference, picked up a back issue of the *Miami Herald* and went directly to Veciana's place. He wasn't home. His wife said she didn't expect him back until evening and didn't know how to reach him. I returned home to another call from Newhall.

"We've found a good photo of Phillips in the last June twenty-third issue of *People* magazine," he said. "It did a feature about his forming that retired intelligence agents group. Do you think you can pick up a copy?" I said I would try because the *Herald* photo, a wire service reproduction, was a poor one, the image a bit washed out. However, after trying several sources, I couldn't locate that back issue of *People*. The public library had already put it into a bound volume and I wouldn't be able to get a reproduction of the article until the next day. I decided to call Veciana later and ask him to join me at the public library in the morning. We could look at the photograph together.

That evening, waiting to talk with Veciana, I glanced at the story in the *Herald* about Phillips announcing his retirement. There were only scant details about his background. It noted that he had been a professional actor, had been recruited by the CIA when he was editing an English-language newspaper in Chile in the early 1950s, had been assigned to posts in Mexico and Venezuela and had been working undercover in Cuba when Castro took over.

Phillips had retired before the Church Committee was formed, before the CIA had admitted to the activities that would garner the Committee its headlines. In defending the Agency at his press conference, Phillips vigorously rebutted the charges kicking around at the time: The CIA *did not* finance the strikes that led to Allende's overthrow; the CIA *never* plotted the assassination of Fidel Castro. Then Phillips made one final point: He said he assumed that many would claim his retirement was phony and that the association he was forming was really a CIA operation. "It is *not*," he declared strongly.

The facts would later reveal he was lying about at least two out of three of those contentions. And he knew it.

When I finally spoke with Veciana that evening he said he did not know the name of David Phillips or remember seeing photographs of the man. He said, sure, he would come to the public library with me the next morning. "I will call Dr. Abella and ask him to come with us also," he said. "Then we can do two things."

After talking with Veciana for weeks about the Kennedy assassination, it appeared that for the first time he was becoming interested in some of the details. One day he told me he had been talking about it with a friend, Dr. Manuel Abella, and Abella recalled seeing a photograph of the crowd in Dealey Plaza taken just prior to the assassination. Abella thought the photo was in *Life* or *Look* magazine—he wasn't sure which—however, he recognized in the crowd the face of a man he knew from Cuba as a Castro agent. I had spoken with Abella and checked back issues of those magazines, but didn't find the crowd shot he described. Veciana decided that now would be the time to take Abella to the library and help him search for the photograph.

The next morning, Dr. Abella, a cigar-chomping pudgy little guy, was waiting with Veciana at his home. We drove downtown to the Dade Public Library in Bayfront Park, the site of the ever-burning Torch of Freedom donated by Miami's Cuban exile community. That morning there was a demonstration in progress—a shouting group of masked Iranian students was calling for the ouster of the Shah. Veciana looked at them, smiled slightly and shook his head. He was used to more demonstrative forms of dissension.

At the periodicals desk, I asked for the bound volume of the *People* we needed and for the bound volumes of *Life* and *Look* which might have crowd photos of Dealey Plaza. We took them to an empty table at one end of the room. Veciana sat down and put on his glasses. I stood beside him and we found the article about Phillips. There was a half-page, black-and-white photo of him standing under a highway sign, obviously taken near Langley. The sign said: "CIA NEXT RIGHT." Phillips was depicted almost full-figured; he was casually dressed, standing with his hands in his pockets, wearing a *guayabera*. The resemblance to the Bishop sketch was clear: the square jaw, the distinctive lower lip, the straight nose, the forehead and yes, the darkened area under the eyes. Only the hairstyle was different.

Veciana looked at the photo. And looked at it. I watched his face for some reaction, but there was none. He kept staring at the photo. "Is it him?" I asked. Veciana didn't answer. He was totally expressionless, his eyes intensely focused on the picture. Finally, he turned the page of the magazine. There were two additional photos of

Phillips, both smaller, both showing Phillips's face less directly and less clearly. Veciana turned back to the large photo. "Is it him?" I asked again. Almost a half a minute had passed and the suspense was pressing on me. Without taking his eyes from the picture, he said, "It is close."

I wanted to shout at him: *It is close?! What the hell do you mean, it is close! Is it him or isn't it him?* But I didn't. Instead, I leaned closer and again asked softly: "Is it him?"

Veciana did not take his eyes off the photo. "Does he have a brother?" he finally asked. The question took me aback.

"I don't know," I said. "But is *he* Bishop?"

Veciana finally shook his head. "It is close, but it is not him."

I remember almost sighing with relief at the end of the suspense. "Are you sure it's not him?" I asked.

"No, it's not him," Veciana said again.

Well, I thought, that sounds pretty definite, and turned to the pile of bound volumes that Dr. Abella was waiting to look through. Then Veciana, still looking at the photo, added: "But I would like to talk with him."

"You would like to talk with Phillips?" I asked, not quite getting his point. "Do you think Phillips is Bishop?"

"No, he is not Bishop," Veciana said, "but he is CIA and maybe he could help."

Maybe he could, I thought, but it was unlikely. I turned to help Abella who was leafing through the other magazines, looking for that crowd shot with the Castro agent. Abella had described the photo precisely, but it was in neither *Life* nor *Look*. Then Abella said maybe it was in *Argosy* or *True*; he remembered seeing articles about the Kennedy assassination in those, also. So I got the bound volumes of those publications and we began looking through them. It took us about fifteen minutes to search through them. Again, we had no luck. Veciana, meanwhile, had remained seated at the table with the *People* magazine opened to the photo of David Phillips. He was studying it very carefully. Just staring at it.

NINETEEN

CONFRONTATION IN RESTON

BEFORE THE SCHWEIKER INVESTIGATION had come to a close, more than a dozen individuals had been considered, however fleetingly, as possibly being the man who called himself Maurice Bishop. The staff of the Church Committee continued to look for Bishop in the area of Army Intelligence, despite my telling them that Veciana was sure about which of his contacts were with the military and that he very much doubted that Bishop was with the military. (Besides allowing itself to be routed to Army Intelligence by the CIA, the Church Committee staff had, on its own, deemed Veciana's being referred to Colonel Kail at the American Embassy significant. Kail, I would later learn, was very much involved in intelligence. But what the staff didn't consider was the possibility that some Army Intelligence personnel actually work for the CIA.)

I continued to show Veciana photographs of individuals sent to me by the Committee staff and others I dug up myself. Some, like de Mohrenschildt, bore a closer resemblance to the Bishop sketch than others, but none came as close as David Phillips. Occasionally, Veciana himself would mention that. Sometimes he would add, "Well, you know, maybe it would help if I could talk with him." Or, "Maybe if I saw him I could tell better." I began getting the impression that Veciana's very definite "no" to that photo of Phillips wasn't all that definite. In addition, the more deeply we dug into Phillips's background, the clearer the pattern of his being in the right place at the right time became. Dave Marston and I began discussing the possibil-

161

ity of bringing Veciana together with Phillips in a direct confrontation. The Committee staff, however, had decided not to call Phillips back for any additional questioning under oath, so whatever we did we had to do on our own, and unofficially.

We did not have the opportunity to have Veciana confront Phillips until September of 1976, just before Schweiker decided to close down his investigation. From my first interview with Veciana until then, I felt as if I were on a very fast train trying to spot a smoking gun in the blur of passing woods. The Church Committee was winding down, and it became clear that only a sensational new revelation, simple enough and obvious enough for the public to instantly grasp its meaning, could force the Committee to start a truly full-scale Kennedy assassination investigation. The Veciana lead was a crack in a door opening onto a new corridor, but time and resources were needed to develop that lead before its ultimate significance could be determined. Nevertheless, in attempting to pursue that lead as best I could over those months, I tried to locate and talk with everyone Veciana had named. But we were hindered by very limited resources. Schweiker's staff budget didn't include travel and expenses for his Subcommittee's investigation and he could not use Committee funds for a staff investigator. So, for instance, we never did get to Veciana's old boss Julio Lobo, who had gone to Spain, or to Customs agent Diosdato, then in California.

Over those same months, there were other pressing leads to pursue. Many of the Organized Crime figures who had been active in pre-Castro Havana, for instance, were in the Miami area, and the contacts I had developed began providing tips worth following up. (One Cuban exile claimed that South Florida Mafia boss Santos Trafficante had predicted Kennedy's assassination; later, that lead would be jumped on hard by the House Assassinations Committee and its Chief Counsel, Organized Crime expert Bob Blakey.) Other leads seemed to come from nowhere, such as when a former employee of Jack Ruby's working in a Miami nightclub, popped up and told me that Ruby was afraid the Warren Commission would discover he had been running guns to Cuba. From each new lead dangled a dozen strings which required immediate follow-up. I was kept very busy.

Meanwhile, at the end of June of 1976, the Church Committee had issued *Book V—The Investigation of the Assassination of President John F. Kennedy: Performance of the Intelligence Agencies* or, as the press called it, the Schweiker Report. Marston air-expressed an advance copy to me the night before Schweiker was scheduled to release it at a major press conference. I thought the report was of historical significance as the first official Government acknowledgment of the invalidity of the Warren Commission Report, but I objected to its overemphasis of the Castro retaliation theory. (Just because the Warren Commission had not been informed of the CIA's Castro assassination plots did not automatically make Kennedy's assassination Castro's revenge.) I was discussing that with Marston on the telephone when Schweiker returned from his press conference. Marston asked Schweiker to pick up the line.

"We've got one of your standard skeptics here, Senator," he said.

"I thought all our skeptics were at the news conference!" Schweiker yelled in mock anguish.

I congratulated him on the report, but told him I thought the Warren Commission critics were going to have what I thought was a legitimate objection. "How could the Committee have failed to pursue the possible relationship of Oswald to the intelligence agencies," I asked, "when the Committee discovered the intelligence agencies admitted a cover-up with the Warren Commission?"

"Because," said Schweiker, "the agencies took the position that they had no relationship with Oswald. And there were no documents in their files, they said, which reveal that there was. We pressed them on that several times and each time they said they had nothing. We hit a blind alley. I don't disagree with you, but considering the type of probe the Committee was conducting and the limited access to the intelligence agencies' files, there was not much we could do about it."

Schweiker was right. Considering that the Committee staff had conducted virtually no independent investigation and relied almost exclusively on records volunteered by the CIA, getting out the report that he did was a major step forward. He, at any rate, was ecstatic at the press reception of the report.

"We have moved the whole Washington press corps from feeling I was a junior edition of Jim Garrison to now considering me a valid Warren Commission critic," he chimed.

Despite the direction his report had taken, Schweiker was anxious for me to keep quietly pursuing the Veciana lead. He said he didn't know how long he could continue such an unofficial investigation, but he felt there were still many things we could do, even on our own, before we gave up.

Late in July, I went to Puerto Rico and came back with some significant new pieces of information. I had found a few of the witnesses I had been looking for and had a long and fruitful conversation with Manolo Ray, the head of the anti-Castro organization Veciana had joined in Cuba and, later, the founder of *JURE*, the group to which Silvia Odio had belonged. I had just flown into Miami International and was dragging my way through the airport when I passed a newsstand and noticed the headlines: Ronald Reagan had chosen Richard Schweiker as his Vice Presidential running mate.

The next morning I was on the line with Troy Gustavson, then Schweiker's press secretary. (With Marston leaving for the U.S. Attorney's job in Philadelphia, Gustavson was taking over as my Kennedy liaison.) "I imagine you've seen the papers," he said. "Were you flabbergasted?" That was a good word. "We all were," he said. "Only Schweiker and Newhall knew about it since Tuesday. Schweiker was on vacation in New Jersey when he got the call from Reagan's campaign manager who said he wanted to meet him in Washington. The Senator and Newhall kicked it around and decided it was the last chance for the moderate wing of the party. Schweiker's really psyched up about it."

I wondered what it meant in terms of Schweiker's continuing the Kennedy assassination investigation. "I don't know," Gustavson said. "I haven't had a chance to discuss it with him. I know he really has a sincere passion for it but I think a lot will depend on what happens in Kansas City, whether Reagan and he get the nomination. I feel that between now and then he's going to have to gear down. First of all, he's just not going to have the time. Also, I think he's going to question the propriety of continuing it because it's automatically politicized as soon as he becomes a candidate."

We decided to keep on it until Schweiker himself called it off.

By early September, however, things had changed. Reagan had not gotten the nomination and Schweiker had returned to Washington terribly depressed. I've never discussed it with him, but I believe it led him to reevaluate his role in public life. Then, too, partly as a result of the Schweiker Report, a groundswell of support for a new investigation into the Kennedy assassination was beginning in the House of Representatives. If that developed, Schweiker decided, he would end his efforts.

Soon afterwards, I heard from Sarah Lewis in Schweiker's office. Lewis, an assistant to Gustavson, had been handling a lot of the Washington research end of the investigation. She had called to tell me that David Phillips's organization, the Retired Intelligence Officers Association, had scheduled a conference in Reston, Virginia, for the middle of the month. At the time, the group was just about a year old and it had been an instant success. Within months, it claimed a few hundred members. (Later, the organization changed its name to Association of Former Intelligence Officers.)

Sarah Lewis and I decided that we would go to the conference with Antonio Veciana. David Phillips would, we assumed, be a very visible figure there and it would be an excellent opportunity for Veciana to tell us for sure whether or not Phillips was Maurice Bishop.

* * *

David Phillips knew we were coming. At least he knew I was coming. Sarah Lewis had called and made arrangements for three people to attend the major luncheon on the last day of the conference. The tickets, $6.50 each, would be in my name. Phillips said we could pay at the door.

That morning, I met Veciana at the Washington National Airport and we waited for Sarah Lewis to pick us up. Veciana and his wife had driven their oldest daughter to Tampa where she was starting college, and he had flown up from there. I had missed traveling with Veciana, which I always enjoyed, because it gave me the chance to chat with him casually. I guess I also enjoyed being privy to the fact that this soft-faced, mild-mannered business executive, leaning comfortably back in his window seat reading the *Wall Street Journal*, was once one of the most fanatically dedicated anti-Castro terrorists. Occasionally, though, that persona would slip out. I recall, for instance, talking with him on one of our trips to Washington about whether or not the CIA should be involved in domestic operations. "Oh sure, it must," Veciana said matter-of-factly. "Because then what happens if you see someone passing secrets to the enemy? He must be killed. He must." He turned back to reading his newspaper, as if there could be no argument.

Sarah Lewis picked us up in her red Volkswagen. She was a tall, attractive, young woman with short blonde hair and a pleasant smile. "Phillips is expecting us," she said, "although I guess he was puzzled by Senator Schweiker's interest in the conference." Veciana smiled.

Close by the Agency's Langley base, Reston is home to a large bloc of CIA employees. It had been born as a model bedroom community for the Washington bureaucrat, an escape from the blight of the decaying urban core. But times change and Reston is now a massive suburban sprawl with problems of its own, though still tediously neat and well-manicured. The Ramada Inn, where the conference was held, also fits in. A curving complex of white stucco, it is a large, modernistic structure with its own mini-convention facilities. It took us a while to find it, so we arrived late.

There didn't appear to be any former spies lurking around the lobby, but a bulletin board directed us to Bankers' Room "B" and "C" down the center hallway. There were two sets of doors to the double banquet room. The one we came upon first, closer to the lobby, was the entrance to the rear of the room. That was simply because the podium, and the table for honored guests, had been set up at the other end of the expanded room, closer to the second set of doors farther down the hallway. A luncheon-ticket table, we later learned, had been set up outside the rear door, but by the time we arrived it was gone and everyone was already seated at large round tables in the banquet room. We were thinking about quietly slipping in when a stocky fellow with a crew cut asked if we were from Senator Schweiker's office. He said he had been waiting for us and that three seats at Mr. Phillips's table had been kept aside. We apologized for our tardiness and followed him into the room. We would have to pay for our tickets later by mail.

It was a very large crowd in a large room, noisy with chatter, the cacophony of tableware and the bustle of waitresses. We wound our way single file through a curveway of packed tables until we came to the one in the far corner of the room, farthest from the rear door. I immediately recognized Phillips, who was sitting with his back toward us. I was walking ahead of Sarah Lewis and Veciana because I wanted to be in a position to see Phillips's face when he first saw Veciana. The fellow leading us tapped Phillips on the back. Phillips jumped up, whirled around, looked directly at me and, smiling, extended his hand as he introduced himself. He had the rich, well-modulated voice of the theater. I watched his eyes as I shook his hand, told him my name and said I was with Senator Schweiker's office. His eyes never left my face, although Sarah was standing directly behind my right shoulder and Veciana was alongside her. Phillips never even glanced at them.

I turned and said, "I'd like you to meet Sarah Lewis . . ." Phillips smiled a greeting and shook her hand. ". . . and this," I continued, "is Antonio Veciana."

Phillips smiled a quick greeting at Veciana, shook his hand and immediately turned back to me. "I'm glad you could come," he said, "and I'm delighted that Senator Schweiker is showing an interest, but I must admit I don't quite understand why you're here." He said this very cordially and with a nice smile. Then he quickly added, ". . . but, of course, you're most welcome." He gestured to the three empty chairs across the table.

It all happened with such speed that I was taken aback. I had thought I would be able to tell, keen observer that I deemed myself, if Phillips had exhibited even the slightest hint of having recognized Veciana. Not only did Phillips not display that hint, but his eyes had moved on and off of Veciana so quickly—in the flash of a brief handshake—that it was almost as if Veciana was a nonentity. Strange, too, when I thought about it later, that Phillips, when he greeted me, had not even glanced at either of the two people standing just behind me, not even at the pretty girl.

We were seated opposite Phillips at the large round table. I was on Veciana's left, Sarah Lewis on his right. Between Phillips and I were his wife, Gina, an attractive woman who had been a secretary at the CIA, and a United Press International reporter, a bluff, red-faced fellow just back from 21 years as a foreign correspondent. (Revelations about the CIA's use of the press and the fact that the Agency actually had working journalists on its payroll hadn't emerged yet, so it never crossed my mind to be suspicious of this fellow. Not even when he casually asked if I were attending the luncheon for any specific reason.)

As soon as Veciana sat down, he reached into his breast pocket, pulled out his glasses, put them on, folded his arms across his chest and began studying Phillips. Inwardly I cringed. Subtle he wasn't. For almost the entire luncheon, Veciana remained in the same position: erect in his chair, arms folded across his chest, staring at Phillips. Occasionally he picked up his fork and dabbed at the food on his plate. Then he would lean back again, fold his arms and look at Phillips. It made Phillips very nervous; his hands were shaking noticeably. He appeared to deliberately avoid looking at Veciana and remained in animated conversation with both his wife and the fellow to his left, a retired Navy officer.

The table was very large and the room so noisy that, at one point, when Phillips leaned towards me to say something, it was difficult to hear him. I thought he was asking again about what particular interest Senator Schweiker might have in this conference. I said I was there because it gave me the opportunity to meet him, and that we were working on something he might be able to help us with. I suggested that perhaps we could talk about it after the luncheon. He nodded and smiled, but because of the din I wasn't sure he caught everything I said. He went back to chatting with the fellow on his left. Veciana kept staring at him.

I kept looking over at Veciana, trying to get a reaction. I didn't want to appear too obvious by engaging him in a whispered conversation, but the suspense finally got to me. I leaned towards him and whispered, *"What do you think?"* Veciana looked at me, shrugged, and continued staring at Phillips.

When the guest speaker was introduced, I turned in my chair, my back to Phillips. Veciana moved only a bit to the side and kept glancing back at him.

The speaker was Lt. General Samuel V. Wilson, the newly appointed head of the Defense Intelligence Agency. A handsome, broad-shouldered soldier with wavy hair and a ruddy complexion, he wore a chestful of colorful ribbons, topped with the blue Combat Infantryman's Badge. He had seen some action. He was also polished, articulate and smoothly dramatic—right out of Patton's give'em-hell school of military speakers. His speech was a model for the occasion, an aggressive defense against the attacks being launched at the intelligence community, a real *us*-against-*them* speech.

When General Wilson finished, the audience gave him a standing ovation. I stood and clapped also; I always appreciate a good speech. Veciana stood but didn't clap, probably because the General didn't say anything about the need to kill Castro. During the ovation, I took the opportunity to lean towards Veciana and ask once again, "Is he Bishop?" Veciana removed his glasses and put them in his pocket. "No," he said, slowly shaking his head, "it is not him." He paused for a moment, then added, "Well, you know, I would like to talk with him." I said I would try to arrange that.

What I had in mind, once we were sure he wasn't Maurice Bishop, was to approach Phillips and ask directly for his help. I would give him a few details, show him the composite sketch; I had a copy with me in a plain brown envelope.

Phillips, however, was too fast for me. By the time I turned around he had already shot out the door near the podium. As president of the association, I realized, he probably wanted to thank his guest speaker and had raced ahead so as not to get caught in the crowd. I quickly ran toward the rear door to try to head him off, beckoning Veciana and Sarah Lewis to follow.

The hallway was already jammed but I could see Phillips talking with General Wilson. I tried to push my way against the flow of the crowd until I noticed that Phillips, having thanked the General and shaken his hand, was moving back down the hall towards me. "Excuse me, Mr. Phillips," I said as I stopped him, maneuvering him against the wall, "I'd like you to meet Antonio Veciana." I turned but Veciana wasn't there. I had thought that he and Lewis were directly behind me but they had gotten caught in the crowd. It was now obvious to Phillips that I wanted to bring him and Veciana together.

"Well, at any rate," I continued, turning back to Phillips, "as you know, I'm with Senator Schweiker and I thought you might be able to help us with what we've been working on."

"What about?" asked Phillips.

"The Kennedy assassination," I said, a bit surprised at the question.

Phillips smiled. "I'll be glad to talk with any Congressman, or any representative of Congress . . . in Congress."

Veciana suddenly appeared at our side with Sarah Lewis directly behind him. "This is Mr. Veciana," I said again. Veciana immediately asked Phillips in Spanish if he had been in Havana in 1960. Phillips answered in Spanish, yes, he had. Did he know Julio Lobo? Phillips said, yes, he remembered the name. Did he know Rufo Lopez-Fresquet (Castro's Finance minister and a CIA liaison)? Phillips said yes, then quickly asked Veciana, "What was your name again?"

"Antonio Veciana."

"Veciana?" Phillips repeated.

"Don't you know my name?"

Phillips shook his head slowly and, with apparent thoughtfulness, said, "No . . ." Then he asked me in English, "Is he with Schweiker's staff?" Phillips now appeared quite nervous.

"No," I said. "Mr. Veciana has been helping us with our investigation."

"What investigation?"

I found it strange that he didn't quite understand. "The Kennedy assassination," I said again. "That's why I thought if we could talk, I mean nothing official, just off the record if you prefer, you could be of some help. I thought . . ."

He interrupted me: "I'll be glad to talk with any Congressman, or any representative of Congress . . . in Congress." His hands shook. I realized that unintentionally, with the push of the crowd behind us, we had inadvertently cornered him.

"Well, there's an area I thought you might help us with . . ." I began, thinking I could push a little.

His smile was forced. "I told you, I'll be glad to talk with any Congressman, or any representative of Congress . . . in Congress," he repeated. Then, suddenly, he turned testy. "I'm sorry," he said, edging towards an opening in the crowd, "you've caught me at a very inopportune moment. As you can see, this is all very hectic here and I'm quite busy, so if you'll excuse me. . . ." He kept smiling, but he was clearly shaken.

"No," I said, "I didn't mean I wanted to talk with you now, but perhaps if I can give you a call . . ."

The smile was gone. With a dramatic, exasperated sigh, he said once again, now slowly and in mock rote: "I'll be glad to talk with any Congressman, or any representative of Congress . . . in Congress. *Now*, if you'll excuse me . . ." He pushed his way between us.

I retreated. I thanked him and told him I enjoyed the lunch and the guest speaker. He smiled again, said we were most welcome and quickly moved away.

I was not returning to Miami right away, so Veciana was going to fly back alone. On the ride to the airport from Reston he remained strangely silent; we all did. What I recall most clearly is our walk out to the parking lot after we left Phillips. It was a beautiful day, very bright after having been inside. Veciana didn't say a word. His face was expressionless.

"He's not Bishop?" I asked again.

Veciana continued looking straight ahead as he walked. "No, he's not him." A long silence. "But he knows."

He knows? "What do you mean, he knows?" I asked.

"He knows," Veciana repeated, without further explanation.

As we were waiting for Sarah to unlock the door of her Volkswagen, Veciana turned to me and said, "It is strange he didn't know my name. I was very well known."

That's funny, because I was thinking exactly the same thing.

For the next three months I thought a lot about what had happened that day. I saw Veciana only once or twice during that period and occasionally talked with him on the telephone. He didn't seem to want to discuss the incident in detail, but once, when I brought up David Phillips's name, he said again, "He knows." When I asked, "You mean he knows who Maurice Bishop is?" Veciana nodded his head. "He knows," he said. "I would like to talk with him more." I assumed he meant that if he could talk with Phillips at length we would be able to elicit some clues from him as to the identity of the real Maurice Bishop. However, from Phillips's reaction to our request for an informal discussion, I knew that was unlikely.

In October, Schweiker concluded that as a lone Senator he could no longer justify being involved in an investigation of the Kennedy assassination. Also, he was disappointed at not having been appointed to the new Senate Permanent Committee on Intelligence, which had come about at the recommendation of the Church Committee. There had previously been four permanent Senate committees with oversight responsibilities for intelligence activity and the Church Committee's report indicated that those committees had all been in the intelligence agencies' collective pocket. Nevertheless, the intelligence community essentially retained veto power over the membership of the new Senate Intelligence Committee, so Schweiker was cut out.

There were two other key factors which forced Schweiker to wrap up his investigation of the Kennedy assassination. One was the announcement by Senator Daniel Inouye, the chairman of the Intelligence Committee, that the new body would continue the investigation of possible intelligence community involvement in the Kennedy assassination begun by the Church Committee. (Schweiker didn't believe that it actually would, but because Inouye had made the public announcement, it left Schweiker without foundation. And Schweiker was right; the new Committee made a few cursory moves then dropped the subject.) The other factor was that the pressure being brought on the House of Representatives to conduct its own Kennedy assassination investigation was finally having results. The independent researchers who had been pushing for years were now joined by those who thought the Martin Luther King assassination also required a valid, final investigation.

Things came to a head when the Congressional Black Caucus brought Coretta King, the widow of the slain civil rights leader, directly to Tip O'Neill, who was about to become Speaker of the House. Mrs. King put it to him directly: "I have to know what really happened to Martin." So with the Black Caucus and the Warren Commission critics putting political pressure on the House leadership, bills to investigate both the King and Kennedy assassinations, after being locked in committees for the past year, were finally pushed through. And the House Select Committee on Assassinations was begotten.

PART TWO:

THE INVESTIGATION

TWENTY

OFF TO A STUMBLING START

*T*HE SELECT COMMITTEE on Assassinations was born in the septic tank of House politics. For many members it was simply politically inexpedient to oppose it. Early in 1975, two Congressmen had each introduced their own bills to reopen the Kennedy assassination. A fiery Texan named Henry B. Gonzalez, who had been a passenger in Kennedy's Texas motorcade, included in his bill probes into the murders of Robert Kennedy and Martin Luther King. A veteran lawmaker from Virginia, Thomas N. Downing, introduced his bill after he had developed serious doubts about the Warren Commission Report. Both bills were stuck in the Rules Committee for more than a year, until the Black Caucus put pressure on the House leadership. Dropping the Robert Kennedy probe, the bills were merged and in September, 1976, the resolution was passed.

But the seeds of dissension were early sown. Traditionally, the author of a resolution establishing a select committee is named chairman of the committee. Downing, however, was a lame duck; he wasn't running for reelection in 1976. His term would expire three months after the new Committee was formed. Gonzalez, on the other hand, was a barroom-brawling Mexican-American, not especially respected by the House power brokers. Despite Downing's lame-duck status, Carl Albert, in one of his last acts before turning the Speaker's helm over to Tip O'Neill, named Downing chairman of the House Assassinations Committee. That really burned Gonzalez.

The first month of the Committee's life was a harbinger of what was to come. It immediately mired itself in internal squabbling. Downing's first choice for the Committee's chief counsel and staff director was Washington attorney Bernard Fensterwald, an early Warren Commission critic who had established a research clearinghouse and lobbying operation called the Committee to Investigate

Assassinations. Although Fensterwald withdrew himself from consideration after Gonzalez objected to him, later, a story appeared in the *Washington Star* headlined: "Is FENSTERWALD A CIA PLANT?— ASSASSINATION INQUIRY STUMBLING." It was learned that material for the story had been leaked from Gonzalez's office.

Downing and Gonzalez finally got together in early October and settled on Richard Sprague as the Committee's chief counsel. Sprague had gotten national attention with his successful prosecution of United Mine Workers President Tony Boyle for the murder of UMW reformer Joseph Yablonski. As First Assistant District Attorney in Philadelphia, Sprague had run up a record of 69 homicide convictions out of 70 prosecutions, and he was known as tough, tenacious and independent. There was absolutely no doubt in my mind when I heard of Sprague's appointment that the Kennedy assassination would finally get what it needed: a no-holds-barred, honest investigation. Which just goes to show how ignorant of the ways of Washington both Sprague and I were.

Early in November, Sprague had lunch with Senator Schweiker in Washington. Sprague knew, of course, of Schweiker's work on the Church Committee and his Subcommittee, but Schweiker also filled Sprague in on the files his personal staff had compiled. In those files was a fat stack of informal memos reporting what I had dug up over the past year, including rough notes of the Antonio Veciana-Maurice Bishop area of the investigation. Schweiker, anxious to help Sprague as much as possible, arranged to turn some of these files over to him. In a letter to Sprague accompanying the files, Schweiker noted: "Because of my concern for the personal safety of some of the individuals who came forth to my staff, neither my staff nor I have publicly divulged their names. I strongly urge that this confidentiality continue to be respected . . ."

When he took the job, Sprague did so with the stipulation that he would have complete authority to hire his own staff and run the investigation as he saw fit. He proposed setting up two separate staffs, one for Kennedy and one for King; and he insisted on handling both cases as if they were homicide investigations.

Certainly in the annals of the investigations of the Kennedy assassination, it was a novel approach. And, judging from the reaction of many Congressmen, it was a far too radical approach. Especially since Sprague was obviously very serious. He said he needed a staff of at least 200 and an initial annual budget of $6.5 million and he refused to guarantee that would do the job. Sprague had hardly settled into his shabby Washington office in the rat-infested, unrenovated former FBI Records Building when the attacks against him began.

In December, Sprague called me and asked me to come to Washington to talk with him. When I got there I found that he had turned the Schweiker material over to Deputy Chief Counsel Robert Tanenbaum, a veteran homicide attorney from the New York District Attorney's Office, recruited by Sprague to head the Kennedy investigation. Tanenbaum had reviewed the material and suggested that Sprague ask me to join the staff. I told Sprague I would if I could be free to pursue those areas in which I had the most background and which I considered the most potentially productive, especially that of intelligence agency involvement with the anti-Castro exiles in Miami. He said I could.

I had lunch with Sprague and a few of his staffers that day, and we discussed some of the things I had worked on with Schweiker and what I thought needed to be done. But Sprague, despite the fact that he had been on the job for more than two months, seemed less occupied with the substance of the case than he did with other problems. He had gotten blasted in the press by a few Congressmen after word got around that the Committee would probably use such investigative devices as lie-detector tests, voice-stress evaluators and concealed tape recorders. Some lawmakers, including a couple of right-wing, military-establishment supporters, suddenly expressed their grave concern for individual rights and said that Sprague was threatening to trample on the civil rights of people he would investigate. At lunch that day, I commented to Sprague about the heat he seemed to be taking.

Sprague shook his head. "You know, I don't understand it. I've never been in a situation like this before, where I'm getting criticized for things I *might* do. It's nonsense, but I don't know why it's happening." As it was, none of us would find out what was really happening in Washington until much later.

So it was arranged; I would officially join the Committee as a staff investigator on January 1st, 1977. I returned to Miami and got immediately to work renewing the contacts and sources I had let lapse over the previous few months. I had file cases of documents and background material and I began to structure an investigative plan. I couldn't wait to get started. Sprague had convinced me that he planned to conduct a strong investigation and I was never more optimistic in my life. I remember envisioning its scope and its character. There would be a major effort in Miami, with teams of investigators and squads of attorneys. We would have all sorts of sophisticated investigative resources and, even more important, the authority to use them. We would cut our way through the thickets of false leads and misinformation. We would zero in on the hottest evidence and work day and night pursuing its validity. The Warren Commission's legacy of deceit had left a stain on American history and now, finally, the Kennedy assassination would get the investigation it deserved. There would be no more deceptions.

Little did I know.

TWENTY-ONE

PROGRAMMED TO SELF-EXPLODE

WHAT SPRAGUE DISCOVERED when he arrived in Washington was that his first order of business was not to set up an investigation but simply to keep the Assassinations Committee alive. The Committee had been officially established in September. All Congressional committees legally expire at the end of each Congressional year and then, if they are mandated to continue under the terms of their originating resolutions, the new Congress reconstitutes them as a matter of course.

However, as soon as Sprague's intentions to conduct a true, tough investigation were known, the flak began to fly. Fueled by some of the press, including the *New York Times*, rumors started circulating that the reconstitution of the Assassinations Committee might not be as "automatic" as assumed. These attacks increased when Sprague announced his staff plan and budget.

Sprague hadn't pulled his figures out of the air, he had analyzed the total resources that the Warren Commission had available from its own staff, the FBI, the Secret Service, the CIA and the Justice and State Departments. He had also figured that the nature of conducting a truly independent investigation precluded using the investigative forces of these other Government agencies, especially since some of these agencies would be under investigation themselves. With a proposed staff of about 200 and a yearly budget of $6.5 million, the Assassinations Committee would not have far more than the Warren Commission in resources. (The Warren Commission had 83 staffers but used 150 full-time agents from the FBI alone.) Still, the budget sounded big and became fodder for additional attacks on Sprague. He was accused of arrogance; he had made a "mistake" in coming on so strong.

"Several people around here who are familiar with the bureaucratic game told me to first present a smaller budget," Sprague admitted. "They assured me that I could always go back later and plead for more. That's the way they do things in Washington, I was told. Well, I won't play that game." Sprague didn't realize what he was up against.

On January 2nd, the day before the convening of the 95th Congress, there appeared in the *New York Times* a major story headlined: "Counsel in Assassination Inquiry Often Target of Criticism." Written by reporter David Burnham, it was an incredibly crude journalistic hatchet job, reviewing Sprague's seventeen-year career as a Philadelphia prosecutor strictly in terms of the controversies he had provoked. Certainly I was aware that Sprague's record had points worthy of criticism, but Burnham's piece left out the grays and painted Sprague a heavy black. Even the *Philadelphia Bulletin*'s Claude Lewis, not particularly a Sprague fan, winced at Burnham's blatant cut job. "You can dig up dirt on anyone if you look hard enough," noted Lewis.

Intended or not, Burnham's piece had the effect of a well-placed torpedo—it almost blew up the Assassinations Committee. On January 4th, an attempt to pass a resolution reconstituting the Committee by a unanimous-consent voice vote failed. That meant the resolution would have to go through a lengthy bureaucratic labyrinth, including passage through the Rules Committee and a budget review exercise, before the Committee could officially be reconstituted. It would take weeks.

In Miami, unaware of the behind-the-scenes turmoil, I was anxious to get rolling. I kept calling Kennedy investigation chief Bob Tanenbaum with reports and advice.

"Bob, I think it's initially important to coordinate my area with what the rest of the staff is doing," I said. "I imagine the staff is already organized into teams, but I think it's important that a program of regular communication between teams and field investigators be developed." I suggested I come to Washington to get a detailed picture of the staff organization and plans.

Tanenbaum agreed. Only in his early thirties, Tanenbaum had risen quickly in New York DA Frank Hogan's office and was the epitome of the quick-thinking, fast-talking prosecutor. He didn't want me to know how chaotic the mess was becoming in Washington. "Let me work things out on this end," he kept saying, "and we'll plan on getting together. Stay loose."

Stay loose? We were supposed to be rolling on the most important investigation in American history. Why the hell weren't we moving?

Over the next several weeks, my confusion and frustration multiplied. Even now, one can view the series of events that took place in Washington and the behavior of some of the characters involved as simply outrageous, unbelievably stupid and/or breathtakingly asinine. Yet, when you consider what happened in the end, the ultimate fate of Sprague and the Assassinations Committee, it's difficult to believe there wasn't a guiding force, a pattern to the events.

On February 2nd, the House voted to reconstitute the Assassinations Committee—temporarily. Still under sharp attack by certain conservative lawmakers suddenly deeply concerned with civil liberties, the Committee was, as the *Washington Star* put it, "given less than two months to justify its existence under conditions that . . . make it almost impossible to develop new evidence." The House had kept the Committee alive, but gave it just barely enough to cover the already reduced salaries of its staff. (Everyone had taken a 40 percent pay cut while waiting reconstitution.)

In Miami, I was keeping busy, but without a structured investigative plan all I could do was take a scattergun approach to the leads. I continued checking out Veciana's story; pursuing Bishop possibilities; digging into the activities of Santos Trafficante, Norman Rothman and other Organized Crime figures and their possible contacts with Jack Ruby; researching the CIA's role in anti-Castro activities; and I went on meeting with my sources and contacts. More and more, when fresh information or a new lead would come in, I found myself telling someone: "That seems worth checking. As soon as we get some help down here and this thing gets organized, I'll get back to you. Yeah, there are a few problems in Washington, but they'll get ironed out. We're beginning to get organized now."

I didn't realize the chaos was just beginning. About a week after the Committee was temporarily born again, I received a call from Bob Tanenbaum.

"Well," he sighed, "World War Three has started in Washington. It's Gonzalez versus Sprague. You wouldn't believe it. Gonzalez is taking back his stationery."

His what?

"Let me read you a letter. It's dated February 9th, 1977. 'Dear Dick. Until the Select Committee is properly organized and its rules established, a number of steps are necessary. Accordingly, I hereby request and direct that you provide me at the earliest practical time, but no later than noon Friday, February 11th, your written assurance as given verbally to the Committee yesterday that, failing to recommend necessary reductions in force, you guarantee compliance with the financial limits imposed on the Committee. . . . Owing to an evident inability of the Committee in past times to adequately control the use of its letterhead and franked materials, and in the absence of any present controls on such materials, you are directed to return to me immediately any and all letterhead material bearing my name. You are reminded that no expense or financial obligation whatever may be made in my name, nor shall any vouchers or other commitment obligating the Committee to expend funds be made without my prior knowledge and personal, specific and written authorization . . . ' ''

With no recourse but to view it in the larger terms of human folly, Tanenbaum roared with laughter. "What an asshole!" he shouted. But it really wasn't funny. Since all Congressional committees use the postal franking privileges of its chairman, and every expense voucher, travel order and most directives and requests to other Government agencies are made under the chairman's signature, Gonzalez, in effect, was stopping the operation of the Committee.

Gonzalez had been furious at not being named chairman of the Committee when it was originally formed. He automatically stepped into the post, however, when Downing retired and the new Congress convened in January. (It was, of course, something of a Catch-22 position since the Committee, not yet reconstituted, was officially nonexistent.) Gonzalez, however, wanted more than just the title. He wanted control and the power to stack the staff with his own people. Sprague wasn't about to give him that.

In December, Gonzalez had told Sprague that, under the formula in the Congressional Rules, the Committee could operate with a budget of $150,000 a month until it was officially reconstituted. On that basis, Sprague began beefing up his original start-up staff with new additions, all of whom were put on the payroll January 1st. I was in that group. Gonzalez, however, had been mistaken about the Committee's budget. The rules actually permitted it only $84,337 a month in expenses while awaiting reconstitution. When Gonzalez was called on the carpet by the Rules Committee for the budget over-run, he said that Sprague had hired the new staffers without his knowledge or permission.

At a meeting of the members of the Assassinations Committee on February 8th, Gonzalez repeated his charges against Sprague and ordered Sprague to fire the people he had just hired. Sprague denied Gonzalez's accusations and refused to fire anyone. The other Committee members backed Sprague. Gonzalez fumed. The next day he wrote the letter cutting off the staff's resources and demanding the return of his stationery.

"And we just got another note from Gonzalez today," Tanenbaum added. "Listen to this: 'Dear Mr. Sprague. You called me at 10:10

yesterday morning. I was out. I returned the call at 11:30. You were not in. You were at a staff meeting. Your secretary said she would get you if it were important. I said, "I don't know if it's important. I'm returning his call." I hung up. I then met the President of the United States. I am the Chairman. You are my employee. Do not forget that.' ''

Tanenbaum had a problem reading that note to me because he was laughing so hard.

The next day, I received my own letter from Chairman Gonzalez. It was a form letter sent to all staffers, without the backing of the Committee:

> This is to convey to you my profound regret regarding the circumstances which surround your present employment. . . .
>
> It is highly deplorable that the person most responsible for your employment did not advise you of the possible difficulty in getting the Committee reconstituted.
>
> As you know, I was not the Chairman during the 94th Congress, but due to errors which have been made under the former Chairman, it has been a long and hard struggle getting the Committee reconstituted . . . and it is only for a very limited basis, through March 31, and for a very limited budget . . .
>
> No one likes a reduction in personnel, but . . . I hope that as soon as possible I will be able to convey to you what the future status of personnel will be with the Select Committee.

Gonzalez kept on swinging. He went to the Attorney General and recommended that Committee staff members who, while waiting for the investigation to get structured, had begun researching the FBI files, be denied access to those files. (It was probably the first time in Congressional history that a Committee Chairman wanted *non*cooperation.) Next, Gonzalez cut off the long-distance telephone calls, thereby isolating the only investigator the Committee had in the field at the time—me.

Sprague later put it succinctly: "Gonzalez went berserk."

Gonzalez finally threw what he thought was his Sunday punch: He fired Sprague. In a hand-delivered letter, Gonzalez charged that Sprague "has engaged in a course of conduct that is wholly intolerable for any employee of the House," and ordered him to vacate his office by 5 p.m. that day. Gonzalez had uniformed Capitol Police officers arrive at the staff offices with orders to physically evict Sprague if he wasn't out. Tanenbaum later told me he and other large staff members actually formed a circle around Sprague to prevent that. But a couple of hours after Gonzalez had sent the letter, the Committee's eleven members signed their own letter directing Sprague to ignore Gonzalez.

What was supposed to be an investigation into one of the most significant and tragic events in this country's history had turned into, as George Lardner of the *Washington Post* put it, "an opéra bouffe." Editorial cartoonists around the country were having a ball. "Pardon me, is this the offices of the . . . nice shot! . . . House Assassinations Committee?" asked an Oliphant character walking in a roomful of stomping, swinging, kicking, brawling lawmakers.

Then Gonzalez went one step too far. At an open meeting of the Committee, he attacked the second-ranking Democrat, Congressman Richardson Preyer, head of the Kennedy Subcommittee. Judge Preyer, a Southern, soft-spoken, former jurist known for his fair-minded, liberal intellect, was one of the House's most respected members. When Gonzalez began flying off the handle, Preyer suggested the Committee adjourn until some problems were ironed out. Gonzalez exploded. "I'm the Chairman! I know you want to be chairman and you're trying to get rid of me!" he yelled at Preyer.

According to Bob Tanenbaum, who was there: "Preyer's head actually jerked back. It looked like a shot from the front, but it was really a neurophysical reaction. It was really an embarrassing moment for the old guy."

Preyer recovered and said quietly, "I do not seek the chairmanship, nor do I want it. I have a motion that we adjourn." The Committee quickly backed him and the members hurried away—except for Gonzalez, who held an impromptu press conference at which he called Sprague "a rattlesnake."

The next day I received a call from Tanenbaum. "Preyer and the other members of the Committee are going to House Speaker O'Neill to ask him to remove Gonzalez from the chairmanship," he said. "We're down to the final act. If Gonzalez is not removed, we're leaving. There's no way we can go on with this man. He's gone mad."

As the news filtered down to me in Miami—through calls made on the WATS line of non-Committee telephones—I became increasingly dumbfounded. While I had read of the scandalous and ridiculous or often just petty behavior of our Washington lawmakers in so-called behind-the-scenes press reports and gossip columns through the years, I always thought they were exaggerated or overly dramatized. But there I was, privy to the inside skinny, and I couldn't believe it was actually happening.

Confronted with the unprecedented situation of Committee members rebelling against their own Chairman, Tip O'Neill waffled. Appearing on a *Face the Nation* telecast, O'Neill said he lacked the power to remove a Select Committee Chairman. He also said the

Assassinations Committee's problems would probably be worked out and that he believed it would stay in business beyond its March 31st deadline.

A cryptic statement, a bit confusing, perhaps, but there must have been some behind-the-scenes pressure brought on Gonzalez. "They tell us that Gonzalez is going to go," Tanenbaum reported to me, "but I think the bastards are lying to us. I think what they're really angling for is a trade-off. If Gonzalez goes, then Sprague will have to go." Although it wasn't immediately apparent, Tanenbaum was right about the bastards.

Chairman Gonzalez resigned from his post—and the Assassinations Committee—in the first week of March. He then flew home to San Antonio and gave a long, raging "exclusive" interview to home-town newsman Paul Thompson of the *Express-News*.

In that interview, Gonzalez ranted wildly about the "arrogant, self-serving power broker" Dick Sprague, a "rattlesnake" who "ran amuck." Gonzalez himself was running amuck, but amid his bizarre ragings, a few of his assessments had the insights of a veteran insider. He questioned, for instance, the composition of the Assassinations Committee itself, which included members who had initially voted against opening a Kennedy assassination inquiry. (Ohio Republican Representative Sam Devine, for instance, had voted twice against creating the Committee.)

"The Committee was programmed to self-destruct," claimed Gonzalez. He saw his unsuccessful entreaties to Tip O'Neill to help fire Sprague as a sign that O'Neill, who was very close to the Kennedy family and, therefore, fearful of exposing Jack Kennedy's personal peccadilloes, never really wanted an investigation.

"I'm aware at last," said Gonzalez, "that the House leadership never had intended for the JFK investigation to fly, and indeed had prefabricated the whole thing for the skids."

The day after that interview appeared in the San Antonio newspaper, I received a call in Miami from Associated Press reporter John Hopkins. "Have you ever been in Washington?" he asked. I said, sure I've been to Washington, why? "Because Gonzalez gave an interview in Texas in which he claimed you've never been to Washington," Hopkins said. "He said he didn't know what you did in Miami and Sprague wouldn't tell him."

Hopkins also told me that Gonzalez claimed that he was forced out of the investigation by "vast and powerful forces, including the country's most sophisticated criminal element."

"By the way," Hopkins asked, "do you have any connections with Organized Crime?"

WHAT?

"In that interview," Hopkins said, "Gonzalez claimed you are supposed to have underworld connections."

I had never met Gonzalez and I doubt that he knew anything about me personally. But he did know my name from the list of new staffers whom Sprague had hired. Gonzalez was making assumptions strictly on the basis of my name. That steamed me. I don't think I've been more angry in my life with someone I had never met. If Gonzalez had lived in Miami, when he awoke the next morning he would have found a horse's head in his bed.

TWENTY-TWO

CHAOS IN WASHINGTON, DEATH IN MANALAPAN

*I*T WAS NEARING the end of March, 1977. Once again the Assassinations Committee was due to die. The resignation of Gonzalez and the appointment of the new chairman, Louis Stokes, a big, balding, relaxed, Democrat from Ohio who was one of the leaders of the Black Caucus, ended the internal feuding and gave the Committee and its staff the chance to concentrate on ending the struggle for survival—its single priority since its birth.

Investigating the assassinations of John F. Kennedy and Martin Luther King? Oh yeah, that's what Congress expected the Committee to be doing while it kept it in a financial armlock, bombed it with criticism and put increasing pressure on it to perform. At one point in the Committee's struggle for survival, the chairman of the Rules Committee, James Delaney, a Democrat from New York, carped: "I'd like to know if they have anything or if this is just a plain witch hunt. I don't know if it's a witch hunt or not." Speaker Tip O'Neill said he thought the Committee would have to produce "something of a sensational nature" to survive.

All too quickly, the lesson of the Warren Commission had been lost and all Sprague and Tanenbaum and the other staff directors could do for the first six months was to try to keep the Committee alive. Congress needed quick cosmetics to publicly justify funding the investigation, so the Committee had to *look* good. The Committee had to *look* as if it were making progress, had to *look* as if it were digging up sensational new revelations. If it didn't perform, there were many members of Congress ready to cut off its gonads.

Under such conditions, it is no wonder that within the Committee staff itself problems began to arise. The staff was pressuring Tanenbaum and Sprague to ward off the attacks from the political front. And Tanenbaum was being pressured by armies of both legitimate researchers and misinformation purveyors, flooding him with data while, at the same time, he was trying to acquaint himself with the incredibly intricate details of the Kennedy case. He was under pressure from the staff to begin a substantive investigation; and he was under pressure from Congress and the press to come up with sensational revelations. Then, of course, Chairman Gonzalez seemed to be doing what he could to prevent him from organizing an investigation.

Tanenbaum became paranoid. He took a small group of staff members into his confidence and distrusted everyone else. His paranoia was reinforced when one staff member was revealed to be feeding Gonzalez reports of Sprague's confidential talks to the staff. That, while having to live under the Sword of Damocles for six months, produced a good deal of squabbling and petty bickering among the staff members. Some young staffers were legitimately concerned about the direction of the investigation and its lack of established priorities but many, some veteran Washington hands among them, were worried that if the Committee did not get reconstituted, there would be no work details to put on their resumés. They began writing memos detailing their concerns and urging the implementation of courses of action they suggested. These became known as "C.Y.A." memos, for "Cover Your Ass."

Isolated in Miami, without authorization or funds to go to Washington, I didn't know what the hell was really going on. But at least I was able to function a bit on my own. I put up a good front for the people I was talking with and randomly chipped away at the mountain of work to be done. On the other hand, the staff of investigators stuck in Washington were, for the most part, spinning their wheels. All they could do was handle what came across the transom.

Cliff Fenton, a top New York homicide detective was brought in by Tanenbaum as Chief Investigator. Like all of the Committee's other ex-badges from the Big Apple, he was a sharp dresser. Hefty and easy-moving, Fenton seemed a mellow type of guy and spoke with a chuckle that was indefensibly contagious—I often envision him back in Manhattan rambling into the lockup with a killer in tow, the guy chuckling right along with Fenton as he's led to his cell. But Fenton was a shrewd, streetwise cop who knew only one way to handle an investigation: Put men out to investigate. Before Gonzalez cut off authorization to travel, Fenton had sent a few of his men out to take random shots at a few of the leads that came in. They came back with enough to convince him that, if he had his way, this would be an investigation heavy with field work. Fenton never got his way. So, especially in the beginning, he had the rough job of keeping his men busy in Washington. Accustomed to being on the street, they got itchy inside. But since only one or two had any background familiarity with the Kennedy case, Fenton suggested they spend their time reading the shelves of books that had been written on the subject, mostly by Warren Commission critics. It was, however, a case of the blind leading the blind. One of the more popular books circulating around the office was a large, softcover volume by Texans Gary Shaw and Larry Harris called *Cover-Up*. It had a lot of pictures in it.

Although the Committee had been in existence for almost six months, it was nowhere close to being able to function as an effective investigative body. But I didn't fully realize that until the last days in March, just before the question of its reconstitution was due to come up again on the floor of the House.

Late Monday afternoon, on March 28th, I received a call from Tanenbaum. The House was scheduled to vote that Wednesday on the reauthorization bill and the Committee members as well as the top staff counsel had been spending most of their time lobbying among the individual lawmakers for support. As they discovered, while many of the Congressmen didn't care for Gonzalez, he was part of the club. Some members even resented Sprague—viewed by a least one Congressman as "just a clerk"—for having beaten out Gonzalez. That Monday, Gonzalez himself had been on the House floor ranting again about Sprague's "insubordination" and even distributing copies of a "Dear Colleague" letter to every House member urging that the Committee be dropped. He was thirsting for revenge.

I asked Tanenbaum how it looked.

"It depends on who you talk to what time of the day." He did not sound optimistic. "Anyway, Wednesday is the day. We'll know one way or the other."

We talked about the situation for a while and then I told Tanenbaum that while waiting around, I had discovered a CIA agent named J. Walton Moore running an overt domestic division office in Dallas. Moore had been there since the time of the Kennedy assassination and, there were some telling hints in his personality and activities. On the off-chance that Moore might be Maurice Bishop, I asked a friend of mine, a local reporter, to have a surreptitious photograph of Moore taken so I could show it to Veciana. (As it turned out, Moore did not resemble Bishop and Veciana confirmed that he wasn't.)

At any rate, I was telling Tanenbaum of my plans to have the photograph taken. I told him that Moore was additionally interesting because he had been in touch with George de Mohrenschildt, a much-traveled oil consultant with mysterious connections. As mentioned earlier, while living in Dallas, de Mohrenschildt had befriended the Oswalds as soon as they had returned from Russia.

"By the way," Tanenbaum said, "I just got a call from the Dutch journalist, Willem Oltmans. He's the guy I was telling you about."

But Tanenbaum needn't have, because Oltmans had already gone national—doing various television interviews, and then going to Washington to tell his story to the Committee. He had befriended de Mohrenschildt and claimed that de Mohrenschildt had confessed that he was part of a "Dallas conspiracy" of oil men and Cuban exiles with "a blood debt to settle." De Mohrenschildt admitted, Oltmans said, that Oswald "acted at his guidance and instruction."

De Mohrenschildt had apparently suffered a nervous breakdown at the time he was talking with Oltmans, but he left a hospital in Dallas to travel with Oltmans to Europe reportedly to negotiate book and magazine rights to his story. Then in Brussels, Oltmans claimed, de Mohrenschildt ran away from him and disappeared.

Now Tanenbaum told me that Oltmans had just called him from California. Oltmans said that in tracking de Mohrenschildt he found that de Mohrenschildt could be reached in Florida. Tanenbaum gave me the phone number. Now Tanenbaum really had something for me.

That afternoon, I checked out the number. It was listed to a Mrs. C.E. Tilton III in Manalapan, a small strip of a town on the ocean south of Palm Beach noted for its wealthy residents. Mrs. Tilton, I discovered, was the sister of one of de Mohrenschildt's former wives. I decided it would be best if I could contact him directly rather than by telephone and so it was early on March 29th, 1977, when I went looking for George de Mohrenschildt in Manalapan.

The house was hidden behind a barrier of high hedges and I hadn't noticed any numbers, so I wasn't sure I had the right place when I pulled into the narrow driveway. It was a strangely grim house for that narrow, monied stretch of Florida coastline, where the mansions are usually chic pastel modern or classy traditional white. But this was a large, two-story New England-type structure of dark cedar shingles and drab green trim. To the rear was a mansard-roofed building containing a series of garages.

As I got out of the car, a young woman emerged unexpectedly from behind the building. She was strikingly beautiful, tall and dark with a smooth sculpted face, long raven hair and deep brown eyes. She wore a tight black leotard and moved with the supple, sensuous ease of a dancer. Her tan body glowed with a sheen of perspiration;

she had obviously been exercising. She wiped her brow and arms with a small towel.

"Excuse me," I said as I approached her. "Is this the Tilton home?"

"Yes, it is," she said. Her expression was cool.

"I'm looking for George de Mohrenschildt."

She hesitated a moment, her eyes cautious, probing.

"He's not in at the moment. I'm his daughter, Alexandra. May I help you?"

I told her my name and why I was there. There was no indication that she was surprised. She said her father was in Palm Beach and, no, she didn't know when he would return or how to get in touch with him. She added, however, that he was certain to be home in the evening and that I could reach him if I called at about eight o'clock. She gave me the telephone number, which I already had.

"I'd appreciate it," I said, "if you would tell him that I'll be calling and would like to see him." We hadn't yet been issued official identification so my only credentials were old business cards which identified me as a staff investigator for U.S. Senator Richard Schweiker. I crossed out Schweiker's name on one and wrote above it, "House Select Committee on Assassinations." She took it and said she would tell her father to expect my call.

The drive from Manalapan to Miami takes about an hour and a half by the slower, more scenic, oceanside road. I was in no hurry. I was feeling elated. We were *doing* something! We were getting somewhere! Despite Tanenbaum's fears, I finally began to feel the investigation would get on track. After all, I had just jumped right into a crucial area of evidence in the case. By sheer luck one of the most important witnesses—perhaps *the* most important witness—was in my territory. I would be the one who would question George de Mohrenschildt and later, perhaps, lead a team into a comprehensive investigation of his possible role in the assassination of President Kennedy.

You have to know something about the mysterious George de Mohrenschildt to understand how I felt. He was one of the most fascinating characters to pop up in the original Warren Commission investigation. Born in Russia in 1911, the son of a Czarist official who later became a wealthy landowner in Poland, de Mohrenschildt received a doctorate in commerce from the University of Liege in Belgium. He came to the United States in 1938 and, with his aristocratic pedigree—he liked to be called the Baron—was able to maneuver his way into the international social set, including a friendship with Mrs. John V. Bouvier, Jacqueline Kennedy's mother. De Mohrenschildt also married well, always at the upper end of the social scale. His first wife was Palm Beach resident Dorothy Pierson; his second was the daughter of a high State Department official; and his third was Chestnut Hill socialite Wynne Sharples. He married Jeanne LeGon, his fourth wife, in 1959 in Dallas. Her Russian father had been director of the Far Eastern Railroad and was connected with Nationalist politics in China. Her brother Sergio had worked on the supersecret Manhattan atomic bomb project.

During World War II, de Mohrenschildt's roamings stirred rumors of spying and he later admitted a connection with the French intelligence service. In 1944, he went to Texas, got a master's degree in petroleum engineering and began developing close ties to the top tycoons of Texas oil, among them H.L. Hunt. He then began traveling around the world as a consultant for various Texas oil companies. In 1961, he showed up at a Guatemalan camp being used by the CIA to train Cuban exiles for the Bay of Pigs invasion. (He and his fourth wife were supposedly on a walking tour of South America.) De Mohrenschildt also worked for a period as a consultant in Yugoslavia for the International Cooperation Administration, a branch of the U.S. Government's Agency for International Development. A CIA memo written at the time by Deputy Director Richard Helms credits de Mohrenschildt with providing valuable foreign intelligence.

Given his background, it seemed strange that de Mohrenschildt would have spontaneously befriended someone with the look of a working-class drifter like Lee Harvey Oswald. He introduced the ex-Marine defector, recently returned from Russia, to Dallas's staunchly anti-Communist White Russian community and helped get him a job with a firm that did aerial photo analysis and map printing for the military. When Gary Taylor, who had been married to de Mohrenschildt's daughter Alexandra, was asked by a Warren Commission counsel if he thought de Mohrenschildt had any influence over Oswald, Taylor replied: "Yes, there seemed to be a great deal of influence there." Asked at the end of his questioning if he had any further comments that might help the Commission, Taylor said, "Well, the only thing that occurred to me was that—uh—and I guess it was from the beginning—that if there was any assistance or plotters in the assassination that it was, in my opinion, most probably the de Mohrenschildts'." The Warren Commission, however, did little to explore the contention.

So I had good reason to be excited about the opportunity I had before me and when I got back to Miami I quickly called the Committee's chief investigator, Cliff Fenton, and told him what had happened. I said I would get in touch with de Mohrenschildt that evening and probably set up an appointment to question him the next morning. "Fine, fine," Fenton said. "Well, you just keep on it." He was obviously preoccupied with the vote the next day. "This is crazy up here, just plain crazy," he said with his characteristic chuckle. "I have never seen anything like this place." I was disappointed he wasn't more excited, but I couldn't believe that the Kennedy assassination investigation would succumb to petty political bickering. And now, of course, I had found George de Mohrenschildt.

About 6:30 that evening I received a call from Bill O'Reilly, a friend who was then a television reporter in Dallas. "Funny thing happened," he said. "We just aired a story that came over the wire about a Dutch journalist saying the Assassinations Committee has finally located de Mohrenschildt in South Florida. Now de Mohrenschildt's attorney, a guy named Pat Russell, he calls and says de Mohrenschildt committed suicide this afternoon. Is that true?"

Less than a minute after I was hit by that report, my telephone rang again. It was Palm Beach State Attorney Dave Bludworth calling. He said my card had been found in de Mohrenschildt's shirt pocket. About four hours after I had been there, de Mohrenschildt had returned to Nancy Tilton's house. His daughter told him of my visit and gave him my card. He put the card in his pocket and, according to Alexandra, did not seem upset, but shortly afterwards he said he was going upstairs to rest. What de Mohrenschildt then apparently did was take a .20-gauge shotgun that Mrs. Tilton kept beside her bed for protection. He sat down in a soft chair, put the stock of the shotgun on the floor and the end of the barrel in his mouth, leaned forward and pulled the trigger.

As soon as I had confirmed de Mohrenschildt's death, I called Richard Sprague. It was about 7 p.m. Sprague was shocked. He suggested I get on the scene immediately while he attempted to put a team of staff investigators together to help me and contacted the Congressional Committee members to ready subpoenas. From the little I knew then, there appeared to be some elements that needed close checking before we could accept the death as a definite suicide. Sprague said he would get back to me as soon as the team was ready to move. Time was important.

Sprague, however, was unable to do anything and he never did get back to me. I had, of course, expected to see Committee counsels and investigators descending on the scene, slapping witnesses with subpoenas for later sworn testimony. What happened instead was that two days after the incident, a junior counsel and a recently hired investigator with little knowledge of who de Mohrenschildt even was, arrived to help me for a couple of days in my frenetic efforts. If it hadn't been for the quick assistance of Palm Beach State Attorney Dave Bludworth and Detective Chief Dick Sheets in securing some of de Mohrenschildt's documents, the Committee would have gotten no more than the newspaper reporters did. As it was, no subpoenas were ever served and no testimony ever taken from at least two important witnesses: de Mohrenschildt's daughter Alexandra and Edward J. Epstein.

I would later learn that as I was talking with Alexandra de Mohrenschildt, her father was in a hotel room in Palm Beach being interviewed by a freelance writer name Edward J. Epstein. Although the author of *Inquest*, one of the first books critical of the Warren Commission, Epstein's increasing contacts with the CIA were considered suspicious by many of his fellow critics. In addition, Epstein was then working under a lucrative contract from *Reader's Digest*—a publication that had done cooperative projects with the Agency—to write a book that would suggest that Lee Harvey Oswald was an agent of the KGB. (Epstein flew out of Palm Beach before I could question him.)

While de Mohrenschildt may have been one of the most important witnesses in the Kennedy assassination investigation, in Washington his death was viewed not as a tremendous setback for the investigation, but as a publicity break that might help the Assassinations Committee survive.

What happened in Washington was this: After I had notified Dick Sprague of de Mohrenschildt's death, I waited for him to call back. Numerous times that evening and well beyond midnight, as I ran between Manalapan, the medical examiner's office and the State Attorney's office in West Palm Beach, I attempted to reach him or Tanenbaum or Fenton or *anyone* who knew what the hell was going on in Washington. Talking with State Attorney Bludworth—who had cooperatively assumed that a Federal panel looking into the Kennedy assassination should be given priority in the case—I tried to give him the impression that the Committee was geared up and ready to move in at any moment, but as time went by and no official word came through he became increasingly confused. So did I. The only one I was able to reach at the Committee's offices was a junior counsel who knew only that Sprague and the staff's top echelon had been urgently called to Chairman Stokes's office.

The next morning, headlines in Washington blared the news of what had happened that night: Sprague quit.

I would learn the details later. Despite the Assassinations Committee finally getting unified with the departure of Congressman Gonzalez, an early straw count indicated that the House still might not approve continuing the probe. As one of the old guard told Committee member Bob Edgar: "You guys dumped Gonzalez. I don't know Sprague at all, but if you don't dump him too, you guys are dead in the water.''

Sensing that, Sprague had early on offered to resign if it meant the difference in keeping the Committee alive. Chairman Stokes assured him that would not be necessary and that the Committee would stick with him. Then, in the last hours of the evening before the House vote, Stokes called Sprague to his office. Repeatedly, Stokes reviewed the situation and each time painted it in gloomier terms. Finally, near midnight, Sprague realized that, despite Stokes's earlier assurances of support, the ground was being shoveled out from beneath him.

"Do you want me to resign now?" Sprague asked. Stokes put his head down and remained silent. Bristling, Sprague stood up.

"Gentlemen," he said, "it's clear it's in everyone's best interest if I resign." He then called his secretary and dictated a two-sentence letter of resignation.

Sprague drove home to Philadelphia at 2 a.m., about the time I was driving back to Miami from Dave Bludworth's office in Palm Beach, wondering what the hell was going on in Washington. By 8:00 the next morning, while I was once again trying to contact someone at the Committee, Sprague was on a plane to Acapulco.

That day, after four hours of stormy debate, the House voted to continue the Assassinations Committee at a budget of $2.5 million for the year. The death of de Mohrenschildt and Sprague's resignation had garnered enough votes.

TWENTY-THREE

TRUTH AND CONSEQUENCES

*T*HE KEY FACTORS that drove Richard Sprague to resign as Staff Director and Chief Counsel of the Assassinations Committee seemed, at the time, to be clear and straightforward. His proposed use of certain investigative equipment such as lie detectors, his demand for an expensive, unrestricted investigation, his refusal to play politics with Chairman Gonzalez—these were the apparent grounds for the vociferous criticism which, in the long run, was debilitating to the Committee's efforts to get on with its job. However, after his resignation and a brief respite from the turmoil of Washington, Sprague was able to view his experience in a broader perspective.

Shortly after he returned from Acapulco, he was interviewed by Robert Sam Anson of *New Times* magazine. Sprague admitted that, with the barrages of criticism that had been flying at him from all directions, he and the staff had little time to actually investigate. By his reckoning, he said, he spent "point zero one percent" of his time examining the actual evidence. Yet, he told Anson, if he had it to do over again, he would begin his investigation of the Kennedy assassination by probing "Oswald's ties to the Central Intelligence Agency."

Later, I asked Sprague why he had come to that conclusion. "Well," he said, "when I first thought about it I decided that the House leadership really hadn't intended for there to be an investigation. The Committee was set up to appease the Black Caucus in an election year. I still believe that was a factor. But when I looked back at what happened, it suddenly became very clear that the problems

195

began only after I ran up against the CIA. That's when my troubles really started.''

In the early months of the Committee's life, Sprague's critics both in Congress and in the press were not only keeping him busy dodging the shots, they were also demanding that the Committee produce some sensational new evidence to justify its continuance. Sprague, therefore, was forced to take some wild swings at what appeared to be a few obvious targets. One area that very clearly needed closer examination was the CIA's handling of the initial investigation of Lee Harvey Oswald's activities in Mexico City.

According to the information supplied to the Warren Commission by the CIA, a man who identified himself as Oswald visited the Cuban consulate in Mexico City on September 27th, 1963. (The probable date of Oswald's appearance at Silvia Odio's home in Dallas, the House Assassinations Committee would later conclude.) The Agency told the Commission that Oswald had been in Mexico City from September 26th to October 3rd and, during that time, Oswald made a number of visits to both the Cuban Embassy and the Russian Embassy, attempting to get an in-transit visa to Russia by way of Cuba. The CIA also claimed that when Oswald visited the Russian Embassy he spoke with a Soviet consul who was really a KGB intelligence officer.

It was later learned, however, that CIA headquarters in Washington was not informed of the incident until October 9th, and then told only that Oswald had contacted the Soviet Embassy on October 1st. The CIA station in Mexico City also told headquarters that it had obtained photographs of Oswald visiting the Embassy and described the man in the photos as approximately 35 years old, six feet tall, with an athletic build and a receding hairline.

When the Warren Commission asked the CIA for photos of Oswald taken in Mexico City, the ones it produced depicted the man described in the original teletype, who was obviously not Oswald. Notified of this discrepancy, the CIA said simply that it had made a mistake and that there were no photographs of Oswald taken in Mexico City; it never identified the man in the photos. As it turned out, the CIA was able to produce for the Warren Commission very little hard evidence regarding Oswald's activities in Mexico City. "For example," Commission Counsel J. Lee Rankin complained, "they had no record of Oswald's daily movements while in Mexico City, nor could they confirm the date of his departure or his mode of travels."

When Sprague first approached this area, he discovered that the CIA officer in charge of reporting such information from Mexico City at the time of Oswald's visit was former Bay of Pigs propaganda chief David Atlee Phillips.

In his autobiography, David Phillips devotes just a few pages to the Kennedy assassination and the Mexico City incident and blames the cable discrepancy on an underling's mistake. He explains the lack of an Oswald photograph on the CIA's inability to maintain camera coverage of the Cuban and Russian embassies on an around-the-clock and weekend basis—a peculiar deficiency during a period so soon after the Cuban missile crisis.

Sprague called David Phillips to testify before the Assassinations Committee in November, 1976. Phillips said that the CIA had monitored and taped Oswald's conversations with the Soviet Embassy in Mexico City, but that the tape was transcribed by a CIA employee who had mistakenly coupled it with a photograph of a person who was not Oswald. Phillips said that the actual recording had been routinely destroyed about a week after it was received.

Sprague subsequently discovered an FBI memorandum to the Secret Service dated November 23rd, 1963, referring to the CIA's notifying them about the man who had visited the Russian Embassy. The memo noted that "Special Agents of this Bureau who have conversed with Oswald in Dallas, Tex., have observed photographs of the individual referred to above and have listened to a recording of his voice. These Special Agents are of the opinion that the above-referred-to individual was not Lee Harvey Oswald."

Sprague was intrigued: How could the FBI agents have listened to a tape recording in November when Phillips said it had been destroyed in October? Sprague decided to push for an answer. He wanted complete information about the CIA's operation in Mexico City and total access to all its employees who may have had anything to do with the photographs, tape recordings and transcripts. The Agency balked. Sprague pushed harder. Finally the Agency said that Sprague could have access to the information if he would sign a CIA Secrecy Agreement.

Sprague refused. He contended that would be in direct conflict with the House Resolution which established the Assassinations Committee and authorized it to investigate the agencies of the United States Government.

"How," he asked, "can I possibly sign an agreement with an agency I'm supposed to be investigating?" He indicated he would subpoena the CIA's records.

Shortly afterwards, the first attempt to get the Assassinations Committee reconstituted was blocked. One of its critics was Representative Robert Michel of Illinois, who objected to the scope of the

Committee's mandate. "With the proposed mandate," Michel harped, "that Committee could begin a whole new investigation of the Central Intelligence Agency!"

That, says Sprague, is exactly what he intended to do.

And that, he also now contends, was the beginning of his fall.

TWENTY-FOUR

INSIDE BETRAYALS AND DIRTY DEALS

ALTHOUGH I HAD KEPT in touch with Antonio Veciana after the end of Senator Schweiker's investigation, I called him on New Year's Day, 1977, to inform him that I had officially joined the House Select Committee on Assassinations. I told him that Schweiker's office had turned my files over to the new Committee and that I thought it would be much more effective than the old Church Committee or the Schweiker Subcommittee because it would have more resources and would be very independent. It was my first day on the job.

Veciana and I chatted a bit and then he asked if I knew that he had been called back to Washington to appear before the new Senate Permanent Committee on Intelligence. I hadn't known.

"I was three days in Washington," Veciana said. "They asked me a lot of questions. There were different people there now and I think some were with the FBI. They asked me not only about the Kennedy assassination but also about the Cuban cause here in Miami, about the bombings here and what was going on."

I asked whether he was questioned again about Maurice Bishop.

"Yes, a little," he said. "They showed me some more pictures, but they were not Bishop."

We chatted some more and then I said that I would be back in touch as soon as the Committee got organized—any day now.

"Well, if I can help you, don't hesitate to call," he said. From his initial leeriness, Veciana's feelings about me had obviously grown to one of trust.

Two weeks later that trust was almost shattered.

I got a call late one Friday afternoon from Troy Gustavson in Schweiker's office. "Veciana's cover has been blown," he said. "The whole story is going to be in Jack Anderson's column next Wednesday."

I suddenly felt a blade burning deep into my back. It was a very personal reaction. Someone, somewhere had betrayed me.

Gustavson told me he had just gotten a call from George Lardner of the *Washington Post*. Lardner had seen advance copies of the two Jack Anderson columns which the *Post* was scheduled to run the following Wednesday and Thursday. Although Veciana's name was not mentioned—Anderson called him "mysterious witness Mr. X"— the second column detailed his relationship with a "Morris" Bishop. "Morris" was how I had spelled Bishop's first name in my rough notes of my interviews with Veciana. Anderson obviously had copies of those notes.

I was furious—furious at the leak and at Anderson. My old journalistic appreciation of a news scoop went out the window. Didn't Anderson have any regard for Veciana's life? Lardner, who had covered the Kennedy assassination and the intelligence community for years, had immediately recognized "Mr. X" as Veciana because Anderson had clearly pinpointed him as the founder of Alpha 66 and the organizer of the Castro assassination attempts in 1961 and 1971. Every Cuban exile in Miami could easily identify Veciana as that person. Now Anderson had marked Veciana as a tool of the CIA and a man who, in turn, had secretly used his fellow exiles as tools of a government which, in the end, had betrayed them. Bombs had gone off in Little Havana for less reason than that.

If Anderson had copies of my original notes, they could have only come from one of four sources: from me, from Schweiker's office, from the new Senate Intelligence Committee (which had inherited all the Church Committee files) or from the House Assassinations Committee. The last had the strongest motivation. After all, at that time the Committee was fighting for its life. It had just failed to be automatically reconstituted and was scheduled to clear its first key hurdle, the House Rules Committee, the following week; and certain Congressmen were crying for evidence of its effectiveness. Anderson's column about our coup in uncovering a "Mr. X" who had met with Oswald could be the kind of publicity boost that might just push the Rules Committee into positive action.

I was still seething with anger when I called Tanenbaum. Then I was taken aback at what appeared to be his genuine shock at the news. He swore that the leak did not come from him or Sprague. In fact, he said, Sprague was at that moment meeting with Schweiker and probably hearing about the Anderson columns for the first time.

"I really think this is an attempt to sabotage us," Tanenbaum said. "We had already gotten word that certain Senators are trying to zing us and the Senate Committee is not being cooperative at all."

In the end, I could not conclusively prove to my satisfaction where Anderson had gotten copies of my notes. I knew for sure that they hadn't come from me or from Schweiker's office. The staff counsel on the new Senate Intelligence Committee who had recently interviewed Veciana, assured me that they hadn't come from him, either.

"It's extremely damaging here," he said, "and I think blows any chance of ever getting to the bottom of the thing. Also, you know we're not going to be able to deal with the Miami Cuban community at all now. Once you blow your sources down there you're cooked."

I knew that damn well, and it increased my fury. There was no assessing the damage that leak could do to my effectiveness as an investigator. Why would any of my sources trust me now? Why should Veciana ever again believe he could tell me anything confidentially? Why should he continue to cooperate at all?

Setting up a meeting with Veciana to tell him about the coming Anderson columns was one of the most difficult things I have ever had to force myself to do. He could accuse me of betraying him and I could not prove that I hadn't. Veciana, however, told me he was not angry at me, but he was very concerned about his own safety. He once again had become active in the anti-Castro movement and it became obvious as we talked that he was extremely worried about the reaction among his close associates. His effectiveness was based on their long trust in him. "It is very bad for me," he said. "It is good that I am going away for a while." He had previously scheduled a lengthy business trip to California.

Veciana and I spent the evening conjecturing about the source of the leak. He told me that he still trusted me personally and believed that I wouldn't have broken his confidence. At first he leaned toward the new Senate Committee as the source because in his recent visit to Washington he had been questioned by some men who were obviously in intelligence, but whose agency associations weren't identified. Then he thought about it and said, "Yet the Senate and Schweiker had my information for almost a year and it was not leaked. I think maybe it was the House Committee."

I eventually came to agree with him. In questioning Tanenbaum further he admitted he had briefed at least six of the twelve members of the Assassinations Committee on the details of the Veciana story

and that copies of my rough notes had been put into the file system—
which meant the entire staff could have had access to them. Tanenbaum, however, expressed the feeling that perhaps it was the CIA
itself which engineered the leak in order to damage the Committee's
credibility.

"Well, if so, it was damn successful," I said. But Tanenbaum was
not nearly as agitated about it as I was, and he repeatedly tried to
calm me down. "Well, at least Veciana's name wasn't mentioned,"
he said, "and at least your name wasn't mentioned. So consider the
bright side and perk up a little bit. Think of the problems I have up
here, and we're not even in business yet. At least you're down there
in the Sunshine State. Be happy, man! Hang in there!"

I hung in there, but to me that leak was like a lightning bolt from
the black cloud of politics which had overhung the Assassinations
Committee from the beginning. The risk to Veciana's life wasn't
considered, the damage to my effectiveness as an investigator wasn't
considered and the irreparable harm it did to the investigation itself
wasn't considered. Only the survival of the Committee was considered. I would have to remember that, I told myself, in dealing with
my confidential sources in the future. As long as I was working for
Congress, I could never again ask for anyone's implicit trust. A hell
of a way to have to work.

Some months later, after Bob Tanenbaum himself had resigned,
he called together his closest associates on the staff and gave us these
final words of advice: "The one thing you have to remember about
this town is to stick together and watch your ass."

The House Select Committee on Assassinations was formed in September, 1976. On March 30th, 1977, Richard Sprague resigned as its
Chief Counsel, one day before the House vote on the Committee's
reauthorization. The new Chief Counsel, Professor G. Robert Blakey
of Cornell University, was not appointed until June 20th, 1977. During
the entire nine-month period of the Committee's existence, the staff—
contrary to the reports to Congress detailing its "progress"—was on
a slow treadmill. Only when politics and finances permitted, could
Chief Investigator Cliff Fenton send some of his men into Dallas to
check out a lead. Yet, even with such a snapshot approach, more
often than not they returned with evidence that hadn't previously
been known or information from a witness who hadn't previously
been interviewed. This indicated that the Kennedy case was still,
despite the years, ripe for a basic street-level investigation. But
without a structured approach, without knowledgeable analysts to
evaluate and chart the raw data and provide direction for the next
step, the Committee was running in place.

Deputy Chief Counsel Bob Tanenbaum had been to Miami Beach on his honeymoon. His image of his Miami-based investigator was of a guy in mirrored glasses sitting around the pool at the Fontainebleau, sipping a daiquiri and watching the bikinis go by. I did that, I told him, only on sunny days.

As I said, I had been moving on my own, and I regularly sent lengthy memos detailing developments in the areas I was pursuing. Eventually, as the file copies of my memos grew thicker and the responses from Washington grew thinner, I began getting the feeling I was being a pain in the ass. I would later learn that both Tanenbaum and Fenton were secreting most of my memos in the back of their file drawers, fearful of information leaking out, each doubtful that any real investigation would ever start.

Finally, in the middle of April, I was authorized to take my first trip to Washington as an official Committee staffer. My fellow staffers greeted me as if I were an envied celebrity, the lucky guy out in the field while the rest of the staff was pinned down at the fort. I had finished the personnel-paperwork process—and received my official identification badge—when Tanenbaum returned from a staff meeting. He proudly told me that the staff had decided that I was its most important member because I was its only working investigator—a scant compliment.

And the staff was in sorry shape. It had been on the brink of the abyss for too long; morale was horrendous and bitching was rife. Many of the junior counsel complained to me that Tanenbaum treated them like children. Tanenbaum complained to me that many of the junior counsel *were* children. "They can't figure out a thing for themselves," he moaned.

The months of enforced wheel-spinning had gotten on everyone's nerves. No matter what the staffers did to keep themselves busy, they knew that until a new director was appointed and assigned them coordinated projects, their work might be meaningless. Besides, without plans, no one knew where to start. To many, however, the greatest frustration came when Tanenbaum ordered the staff to outline all 26 volumes of Warren Commission evidence. "Next we'll have to tear the pages out, shuffle them and put them back in order," one staffer wisecracked to me.

Before Sprague resigned, he had asked Tanenbaum to stay on and take his slot. Tanenbaum said, no way. He had agreed that the terms of their pyrrhic victory over Gonzalez had forced Sprague to appease the politicians and resign, too. Tanenbaum told me, "I agreed to stay for the transition, but I couldn't take the job after I just agreed with Dick that he had to resign. I couldn't live with myself if I did that."

Later, Tanenbaum would tell me that his disillusionment with

Washington had begun much earlier. A University of California graduate, Tanenbaum had come out of Berkeley's hotbed of student
activism all fired up and anxious to right the world's injustices. He
had joined Frank Hogan's District Attorney's Office in New York
because it had a national reputation for aggressiveness and honesty
and it was a place to see plenty of action. Big Bob Tanenbaum loved
his action hellbent fast and straight up, like the way he played
basketball when he was a college star, and he wasn't cut out for shifty
politicking. One of the reasons he had accepted the Assassinations
Committee job was because he felt that Robert Morgenthau, the new
Manhattan DA, had let politics slip into the office and he lost respect
for the man. (As Tanenbaum subtly put it: "I decided he would be a
fire hydrant in Canarsie if his father wasn't Henry Morgenthau.")

Tanenbaum left Washington believing that Congress is the last
place to put responsibility for a Kennedy investigation—or any investigation, for that matter. As a case in point, he likes to recall his initial
impression of life inside Washington's power center: "The first meeting I went to with the Congressmen was before we were assigned
office space," he recalls. "And that's all they seemed to care about.
They weren't concerned about the big picture, about what we were
trying to do. I was waiting to hear about how they wanted to conduct
the investigation, what parameters they wanted to establish, how it
was going to be organized. There was none of that. They were
bickering about office space and parking spaces and paper clips and
supplies and scurrying all around on penny-ante little missions. It sort
of hit me, is this what it's all about? Then it degenerated after that."

In the period after Chairman Henry Gonzalez had resigned and
Dick Sprague was still Chief Counsel, Tanenbaum was asked by the
Committee's new chairman, Louis Stokes, to do some lobbying to
help get the Committee reconstituted. A series of informal dinners
were scheduled for Tanenbaum and other key members of the staff to
meet with small groups of Congressmen to persuade them to support
the Committee.

"So we're going out to dinner with these members of Congress,"
Tanenbaum recalled, "and one night we're scheduled to go out with a
group that includes this guy from Ohio, John Ashbrook. I remember
we went to a restaurant called The Chicken Place in Maryland. I had
a couple of my staff people with me. So after I gave them my pitch,
Ashbrook takes me aside and says, 'You know, we checked you out
and you're OK.' I'm thinking, what the hell does he mean, I'm OK?
I've got no background, I finished law school and I went into the DA's
office. And then he says, 'Well, we really don't mind funding the
Kennedy assassination, although I didn't think much of the man,

but . . .' and these are his exact words, ". . . we'll be damned if we're going to fund that nigger King's.'

"I just turned away. I told my staff, 'I gotta go, I can't take any more of this shit.' I left them there. When I got back home I called Dick and told him the whole story. I told him, 'I had enough of this. If they don't want to fund this fuckin' thing I don't give a shit.' Sure I cared, but at the same time I didn't want it to be a forced situation where you wouldn't be able to do your job.''

Of course that wasn't the end of it. The next morning, Tanenbaum received a call from Jack Anderson. (Tanenbaum does a good imitation of Anderson's clipped voice of authority.)

" 'Jack Anderson here.'

" 'Yeah, Jack.'

" 'I understand that John Ashbrook of Ohio . . . '

" 'Johnstown, Ohio.'

" 'Uh, yes, Johnstown, Ohio. I understand that John Ashbrook of Johnstown, Ohio, referred to Martin Luther King as a nigga. Is that true?'

" 'Let me tell you something, Jack. First of all, it was a private dinner. Secondly, I'm not getting into a confirming or denying routine with you. I'm not going to comment on anything that occurred at a private dinner.'

" 'Well, would you confirm . . . '

" 'No, Jack, I won't confirm or deny anything.'

"He hangs up.''

Seconds later, Tanenbaum received a call from Congressman Ashbrook:

" 'You may be getting a call from Jack Anderson . . . '

" 'I already got it.'

" 'You did? What did you say?'

" 'What I said is none of your business.'

" 'What do you *mean* it's none of my business?'

" 'It's none of your business.'

" 'Well, uh, ahh . . . the most important thing I want to communicate with you is this. I want you to tell him that I never said that word about Martin Luther King.'

" 'You mean when you called him a nigger?'

" 'I don't remember saying that!'

" 'You did. I heard it and my staff with me heard it.'

" 'Well, I'm telling you . . . '

" 'No, I'm telling you that whatever I said to Jack Anderson is none of your business, but I'm not going to lie to anyone.'

" 'I'm *ordering* you to tell Jack Anderson that John Ashbrook never said that King was a nigger!'

" 'Well, you call up Lou Stokes and you tell him you want me fired because I refuse to lie about you calling Martin Luther King a nigger. OK? Thank you.'

"And I hung up the phone and never heard from the guy again."

Although he was frustrated that he would never be able to conduct the investigation into the assassination of President Kennedy the way he had wanted to, when Bob Tanenbaum left Washington, he wasn't totally sorry to go.

After he departed, Tanenbaum went to California and got into private practice. (He also took to writing novels based on his experiences as a New York prosecutor and, in his spare time, successfully ran for mayor of Beverly Hills.) But before leaving, Tanenbaum maneuvered to get another staff investigator to come to Miami and work with me.

The Miami branch of the Assassinations Committee became a two-man operation when Al Gonzales came down in August. A former cohort of Chief Investigator Fenton's on the New York Police Department, Gonzales had retired as a top detective and then worked for a while for the New York State Special Commission investigating the Attica riot. When Castro made his first visits to the United Nations after coming to power in 1959, Gonzales was picked to be his special bodyguard. Al was a native New Yorker, not of Cuban heritage, but Fidel took a liking to him, insisted that Al remain at his side, put his arm around him and invited him to be his personal guest in Cuba. Castro called him *El Grande*. Al was about six foot four and weighed 270 solid pounds. I felt a little more secure in Little Havana after Al joined me.

TWENTY-FIVE

NEW PRIORITIES, SAME OLD GAME

I DID NOT MEET G. Robert Blakey, the new staff boss of the House Assassinations Committee, until right before Bob Tanenbaum resigned late in July of 1977. Just before Blakey's arrival, Tanenbaum had begun to get some structure into an investigation that had been kept in disarray by the forces of political priorities. Various special projects—such as compiling a list of Dealey Plaza witnesses, arranging autopsy and ballistic studies, preparing photo analysis and starting file research—were beginning to give the staff something real to do and we were finally moving forward. Tanenbaum had also come to the conclusion that, just as Miami was an obvious lode of information, so was New Orleans. As controversial and denigrated as Jim Garrison's investigation there had been, it had produced some intriguing and apparently valid new information that needed to be pursued. New Orleans had been an important base for both anti-Castro and Organized Crime activity, and it was there Oswald had most of his known contacts with anti-Castro Cubans. Both Tanenbaum and Cliff Fenton decided the Committee needed local guys on the street there as much as it did in Miami. So Fenton made some contacts and borrowed two streetwise cops from the New Orleans Police Department. They were an odd couple: Bob Buras was a tough ex-Marine, a serious, Scripture-quoting, born-again Christian; L.J. Delsa was an amiable, beer-guzzling, former undercover narc with excellent contacts in the French Quarter; strangely, they clicked together. They were, besides Al Gonzales and myself, the Committee's only "outside" investigators.

(Buras and Delsa would later get themselves in hot water with the Committee when they gave a witness a lie-detector test without authorization. They made the mistake of thinking they were conducting a real investigation.)

While we were finally moving, it was still maddeningly slow. It was late in June when I received a call from Tanenbaum who said, "I'm going to give you an investigative plan. I'm getting it together now."

"Hey, that's great, Bob," I said. "I've got to cut back on my tanning time anyway, I just hit my perfect shade."

Tanenbaum ignored my stab at cynical humor. "Yeah, that's what I'm going to do," he said. "Blakey starts officially on Friday and I want you to come up next week to meet him. Meanwhile, I tried to talk to him about getting organized but instead he gave me this little book he wrote called *Techniques in the Investigation and Prosecution of Organized Crime*. He told me, 'When I talk about an investigative plan, I want you to know my lingo.' Then he hands me this cockamamie book."

The next week I was in Washington sitting in Tanenbaum's office when Blakey stuck his head in the door. "Come in, Bob," Tanenbaum called. "We're just getting a briefing on the Miami situation."

Actually, Tanenbaum had been telling me about a job interview he had that afternoon at the Justice Department. Blakey strolled in, introduced himself, slouched in a chair, leaned back and put his scruffy brown loafers up on Tanenbaum's desk. Damn, if he didn't look like a real Ivy League professor: baggy, pin-striped gray suit, button-down blue Oxford shirt and archaic green slim-jim tie. He wasn't a big man, but his slight paunch, soft, pale face and receding hairline made him look older than his 41 years. Under heavy, gray-flecked brows, he had strikingly clear blue eyes and he exuded a casual self-confidence. When I told him about what we were doing in Miami, he expressed keen interest, particularly about Santos Trafficante and his involvement in the areas I was investigating. Blakey then began talking about his days with the Organized Crime and Racketeering Section of the Justice Department.

"You want to hear something ironic?" he said. "My last meeting with Bobby Kennedy was on November 22nd, 1963. He was running late for a luncheon appointment and had to hurry off. He said we'd finish up when he returned. He never returned. At lunch he got word of his brother's death in Dallas."

Among my first impressions of Bob Blakey was that he was very knowledgeable in the ways of the Washington bureaucracy. It was obvious that he knew how to take over an operation because the first thing he did when he arrived was nothing. That, as they tell you in the military, is exactly what a new commander should do when he is assigned a unit: Do nothing but walk around, look around, listen carefully and ask questions. Then you'll know how to move for control quickly and firmly.

Despite his soft-spoken, casual, sometimes even whimsical demeanor (he invaded the home of some staff researchers on Halloween Eve dressed as Count Dracula), Blakey turned out to be a very cunning intellectual strategist who seemed to take quiet pride in his ability to manipulate both people and situations. His foil, at times, was the man he brought in to replace Tanenbaum as Deputy Chief Counsel in charge of what was called the Kennedy Task Force, Gary Cornwell.* A 32-year-old Justice Department prosecutor out of the Kansas City Organized Crime Strike Force, Cornwell was a cocky, stocky, stumpy Texan who exuded a brash pragmatism. He talked fast, loud and Texan, smoked pipes and big cigars, drove a Datsun 280Z, wore cowboy boots and appreciated both hard rock and Willie Nelson. I had to like the guy.

But, contrasts in character that they were, professionally both Blakey and Cornwell viewed their roles in the same limited perspective: They were the hired hands of the twelve Congressional Committee members and the priorities of their job were governed strictly by the desires of those members.

By the time Bob Blakey was offered the position as Committee Chief Counsel—a few nationally known figures, including former Watergate prosecutor Archibald Cox and former Supreme Court Justice Arthur Goldberg, had reportedly refused it—the public tumult the Committee had endured convinced most of its members that they were trapped in a no-win situation. They couldn't get out of it without losing some political face, so they had to get it over with as soon as possible. When Chairman Stokes offered Blakey the job, he told him that he wanted the Committee's business wrapped up within its two-year lifespan and the final report finished by the end of the 1978 Congressional year.

The two-year limitation was arbitrary and artificial but, somewhere along the line, it became written in stone. Dick Sprague admitted to some of the blame. "When I first came to Washington," he later told *Gallery* magazine writer Jerry Policoff, "I was asked how long it would take. And my response was, to properly investigate murder you can never put a time limit on it. If you ask me what I

---

*The Martin Luther King Task Force had a parallel staff of deputies, counsels, investigators and researchers. There was a joint administrative section and a parade of temporary consultants, and although the number on the Committee's staff fluctuated, it never topped 118.

think ought to be the time to get the job done, my estimate would be two years. If you've got an outside limit, and people who are being investigated know that, they can stall you for that length of time and defeat the investigation.''

Sprague's fear of delaying tactics was based on precedent. That's what the CIA had pulled on the Warren Commission. When the Agency was being pressed about its Mexico City operations, an internal memorandum written to Deputy Director Richard Helms noted: "Unless you feel otherwise, Jim [Angleton] would prefer to wait out the Commission on the matter. . . ." (Angleton was the longtime chief of the CIA's Counter-Intelligence Division which, strangely enough, was the unit handling the Agency's dealing with the Warren Commission.)

At his first general staff meeting late in August, 1977, the new Chief Counsel of the House Select Committee on Assassinations pointedly announced that he had taken the job with the stipulation and the promise to Chairman Stokes that the staff would finish its investigation and produce a report by December 31st, 1978. There was absolutely no possibility, Blakey said, that the Committee would be extended beyond that time.

And with that pronouncement, I got a revealing insight into Bob Blakey's character. It also indicated how he viewed the importance of John F. Kennedy's assassination: He saw nothing incongruous in accepting a basic and crucial limitation to conducting "a full and complete investigation" of one of the most important events in this country's history.

Yet, I really didn't believe Blakey. I felt that once we started rolling, once we started accumulating evidence that demanded further investigation, well, then Blakey, with the backing of the staff, would stand up to the Committee and the Committee would stand up to Congress and Congress would be forced to give us more time and money. The Kennedy assassination was just too important. We *had* to go all the way.

At that initial staff meeting Blakey also established the parameters of the Committee's operations. In clear, simple and carefully defined terms reminiscent of a Political Science 101 lecture to a class of frosh, he explained the differences between the functions of a legislative body and the goals of a law-enforcement agency. Our primary duty, he pointed out, was not to conduct a criminal investigation. We were limited by the powers and privileges granted to Congress by the Constitution. Our investigative powers were merely an auxiliary of the legislative function. We were not out to produce indictments. We had no legal sanction to arrest or imprison anyone. Our goals were to gather evidence to be presented at public hearings and, after that, produce a final report.

There was no doubt that Bob Blakey knew what he was about. Not only was it apparent that the staff would finally get truly organized, it was also clear that organization itself would be the essence of its being. That became even clearer when I went back to Washington a few weeks later for another general staff meeting. By that time every staff member had received newly arrived Deputy Counsel Cornwell's first memorandum. It said, in full:

> Attached hereto is copy of House Resolution 222. Please familiarize yourself with this document.

That was the resolution that had created the Committee almost one year before. (Actually, it was the duplicate; the Resolution was given a new number when the Committee was reconstituted.) At the time, many staffers—especially the youthfully cynical junior counsel—took Cornwell's premier memo as silly and gratuitous. But Cornwell was laying the very first block in what both he and Blakey took to be their ultimate goal: To Build a Record. That was the essential message of our second general staff meeting. It dealt with the whys and hows of record-building: information processing and staff procedures, rules and regulations, the standardization of operations and documentation production.

I remember returning home after that meeting feeling as if I had just been smothered under a blanket of verbal fog. The investigators had been given a lengthy memorandum titled "Investigative Techniques and Procedures." Blakey called it "a summary of specific guidelines." For instance, among the compelling points listed under "Travel" were: "Call the office every day between the hours of 10:00 and 12 noon." And: "Be sure you stay at a reputable hotel."

An even lengthier directive distributed to all staff members was "General Operating Procedures." Attached to it were sample forms for an Outside Contact Report, a Document Log, a Routing Slip, an Investigation Interview Schedule and other standardized reports. Point 9 is illustrative of the type of detailed control Blakey wanted.

> (9.) All correspondence intended for transmittal to anyone outside of the staff will first be discussed (orally, or with the aid of a rough draft, as the case may require) by the staff attorney, researcher, or investigator with his immediate supervisor, (the Assistant Deputy Chief Counsel, Chief Investigator, or Assistant Chief Researcher) and then will be typed in final form, proofed and (if appropriate) signed. The completed letter ready for mailing, together with all supporting documents will then be

submitted, first, to the staff member's immediate supervisor, and ultimately to the Deputy Chief Counsel for review. When approved by the
Deputy Chief Counsel, the letter will be delivered by the Deputy Chief
Counsel's secretary to Security for copying. Unless otherwise specifically authorized, two copies of each such piece of correspondence will
be made in all cases except Agency requests, where three copies will be
made. One copy will be treated as an "original document," and one copy
will be treated as a "working copy" and returned to its author (See
Document Handling procedures below.) With respect to Agency requests, the third copy will be delivered to the Chief of Legal Staff for
filing in the Agency Requests File. The original (signed) letter will be
delivered to the Chief Counsel for approval (and/or signature), and then
mailed by the Chief Counsel's secretary.

Although I recognized that there was a point to this and, in fact,
felt the staff was in dire need of organizational control, it bothered
me. Blakey seemed far more interested in the character of the record
of the investigation than he was in the character of its substance. And
I was already concerned because, just prior to that general staff
meeting about procedures, Cornwell had called me into his office and
told me he wanted to talk to me about the nature of my reports.

When I was working for Senator Schweiker, he was not concerned
with formal reporting procedures, he was interested in my spending
the time developing information that might help resolve the Kennedy
assassination. I was in almost daily telephone contact with the staffers
in his office who were working the case, and I regularly forwarded
informal reports detailing and analyzing the information I was uncovering. I felt these reports were necessary to put the information in
perspective and provide a groundwork for discussing where we were
and where we were going. Facts can sometimes be misleading and
can, as critic Dwight MacDonald said, take on different hues and
tones according to the light in which they are viewed. When I joined
the House Committee, I thought similar analytical reports would be
especially useful since no other investigator had my experience in the
case.

Now Cornwell told me to cease and desist.

"I want your reports to be strictly factual," he said. "Just give us
the information. I don't want any of your analysis going into the
record."

"Now wait a minute, Gary," I objected. "Remember we're talking
about Miami. How can I report simply what I'm told without analyzing the validity of the source of the information. In Miami we're
dealing with many politically radical Cubans and soldiers of fortune

who are notorious disseminators of misinformation. To report their droppings as gospel would produce a misleading record."

"I realize that," Cornwell said, "but all I want from you is the straight, unadorned information. If you feel you have to analyze the information, put it on separate yellow paper and I'll tell the mail room not to log it in."

That didn't quite answer the point of my objection, but I came to refer to the procedure as the "Yellow Paper Ploy."

On the plane flying back to Miami after that staff meeting, I thought that for the first time, I was really beginning to understand what it's like to work in Washington. Blakey obviously knew: What's important is not what you do, but how what you do *looks* while you're doing it, how it *looks* after you've done it, and how it will eventually *look* in relation to how everything else you've done *looks*. The inside of government is a funny house of mirrors and it was instant frustration. But we couldn't say the hell with it and walk off the court—it was the only game in town. I could only hope that, in the long run, what we *did* would be as important as how we looked.

There is no doubt that what Blakey produced *looks* impressive. In its final published reports, a compilation of the Committee's legal memoranda alone took a separate hefty volume of 925 pages. And the Committee turned over to the National Archives more than 800 boxes of files—many times more than the Warren Commission produced. That, of course, *looks* impressive. That was one of Blakey's priorities. Yet Blakey moved to make sure that the information in those files would be kept from public scrutiny for 50 years.

The hypocrisy of it all was palpable. "It is essential," said a statement issued by members of the Assassinations Committee shortly after it was formed, "not only that persons be able to judge the performance of the executive agencies, but that they be able to judge this Committee's performance as well. Such is the very essence of representative democracy."

Despite that promise of conducting an investigation the public would be able to freely scrutinize, by the time the Committee's report was released, Blakey had already quietly arranged to lock up all the documents and files it didn't publish. In addition, Blakey had Chairman Louis Stokes ask the Justice Department, the FBI and the CIA to treat the records that they had supplied the Committee in the same fashion as "Congressional material" not to be released to the public. This included documents which private researchers had previously requested and would have likely received under the Freedom of Information Act.

Although, Oliver Stone's movie *JFK* produced tremendous public

pressure for Congress to release all the Kennedy records, the procedural process that might ultimately open them to public scrutiny has
enough diversionary elements built in to prevent total scrutiny of the
most important documents, including key CIA records. As far as the
Assassinations Committee's internal memoranda, they would reveal
less about the substance of the Kennedy investigation than about its
shortcomings. Which, I believe, is why Blakey wanted them locked
up in the first place.

TWENTY-SIX

SPOOKS, RATS AND 'REALITY'

BY THE END of its first year of operation, the House Assassinations Committee was fumbling its way forward. We were, at least, well organized. With the exception of those in the administrative, legal and documents-handling sections, the staff was divided into five major "Teams." Each team had two or three attorneys, researchers and investigators. The "outside" investigators in New Orleans and Miami were at the disposal of all the teams. In Miami, Al Gonzales and I worked mostly with Team Two, which had the Organized Crime and Jack Ruby areas, and with Team Three, which had anti-Castro Cubans and New Orleans.

Bob Blakey spent his first few months as Chief Counsel and Staff Director establishing protocol, cranking up the record-building machinery and formulating "working relationships" with other Government agencies. He did, however, at an early staff meeting, outline the Committee's specific goals and direction.

For the first few months, he said, each team would thoroughly review its areas of investigation—he called it "foraging." The second phase, he said, would entail defining the priority "issues": that is, deciding the crucial questions in each area. ("Issue" was the favorite word among Washington lawyers. They used it to mean "question.") The third phase would be the concentrated investigation of those key questions. After that would come the public hearings and then we would write the report.

It all made a good deal of sense and it finally appeared that a real investigation might be getting under way. However, when Blakey began concerning himself with the substance of the case, an indication of his attitude towards the various methods of investigation became clear.

Compared to his interest in the empirical aspects of the investigation—what the investigators on the street were actually coming up with—Blakey spent a disproportionate share of his time looking after the scientific examination of the evidence. He had the academician's view that this would have the "greatest reliability," which is undoubtedly why so much time and money were spent on such things as neutron-activation analysis, acoustics studies, ballistic and trajectory analysis and other scientific studies. But science, like statistics, can lie and two scientists often read the same results in opposite ways. It happened, for instance, with the Assassinations Committee's panel of forensic pathologists: One eminent doctor totally disagreed with his eminent peers, who had all endorsed the Warren Commission's single-bullet theory.

What is particularly important about that dissent, by the way, is that it was not based on fine-point technicalities or subtle differences in methodology, as such dissents often are. It was much harder and more definitive than that, and it came from the President of the American Academy of Forensic Sciences, Dr. Cyril Wecht. As Chief Coroner of Allegheny County in Pittsburgh, Dr. Wecht had done thousands of homicide autopsies and, in his lengthy and detailed dissent, he did not mince words:

> Despite the semantical sophistry and intellectual gymnastics of the forensic pathology panel report, it is clear that the single-bullet theory can no longer be maintained as an explanation for the bullet wounds in JFK's back and neck, and all the bullet wounds in Gov. John B. Connally. The angles at which these two men were hit do not permit a straight line trajectory (or near straight line trajectory) of Commission exhibit 399 (the so-called magic bullet) to be established. Indeed, quite the opposite is true. In order to accept the single-bullet theory, it is necessary to have the bullet move at different vertical and horizontal angles, a path of flight that has never been experienced or suggested for any bullet known to mankind.

So much for the great reliability of scientific analysis.

One critical problem, which Blakey largely dismissed, was that some of the evidence being scientifically evaluated couldn't be authenticated as being *original* evidence—the chain of custody could never be proven in any court. The state of security in which some of the evidence was kept was incredibly lax. In 1972, for instance, it was discovered that someone had gotten into the National Archives' security area and taken President Kennedy's brain and a set of microscope tissue slides that might have conclusively shown the direction of the fatal bullet. Although hints have come from the Kennedy family that Robert Kennedy wanted the brain in order to bury his brother's body properly, that doesn't explain the theft of the slides as well. And stored in the same security area were other crucial pieces of evidence which were not taken. These included the photos and x-rays which the Assassinations Committee relied on to corroborate the single-bullet theory.

Blakey's main problem with his experts was keeping control of them, especially when their findings threatened to throw the investigative plan, with its time and budget limitations and restricted priorities, completely out of whack. One who gave him a major headache was a photographic consultant named Robert Groden.

Groden had played a major role in getting the American people to grasp the significance of the Zapruder film. *Life* magazine had bought the original film from Abraham Zapruder, reportedly for $150,000, and then held it tightly for years. The Warren Commission, working only from frame-by-frame slides supplied by the magazine, printed black-and-white photographs from individual frames in its Report, but deliberately omitted key frames. In its issue of October 2nd, 1964, released four days earlier to coincide with the Warren Report's publication, *Life* itself printed large color stills. The caption of one described how the fatal shot had "snapped the President's head to one side." The editors, however, quickly realized that was in conflict with the Warren Report, so they stopped the presses and changed the caption to make it consistent with the Report: " . . . the bullet . . . caused the front part of the head to explode forward." But then, of course, the photograph contradicted it. Again the presses were stopped and, at tremendous expense, the pages replated. This time all the captions were consistent and the contradictory photo was omitted. (Now all three editions of *Life* are collector's items.) Although it had reproduced still frames, *Life* would not allow the Zapruder film to be shown to the public. The lords of Henry Luce's publication, which had a long history of cooperation with the Government, obviously felt it would cause trouble because it is so apparent that the killing shot came from the right front.

However, when Robert Groden was working in New York in the motion picture optical field, he developed a contact who bootlegged him a copy of the Zapruder film. For years, Groden worked on techniques that would optically enhance each of the shaky frames. (Zapruder, standing on a parapet in front of the grassy knoll, was a nervous older man with vertigo.) When he found one that produced optimum results, he patented it and called it "Grodenscopy."

Groden's enhanced version of the film eventually wound up on national television and, for the first time, the American people got a dramatic illustration of what the Warren Commission critics had been saying. The publicity led Virginia Representative Thomas Downing to view the film and he was shocked enough to introduce the first bill to establish a House Committee to investigate the Kennedy assassination. When the Committee was finally formed a year later, Downing hired Groden as a photographic consultant. He was still in that slot when Chief Counsel Bob Blakey arrived.

Groden caused Blakey some problems. "One of the first things I did," Groden recalls, "was ask to see the autopsy photographs in the National Archives. I wanted to find out how it was the Warren Commission concluded the shots came from the rear when all the doctors at Parkland Hospital, every one of them, wrote in their reports that Kennedy's head was blasted out. When I saw the autopsy photographs I was shocked. After years in photo optic work I knew what I saw, and what I saw was a matte line in the photograph of the back of the President's head. That's when two photographic elements come together visually and there's an overlap. I saw a soft edged matte insertion forgery of very high quality which made it appear as if there were a small wound of entry in the rear of the President's head."

Groden did some photo-optical tests on copies of the photographs to confirm what he saw. "Then," he says, "I wrote a report about it to Blakey saying that based on my professional opinion the autopsy photographs of the President's head had been retouched."

A week after Groden submitted that report, a very strange incident occurred at Committee headquarters. Blakey's negotiations with the CIA to give Committee staffers access to the Agency's records were evolving. The Agency had agreed that certain records could, for the sake of convenience, be brought to Committee offices, and a special security room was set up and kept under the guard of a CIA representative. In an adjoining but equally secure room was a safe containing the autopsy photographs and x-rays and some of the ballistic evidence. Even the Committee staff couldn't touch them without Blakey's permission and each visit to the safe was meticulously logged. One day, a staffer, with authorization, removed some photographs for study in another office and closed the safe but neglected to lock it. When she returned, she noted that one of the autopsy photographs, instead of being in its plastic jacket in its book, was loose and lying on top. It was as if someone had removed it for examination and then, perhaps hearing her return, quickly tossed the photograph back without out putting it back in its protective jacket. Blakey called the FBI and a fingerprint check revealed that the person who had touched the photograph was Regis Blahut, the CIA's security representative. Confronted, Blahut first denied and then, after failing three polygraph tests, admitted he had handled the autopsy photo. Blakey later attributed Blahut's act to "curiosity," but Blahut blurted to a reporter, "There are other things involved that are detrimental to other things." The CIA fired him but, in the end, the Committee never did find out what that incident was really all about, or whether it was related to any of Bob Groden's claims.

Meanwhile, Blakey hadn't responded to Groden's report, and Groden was getting frustrated. He then suggested to Blakey that he bring the original autopsy photos and x-rays to Dallas and show them to the doctors at Parkland Hospital who had handled Kennedy. Recalls Groden: "Blakey said that would be too dangerous. He said, 'Suppose there was a plane crash or suppose they got stolen.' I then suggested he bring the key Parkland doctors to Washington to study the photos. He said that would be too expensive. Blakey never really confronted my contention that we were dealing with false autopsy photographs."

Groden was also involved in helping the acoustics consultants synchronize the sounds of gunshots (recorded on a police Dictabelt tape when a motorcycle cop accidentally left his mike open in Dealey Plaza) with the sequence of frames on the Zapruder film. Groden came up with the technique of using magnetic film tape with a recording magnetic film projector to match the sounds with the film and the results, he says, convinced him that the third shot had struck Kennedy from the front. But Blakey was adamant and the Committee concluded that Oswald had fired three shots at the President from the rear, with only the second and third shots hitting, thus keeping the single-bullet theory intact.

Says Groden: "Blakey suppressed my results. He refused to let me present my evidence to the Committee. I was a consultant who wasn't permitted to consult."

Blakey had settled on an interpretation of the acoustics results, but then his reliance on scientific testing got him into real trouble. If Oswald had fired three shots from the Depository, as the acoustics results were supposed to indicate, the gap between the first and second shots was only 1.66 seconds. In the Warren Commission's tests, the fastest that FBI marksmen could fire a Mannlicher-Carcano rifle was 2.3 seconds. Blakey decided to repeat the tests with professional firearms consultants. But this time, the marksmen did not use a telescopic sight like the one on Oswald's rifle (which, by the way, wasn't aligned properly), but only the rifle's own iron sights. Three tests resulted in firings of 1.65, 1.75 and over 2 seconds. The target was hit on the two fastest times, but the only way that rifle could be fired fast enough was simply to point-aim it without using the sights. That was fast enough, but no one came close to hitting the target on the second shot. And while all this testing was done with the same model Mannlicher-Carcano that Oswald used, it was not the actual weapon, because the bolt on his rifle tended to stick. As one of the testers for the Warren Commission reported: "The pressure to open the bolt was so great that we tended to move the rifle off the target."

That, in itself, meant that all the House Committee's firing tests were ludicrous.

I eventually came to believe that Blakey's initial dependence on scientific analysis was partially the result of his lack of confidence in the investigative staff. Although Blakey was eventually able to stack the staff counsel positions with people he hired himself—Cornell Law grads and individuals with backgrounds in prosecuting Organized Crime—most of the investigative staff had already been hired before he arrived. And because former Chief Counsel Sprague had viewed the Kennedy assassination as a homicide case, almost all the investigators were from police homicide squads, the largest number from New York City. Blakey's past associations had been with law enforcement personnel of more sophisticated breeding—mostly FBI agents and Internal Revenue specialists. Now here he was, stuck with a bunch of street cops. The way Blakey eventually structured the investigation indicated that he thought little of his investigative staff's potential effectiveness. So they were never given a chance.

In Miami, working pretty much on our own, Al Gonzales and I were making progress in what we considered potentially the hottest area, the association of anti-Castro activists with intelligence operatives. Then suddenly from Washington came word that we were about to be rocked by a new strategy directive from Blakey. The warning came from Edwin Lopez, a young researcher who had accompanied me on the trip to New York to meet Marita Lorenz. Lopez, a very bright guy who was attacking his job with youthful fervor, was one of the group of law-school students Blakey had brought from Cornell. Out of New York's Puerto Rican *barrio*, Lopez was a brilliant free spirit with an infectious smile, long curly locks, baggy jeans and flip-flops. He was only 21 but looked 16. Lopez was calling to tell me that Team Three had a major meeting with Deputy Chief Cornwell that morning.

"I think we may have some problems," Lopez said. "In our discussion with him, Gary craftily manipulated the conversation around to Miami. Then he asked, 'What the hell are those guys *doing* down there? Someone call Fonzi and ask him to answer the question in twenty words or less.' So I raised my hand and said that I could answer the question in five words: 'Trying to solve the case.' Then he said, 'Well, those guys are running around down there and they're never going to come up with anything we can resolve in time. I've got to bring them into our framework.' "

Lopez sounded very concerned. "To tell you the truth," he said, "that really shocked me. I couldn't believe he didn't know what you guys are doing down there."

I couldn't believe it either, and didn't. Cornwell had to be aware of exactly what we were doing if he read our reports—both formal and yellow-paper—which were flowing across his desk. I didn't believe he wasn't well aware of the importance of Miami. What the critics had come to call "the Cubanization of Oswald" is one of the major mysteries of the Kennedy case. Although he assumed a pro-Castro public posture, Oswald's contacts were mostly with anti-Castro activists. Miami was the heart of anti-Castro activism and the headquarters of the groups with which Oswald had contact. Cornwell knew all that very well. I wondered what he meant when he talked about bringing the Miami investigators "into our framework."

Shortly afterwards, Al Gonzales and I were called back to Washington for a major meeting. Eddie Lopez met us at the airport, a dour expression on his usually grinning countenance.

"No one is very happy around here," he said. "There's been a new operating procedure directive. Cliff Fenton has had to call all his investigators back from Dallas and they've been hanging around the office now for more than two weeks. Blakey and Cornwell have told us that everything will stop until we develop what they call the 'key issues.' By that they mean questions which can be resolved by June. By then, they said, the investigation must be over because we have to prepare for the public hearings and then the final report."

I couldn't quite grasp what Lopez was saying. Either I didn't want to believe it or I was hung up on the basic incongruity of developing "key issues" resolvable by June. Lopez said that the general staff meeting was scheduled for the next afternoon, but I was too anxious to wait. With a few members from Team Three and Chief Investigator Fenton, we arranged to meet with Cornwell that morning.

The Assassinations Committee staff worked out of what was called House Annex No. 2, the former FBI Records Building, just southwest of the Capitol. (It was undergoing renovations for the entire two years of the Committee's life and scurrying rats became such a frequent sight that staffers took to yelling at them for not wearing their I.D. cards.) Cornwell had a large corner office with leather chairs and couches and a long conference table in front of his big desk. One set of windows had a bleak view of a grimy stone viaduct which carried Amtrak's railroad tracks around the southern edge of the city.

The other set offered a more inspiring vista: the impressive grandeur of the three main House office buildings, set on the incline of Independence Avenue and looming above their white marble massiveness, the golden dome of the Capitol.

Cornwell said he thought we had foraged enough. "I have the feeling," he said, "that if we go on the way we are we would have a great deal more information but, come time to write the report, we'd be no further along than we are now in terms of reaching conclusions. You have to remember that our ultimate goal is to get a report written."

What he and Blakey did not want, Cornwell said, was a report that would cause the public to say, "You mean we spent $5 million on *that?*" They did not want a report that would have the Committee concluding, in effect, that if it had so much more time and so much more money it might then come up with some definite answers.

Therefore, Cornwell said, in order for the report to reach *some* definite conclusion, the character of the investigation would have to change. The investigation would now be structured around what he called "linchpin" issues. Those issues, he said, would of necessity have to be selected with certain criteria in mind. There would be no broad, encompassing questions to which we *probably* wouldn't find the answers—or *knew* we would not find the answers—within the scope of our time and resource limits.

That was the key. We only had so much time and so much money remaining before we had to get out a report. "We must remember," Cornwell said, "that Congress gave us a job to do and dictated the time and resources in which to do it. That's the legislative world. Granted, it may not be the real world, but it's the world in which we have to live."

With his hint of a Texas drawl and his talent to articulate his thoughts quickly, Cornwell had a prosecutor's ability to exude reason and rationality regardless of what he was saying. I remember sitting slouched in that big leather couch, scribbling some notes and waiting for what he had just said to sink in.

Then it dawned on me: "Realistically, that doesn't make any *sense!*" I almost yelled, struck by my sudden realization.

Cornwell let go a loud whoop of a laugh. "Reality is irrelevant!" he yelled back with a big grin.

"Com'on, Gary, I'm serious," I said. "Are you telling us that we won't be able to pursue any questions in this case, regardless of how important we think they are, unless we *know* we can thoroughly investigate them in a few months?"

"I am serious," said Cornwell. "And I'm not being flip when I say reality is irrelevant here. I told you, this is not the real world we're dealing with, this is the legislative world. We have to live with it.''

Bill Triplett, the leader of Team Three, was a soft-spoken, pipe-smoking young attorney whose career had been spent almost entirely in Government bureaucracies. He puffed his pipe, cleared his throat and said, "Well, Gary, I have to express strong dissatisfaction with that approach." He said he felt that in his team's area, the anti-Castro exiles, that kind of restrictive approach would make it almost impossible to pursue a real investigation.

Cornwell disagreed. "I'm sure you guys can come up with some real good linchpin issues after you think about it," he said.

Investigator L.J. Delsa had come up from New Orleans for the meeting. With his shiny, tasseled loafers, dapper three-piece suit, mod moustache and styled hair, Delsa looked like the TV version of the cool detective. He kept his smarts hidden under the thin veil of a down-home *Lo-o-o-zeeanna* accent.

"Well now, down in *N'Arrlnns*," he said, "we got some *eeessshews* that need a good lookin' into." He began detailing what he considered a crucial area that was still unexplored.

Cornwell interrupted him. "No, no, no." He shook his head, frustrated with Delsa for not getting his point. "You don't have *time* to do that! Like I said, that's the real world. That's irrelevant. This is the legislative world.''

Sitting there staring over Cornwell's desk and out the window at the marble buildings and the Capitol dome, I felt the strange sensation of slowly becoming detached, floating above the very scene in which I sat. Thousands of Americans were working in those Government buildings, and thousands more were in other buildings all over the country, millions going about their daily business, and I saw myself sitting in this office with this small group of people making decisions that would become a part of the history and maybe the future of those people.

I don't know why that awesome thought struck me then, but I remember that it did. And I remember thinking that I should be feeling a certain satisfaction, a touch of pride in being there, sitting there in that office, having a role in something as historically significant as the Kennedy assassination investigation.

But I didn't. I felt, rather, a certain uneasiness, as if I were part of something devious. I'm not sure what those people out there expected, but it crossed my mind that, sitting in that office what we were doing was planning to deceive them. Those people out there thought we were investigating the assassination of President Kennedy. We were planning to get out a report.

* * *

By the time of the general staff meeting the next afternoon, all the teams in the JFK task force had gotten the word of the new investigative approach. Cornwell had held special conferences with each team. The big meeting was held in one of the large conference rooms on the fourth floor, above the staff offices, yet it still felt crowded with a few dozen people jammed into it. Cornwell sat at the head of a long conference table, a big cigar in his mouth, looking tweedy in an elbow-patch jacket. His chair was tilted back and, characteristically, his boots were up on the edge of the table. Blakey, in an uncharacteristic candy-yellow corduroy suit, had stationed himself against the wall behind Cornwell.

The room quickly grew still when Cornwell called for attention. "*Allll*right," he drawled. "I understand there's been a lot of bitching about the procedures we've instituted, so we'll let anyone who has any critical comments to make speak up."

He blew smoke from his cigar, put a Cheshire grin on his face and slowly looked around the silent room. One of the document clerks raised her hand and said she had a complaint about the new system of getting copies made. There was a discussion about that, and then someone else complained about another administrative wrinkle. Finally, Cornwell, mischievous grin still on his face and mock disappointment in his voice, said, "Gee, I thought someone would raise the *big* issue."

"All right," John Hornbeck piped up from the back of the room, "I'll raise the *big* issue." Hornbeck was the leader of Team Two, the Organized Crime unit. Sandy-haired and ruddy-faced, he had the open, ingenuous style of a "Doonesbury" good guy and impressive credentials as an Organized Crime prosecutor in Denver. (He would eventually resign early, disgusted with what he called the "craziness" of Washington, and flee back to his mountain home and his horses.)

"The big issue," Hornbeck said, "is whether this investigation is going to be conducted in terms of restricted issues, in terms of getting out a report, or is it going to be a true, wide-ranging investigation?"

That summed it up. Cornwell answered it by repeating what he had told the individual teams: We were done foraging; we were not living in the real world, we were living in the legislative world; we had to get the report out.

Then Blakey spoke up. "Listen," he said, "I've laid this all out to you from the beginning. I said we would spend the first months looking at the entire spectrum of the case and defining our goals. Well, we reached the point where we must start moving on the report. Our main priority is the report. Now you may say I'm trying to cover my ass, but you don't have to worry about me covering my ass because I know how a report should be written. I know how to make a report *look* good. But I want more than that. I also want the report to *be* good. I just don't see a conflict in getting the investigation now boiled down to certain basic issues in attempting to solve the case."

If he believed that, Blakey was perhaps the only one in that room who didn't see the conflict. I looked toward Chief Investigator Cliff Fenton sitting in a corner. He was leaning forward, his hands clasped between his knees, his eyes staring down at the floor, his head slowly moving back and forth. He was in a tough spot. His investigators would not be able to get back out until each team had developed its key issues and had them approved by Cornwell and Blakey. Then a specific "investigative plan," detailing who would be interviewed and when, had to be drawn up from the issues and that, too, would have to be approved. It would be weeks before the investigators could get back on the case.

And so it was. Confined to Washington, with the leads they had been developing in Dallas left dangling, Fenton's investigators began growing stir crazy. There are only so many coffee breaks a man can take a day. Fenton tried to keep up a good front and maintain their morale but, inside, he was seething with anger himself.

One day he burst into Blakey's office.

"What are you *doing* to me?" he demanded. "Those are professional people out there! This is damn embarrassing to me."

Blakey calmed him down, but the attitude of the investigators degenerated to the point where Fenton was forced to call a special meeting.

He sat at the head of the table with a smile on his face. "All right, all right," he said. "I got to admit that I've never seen an investigation conducted like this. But that don't mean it won't work."

In response, there was a general snort.

"All I'm saying," Fenton continued, "is that we've got to give it a chance. I don't want anyone around here starting to feel they're just working for the money. Just because we've never seen it done this way before, that don't mean it won't work. Try to remember that."

"The way it looks to me," said Clarence Day, a homicide veteran from Washington, "is that this investigation is over."

There was a loud murmur of affirmation from the rest of the guys.

"Well, I've got to admit," Fenton chuckled, "I'm sort of flabbergasted. In fact, I'm totally flabbergasted. But, between us, I can tell you now we've been promised something. We've been promised that as soon as we're done with this 'issues' business at the end of May, while everyone else is busy with the public hearings and getting the report written, we'll be able to continue the investigation and cover it in any way we want. We got a promise on that. So that if anyone comes up with something that doesn't fit into the 'issues' thing, just let me know and I'll make sure we get to it when we start moving the way we should be. OK?''

That seemed to lift a bit the depression that had hung over the group from the start, although the meeting did end with an extemporaneous chorus of a country song popular at the time: ''Take This Job and Shove It.''

TWENTY-SEVEN

GOOD GUYS, BAD GUYS AND THE CIA

AFTER THE BIG MEETING with Blakey and Cornwell, I remained in Washington to help the anti-Castro team formulate its issues. It quickly became obvious that each team had to limit not only the type of questions it could investigate, but also the number of questions. It was already March of 1978. Since the public hearings were scheduled for September, our "full and complete" investigation would now have to be done in five months.

For the next few weeks, the staff worked late into the night to develop issues that covered the most important questions but still could be wrapped up within the time and budget limitations. Some teams could do that easier than others. The ones handling the ballistics and autopsy projects, for instance, already knew what questions they needed to ask their panels of experts.

The anti-Castro area was one of the toughest for which to develop questions which could be fully explored in a limited amount of time. Yet, as I've said, Oswald's association with anti-Castro Cubans was one of the key mysteries of the Kennedy assassination. Our work in Miami was opening long-closed doors—many of them marked "CIA"—and it was just as likely that continuing the investigation would lead to more questions, not answers. About that, Blakey and Cornwell were right. Yet, if those questions were relevant to an answer to the Kennedy assassination, how could they be ignored? That was the circle we kept finding ourselves running around in as we attempted to develop acceptable issues.

The first question I tried to get approved was the one that my experience in the case had shown to be the priority: Was there an intelligence agency connection through anti-Castro Cubans and Oswald to the Kennedy assassination?

Of course I knew that question would never pass muster because of the investigative effort it would require. By the very nature of its operations, an intelligence agency doesn't leave authentic tracks. One has to look for patterns. What I wanted to pursue involved the pattern of what had already been identified as misinformation—almost all of it linking Oswald to Castro—which was born in Miami immediately after the assassination. That, I figured, would also give me the opening to pursue what Veciana had told me, since Bishop had asked him to help create the phony story of Oswald meeting with the cousin in Castro's intelligence service.

Cornwell rejected the issue. I was back in Miami when Eddie Lopez broke the news.

"Cornwell said that issue wouldn't prove anything," Lopez told me. "He said all it would do is raise the question of whether or not an intelligence agency was monitoring Oswald for one reason or other and after the assassination was trying to disassociate from him. So I said to Gary, 'But don't you see how much closer we'd be if we could prove that?' And he said, ' "Closer" is not good enough. We can't put "closer" into a report.' "

In the end, struggling to concoct anti-Castro issues that would get approved, we fell into a trap that Blakey had set. Other teams also wound up in the same trap. It sprung from our attempt to structure a question that would be vital, answerable within the time and resources allowed and, at the same time, broad enough to permit the widest scope of investigation. We didn't realize that those prerequisites combined to produce results that might look good but were actually superficial.

For instance, one of the approved issues for our team was this: Was Lee Harvey Oswald associated with any actively militant anti-Castro groups possessing the capability, motivation and resources to assassinate the President?

I initially thought that question would leave open the most investigative doors for me and Al Gonzales in Miami. We found, however, that although the issue was broad, we were bound by the "investigative plan," which was to cover the issue adequately enough to provide material for the final report. So we couldn't pursue any one part of it in depth—we barely had time enough to touch all the bases. In this case, for instance, the investigative plan required our finding at least three leaders from each selected anti-Castro group, interviewing them about any possible contact with Oswald, accepting their answers without further corroboration and then moving on to the next group. Every team's investigation was rife with such superficiality. So, in the end, the report's conclusions were drawn from the usually less-than-solid information derived from those superficial contacts.

At the time, of course, we simply had mixed feelings about what was happening—at least *something* was happening. Those of us who had been aboard the Committee boat while its sails flapped in irons for a year felt enormously grateful that we were moving. Blakey had sailed us into much smoother waters. Oh sure, over coffee in the basement cafeteria or late-night drinks at the Market Inn we speculated about the dark sides of Blakey's possible motivations but, at the time, most of us basically felt he was doing the job as he legitimately thought it should be done.

Certainly we had no reason to suspect otherwise. Besides, Bob Blakey was a nice enough guy. A Notre Dame grad, a good family man with seven children, a man who had always worn a white hat in the war against the bad guys. His intellectual brilliance justified the hint of arrogance, but still he was easy to talk with, had a good sense of humor and knew when to listen. I liked him. In fact, although I objected to the limitations imposed on the investigation, early on I defended Blakey.

Immediately after coming aboard, Blakey had imposed a curtain of silence on the staff, forbidding anyone from talking to outsiders about details of the Committee's operations. I thought it was a good idea, considering some of the distorted press we had gotten. However, as staff discontent grew, leaks began to occur. I learned, for instance, that freelance writers Scott Malone and Jerry Policoff were preparing a scathing article about Blakey for *New Times* magazine. They were blasting Blakey for returning $425,000 of first-year Committee funding to the Treasury while staffers thought the investigation was being hindered for lack of funds. They also were hitting Blakey for firing an excellent researcher under the false guise of "poor work quality" when the researcher's only sin was being too close to certain critics. They were charging Blakey with being suspiciously cozy with the CIA, making agreements with the Agency severely restricting the staff's use of intelligence information. And they were accusing him of Machiavellian scheming in inviting key critics in as consultants and then forcing them to sign nondisclosure agreements in an attempt, they said, to preempt future criticism.

Perhaps most upsetting was their claim that Blakey was really a wolf in sheep's clothing. Malone and Policoff had discovered that Blakey had once filed an affidavit in support of a libel suit brought against *Penthouse* magazine by an alleged racket-connected Nevada resort owner named Moe Dalitz.

I remember telling Policoff that, despite my reverence for freedom of the press, it somehow bothered me that the piece was going to run. However, Policoff, considered one of the more moderate and level-headed of the independent researchers, was truly becoming convinced that Blakey was a devious character with sinister motives.

"I just can't buy that," I said. "Whether or not he's making the right decision is a point that can be argued, but I believe he's sincere when he explains his reasons for them. Besides, what do you accomplish by attacking Blakey now? You'll only be hurting the work of the Committee. We may not be doing everything right or as well as we should be, but we are doing them. We're the only game in town." Hope dies hard. I wouldn't let mine go easy.

Shortly after the *New Times* article appeared, a rumor spread that Blakey would be offered a top job in the Justice Department when he wrapped up his Committee work. Suddenly that rumor burst into a flame, ignited by what became known as "the Ortiz manuscript" flap.

About six months earlier, on a tip from an Assistant U.S. Attorney who had worked in Miami, Al Gonzales and I had interviewed a Miami lawyer who represented a Puerto Rican named Antullo Ramirez Ortiz. Ortiz, as he called himself, was in a Federal prison serving time for having hijacked a plane to Cuba in 1961. Castro had released him from Cuba in 1975 and Ortiz voluntarily surrendered to the FBI when he returned to the United States.

According to the lawyer, Ortiz had an incredible story: While being held in Cuba, Ortiz had been assigned to work around the headquarters of the Cuban DGI, the intelligence service. As such, he had the opportunity to surreptitiously check his own file and in his search, he came across a neighboring file marked "Oswaldo/Kennedy." Ortiz claimed the file revealed that President Kennedy had been killed by a "hit team" from Moscow.

While in prison in the United States, Ortiz had produced a manuscript of his adventures, including his discovery of the Kennedy file. The Miami attorney had a copy of the manuscript, written in Spanish, which he was in the process of trying to market through a New York literary agent. With the permission of Ortiz, who was in a prison on the West Coast, the attorney gave us a copy of the manuscript.

Gonzales took the manuscript home that evening and read it. I called him the next morning.

"Al," I said, "drawing on your fathomless depth of experience, as well as your capacious repository of literary and factual knowledge, what is your assessment of the manuscript's substantive merits?"

"Bullshit," said Al.

I agreed. In fact, after checking further on Ortiz's background, thought it possible he might have had some association with American intelligence. (He had served in the U.S. Army, had gone to Cuba to help smuggle arms to Castro before the Revolution and had once worked for a major defense contractor in California.) Nevertheless, Gonzales thought that staff researcher Eddie Lopez would have a better grasp of Ortiz's Spanish idiom, so he expressed the manuscript to Washington. Lopez read it, wrote a summary, and turned both the summary and the manuscript over to Blakey. He later told me he had the same opinion about it as Gonzales.

Sometime later, I asked Lopez if he had ever had any reaction from Blakey about the Ortiz manuscript. No, he said, and he wondered why he hadn't. Even if it were disinformation—especially if it were—it would be important, particularly if we could trace it to an intelligence source. That alone made it a sensitive item. I made a note to ask Blakey about it.

I didn't have to. Late one Sunday evening, I received the only telephone call I ever got from Bob Blakey. There was a very nervous edge to his voice.

"Talk to me," he said. "Tell me everything you know about how we came in contact with the Ortiz manuscript."

At the moment, it was not very fresh in my memory, but I eventually pieced together the details.

"All right," he said, "I just wanted to refresh my own recollection about it. I'll tell you why I asked." He said that on Friday afternoon one of columnist Jack Anderson's legmen had called him to check out a rumor. The rumor, Blakey said, was that he had sold out to the CIA in return for a high Justice Department post. An example of the sellout, he said, was the fact that he had turned the Ortiz manuscript over to the CIA.

Blakey asked if I had heard any such allegations. I told him I had not. "Well, anyway," he said, "if you hear it, it ain't true." He laughed.

What Blakey hadn't acknowledged to me was that he had, in fact, turned the Ortiz manuscript over to the CIA. He subsequently admitted that when Al Gonzales stopped him in the Committee hallway and specifically asked what happened to it. Blakey claimed he had sent it to the CIA because the Agency had linguists who could more accurately translate Ortiz's idiom than Lopez could.

Later, I asked Al Gonzales what he thought of Blakey's explanation.

"Bullshit," said Al.

Well, I didn't know. But I thought it was a plain dumb thing to do, to act as if the CIA were a partner in the House Committee's probe, not one of the subjects of its investigation. I didn't want to believe that Blakey's relationship with the CIA was getting a bit too cozy. I didn't want to believe it, but eventually I had to.

TWENTY-EIGHT

SOME KIND OF INVESTIGATION

*E*ARLY IN May, 1978, a trim, swarthy man with dark, penetrating eyes and heavy brows, wearing a finely tailored, double-breasted brown suit, appeared before an executive session of the House Select Committee on Assassinations. Ten members of the Committee staff were present, but only three Congressmen. The witness, who will here be called Carlos, had come from Miami in answer to a subpoena. His attorney, who was not present, had earlier indicated to Committee counsel Bill Triplett that the witness desired immunity from charges if, during his testimony, he incriminated himself in any illegal acts. Triplett told the witness that if at any point in the questioning he desired to invoke that immunity, he could do so by first refusing to answer a question on the basis of his Constitutional rights under the Fifth Amendment. That he never did was, I thought, an indication of how well protected he felt.

Committee Counsel Triplett then handed Carlos a document called JFK Exhibit 94.

"We have a translator available if you have any problems reading it," Triplett said.

"I can read it," the witness said. He read carefully. "Thank you," he said, returning the document. "I have read it."

"Do you understand," Triplett said, pointing at the document, "that should you feel bound by any prior oath to the CIA, that this effectively relieves you of that responsibility for the purposes of this hearing? Is that your understanding?"

Senator Richard S. Schweiker, chairman of the Senate's JFK Subcommittee, hired Gaeton Fonzi to investigate the links between the CIA and anti-Castro Cubans when he discovered that "the fingerprints of intelligence were all over Oswald's background." UPI/BETTMANN

Arlen Specter was a young, ambitious Assistant District Attorney in Philadelphia when he joined the Warren Commission. With Navy Captain James Humes, the doctor who led the Kennedy autopsy, Specter devised the single-bullet theory to eliminate the possibility of a conspiracy. Questioned by investigator Fonzi, he admitted there was conflicting evidence that "gave us a lot of concern." Specter's inability to resolve the contradictions led Fonzi to his initial surmise of a conspiracy. UPI/BETTMANN

Richard Sprague, the first Chief Counsel of the House Assassinations Committee, was immediately bombarded with criticism from the media and Congress when he called for an unrestricted investigation and refused to play the Washington political game. Within six months, he was forced to resign. "But when I looked back at what happened," he later said, "it suddenly became very clear that the problems began only after I ran up against the CIA." UPI/BETTMANN

Chief Counsel G. Robert Blakey (shown here between Assassinations Committee Chairman Louis Stokes and JFK Subcommittee Chairman Richardson Preyer) early told his staff that the Committee had two priorities: to get a final report written by the deadline and to keep the investigation within its budgetary limitations.
UPI/BETTMANN

MR. PREYER

Chief Investigator Cliff Fenton [right], once a top-ranked New York homicide detective, had a tough time keeping up the morale of his staff investigators. After being told he would be given the freedom to conduct a wide-ranging probe after the required "restricted issues" were handled for report purposes, almost all his staff was fired in a sudden "budget crisis." (In photo with Fenton are two of his top men: Jack Moriarty and Jim Kelly [in dark glasses]. Kelly, with contacts into the intelligence community, slipped Fonzi the "Highly Sensitive" document naming key Agency operatives.)
FONZI

Clare Boothe Luce, former U.S. Ambassador to Italy and wealthy widow of Time, Inc. founder Henry Luce, was early involved in dispensing information indicating that Castro was involved in Kennedy's assassination. Later she threw a red herring in the path of both Senate and House assassination committee investigators, consuming many fruitless hours. Fonzi discovered that Luce was a close associate of CIA disinformation specialist David Phillips and was on the board of his Association of Retired Intelligence Officers.
UPI/BETTMANN

Above left, Marita Lorenz was nineteen years old when she met Fidel Castro and had an affair with the Cuban dictator. She was later recruited by Frank Sturgis to spy for the CIA and attempted to poison her former lover. In testimony before the Assassinations Committee, she claimed she traveled to Dallas with a group of CIA operatives and anti-Castro Cubans planning to kill Kennedy. Part of her testimony might have been considered valid if she hadn't lured Committee investigator Fonzi into the middle of a wild encounter she had with Sturgis. *Right,* young John Rosselli started as a street hood in Al Capone's Chicago mob. He later became the CIA's key player in the Agency's alliance with Organized Crime to kill Castro. One witness saw Rosselli training an assassinaiton team at the CIA's secret JM/WAVE base in Miami and reporting directly to the station's chief of operations, David Sanchez Morales. In 1976, shortly after his secret testimony to Senator Schweiker's Kennedy Subcommittee, Rosselli's mutilated body was found in an oil drum floating in Biscayne Bay.

Below, former Chilean Foreign and Defense Minister Orlando Letelier and a colleague were killed on Embassy Row in Washington, D.C. when a planted bomb exploded under his car. The death order had come from the Chilean military junta which had overthrown elected President Salvadore Allende with the help of the CIA and David Phillips's secret Track II program. Both the head of the assassination team, an American-born member of the Chilean intelligence service, and some of the anti-Castro Cubans involved, had links to Phillips and the CIA. Phillips was involved in disseminating derogatory information about Letelier after the bombing.   UPI/BETTMANN

Former Army Captain Bradley Earl Ayers was assigned to train anti-Castro Cubans at the CIA's JM/WAVE station in Miami during Kennedy's secret war against Castro after the Bay of Pigs. Ayers revelations about David Morales, the Chief of Operations at the station, led Assassinations Committee investigator Fonzi to probe the relationship between Morales and David Phillips and uncover their link to the Kennedy assassination.

PHOTO COURTESY OF BRAD AYERS

On the orders of the CIA strategist he knew as Maurice Bishop, the youthful Antonio Veciana founded Alpha 66 in 1962 and made it the most militant and effective of all anti-Castro groups. Veciana himself gained a reputation as a terrorist and, at one point, was ordered confined to Miami by Federal authorities. Yet, with the help of Bishop, he obtained a job on the U.S. Government payroll as a banking consultant in La Paz, Bolivia, for the Agency for International Development.
FONZI

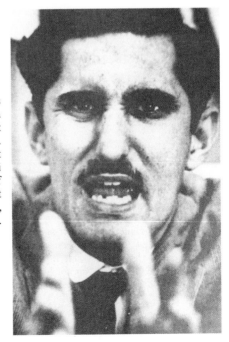

Mitchell Livingston WerBell III was among the more colorful characters to emerge in the Kennedy assassination investigation. A member of the Old Boy network of America's intelligence service, he was an expert on "silent-kill" devices and the principal supplier of the CIA's most sophisticated weapons. Drinking heavily in an interview with Committee investigator Fonzi, he let slip a startling revelation about Jack Ruby.
UPI/BETTMANN

The Assassinations Committee discovered that George DeMohrenschildt, a prominent Dallas social figure who had mysteriously befriended a working-class ex-Russian defector, had been asked by the CIA's resident Domestic Contact agent to debrief Oswald. When Committee investigator Fonzi tracked down DeMohrenschildt in South Florida, the longtime CIA asset was found dead before he could be questioned. However, in the skewered world of Washington politics, DeMohrenschildt's sudden death was a factor in keeping the Assassinations Committee alive.
UPI/BETTMANN

When bar-brawling Texas Congressman Henry Gonzalez became chairman of the Assassinations Committee, he immediately got into a battle with Chief Counsel Richard Sprague over control of staff hiring. When he attempted to fire Sprague, the other Committee members rescinded his order. Steamed, Gonzalez resigned and gave his hometown newspaper a blistering interview, complaining of "scams" Sprague pulled, including, he said, hiring "someone by the name of Gaeton Fonzi who's never so much as been in Washington. He is supposed to have underworld connections, this Fonzi, and he's in Miami. What he does down there, nobody knows and Sprague won't tell. He's probably hanging around some slop chute."
UPI/BETTMANN

Author Gaeton Fonzi before the Capitol on one of his frequent trips to Washington while serving as a Staff Investigator for the HSCA.
FONZI

Despite President Kennedy's orders to the CIA after the Cuban missile crisis to shut down all anti-Castro guerilla operations, Alpha 66 leader Antonio Veciana [left] called a press conference with Armando Fleites, secretary general of the Second Front of the Escambray, to proclaim their intention of continuing military raids against Cuba. Veciana later revealed to investigator Fonzi that the idea for the press conference came from his secret spy master, Maurice Bishop, in order to embarrass Kennedy. It was Veciana's report of seeing Bishop with Lee Harvey Oswald in Dallas two months before the assassination that broke new ground in the investigation.   FONZI

Silvia Odio's testimony that she saw Lee Harvey Oswald with two Cubans in Dallas would have negated the report the Warren Commission was preparing that there was no conspiracy. "We're supposed to be closing doors, not opening them," said the Commission's Chief Counsel, J. Lee Rankin in deliberately relying on false or incomplete FBI reports which discredited her testimony. Based on firm evidence developed by Committee investigator Fonzi and counsel Jim McDonald, the Assassinations Committee concluded that Odio was telling the truth, but its financial report ignored the real significance of that conclusion.
JOHN WOODS COLLECTION

A police artist's sketch of spy master Maurice Bishop, the CIA operative who was seen with Lee Harvey Oswald. It was drawn from details provided by Alpha 66's Antonio Veciana, whom Bishop controlled. Since Veciana worked with Bishop over a twelve-year span, it is a chronological as well as a visual composite. When Senator Richard Schweiker saw the sketch, he recognized its close resemblance to David Atlee Phillips, the CIA's former Chief of Western Hemisphere Division.   FONZI

David Atlee Phillips.   FONZI

Watergate conspirator E. Howard Hunt's shadowy presence in the most clandestine and often illegal CIA operations, including a number of assassination plots, down through the years led to his being called to testify before the Assassinations Committee. He changed the details of where he was on November 22, 1963, several times. In his autobiography, Hunt honored his close friend David Phillips by dubbing him with the pseudonym of "Knight." CIA insiders knew that actually was the pseudonym of Hunt's idol, CIA Director Richard Helms.   UPI/BETTMANN

Future Watergate burglar Frank Sturgis was questioned by FBI agents in his Miami home the day after Kennedy's assassination. "They told me I was the one person they felt had the capabilities to do it," Sturgis says. Sturgis remained in close contact with investigator Fonzi during the Assassinations Committee investigation, pushing unconfirmed reports of Castro's participation in the assassination. The Committee probed the possibility that Sturgis may have been one of the three tramps arrested behind the grassy knoll in Dealey Plaza immediately after the assassination, but comparative photo analysis was inconclusive.
FONZI

One of three so-called "tramps" taken into custody in the railroad yard behind the Texas School Book Depository after President Kennedy's assassination. Some researchers believe he resembles veteran CIA asset Frank Sturgis, perhaps wearing a disguise. The Assassinations Committee analysts concluded that, if a disguise was used, no photo comparison would be valid.   FONZI

On November 22, 1963, the CIA sent a photograph to the FBI identifying this man entering the Russian Embassy in Mexico City as Lee Harvey Oswald. It was meant to corroborate an earlier cable sent from its Mexico City station reporting that an American male identifying himself as Oswald contacted the Soviet Embassy on October 1, according to the Agency's "reliable and sensitive source," meaning its wiretap. David Phillips was the CIA agent in charge of disseminating this information in Mexico City. The photo, he later swore, was simply a "mistake," and the wiretap recording had been routinely destroyed. The Assassinations Committee discovered he was lying.   FONZI

Organized Crime boss Santos Trafficante was likely involved in the Kennedy murder, according to Assassinations Committee Chief Counsel G. Robert Blakey, former professor at Cornell Law's Organized Crime Institute. Blakey cited the testimony of anti-Castro Cuban José Alemán, who said that Trafficante told him that Kennedy "is going to be hit." Not mentioned in the Assassinations Committee report is that Alemán was a veteran FBI informant and Trafficante knew it at the time of the alleged conversation.   FONZI

The U.S. Information Agency chief at the U.S Embassy in Havana in 1960 when Antonio Veciana was recruited by CIA operative Maurice Bishop. Paul Bethel was initially suspected of being Bishop by investigator Fonzi. But Veciana said Bethel wasn't Bishop because Bishop had told him to contact Bethel for help when he first established Alpha 66. Bethel told Fonzi, however, that he was a close personal friend of David Phillips. Bethel was the founder of the Citizens Committee to Free Cuba, an Agency front involving many of David Phillips's assets, including Clare Boothe Luce who pushed false Castro-did-it stories immediately after the Kennedy assassination. FONZI

A rare photograph of David Sanchez Morales appeared in a Cuban government propaganda newspaper in 1978. The paper was devoted to revealing the CIA's operations against Cuba, including "the plot to involve Cuba in the assassination of Kennedy." The photo identified Morales as "an officer of the CIA Station in Havana, 1959." David Atlee Phillips was working deep cover in Havana with Morales at the time, posing as a public relations consultant. FONZI

As a youth, David Morales was an all-around high school athlete as well as a member of the Catholic Youth Organization's boxing team. In this classic photo, Morales, seated next to the priest coach, is 17 years old. On Morales's left is Paul Carbajal, one of two brothers who considered Morales as part of their family. Morales, in turn, shared some of his darkest secrets with them.

PHOTO COURTESY OF CARBAJAL FAMILY

Ruben "Rocky" Carbajal stands in front of one of the Indian murals which adorns the facade of his family's El Molina restaurant in Phoenix. David Morales considered himself a member of the Carbajal family and, despite his world-hopping career in the CIA, always returned to El Molina. On his last trip home, Morales told Carbajal he had been feeling ill "ever since I left Washington." Carbajal remains suspicious about Morales's sudden death.   FONZI

So close was he to them, that Joe and Rose Carbajal considered Dave Morales as one of their sons. He returned to Phoenix to help celebrate their 50th anniversary in 1977. Ruben Carbajal took this photo of Morales with his father Joe [center], his mother Rose [right], his brother Paul and his wife and [left] Bob and Florene Walton. It was one night in Washington with Ruben and Bob Walton five years prior that Morales let slip his secret about the Kennedy assassination.   PHOTO COURTESY RUBEN CARBAJAL

(Left) Fonzi on the Grassy Knoll in Dealey Plaza in 1965, while researching his ground-breaking article, "The Warren Commission, the Truth, and Arlen Specter" as Senior Editor of Philadelphia Magazine. (Right) Returning to Dallas in 1978 as a Staff Investigator for the HSCA, Fonzi is seen outside the theater where Oswald was apprehended on November 22, 1963. FONZI

Richard Billings chats with research attorney Jane Downey at Assassination Committee headquarters. Billings, the former *Life* magazine editor who covered CIA activities in Miami during JM/WAVE's operation, later wrote a book with Chief Counsel Blakey about Organized Crime's involvement in the Kennedy assassination. FONZI

Incognito, researcher Betsy Palmer models the new "Reality is Irrelevant" tee-shirts that mysteriously arrived from Miami shortly after Chief Counsel Blakey told his Assassinations Committee staff that it would have to limit the areas of investigation because of time and budget constraints. FONZI

Inconspicuously nestled in a wooded area next to what is now the Metro Zoo, the CIA's JM/WAVE headquarters had a sign on its door that read: Zenith Technical Enterprises. Organizing and supplying the CIA's secret war against Castro, it became the largest employer in South Florida. Run by veteran clandestine boss Theodore Shackley, his chief of operations was David Morales. As head of propaganda and psych warfare activities, David Phillips was a frequent visitor who had all 300 Agency officers handling the anti-Castro Cuban groups reporting to him.   PHOTO COURTESY OF BRAD AYERS

Assassinations Committee Researchers Dan Hardway, Leslie Wizelman and Edwin Lopez were students at Cornell Law when their professor, Bob Blakey, convinced them to take a sabbatical to go with him to Washington. Initially loyal followers, they eventually became disillusioned with Blakey's handling of the investigation. Hardway and Lopez wrote a report on Oswald in Mexico City that the CIA refused to release.   FONZI

"Yes," Carlos said.

Eddie Lopez, who had studied the CIA's files on the witness, was watching from a seat on the side of the room; a slight smile crossed his lips. Carlos had not asked why the Committee should feel that document was relevant to him.

The witness was questioned for more than two hours over morning and afternoon sessions. Some of his testimony contradicted information found by Committee researchers in CIA and FBI documents, but for the most part he denied association with almost all the individuals and activities which formed the basis for his being subpoenaed before the Committee. He was cool, calm and direct. "I never worked for the CIA, I never talked to anybody associated with the CIA."

After the questions and the litany of minimal and negative responses were over, an outside observer might have wondered why the Assassinations Committee decided to select, out of the half-million Cubans in Miami, this particular one.

The Committee staffers responsible for developing the information that brought the witness to Washington were not surprised by the results of the hearing. Nor were they surprised by the witness's attitude of invulnerability—it was justified. They had learned just before the hearing that a certain Federal agency had requested that the witness not be questioned about his activities within a certain time frame. But that, of course, had nothing to do with the Kennedy assassination.

The Committee staffers felt, however, that their efforts had been thwarted long before the witness was called to Washington. They knew that Al Gonzales and I had been deliberately stopped short in developing a vital piece of information. It would have been, we thought, an investigative coup. We were told that our efforts were crushed for valid procedural reasons, but we came away feeling there were other forces involved—forces that went to the heart of Bob Blakey and the Committee's arrangement with the CIA.

It all began when Rolando Otero said he was going to tell me how President Kennedy was assassinated. This was shortly after I began working for the Assassinations Committee and Otero was in the Okaloosa County Jail in the Florida Panhandle. Otero wanted to talk, but he wanted me to know that his knowledge was based on only two factors: secondhand information, and what he had learned about the CIA's tactics and procedures when he worked for the Agency.

Otero said his source had told him that Lee Harvey Oswald was sent to Russia as a CIA agent. The decision to kill Kennedy was made before Oswald's return to the United States. Otero said he had no specific knowledge of the number involved, but his training led him to guess there were between thirty and thirty-five CIA operatives in Dallas on the day Kennedy was killed, including the actual hit team. He figures there was a minimum of three on the hit team, at least one stationed in front of, and another behind, Kennedy. Otero said he understood that most of the final planning and coordination took place at meetings held in the Dallas YMCA Building, and he gave me the names of five Miami men who, according to his source, were involved in the plot. He said he didn't know the roles that four of them played, but the fifth, the one called Carlos, was in contact with Oswald and was posing as a photographer in Dealey Plaza on November 22nd.

I met with Rolando Otero because his attorney, Bob Rosenblatt from the Miami Public Defenders Office, had called and told me Otero wanted to talk with me. I knew of Otero because he had gotten major headlines when he was accused of placing bombs in Federal buildings in the Miami area. I also knew of his association with the most violent anti-Castro terrorists, so I thought it might be worth the trip. A wiry, intense young man, with a wild crop of black curls, Otero burned with an almost visible fervor when he spoke of his hatred for Castro. But he believed that any attempt to blame Castro for the assassination was part of the CIA's ploy to throw the investigation off track. The Agency did the same thing, he said, when it injected the Mafia scenario at the time of the Garrison investigation.

Despite having worked for the CIA, Rolando Otero had no love for the Agency; he had even less for the FBI. He had been tried in Federal Court for nine bombings the Bureau said he committed in Miami in a single three-month period, but he was acquitted and the Federal judge trying the case had specifically chastised the Government for its "weak" case. According to Otero's attorney, the FBI was so embarrassed that it pressured the State into bringing charges and retrying Otero in State court. This time the trial was held in Florida's Panhandle, where red-necked real Americans could tell the difference between the good guys and a crazy Cuban bomber. Despite that, Otero was convicted of only one of the charges, placing a bomb in a locker at Miami Airport. The prosecution's main evidence was a locker handle with Otero's thumb print on it, although, as his attorney argued, the FBI's prime informant himself had enough CIA training to know how to transfer a print.

Otero was scheduled to be sentenced on that one charge the day after I spoke with him. Both he and his attorney were expecting a long term, perhaps ten years. He was sentenced to forty. The next day Otero tried to commit suicide. He was in intensive care for two days, but survived.

The way Otero's situation came about bears a resemblance to the set of circumstances that led to Antonio Veciana's criminal charges and prison sentence. Both men were considered out of control in their determination to assassinate Fidel Castro. Just two years earlier, Otero had been involved in a plot to kill Castro in Venezuela which, he said, was planned without the support or knowledge of the CIA. Among those involved in the attempt were Hector Serrano, Antonio Gonzalez and Ciro Orizondo. The plot failed; then, several months later, Serrano heard that the FBI was going to link him, Gonzalez and Orizondo to Otero and the bombings. Scared, Serrano went to the FBI and told his story.

According to the FBI report, Serrano said that Gonzalez, on hearing about the frame-up, had called Arturo Cobos, described by the FBI as "a Cuban known to have contacts with the CIA." Cobos, said the report, "furnished Gonzalez the name of [the man we are calling Carlos]" and said that he could verify the rumor because he had "contacts on a high level with the CIA in Washington, D.C." When Gonzalez contacted Carlos, he said he would check with his sources. Carlos called back and said it was true, the FBI was going to link them to the bombings. But, Carlos said, the CIA was going to help; the Agency was sending someone to Miami to help them.

What happened next was this: A fellow who said he was a Treasury agent arrived from, of all places, Minnesota, gathered Otero's friends together and took them to a "safe house" where, he assured them, they would be safe from the FBI. He held them there for a couple of days during which time they were visited by the man who was the Government's key witness against Otero, Ricardo Morales. "The Monkey"—*El Mono*—as Morales was known, filled them in on the "details" of Otero's involvement in the bombings. Meantime, the Treasury agent went to Otero's apartment and collected a couple of tape recorders, a typewriter and a few other items and then flew out of town. That's the last anyone saw of the equipment or the Treasury agent.

In checking out that story, I discovered there was, indeed, such a Treasury agent in Minnesota and I called him. He told me he had worked for the Alcohol, Tobacco Tax & Firearms Division in Miami for many years and that he had received a call from an old informant about the situation with Otero—Carlos. So he flew into Miami to help out.

"Help out who?" I asked.

"That's all I can say now," he answered.

It was all very strange but what I could make of it was this: The Treasury agent (or whoever he really worked for) wanted to make sure that, while Morales was helping the FBI build its case against Otero, the Bureau didn't stumble across any untutored witnesses, or evidence that would have knocked the case out early. Hence the quick visit to Miami, the safe-house scenario and the gathering of "evidence."

The principal orchestrator of the scheme to get Otero out of circulation was the main prosecution witness himself, Ricardo "the Monkey" Morales. Despite his nickname, Morales was a suave, handsome fellow, a regular at Miami's fanciest clubs. (He would eventually be assassinated by the manager of a classy bar on Key Biscayne in what the police said was an act of self defense.) Once a member of Castro's intelligence service, he defected and became an explosives expert and contract agent for the CIA, working for the Agency throughout Latin America and in the Congo. He was certainly one of the CIA's elite operatives. During Otero's Federal trial, the defense wasn't able to question Morales because, according to the prosecutor, "he was unavailable." He was busy in Caracas working as a deputy to the chief of the Venezuelan secret police. (I would later learn that the chief was on the CIA's payroll at the time, as was Morales.)

I was, of course, very skeptical of this story. I felt it hung on very weak hooks. The common thread in this whole tangle was the mysterious Carlos, who Otero's source said was the link to the Kennedy assassination. Otero's source—to whom we gave the code name of Ten-One*—claimed to have gotten that information directly from Carlos. But Ten-One was only a small-time con man whose name had never surfaced in the circles of associates of major anti-Castro activists. And the real name of "Carlos," Ten-One's alleged source, was another I had never heard before. That didn't mean much in itself, but if he had played a role, where were all the important links, the connections? They would have to be there.

I found Ten-One in the Florida City state prison, on the edge of the Everglades south of Miami. Otero had known him casually but they had met again when Otero was being temporarily held in the Broward County jail. When Otero saw him, Ten-One was in for carrying a fraudulent driver's license. Then, while awaiting trial, he was picked up on bad check charges. Joe Mazur, a detective in the Broward State Attorney's Office, had helped me find Ten-One and, since Mazur knew him, offered to be my cover when I approached him. I didn't want him to know my interest in the Kennedy assassina-

---

*We developed a code name for Ten-One which Al Gonzales and I used in our reports to Washington. Aside from a Federal employee whose job we wanted to protect, Ten-One was the only source we used a code with even in our phone conversations. We felt we had been burned by the leaks about Veciana in the Jack Anderson columns and we wanted to be sure there would be no Committee leaks of Ten-One's true name. If there were, Ten-One would be dead because he led us to a level of international intrigue we weren't looking for.

tion on our initial contact, so on our first visit Mazur introduced me simply as "one of my associates." I had briefed Mazur, a bright, gregarious cop with a deceptively easy style, who asked most of the questions. Mazur's chatty, rambling and circuitous manner was subtle and effective.

Ten-One, it turned out, was far more than a small-time con man. In 1965, he was fighting with the Marxist rebels against the right-wing regime in the Dominican Republic when President Johnson sent in the U.S. Marines. Ten-One crossed the line to join the American forces, bringing with him an armload of charts, plans and intelligence documents that made him an instant hero to the CIA. He was immediately flown to Jamaica for safekeeping where he was introduced to Paul Bethel who debriefed him. (As mentioned earlier, I had spoken to Bethel a few times in the course of my investigation. An extreme right-winger, Bethel was the former press attaché in Havana and a close friend of David Atlee Phillips.) Bethel then flew Ten-One to Miami to meet with U.S. Senator Thomas Dodd of the Internal Security Subcommittee. Dodd was holding hearings on the spread of Communism throughout the Caribbean and Latin America and Ten-One, with the inside skinny from behind enemy lines, told him what he wanted to hear: It was true, there was tremendous Communist infiltration into the Caribbean, hundreds of rebel leaders had been training in Cuba, Red China and Russia. Ten-One was brought to Washington, where he wound up in meetings with the top brass in the National Security Council. He had become a minor inside celebrity and a valuable informant.

More interesting to me than Ten-One's celebrity was that when he crossed over in the Dominican Republic, one of the first Americans he met was a mustachioed, cocky little bantam of a guy, dressed in full battle fatigues and carrying a swagger stick. It was the colorful rapid-fire arms dealer and guerrilla school headmaster out of Powder Springs, Georgia, Mitchell Livingston WerBell III.

Ten-One wound up in Powder Springs. A man with many trades and contacts, Ten-One made himself useful providing travel documents and passports for WerBell and his operatives. It was through WerBell that Ten-One met Carlos, who was one of WerBell's numerous "representatives." (So was Gerry Patrick Hemming, cofounder with Frank Sturgis of the International Anti-Communist Brigade; and Ken Burnstine, a celebrated South Florida real estate developer who pioneered the mass importation of marijuana through a scheduled fleet of his private cargo planes. Burnstine was later going to be the Government's prime witness in a drug case against WerBell, but his plane exploded before he could testify.)

When Joe Mazur and I first sat down with Ten-One in the Florida

City prison we were wondering how we could get him talking about his association with Carlos, but we didn't realize how badly Ten-One wanted to get out of jail. He felt a victim of the prison system, which erroneously recorded his two eighteen-month sentences to run consecutively, not concurrently. He had already served ten months and thought he should get out on work release. Mazur suggested we might be able to help him if he was cooperative. Ten-One knew what he meant.

"As a matter of fact," he said, "there is someone you might be interested in. He was heavy into handling explosives for a while. This guy is what I would call a big chief. I was associated with him for about two years, indirectly, through Mitch WerBell. This man was working for WerBell back in 1963. As a matter of fact, he was involved to some degree in the Jack Kennedy thing. . . . " He let his voice slip to a mumble.

"The Jack Kennedy thing?" asked Mazur.

"That's another story," said Ten-One, "but you want to check out [Carlos]. I know he's on my FBI report because my lawyer showed it to me. They have me as his 'associate.' Evidently, when I was seeing him, they had him under surveillance, otherwise they wouldn't have made the connection. What you might be interested in is I've gotten word he's now putting something together, some kind of underground organization. For what, I don't know."

On that visit we couldn't comfortably bring the conversation back to the Kennedy assassination. But on the second visit, about a week later, we decided to tell Ten-One about my connection to the Assassinations Committee. Still, wanting to protect Otero as a source, I didn't directly ask Ten-One about what Otero had said about Carlos and the link to the Kennedy assassination. And Ten-One, perhaps not wanting to play all his cards, never got very detailed. "I wouldn't put anything past [Carlos]," he said, "since I know that's the kind of business he's involved in. Perhaps he told me he was in Dallas because he wanted me to think he was a Government agent." Ten-One did say that Carlos told him about some photographs he had taken in Dallas, but not that they were taken on the day Kennedy was shot. "He led me to believe he had some photographs from down there," Ten-One said, "but I don't know from when. He said they were in a bank vault because he said they were too hot. I know he took them himself because he's a good photographer. He had two 35-millimeter cameras, a Nikon and a Minolta, and a few lenses."

Ten-One also told me: "The more I think about it, if [Carlos] was involved in any way, then Mitch must have been. At one time they were both involved in getting people. Once they were looking for two guys from the Dominican Republic, one of them Hector Aristy, who later surfaced in Red China. Then a Frenchman named Jean Pierre Andre. Mitch found Andre and Andre is no longer among the living. And I know the Company wanted those men."

I asked Ten-One if Carlos ever said anything about Oswald killing Kennedy. "Oh, sure," he said, "he doesn't believe it. He doesn't believe it because he knows some of the people involved in it. He said he knows some of the people who were involved because they were talking about it before it even happened."

That was as close as Ten-One would ever come to telling us the details he reportedly gave Otero. Anyway, Al Gonzales and I decided to help Ten-One get out of prison on a work-release program. Ten-One had agreed to get back in touch with Carlos. It was no problem getting Ten-One released because there actually *was* an administrative error in his sentencing records. We asked a local judge to review the records and the judge released him immediately.

Meanwhile, we had done some research into Carlos's background. We found he was closely associated with the most violent element of the anti-Castro activists, but almost always in a behind-the-scenes role. Ten-One's claim that Carlos was "heavy into handling explosives" was repeated in a Miami Police report on the arrest of a Cuban activist for bombing a boat. The activist said Carlos had supplied the C-4 explosives used in the bombing. Then, when two of CORU's members were arrested in Mexico in a failed attempt to kidnap the Cuban consul, it was Carlos who went to offer the authorities a deal: to keep terrorist activities out of Mexico in exchange for light treatment of the two. They later escaped. (CORU was an umbrella organization of terrorist groups formed in the mid-Seventies; its significance will be detailed later.) We also discovered that, earlier, Carlos had openly exhibited an interest in the Kennedy assassination; he was among several individuals from Miami who turned up in New Orleans to volunteer their services in Jim Garrison's investigation. (It was known, of course, from former CIA officer Victor Marchetti that Director Richard Helms had told his staff to look for ways to monkey wrench Garrison's investigation. But it was the House Committee that discovered the CIA had planted a number of agents on Garrison's staff.)

As soon as he was released, Ten-One easily reestablished contact with Carlos. With his ability to provide certain equipment necessary for a covert operation, Ten-One was an obvious asset. And, from what we would learn, Carlos's operation could use someone with such talents, although it took a few months for Ten-One to earn the trust of the group. One weekend, for instance, Ten-One was invited to a meeting of the group. To get there, he waited for a call at a certain time at a particular telephone booth. His first set of instructions took him to another telephone booth. His second set to another and his third to yet another. Then he was told the meeting had been postponed. Ten-One told us he felt it was a test and that he was likely being watched to see if he was making any calls or had any contacts between instructions.

Just as in an intelligence operation where an individual participant is given as limited a view as possible of the overall plan, Ten-One was not privy to the details of the mission of Carlos and his associates. But what he did learn shocked us and sent nervous jitters through the Committee's staff bosses in Washington. According to Ten-One's reports, we had stumbled upon an assassination operation.

Ten-One learned of the plans one night over dinner at the Versailles in Little Havana with a man named Emilio, the coordinator of the operation. Emilio told Ten-One that a team was being formed to put the late dictator Rafael Trujillo's millionaire son, Rhadames, back in power in the Dominican Republic. Later, in talking directly with Carlos, Ten-One said he got the impression that Mitch WerBell was also in on it. "If Mitch is involved," said Ten-One, "that means the CIA is connected or at least has knowledge." According to Ten-One's reading of the situation, the aging Dominican President, Joaquín Balaguer, was beginning to run the country as his personal fiefdom, down to having nightly meetings to decide where the country's money would be spent the next day. Balaguer was not being as cooperative with U.S. interests as he had been and, strategically, the U.S. had to keep a handle on the situation to prevent other foreign interests from exploring the vast offshore oil potential of the island.

All of this did not, of course, have anything to do with the Kennedy assassination and Al Gonzales and I would not have encouraged Ten-One in his role except for one bit of information he brought us: There were two men in the operation who fit the descriptions of "Angel" and "Leopoldo," the two men Silvia Odio said had visited her apartment in Dallas with Oswald.

Our reports to Committee Chief Counsel Bob Blakey documented our activities with Ten-One and we also kept Chief Investigator Cliff Fenton posted. Fenton encouraged us but was a little nervous that we may have stumbled into an intelligence operation the depth and breadth of which we could not see, one perhaps controlled by those who had the power to unleash destructive forces against the Committee.

Nevertheless, Al Gonzales and I thought our limited goal of trying to identify the two men who might be connected to the Odio incident was important. Ideally, we needed photographs. As time went by, the meetings of this group were more frequent and Ten-One, although not invited to all of them, knew when they came up. (The group met in the back rooms of a classy boutique on Miracle Mile in Coral Gables. Carlos had two women running it for him as a front, and it also gave him an excuse to make frequent "buying" trips to Latin America.) Then Ten-One told us a meeting was scheduled that would include the two men we wanted to photograph. I quickly called a contact at the Metro Dade Organized Crime squad and asked if his unit would do us a favor. Sure, it would be glad to cooperate, my contact said, and would provide a well-disguised surveillance van to take surreptitious photographs of our subjects.

Al and I were excited. Over the years Silvia Odio had been shown hundreds of photographs but few were even close to the descriptions she had provided. From Ten-One's reports, and the fact that they were closely linked to relevant operations, we thought we might have finally stumbled on a hit.

We may have. We'll never know. After we had made all the arrangements for the surveillance van to be in place on the day of the meeting, Al Gonzales called Chief Investigator Cliff Fenton and told him of our plans.

"Hey, now wait a minute, Al," Fenton said, "just wait a minute. I know you guys are trying to do your job down there but, hey, you might be getting into something bigger than all of us. Let me check with the guys upstairs and get back to you. Just hold off for now, OK?"

It didn't take long for Fenton to call back.

"Call it off, Al," he said. "Call it off quick! The shit hit the fan up here when I told Cornwell and Blakey what you guys were doing. They blew their tops. They said we are not *authorized* to do that kind of stuff!"

Al couldn't believe it.

"What kind of *stuff*?" Al fumed. "We're trying to find some answers in this case, Cliff. What kind of an investigation are we supposed to be doing?"

It was a bit embarrassing calling my contact at the Organized Crime squad to tell him we had to call it off. When he asked why, I told him the truth. He asked me almost the same question Al had asked Fenton: "What kind of investigation are you guys doing?" It was a question that would long echo in my mind.

After our aborted attempt to take surveillance photos, Al and I raised enough fuss to convince Blakey that the Committee should at least question Carlos under oath. A subpoena was prepared and Al served it on him. A few days later, Ten-One called and said that something strange was happening. Everybody in the group was taking off, leaving town. He said he got word that the operation was being put on hold and he asked if I knew what was happening. I could guess; but I didn't tell him. I also didn't tell him that, just for the hell of it, Al and I had checked the telephone calls the witness had made immediately after he received the subpoena to testify before the Committee. He had made a lot of calls but the one that stuck out was the one to McLean, Virginia. I knew that billings on calls to CIA headquarters are listed under that town, but I didn't bother to check the listing of the specific number Carlos had called. We weren't doing that kind of an investigation.

TWENTY-NINE

A MASSACRE FROM WITHIN

*F*RUSTRATED AS THE STAFF was becoming with the limitations being imposed on the investigation, in retrospect we shouldn't have been surprised. The restricted-issues approach was itself creating limitations and keeping them well defined. Still, it was early June before we began to realize this approach had another important element built in.

Even though the issues selected had narrowed the breadth of the investigation, it was obvious in most areas that the investigative plan still wouldn't be completed. But that didn't really matter. The investigative plan itself only called for touching all the bases—the Committee version of covering its ass—so the report could be written simply on the basis of the effort made. It generated an underlying philosophy: Why take the time to go all the way down the road when you already know what it looks like from here? Or can guess what it looks like and maybe come pretty close. Whatever, this isn't the real world, reality is irrelevant.

I don't know if Blakey finally recognized the futility of our trying to continue a valid investigation within his restricted issues. If he did, he couldn't admit it, so I also don't know whether that was a factor in what happened next. All the staff heard at first was the rumor of momentous change in the wind.

At the time, Al Gonzales and I were in Caracas, primarily to talk with a witness who was too important to be dumped from any investigative plan: Dr. Orlando Bosch, the best-known and most violent of anti-Castro terrorists. Bosch was being held by the Venezuelan government for blowing up a Cubana Airlines plane and killing 73 persons. The "issue" question we were to ask Bosch was whether he or his anti-Castro group ever had any association with Lee Harvey Oswald. We obviously were on a mission of going through the motions for the record, touching the bases. Bosch was not under oath and under no compulsion to tell us the truth. In fact, he could tell us whatever fanciful story he wanted to tell us. Without the time or resources to check on what he said, we were mere conveyors for the record of whatever lies or propaganda he wanted to get out.

Nevertheless, sitting in our hotel room one evening near the end of our stay, both Gonzales and I were feeling elated about what we had accomplished in Caracas. We had found and talked with two other important witnesses, individuals Antonio Veciana had named as being involved with him in the planning of the Castro assassination attempt in Chile in 1971. Interviewing them led us to believe Veciana was telling the truth about that plot. So Al decided we should call Washington to tell Cliff Fenton the news of our progress. When he hung up, he didn't look too happy.

"It's hitting the fan again up there," he said. "Cliff said that Blakey just discovered that there was some kind of miscalculation in the way they were keeping the financial records and that the Committee is running way the hell over budget."

"What's that mean," I asked, "that they can't afford to bring us home?"

"No such luck," said Gonzales. "Cliff thinks that maybe Blakey is going to use that as an excuse to make some staff cuts."

Fenton was right on target. At a special staff meeting shortly afterwards, Blakey went into a long explanation of what had happened. He and Tom Howarth, the Committee's budget officer, had just spent days going over the books, he said, and they were astounded at what they discovered. Their budget projections had been way off base. Now there was no way that the final phases of the Committee's work—specifically, the public hearings and the report writing—could be completed without major budget cuts. Some of the staff, announced Blakey, would have to be let go.

Al Gonzales and I couldn't get back to Washington until after the massacre. In the weeks between Blakey's announcement and the firing, morale and work production plummeted to near zero.

"You can imagine what it's like up here," one of the secretaries told me when I called. "The general attitude is, why should I do anything if I'm going to be fired? Everybody is feeling just terrific."

Whenever they felt the administration's edicts began to border on the absurd, a few stealthy jokesters had taken to posting on the bulletin board obviously phony memos from Chief Counsel Blakey. The coming staff cuts had produced the latest posting, a parody of Blakey's passion for scientific analysis. The memo said that a decision had been made about which individuals would be let go in consultation with a panel of experts who had established the proper scientific postulations for the decision: "All Leos, Cancers, Pisces and Tauruses are hereby dismissed."

There was no humor in the real dismissals. In fact, some were shocked at the character of the cuts: Of the 25 staffers given their walking papers, the majority were investigators. In June, just before the cut, the Committee employed 118 persons; in the end, only 83 staffers remained. Of those, only four were Kennedy assassination investigators.

Cliff Fenton took the massacre of his staff with a good deal of bitterness. "It's a catastrophe," he said. "They really bagged me. They kept promising me that we would be able to swing the way we wanted after we finished the work plan at the end of June. That's why I kept telling everybody whenever they started bitching that this wasn't the real investigation, 'All right, just finish the work plans, just finish the work plans.' But had they told me the whole investigation was going to be over in June, well, you know, we would've tried some slippin' and slidin' and maybe got a few things done. Now suddenly everything's off. They checkmated me."

I lost my partner in the cut. Al Gonzales was especially angry because he thought we were making progress and he didn't believe Blakey's reasons. In addition, he had moved his family from New York and was looking to buy a house. "I knew it was coming," he kept saying. "They really didn't want an investigation."

Al had actually started moving toward that opinion earlier. It had particularly bothered him that he was not invited to join Blakey, a select few staffers and a couple of the Committee members on a trip to Cuba to interview Castro. When Al was hired by the Committee, he was told by then-Deputy Counsel Bob Tanenbaum that his early acquaintance with Castro as his New York bodyguard would be utilized by the Committee to establish a rapport. And if Castro cooperated, he could be a valuable new source of information.

But Blakey deliberately kept Al Gonzales off the Cuba trip, saying he specifically didn't want to bring anyone who knew Castro; he wanted the Committee's record to reflect that it was totally objective in its approach to the Cuban leader. Al thought that was asinine. He was convinced that the brief friendship he had developed with Castro in New York might open doors of trust that would be valuable. As it turned out, Castro was cooperative with the Committee, but Eddie Lopez, who did go on the trip, believes that Castro might have been more forthcoming, especially in providing access to Cuban intelligence documents. Gonzales remained upset with Blakey. "I don't think he really wanted to get all the information possible," Al concluded. "He wanted to make the trip more for the record."

It was a couple of weeks after we returned to Miami from Caracas before Al and I could get back to Washington and, by that time, we knew Al was among those being let go. As soon as we arrived, Deputy Chief Gary Cornwell called us into his office for a private conference to try to assuage Al's obvious bitterness.

Cornwell had a nervous little smile on his face. Gonzales is a very big man, normally very gentle and very quiet, but his heavy-lidded eyes had a way of narrowing and exuding a seething inner intensity when he was angry. Completely filling his chair, he looked less like a docile detective than an intimidating sumo wrestler.

"I just want to tell you fellas what I told everyone else," Cornwell said, "because I don't want you to be upset by all this or take it personal."

He was on a trip, Cornwell said, when he got a call from Blakey saying that he had just gone over the books and discovered that the Committee was in a financial jam. Cornwell said that when he returned, he decided the situation boiled down to a single issue: Was Blakey telling him the truth or did he have other motivations in cutting the staff? Cornwell claimed he then reviewed the books himself and found that Blakey was right, something had just gone wrong in keeping track of the budget.

Gonzales sat and listened and said nothing, his eyes still angry slits. Cornwell sounded sincere.

"Al," he said, "I just want you to know if there was any way we could have kept you on the staff, just one more guy, you would have been it. You've been doing a helluva job and I want you to know we appreciated it and I don't think you should personally feel bad about it." Cornwell tried a conciliatory grin.

Gonzales sat silent for a moment then said, very softly: "I feel like I've been screwed."

Before they departed, Bob Blakey agreed to the idea of giving each of the investigators being fired a special award for meritorious service. The idea came from the investigators themselves. They did, after all, now have to go out and hustle up new jobs and such an award would stand out as a gold star on their resumés. And so it was arranged that the Chairman of the Committee would present to each investigator a large, very lovely wooden plaque with a beautifully engraved brass plate. The investigator's name was elegantly etched in and, below it, was the notation that he had provided "outstanding service" in the investigation.

Although I wasn't among those being fired, I also received an award. I keep it aboard my sailboat where it can be enviably observed by my faithful crew while they do their duty. It's hanging in the head.

THIRTY

SETTING UP THE
SCENARIO

*I*N THE MONTHS BETWEEN the firings in June and the scheduled demise of the Committee at the end of December, Bob Blakey directed his attention almost totally to two things: the public hearings and the writing of the report.

As Blakey had told the staff at his very first briefing almost a year earlier, he viewed the public hearings as one of the most important functions of the Committee. Blakey's hyped-up concern for the hearings came as a revelation to me and was an early indication of how very astute he was about the ways of Washington. Naively, I had always assumed that Congressional public hearings were for the public. So I had thought that the Assassinations Committee's public hearings would be our opportunity to present to the American people the first objective overview of the Kennedy assassination. The way I saw it, if the hearings had a political purpose, it would be to educate and rouse the public to demand that its government produce a firm and final conclusion to one of the most significant events in our country's history. In my mind, such public hearings act to fulfill one of the basic tenets of a democracy—you know, all those platitudes you learned in civics class in high school.

But Washington teaches its own civics lessons and I learned that Congressional public hearings are not for the public but for Congress. They are designed to provide the Committee members with as much exposure as possible, and give the public the impression that its Congressmen are serious about what they're doing and that they have not been squandering the taxpayer's money. Hearings are primarily designed, in other words, to be politically rewarding.

If the public hearings of the House Select Committee on Assassinations had revealed even a hint of what the Committee had actually been doing for the preceding year and a half, the hearings would have been great fodder for commercial television, a show that might fit, stylistically, somewhere between *Saturday Night Live* and *Dallas* (the soap opera, not the city). But, of course, the hearings couldn't reveal the truth. Instead, what they cleverly did was prepare the public for the Committee's final report.

Admittedly, my special disappointment in the structure of the public hearing came as a result of my own intentions to use them to inform the public of those areas I was familiar with and knew were particularly important. I saw the hearings as an opportunity to make what we had been doing worthwhile.

Chief Counsel Blakey had begun prep work for the public hearings almost immediately after joining the Committee. The hearings were scheduled for September, 1978, and memoranda concerning staff procedure for them were pouring forth as early as November, 1977. It was, however, my understanding that no firm decisions would be made about which witnesses to call until just several weeks before the hearings.

Sometime later, I had a discussion about the public hearings with a Senior Counsel staffer named Jim McDonald. McDonald's hiring was an indication of how much weight Blakey was giving to the presentation of the hearings. A former Organized Crime consultant to Florida Governor Reubin Askew, McDonald had just joined a prestigious Miami law firm when Blakey convinced him to delay starting his new job and to take temporary duty with the Committee—with the promise that he could leave after the hearings. McDonald, a former FBI agent, was clean-cut and boyish, bright and articulate. Blakey felt he would look good on television.

McDonald was with the Committee only five months but, as a result of staff attorney attrition, he ended up in charge of two key teams: Team Two, the Organized Crime unit; and Team Three, the anti-Castro Cuban unit. This gave him a special insight.

"When I got to Washington," McDonald recalled, "none of the staffers had a focus on what the hearings were going to be about. And as the summer dragged on we began to realize that we didn't have a heck of a lot to present at a public hearing. I remember that was the big topic of discussion in each team: What are we going to put on that's meaningful? What new evidence could we present? We didn't want to trot out the old Warren Commission stuff. Then sometime in

July, I guess it was, Blakey and Cornwell got together and we were all handed an outline of exactly what the hearings would contain."

According to that original outline, the area of anti-Castro activities would be given a proportional share of public exposure. "Under that area are listed Odio and Veciana," McDonald had told me at the time, "but I'm wondering if that's going to be misleading. I'm afraid the impression may come from their appearance that the Committee is trying to link anti-Castro Cubans directly to the assassination. There's no evidence to that."

I agreed. In fact, I pointed out, the Veciana incident indicates that Oswald's association was not with anti-Castro Cubans but with the intelligence community. Obviously, that area was particularly sensitive. The possibility of Oswald's association with the Central Intelligence Agency was going to be handled in a circuitous way at the hearings, as part of the presentation concerning the performance of the Federal agencies' response to the Kennedy assassination.

Nevertheless, I was pleased with the proposed structure of the hearings as far as my area was concerned because, prior to calling the witnesses, an introductory narrative would be read by Blakey. McDonald agreed that I would write the background narrative introducing the whole anti-Castro Cuban area of the investigation, as well as individual introductions for Silvia Odio and Antonio Veciana. I wanted the public to grasp the significance of Odio's and Veciana's testimony in its proper context, so I couldn't ask for more.

McDonald and I worked closely in preparing for this aspect of the public hearings. We both felt we had only one major problem: to convince Silvia Odio to testify publicly. After talking with her, McDonald concluded that she would make an impressively credible witness. In fact, McDonald himself had developed a witness in Dallas, Dr. Burton Einspruch, Odio's psychiatrist, who corroborated that she had told him—*prior* to the Kennedy assassination—of the mysterious visit by Oswald and his two companions. That's the kind of evidence a trial attorney appreciates.

Silvia Odio had never been an eager witness. The FBI had discovered her only coincidentally and her experience with the Warren Commission had left her distrustful. She had hidden from the Kennedy researchers and even turned down large sums of money from checkbook journalists. She was fearful that any fresh publicity would wreak havoc on the stability she had struggled to achieve, and now, she was terrified for her safety.

It had taken me a while to cultivate her trust. When I first met Odio while working for Senator Schweiker, I could honestly promise her confidentiality. Now I was no longer in control. And yet—perhaps because of her Cuban experience—she had a deeper belief in the democratic system than most Americans. So I thought I could convince her that it was more important than ever that she testify publicly.

"I have been dreading that you would call," she said when I telephoned. "Please don't let them call me for public hearings. I'm not ready to upset my whole life again."

"Well," I said, "Jim McDonald is coming down next week and perhaps we can have lunch together and talk about it." She had liked McDonald when she met him.

"But *why* do I have to do it?" she asked. "You have the story, the FBI has the story. I have repeated it so many times before. You have my sworn statements and you and Jim spent four hours taking my deposition. If the Congressmen want to see me privately, I'll be glad to see them privately. Tell me, please, *please* tell me why I have to go through it all over again? *Why?*"

I understood her fears very well and had a tough time giving good answers to her questions, but she eventually agreed to have lunch with McDonald and me the next week. As a matter of formality, McDonald was bringing down subpoenas for both her and Veciana, but the last thing I wanted was to force Silvia Odio to testify. If I couldn't convince her to come to Washington voluntarily, I would not be part of any legal coercion.

When I approached Antonio Veciana, he was also reluctant to make a public appearance. Although our personal relationship was still good and he had accepted the loss of anonymity resulting from the Jack Anderson columns, his view of the Committee's motives had changed drastically when Blakey and his crew went to Cuba. (At this point, Veciana had been out of prison for more than a year and was intensively back into anti-Castro operations with his exile-cohorts. I believed that he had become an insider in a small exile power group— like the little-known generals who really control the Pentagon—that was continuing the war against Castro. The group planned strategy for penetration and counterintelligence operations on the highest levels and its successes were quietly effective.)

"Well, of course I will go because I must go," Veciana said when I asked him to testify. "But I have already given three times sworn statements about Bishop, twice before the Senate Committee and once before the House Committee. They already have my sworn statements. I cannot change my sworn statements. So what good is it for me to go to Washington again?"

I knew exactly what Veciana meant. He had sworn that David Phillips was not Maurice Bishop and he was letting me know he could not change that. I assured Veciana we did not want him to change his sworn statements but that his appearing before the Committee would indicate that his testimony was being given a good deal of weight. In fact, I said, Chief Counsel Blakey himself would be declaring to the American people that Veciana's story appeared credible. (I could say that because I had already written the introduction Blakey would read.) At any rate, from his experience with Government, Veciana knew he couldn't avoid the Committee's command request.

I reported all this to McDonald and added: "I think we're going to have problems with Silvia. It's going to take all your persuasive abilities as a trial attorney to convince her."

"Leave it to ol' Jim," said McDonald, never short of confidence or enthusiasm.

The Miamarina, a port of call for yachts from around the world, is in Bayfront Park in downtown Miami. A large circular restaurant sits at the core of its finger piers and from its elevated patio, against a backdrop of palms and blue sky, luncheon diners can survey the rows of salty sailing craft rolling restlessly on their lines and hear the siren song of their slapping halyards.

It was a lousy spot to try to convince someone to go to Washington. Jim McDonald and I spent a couple of hours there telling Silvia Odio why we thought her public appearance before the Assassinations Committee was so important. McDonald did most of the talking. I thought Odio's objections were much too valid, so I kept relatively silent. Nevertheless, we eventually convinced her the American people had the right to hear her story as she presented it, not as the Warren Commission had distorted it.

"All right, I'll go," she finally said. "But only because I trust you and I agree it's important for the people to know what happened. I must be crazy letting you two talk me into this, but I believe in you."

Shortly afterwards, I began making arrangements to bring Silvia Odio and Antonio Veciana to Washington. Veciana had business to attend to, but did a little schedule juggling for the trip. Odio received permission to take a leave of absence from work and she and her husband, who was accompanying her at his own expense, made reservations at a Washington hotel. Meanwhile, I got busy finishing up the piece that Blakey would read to introduce the anti-Castro Cuban area of the investigation.

In the first weeks of the Committee's public hearings long days were devoted to the detailed presentation of the scientific analyses done on what was left of the physical evidence in the case. Even longer days were devoted to Government officials talking about the relationships various Federal agencies had had with the Warren Commission. The hearings were reported in all the major newspapers and on national television's evening news. There was not as much publicity, however, as Blakey had counted on. The largest radio and television networks had decided that the Committee's public hearings were probably not going to provide anything really new or sensational and dropped plans for live coverage. Not even Blakey's personal, impassioned pleas to the networks' top executives could induce them to change their minds. Only National Public Radio covered the hearings live, but not on a fulltime basis.

An attempt was made to jiggle the public's attention by calling as witnesses such well-known figures as Governor and Mrs. John Connally, Marina Oswald, former CIA Director Richard Helms and ex-President Gerald Ford, but their testimony provided little of lasting interest, certainly no new revelations.

The last week of the hearings was set aside to cover the basic issue of whether or not the assaassination had been a conspiracy. Hopefully, conspiracy-theory week would grab a little more attention. Yet, when I reviewed the schedule, I thought it had an obvious prejudice: One day was devoted to what Blakey termed "flakey" theories (such as the "umbrella man" theory, which had Kennedy shot by a man wielding a weapon hidden in an umbrella); one day was scheduled for the anti-Castro Cuban area; and three days were to be devoted to exploring the possible connections of Organized Crime to the assassination.

Chief Investigator Cliff Fenton came to Miami just hours before I was scheduled to leave for Washington. Fenton had brought with him a subpoena for Organized Crime figure Santos Trafficante, a gentle-looking little old man who lived in North Miami. Although his link to the assassination was tenuous, Trafficante's appearance was planned to give the Committee's last days of public hearings a final shot of media "sex appeal"—a term Blakey liked to use.

Fenton not only brought Trafficante's subpoena, but some lousy news for me: There would be no witnesses called in the anti-Castro area. A day was being lopped off the last week of hearings—Friday is not a day when Congressmen like to hang around Washington—and the Organized Crime presentation was being allotted additional time. I was directed to tell Silvia Odio and Antonio Veciana to cancel their trips to Washington.

My reaction was not favorable. I was, to put it mildly, very upset. Not to worry, I was told. Although no witnesses would be called, there would still be a public presentation of the anti-Castro Cuban area and Blakey would still read the narrative detailing the stories of Odio and Veciana. National radio and television would carry it, and the public would finally learn about an important part of the Kennedy assassination picture. In fact, I was told, when I got to Washington I would now have time to revise the narrative, add to the details and make the presentation that much stronger.

When I informed Veciana about the change in plans, he was

surprised and confused. "I don't understand," he said. "Why did they make me a subpoena and now they say they don't want me?"

Veciana was a man trained to look for hidden motives and mirror images in the course of events and his suspicions were very finely tuned. I told him what I had been told: The Committee had run out of time, but his story would still be presented in narration. Extra time was needed to present the Organized Crime aspect of the investigation. He found my explanation inadequate. "I think there is more to it than that," he said.

(Veciana would later tell me the basis for his suspicions. His inside sources in the Miami FBI office told him that the FBI had a confidential informant who had claimed that Veciana was a Castro agent. The FBI told that to the Committee, and that's why he was not called, Veciana said. It was the informant, added Veciana, who was the real Castro agent. I was never able to check this out, but knowing Blakey's reverence for FBI information, that scenario wouldn't surprise me.)

Then I told Silvia Odio. McDonald and I had convinced her that her testimony was absolutely necessary, appealing to her devotion to lofty ideals and principles. She did not take the news the way Veciana did.

"My God, this is incredible," she said, "after all the hell I've been putting myself through." She paused, unable to express the depth of her reaction. "I feel a tremendous anger," she finally said softly. "Well, this is the end for me. I don't want to have anything more to do with any more investigations or anything that has to do with the Government at all. Of course, I'm glad in a way that I don't have to go through the public exposure, but now I really know that they don't want to know. They don't really want to know because they don't have any answers for the American public. They should never have started this charade in the first place."

Her anger, she said, was not directed at me, but perhaps, in part, it should have been. I just listened; I could not answer her. In my gut, I knew she was right.

THIRTY-ONE

SLIP-SLIDING AWAY
FROM THE CIA

*I*N RETROSPECT, it's clear that the last week of the Assassinations Committee's public hearings was designed to leave the overwhelming impression that Organized Crime was involved in the murder of President Kennedy. And, again in retrospect, it appears that this was a deliberate attempt to set up the American public for what was coming in the final report. The results of the acoustic tests—which found that more than three shots were fired, thus dictating the conclusion that there was a conspiracy—were already well known. So the public hearings became an opportunity for Blakey, who had to pin the conspiracy on someone, to pin it on the Mob. Then, too, his Organized Crime expertise would come in handy in structuring a final report that had "sex appeal" and the appearance of substance. (Unfortunately for Blakey, the results of the acoustics tests, which had seemed so sure, would start causing him major headaches during the hearings, which would continue through the writing of the report.)

Most of the members of the Committee's Organized Crime team never bought Blakey's theory. "I remember that as being a constant battle at our meetings," Jim McDonald later recalled. "Most of us on the team felt we never made the link. Maybe Blakey's O.C. consultant Ralph Salerno made the link, but that's Ralph Salerno. The team never made the link. But at our meetings it was obvious that Blakey wanted that. He wanted to make the link more than anything else."

Blakey seems to have made the link well before the acoustic results dictated the need for a conspiracy theory. "When Blakey sold me on joining the Committee," McDonald remembers, "we had a long discussion over the phone. This was in late February. He was intimating he had some new evidence and he finally asked me, 'Well, who do you think killed Kennedy?' I said I didn't know. And he said, 'Think. Think about it.' And I guessed, 'Castro? Cuban exiles? I really don't know.' '*Think!*' he said. 'It's so obvious!' By that time I was just confused. Finally he blurted out, '*Organized Crime killed Kennedy!*' "*

---

*Perhaps no better example of Blakey's inclination toward providing the public a veneer of Organized Crime involvement is his handling of one witness whose credibility had some serious shortcomings. With a ritualistic fanfare of security worthy of a Mafia kingpin turned Government informant, the U.S. Marshals Service brought José Alemán to testify during the public hearings of the Assassinations Committee on September 27th, 1978. I had first interviewed Alemán in August of 1976, after an article appeared in the the *Washington Post* written by George Crile, then a freelance writer (now a CBS Television feature producer) known to have close sources within the CIA. Alemán confirmed what Crile had reported: that Organized Crime boss Santos Trafficante had told him before the assassination that Kennedy was "going to be hit." A few weeks before Alemán's public testimony, Chief Counsel Bob Blakey sent Organized Crime team counsel Andy Purdy to Miami and Alemán repeated to Andy and me what he said Trafficante had told him. And he also reaffirmed that he had the impression that Trafficante was not just conjecturing, he actually knew a plan was in the works. But when he testified in public before the Committee, the hearing room lined with armed U.S. Marshals, Alemán backed down, claimed he was in fear of his life and said perhaps he misunderstood Trafficante and what the Mob boss probably meant was that Kennedy was going to be hit by "a lot of Republican votes" in the 1964 election. That display of cowering trepidation likely enhanced Alemán's credibility and his quote of Trafficante—"he is going to be hit"—has since worked its way into every Kennedy assassination book with a "Mob-did-it" theme, including Blakey's.

The truth about Alemán's story—and its source—never got into the Assassinations Committee's report. José Alemán was the son of José Manuel Alemán, one of the most politically powerful and wealthiest men in Cuba in the 1940s. Nominally the minister of education, the elder Alemán showed his smarts by backing up a truck to the Cuban treasury and making off with the country's foreign reserves. He took his money to Florida and, by the time he died in 1950, he owned rows of ocean-front hotels, a large piece of Key Biscayne, Miami Stadium and other interests worth about $20 million. Young José blew it all. In the summer of 1962, when Alemán was down to his last and fast-fading Miami Beach hotel, the Scott-Bryant, and was looking for a bail-out, a friend introduced him to Santos Trafficante who arranged a $1.5 million loan through the Teamsters. (Alemán told me that, in return, Trafficante wanted a connection to Alemán's friend, Juan Bosch, the president of the Dominican Republic, where the Mob boss wanted a casino.) Thereafter, Trafficante would drop by the hotel and, in the privacy of Alemán's office, shoot the breeze. It was in one of those discussions, with Trafficante rambling about democracy and communism and Castro, that the subject of Kennedy's future came up. Alemán said, he had remarked that Kennedy was likely a shoo-in at the next election, when Trafficante indicated the President might not last until then. Alemán said he began to argue the point when Trafficante interrupted him. "No, José," he said. "He's going to be hit." That story, as Alemán told it to me, was essentially what George Crile had written in the *Washington Post*.

In addition to pushing an Organized Crime conspiracy, the Committee's public hearings had another significant characteristic. Although Blakey's press releases had claimed the hearings would cover the area, they never truly delved into most of the evidence dealing with connections between Lee Harvey Oswald and the Central Intelligence Agency.

Blakey acknowledged that and said the reason had to do with the arrangements he had made with the CIA in order to gain access to its files. One of the stipulations was that all information the Committee obtained from the CIA and wanted to use in its final report would be reviewed by the CIA prior to its publication. It was then, Blakey told the staff, that we would argue with the CIA for release of the information on a point-by-point basis. Therefore, Blakey said, he didn't want to present any information in the public hearings which might lead to a premature skirmish with the Agency. Initially I thought Blakey was perhaps overcautious, but then I had an experience with him in which he leaned over ridiculously, maybe even suspiciously, backwards.

However, Crile's piece went further. After Trafficante told Alemán about a Kennedy hit, Crile reported, three Cubans who Alemán "had known in Havana and . . . had gone to work for Castro after the Revolution, appeared in Miami and then left for Texas. He [Alemán] suspected them of being Cuban agents. . . ." The impression Crile gave, of course, was that those Cuban agents were on their way to Dallas and likely involved in fulfilling Trafficante's prophecy.

When I spoke with Crile, I learned that one of Alemán's closest associates was Eugenio Martinez, who also happened to be a regular source for Crile. Martinez was well known among Miami's Cubans for his many daring and heroic raids during the height of JM/WAVE's secret war on Cuba. Martinez was still on the CIA payroll when he was involved in the Watergate burglary. I also learned from Crile that his depiction of the three mysterious "Cuban agents" who passed through Miami on the way to Dallas was misleading. One of them was actually a former Worcester Academy school chum of Alemán; another was killed in a plane crash before the assassination.

With additional research, I learned there was a major factor that weighed heavily against the significance of Trafficante's alleged quote. In 1958, Alemán had been recruited by the FBI as an informant and, in fact, testified against Norman Rothman. Involved in arms smuggling and counterfeiting, Rothman was a major figure in the Mob. (At one point, Meyer Lansky had put him in charge of all slot machine distribution in Cuba.) After his testimony in the Rothman trial, Alemán's relationship with the FBI grew even closer. One would have to assume then that Santos Trafficante—known to be so discreet in conducting his illegal activities that he never spent a full day in a U.S. jail—made a very indiscreet comment to someone he knew to be an FBI informant. And although the date he allegedly made that comment was buried during the Committee's public hearings in the sensationalism of its substance, it actually occurred more than a year before Kennedy's assassination.

José Alemán, by the way, died in August, 1983, in a volley of Miami police gunfire after he had shot four of his relatives, killing an aunt and seriously wounding his six-year-old cousin. Alemán was reportedly shouting epithets against Communism and the Castro regime when he died.

When I finally got to Washington during that last week of the public hearings, I immediately set about expanding the anti-Castro narrative that Blakey was scheduled to present. Since Odio and Veciana weren't going to be there, I was more intent than ever that their stories be told to the American people. If Blakey presented them properly, their stories might still have some impact. So I wrapped up the narrative and put it into the system for approval. Subsequently, neither Cornwell nor Blakey indicated they wanted to discuss any part of it with me. But the night before it was to be presented, I checked the final typed draft and noticed that a very significant fact had been eliminated from the Veciana narrative, an omission that went directly to the heart of his credibility.

Deleted from Veciana's story was the fact that the State Department had confirmed his employment by the United States Government, that he had worked for the Agency for International Development as a bank consultant in La Paz, Bolivia, and that his application for the job had been accepted and approved, although he had never signed it. That indicated that someone connected to the U.S. Government had pulled some strings for him. The point lent credibility to his contention that his AID job was just a cover for the counterintelligence work he was doing on behalf of Maurice Bishop.

I walked into Blakey's office and asked him why such an important point had been eliminated. Blakey said it was because he didn't want to get into a hassle with the CIA before it was necessary. After the final report was written, he declared, if we felt it necessary we could have a knock-down-drag-out fight with the Agency over what information should be released.

I found it interesting that Blakey was assuming that the CIA would be sensitive to evidence indicating it had been involved in pulling strings for Veciana. But Blakey's caution, I explained, was unneccessary in this instance because this bit of information had not come from the CIA, it had been developed when I worked for Senator Schweiker, and I had brought it to the Assassinations Committee myself. The information had originally come from the State Department and it was not classified in any way.

Blakey pretended to miss my point. "Well, in any case," he said, "we've just got too much to do to get into a hassle with the Agency at this point." He quickly dismissed me and turned to other staffers waiting to see him.

The next day, when it came time to present the anti-Castro Cuban narrative and the stories of Silvia Odio and Antonio Veciana to the American public, Blakey turned to Congressman Stokes and said: "Mr. Chairman, in light of the time pressures that the Committee is operating under today, I would like to ask permission that the narration on the anti-Castro Cubans be inserted into the record as if read."

At the conclusion of its public hearings, the House Select Committee on Assassinations had been in existence for more than two years. Officially, it had but three months left. During that time, its dwindling staff, characterized by a numb and glassy-eyed determination to simply finish its job, worked into the night on the various team summaries for the final report.

In those last months, Chief Counsel Blakey's preoccupation was with the results of the acoustics tests. A police radio tape of the sounds in Dealey Plaza when Kennedy was shot had been analyzed by an acoustics expert, Dr. James E. Barger, from the firm that had been appointed by Judge John Sirica to examine the eighteen-minute gap in the Watergate tape. There was no doubt that the tape recordings, as analyzed, indicated that more than three shots were fired, likely even more than four. In a conference with Blakey and Cornwell the evening before his scheduled appearance at the public hearings, Dr. Barger had held strong to that opinion—and that meant conspiracy. Blakey was ecstatic that the hearings would finally have the sex appeal that Congressmen so appreciate. The next day, however, under the pressure of the public spotlight and feeling very much alone as the only witness testifying on the matter, Dr. Barger toned down his conclusion to a "50–50 chance" of a fourth shot.

Cornwell stomped back to the offices from the hearing room cursing a blue streak and yelling as if he had been personally betrayed. Blakey's administrative flunky, Charlie Mathews, threw his arms in the air and shouted, "He didn't testify to what we *paid* him to testify to!"

Blakey would later claim that when he came to the Assassinations Committee he felt that a conspiracy was "highly unlikely." In fact, many on the staff appeared quite upset when Blakey early on appeared to be ready to confirm the Warren Commission's conclusions, despite all the contradictions.** But then, when the acoustics results finally

---

**Among those who were most upset were the three law students Blakey had brought with him from Cornell by convincing them that a year's sabbatical from school would provide them with invaluable experience in how government worked. It was not what they expected. Originally his devoted partisans, they were quickily disillusioned. Blakey told them their criticisms were "immature." One, Leslie Wizelman, who had been initially assigned to thoroughly review the Warren Commission's findings, was in Washington only four months when she sent Blakey a memo headed "The Future of My Immaturity." In it, she wrote: "I find myself greatly frustrated about my role on this Committee. I will have very serious difficulties writing a report that concludes the Warren Commission was right. I simply do not believe it. It appears that certain theories have been developed and conclusions have been established. It would be interesting to have someone . . . tell us upon what they are based. In addition, it would

gave Blakey the hook onto which he could hang his Organized Crime conspiracy theory, he wasn't about to let it slip out of his hands. So he hired auxiliary experts and conducted additional field tests in Dallas, and he got it. The Assassinations Committee was able to conclude that there was a "95 percent probability" that a fourth shot was fired from the grassy knoll.***

Of course, one problem with concluding that there *was* a conspiracy is that it ignored the fact that such a conclusion impugned the validity of a lot of the physical evidence which the Committee had spent a couple of hundred thousand dollars scientifically analyzing. And it also raises the question of whether many of the pieces of evidence—including the autopsy photos, the x-rays and the bullet fragments—so scientifically analyzed were really authentic or, as some critics were charging, concocted or tampered with. In the end, the Assassinations Committee's final report quiveringly declared: "President John F. Kennedy was probably assassinated as the result of a conspiracy."

Thus spoke the Congressmen. Then dutifully closed up shop. And G. Robert Blakey, before he assumed a new, prestigious post at Notre Dame's Law School, sat down with Dick Billings, the former *Life* magazine editor who had helped Blakey write the final version of the Committee's report, and together they wrote a book about how the Committee concluded that Organized Crime killed President Kennedy. The book had the tone of authenticity because they had access to Committee files and documents that Blakey had arranged would be withheld from the public for fifty years.

---

be very interesting to know if we are going to actively investigate the Kennedy assassination."

***The debate over the accuracy and methodology of the Committee's acoustic results is still in progress. The National Academy of Sciences reviewed the tape of the gun shots and decided the sounds were not all gun shots, perhaps just static. Committee expert Dr. Barger defended his analysis, claiming his methodology was much less subject to error than the Academy's. Blakey, too, blasted the Academy for, ironically, failing to do a complete enough study. In a memorandum printed in the Congressional Record three years after the Committee's report, Blakey also pointed out that the Committee's findings of a shot from the grassy knoll was based on factors other than just the sounds from the police radio tape, including testimony of witnesses near the grassy knoll who heard and saw signs of gun fire. That, of course, contradicts Blakey's position prior to receiving the results of the Committee's acoustics tests, when he was ready to dismiss such evidence outright and have the final report declare there was no conspiracy.

THIRTY-TWO

SIGNALS FROM 'THE NIGHT WATCH'

So FAR, what we've been dealing with is how the Assassinations Committee went in the direction it did. The question that remains is: Why?

The answer goes far beyond a predisposition on the part of the Committee's Chief Counsel, beyond the narrow, self-centered political perspective of Congress. The answer goes to the heart of what the U.S. Government doesn't want to tell the American people about the assassination of President Kennedy. That's the other part of the story, the part that explains why a critical area of evidence was given only token consideration.

Antonio Veciana, a relevant and credible witness, had alleged that an intelligence operative who used the name of Maurice Bishop was associating with Lee Harvey Oswald immediately before President Kennedy was assassinated. That was evidence in the realm of the Committee's mandate and it screamed for attention. It was evidence which demanded that an intensive and thorough effort be made to prove or disprove it.

That never happened. The early political and organizational chaos, the establishment of priorities not related to the substance of the case, the subsequent restrictions imposed upon the selection of key issues, the diffusion and then decimation of investigative resources, the preference for concentrating efforts on Organized Crime rather than taking on the intelligence establishment—all were factors which dictated the Assassinations Committee's ultimate handling of and its conclusions about the revelations of Antonio Veciana.

And so, because it did not conduct "a full and complete" investigation, the Committee had to distort the facts in its final report in order to justify its conclusion—and cover its ass.

For $5.5 million, the American people should have at least gotten the bare facts.

On September 20th, 1976, I wrote an informal memorandum to Senator Richard Schweiker detailing exactly what happened when Antonio Veciana, Sarah Lewis and I met David Atlee Phillips at the luncheon meeting of the Association of Retired Intelligence Officers in Reston. The memo eventually became Document No. 013455 in the files of the House Select Committee on Assassinations.

It began: "Instead of finally resolving anything, the confrontation between Veciana and David Phillips on Friday in Reston only raised a lot more questions in my mind. . . ."

It concluded: "I must admit I have some strange feelings about all this. As you know, as a result of having spent so many hours with him and going over his story in such detail . . . I'm convinced that Veciana is telling us the truth about his contacts with Bishop, but now, for the first time, I have some doubts about Veciana's credibility when it comes to Phillips. . . ."

The memo noted that Veciana's attitude appeared to have changed from when I had first met him six months earlier, largely as a result of his getting involved again in the intrigues of Miami's anti-Castro strategists. The memo then speculated: "Veciana may now feel that it won't pay to identify Bishop and, in fact, if Bishop knows he can do so at any moment, he might find that an incentive to get back into action with Veciana. . . . They may both feel that they can wait for all this to blow over, even if it's a year or two. . . ."

A few months later, confirmation of Veciana's anti-Castro activity came when an informant told me that Veciana had recently undertaken a secret mission to Latin America to deliver an explosive device. Another indication came when the FBI told Veciana that it had information that an attempt was going to be made on his life. Declaring Castro the perpetrator of the plan, Veciana publicized the warning and thus, he claimed, aborted the attempt. Then Veciana told me that he very much wanted to get back in touch with Maurice Bishop.

As for David Atlee Phillips—well, it was becoming clear that it was more than coincidental how incredibly well he fit the puzzle named Maurice Bishop. Senator Schweiker was the first to observe that the composite sketch of Bishop was a very close likeness of Phillips. In addition, specific details about Bishop revealed by Veciana long before David Phillips had popped up had left an impression on me. One was the very unusual physical characteristic they shared—the dark, weathered, ellipses under their eyes. Another was Veciana's assumption that Bishop was a Texan. David Phillips grew up in Texas and still had family living in Fort Worth.

Then, early in 1977, David Phillips's fascinating "autobiography" appeared: *The Night Watch—25 Years of Peculiar Service* [Atheneum, N.Y.]. It would be misleading to characterize any published work by a competent intelligence agent as "revealing," especially one written by an expert in counterintelligence and propaganda. And David Phillips did, indeed, have a reputation among his peers as *the* expert in the field. His book does, however, provide relevant benchmarks.

David Atlee Phillips was born on Halloween, 1922, in Fort Worth. His father died when he was five, leaving his family a portfolio of oil stocks, lifetime membership in the country club he had founded and a house on the fourth green. The stocks collapsed in '29, but young David's mother went to work and sent him off to William and Mary College in Virginia. Phillips paints himself as a bit of a Fitzgeraldian party boy who, before the next term came around, was back home plodding through Texas Christian University for a period, and then selling cemetery plots.

More than anything, however, David Phillips wanted to be an actor. He spent a couple of years bumming around New York in the effort, but his road to glory was detoured by World War II, a stint in a German prison camp and a daring escape. After the war, he tried professional acting again, this time with a bit more success, and joined a couple of touring road shows for a while. Whenever possible during his Agency career, wherever he was stationed, Phillips would invariably start or join a little theater group.

In 1948, Phillips married his first wife, Helen Hausman Haasch, an airline stewardess. With a $200-a-month stipend from a producer's option on a play he wrote (it was never produced), he and his bride decided to go to Chile to live cheaply.

Life in Chile was made easier, Phillips said, because both he and his wife could speak the language. He had studied it casually in college and seriously while visiting Mexico. One of the reasons he was recruited by the CIA, Phillips claimed, was because of his fluent Spanish.

At first, Phillips wrote plays, attended classes at the University of Chile and joined a local theater group. Then came the opportunity to buy, with borrowed money, a small newspaper, *The South Pacific Mail,* and some secondhand presses for commercial printing. It was the purchase of the presses by an American, Phillips said, which attracted the interest of the CIA's chief of station in Santiago. Phillips was recruited to be a "part-time" agent at $50 a month. His salary was deposited in a Texas bank after going through a cover company in New York.

Eventually, Phillips was sent to New York for special training. In his book, he revealed the depth of secrecy which the CIA impresses upon its deep-cover recruits: "My training officer . . . took me to a brownstone in the East Seventies. It was a CIA safe house for training overseas personnel who were undercover, or anyone whose job was so sensitive that he was not allowed to visit Washington or the Agency training retreat in nearby Virginia. There were other agents in the safe house, but I never saw them. When I went to the john my instructor would check first to be sure it was not occupied by another student."

Phillips's three-week training session appears to have been a model for Antonio Veciana's training program in Cuba. Initially, Phillips was taught the tools of basic tradecraft—how to conduct surveillance and counter surveillance, set up clandestine meetings, employ deception techniques and run "dark alley" operations. Phillips was then told he had the qualifications the Agency looked for in a propaganda specialist and his training thereafter concentrated on the techniques of propaganda and political action. Phillips described it as a "freshman course." He noted: "It was some years later before I graduated into the more esoteric graduate schools of tradecrafts."

David Atlee Phillips thus began his journey into what would eventually be the deepest realms of the CIA's machinations and, from there, up the ladder of its bureaucracy to the highest operational echelons. His successes as an agent, some which are detailed in his book and some only obliquely hinted at, were mainly in the area of propaganda, psychological warfare and counterintelligence.

It was a swift rise. Only recently a part-time recruit in Chile, Phillips was selected by the Agency to play an important role in overthrowing Jacobo Arbenz's leftist regime in Guatemala in 1954. Phillips's task was to help set up a clandestine radio station in Mexico—the Voice of Liberation—and, while pretending to be broadcasting from within Guatemala, orchestrate a crescendo of false reports about legions of rebels which didn't exist and major battles which never took place. Under such a propaganda barrage, the Arbenz government fled the country before many real bullets could fly. Phillips later termed the technique, which he would use again, "the big lie."*

---

*In this, his first major assignment for the CIA, Phillips demonstrated a particular propensity for the mirror images so prevalent in counterintelligence tradecraft. For instance, part of the Voice of Liberation's mission was to generate disinformation that would foment a confusing array of rumors among the populace. One typical broadcast assured listeners: "It is not true that the waters of Lake Atitlán have been poisoned."

It was during the Guatemala operation that Phillips made some of the Agency contacts and close associations which would endure throughout his career. Among them was E. Howard Hunt. In his autobiography, Phillips describes Hunt as being "friendly, anxious to help me and considerate." (Phillips's kind characterization of Hunt is in marked contrast to the published and unpublished opinions of many of Hunt's CIA colleagues, most of whom refer to Hunt less than admiringly. Former CIA Deputy Director Ray Cline, for instance, considered Hunt eccentric and noted that he "had the reputation of being something of a zealot.") Phillips would later work very closely with Hunt during the planning of the Bay of Pigs invasion and in other, less visible, operations.

Although Phillips moved up to the highest rungs of the CIA ladder, he spent most of his career in the field, giving him a flexibility and a freedom of movement that a desk-bound Washington officer would not have. Even when headquartered in Washington as propaganda chief of the Bay of Pigs operations, Phillips regularly flew into Miami to check on the activities of the various front groups. He also played a major role in the Agency's actions in the Dominican Republic (where Mitch WerBell, assassination weapons expert, was a mysterious but prominent figure). Aside from a year and a half in Lebanon, Phillips's entire career was spent fighting the Communist menace in the Caribbean and Latin America. And most of the time, his sights were on the man the CIA considered the greatest Communist threat the hemisphere had ever known: Fidel Castro.

Keeping Veciana's story in mind, my attention was attracted by certain segments of Phillips's career. In a frayed and yellowing copy of the 1960 edition of the *Anglo-American Directory of Cuba*, there is a listing on page 92: "PHILLIPS, David Atlee (Amer.): . . . Public relations counselor, David A. Phillips Associates. . . ." In that pose, Phillips was a deep-cover operative in Havana, hobnobbing with media executives and newspaper reporters, lunching with the local businessmen and, ostensibly, pitching stories or clients. "My favorite luncheon place," he wrote, "was the Floridita restaurant in colonial Havana." Once he saw Hemingway there.

Phillips admitted that after he hung up his shingle as a public relations counselor, "No one rushed the door in any event, nor did I solicit clients." He noted, though, that he did eventually wind up with at least one client with which he briefly worked a trade for French lessons: the Berlitz Language School. In his book, however, Phillips discussed very little of what he actually did in Havana as a covert operative, saying only that he "put in a full day for CIA," and that he "handled" agents.

Another aspect of Phillips's career which interested me was his tour of duty in Mexico City in the early Sixties. The CIA had told the Warren Commission that Oswald had visited both the Cuban and Russian embassies there in attempts to get visas to travel to those countries. There was also a number of unsubstantiated reports which flowed out of Mexico City immediately following the Kennedy assassination, pointing to Castro or the Soviets as the instigators. Understanding what really happened in Mexico City was critical to solving the mystery of Kennedy's death.

From 1961 through the fall of 1963, Phillips was Chief of Covert Action in Mexico City. It is impossible to overemphasize the importance of Mexico City in the "Spy versus Spy" games going on at that time. It was the only place in the Western Hemisphere where every Communist country and every democratic country had an embassy, and it was a hotbed of intrigue. The Americans alone had fully staffed stations for the FBI, Army Intelligence and the CIA. To be the Chief of Covert Action in Mexico City was a prestigious job indeed. How well Phillips did his work is revealed by the fact that barely two years into his assignment—just prior to the Kennedy assassination—he was made Chief of Cuban Operations there. In both jobs his main activities were in propaganda, dirty tricks and counterintelligence, and his central focus was on maintaining a watch on Castro's intelligence agents, many of whom worked out of the Cuban Embassy.

The Assassinations Committee's first Chief Counsel, Richard Sprague, had run into a roadblock when he attempted to probe Phillips's activities in Mexico City. After G. Robert Blakey became Chief Counsel, an arrangement was made with the Agency to give Committee staffers who signed the CIA Secrecy Agreement access to previously restricted files (although there was a stipulation, which gave the Agency censorship rights over any information the Committee wanted to make public). The Committee was interested in a number of questions related to what Phillips actually did in monitoring Lee Harvey Oswald's actions in Mexico City: If Oswald was observed going into the Cuban and Soviet embassies, as the CIA said he was, where were the Agency's surveillance photos? If Oswald was heard talking with a Soviet intelligence officer, as the CIA said he was, where were the Agency's tape recordings of the conversation? Why did the CIA send a photograph to the Warren Commission of a man it said was Oswald when it was obviously not Oswald? Those were just some of the questions that fell directly into David Phillips's area of responsibility. He had to know the answers. And if he didn't, why didn't he?

Despite the fact that the Assassinations Committee did not answer all those questions in its final report, it nevertheless came to conclusions. And most of them are masterpieces of definitive statements injected with contradicting qualifiers, revealing more about the Committee's investigation and its relationship to the CIA than do all its pages of exposition and conclusions. For instance (italics added): *"Despite the unanswered questions*, the weight of the evidence supported the conclusion that Oswald was the individual who visited the Soviet Embassy and Cuban Consulate." It dismisses the Agency's handling of the Oswald case prior to the assassination as simply "deficient," and yet admits that *"the Committee was unable to determine* whether the CIA did in fact come into possession of a photograph of Oswald taken during his visits to the Soviet Embassy and Cuban Consulate in Mexico City, or whether Oswald had any associates in Mexico City."

The question of Phillips's veracity is not addressed in the Committee's final report. (In fact, David Phillips's name is not even mentioned in the report; it appears only in an appendix volume.) However, noted in one of the footnotes to the report is an important document titled, *Lee Harvey Oswald, the CIA and Mexico City*. This is a 300-page, comprehensive staff report written by two of the Committee's best researchers, Dan Hardway and Eddie Lopez. The CIA classified it as being much too sensitive for release to the public.

PART THREE

A VERY PECULIAR SERVICE

THIRTY-THREE

SQUIRMING OUT OF THE BOX

IN MY SEARCH for the real Maurice Bishop, the more I learned about David Atlee Phillips, the more I was struck by how snugly he fit the outline. Phillips's physical description, his interests, his job assignments; all were unwaveringly along the lines of almost everything Antonio Veciana had told me about Bishop, well before we even knew there was a David Phillips. Could this all be mere coincidence?

Of course it could—especially if there were other, conflicting factors which militated against the possibility. But there weren't. To the contrary, other aspects of Phillips's career made the fit even tighter. In 1968, for instance, at Bishop's suggestion and with his help, Veciana got his U.S. Government job with the Agency for International Development as a banking consultant in Bolivia. It was at that time, said Veciana, that his activities with Bishop went beyond schemes directed specifically against Castro to include strategies aimed at countering Communism throughout Latin America.

That's exactly when Phillips took on such responsibilities. Late in 1967, David Phillips had returned to Washington to accept a new assignment—Chief of the Cuban Operations Group of the CIA's Western Hemisphere Division. "Although I would report to the head of the Latin American affairs," he noted in his autobiography, "my responsibilities were worldwide: To keep tabs on Cuban preoccupations in Europe, Africa, Asia and the Middle East and in more than twenty countries in Latin America and the Caribbean, as well as to manage CIA espionage operations in Cuba. Professionally, it was a prestigious but demanding assignment.''

In my mind, however, the most significant of Phillips's ''responsibilities'' were those that had to do with Chile.

This from my notes from a tape-recorded interview with Antonio Veciana on March 16th, 1976, before we discovered Phillips:

> [Veciana says] although all of Bishop's plans against Castro failed, there were other plans, against other people, that didn't fail. He knows—he says there is no doubt—that Bishop was involved in the plan to dispose of Allende in Chile. That was one of his jobs. He knows that by the contacts in Chile that Bishop had. ''All the connections I had in Chile were given to me by Bishop.''

For instance, in the plot to kill Castro in Chile in 1971, one part of the plan called for the Chilean military to grab the assassins before Castro's own forces could get hold of them or kill them. That, said Veciana, had been arranged by Bishop. It was a strong indication that Bishop contacts in the Chilean military went very high.

In December, 1975, the Senate's Church Committee issued a staff report titled *Covert Action in Chile: 1963–1973*. It said:

> Was the United States directly involved, covertly, in the 1973 coup in Chile? The Committee has found no evidence that it was. However, the United States sought in 1970 to foment a military coup in Chile; after 1970 it adopted a policy, both overt and covert, of opposition to Allende; *and it remained in intelligence contact with the Chilean military, including officers who were participating in coup plotting.* [Italics added]

The Church report also noted that the CIA did not consult its Congressional oversight committees, as required by law, on most of its Chilean covert action projects. And while many were approved by President Nixon's executive oversight group (called the 40 Committee), some projects did not even have this cursory overview. As the Senate's report said: ''Congressional oversight committees were not consulted about projects which were not reviewed by the full 40 Committee. One of these was the Track II attempt to foment a military coup. . . .'' The chief of the Track II project was David Atlee Phillips.

Another relevant fact noted in that report was the huge amount of money available to the CIA's covert operatives in Chile. Of the total of $13 million the CIA poured into that country, more than $8 million was spent in the three years between the 1970 election and the military coup which toppled Allende. Since most of that was spent on propaganda and slipped to assets in media operations, Phillips had access to a great deal of cash. However, when Phillips testified in executive session before the House Select Committee on Assassinations, he scoffed at Veciana's contention that he was paid $253,000 in cash at the termination of his relationship with Maurice Bishop. Phillips said that was too large a sum of money for the CIA to pay out unvouchered or "off the books." As Chief of the Agency's Western Hemisphere Division, he said, "I would have had to know about it."

Veciana had told me that the beginning of the end of his relationship with Bishop came with the discovery of the unauthorized subplot to blame Russian agents for the Castro assassination attempt in Chile in 1971. I began to suspect that was only part of the reason when a close associate of Veciana's told me, and Veciana himself later admitted, that he was pushing to continue the efforts to kill Castro, and with ever more daring schemes. Bishop did not approve. That is the reason Veciana initially thought he was put out of action.

Another factor may have also played a part. In 1973, Phillips got promoted to his top Agency position. In his autobiography, Phillips told a self-effacing story about an incident which occurred shortly after he took over as Western Hemisphere Division boss—the highest level to which a CIA officer can climb without Presidential appointment. One weekend he received a report that a CIA agent had walked into the Chilean Embassy in Mexico City and offered information about a secret Agency plan. Phillips rushed to his office on Sunday and spent the entire day checking out the report, finally learning that the so-called defecting agent was a phony. On Monday morning, he writes, he was gently chastised by his superior, whom he calls "Abe," for not delegating the task to the proper subordinate. "The Division Chief had to delegate even the most intriguing cases and allow others to enjoy the excitement of running operations . . ."

"Abe was right," Phillips admitted. "I soon found that 95 percent of my time must be devoted to mundane management matters and only a precious few moments to the more interesting development and direction of operations." Perhaps, then, Phillips realized that the job of keeping tabs on Veciana was taking more time than he could now devote to it, so he cut Veciana loose.

When Phillips's book, *The Night Watch*, was published, it became an irresistible exercise for me to scrutinize it for clues. Although his autobiography couldn't avoid a few broad revelations, it was cleverly constructed to reveal as little information as possible about the details of his many covert actions. Yet the question that the book evokes, more in essence than in substance, is whether or not this autobiography is, in itself, a charade, or did it merely a reflect the charade that was Phillips's life? (I came to suspect that Phillips may, indeed, have been one of the very best covert agents the CIA ever had. His former wife once told a friend, "He lies in his sleep.") Indeed, his book may inadvertently contain just one mirror too many and, finally, reflect a man who was simply duplicitous.

Phillips, for instance, portrayed himself as a moderate liberal; he claimed that he had voted for George McGovern and for Hubert Humphrey when they were Presidential candidates. He also would have his readers believe that he possessed a levelheaded moral and philosophical objectivity, that he was a man who agonized much over the ethical and legal implications of his covert operations. Yet his career was rich with Agency honors, rewards and promotions for his repeated successes as a dirty-tricks expert. And he boasted openly about his role in dislodging democratically elected left-wing governments, as in Chile. Moreover, the real David Phillips was closely associated with top figures in the military-industrial complex, as well as with the most hawkish of the nation's right-wing power brokers.

For instance, as previously noted, I discovered that his friendship with Clare Boothe Luce extends to her board position on his Association of Former Intelligence Officers. This was an advantageous relationship for Phillips because, as the wife of Time, Inc. board chairman Henry Luce, she was an influential figure in the operations of her husband's publications. I recall talking with former *Life* correspondent Andrew St. George early in 1976, before I had even heard the name David Phillips. St. George told me that one of the many ways in which *Life* was cooperating with the CIA was in its boosting of Alpha 66. "We would run these various stories and reports which made it appear much larger and much more important an organization than it in fact was."

One point in Phillips's autobiography that was particularly relevant for me was how he handled the question of his involvement in or knowledge of assassination plots against Fidel Castro.

During the heyday of the CIA's operations against Castro, David Phillips was one of the most important figures in the Agency's anti-Castro plotting. Yet, in his autobiography, Phillips surprisingly claimed a lack of awareness of any assassination plans and, in fact, relegated the point to a footnote:

> I have often been asked how it was possible that I did not know of the Castro assassination schemes. The question is usually predicated on the assumption that when I became Chief of Cuban Operations and then head of all Latin American Affairs someone would have told me, or I would have read about the endeavors in documents in my safe. The fact is that those few CIA officers involved did not discuss their participation even with senior officers not in the chain of command at the time of the

plots. And highly sensitive papers are not retained in a division chief's office. . . .

In his book, Phillips did, by the way, admit knowing of a coup plot by anti-Castro rebels, which occurred while he was still a deep-cover operative in Havana. He says he was asked by his case officer to undertake a "special" mission and approach the rebel group as an American anxious to assist anyone plotting against Castro. He was to find out the details of the plan and report back. Phillips said he cultivated one of the conspirators, attended a secret conclave of the group and reported that he thought the plot would fail. Shortly afterwards, a Castro informant broke up the scheme and several of the plotters were arrested.

One detail in this story that drew my interest was Phillips's thoughts on the various methods by which he could approach the plotters: "It would be tricky," he wrote. "I could approach and cultivate one of the conspirators using a false identity, perhaps in disguise." Disguises, I have learned, do not have to be blatant or sophisticated; sometimes they're just subtle enough to avoid instant recognition. Phillips was an actor, so using disguises makes a lot of sense. But I also found it interesting that it was a ploy favored by one of Phillips's admired associates: E. Howard Hunt. Hunt has admitted repeatedly using disguises in his covert work. And while on his White House Plumbers operations, Hunt still drew them from the resources of the CIA's Technical Services Bureau.

Because his testimony was already on record with the Church Committee and so couldn't be brushed aside, because he did fit into the "issues plan" (albeit in an oblique way), and because it was an area I kept pushing, Antonio Veciana was finally brought to Washington on April 25th, 1978 to testify in executive session before the House Select Committee on Assassination. David Phillips was scheduled to testify immediately after Veciana. That was not coincidental. I was hoping that Veciana and Phillips might encounter each other in the hallway outside the hearing room.

That day, Veciana again testified under oath that David Phillips was not the person he knew as Maurice Bishop. He admitted, however, that there was a "physical similarity."

When Veciana was finished, I walked out by his side. I saw Phillips talking with someone immediately outside the door. He glanced up, looked at Veciana, glanced at me and quickly turned back to his conversation. Veciana also spotted Phillips. He leaned over to me and said with a half-smile on his face, "There's David Phillips."

After I had escorted Veciana out of the building, I returned to the hearing room to listen to Phillips. He was again being questioned about his knowledge of Oswald's activities in Mexico City and the validity of his previous testimony. Then the questioning came around to Veciana and Bishop.

David Phillips said he never, ever used the name of Maurice Bishop. (Although CIA covert operatives have registered pseudonyms, most also use operational aliases with their field contacts. These are not registered and are changed at will.) Phillips also said he did not know of anyone in the CIA who used the name Maurice Bishop. When asked if he knew Antonio Veciana, Phillips came on strong, his voice edged with a controlled restraint, as if he were getting sick and tired of having to put up with such nonsense. He said he had seen Veciana only twice in his life, the second time that very morning as Veciana was emerging from the hearing room. The first time he met Veciana, Phillips said, was at a meeting of the Association of Former Intelligence Officers in Reston.

I was facing Phillips's right side, sitting at a staff table, a level below the U-shaped Congressional dais. Kennedy Subcommittee Chairman Richardson Preyer, the white-haired North Carolina Representative, was presiding. As I listened I was struck by how credible Phillips sounded as he began to speak about an incident with which I was personally familiar.

Phillips said that Veciana was brought to the Reston meeting by an investigator from Senator Schweiker's office but that he was not introduced to Veciana by name. Veciana, he said, was introduced to him only as "the driver." He said that Veciana asked him some questions in Spanish, and he had the feeling that Veciana did that in order to hear his accent. But he did not say what questions Veciana asked him. At the time, Phillips said, he did not know who Veciana was or why Schweiker's office had sent him to the meeting. Later, of course, he said, he read about Veciana in Jack Anderson's column.

I was shocked. An impulse flashed through me to jump up and shout: *"That's not true!"* I had personally introduced them *twice* at the luncheon in Reston. In fact, Phillips had even asked Veciana, "What was your name again?" and Veciana had told him. And when Veciana had asked Phillips if he remembered him, Phillips had said no, that he didn't.

I was there. Veciana was there. Sarah Lewis was there. It was documented in my reports, written immediately afterwards. What was Phillips trying to pull? This was *sworn* testimony. I was dumbfounded.

Of course, thinking about it, I realized what a box Phillips was in. At the Reston encounter, he had been caught by surprise and, when hit immediately with Veciana's name, his first reaction was defensive, to deny any knowledge of Veciana. That was a terrible blunder for a man whose whole career had been devoted to anti-Castro operations. Phillips had no choice but to cover it up by denying he was ever introduced to Veciana by name.

Phillips obviously thought—or knew—he could get away with that brazen ploy. And he was right.

Later, I talked to Chief Counsel Bob Blakey. "Do you realize that David Phillips lied in his testimony," I said. I thought, *Now* we had him.

Blakey raised his eyebrows. "Oh, really," he said. "What about?"

I gave him the details. He listened carefully, thought silently for a moment, shrugged his shoulders and walked away.

THIRTY-FOUR

SHOW & TELL IN MEXICO CITY

I WATCHED AS David Phillips, his hands shaking noticeably, lit his third cigarette. He had forgotten he had two already burning, hardly touched, sitting on the lip of the ashtray. It was August, 1978, and Phillips had been called in to the Assassinations Committee headquarters for "informal" questioning about his activities in Mexico City. He had already appeared twice before the Committee in executive sessions. In his initial appearance late in 1976, shortly after the Committee was formed, Phillips was questioned by the Committee's then-Chief Counsel Richard Sprague about the CIA's Mexico City activities. It was, unfortunately but of necessity, a superficial interrogation because the Agency had refused to provide documents related to Phillips's role there. Phillips's second executive session, in April 1978, dealt mostly with questions generated by Antonio Veciana's testimony earlier that same day and indications that Phillips was "Maurice Bishop." However, Phillips had responded to a request for informal questioning by the staff—aware, of course, that he could be subpoenaed if he refused—and voluntarily appeared at Committee headquarters for an "off the record" session. The questioning would center on Mexico City. It was a key piece of the Oswald puzzle, so knowing what Phillips did or didn't do there was important.

Although I wasn't directly involved in the Mexico City aspect of the investigation, I was interested in it for several interlocking reasons: Although the CIA Station Chief there at the time was the late Win Scott, an enigmatic fellow who played his cards close to the vest and let his agents roll free, Phillips ran most of the operations, first as Chief of Covert Actions and, later, Chief of Cuban Operations. That meant that *if* Oswald was in Mexico City and *if* he were involved in any intelligence activity, whether pro- or anti-Castro, Phillips would have been either a player, or he would have known about it.

In addition, as the person directly responsible for monitoring Cuban spy activity in Mexico City, Phillips had to know that Guillermo Ruíz, Antonio Veciana's cousin, was a ranking Cuban intelligence officer there. Maurice Bishop had told Veciana he knew of Ruíz and his position and had attempted, through Veciana, to plant a false story linking Oswald to Ruíz. That smacked of a ploy straight out of a propaganda expert's bag of tricks. Another factor focusing attention on Phillips was his expertise in counterintelligence misinformation ploys and his success in using them. Immediately after the Kennedy assassination, Mexico City was a source of stories, all of which were impossible to document, pointing to a Castro or Soviet connection to Oswald. At least one of these Mexico City stories was planted to get the attention of higher authorities.

After Oswald was murdered by Jack Ruby, a young Nicaraguan named Gilberto Alvarado Ugarte walked into the American Embassy and insisted he had a story to tell Ambassador Thomas Mann. Alvarado claimed that he had gone to the Cuban Embassy in September and, while waiting to conduct some business, had seen three persons talking on a patio a few feet away. One was Lee Harvey Oswald, another a tall, thin Negro with reddish hair and the third a Cuban from the consulate. Alvarado said he saw the Cuban give the Negro a large sum of money and then heard the Negro tell Oswald, "I want to kill the man." Oswald replied, "You're not man enough. I can do it." The Negro then gave Oswald $5000 in large denomination American bills. Their conversation, said Alvarado, was in both Spanish and English.

The story caused quite a stir with Ambassador Mann, a hard-boiled anti-Communist who, even before Alvarado showed up, was pushing the FBI to investigate a Castro link to the assassination. It would later become one of the first pieces of "evidence" to plant the seed of suspicion of a foreign conspiracy in President Johnson's mind, a fear he used to push Earl Warren into the job of assuring the American people there was no conspiracy. The seed was planted, but the story never did check out. Alvarado subsequently retracted his story, saying he had fabricated it because he wanted to get to the United States to join the anti-Castro activists. Then he recanted his retraction; and then, failing a polygraph test given by the Mexican police, again confessed he had lied. Nevertheless, Alvarado's claims were brought to the attention of the Warren Commission by CIA boss

Richard Helms. In its final Report, the Commission devoted two entire pages to Alvarado's story.

The Warren Commission, however, had never really considered the source of the story: Alvarado, it was later discovered, was an agent of the Nicaraguan intelligence service. Nicaraguan dictator Anastasio Somoza was one of the CIA's most powerful and well-paid assets, having permitted the Agency to use his country as a training camp and assembly grounds for a second Cuban invasion after the Bay of Pigs failure. In fact, at the time of the Kennedy assassination, the Bay of Pigs' military chief, Manuel Artime (dubbed "the CIA's Golden Boy") was still running guerrilla raids out of two training bases in Nicaragua and holding on to a huge arsenal of equipment. (After the bases were closed, Artime became partners with Somoza in the beef-exporting business.) Also at that time, Artime was involved in a Castro assassination plot with his personal friend and Miami Shores neighbor, E. Howard Hunt. (Hunt, you may recall, was a highly regarded friend of Phillips, and Phillips's first wife, Helen, has said that Hunt was a frequent visitor to their house in Mexico City.)

The type of incident the Alvarado fabrication represents has the clear hallmarks of a counterintelligence scheme, a shrewd ploy loaded with diverse angles, from the ridiculous to the sublime. However ludicrous the scenario, it requires time and effort to investigate and, although discredited, in the end it leaves ripples, further muddying already murky waters.

As a Nicaraguan intelligent agent working out of Mexico City, Alvarado was one of David Phillips's assets. There may have been others more strategically placed. For instance, the CIA had provided the Assassinations Committee with this "blind" memorandum, meaning it came without notation of origin or destination:

1. A reliable source reported that on November 22, 1963, several hours after the assassination of President John F. Kennedy, Luisa Calderon Carralero, a Cuban employee of the Cuban embassy in Mexico City, and believed to be a member of the Cuban Directorate General of Intelligence (DGI), discussed news of the assassination with an acquaintance. Initially, when asked if she had heard the latest news, Calderon replied, in what appeared to be a joking manner, "Yes, of course, I knew almost before Kennedy."

2. After further discussion of the news accounts about the assassination, the acquaintance asked Calderon what else she had learned. Calderon replied that they [assumed to refer to personnel of the Cuban Embassy] learned about it a little while ago.

When Blakey and a few of the Committee staffers went to Cuba to talk with Castro, they attempted to interview Calderon. She refused to be questioned, saying she was ill, but she did respond to written questions and denied any foreknowledge of the assassination. The Assassinations Committee was never able to confirm if Calderon was one of the double agents the CIA had in the Cuban Consulate but, if so, she would have been one of David Phillips's assets. (Phillips, citing loss of memory, would only acknowledge that her name was "familiar.") The point of the original story, however, remained on the record: Cuban intelligence could have had something to do with Kennedy's assassination.

Yet the pattern of misinformation flowing out of Mexico City is only a small part of what makes that area the most intriguing of the mystery. Its relation to the assassination is abundant with mirror images and infused with contradictions so compelling they smack of deliberate design. The very existence of that design may portend the answer.

The Warren Report said: "Oswald departed from New Orleans probably about noon on September 25 and arrived in Mexico City at about 10 a.m. on September 27." (That was the same period when Silvia Odio said, "Leon Oswald" and the two Latin men had arrived at her apartment in Dallas.) The FBI reports to the Warren Commission indicate that Lee Harvey Oswald boarded a connecting Continental Trailways bus in the early morning hours of September 26, 1963, somewhere in southern Texas. He appeared determined to make himself memorable to his fellow passengers, introducing himself to two young Australian girls riding in the back and, moving about the bus, to an older couple from England. He was exceptionally gregarious, even a bit gabby, talking at length about his times in the Marines and his life in the Soviet Union. He mentioned he was with the Fair Play for Cuba Committee in New Orleans and that he was traveling through Mexico to get to Cuba—he said he even hoped to see Fidel.

The Warren Commission reported that a "Lee Harvey Oswald" registered at the Hotel Comercio, spent his leisure hours alone, perhaps went to a movie or a bullfight and had a few cheap meals at a restaurant near the hotel. (The Commission did not include in its report the fact that another resident of the hotel told the FBI that he had seen Oswald with four Cubans, one of whom had come from Florida.) The Commission concluded that after six days in Mexico City, Oswald returned to the United States by bus.

What Oswald actually did during those six days is a puzzle. In fact, part of the puzzle is whether or not it was the real Oswald in Mexico City.

According to the Warren Report, just before lunchtime on September 27th, a young American walked into the Cuban Consul's office in

Mexico City. Hesitantly, he asked the Consul's assistant, a Mexican woman named Silvia Duran, if she spoke English. She did. He said his name was Lee Harvey Oswald and that he needed a transit visa through Cuba to go to the Soviet Union. He said he was in a hurry because he wanted to leave within three days and stay a couple of weeks in Cuba. He had plenty of credentials—passports, documents from the Soviet Union, correspondence with the American Communist Party, his membership in the Fair Play for Cuba Committee—and claimed he should be accepted as "a friend of the Cuban Revolution."

Silvia Duran was suspicious of the young man's overstated allegiance to Communism. She told him she couldn't give him a transit visa through Cuba without his having permission from the Soviet Embassy for travel to Russia. He would also need photographs for his visa application and she directed him to a nearby passport photo studio.

The American returned a few hours later with the pictures. Duran accepted his application, not paying much attention to it, and told him it would take about a week to process. The man got upset. "Impossible," he said. "I can only stay in Mexico for three days." Duran said she couldn't do anything about it and the man left.

He returned again early in the evening, just after the Consulate had closed to the public, and managed to talk his way into seeing Duran again. Now he said he had been to the Soviet Embassy and was told that his Soviet visa would be granted, so the Cubans could issue him their visa immediately. Duran decided to check the Soviets herself, called the Russian Embassy and was told they knew about Oswald but approval from Moscow could take three or four months. (Whether or not Oswald himself talked to the Russians at this point is a question: Duran says he didn't, but the CIA has transcripts of tapes indicating that at one point in her call to the Soviets she handed the telephone to Oswald. He did speak to them, reportedly in broken Russian, which is curious because Oswald actually spoke the language very well.) So when Duran reiterated that she couldn't issue a Cuban visa without Russian consent, the American got irate, started yelling, said his tourist permit in Mexico was about to expire and he had to get to Russia immediately. Duran was forced to call the Cuban Consul, Eusebio Azcue, out of his office. Azcue and the young man argued and Azcue ordered him out of the building.

The source of that information—and almost all the other information the Warren Commission received about Oswald's activities in Mexico City—was the CIA. The Agency let it be known that its "highly confidential and reliable sources" included telephone taps, wall bugs and inside informants. The CIA told the Commission of Oswald's visits to the Cuban consulate and said it had photographs of

Oswald visiting the Soviet Embassy and tape recordings of Oswald telephoning the Soviets and asking for a "Comrade Kostin." (That, the Agency said, was a code name for Valery Kostikov, a Russian officer in charge of the KGB's Department Thirteenth, which was responsible for assassinations and sabotage.) The CIA said its tape recording revealed that Oswald asked Kostin, "Are there any messages for me?"

The CIA also got the cooperation of the Mexican Security Police, who interrogated Silvia Duran and obtained her confirmation of Oswald's visit. All the CIA's documentation was forwarded to the Warren Commission by Richard Helms, the Deputy Director for Plans.

The Warren Commission was obviously impressed with the Agency's claim of having documentation for such dynamite revelations but, in the end, the CIA never gave the Warren Commission any photographs or tape recordings of Oswald in Mexico City.

On the day that President Kennedy was assassinated, the CIA sent one of the photographs it had taken of "Oswald" in Mexico City to the FBI. The photo was of a man who was husky, beefy-faced, balding and clearly not Lee Harvey Oswald. The CIA later told the Warren Commission there had simply been a "mix-up" and that it could explain it. It never did. The man in the photograph was never identified.

The CIA maintained complete, back and front, photographic surveillance on both the Cuban and Soviet embassy compounds. Presumably, the cameras were working properly in early October, 1963, when they photographed an American visiting the Soviet Embassy. That presumption is based on a cable CIA headquarters sent on October 10, 1963, to the FBI, the Navy and the Department of State:

> On 1 October 1963 a reliable and sensitive source in Mexico reported that an American male, who identified himself as Lee OSWALD, contacted the Soviet Embassy in Mexico City inquiring whether the Embassy had received any news concerning a telegram which had been sent to Washington. The American was described as approximately 35 years old, with an athletic build, about six feet tall, with a receding hairline.
>
> It is believed that OSWALD may be identical to Lee Henry [sic] Oswald, born on 18 October, 1939, in New Orleans, Louisiana. A former Marine who defected to the Soviet Union in October 1959 and later made arrangements through the United States embassy in Moscow to return to the United States with his Russian-born wife, Marina Nikolaevna Pusakova [sic], and their child.

The description of the "Oswald" in the cable did not, of course, fit the real Lee Harvey Oswald. It did, however, fit the description of the man in the photograph the CIA sent to the other agencies on November 22nd. Didn't the CIA know what Oswald looked like? The Agency certainly acted as if it had no idea because on October 4th, three days after the photo of the unidentified man was taken, the CIA asked the Office of Naval Intelligence to forward it two of its most recent photographs of Oswald. By November 22nd, the Navy had not yet sent them.

What makes this all relevant to David Atlee Phillips? As head of Cuban Operations in Mexico City, he was the person responsible for the surveillance, the photographs and all the cables being sent around.

The day after the assassination, Phillips had lunch with his good friend Carl Migdale, chief of the *U.S. News & World Report*'s Mexico City bureau. "Thank God," Phillips told Migdale, "that we reported on Oswald being here in September, otherwise my organization might be in danger of being eliminated." While he didn't explain what he meant by that, it's interesting that Phillips made sure a reporter was among the first to know of Oswald's visit.

From the start, the House Assassinations Committee recognized that penetrating the riddle of both Oswald's and the CIA's activities in Mexico City was critical to its investigation. When Dick Sprague had attempted to check out certain points in Phillips's testimony, the CIA threw up an effective roadblock, refused Sprague access to the files unless he signed the CIA's secrecy oath. Sprague declared that would be in direct conflict with his mandate, which included considering the CIA as a possible target of his investigation. Today, Sprague still feels it wasn't coincidental that the increase in the political and media attacks that eventually forced him out began after he threatened to fight the CIA all the way.

In its final report, the House Assassinations Committee appeared to come to a definitive conclusion about Oswald's activities in Mexico City. "The Committee found no evidence of any relationship between Oswald and the CIA." But Chief Counsel Blakey, the guiding proponent of that conclusion, knew that the Committee's principal researchers and investigators working the Mexico City area believed there was a slew of "evidence" to indicate that the CIA was very much involved in Oswald's activities.*

---

*One of the most interesting and, certainly, insightful comments made about the mystery of Mexico City came when Assassinations Committee Chairman Lou Stokes asked Fidel Castro about it. "You see, it was always very much suspicious to me," Castro said, "that a person who later appeared to be involved in Kennedy's death would have requested a visa from Cuba. Because, I said to myself—what would have happened had by any chance that man come to Cuba—visited Cuba—gone back to the

When David Phillips was first called before the Assassinations Committee by Dick Sprague, he was asked about the Oswald photo "mix-up." He said that on the day that Oswald visited the Soviet Embassy, the CIA's monitoring cameras weren't functioning. It was about that time, he said, that the tap on the Soviet Embassy's telephones picked up a call from someone who identified himself as "Lee Henry Oswald." The caller was concerned about the status of his application for a visa to visit the Soviet Union through Cuba. Phillips said the conversation was deemed important enough to forward to CIA headquarters and that the agent in charge of writing and sending the cable was given a transcript of the taped call and photographs of "an American" entering the Soviet Embassy at about the same time. The agent, claimed Phillips, mistakenly based his description of the caller on the photograph he was given, resulting in an inaccurate description of Oswald in the October 1st cable. Then, according to Phillips, the actual tape recording on which the transcript was based was destroyed by recycling about a week after it was received. (That would be about one month before the assassination.)

In an interview with Ronald Kessler of the *Washington Post* a few days before his Committee testimony, Phillips was a bit more dramatic. He said he had heard the tape and saw the transcript and that Oswald was trying to make a deal with the Soviets. Phillips recalled that Oswald told them, "I have information you would be interested in, and I know you can pay my way."

There was a problem with Phillips's claim that the tape recording had been routinely destroyed sometime in the middle of October. There is a memo dated November 23rd, 1963, from J. Edgar Hoover to Secret Service Chief James Rowley:

> The Central Intelligence Agency advised that on October 1, 1963, an extremely sensitive source had reported that an individual identifying himself as Lee Oswald contacted the Soviet Embassy in Mexico City inquiring as to any messages. Special Agents of this Bureau, who have conversed with Oswald in Dallas, Texas, have observed photographs of the individual referred to above and have listened to a recording of his voice. These Special Agents are of the opinion that the above-referred-to individual was not Lee Harvey Oswald.

How could the FBI agents *listen* to a tape recording that had been destroyed a month before? The House Committee solved that problem

States and then appeared involved in Kennedy's death? That would have really been a provocation—a gigantic provocation. . . . That is why it has always been something— a very obscure thing—something suspicious—because I interpreted it as a deliberate attempt to link Cuba with Kennedy's death."

by relying on the testimony of Gordon Shanklin, the FBI Special Agent-in-Charge in Dallas. Shanklin, who was backed by a couple of his fellow agents on this point, said the FBI report was mistaken, that the CIA had only sent photographs and the typed transcript, not a tape recording. That meant, of course, that Hoover's memo to another ranking agency boss simply contained a gross error. However, Shanklin was the original source of Hoover's memo and it's difficult to believe he didn't know the difference between reading a transcript and listening to a tape. (Shanklin's credibility has been called into question on another matter, when he reportedly ordered an FBI subordinate to destroy a note he had received from Oswald.**) Some researchers believe that Shanklin's claim that the CIA did not send a tape recording may be accurate but misleading. It's possible, they suggest, that the FBI agents simply listened to the tape as it was transmitted by telephone on a secure line.

Despite such a major discrepancy, and the fact that the occurrence couldn't be documented, the Assassinations Committee concluded that the tape had, indeed, been "routinely" destroyed.*** It also

---

**During the Church Senate Committee probe in 1975, the FBI finally admitted that Oswald had delivered a secret note to agent James Hosty at its Dallas office several days before the assassination. The note allegedly contained a threat against the FBI for harassing him. When Oswald was shot to death by Jack Ruby, Hosty ripped up the note and flushed it down the toilet. He claimed he was ordered to do that by Shanklin, his immediate superior. Shanklin denied it, but Shanklin's boss, assistant FBI Director William Sullivan, testified that Shanklin had often discussed an "internal problem" over a message from Oswald.

***Considering that the Committee knew David Phillips had lied under oath on other matters—specifically, about his activities at CIA's Mexico City station (as I'll detail later) and about his encounters with Alpha 66 leader Antonio Veciana—it's incredible that Chief Counsel Bob Blakey would have the Committee conclude Phillips was telling the truth about the tapes. Historically, that's likely to be one of the Committee's major embarrassments. In fact, Phillips's testimony concerning the "routine" destruction of the Oswald tapes is turning out to be the major crack in the wall of fabrications he built around his role in Mexico City. Researchers have recently developed evidence which raises fundamental questions about the validity of the information the CIA provided to both the Warren Commission and the Assassinations Committee.

Late in 1991, researchers Joseph Heyer and Jennifer Gers wrote to Warren Commission member William Coleman about a trip to Mexico City he took with Commission attorney W. David Slawson while handling the Commission's investigation into the possible involvement of foreign governments in the assassination. They were concentrating, of course, on Fidel Castro. The researchers asked Coleman about Oswald's activities in Mexico City. In a reply dated December 18th, 1991, Coleman wrote: "The Warren Commission had access to records which showed that Lee Harvey Oswald had contacted the Soviet Embassy and . . . the Cuban Embassy. We read the transcripts of what was actually said and *we heard the words being spoken.*" [Italics added]

Attempting to follow up, Gary Rowell, publisher of the JFK research journal *The Investigator,* attempted to question Slawson about the Oswald tapes. Slawson put

definitely concluded that Lee Harvey Oswald did appear at the Cuban and Soviet embassies, although the evidence supporting that finding was also anything but definitive. Said the final report:

> The Committee weighed the evidence on both sides of the Oswald-at-the-Cuban-consulate issue:
>
> That it was Oswald was indicated by the testimony of Silvia Duran and Alfredo Mirabal, who was in the process of succeeding Azcue as Cuban consul when the visit occurred in late September 1963. They both identified Oswald from the post-assassination photographs as the man who applied for a Cuban visa.
>
> That it was not Oswald was a possibility raised by the Committee's inability to secure a photograph of him entering or leaving the Soviet Embassy or the Cuban consulate. The Committee obtained evidence from the Cuban Government that such photographs were being taken routinely in 1963. Further, the Committee found that Oswald paid at least five visits to the Soviet Embassy or the Cuban consulate.

Not mentioned in that summary is that the Committee dismissed the testimony it had obtained from the former Cuban consul, Eusebio Azcue. Yet it was Azcue who, like Duran, had direct contact with the American. Mirabal only saw the action briefly from an adjoining office. Perhaps, it conjectured, "there was a sinister connection between Oswald and the Castro regime that Azcue was attempting to conceal."

Azcue told the Committee that, having returned to Cuba prior to

---

him off. So Rowell had his daughter Amanda write to Slawson concerning a school project on the Kennedy assassination. In a December 4, 1992 reply, Slawson states:

"Yes, I listened to the tape of Lee Harvey Oswald's telephone conversations with the Soviet Embassy in Mexico City. I did not feel that the voice sounded any different from what I expected his would sound like."

Yet Slawson devotes the rest of the letter explaining why it would be impossible to definitely ascertain whether or not it was really Oswald's voice. Among the points he makes is that wiretaps in the early 1960s did not give good sound reproductions and were "scratchy and full of static." He also notes that Oswald may have been disguising his voice, since he had repeatedly been warned by the Soviet official with whom he talked that "he should assume that the CIA was listening."

That confirmation of the existence of the Oswald tapes as late as the middle of 1964, contradicting Phillips's sworn testimony that they were destroyed within weeks of the assassination, generates serious questions: Would Phillips have deliberately taken the risk of committing perjury in both 1975 and 1978 if he *knew* the tapes had not been destroyed by then? Was Phillips certain that the tapes were destroyed because Phillips himself had a role in destroying them? Were the tapes destroyed because it wasn't really Oswald's voice on them? If the tapes were destroyed *after* the Warren Commission members heard them, was it because the CIA feared future investigations might do what the Warren Commission didn't do—that is, subject them to authentications tests? And, finally, if the tapes were fraudulent, were they produced under the direction of the one specialist in the CIA who had the most experience in such communication ruses and psych warfare schemes, David Atlee Phillips himself?

the Kennedy assassination, he had assumed that the Lee Harvey Oswald arrested in Dallas was the same man he had encountered in Mexico City. It was only later when he went to a movie and saw a newsreel which included close-ups of Oswald in custody that Azcue realized that the man he met at the consulate "in no way resembled" Oswald. That man, said Azcue, was perhaps 35 years old and had dark blond hair. Although Azcue acknowledged it was Oswald's photo on the visa application, he told Blakey and the Committee members, he could "almost assure" them that the clothing Oswald wore in the photo wasn't the same as the clothing worn by the man he had encountered at the Consulate. (The FBI checked all the photo studios within miles of the Consulate and couldn't find one where Oswald had his photo taken.)

On the other hand, Silvia Duran said that the man she saw was Oswald, although her description didn't quite fit the real Oswald either. She, too, described him as older, much shorter, with lighter hair and a heftier build. The Assassinations Committee, however, was well aware of a factor that called into question the validity of Duran's testimony—her arrest by the Mexican Security police soon after the assassination. The CIA had provided the Warren Commission with reports of her interrogation, but didn't tell the Commission it was involved in having her arrested and held incommunicado for several days.

This from a CIA cable at the time:

> Arrest of Silvia Duran is extremely serious matter which could prejudice U.S. freedom of action on entire question of Cuban responsibility. . . . With full regard for Mexican interests, request you ensure that her arrest is kept absolutely secret, that no information from her is published or leaked, that all such info is cabled to us, and that fact of her arrest and her statements are not spread to leftist or disloyal circles in the Mexican government.

Silvia Duran was, according to her own written account, brutally arrested by the Mexican police. Lured to her brother-in-law's house, she was confronted by a squad of plainclothes policemen. She tried to make a telephone call but one of them grabbed her. When she struggled, two of them jumped on her and threw her down. With hands clamping her arms and mouth, she was led to a pickup truck and driven to Security Forces headquarters. There she was interrogated by five agents. "One in shirtsleeves with the face of a bulldog who puts his foot on the chair and blows smoke in my face. 'Are you a Communist?' he asks. More than talking he is barking. . . . After five hours of his interrogation the light seems as bright as the sun, my eyes and throat burn me. . . . 'Did you have sexual relations with Oswald?'. . . .''

After eight hours of this, Duran identified Oswald as the person who came into the Cuban consulate. When she was released, however, she began talking a bit too much about her experiences, which prompted the CIA to send another cable directing its Mexico City station to employ its assets in the Mexican police to arrest her again:

> . . . to be certain that there is no misunderstanding between us, we want to insure that Silvia Duran gets no impression that Americans are behind her rearrest. In other words we want Mexican authorities to take responsibility for the whole affair.

After the House Assassinations Committee report was released, author Anthony Summers tracked down Silvia Duran in Mexico. A journalist from Ireland, Summers had been involved in the production of a British Broadcasting television special on the Kennedy assassination. Having gotten a contract from McGraw-Hill to write a book on the subject, Summers, a forceful investigator, was doing a lot of fieldwork.

Silvia Duran had long before left her job at the Cuban Consulate and was working in a local Social Security office. She told Summers that her identification of Oswald had come largely from her recollection of the name, not from pictures she had seen. Summers had come with film footage of Oswald being interviewed in New Orleans after he was handing out pro-Castro leaflets and showed it to Silvia Duran. She said, "I was not sure if it was Oswald or not . . . the man on the film is not like the man I saw here in Mexico City."

In her own notes detailing the incident, Duran had written that the American at the consulate was not much taller than herself—she's less than five feet four inches—with blond hair and "blue or green eyes." (Oswald was near five-ten, had dark hair and brown eyes.) That was consistent with the description she had given the Assassinations Committee.

On that trip, Summers also spoke with a man named Oscar Contreras, who said he met a blond American calling himself Oswald in Mexico City in the fall of 1963. Committee investigators were never able to pin down Contreras. And Blakey, in his presentation to the Committee, made it appear that Contreras was deliberately avoiding them. Yet Summers found him quite easily in Tampico, where he is the editor of the local newspaper, *El Mundo*.

Contreras was then a law student at the National University and active in left-wing politics. He belonged to a pro-Castro student group and had contacts in the Cuban Embassy. One evening in the last week of September, Contreras and three friends from his political group emerged from a discussion meeting and stopped by the school cafeteria. An American sitting at a nearby table struck up a conversation, introducing himself as Lee Harvey Oswald. Contreras and his friends thought that was funny because "Harvey" and "Oswald" were rabbits in a Mexican cartoon popular at the time. Soon their newfound American friend was telling them of his problems trying to get to Cuba. He asked if they could help him through their contacts in the Cuban Consulate.

Later that evening, Contreras did call Ascue, whom he knew, as well as another friend who was a Cuban intelligence officer at the Embassy. Both advised him to stay away from the American. They told him they had become suspicious of the man and said he might be a provocateur attempting to penetrate left-wing groups. The next day, Contreras and his friends told Oswald that the Cubans did not trust him and that he would probably not be given a visa. Oswald, nevertheless, kept trying to ingratiate himself with them and, in fact, joined them in an all-night bull session. He left the next morning and that, said Contreras, was the last he saw of Oswald.

Contreras told Summers that he now doubts that the man really was Oswald. He, too, said the man he met was over thirty, light-haired and fairly short. Contreras, not very tall himself, remembers looking down on "Oswald the Rabbit."

What most intrigues me about this incident is that "Oswald" approached Contreras and his friends. He obviously knew they were members of a pro-Castro student group and that they had friends and contacts in the Cuban consulate. It seems like it was a set up. (And just as David Phillips, head of the CIA's Cuban Ops in Mexico City, had to have known about Antonio Veciana's cousin in Cuban intelligence, so he must have had knowledge of—and probably agents in—every pro-Castro group in Mexico. That was part of his job.)

In concluding that there were no traces of an intelligence connection to Oswald's activities in Mexico City, the Assassinations Committee swallowed a host of incredible claims by the CIA.

Is it credible, for instance, that at a time when relationships between the U.S. and Cuba and the Soviet Union were still tense, that the CIA would have permitted its surveillance cameras to remain nonfunctional for any length of time or be put off-line over the weekends? Or how, if the cameras were functioning, could they have missed Oswald on every one of his five trips to the Cuban and Soviet compounds?

The CIA had told the Warren Commission that, after it discovered on October 1st that "Lee Henry Oswald" had visited the Soviet Embassy, it had to ask Naval Intelligence for photos of Oswald to match against the photo of the man its surveillance cameras had captured. Is it really possible that the Central Intelligence Agency didn't have a photograph in its files of a former Marine who had defected to Russia? And if the CIA didn't have a photo of an American defector in its files, then there are only two possible explanations: The Agency was incredibly negligent or Oswald wasn't truly a defector.

Yet, after telling the Warren Commission it had no photo, the Agency later delivered to the Commission a folder on Oswald containing "exact copies of all material in this file up to early October 1963." In the folder were two newspaper clippings reporting Oswald's defection to the Soviet Union in 1959. Both featured very large photographs of the real Oswald.

It was against that background of Agency deceptions and inconsistencies that researchers Dan Hardway and Charles Berk and I sat down for our informal session with David Phillips that summer afternoon at Committee headquarters. Phillips was unaware of what direction the questioning was going to take and, it became apparent later, had obviously thought he was going to be grilled again about his being Maurice Bishop. His appearance at the Committee in executive session in which he testified he was not Bishop, and then lied about never having been introduced to Veciana by name, had occurred only a few months earlier. So it was natural he would assume we wanted to press him a bit more. That he was ready for. What he wasn't ready for was Dan Hardway's deep grilling about Mexico City.

It was Hardway's session all the way. (It was Committee procedure in "informal" interviews to have only one staffer ask all the questions in order to preclude charges of intimidation.) Eddie Lopez, Hardway's research partner in the Mexico City area was out of town; Chuck Berk was there because he was on the team investigating the pro-Castro links to the assassination. (Berk was also interested in CIA procedures and methods, something we were constantly trying to figure out in order to evaluate the credibility of the Agency's responses to our inquiries.) I had heard about the session only by chance that morning—an indication of the compartmentalization structured into the investigation—and took the opportunity to sit in.

Danny Hardway didn't look like much of a threat. He was one of the group of law students Blakey had brought to Washington to be his trusted, pre-washed, tight clique of loyalists—or so he thought. Instead, they soon evolved into the staff's Young Turks. Sincere and determined, they became annoying bugs in his ear. They were also giving the CIA fits. They encamped themselves at Langley for weeks at a time, laboriously creeping through drawers of records and documents, deciphering filing codes and cross-references, demanding more than the Agency was willing to admit it had and asking troublesome questions. (At one point, the Agency tried to blackball Eddie Lopez, a particular irritant, by formally complaining to Blakey about Eddie's plopping through its hallowed hallways in his flip-flops.)

Phillips and Hardway made quite a contrast in the small room the four of us had squeezed into. The former Chief of the Western Hemisphere Division, tanned, precisely groomed, wore a dark gray executive suit, white shirt, conservative blue tie, polished black wingtips. He sat back in his chair, legs casually crossed, relaxed and seemingly nonchalant. At first, there was only a slight shaking of his hand when he raised his cigarette to his lips for long, deep drags.

Danny Hardway wore a red plaid cotton shirt and a pair of faded jeans. He had a nervous habit of brushing his lengthy, straight black hair away from his eyes. His young voice had an edgy, but easy West Virgin-ny twang.

"Mr. Phillips," Hardway began, "I'm sure you're familiar with the letter of agreement the Committee has from the Agency to allow you to feel free to answer our questions regardless of any secrecy oath you may have executed. We have a copy of the letter if you'd like to review it."

Phillips shook his head, took a drag of his cigarette and said that wasn't necessary, he remembered it.

Hardway began with seemingly random, general questions, asking Phillips about his subordinates and the set up of his "propaganda shop" while he was chief of covert action in Mexico City. But Hardway wasn't winging it; he had been in on earlier interviews with Phillips and had reviewed every word of Phillips's previous responses against the files and information from other CIA agents. Hardway had prepared a detailed background and briefing book to outline the unresolved issues. And he had summed up our witness in his book: "Since the time that Mr. Phillips testified the HSCA staff has developed information that tends to show that his prior testimony was substantially incorrect on many points." In other words, Phillips had probably lied.

As Hardway took Phillips deeper and deeper into his previous testimony, Phillips became more uneasy, shifting in his chair, lighting yet another cigarette, forgetting the one resting on the edge of the ashtray.

The first area Hardway pressed Phillips on dealt with all those stories that came out of Mexico City and Miami connecting Oswald with Castro or Soviet intelligence, effectively creating Oswald's image as a Communist sympathizer. Hardway's research had indicated that most of the individuals originating the reports were David Phillips's assets. In his previous testimony, Phillips had attempted to distance himself, claiming these assets were run by other CIA agents. Now Phillips, realizing that Hardway had documentation from the Agency contradicting that, started to squirm. (After the session, Hardway told me, "I'm firmly convinced now that he ran the red-herring, disinformation aspects of the plot. The thing that got him so nervous was when I started mentioning all the anti-Castro Cubans who were in reports filed with the FBI for the Warren Commission and every one of them had a tie I could trace back to him. That's what got him very upset. He knew the whole thing could unravel.")

There were other points Phillips had trouble explaining. For instance, in trying to justify the fact that he had learned of Oswald's contact with the Soviet Embassy on October 1st but had not sent CIA headquarters a cable about it until October 8th, Phillips said the delay was caused by the Agency's tape transcribers, a team who worked outside the station. Phillips portrayed himself as the tenacious supervisor constantly pressing them to get the transcripts finished and get the cable out to headquarters. He said the tapes and transcripts were delivered and picked up by a fellow officer at the station, a woman named Anne. He remembered reading the transcripts when they were done and learning Oswald offered information to the Russians. Phillips also specifically remembered signing off on the cable.

Phillips was unaware of the contradictory information Hardway and Ed Lopez had dug up at the Agency. They read the transcripts and found no indication of Oswald making any such offer. The routing schedule on the transcripts indicated they weren't even sent to Phillips. His former associate Anne denied she had delivered and picked up the tapes and transcripts. And, during the period Phillips said he was involved in all this, the Agency's records indicated he was on temporary duty leave in Miami and Washington.

Hardway told me that, based on the research he had done tracking the routing of the cables and the lack of credible answers about them from Phillips, he believed there was a strong possibility the cables were created after the fact.

In questioning Phillips, Hardway was also working from information that had been dug up on a couple of secret trips to Mexico City made by Lopez and investigator Harold Leap. Without the Agency's permission, they had located and interviewed a couple of CIA assets who had worked inside the Cuban Consulate at the time. The Agency never revealed this to the Warren Commission, but it actually had planted spies within the Cuban compound. That may be relevant to the fact that, in the end, the only "proof" that the real Oswald was inside the Cuban Consulate were his photograph and his signature on his visa application. Anyone working inside the consulate would have had access to the drawer in which Duran had filed Oswald's visa application before a copy was sent to Cuba. The CIA's assets also told Lopez and Leap that the consensus among employees within the Cuban Consulate after the Kennedy assassination was that it wasn't Oswald who had been there. The assets said they reported that to the Agency but there were no documents in the CIA files noting that fact.

While in Mexico City, Lopez and Leap also spoke with the Agency personnel who had listened to and were involved in translating and transcribing the tape of the man who called the Soviet Embassy. They said that after Oswald's arrest, when they heard his voice on radio and telecasts, it wasn't the same voice they remembered from the tape. The man who called the Embassy had a huskier voice and didn't speak as fast as Oswald and, perhaps most revealing, spoke in very poor, broken Russian. (Oswald's Russian wasn't excellent, but Marina Oswald later said that when she first met Oswald in Minsk, she thought his accent was from another part of the Soviet Union.)

Phillips seemed to become especially nervous when Hardway began questioning him about the lack of photographs of Oswald. He maintained that the surveillance cameras at both the Soviet and Cuban Embassies were not functioning at the time of Oswald's visits. Phillips stuck to the story that the Agency didn't maintain an around-the-clock and weekend surveillance of the Soviet Embassy. He also said that the Cuban Embassy camera happened to be malfunctioning during the time of Oswald's visit. So despite the fact that Oswald had allegedly made at least five visits to the Cuban Consulate and Soviet Embassy, there were no photographs to prove it. (At one point, the Agency had said it was testing a new type of automatic surveillance camera on the Cuban Embassy the week that Oswald was visiting and that none of the test photos were retained. It gave no reason why they weren't.)

Ed Lopez later told me that his and Leap's Mexico City research clearly revealed that Phillips was lying. "When we talked to one of the photographers who worked the cameras in Mexico City, he told us that they were working twenty or thirty days in a row at that time, without a day off, so there had to have been weekend coverage. When we asked about the cameras being broken, he laughed. He said, 'Well, of course, we would have more than one camera. We never just had one camera.' "

There was, in fact, plenty of evidence that the cameras trained on the Cuban Consulate *were* functioning throughout the period Oswald was allegedly in Mexico City.

"We definitely saw photos from the period Phillips said the cameras were not working," Lopez said. "The CIA showed us hundreds of photographs. We looked at every one carefully. We had at least three binders of contact prints and they covered a period from about the last week in September until the middle of October. There was no photograph of Oswald.''

Perhaps the most intriguing confirmation that the cameras and the Agency's personnel were all working came during the Committee members' visit to Cuba. The Cuban intelligence service showed them its own photographs of the American photographers shooting from their hideaway across the street from the Cuban Embassy. It was the mirror image of the spy game come alive.

In the end, Phillips couldn't explain the contradictions in his testimony about the Agency's surveillance capabilities or why, if the cameras at the Soviet Embassy *were* working on October 1st when it photographed the unidentified man passed off as Oswald, there was no photograph of the real Oswald.

Lopez and Leap uncovered other revealing information in Mexico from the CIA officer who was Deputy Chief of the station at the time. "He told us," Lopez reported, "that Phillips was really a bizarre character. He was a loner and reported only to the station chief, Win Scott. But Scott just let him do whatever he wanted. He was really autonomous. He said he thought that Phillips was running his own operations that no one else knew about. He did know that whenever Phillips was working on an operation he was careful not to leave his fingerprints anywhere. That's the word he used: 'fingerprints.' ''

In another intriguing revelation, the former Deputy Chief remembered being called into Win Scott's office one day. With Scott was another station officer. It could have been Phillips, he said, but he isn't positive. There he was shown a photograph of Lee Harvey Oswald. Two or three other people were in the photo, the Deputy remembered, and the discussion centered on who Oswald was and who the other people were. He didn't remember if the photo was taken in front of the Cuban or Soviet Embassy or not, or if this incident took place before or after the Kennedy assassination. The Deputy did say that the photo was considered sensitive enough for Win Scott to keep it in his private safe. (Carl Migdale, the reporter who was a close friend of both Scott and Phillips, said Scott one day boasted, "I've got all the family jewels in that safe.")

Win Scott was part of the OSS Old Boys clique of officers who controlled the Agency. He was very close to Richard Helms, Deputy Director of Plans in the early Sixties and, later, CIA Director. Retired in 1969, Scott remained in Mexico and worked on his memoirs. Then, in April, 1971, Scott climbed a gangplank in his back yard to look at a brick wall that was being built. He slipped and fell into his rosebushes. He got up, said he was fine. Two days later his wife found him dead, slumped in his chair at the breakfast table. Within hours, the CIA's spookiest of spooks, James Angleton, the eccentric epitome of John le Carré's Smiley, arrived to collect everything that Scott had kept in his safe. When the Assassinations Committee asked Angleton if he had retrieved a photo of Oswald, Angleton denied that he had. "That story," he said, "is poppycock!" (Angleton, who was the CIA's Chief of Counterintelligence, had also been the CIA's liaison with the Warren Commission.****)

In handling the Mexico City maze in its final report, the House Assassinations Committee did a tricky juke step away from dealing with David Phillips's lies. Neither did it deal with the significance of the complex web of deception and confusion the CIA had woven. It simply built a conclusion keystoned with a paradox:

> The Committee was unable to determine whether the CIA did in fact come into possession of a photograph of Oswald taken during his visits to the Soviet Embassy and Cuban consulate in Mexico City, or whether Oswald had any associates in Mexico City. *Nevertheless, other information provided by the CIA* [italics added] as well as evidence obtained from Cuban and Mexican sources, enabled the Committee to conclude that the individual who presented himself as Lee Harvey Oswald at the Cuban consulate in Mexico was not an imposter.

That deduction was rife with wishful thinking. There was no "other information provided by the CIA." If the Agency revealed any convincing information exclusively to Chief Counsel Bob Blakey, he never mentioned it to Hardway or Lopez, the researchers who wrote the final report on Mexico City. And there was no reason for him not to give them that information if he had it. After all, Blakey had to have realized that the CIA would never allow the public release of the Mexico City report.

When David Phillips had arrived at the Committee for the informal session, he was the epitome of the cool, charmingly casual, self-

---

****Clare Boothe Luce, who should know, once wrote to James Jesus Angleton: "There's no doubt you are easily the most interesting and fascinating figure the intelligence world has produced, and a living legend." I saw Angleton in the Committee hallways frequently, a tall, permanently stooped, bony-faced figure with thick glasses, somber in his trademark long black coat and black homburg, his black umbrella and a copy of the *New York Times* always under his arm. (I was told he was there to review and correct his testimony, a right given all Committee witnesses.) Angleton, a passionate breeder of orchids and lover of T.S. Eliot's poetry, ran the Agency's most secret closet, its counterspy ops. He devoted much of his career to a belief that the Agency had been infiltrated by a Russian "mole." That passion eventually produced a bitter internal battle among the hierarchy and Angleton was fired by CIA Director William Colby in December, 1974. "I never knew what he was doing," Colby said. Angleton died of cancer on May 11, 1987.

assured CIA agent. Near the end, he looked weary and shaken. He had sucked his way through an ashtray full of cigarettes, obviously caught off guard by the depth of Hardway's detailed information about the Agency's activities in Mexico City. Phillips had not expected to be confronted with the perjuries of his previous testimony.

Then something strange happened when Hardway moved the interrogation off the Mexico City area and into the area dealing with Antonio Veciana and Maurice Bishop. At my suggestion, Hardway had earlier asked Phillips some questions that were relevant but not obviously linked to that area, and Phillips's descriptions of his activities were tightly relevant to what we knew about Maurice Bishop. For instance, Phillips admitted that aside from the projects that he ran out of his propaganda shop in Mexico City, he was also using assets he had developed prior to his posting there. He said he had traveled to Miami regularly and had often seen people he had known from his days in Havana, including those he was running as assets himself. He also admitted that one of the primary activities of his Cuban Ops shop was to identify the Cuban intelligence officers in the Cuban Embassy, along with their functions and assignments.

However, the very first question that was clearly related to Antonio Veciana brought an abrupt change, almost a character transformation, in Phillips. Hardway had asked about his relationship with Julio Lobo, the Cuban millionaire in whose bank Veciana had worked in Havana and who, it was later learned, had a close association with the CIA, even serving as a front in negotiating the release of the Bay of Pigs prisoners. At that question, Phillips rose in his chair.

"Now I've had enough!" he said forcefully. His nervousness now gone, his demeanor strong. "I've covered this area numerous times in my testimony and depositions. Do you think I appreciate living with the fear and tension of possibly being called before the television cameras and have this Veciana fellow stand up and point his finger at me and say that I'm Bishop and that he saw me with Oswald? Now I'd like to know once and for all if Veciana's ridiculous story is still being considered and if any conclusive decision has been made about it. I'm just sick and tired of having to live with this nonsense!"

Hardway firmly told Phillips we had no authority to provide him with any information about the Committee's activities, but Phillips's dramatic response surprised us. Grilled about Mexico City, he had been tentative in many responses, uncomfortable and fidgety, even a bit sweaty. Suddenly he had changed at the first question related to Veciana and the Maurice Bishop story. His response was so strong and structured, it almost appeared he had rehearsed it. But I shouldn't have been surprised. I had forgotten that David Phillips, at every station he was ever posted to in his career, had always gotten involved in acting in a little theater group. He was a natural.

THIRTY-FIVE

POLISHING THE BADGE
OF HONOR

SHORTLY AFTER THE Bay of Pigs operation, President John F. Kennedy confided to his adviser Arthur Schlesinger, Jr., that after he took office he should not have retained Allen Dulles as CIA Director. "I can't estimate his meaning when he tells me things," said Kennedy.

Immediately after he was appointed to the Warren Commission to investigate Kennedy's assassination, Allen Dulles told columnist Murray Kempton he was confident that the Commission would find no evidence of a conspiracy.

At an early meeting of the Warren Commission, the members discussed what Chief Counsel F. Lee Rankin called "this dirty rumor" that Oswald may have been an FBI informant.

"This is a terribly hard thing to disprove, you know," said Allen Dulles. "How do you disprove a fellow was not your agent? How do you disprove it?"

Louisiana Congressman Hale Boggs then asked, "You could disprove it, couldn't you?"

"No," said Dulles.

"Did you have agents about whom you had no record whatsoever?" asked Boggs.

"The records might not be on paper," said Dulles.

Boggs then asked about an agent who did not have a contract but was recruited by someone from the CIA. "The man who recruited him would know, wouldn't he?" asked Boggs.

"Yes, but he wouldn't tell," said Dulles.

Commission Chairman Earl Warren appeared a bit taken aback. "Wouldn't tell it under oath?" he asked.

"I wouldn't think he would tell it under oath, no," answered Dulles.

It was a revealing admission given, as it was, from a loyal CIA officer's perspective. This same perspective was held by former CIA Director Richard Helms, who called his conviction for perjury before Congress a "badge of honor."

At the time when Chief Counsel Bob Blakey was making arrangements with the CIA for access to its files, one staff member raised the question of whether or not, in the absence of access to the file system itself, we could tell if the Agency was being honest with us in response to requests for all the files on a particular subject.

"You don't think they'd lie to me, do you?" Blakey responded. "I've been working with those people for twenty years."

Of all the factors which dictated the Assassinations Committee's ultimate disposal of the revelations of Antonio Veciana and produced its conclusions about David Phillips and Maurice Bishop, there was one of pivotal influence: the Committee's relationship with the Central Intelligence Agency.

At one of our early staff meetings, Blakey revealed what our strategy would be in dealing with the CIA: It will be "realistic," he said. He was in the delicate process of negotiating a "working arrangement" with the Agency, one that would give us unprecedented access to its files. Meanwhile, Blakey said, we have to keep in mind certain very real factors: First, we are a *temporary* Congressional investigative entity with a limited time to do our job; then we will disappear. The CIA will be around long after we're gone. Our attitude, said Blakey, will be one of sympathy to the CIA's overall mission and its continuing role. That's the attitude, he said, we shall manifest in all our dealings with the Agency. For our report, Blakey said, we will keep a record of how the Agency complies with our requests for files. The record is what's important.

"The thing to do now," said Blakey, "is be nice to the Agency. Ask for things in a nice way. If you have difficulty, deal with them in a nice way, don't buck them head-on at this point. That may result in the battle being lost on the beaches."*

---

*Blakey may have avoided losing the battle on the beaches, but there was little the Committee staffers could do when, even after nominally achieving the Agency's cooperation, they ran into what appeared to be deliberate stalling tactics, making Blakey's reminder that we were a *temporary* Congressional entity very relevant. One day, researcher Leslie Wizelman, on a visit to the Agency to review the files of former Bay of Pigs military leader Manuel Artime, who later worked for the CIA in a number of anti-Castro operations (including an assassination attempt), became so frustrated with what she considered the Agency's deliberate procrastination, she returned to

Unlike his predecessor Dick Sprague, Bob Blakey saw nothing ludicrous in seeking a "working arrangement" with one of the subjects of the Committee's investigation. Neither did he view House Resolution 222 authorizing the Committee to conduct a "full and complete investigation" as being in conflict with the CIA's refusal to provide total access to information except on its own terms.

Our arrangement with the Agency evolved over several months, most of the steps negotiated personally by Blakey and CIA Director Stansfield Turner. Ultimately, every Committee staff member who signed the CIA Secrecy Agreement got access to the Agency's classified files. No other Congressional committee had ever reviewed these files without the Agency first deleting what it called its "sensitive sources and methods," which identified how the information was obtained. Knowledge of such sources and methods was often more important than the information itself.

Blakey was exceptionally proud of his arrangement with the Agency and, in a sense, he had a right to be. Although the Agency had the final say in what information obtained from its files could be published, the Committee's final report and, more significantly, its appendix volumes were liberally documented with Agency file material. Even now, independent Kennedy assassination researchers are still discovering a cornucopia of new information in that published material, even if it reflects an incomplete investigation and raises more questions than it answers.

Yet, in the end, Blakey was suckered. Although in his periodic reports to the staff he pictured himself as a bulldog, snapping at the Agency at every instance of evasiveness or recalcitrance, he was

---

Committee headquarters and put the notes she had doodled while she was waiting into what was ironically called an "Outside Contact Report":

"After being told to review Artime's files at the Agency, I called Karen yesterday and asked her if it would okay to review the files today. She informed me that it was okay. I arrived at the Agency at 9:15 A.M. I called Barbara and asked her to bring me Artime's files. After approximately 30 minutes, Barbara arrived without the files. She informed me that she thought they were in her office, but when she looked they were not there. I asked her if she had been told yesterday that I would be out to review the files. She said, 'Yes.'

"It is 10:30 now and I still have no files. More later.

"Oh, I forgot one thing. This morning when I requested my list of cryptonyms [the CIA's code names for operations], Karen told me she's having trouble locating them. She has not yet found them.

"I was just informed they found my cryptonyms (10:45), but still no files.

"Sorry, it was a mistake, they did not find my crypts. It is now 11:00 and Bill [the supervisor] is out of the office and therefore there's nothing that can be done about getting me Artime's files.

"Finally received 3 files at 11:25 A.M. and my cryptonyms at 2 P.M."

actually acting on two erroneous assumptions: First, that access to CIA files meant that the Committee would have access not only to *all* CIA files but also to the information which would enable us to search knowledgeably and comprehensively through those files; and, second, that the CIA files themselves reflected a complete and accurate record, including whether or not the Agency or any of its personnel were involved in the Kennedy assassination.

Most staffers felt that Blakey's assumptions were either gullible—he was, after all, working on the Agency's turf—or deliberately Machiavellian. In either case, it's quite obvious he made those assumptions because they were necessary to produce the kind of final report he had in mind. While Blakey liked to give the impression that he was cleverly manipulating the Agency to our ends, for him "our ends" meant an impressively thick final report heavy with references to CIA documents. Plenty of sex appeal in that.

After the Committee's report was released, Blakey told a journalist that he had seen certain CIA files which were not shown to anyone else on the Committee's staff. That certainly made me wonder who was manipulating whom. But the most revealing indication of the CIA's toying with Blakey came in an internal memorandum that slipped out during the course of a 1981 lawsuit brought under the Freedom of Information Act by Washington attorney Jim Lesar of the Assassination Archives and Research Center. The memorandum recorded a visit by Blakey to the Agency very late in the ballgame. Although heavy with deletions, it provided this insight: "Mr. Blakey examined only that material held [deletion]. He apparently did not go elsewhere within the Agency, [deletion], to examine their holdings."

Did the CIA ever tell Blakey about these other "holdings"?

The Assassinations Committee staff reportedly examined nine four-drawer safes, eight drawers of which contained Oswald's 201 file. But, reveals the CIA memorandum, "Oswald's 201 file was not completely reviewed by HSCA staff members."

When, in preparation for his book *Reasonable Doubt* [Holt, Rinehart, Winston, 1985], Henry Hurt asked Blakey about the failure to review all of Oswald's 201 file, Blakey said: "My memory is that we did it. If the CIA says we did not, its records are incomplete."

Yet the CIA memorandum contains that amazing admission: The Agency has file drawers of material it did not provide to either the staff of the Assassinations Committee or to Blakey himself.

Bob Blakey's reverence for the CIA as an institution permitted the Agency to impose its priorities on the Committee's mandate. And the CIA's priorities did not have anything to do with determining the facts of President Kennedy's assassination. The Committee's relationship with the CIA totally ignored the insights provided by Allen Dulles and Richard Helms.**

Before the Committee's investigation got underway, I had a revealing discussion with a former high-ranking CIA officer. He had retired to Florida and, having lost the narrow focus of the career insider, he had slowly begun viewing the Agency in a new light. He told me that the CIA's response to the coming investigation would be "predictable." It would react the way it has always reacted: A "task force" of key personnel would be formed to "handle and contain" the inquiry. He cited the Agency's response to both the Rockefeller Commission and the Church Committee as examples. He said the "clandestine mentality" that is drilled into CIA operatives until it is instinctual would permit most of them to commit perjury because, in their view, their secrecy oath supersedes any other.

"You represent the United States Congress," he said. "But what the hell is that to the CIA?"

"But what the hell is that to the CIA?" It was hard to believe that someone from the inside was being so brutally candid. What the hell are the lawfully elected representatives of the people in a democracy? Obviously not as important as maintaining the institutional sanctity of the CIA.

I think of that statement when I recall what subsequently occurred, especially in our pursuit of the truth about David Phillips's activities. And then I think of the incredible admission buried in the Committee's final report:

> . . . the Agency's strict compartmentalization and the complexity of its enormous filing system . . . have the . . . effect of making congressional inquiry difficult. For example, CIA personnel testified to the Committee that a review of Agency files would not always indicate whether an individual was affiliated with the Agency in any capacity. Nor was there always an independent means of verifying that all materials requested from the Agency had, in fact, been provided.

That was an admission that stands in stark contrast to Blakey's public statements *after* the report was issued. Within months Blakey

---

**Perhaps too late, Blakey was given a powerful insight into the disdain with which the Agency really viewed the Committee's efforts. The *Washington Post*'s George Lardner was among the group of reporters who chatted with ex-CIA director Richard Helms during a recess in his executive-session testimony before the Assassinations Committee. Lardner later wrote: "Helms told reporters during a break that no one would ever know who or what Lee Harvey Oswald . . . represented. Asked whether the CIA knew of any ties Oswald had with either the KGB or the CIA, Helms paused and with a laugh said, 'I don't remember.' Pressed on the point, he told a reporter, 'Your questions are almost as dumb as the Committee's.' "

was denigrating that conclusion. For example, that summer Blakey was interviewed at Cornell by reporter Chris Stanley of DIR Broadcasting of New York City. Among his declarations: "In point of fact, the Committee ultimately obtained from the CIA every single document that it wanted. No limitations were put on it. We got deeper and wider in the Agency files than any other Congressional committee in the history of Congress—bar none. . . ."

So although the Committee report admits there was no way of verifying that the CIA wasn't lying to us about producing all its files or that it was telling us the truth about its affiliations with certain individuals we asked about, Blakey still asserts his belief in the Agency's veracity.

Would the CIA lie to Congress? Let's see, we'll take an answer from those three gentlemen sitting in this back room of history here. Who would like to respond first? Mr. Dulles? Mr. Helms? Mr. Phillips?

THIRTY-SIX

THE NAME GAME

IN July of 1977, two months after he had written his first column about "Mr. X" and his revelations concerning "Morris" Bishop, Jack Anderson brought the subject up again. He wrote:

> The Central Intelligence Agency had no comment last May when we quoted from House investigative files that the CIA was in contact with Lee Harvey Oswald in Dallas on the eve of the John F. Kennedy assassination.
> . . . The CIA, though maintaining official silence, reacted to our story in an internal memo. We have obtained a copy of the memo. . . .
> This memo . . . is addressed to the CIA's Deputy Director for Operations. It states: "The Jack Anderson column of 6 May 1977 alluded to 'the CIA man, Morris Bishop,' in Dallas. . . . The CIA did not have contact in Dallas with Lee Harvey Oswald. . . . We have run exhaustive traces to identify Morris Bishop without success. The name Morris Bishop has never been used as a registered alias or pseudonym nor has anyone with the name ever been employed by the CIA."

It was not until March 2nd, 1978—almost ten months after Jack Anderson first blew the lid of secrecy off the existence of an intelligence operative named Bishop—that the House Select Committee on Assassinations finally got around to officially asking the CIA to check all its files and index references for a Maurice Bishop. On March 31st, the CIA informed the Committee that its Office of the Inspector

General, its Office of the General Counsel, its Office of Personnel and the Deputy Directorate of Operations had no records of a Maurice Bishop and that a search of David Phillips's files did not indicate he had ever registered the alias of Maurice Bishop.

I was the only staff investigator on the Assassinations Committee with a journalism background. As such, I was particularly mindful of Blakey's early directive that all the activities of the Committee, classified or not, be kept confidential. Some of my best friends were journalists and I was in touch with them regularly. In addition, some of them had been doing important and very effective research into the Kennedy assassination themselves and were excellent sources of information. For that reason, I refused to restrict my contacts with them but, at the same time, knew that I had to be particularly careful not to leak any Committee information.

One of the journalists with whom I was in regular contact was a tall, cocky young freelancer named Scott Malone. Malone had stirred Blakey's ire by being annoyingly pushy while questioning him about a piece in *New Times* magazine and Blakey had declared him *persona non grata* at Committee offices. But Malone was a good digger and a hustler. Along with Irish journalist Anthony Summers, he helped produce a BBC television special about the Kennedy assassination and one day, while working on that, he wound up in Miami to interview Robert McKeown.

In the mid-Fifties, McKeown had a successful business in Cuba, but he was forced out by Batista and was eventually arrested in Texas with a house full of arms and munitions he was planning to smuggle to a mountain rebel named Fidel Castro. Actually, McKeown was a front for Carlos Prío, the Mob-connected former Cuban President for whom Frank Sturgis was also working. After the Kennedy assassination, the FBI discovered that Jack Ruby had once contacted McKeown to ask for a letter of introduction to Castro. McKeown has given a variety of reasons for Ruby's wanting the introduction. He has said that Ruby wanted to sell Castro a shipment of jeeps and he has said that Ruby wanted to obtain the release of some friends Castro had imprisoned. In an interview I had with McKeown while I was working for Senator Schweiker, McKeown expanded on his Ruby stories, claiming, among other things, that Ruby had also had access to a load of slot machines hidden in the mountains of New Mexico. (McKeown would also later claim he had been visited by Oswald. By then McKeown was an old man, sickly and in need of money. The last time I saw him he said Mark Lane was going to get him a big book contract.)

At any rate, after Scott Malone talked to McKeown I met him for lunch to find out if McKeown had revealed anything new. He hadn't, but as we were finishing our lunch, Malone casually mentioned that McKeown told him he had met a fellow at his bridge club who used to be involved in anti-Castro activities back in the early Sixties. Malone thought the fellow might be of some help to me and gave me his name.

That was in January, some months prior to the firing of most the Assassinations Committee's investigative staff in June, so I still had Al Gonzales working with me in Miami. Gonzales tracked down McKeown's friend in Coral Gables and one morning, when we were in the neighborhood, we dropped in. We wouldn't have been so casual about it if we had known how important he was going to be.

In the report I later wrote, he was given the name of Ron Cross, for a variety of reasons. Cross, we discovered, had been a CIA case officer at the Agency's JM/WAVE station during the height of its anti-Castro activities. He handled some Cuban exile units and helped organize a rebel group that, although not near the size and effectiveness of Alpha 66, was among the most active. Early in his career, while posing as an American businessman (the classic CIA cover story), Cross had pulled an operational coup by infiltrating Castro's mountain stronghold before the big *barbudo* seized power. There Cross ran into my old pals, the ubiquitous freelancer Andrew St. George (who confidentially asked Cross who he "really" worked for), and the daring gun runner Frank Sturgis.

Cross, retired from the Agency since 1964, was a thin, tanned, soft-spoken fellow. Although we had spoken to other cooperative former CIA officers, he was surprisingly candid. Then, at the end of our long first meeting with him, he volunteered that he was a member of Alcoholics Anonymous. "I want you to know that," he said, "in case someone happens to remark, 'Oh, I know that old drunk.' Well, once a time ago, I was an old drunk." Both he and his wife, an attractive, dark-haired woman who seemed particularly attentive to him, said the stress of intelligence work had caused the problem. I was impressed with Cross's admission, but I later learned that excruciating honesty is a requisite to being a successful member of AA.

Cross was a gold mine of information. He provided us not only with specific details about the operations of the groups he handled, he also gave us a broad insight into the structure and activities of the JM/WAVE station, including the duties of, and the relationships among, the station's top personnel. He mentioned, for instance, that E. Howard Hunt occasionally came by the headquarters. ("He would come in, puff on his pipe and look down his nose at the case officers.")

Gonzales and I held back from asking him certain questions, for fear of revealing what we knew. We were leery. Stumbling on Cross, we both quickly realized, was a stroke of dumb luck. In our particular areas of interest, Cross had been in the right place at the right time. But we wanted to check him out a bit. Trusting souls we never were.

We did, however, ask him about David Phillips. Sure, Cross said, he knew Phillips. He said that Phillips, working through the JM/WAVE case officers, had coordinated the propaganda operations of all the Cuban exile groups the Agency was running. He added that Phillips worked mostly out of Washington but flew in and out of Miami frequently. The officers worked with Phillips's direct subordinate at the station on a daily basis, a fellow who used the name of Doug Gupton.

Over the next few weeks, both Gonzales and I were in frequent touch with Cross as we attempted to check out the validity of both the man and the information. He appeared to be straight. We then decided to test him.

One day Gonzales called him and told him we were working on something that required confirmation of the pseudonyms or aliases used by certain CIA officers at the JM/WAVE station. He threw three name at Cross: "Bishop," "Knight," and a third, the true name of an officer who had actually worked out of the Havana station.

Off the top of his head, Cross said, he believed that "Bishop" was the name used by David Phillips; "Knight" was a name that E. Howard Hunt occasionally used; and, he said, we must be mistaken about the third name being an alias because that was the true name of a fellow he had known in Havana.

Cross added that within the next few days he would likely be talking with a few of the Cuban exile agents who had worked with him. In chatting with them about the old days, perhaps, he said, his memory would be refreshed and he could give us a more definite answer.

Several days later, Al Gonzales dropped in on Cross to see if his memory had been refreshed. Well, Cross said, it had been, a bit. He said he still was not definite about whether Hunt had used the "Knight" alias but was still sure that the third name was a true name. And now, Cross said, he was "almost certain" that David Phillips had used the name of "Maurice Bishop."

That surprised us. We had not given Cross Bishop's first name.

There was another interesting fillip to what Cross told us. In his memoir, *Give Us This Day*, E. Howard Hunt anoints the "Propaganda Chief" of the CIA's anti-Castro operations—"an officer who had worked for me brilliantly on the Guatemala Project"—with the pseudonym of "Knight."

In his own autobiography, David Phillips admits that Hunt is referring to him and, flipping the mirror a few times, adds: "Bestowing the name of Knight was the ultimate accolade—people who have worked in the CIA will recall that pseudonym belonged to one of the Agency's most senior officers, a man Howard idolized." (In Thomas Powers's biography of Richard Helms, *The Man Who Kept the Secrets* [Alfred A. Knopf, 1979], the owner of the Knight alias was revealed to be former CIA Director Helms, Hunt's boss. Those who know E. Howard Hunt have no doubt that, in actuality, Hunt himself would have occasionally donned the pseudonym of his idol. Such are the games spooks play.)

Over the next few weeks, we continued checking out Cross himself and spoke with a number of Cuban exiles who had worked with him, as well as others who had known him. We found no discrepancies in anything he had told us. I felt, however, that I should once again confirm his recollection about Maurice Bishop. One day, after a lengthy conversation about other areas of the JM/WAVE operation, I offhandedly said, "Oh, by the way, we're still checking into some of the cover names that were used at the time. Do you recall Al Gonzales asking you about 'Knight' and 'Bishop'?"

Yes, Cross said, he had been giving it some thought and he was fairly sure now that Hunt did use the Knight alias. He also said he was now "almost positive" that David Phillips used the name of Bishop. The reason for that was he had been thinking about Phillips's assistant at the JM/WAVE station, that fellow Doug Gupton. Cross said he now recalled that when discussing special field and agent problems Gupton at times said, "Well, I guess Mr. Bishop will have to talk with him." "And, of course," Cross said, "I knew he was referring to his boss, Dave Phillips."

There's an irony here: If Al Gonzales and I had known for a fact—and reported it to Washington—that Ron Cross was a retired employee of the Central Intelligence Agency, we would not have been able to interview him for weeks, perhaps months. As part of Blakey's "working arrangement" with the Agency, it was agreed that the CIA would clear and arrange all interviews with both its present and former employees. That, of course, permitted the Agency to keep track of exactly where the Committee's investigation was going. As a result of that arrangement, almost every one of these interviews was conducted at CIA headquarters, where there was always an Agency liaison present to monitor it.

So there was no way we could avoid going through the CIA to locate and interview the man whom Cross had identified as David Phillips's assistant at JM/WAVE. Still, it was more than six months after Cross's revelations that the Assassinations Committee got around to interviewing Doug Gupton, who had recently retired from the CIA. The interview took place at the Agency's headquarters.

Gupton acknowledged that he had worked at JM/WAVE when Cross said he had and that his immediate superior was David Phillips, who was stationed in Washington. He also acknowledged that he worked with Ron Cross daily.

Gupton said that Phillips was actually in charge of two sets of operations. Gupton's was the one run out of Miami and, he said, he kept Phillips fully informed. Explaining their working relationship, Gupton said they were in regular contact by telephone and cable. Phillips, he confirmed, also visited Miami "quite often."

The other set of operations, Phillips ran personally out of Washington and, Gupton said, Phillips did not keep him briefed about those, so he didn't know anything about their specifics or what contacts Phillips used. Gupton did believe, however, that Phillips used many of his old contacts from Havana in these activities.

Then Gupton was asked if he knew whether or not either E. Howard Hunt or David Phillips ever used the cover name of "Knight." Gupton said he did not know.

When asked if David Phillips ever used "Maurice Bishop" as a cover name, Gupton said, "I don't recall."

When told that Ron Cross said he specifically remembered Gupton referring to David Phillips as "Mr. Bishop," Gupton remained silent for a moment, looked down at his lap and said, "Well, maybe I did. I don't remember."

Gupton was then shown the composite sketch of Maurice Bishop. No, he said, it didn't look like anyone he knew.

The House Select Committee on Assassinations issued 542 subpoenas for individuals to appear before it or provide material evidence. It actually took sworn testimony in depositions, at public hearings or in executive sessions from 335 witnesses. Despite the significance of their statements, the Committee never questioned Ron Cross or Doug Gupton under oath.

THIRTY-SEVEN

'UNCLE DAVID' AND THE TIES THAT BIND

*N*EAR THE END of his testimony before the Assassinations Committee in April, 1978, David Phillips was shown the composite sketch of Maurice Bishop. Since I had not had the chance to show it to him at the luncheon in Reston, I assumed it was the first time he had seen it. Phillips put on his glasses and studied the sketch for a moment. Slowly he nodded his head. "It does look like me," he said. He paused for a moment and, with a whimsical smile, added, "Actually, it looks more like my brother." He said his brother was a lawyer in Texas.

It was about a month later that I received a call from Leslie Wizelman. A researcher on the Organized Crime team, she was one of Blakey's bright young Cornell Law students. "I have a neat story to tell you," she said. "I'm going down to Texas next week, so today I called the Tarrant County Crime Commission in Fort Worth just to see if they had any files that might be helpful. I wanted to speak to the director and asked the secretary what his name was. She said, 'Mr. Edwin Phillips.' Well, it immediately struck me that it might just be David Phillips's brother. He wasn't there but he called me back later. He was real friendly. While I was asking him if he had files on the specific individuals we were interested in, I kept wondering how I could ask him if he was David Phillips's brother. He was very nice and he thought he had some files that might help us and said he'd be more than happy to cooperate. Then he said, 'I think I should tell you that I'm David Phillips's brother, someone your Committee has spoken with.' He asked if I knew that. I admitted I had been wondering if there were a relationship. Then he said that he makes it a point to keep up with what the Committee is doing and that his brother David, after he testified, asked him to search his Crime Commission files to see if he had anything on CIA activities in Dallas or on a Maurice Bishop. He said he did and, of course, he didn't find anything. Now that's some kind of a coincidence, isn't it?''

That was, indeed, some kind of coincidence. And while I could not forget that David Phillips career was as a misinformation expert, I also could not forget his comment about his brother looking more like Maurice Bishop than he did. A sincere investigative effort would have required that such information be checked out immediately, if only for the record. But this was the Assassinations Committee and I knew no one would do it if I didn't do it myself. All I had to do was figure out some way to get to Texas.

Although there were a number of witnesses in Dallas I had long wanted to interview because of their Miami connections, my requests for travel authorization to Texas kept getting bogged in the bureaucracy. In addition, the priorities of the Organized Crime area were being pressed upon me, including searching for old Mob figures who might expire, one way or the other, before we could officially interview them. Chief Investigator Cliff Fenton had said he wanted all his investigators to get to Dallas eventually and promised that when the "issues" plan was wrapped up, we would flood the place. But then came the mass firings in June and in the end there were only four of us left. It is hard to flood a place with four guys.

By the end of July, 1978, with the investigative staff a remnant of its former self, junior and senior counsel and researchers were frantically flitting around the country in an attempt to fill all of the increasingly obvious gaps in the investigative plan. The idea was to get a contact, sworn deposition or an interview on the record—the quality or substance didn't matter. After all, the real investigation had already ended with the firing of the investigators.

The way it worked was this: If someone was going to California, for instance, to interview a witness associated with a team's issue, he or she was also asked to interview any other witnesses who happened to be in the area. It did not matter whether the staffer doing the interview was familiar with the details of that other team's issues. More often than not, the staffer wasn't and wouldn't have time to be adequately briefed. There are a number of interview reports from this period which will clearly indicate when and if they are ever made available to the public—that the interviewer really didn't know what the hell the questions meant, and had no idea if the answers needed follow-up questions or if they were even relevant.

"This is ridiculous," staff counsel Jim McDonald told me one day. "They've got me taking depositions and interviewing all these people in Dallas and you're the guy with the background on a lot of them. You've got to go to Dallas with me. I'm going to insist on it."

So in the final months of the life of the Assassinations Committee, the only remaining investigator who had not yet officially been to the scene of the crime got to visit it. (I had, of course, been to Dallas before I joined the Committee, but that didn't count on the Committee's record.) I told Leslie Wizelman I was going.

"Oh, good," she said, "you can drop in on Edwin Phillips and ask him if he has those Crime Commission files ready for me yet. He was supposed to have them by the end of June, but every time I call he tells me they're not quite complete yet. You can pick them up for me if they're ready. Besides, you'll enjoy meeting him. He's really friendly."

I spent a few days in Dallas helping Jim McDonald with witness depositions, most of which had to do with Jack Ruby. I did, however, get to talk with a few people I had wanted to meet, including the retired Colonel Sam Kail, the military attaché at the American Embassy in Havana in 1960, and the man to whom Maurice Bishop had referred Veciana.

Kail, a trim and tanned ex-infantryman, was affable and appeared cooperative. He said he remembered Veciana's calling him not long ago and asking him about Maurice Bishop. He said he didn't remember Veciana visiting him at the Embassy but, as military attaché, he had "hordes" of Cubans streaming through his office with all sorts of plans and plots. "I think it would be a miracle if I could recall him," he said.

Kail also said, however, that some CIA officers attached to the Embassy would frequently use his name without telling him and sometimes they even posed as him. Then, he said, some of the Cubans the agents had seen would come back to the Embassy, ask for Colonel Kail and tell him he wasn't the Colonel Kail they had met.

As military attaché, Kail said, his main function was in intelligence.* After the Bay of Pigs, he was assigned to an Army detachment

---

*Sam Kail seems to have had an on-going role as a CIA liaison. Discovered in the CIA's files on George de Mohrenschildt, which revealed that "the Baron" had served as the Agency's debriefer of Oswald when the Marine defector returned from Russia, was a notation that Kail had instigated a May, 1963, meeting between de Mohrenschildt and a CIA staff officer in Washington, D.C. The month before, de Mohrenschildt had moved to Haiti to get into business with Clemard Joseph Charles, a key adviser to Haitian President "Papa Doc" Duvalier. Kail thought Duvalier would be useful to the CIA in Operation Mongoose, the code-name for its JM/WAVE-based efforts to overthrow Castro. De Mohrenschildt had a tight relationship with Charles, who reportedly

in Miami debriefing Cuban refugees. Asked about his relationship with the CIA's JM/WAVE station, Kail said, "I suspect they paid our bills." However, he added that he had no contact with David Phillips and had never met him.

The fact that Kail was operating in the intelligence area was, I thought, important in determining Veciana's credibility about his early contacts with Maurice Bishop. Also significant was Kail's reconfirming a detail that seems minor but becomes important in judging Veciana's memory and credibility. Veciana said that he recalled Kail telling him he was going home to Dallas for Christmas in 1960. Yes, Kail said, he did get home for Christmas that year.

There was so much to do in such a short time in Dallas I did not think I would get the chance to meet Edwin Phillips. At the last moment, however, an urgent call from Washington extended my stay in Dallas. We needed an interview with a witness who had been a friend of the Oswalds. The witness was outside my investigative area and not someone I knew a lot about, but if neglected, it would have left too glaring a gap in the investigative plan. I did not have with me the necessary background files and records to conduct a meaningful interview, which meant my encounter with the witness would necessarily be brief, strictly for the record and embarrassingly superficial. That's how bad things got at the end.

It was late in the afternoon when I called on Edwin Phillips. His rather unpretentious office in downtown Fort Worth was in the Electric Service Building, a staid old structure. His secretary, a matronly woman with pale skin, rosy cheeks and an impeccably neat permanent, was friendly and charming and we chatted amiably while I waited in the anteroom for Phillips to finish a telephone conversation. Another secretary, a thin, younger, modestly attractive woman,

---

was Duvalier's principal distributor of largess to American politicians. However, considering the fact that the CIA had maintained an interest in Charles since the early Sixties, it's possible that Charles was a conduit of funds for the CIA. Late in 1963, several large deposits popped up in de Mohrenschildt's Haitian bank account, including one for two hundred thousand dollars from a Bahamian bank. This occurred when de Mohrenschildt and Charles were supposedly running a sisal plantation, a derelict operation they never went near.

Quite recently, into this intertwining connection of characters came someone whom I had not previously associated with de Mohrenschildt or anyone directly linked to Oswald. He was discovered by one of the most diligent of private researchers, Peggy Adler Robohm, who in checking Clemard Charles's numerous corporate fronts, discovered the St. Charles Pacific Peace Organization, incorporated in 1988 as a non-profit entity with the power to raise money to do all kinds of profit making activities—as long as it included "elevating the standards of health"—without having to pay taxes. The Treasurer of the Corporation was listed as Frank Sturgis.

smiled a greeting as she passed, and we exchanged pleasantries. Leslie Wizelman was right, I thought, this was a friendly place.

Edwin Phillips greeted me effusively as he emerged from his office. "Well, well, it sure *is* a pleasure to see you," he said. "You come right on in now." He shook my hand and guided me in.

He was obviously older than David Phillips, shorter, paunchier and more jowly. There was no doubt that they were brothers, but Edwin Phillips's resemblance to the Maurice Bishop sketch was in no way as close as David's.

Seated in his high-backed black leather chair, surrounded by the old-fashioned scrolled-mahogany furniture, attired in a dark conservative suit and vest, Edwin Phillips reminded me of a down-home Texas politician: fast-talkin', drawlin', back-slappin' friendly and sharp as an ol' hoot-owl.

I didn't get a chance to do much explaining. I said I happened to be in the area and I dropped by, really, for only two reasons. The first was that Leslie Wizelman had asked me to check on the files and see if they were ready yet.

Phillips hemmed and hawed a bit as he began rummaging and flipping through the piles of papers on his desk, and said well, yes sir, he had gotten together the files and they were right here somewhere, but he hadn't a chance to organize them yet and he wasn't about to give them to Leslie in the mess they were in, no sir, but he was gonna get to them right soon now and he'd have them ready for her in another week or two for sure.

"Now that Leslie, she is a mighty fine little gal," he said. "Ah admire her, ah do. And ah respect her, an' ah respect the work she's doin', but ah tol' her as soon as she walked in here, ah tol' her, you know ah'm David Phillips's brother, an' you people have been talkin' to David and, well, David's my younger brother an' ah always kinda looked after David. . . ."

Edwin Phillips said that David had called him and told him about his testimony before the Committee and told him what had happened, about how the Committee had gotten him mixed up with this fellow Maurice Bishop. He said David told him that he was shown a sketch of this Maurice Bishop and David told him that when he saw it his mouth just dropped, he was so surprised at how much of a resemblance there was.

"But David told me," said Edwin Phillips, "that he said the sketch looked more like me than him." He laughed. "Ah told David that ah resented his takin' advantage of our fiduciary and fraternal relationship." He laughed again. "You know, ah always kinda looked after David."

Well, I said, that was the other reason I came by. Being that I was in the neighborhood, I thought he might just get a kick out of taking a look at the sketch himself. Maybe he would be interested in seeing it, I said; I just happened to have it with me.

Phillips seemed genuinely delighted. "Well, that's mighty nice of you," he said. "Ah do appreciate your thoughtfulness."

I reached over and handed him the sketch. He leaned forward in his chair and looked at it closely.

"Ah am *astonished*!" He almost shouted. "Ah am astonished! Why that *is* amazin'! That certainly *does* look like David!"

He kept staring at the sketch and shaking his head in amazement. "Well, now," he said, "ah'm gonna kid David about that. That does look a *lot* more like David than it does me, don't it now?"

Well, I admitted, there is a resemblance. Edwin Phillips couldn't get over it. He went on about how David told him about this Cuban fellow who said he saw this Maurice Bishop with Oswald and how the Committee had asked David about it. I got the strong impression that David Phillips had briefed his brother in exceptional detail about his testimony.

Edwin Phillips thanked me again for dropping by, said it was mighty nice of me to go out of my way. Well, I said, I thought he would just get a kick out of seeing the sketch, after what David said about it resembling him and all.

He was laughing about that as he escorted me out of his office and then, as we passed his secretary, began telling her the story and why I had come by.

"Would you mind showing my secretary the sketch?" he asked.

Not at all, I said, pulling it out of my briefcase again.

His secretary put on her glasses and studied the sketch.

"Ah was just tellin' this gentleman how astonished ah was," said Edwin Phillips as she looked at it.

It was his secretary's turn to shake her head in amazement. "That's David," she said simply. "That's David."

"Come take a look at this," Phillips called to the younger woman at the other desk. "This is my daughter Beth," he said, introducing her. "Let's see what she thinks. Does that look more like David or more like me?"

Beth moved behind her father to get a better look. "Why that's Uncle David!" she said. "That *is* Uncle David!"

Now they were all shaking their heads and laughing at the incredible coincidence. It sure struck them as mighty funny. It struck me as funny, too. I found myself chuckling almost all the way back to Washington.

THIRTY-EIGHT

A BROTHERHOOD OF DECEPTION

IN SEPTEMBER, 1978, when only three months remained in the official life of the Assassinations Committee, I was taken out of Miami and brought to Washington to coordinate the writing of the anti-Castro team's section for the "final" report. Chief Counsel Blakey had told us, "This is no time to be opening doors," but I kept trying, partly because I was becoming worried that an effort might be made to dismiss Antonio Veciana's story entirely. Then I recalled that at one point, Veciana had told me there was an intermediary, a woman, who had served as a telephone contact for Bishop whenever Veciana had to leave Miami. By contacting her, Bishop would learn where Veciana was and how to reach him. The fact that Veciana had voluntarily told me about her added to his credibility, but I had not thought that talking with her was a priority in the investigation because, never having met Maurice Bishop, she could not identify him, she could only confirm his existence. But, I figured, now would be the time to do it. Getting this woman's statement on the record would make dismissing Veciana's story a bit more difficult.

Veciana had intially told me he did not want to reveal her identity because he did not want to get her involved in the investigation. She lived in Puerto Rico now, had a family and a good job and he was afraid she might end up with a lot of publicity she didn't need. I couldn't argue with that, but now I told Veciana I needed her name because his credibility was on the line in Washington.

Veciana was reluctant, but when I told him I would consider it a

316

personal favor, well, he said, in that case . . . he would have to ask her first. He would be seeing her in Puerto Rico within the next few weeks and would talk with her about it. I asked Veciana to call me in Washington after he did.

Shortly afterwards, I received a call not from Veciana but from Tony Summers. Summers had discovered Veciana through the Jack Anderson column and had begun to spend a good deal of time with Veciana. An unassuming and charming fellow, the deft Irishman had struck it off well with the Cuban exile.

"I think I have some information that might be of some help to you," Summers said. "I have managed to goad Veciana into revealing the name of his intermediary. He didn't want to, of course, but I began telling him that I thought the information he was providing was balderdash. He's very sensitive, you know, about his credibility, so he told me her name and asked me not to contact her directly without his clearing it first. I thought you ought to know."

Summers said he didn't have the time to check out the woman himself, what with his book deadline, but thought the Committee would want to. Although Summers didn't have the woman's current address in Puerto Rico, I assumed that if Veciana wouldn't give it to me she could easily be found with a bit of research. Still, I was sensitive about my relationship with Veciana and did not want to do anything behind his back. Besides, I felt her cooperation was contingent on his approval, so I called him. "She is very afraid," he said. "She feels she was not involved in anything and she is afraid there would be a lot of publicity that would hurt her family and cause her trouble in her job. I told her then, well, if she will just talk to you and if you can guarantee her there will be no publicity and she will not have to come to Washington, would she do that? She said O.K., she will just talk to you if you can guarantee that. Do you want to talk with her?"

I remember walking with some excitement into Deputy Chief Counsel Gary Cornwell's office. "I think I can locate the intermediary who will confirm the existence of Maurice Bishop," I said. "All I need is a couple of days in Puerto Rico and a promise that she won't get any publicity or be called to Washington."

Initially, Cornwell looked at me with some surprise and excitement himself. Then, as if coming to his bureaucratic senses, he burst into a loud guffaw. *"No way!"* he shouted. Then he turned serious. "Besides." he said, "it's too late. We don't have the time or the money. How far along are you on the report?"

Sure, I was disappointed but, in retrospect, not as disappointed as I should have been. After two years of riding the details, I had no doubt there was a Maurice Bishop. The trip to Puerto Rico would have simply confirmed that.

Simply confirmed? Simply confirmed that Veciana wasn't concocting this fantastic story about an intelligence officer who likely held the key to the Kennedy assassination?

If I had known then how Blakey and the Committee were going to distort Veciana's testimony in the final report, I would have realized how crucial that trip to Puerto Rico was. I might have also realized how absolute confirmation of the existence of a Maurice Bishop would have put the Committee in quite a dilemma, placing a nasty, unavoidable little land mine on the pathway along which the Committee was pushing its conclusions.

Tony Summers wrote his book without speaking with Veciana's and Bishop's go-between, so *Conspiracy* [McGraw-Hill, 1980], published over a year after the Assassinations Committee issued its report, didn't mention the existence of the intermediary. In writing about the question of David Phillips, Summers relied heavily on what I had written about the Committee's investigation into Veciana's story. We kept in touch after his book's publication and one day, about a year later, Summers called and said he finally had the opportunity to go to Puerto Rico. While there, he would track the woman down.

When Summers returned to Miami, he told me a story that made the Committee's failure even more disheartening. He had found the woman and, since her identity still needs protection, we'll call her, as Summers does, Fabiola. She was working as an administrative assistant in a social service office, a woman in her sixties, a grandmother living comfortably with her husband in a suburb of San Juan. She said that until Veciana had called her to ask if she would talk with me, she hadn't been in touch with him for years. They had met in Havana, she said, where she was his secretary at the Banco Financiero. She said she knew that Veciana had begun to disagree with Castro's policies, but didn't know exactly when he became active. She did remember a time when he started taking "language courses" in the evening. (That coincided with the period when Bishop put Veciana through intelligence training with "Mr. Melton," in the building which housed the Berlitz Language School, one of David Phillips's "public relations" clients.)

Fabiola said Veciana never told her about any connection with U.S. intelligence, but she had supported him in his anti-Castro activities and, she said, he trusted her completely. Although she didn't know that anyone besides Veciana was behind the scheme, she did recall an incident when Veciana was working to destabilize Cuba's monetary system—at one point he asked her to hide a half-million dollars for a while. Fabiola said that when she left Cuba in 1961 and found a job in Puerto Rico, Veciana asked if she would act as an answering service for him whenever he left Miami. That was when Summers mentioned several names to her, some of which he fabricated, and asked her if Veciana had ever received calls from any of those individuals. The only name Fabiola remembered was Bishop's.

Fabiola's recollection of calls from a "Mr. Bishop" stretched over the period of time when Veciana said he was working with him. However, Fabiola also recalled another name that was linked to Bishop's in her memory, perhaps because they both sounded Anglo. The other name was "Prewett." It was all a bit vague now, what with the years, but in chatting with Summers she recalled that she assumed both Bishop and Prewett were somehow connected with the American press. And, oh yes, Prewett was a woman.

Without knowing it, of course, Fabiola had put a locking pin in another shackle linking David Phillips and Maurice Bishop. Virginia Prewett* was one of Phillips's most faithful media assets.

Besides publishing her own newsletter, the *Hemisphere Hotline*, Prewett was a columnist for the *Washington Daily News,* specializing in Latin American affairs. Through the Sixties, Prewett's column was syndicated by the North American Newspaper Alliance, whose founder, her close friend Ernest Cuneo, was a veteran of the OSS. Prewett was a favorite of right-wing Congressmen, who regularly inserted her columns into the Congressional Record. During the Cuban missile crisis, when Maurice Bishop directed Veciana to send Alpha 66 raiding parties into Havana harbor to attack Russian ships, Prewett staunchly defended the raids when Kennedy condemned them as "irresponsible acts."

Tony Summers decided to talk with Virginia Prewett after Fabiola had linked her name with Bishop's. Since his book was already published, Summers realized Prewett might connect his inquiries to the Kennedy assassination, so he asked a British friend named David Leigh to accompany him and take the lead in the interview he had arranged. (Leigh was in the U.S. on an exchange program and was working as a reporter for the *Washington Post*.) Prewett was obviously suspicious that two reporters were handling a mundane interview and at times she apparently suspected a question had more than its surface significance. Then she appeared flustered or confused and even began contradicting herself.

Yes, Prewett said, she did remember covering the activities of

---

*Prewett died of a heart ailment in April, 1988, at age 69, three months before David Phillips's death from cancer.

Alpha 66 quite a bit and, yes, she did assume that the group had some CIA backing. She admitted she was in touch with the group's leaders at the time and, when Veciana's name was mentioned, she asked, "Where is he now?" When Bishop's name was mentioned in connection with Alpha 66, she accepted the implication that he was associated with the Agency and said, "Well, you had to move around people like that." Later, as the interview progressed and the questions got more pointed, Prewett began to hedge a bit and, finally, contradicted her initial answers. Veciana? No, she had never met him. Bishop? "Well, I didn't know him personally." David Phillips? Never met him.

Later, when Antonio Veciana was asked about Virginia Prewett he readily admitted having met her a few times. "Virginia," as he called her, seemed to be always interested in what Alpha 66 was doing and he briefed her occasionally on its plans. He specifically remembered meeting her in a hotel more than once when he was working out of Puerto Rico and "probably in Washington."

Sometime later, David Leigh had the opportunity to interview David Phillips, who not only recalled specific meetings with Virginia Prewett in the Dominican Republic—as Chief of Station there in 1965, Phillips was charged with installing a covert political action program and needed media support for Agency propaganda—but he also admitted he knew her quite well.

Leigh was clever—he had brought up Prewett's name in a seemingly irrelevant context. Phillips, of course, was not aware that Veciana's go-between had linked the names of Bishop and Prewett, so he was comfortable admitting a close association with her. Yet, in that passing admission, he had flashed Leigh a glimpse into the character of a man whose entire life was a covert operation.

It had long been curious to me how the moderate-to-liberal pragmatist portrayed in *The Night Watch* had gotten involved with the rabidly right-wing Prewett and friends. And in fact, their relationship was actually very tight. Prewett was deeply involved with anti-Castro extremist groups and her connections may provide a glimpse into David Phillips's reach as an agent and into his true political affinities.

There was, for instance, Prewett's charter membership on the board of directors of the Citizens Committee to Free Cuba.

In the early Sixties, there were a number of "committees" with similar sounding names—Citizens for a Free Cuba, Free Cuba Committee, Crusade to Free Cuba and Cuban Freedom Committee among them—and there was some overlapping of membership. All were formed as conduits for funds for anti-Castro activity; some funding came from private sources, but most came from the CIA. In fact, the Agency itself established some of these committees to funnel money and arms to anti-Castro groups. (Sure, the similar names made for some confusion. Late in the evening of November 22nd, 1963, for instance, at a crowded press conference in Dallas, District Attorney Henry Wade announced that suspect Lee Harvey Oswald was a member of the Free Cuba Committee. Near the back of the crowded room, someone spoke up to correct him, saying, No, it was the Fair Play for Cuba Committee. There was a big difference. The man who corrected Wade was Jack Ruby.)

The front to which Virginia Prewett belonged had the most powerful backers, as well as some curious connections to the Kennedy assassination investigation. A few of its members had been sources for some of the early reports which appeared to be designed to muddy the waters. In fact, immediately after the assassination, one of the first tips received by the FBI carrying the theme that Castro was involved, came from Daniel James, a journalist who, like Virginia Prewett, had worked for Ernest Cuneo. (James had written a book, *Red Design for Americas*, which provided a rationale for overthrowing the Arbenz government in Guatemala.) James's tip, according to the November 23rd, 1963 FBI report, was that a Cuban source had "advised him that Fidel Castro, in early September at a function at the Brazilian Embassy in Havana, remarked that if the United States causes him difficulty he has facilities to 'knock off' United States leaders."

When the Citizens Committee to Free Cuba was formed, Ernest Cuneo, along with Prewett, became a board member and Daniel James became the executive secretary. Its founder and executive director was Paul Bethel. A veteran of the U.S. Information Agency, Bethel's background was in the military, but a lot of his activities smacked of intelligence connections. Among his more interesting assignments: He served in Germany when William Harvey was CIA chief of station there. (Harvey would later become the Agency's point man in Castro assassination plots with the Mob's Johnny Rosselli, Santos Trafficante and Sam Giancana.) Bethel was press officer in Tokyo when Oswald was stationed at the nearby Atsugi U-2 air base. In Havana in 1959, he worked with American soldier of fortune William Morgan in what might have been the Agency's first attempt to overthrow Castro. He was a consultant to the Senate Internal Security Subcommittee when it held its "Communist Threat to the Caribbean" hearings, which dwelt on the alleged infiltration of Communists into the highest echelons of the State Department. Bethel wrote for CIA asset William Buckley's *National Review* and was editor of *Latin American Report*, a monthly dealing mostly with the Communist menace south of the border. And he was among those who ranted the loudest about Kennedy's deal with Khrushchev after the missile crisis. "There is no doubt," he wrote, "that President Kennedy . . . consciously set about the business of stopping all efforts to unhorse Fidel Castro—from outside exile attacks, and from Cuba's internal resistance movement.''

In 1969, Bethel wrote a book titled *The Losers*. In it, he suggests that President Kennedy, Robert Kennedy, Martin Luther King, certain members of Kennedy's cabinet, certain career officers in the State Department and even a cabal of officers in the CIA might have been active or tacit Communist agents. This 614-page book traces Bethel's government career battling "losers" in the bureaucracy who were soft on Communism. Although it covers the early Sixties, Bethel's book makes no mention of the Kennedy assassination.

In my search to get an overview of Miami's anti-Castro activities in the Sixties, Bethel's name had come up several times and, as mentioned earlier, I met him on occasion in his home in Coconut Grove. Bethel had been very active with some Cuban exile groups, including the Student Directorate and Alpha 66. A tall, handsome guy in his late fifties, Bethel was articulate and candid but spoke mostly in generalities.

Later, after the police artist's sketch of Maurice Bishop was drawn, Paul Bethel was the first person who came to my mind as someone who resembled the drawing. He seemed to fit Veciana's physical description and he appeared to have been in some of the right places at the right times, including the American Embassy in Havana, where he was the USIA's press attaché during the period that Veciana met Bishop. So I was anxious to have Veciana confront Bethel to confirm if he were, indeed, Maurice Bishop.

"No," Veciana said when I called him to tell him I thought I had found Bishop. "Paul Bethel is not Bishop. I know Bethel, I have met him."

"How did you meet Bethel?" I asked.

"Bishop sent me to him," he said. "When I first came to Miami, Bishop said here is someone who will help you fight Castro. He was of some help."

Later, Bethel himself told me he was a close friend of David Phillips. When both were in Havana, they were in the same little-theater group. Both were very good actors.*

Among those compatriots Paul Bethel recruited to be founding members of his Citizens Committee to Free Cuba was Clare Boothe Luce, who, it may be remembered, was also a founding member of David Phillips's retired agents organization. (As detailed earlier, while work-

---

*Paul Bethel died of cancer in Miami on May 20th, 1979, two months before the release of the Assassinations Committee's final report.

ing for Senator Schweiker I had spent a good deal of time and effort on a Luce-inspired wild goose chase, trying to confirm an embroidered story she had given Schweiker about Oswald trying to penetrate an anti-Castro group.) Significantly, one of the major backers of Bethel's committee was Luce's "great friend," Miami multimillionaire William Pawley, who had gotten her involved in sponsoring anti-Castro activists. When I started work with the Assassinations Committee, I made Pawley a top candidate for questioning. Unfortunately, his suicide took away that opportunity.

It's the pattern of David Phillips's associations that's relevant, and that pattern takes shape not only in the character of those with whom he worked closely, but also in the spread of alliances that fans out from them. William Pawley was a man who played a high-stakes game. As detailed earlier, he sponsored a fleet of boats for anti-Castro Cuban raiding parties and, in an effort to sabotage President Kennedy's Cuban missile crisis deal with Khrushchev, Pawley provided the yacht for the Cuban raiding party that was going to bring back two Russian missile site technicians. (If the mission hadn't failed, Luce was going to play the story big in *Life* in order to embarrass Kennedy.) Among those with Pawley on a CIA amphibious aircraft accompanying his yacht that night was John Martino, who had worked with the Mob in their lucrative Havana casinos. Martino's membership in the raiding party, and Pawley's dealing with him, reveals a crucial link in the fellowship of covert activists.

In August of 1977, during that disjointed period shortly after Chief Counsel Bob Blakey took the helm of the Assassinations Committee, a call came in from an informant in Fort Worth, Texas, who identified himself only as "Fred." This Fred said he had been in business with the late John Martino, who had died two years earlier after a long illness. Fred claimed Martino had told him that he "worked for the CIA" and that Kennedy was killed by anti-Castro Cubans. Martino had also told him that the assassins knew the President's motorcade route before they went to Dallas. That was all the information that Fred provided. His call was taken by a young Committee lawyer who had not yet acquired a thorough knowledge of the Kennedy case and didn't realize the call's startling implications. He simply wrote a memo about it and put it into the system.

From its inception, the Committee had received numerous calls with "inside information" about the Kennedy assassination. Most were so obviously off-the-wall they were ignored, but a few did have enough substance to bear checking out. The call from Fort Worth would probably have been ignored because of its generality: some guy who allegedly worked for the CIA said anti-Castro Cubans killed Kennedy. But when I read the memo, I recognized John Martino's name. I knew of Martino's relationship to William Pawley and Pawley's to the CIA and David Phillips and what the caller claimed Martino said shocked me. In fact, I had long suspected that John Martino was one of Phillips's assets, because he was among those involved at the time of the Warren Commission in promulgating uncorroborated rumors of Oswald's connections to pro-Castro Cubans in Miami, New Orleans and Mexico City.

John Martino was a relative of Philadelphia Mafia boss Angelo Bruno. He came out of a stint in Atlantic City as an expert at "repairing" casino vending and slot machines. Alan Roth, a Miami Beach developer, told me he first hired Martino when he owned a strip of South Beach real estate and leased a few places for bingo and slot machines. When Roth built the Deauville Hotel in Havana, he leased the casino to Santos Trafficante and Martino went to work there. (It was interesting that Roth admitted Martino's ties to top Mob figures. Roth should know: He was in business with Sammy Kay, who often fronted for Meyer Lansky.)

In July, 1959, Castro arrested Martino. His widow told me it was a case of mistaken identity, they were looking for a Navy officer with the same name. Nevertheless, Martino was held until October, 1962, and was released only after she hired a lawyer recommended by a friend who knew someone who had been in the American Embassy in Havana. She said she didn't have to pay the lawyer because he was being paid by that American Embassy fellow.

When Martino was released, he wrote a book titled *I Was Castro's Prisoner*, published in August, 1963. His collaborator on the book was Nathaniel Weyl, author of *Red Star Over Cuba*, who worked with Frank Sturgis after the Kennedy assassination pushing stories about Oswald in Miami. Weyl was also a member of the Citizens Committee to Free Cuba.

Right after his book's publication, Martino began traveling the country giving anti-Castro lectures, usually sponsored by the John Birch Society and other right-wing organizations. After the assassination, Martino's talks contended that Kennedy's death was the result of an act of retaliation for a CIA attempt on Castro's life. This "according to a source," Martino would say, "high in the Cuban government." Interestingly enough, that was the same story pushed to columnist Jack Anderson by Martino's close pal, Johnny Rosselli, the Mob figure who was actually involved in the CIA plots.

I was never able to corroborate the claim that Martino had said, before he died, that he knew of an anti-Castro, not a pro-Castro link to the Kennedy assassination. I did, however, find that Martino had once been in business with a "Fred" from Fort Worth. He and Fred Claasen were selling guns and bulletproof vests to the Guatemalan government. I tried to track down Claasen but he seemed to have disappeared from Fort Worth. Both Martino's widow and his son, Edward, told me that Martino never talked to them about anti-Castro Cubans being involved in the Kennedy assassination. But, said Ed Martino, who was with his father when he was arrested in Cuba, neither did his father ever reveal the source of his claim that Castro was involved in the Kennedy assassination. Ed Martino did say that his father told him he saw Lee Harvey Oswald passing out pro-Castro leaflets in New Orleans. His father, traveling on his lecture circuit, just happened to be there that day.

The trail that led from Maurice Bishop to Virginia Prewett to the Citizens Committee to Free Cuba produced another individual with close ties to David Phillips. In 1961, when Phillips was handling the propaganda desk for the Bay of Pigs operation and, as such, was in constant contact with friendly media types, there was a reporter on the *Miami News* named Hal Hendrix, whose coverage of the invasion seemed to be deeper and more detailed than any other journalist's, local or national. In 1962, Hendrix's coverage of the Cuban missile crisis was so penetrating and insightful it garnered his paper a Pulitzer Prize. The next year Hendrix got himself promoted to a more prestigious job, covering Latin America for the Scripps-Howard News Service. Still based in Miami, Hendrix's sources remained quite extraordinary. In a piece for Scripps-Howard dated September 23rd, 1963, Hendrix wrote a colorful and detailed description of the coup that toppled Juan Bosch, the leftist president of the Dominican Republic. If Hendrix's report didn't come from inside sources, it was an amazing display of clairvoyance—the coup didn't take place until the following day. Hendrix's close ties with the CIA were so apparent that, according to one staffer, he was sometimes referred to in Scripps-Howard's Washington office as "The Spook." However, that wasn't something Seth Kantor particularly remembered when he called Hendrix in Coral Gables on the afternoon of November 22nd, 1963.

Seth Kantor was the Scripps-Howard representative in the President's press corps that tragic and chaotic day in Dallas. The weight of the news service's coverage fell especially heavy on Kantor because he had worked for a Dallas newspaper and knew the locals. (One local he knew was Jack Ruby. Kantor had met and spoken with Ruby at Parkland Hospital moments before Kennedy was pronounced dead. Ruby later denied he was there and the Warren Commission, eager to squelch any evidence that Ruby's shooting of Oswald wasn't spontaneous, concluded that Kantor was mistaken.) After Oswald was arrested, Kantor checked in with his managing editor in the Washington office and was told to call Hal Hendrix at home in Florida. Hendrix was leaving for an assignment in Latin America, Kantor was told, but had some background information on Oswald he wanted to relay. Kantor called him and Hendrix provided a detailed briefing about Oswald's defection to the Soviet Union and about his activities in New Orleans handing out pro-Castro leaflets. Calling from the hectic Dallas police station, Kantor was too busy with what he was hastily scribbling to bother asking Hendrix where he had gotten the information—or how he had gotten it so soon after Oswald had been arrested and connected to the assassination.

Seth Kantor didn't recognize the significance of what had occurred until years later—although the Government obviously did much sooner. When the Warren Commission published its volumes of evidence it included a document listing the FBI's checks of telephone calls Kantor had made that day. The document, however, was based on an FBI report that was not released. Listed in the original FBI report, but not in the document published in the Warren Commission's volumes of evidence, was Kantor's call to Hal Hendrix. Why had that call to Hendrix been purged?

Some years later, Hendrix went to work for the International Telephone & Telegraph Corporation in Chile. In 1973, a Senate Multinational Corporations Subcommittee began looking at the role the CIA and ITT played in trying to prevent the election of socialist Salvador Allende in 1970. Under oath, Hendrix was asked about the source of a cable he sent to an ITT vice president notifying him that the American Ambassador in Chile had received a green light from the Nixon White House giving him "maximum authority to do all possible—short of a Dominican Republic-type action—to keep Allende from taking power." The cable also said that the Chilean army had been assured of "full material and financial assistance by the U.S." and that ITT had pledged financial support to the anti-Allende forces. As the Church Committee would later learn, David Phillips was in charge of the CIA's anti-Allende operation. But when asked during the 1973 probe about the source of the cable, Hendrix told the Senate investigators that his source was "a Chilean who was a personal friend." He lied. Three years later, a CIA cable was discovered that revealed not only that Hendrix's source was a CIA officer but that the Agency knew he was going to lie.

Hey, what are friends for?

On March 23rd, 1978, I wrote a memo to Chief Counsel Blakey about Hal Hendrix. A front-page story in the *Washington Post* revealed that two executives with ITT had been charged in connection with the Government's probe of CIA ventures in Chile, and that Hendrix had become a Government witness. My memo noted:

The two ITT aides are now charged with conspiring with Hendrix to block the Senate investigation of charges that ITT worked with the CIA to fund opponents of Allende in 1970. Last year, Hendrix pleaded guilty to a misdemeanor charge after being indicted for perjury in his Senate testimony. I suggest it is a most opportune time to subpoena Hendrix before our Committee in the hope of getting some valuable information from him. Considering his recent experience, Hendrix might respond more validly to a subpoenaed interrogation than he would to informal questioning. . . .

I had figured, considering Hendrix's propensity to lie about his CIA activities, there was little chance of his telling the truth. Now, however, having been caught lying once, the pressure to tell the truth under oath might produce valuable evidence, both regarding his knowledge of Oswald's activities and his relationship with David Phillips. I considered Hendrix an extremely important witness.

Unfortunately, it wasn't a good time to ask Blakey to continue pursuing the evidence that pointed to the intelligence community because he was deeply involved in structuring the Committee's public hearings with their accent on Organized Crime. There was never any response to my Hendrix memo.

THIRTY-NINE

A CONFLICT OF RECOLLECTIONS

D AVID PHILLIPS WAS a man of action. In *The Night Watch*, he tells how much he regretted having to spend so much more time behind a desk as he moved up in the Agency's ranks. Phillips loved being on the operational end of the dirty-tricks business, playing the covert-action games, surreptitiously spinning hidden wheels to orchestrate the series of "coincidences" which would bring about a particular counterintelligence objective. And the numerous awards he received indicate just how good he was at it. He tells the story, for instance, of so successfully setting up a top Cuban intelligence officer in Mexico City that Castro was led to believe that the man was involved in private illegal activity and recalled him to Cuba.

But Phillips's "autobiography" is rife with contradictions and paradoxes. On the one hand, he portrays himself as a hesitant spy, on the verge of quitting the Agency a few times, ready to begin "a new career" in public relations, writing or acting. Still, he kept accepting additional responsibilities. ("Albeit reluctantly, I became a manager of money and people. . . . ") The book is infused with the modesty of a dutiful but not very aggressive fellow who was simply lucky. Only indirectly was his job imbued with heroics or quiet valor. In one scene, set in the officer's bar at the CIA training school, a veteran agent interprets the cryptic message of an old Agency hand for a young recruit: "He's trying to tell you that the night watch can be lonely, but that it must be stood." It is that sort of subtle message-sending that characterizes almost all of Phillips's work, professional and personal.

He was also evasive. Although he was in key positions of responsibility at the time, Phillips claims he wasn't in the loop on a couple of the Agency's most infamous operations. This former Chief of Cuban Operations says, for instance, that he was never told about the CIA's relationship with the Mafia or their partnership in Castro assassination attempts.

Reading Phillips's book makes one wonder how someone whose career was a series of lucky breaks and modest successes could rise to the prestigious level of a Division Chief, the penultimate grade in the Agency, just below the presidentially appointed Director and Deputy Director. This became even more of a puzzle when I discovered there was a range of opinion among Phillips's workaday colleagues on his abilities as a professional spy.

One retired CIA officer, who still prefers anonymity, was chief of collections in covert action when Phillips was on the Cuban desk. "There wasn't a period when I could sign off on a cable from him," he said. "I usually had to send them back for some glaring technical errors. He was an incredibly sloppy officer, but he had a keen sense of public relations. Phillips was a grandstander. He was one of those guys who wanted to run countries in his own freewheeling style. We had a lot of guys like that. Howard Hunt was another fellow cut precisely from the same cloth as Dave Phillips. They were romantic adventurers. They couldn't possibly subject themselves to the kind of dry, arid, dispassionate anonymity you have to have if you're going to be a good espionage officer. Phillips was the supreme adventurer, one of a crowd of grandstanders who got into this goddamn CIA and once they got in they found out that in America, the grandstanding country, they could actually play to the galleries. And they've got away with it."

How, then, is Phillips's rise through the ranks explained?

"One of the problems with the Central Intelligence Agency," said the former officer, "is that it operates with two sets of books. It allows men like David Phillips, who could not endure otherwise, to get into positions where they can't be dropped off the line. David Phillips should have been dropped off the line in Mexico but he got under the protection of Des FitzGerald* and reached that certain

---

*In 1962, Desmond FitzGerald, then Chief of the Far Eastern Division, was made head of the CIA's Cuban Task Force W after its former boss, William Harvey, the Agency's handler of the Mafia Castro assassination plots, had been caught still dealing with the Mob even after Robert Kennedy had issued a cease and desist order. But, in 1975, the Church Committee said that FitzGerald himself had headed at least three Castro assassination attempts. In fact, he was meeting for that purpose in Paris with Rolando Cubela, a CIA asset (code-named AMLASH) who was a major in the Cuban army, on the day President Kennedy was killed.

point. Now once you reach that certain point, you can almost do no wrong because you've got too much guilty knowledge inside your head.''

I discovered others in the intelligence community outside the Agency whose views were also in contrast to the well-crafted image Phillips had created. Retired Naval Intelligence Captain Lionel Krisel, who was the Naval attaché at the American Embassy in Havana in the late Fifties, first met Phillips at a party Press Officer Dick Cushings was giving for a fellow he had known in Chile. "Everyone was very impressed with this handsome, dashing fellow and his charming wife," Krisel recalls. "I thought he was just another good-looking guy who was sort of bumming around Latin America because he couldn't make a living in the States. Later, of course, I learned he was undercover as an operative, but to this day I don't know what the hell he was doing there.''

Several years after this encounter, Krisel, a first-rate intelligence analyst, was commissioned by Admiral Arleigh Burke to gather the facts about the Bay of Pigs and write the Navy's official history of that operation. It was a particularly sensitive mission because the CIA, having held the operation very close to its vest and, therefore, having been totally responsible for its failure, was, retroactively, trying to cover its ass by attempting to diffuse the blame among all the military services. Throughout the years of his research for the as-yet-unreleased report, Krisel and his wife, Marcella, who worked with him on the project, felt they were being monitored by the Agency. In fact, they have some evidence that their telephones were tapped.

At one point, the Krisels felt that Phillips tried to take advantage of their acquaintance from their Havana days by attempting to weasel information from them about their research. The Krisels were invited to dinner one evening at the home of Clair Boonstra, a former Ambassador to Costa Rica who had been economic affairs counselor at the American Embassy in Cuba when the Krisels were there. When they arrived at Boonstra's home, the Krisels were introduced to "an old friend from Havana," David Phillips, who was by then Chief of the CIA's Western Hemisphere Division. With Phillips was his second wife, the former Virginia Simmons. Gina, as she was called, was delighted to hear that Krisel knew her father, also a Naval officer and Academy graduate. That, the Krisels felt, was a factor in the discomfort that Gina Phillips later exhibited. Marcella Krisel kept detailed notes of the evening.

When Phillips first arrived, she reported, the phone rang for him immediately. "When Margaret [Mrs. Boonstra] said, 'If you want to be real private, use the phone in the bedroom,' he said that would not be necessary. Just the call itself was no doubt the message.

"After we finished dinner, Dave said, 'Now we must talk about the Bay of Pigs.' Gina said, 'If that's the case, I'm leaving the room because it's making me nervous.' Lionel said it would be better to discuss it with Dave at another time. The question was: Was she nervous because in her natural loyalty for the Navy she was uneasy knowing that her husband was either about to try to get information from us for the CIA, or we were bugged and she knew it? Dave had another phone call just as we were leaving and then told his wife he would have to go by his office before going home."

Lionel Krisel, adding to his wife's observations, notes that a van pulled up and parked in front of the house shortly after the Phillipses arrived. He believes the van had an audio-surveillance mission and the telephone calls Phillips received were related to that. The fact that Krisel, a respected, high-ranking Naval Intelligence officer, suspected David Phillips of such deception reflects the reputation this veteran CIA operator had in the intelligence community.

In probing Phillips deeper, I began to feel he was more than one character. There was, in fact, more than one side to both the personal and the professional David Phillips. In his book, he portrays himself as something of a family man, concerned for his children, but his first marriage was a disaster because he was such a hard-drinking womanizer. And professionally, I would discover, he was not simply another diffident duty officer but an active player in a small clique within the CIA hierarchy who were almost autonomous in their operational capabilities. He was the protege of a brotherhood sprung from the Old Boys network of OSS veterans, who held the operational reins of the Agency. If he weren't, he would never have climbed so far and so high and he would never have survived his free-wheeling reputation among the nose-to-the-grindstone professionals who believed that the most effective agent was an anonymous cog in a silent, synchronized intelligence machine, not an autonomous "grandstander."

Until I casually dropped in to visit his brother Edwin, David Phillips might have assumed that the Assassinations Committee had ceased its efforts to identify Maurice Bishop. He had been questioned under oath, Antonio Veciana had been questioned under oath, and the CIA had checked its files and declared that no agent or officer had ever officially used the name Maurice Bishop. But my visiting his brother signaled Phillips that the Committee had not dismissed the possibility that he was the man Veciana said he saw with Lee Harvey Oswald in Dallas.

Shortly after I returned from Texas, there was a series of meetings in Washington to brief the staff for the preparation of the final Committee report. Dan Hardway greeted me as I walked into the office. (At the time, he and Ed Lopez were working on their secret report about Mexico City, which the CIA would not allow the Committee to publish.)

"Hey," Hardway called in his dulcet mountain twang, "we got an interview comin' up at the Agency you might be interested in." Hardway said that in the course of his file research at the CIA he had uncovered the existence of a deep-cover operative he wanted to talk with. The guy turned out to have worked deep cover and been involved in such sensitive operations that the CIA was reluctant to let the Committee interview him. Pushed a bit, the Agency relented, but insisted on special security measures for the interview, including limiting the number of Committee staffers who could see him.

"Turns out this fella worked with Dave Phillips quite a bit," Hardway said, "and probably was a good friend of his. Got any questions you want me to ask him?"

Yeah, I did, but the fella—who will here be named Bart Henry— turned out to be a closer friend of Phillips than Hardway suspected; so close, in fact, that he might have revealed something special about the bond that exists among covert operatives.

Bart Henry had been a CIA agent for almost twenty years. He specifically said that he worked very close to David Phillips—in fact on a "day-to-day" basis—on Cuban operations between 1960 and 1964. He said he thought of Phillips as one of the best agents the CIA ever had, characterized him as an "excellent intelligence officer," and admitted he was "a personal friend."

When Henry was asked if he knew an individual named Maurice Bishop, he shocked his interviewers by saying that he did. When asked to explain his relationship with Bishop, Henry said: "Again, Mr. Bishop was in the organization but I had no personal day-to-day open relationship with him. Phillips, yes; Bishop, no. I knew them both."

Strangely, however, Henry couldn't describe Bishop's physical characteristics. He then said he had only seen him "two or three times" in the "hallway or cafeteria" at CIA headquarters in Langley. The times he saw Bishop, Henry said, were between 1960 and 1964, when he himself was in Cuban operations, although, he said, he did not know if Bishop also worked in that area. Henry said he thought Bishop worked in the Western Hemisphere Division and that he had a position "higher than me." When pushed for further detail, Henry could not be more specific.

If he did not really know Bishop, Henry was asked, how did he know that the person he saw at CIA headquarters was, indeed, Maurice Bishop? His answer: "Someone might have said, 'That is

Maurice Bishop,' and it was different from Dave Phillips or . . . guys that I know.''

The interview went on into other areas and then, just before it ended, Henry was shown the composite sketch of Bishop without being told who it was. No, he said, it didn't remind him of anyone he knew.

I reviewed the transcript of that interview several times. A few of Henry's contentions, I thought, were difficult to believe. First of all, I had been in on a number of interviews and file searches at Langley. Having glimpsed just the surface mechanisms of the CIA's rigid security procedures, and felt the heavy, stultifying silence in its hallways, I doubted very much that Maurice Bishop would have been so casually pointed out by name—especially not in the Agency's special cafeteria reserved for covert operatives. Henry's scenario rubbed against the Agency's "need-to-know" secrecy rule. (In fact, David Phillips himself reveals in his autobiography how for years he assumed that the Chief of Counterintelligence, James Angleton, was a person once pointed out to him in the hallway at headquarters and then, when he was assigned to work for Angleton, was quite shocked to be introduced to someone else.)

In further review of Bart Henry's transcript, however, I was struck by something much more fascinating: In answering questions about Maurice Bishop, he repeatedly mentioned David Phillips's name in the same sentence. Henry wanted us very much to know that, yes, he knew Maurice Bishop and he knew David Phillips and they were two different individuals.

Confirmation of my suspicions of Bart Henry's objective would come a few weeks later, following another surprising development in the search for Maurice Bishop.

About a week after the interview with Bart Henry, a young senior counsel named Bob Genzman happened to be on the West Coast taking a deposition from former CIA Director John A. McCone. A wealthy former shipbuilder, McCone had been appointed by President Kennedy in 1961 and was in the post when Kennedy was killed. Genzman's team was not working the anti-Castro area and so he was not intimately familiar with the details of the Veciana revelations about Maurice Bishop. Nevertheless, Bishop's name was put on a list which Genzman was asked to run by McCone in order to get his response—just for the record, of course. Here's the way Genzman's questions and McCone's answers were recorded in the deposition:

Q: Do you know or did you know Maurice Bishop?
A: Yes.

Q: Was he an Agency employee?
A: I believe so.
Q: Do you know what his duties were in 1963?
A: No.
Q: For instance, do you know whether Maurice Bishop worked in the Western Hemisphere Division or whether he worked in some other division of the CIA?
A: I do not know. I do not recall. I knew at the time but I do not recall.
Q: Do you know whether Maurice Bishop used any pseudonyms?
A: No, I do not know that.

When Genzman returned to Washington he told me how surprised he was at McCone's positive response to the Bishop name. "I only wish I were more familiar with the details of the Bishop story so I could have asked him more specific questions," he said, "but he didn't seem to remember much else. I got the impression he just somehow recalled the name from his days at the Agency and that was about it. I believed him."

Initially, I found it difficult to fit McCone's recollection of the name of Maurice Bishop—and that was basically all he really remembered—into the model of the evidentiary structure which was emerging. Then, as I dug deeper, the role of John McCone himself appeared to provide a perspective.

David Phillips obviously didn't appreciate the appointment of McCone as CIA Director, describing McCone as an "outsider" without experience in clandestine operations. "In his first appearances at Langley," Phillips wrote in his autobiography, "he left an impression of austerity, remoteness and implacability."

Although McCone was the Director of the CIA, the fraternity never accepted him. McCone was appointed after Kennedy had fired Allen Dulles, the dean of the Old Boys network, and McCone immediately put a greater emphasis on intelligence analysis and estimates and placed more stringent controls on covert operations. As a result, the brotherhood of insiders who actually ran the Agency kept McCone in the dark about the CIA's most sensitive operations. Later, for instance, Richard Helms, who was McCone's Deputy Director of Plans and head of the dirty tricks department, admitted he never told McCone about any of the Agency's plans to kill Castro, or about the CIA's working relationship with the Mafia.

The CIA has admitted participating in some plots to assassinate Fidel Castro. While there is nothing in the Agency's own records to support the contention, there is plenty of independent evidence to suggest that the CIA—or some of its operatives acting "unofficially"— was also involved in "off-the-book" plots to kill Castro. It makes sense—the initial *raison d'être* of Maurice Bishop's relationship with Antonio Veciana, for instance, was to assassinate Castro.

Is it possible that Director McCone was told of Maurice Bishop without being told the specific nature of his operations? Could that account for what appeared to be McCone's vague familiarity with the name?

Having gotten the surprising confirmation of the existence of a Maurice Bishop from both John McCone and Bart Henry, the Assassinations Committee asked the CIA to once again search its files for any references to a Maurice Bishop. Chief Counsel Blakey said he also wanted a written reply from the Agency indicating whether an individual using either the true name or pseudonym of Maurice Bishop had ever been associated in any capacity with the CIA.

Less than two weeks later, the Committee received an answer. The results of its file search for Maurice Bishop, said the CIA, were again negative. "No person with such a name has a connection with the CIA," said the reply. "Quite frankly," it added, "it is our belief—from our earlier check, reinforced by this one—that such a man did not exist, so far as CIA connections are concerned."

It was later revealed, however, that the CIA had gone beyond just another checking of its files. The Agency itself, it turned out, had been puzzled by the responses the Committee had received from John McCone and Bart Henry. On October 19th, 1978, Chief Counsel Blakey received a letter from the Agency's chief liaison with the Committee:

> This is to advise you that I have interviewed Mr. McCone and a retired employee [Bart Henry] concerning their recollections about an alleged CIA employee reportedly using the name of Maurice Bishop.
>
> We assembled photographs of the persons with the surname of Bishop who had employment relationships of some type with the CIA during the 1960's, to see if either Mr. McCone or the employee would recognize one of them.
>
> Mr. McCone did not feel it necessary to review those photographs, stating that I should inform you that he had been in error. . . .
>
> The employee continues to recall a person of whom he knew who was known as Maurice Bishop. He cannot state the organizational connection or responsibilities of the individual, not knowing him personally, and feels that the person in question was pointed out to him by someone, perhaps a secretary. He is unable, however, to recognize any of the photographs mentioned above. . . .
>
> It should be noted that the employee's statements to the effect that it is usual for employees to use aliases at Headquarters is in error. . . .
>
> In summary, Mr. McCone withdraws his statements on this point.

The employee continues to recall such a name, but the nature of his recollection is not very clear or precise . . .

That, to me, was an astonishingly revealing letter. The Agency had obviously gone to John McCone and told him that there was no official record of a Maurice Bishop in its files and McCone, who had only a vague recollection of the name to begin with and no ulterior motive, simply said, in effect, O.K., boys, I guess I was wrong. Bart Henry, on the other hand, couldn't very well back down from his contention. He had a personal friend to consider.

David Atlee Phillips, former Chief of the Western Hemisphere Division of the CIA, lied under oath to the House Select Committee on Assassinations—and he got away with it. In its final report, the Committee slipped in that fact obliquely, relegating it to a footnote. This was a devious way to cover its ass; it also illustrated the Committee's readiness to dismiss evidence that would contradict the final report.

That it disregarded Phillips's perjury confirms the Committee's tacit decision not to pursue the truth *wherever* it might lead—especially if it headed toward the CIA. Chief Counsel Blakey had, after all, a very delicate "working agreement" with the Agency.

David Phillips represented the most crucial investigative link ever developed between the Central Intelligence Agency and the assassination of President Kennedy. His seemingly "coincidental" emergence in more than one meaningful area demanded an in-depth probe. The Committee deliberately avoided doing that. It never put pressure on the Agency to resolve the "inconsistencies" of Phillips's testimony about his role in Mexico City and his covert relationship to anti-Castro activities. I felt the CIA should be made to reveal not only every facet of Phillips's career, but also to produce all its files on every CIA asset or associate who had ever worked with Phillips. And because the Committee had given a couple of Phillips's closest Agency buddies the option of lying by not questioning them under oath, I wanted all future interrogations to be by sworn testimony.

My prodding was an annoyance. Chief Counsel Bob Blakey would later tell journalist Tony Summers that he had been privately briefed by the CIA about the issue. So, while he personally accepted the notion that David Phillips was, indeed, Maurice Bishop, he didn't believe that Veciana ever saw Oswald. It was as if he had never read in my reports how Oswald's name had surfaced in a totally incidental manner during my first interview with Veciana, who wasn't then aware that I was primarily interested in the Kennedy assassination. Further, Blakey's unfounded assumption that Veciana was deliberately planting misinformation was itself loaded with ramifications demanding a broader investigation. But a broader investigation was the last thing that Blakey and the Committee wanted or would permit. My insistence that we go after the Phillips-Bishop connection, Blakey would later claim to the media, was like Captain Ahab's obsession with the Great White Whale. But Blakey didn't get the point: Moby Dick was a helluva lot more than just another fish in the ocean.

FORTY

MURDER THROUGH A FOREST OF MIRRORS

*I*N 1988, nine years after the Committee's final report was released, David Atlee Phillips died in his home in Bethesda, Maryland, after a dreadfully long fight with cancer. He was 65. His death seemed anticlimactic. The Assassinations Committee had blown a pivotal opportunity in not conducting a full and complete investigation into the role of David Phillips in the Kennedy assassination. Independent research done since then, by myself and others, and without the power and resources of the Government, has gone deeper than the Committee ever wanted to go. Now the enormity of the Committee's failure can be even more clearly documented.

Phillips was a chameleon of a man whose character and career should have been probed in multiple contexts. That contention is not the result of hindsight: The Committee had indications that Phillips was involved in more virulent operations and with more deadly associates than the Agency had revealed. Ironically, this man—anonymously referred to in the Committee's final report as "the retired CIA officer"—was enmeshed in some mysterious exploits at the very time the Committee's investigation was in progress.

On the morning of September 21st, 1976, four days after the House of Representatives passed Resolution 1540 which established the Select Committee on Assassinations, former Chilean Foreign and Defense Minister Orlando Letelier drove down Massachusetts Avenue in Washington, D.C., on his way to work at the Institute for Policy

Studies. With him were two colleagues, newlyweds Ronni and Michael Moffitt, both 25 years old. As the blue Chevelle entered Sheridan Circle and moved by the ranks of stately former mansions and townhouses along Embassy Row, a remote-controlled bomb fastened under the car exploded with a concussive boom, lifting the car, blowing off the driver's door and crumbling the roof. The car crashed down onto a Volkswagen parked in front of the Rumanian Embassy and smoldered amid shattered glass and charred debris. There was a large hole in the car's front floor panel; Letelier's body was wedged backwards in the mangled metal, his legs blown off. Ronni Moffitt staggered out of the car and collapsed, her carotid artery severed by shrapnel. Michael Moffitt was blown out of the car, miraculously with no serious injury. Only he would survive.

There was no question that the plan to assassinate Letelier was conceived in Chile. At 44, a tall, handsome man, a poet, a lawyer, an economist, an associate of the Inter-American Development Bank and Ambassador to the U.S., Letelier had been Chile's Defense Minister when Salvador Allende was overthrown and murdered by the junta generals in September of 1973. The junta generals had gotten into power with the help of the CIA and David Phillips's Track II program.* More than 10,000 were shot or tortured to death in the years following the coup. Letelier was arrested, tortured and shipped to a concentration camp on a barren island in the Straits of Magellan where he was put to work cracking rocks. Isabel Letelier, with the wives of other former ministers, organized a worldwide movement to free him and on the first anniversary of the coup, hoping to mute increasing international criticism, General Augusto Pinochet released Letelier and permitted him to leave the country.

---

*Track II, as the name implies, was part of a two-track program emanating from the highest echelons of the U.S. government to prevent Salvatore Allende from taking power. Having won the election with a plurality of the votes, Allende's presidency needed confirmation by the Chilean congress. Track I was more or less "overt," created to manipulate the congress into voting down Allende's election. Track II was the CIA's top-secret effort to induce a military coup. This program was so closely held that Phillips, who was recalled to Washington from his posting in Brazil to take the helm, was given an office in a mail room so no one at Langley would suspect the importance of his mission.

Track I was officially disbanded in mid-October 1970, about a month after it began. Ostensibly, the U.S. Government was calling a halt to all involvement in the Chilean election because of the botched kidnapping of Chilean armed forces chief General Rene Schneider by officers eager for a coup. (Schneider was killed in the attempt.) However, Track II lived on—funding right-wing newspapers and opposition groups, and likely funding a national truckers' strike. (The truckers managed well, despite having no strike fund and no visible means of support.) Between March of 1970 and October 1973, David Phillips had control of an $8.8 million CIA budget for Chile.

That was the General's mistake. Letelier was soon speaking out and traveling widely through Europe and Latin America meeting with influential friends, labor leaders and government ministers, urging a boycott of Chile and the cancellation of loans and trade credits. However effective he actually was, the Chilean generals began perceiving him as more than just a thorn in their side, but as a real threat, a rebel leader rallying a growing body of opposition to their government.

Not only did David Phillips have contacts which went back many years among the top Chilean military leaders who ordered the Letelier hit and were responsible for carrying it out, he likely had a role in helping them retain power through his skilled intervention in the aftermath of Letelier's murder. And, among Phillips's network of anti-Castro Cubans, who were trained as assets while Phillips was head of psych ops at the JM/WAVE station in Miami, was a group of terrorists who would later be directly linked to the Letelier assassination.

The interconnections among these men are Byzantine, stretching over dozens of years and thousands of miles and Chile is a signpost pointing a way through the forest of mirrors. Following these connections is crucial to understanding why the Assassinations Committee should have considered David Atlee Phillips a priority—perhaps *the* priority—in its investigation.

Consider this: David Atlee Phillips had begun his CIA career in Chile as a $50-a-month part-time agent. He had retained friendships and contacts through the years and was the CIA's resident Latin America expert. As mentioned previously, he was pulled from his post as CIA Chief of Station in Brazil to nurture the CIA's Track II program, which was of the utmost importance to the U.S. Government. (Just prior to Allende's election, Henry Kissinger had told the National Security Council, "I don't see why we need to stand by and watch a country go Communist because of the irresponsibility of its own people.") Although Phillips returned to South America—from Brazil he went to Venezuela—he was again recalled to Washington in June of 1973 and was made Chief of the Western Hemisphere Division just as the anti-Allende campaign was succeeding in Nixon's goal of "making the economy scream." That September, Allende was killed and General Augusto Pinochet and the junta took power.

In October, one month after Letelier's car was bombed in Washington, the mid-air explosion of a Cubana Airlines plane flying out of Barbados killed all 73 persons aboard, including a score of South Americans and all 24 of the young athletes on Cuba's gold-medal fencing team. Trinidad police arrested two Venezuelans, Freddy Lugo and Hernan Ricardo, who had been traveling on the first leg of the trip under assumed names. Ricardo, who worked for Luis Posada's security agency, admitted that he and Lugo had planted two bombs on the plane. He said that Posada and Dr. Orlando Bosch were the masterminds. Ricardo and Lugo were turned over to the Venezuelan police and Posada and Bosch were arrested. Interestingly, when the police raided Posada's office, they discovered a map of Washington showing Letelier's daily route to work.

It was Luis Posada who had earlier worked with Antonio Veciana to organize the Castro assassination attempt directed by Maurice Bishop in Chile in 1971. At the time, Posada was working for the Venezuelan secret police, known as *DISIP*, and was also, I would later learn, on the CIA payroll—as he had been ever since he left the CIA training post at Fort Benning, Georgia. In 1975, Posada ostensibly left *DISIP* to set up his own private security agency.

Despite worldwide condemnation of the plane bombing, the arrest of Posada and Bosch actually put the Venezuelan government in a bind. Posada was little known publicly, but former baby doctor Orlando Bosch was probably the most famous Cuban exile of all. He was an extreme and very vocal anti-Castro fanatic. "Bosch," the *Boston Globe* once editorialized, "is in a class with terrorists such as Abu Nidal." Yet the Venezuelan government had given Bosch safe haven in Caracas while he was a fugitive from the United States Government. (He had left the country while on parole after serving time for firing a bazooka at a Polish ship that was docked in Miami Harbor while en route to Cuba.) The Venezuelan government was further embarrassed because Posada had earlier been on the payroll of its own secret police.

By June of 1978, Posada and Bosch were still being held in a Venezuelan jail without yet having been brought to trial—although the actual bombers, Ricardo and Lugo, had been convicted and were serving twenty-year sentences. At the time, I wasn't aware that David Phillips had any association with either the Letelier murder or the airline bombing, but both Posada and Bosch were on the list of witnesses Al Gonzales and I had requested to interview for the Assassinations Committee investigation. But we had been kept busy with other matters and couldn't get permission to go to Venezuela until somewhat late in the game. Finally, considering Veciana's report of Posada's involvement in the aborted attempt on Castro in Chile, and Marita Lorenz's story of Bosch's direct involvement in the Kennedy assassination, Bob Blakey decided that those two witnesses were, after all, bases that had to be touched for the sake of the final report's appearance of thoroughness. The fact that Posada's and Bosch's statements and their answers would not be taken under oath was irrelevant. Having them on the record was important. This, after all, was the last investigation.

Gonzales and I interviewed Posada and Bosch individually in a small visiting room in the Cuartel San Carlos, a place that looked more like an old Spanish monastic retreat than a prison. It was relatively clean and seemed to be run rather casually by the Venezuelan Air Force.

Bosch was brought out first, escorted by a lieutenant of the guard. The former pediatrician is a small man with broad, dark brows, heavy jowls and a strong chin. He wore thick glasses and looked tired and pale. Although neatly dressed he exuded an air of dishevelment, like an intellectually immersed college professor. He was cordial, expressed no reluctance to cooperate and, at the end, said he would be willing to sign a deposition or sworn statement to everything he had told us. Al Gonzales's long and gritty education as a homicide detective has given him a better than fair sense of a witness's credibility, but both he and I were taken aback by Bosch's seeming lack of evasiveness. He was a true ideologue and quite proud of it.

We questioned Bosch extensively about his activities and associates, including his relationship with the CIA. He said he ran an anti-Castro training camp for the Agency in Homestead, Florida, shortly after the Bay of Pigs. His liaison agent was a "Mr. Williams." When Bosch became suspicious that the U.S. Government was deceiving him about planning another invasion of Cuba, Williams warned him about reacting too strongly. "He told me, 'Be careful, they will betray you.'"

And Bosch felt he was betrayed. He said he wrote a pamphlet, titled *The Tragedy of Cuba,* accusing the United States of misleading the Cuban exiles, and sent a copy to President Kennedy. Bosch included a letter saying if he didn't get a promise of action from Kennedy he would publish the pamphlet and close down the camp. Receiving no reply, he had five thousand copies of the pamphlet printed and then shut down the operation. "Since then, I have had nothing to do with the CIA," he said.

Considering his ideological perspective, Bosch's assessment of the Kennedy assassination surprised us, although it was the same as Antonio Veciana's. Bosch said he had never studied the details but, unlike many of his fellow Miami exiles eager to stir up a U.S. reaction against the Cuban dictator, Bosch said he didn't believe that Castro was involved. "What could Castro gain by doing that?" Bosch asked. "It was too risky a thing and he had nothing to win. Whatever you can say about Castro, it is true, but he is not stupid." Bosch, who has devoted his life to fighting Castro, knows that well.

Asked about the allegation made by Marita Lorenz that he was involved in the Kennedy assassination, Bosch said he had heard about it on television news in Venezuela. (Lorenz, you may recall, claimed that Bosch was part of a group she had traveled with to Dallas a few days before the assassination. She also said that Bosch was present in a motel in Dallas when Kennedy's murder was planned.) Bosch dismissed it all with a wave of his hand. "I've never been farther west than New Orleans," he said. Bosch said he first met Lorenz when she was brought to his house by a pilot named Alex Rorke, an associate of Frank Sturgis, with whom Bosch said he worked frequently. Bosch described how they were planning an air raid over Cuba at the time and Lorenz wanted to be involved. Subsequently, Bosch said, Lorenz called him a few times asking to take part in his anti-Castro actions. He turned her down. "I could not understand why a girl like her wanted to get involved in these kinds of things," he said.

We asked Bosch about Antonio Veciana, whom he called "a good friend." He said he knew that Veciana was instrumental in organizing the assassination plot against Castro in 1971. "We do not call it an assassination attempt," said Bosch. "We call it a 'justice action'." More significant, he was familiar with the details of the plot. "That was the best chance we had, Castro in Chile. There were these two guys right in front of Castro with the machine gun hidden in the camera. Right in front of him with a machine gun from here to there, but these two guys, these two—I want to qualify them—*bastards*, were in front of him and one was scared and the other was chicken. Right in front of Castro!" Bosch shook his head in dejection, his shoulders sagged with the weight of his sorrow for the lost opportunity.

Although Bosch knew all about the failed "justice action," he said he did not learn of the details from Veciana. "A friend told me exactly what happened," said Bosch. Al and I assumed that "friend" was his prison pal and co-conspirator in the airline bombing, Luis Posada. Bosch, however, said he wasn't aware of Veciana being involved with any American intelligence agent in the planning, and that Veciana had never mentioned a Maurice Bishop to him. "This Bishop you ask about, I do not know," he said. "But I believe it could be true because Veciana is an action man and to do all the things he did you have to have a lot of connections, and that's not too easy."

The candid assessments offered by Orlando Bosch were in striking contrast to what we got from Luis Posada. He strolled into the room casually self-assured, a good-looking guy in his late forties, tanned and tall with no hint of prison pallor. His brown hair was trimmed and styled, his shirt tailored, his trousers sharply creased. Prison life seemed to agree with him.

Posada put his feet up on the desk, smiled and admitted to very little. Yes, he said he knew Antonio Veciana but not well, may have met the man twice briefly. No, he wasn't involved in any plan to assassinate Castro. "Veciana is like most Cubans," he said. "They talk too much and make up stories."

Posada was deliberately vague about the chronology of his association with the CIA. "All Cubans work for the CIA," he laughed. He admitted taking the Agency's secrecy oath after leaving Fort Benning but said he didn't remember when he left the Agency's employ.

Didn't remember?

He laughed again.

What we didn't know at the time was that Posada was a major figure in an international game of intrigue then in progress.** It was more than intrigue, it was a kaleidoscope of deceptive allegiances among the world's most cunning intelligence operatives. Only years later, when time and more probing cleared some of the fog, would I be able to glimpse the larger pattern. It is, of course, in that larger pattern where men on the level of David Atlee Phillips leave their marks.

The records, for instance, indicate that Luis Posada was dropped by the CIA in 1967. However, I would later learn that it was in the summer of that same year when Posada was drinking a beer with a friend at the Centro Vasco, a popular Basque restaurant on Miami's Calle Ocho, when a strange man in a dark suit approached him. Where the man came from or who sent him, Posada claims he doesn't know, but the man brought with him an offer for Posada to join *DISIP*. The offer came at a time when Castro, his eye on Venezuela's rich oil reserves, had dispatched scores of his own covert agents to organize the country's leftist guerrillas and the CIA was tracking that activity very closely.

By 1971, Posada, using the *nom de guerre* of Comisario Basilio, was chief of *DISIP*'s security division, in charge of surveillance and counterintelligence. The Cuban Embassy in Caracas came under permanent watch—its phones tapped, personnel tailed and civilian employees cultivated as informants. But there was a lot of local political spying which Posada also enjoyed, so much so that he made the mistake of gossiping about a salacious conversation that had been recorded between a young politician and his mistress. The politician never forgave him for wagging his tongue about that and when Carlos André Perez later became President of Venezuela, Posada was out of

---

**In retrospect, we did get an indication that something was in progress by Posada's denial that he knew David Phillips. When we later questioned Phillips, he knew we had access to the records and he did not know of Posada's denial, so Phillips admitted that Posada had been one of his operatives and had worked with him closely on Chilean activities.

a job. It was then that he opened his private security agency. To prepare himself, he became qualified as a polygraph expert at what he told us was "a private school outside of Washington."

After Posada, President Perez appointed another Cuban exile to be chief of state security. Orlando Garcia Vasquez, a dapper fellow with a gleaming bald head and an immaculately trimmed black beard, was the man Al Gonzales and I had to see to arrange our prison interviews with Posada and Bosch. In the process, we spent some time with Garcia in his *DISIP* headquarters, drinking coffee and chatting amiably. We were impressed with his six telephones, his gold Rolex, his two heavy gold rings (one diamond encrusted), his thick gold chain, his fancy silk shirt and his maroon cashmere sport jacket. Quite friendly, he seemed particularly interested in our interest in his prisoners. At the time, we didn't know that Orlando Garcia, besides being the head of the Venezuela secret police, was also on the CIA's payroll.

But as it turned out, these interviews merely skirted the edges. Probe a little more deeply and the forest of mirrors multiplies. In 1974, when Orlando Bosch jumped parole and fled the U.S., *DISIP* chief Garcia and his deputy, Ricardo "The Monkey" Morales invited Bosch to take refuge in Caracas. (You may recall that Morales, a Cuban exile and a veteran informant for the CIA, the FBI and the DEA, was the Government's "unavailable" witness in Rolando Otero's trial for an airport locker bombing in Miami.) But Bosch was expelled from Venezuela late that year after he was charged with two bombings, so Garcia had to slip him back into the country in secret. From there, Bosch skipped over to Chile and was feted by the junta.

David Phillips was in the thick of Latin American affairs in December, 1974, when Orlando Bosch, along with fellow anti-Castro terrorists Guillermo Novo and José Dionisio Suárez, visited Chile—at the invitation of and on the tab of the junta generals—and worked out a mutual assistance pact with General Pinochet. Chile would supply Bosch's militants with arms, explosives, false passports and a safe haven from which to operate. In return, the Cuban exiles would generate pro-Pinochet propaganda and help *DINA*, the Chilean secret police, get rid of Pinochet's exiled enemies, who were stirring up world opposition to his regime. It wasn't long before the results of Bosch's pact with Pinochet began to surface.

Phillips formally departed from the Agency in May, 1975, leaving responsibility for the Western Hemisphere behind. But he set up the Association of Former Intelligence Officers, and in doing so, actually positioned himself closer to the intelligence community. Phillips maintained contact with his closest associates in the Agency, including the man aware of every covert affair in progress—deputy director of operations Ted Shackley. Phillips's ties to Shackley went back decades and included their close working relationship at JM/WAVE, which Shackley headed.***

Then, in the summer of 1976, at a mountain resort near Bonao, Dominican Republic, twenty men representing the most militant Cuban exile groups held a secret meeting. It was a personal triumph for Orlando Bosch to bring together these fractious players in a coalition called Commando of United Revolutionary Organizations, or CORU. Attending that meeting were several friends of Bosch including the brothers Ignacio and Guillermo Novo and José Dionisio Suárez. These three men would later be charged in the Letelier assassination. (You may also recall that Marita Lorenz claimed the Novo brothers were along for the ride to Dallas.) Also present were Luis Posada and the *DISIP* chief's top gun, Ricardo Morales.

In the ten months after that meeting, CORU took credit for more than fifty acts of violence, including bombings, kidnappings and assassinations in Miami, New York, Panama, Brazil, Mexico and Argentina. As Bosch would later boast to *New Times* journalist Blake Fleetwood: "Everything was planned there." It was during this period that the Letelier assassination and the Cubana airlines bombing took place.

The Letelier assassination was not a CORU operation, although a few of the players were involved. But it was done for Chile and it was done with open arrogance. In daylight, on the streets of our nation's capital, in sight of hundreds of people and a dozen foreign embassies, brazen terrorists dared to carry out an outrageous gangland-style execution.

Since the first suspects to pop up were the Chilean secret police and radical anti-Castro Cubans, the CIA had reason enough to be—at the least—embarrassed by the incident. The Agency's close working relationship with Chile's intelligence service was well known and it was a matter of record that it was responsible for training Cuban exiles in the most sophisticated techniques of terrorism. So it seemed rational that the Agency would undertake a measure of damage control, and it seemed natural that the Agency would call upon the

---

***There is a sidebar to these interlocking circles of associations that's relevant to David Phillips's character and his lifelong charade. He had always presented himself as a pragmatic liberal—in fact a Democrat, although more politically moderate. He portrayed himself as an independent thinker who, while a defender of the Agency's subversive activities was unaligned with its militantly conservative elements. Yet those same elements maintained operational control of the CIA during those years when Phillips himself was rising to the highest ranks of the Agency. He was very much a part of the Old Boys network, the dominant insiders whose leaders were OSSers Allen Dulles and William Casey, those icons of Cold War zealousness. David Phillips was close to both men.

one man who had developed the best contacts and who was its most sophisticated, subtle and successful media expert and manipulator: David Atlee Phillips.

Soon a series of stories were planted in the press. *Newsweek*'s "Periscope" column said: "After studying FBI and other field investigations, the CIA has concluded that the Chilean secret police were not involved in the death of Orlando Letelier. . . ."

Jeremiah O'Leary, a *Washington Star* reporter long close to David Phillips, wrote: "Probers are not ruling out the theory that Letelier might just as well have been killed by leftist extremists to create a martyr as by rightist conspirators."

Reported the *Washington Post*: "CIA officials say . . . they believe that operatives of the present Chilean military junta did not take part in Letelier's killing, according to informed sources. CIA Director Bush expressed this view in a conversation late last week with Secretary of State Kissinger, the sources said. What evidence the CIA has obtained to support his initial conclusion was not disclosed."

One of the more interesting interpretations of the case came from a "Special Report" produced by the Council for Inter-American Security, a right-wing think tank, and distributed to the national media. It was written by Virginia Prewett, the journalist who had a special relationship with David Phillips. The piece Prewett wrote about the Letelier bombing indicates why she was one of Phillips's most effective media assets.

Prewett's "Special Report" was actually a diatribe against the Washington press for initially assuming that Chilean generals were involved in murdering Letelier. She, too, suggested that Letelier may have been sacrificed by leftists to turn world opinion and U.S. policy against the Pinochet regime. "Letelier was headquartered at and operated under the aegis of the radical leftist Institute for Policy Studies," she noted darkly. "Since the days of Stalin and Trotsky, intramural strife and expenditure of human life for political ends have been commonplace within the left."

However, extreme pressure on the U.S. Government from Letelier's associates at the Institute for Policy Studies drove a small group of dedicated individuals in the U.S. Attorney's office and the FBI to successfully pursue the case, despite the obstacles and false markers placed along the path by their own Government. Here's what they eventually were able to prove:

The orders to kill Letelier did, indeed, come from the highest levels of the Chilean government, through the head of *DINA*. Two high-level *DINA* officers carrying false passports were sent to the U.S. and they, in turn, contacted the anti-Castro Cubans who carried out the assassination. But the designer of the plan itself, the bomb maker and bomb planter, was the *DINA* agent in charge, Iowa-born electronics expert Michael Townley. Thirty-eight years old, tall and lanky with longish brown hair and a droopy moustache, Townley was the son of an American business executive who wound up as general manager of the Ford Motor plant in Santiago, Chile. Young Michael went back to the States to attend boarding school in Florida. He later worked as a mechanic among the Miami's Cuban exiles and returned to Chile just before Allende's election. He immediately became involved with the most radical opposition which, after Allende's overthrow, led to his connection with *DINA*.

Both Townley and the CIA deny he was an agent, but Townley admitted contacting the Agency before he returned to Chile. Agency records also show he was given "Preliminary Operational Approval," the green light to be used as an asset. The Agency claims that approval was later canceled, but has never satisfactorily explained why.

Townley eventually made a deal and testified against his *DINA* bosses and the five anti-Castro Cubans involved. He received a ten-year sentence, served five and is now living under the Government's witness protection plan. General Pinochet refused to let the *DINA* bosses be extradited and the Chilean military courts refused jurisdiction. Three of the five Cubans tried were convicted but their convictions were overturned for procedural error on appeal. (The other two had fled but were eventually caught; the last one arrested in 1991. Both pleaded guilty and each given a twelve-year sentence.) As part of an informal agreement with Townley, the Government agreed not to pursue his business relationship with his father, J. Vernon Townley, who had become a vice president of a major South Florida bank. (Townley and son had set up a corporation, called PROCIN, which imported chemicals which Michael Townley used to manufacture poison gas. Michael Townley had used the pseudonym of Kenneth Enyard on the corporation papers.)

While there are no available records which indicate that David Phillips had any operational association with Michael Townley, it's quite likely. Townley, for instance, ran a clandestine radio station to broadcast anti-Allende propaganda during the period Phillips ran the CIA's anti-Allende operation. What is known is that Phillips and J. Vernon Townley were well acquainted in Chile. Both were active in the urbane Latin American subculture of American diplomats and affluent U.S. corporate executives and they were buddies at the same social club in Santiago.

The first real evidence I had of Phillips's ongoing intelligence activity beyond his "retirement" came after the demise of the House Assassinations Committee, when I received a call from someone who said, "I think we have a mutual interest in David Phillips." It was Saul

Landau, a senior fellow at the Institute for Policy Studies, who had worked with Orlando Letelier. Landau and *Washington Post* reporter John Dinges were researching a book about the murder and found that Phillips had injected himself into the case. Landau couldn't understand why.

Somehow, according to the sources developed by Landau and Dinges, Phillips had obtained copies of papers that had been in Letelier's briefcase and was involved in distributing them to selected journalists and friendly legislators. The briefcase had been found on the scene of the bombing by a Washington homicide detective who happened to have a Latin background and was acquainted with Phillips. (The CIA and the Washington D.C. Police Department had an established relationship through a cooperative training program.) Among the items in the briefcase was a letter to Letelier from Salvador Allende's daughter, Beatriz, who had been given safe haven in Cuba. That was a juicy morsel Phillips and his media assets blew to distorted proportions. Pointing to Beatriz Allende's note, which said that she was sending Letelier pamphlets documenting human rights violations by the junta generals, columnist Virginia Prewett's "Special Report" concluded that the briefcase documents "revealed that Havana was manufacturing propaganda on 'human rights violations' in Chile for Letelier to use at the UN and elsewhere."

But one of the oddest and—considering she was among David Phillips's closest media assets—perhaps most relevant points in Prewett's piece on the Letelier murder was a reference to the Kennedy assassination. Apparently believing—or being told—that the image of Lee Harvey Oswald as the "lone nut assassin" could use repolishing, Prewett noted: "There are curious apparent similarities between Townley and Lee Harvey Oswald. Behind his drooping walrus moustache, Townley's photographs reveal the same 'loser' look. . . . His background of apparent ambivalence between leftist and rightist political extremes is similar to Oswald's." Strained as it was, that observation was clearly designed to do double duty.

Although Saul Landau and John Dinges had discovered Phillips's role in distributing the briefcase documents, Landau said he kept wondering whether Phillips's involvement went beyond simply using his skills in propaganda and media manipulation. That suspicion came out of indications that the CIA had advance information that Letelier was going to be hit.

Six weeks before the Letelier murder, the U.S. Ambassador in Paraguay, George W. Landau (no relation to Saul Landau), received a call from a top aide of Paraguayan President Alfredo Stroessner who said he was relaying a request directly from Chilean General Augusto Pinochet. The aide said that he needed visas immediately for two

Chilean army officers using Paraguayan passports to travel to Washington on an intelligence mission. He said the mission had been cleared with the CIA station in Santiago and that the two men would be in touch with CIA Deputy Director Vernon Walters in Washington.

Ambassador Landau knew it was an established practice of the CIA to cooperate with the intelligence services of "friendly" countries, including the granting of visas through the State Department for intelligence missions. Still, Landau was suspicious. Although he immediately granted the request, he took the precaution of having the Chilean officers' false Paraguayan passports photographed. Landau then sent a top-secret cable to CIA Deputy Director Walters asking him to confirm that the Chilean intelligence mission had been coordinated with the CIA. By diplomatic pouch, he also sent the CIA copies of the false Paraguayan passports which contained the photographs of "Juan Williams" and "Alejandro Romeral," the false names under which the two Chilean agents would be traveling. (One passport was particularly suspicious because it showed the photo of a tall, light-skinned man who gave as his birthplace a remote Paraguayan village where short, dark-skinned Indians lived.)

When Ambassador Landau's cable reached the CIA, Deputy Director Walters was on vacation in Florida, so it went directly to the desk of Director George Bush—at least Bush's initials were stamped on the cable. Today, authors Saul Landau and John Dinges believe that Bush never looked at it or, in his "out-of-the-loop" management style of running the Agency, didn't realize the significance of the cable. According to their sources, Bush passed it on to the Deputy Director of Operations, Ted Shackley. Apparently, Shackley simply sat on it until Walters returned. Finally, more than a week after Ambassador Landau's request for confirmation, Walters replied that he was "not aware" of the Chilean mission and wanted nothing to do with it.

The Chilean secret intelligence officer "Juan Williams" was Michael Townley; "Romeral" was an associate named Armando Larios. The CIA had their photographs when they arrived in the United States to kill Letelier.

The CIA was also aware that the Chilean secret police had formed an alliance with five other Latin American intelligence agencies, Paraguay among them, called Operation Condor. The purpose of the alliance was to assist each other in dirty missions, including assassinations. Considering its own close association with the Chilean agency (Deputy Director Walters was a personal friend of *DINA* chief Manuel Contreras), the CIA likely also knew that Michael Townley had been sent on at least two previous assassination missions outside Chile, one of which was successful.

Two weeks after the Letelier murder, the assistant U.S. Attorney and the FBI agent assigned to the case met with CIA Director Bush. Although Bush did suggest that Operation Condor may have some bearing on the Letelier case, he did not say a word about the "Williams" or "Romeral" photographs the CIA had in its possession, nor anything about the Paraguayan visa request. Even when the investigators later became aware of the photographs through the State Department, the CIA never volunteered that it had prior knowledge of the assassination team entering the U.S.

In fact, instead of providing information that pointed the finger of suspicion at *DINA* and Chile, the CIA apparently called out its misinformation forces and planted a series of false stories in the press.

Today the IPS's Saul Landau maintains that David Phillips, because of his close association with then-CIA clandestine ops director Shackley and his role in the misinformation campaign surrounding Letelier's death, most likely had prior knowledge that the assassination was coming down. "They could have stopped it," Landau says. "Wouldn't you think that any decent human being would have called Letelier and said, 'Look, you're a target, be careful.' Their information was solid. Chilean agents traveling under the cover of another country's passports was the standard operational procedure of Operation Condor's earlier assassination attempts. That cable from Ambassador Landau was a red flag which the CIA, for some reason, decided to hide. And David Phillips knew it."

A couple of days after the killings of Letelier and Moffitt, David Phillips returned a call from John Marks. Marks had been on the State Department's intelligence staff but had resigned and become a critic of the spy community. (With former CIA staffer Victor Marchetti, he co-authored *The CIA and the Cult of Intelligence* [Knopf, 1974].) Marks had known the murder victims, and he knew Phillips.

"I came home late last night," Phillips said, "and there was a note on the freezer door in the kitchen with your name. Did you call?"

"I'm very concerned about the Letelier business," said Marks.

"I can understand," said Phillips.

Marks's voice was unsteady, he was still very shaken by the news. "I knew him and the people who were killed with him. And it would seem to me that the circumstantial evidence points to an involvement of the Chilean government, through *DINA*. I mean, I would suppose you, too, would be shocked by what was going on."

"That's correct," said Phillips.

"Well, I'm hoping, because I think I have some knowledge of the very close liaison arrangement, and penetrations on top of that, with *DINA*, that there would be information available on your side of the river, so to speak. Dave, I think it's in everyone's interest that this thing get broken.''

"I'll tell you this," said Phillips, "if I find out anything that I think will help solve the murder of a man in Washington, D.C., I'll collaborate with you in seeing that the information gets where it should be.''

"I mean, it's my feeling that this raises the stakes in a way that it shouldn't be raised, this kind of violence," Marks went on. "I could have been riding in that car, Dave. People I knew were riding in it.''

"Was it just accidental that the other people were there?" asked Phillips.

"Yeah. And when you consider . . . I mean it's almost certainly a radio-controlled bomb . . . I mean, it just goes to show the kind of thuggery we're dealing with.''

"Of course, that's not new in Latin America," the former chief of the Western Hemisphere Division reminded him.

"I mean it would be inconceivable to me," said Marks, "that *DINA* could put together such an operation without, well, not necessarily liaison channels but at least penetration channels having some idea that something like this was up." (Marks was referring not only to the CIA's formal liaisons with the Chilean secret police but also to the covert agents it had within *DINA* itself. He was saying the obvious: The Agency *had* to have known.)

"Well," said Phillips coolly, "in this, as in all things, it would be good to have some evidence. But, John, I'll assure you that if I come up with anything, not only for my own personal conscience but for every good reason, I'll let you know anything that might be helpful.''

He sounded very sincere. Why would David Phillips lie about something as serious as murder?

FORTY-ONE

THE CRACK IN THE COVERT WEB

STAFF INVESTIGATOR Jim Kelly reminded me of Sergeant Joe Friday of the old *Dragnet* TV series, except Kelly was less swarthy, had a moonish face and less hair. Actually, he didn't look at all like Friday, but he had those eyes, the cool, slow-blinking, phlegmatic, inscrutable eyes of the classic detective. He spoke in a mumble-whisper, as if everything he said were classified and the walls were listening. But he was a bright guy and a damn good investigator, plodding, sincere and thorough and, word had it, with exceptional inside sources. He was among the few JFK staff investigators who came from a Capitol Hill background, having worked for other Congressional committees. After getting to know him, I dismissed my suspicions about his having a covert association with the intelligence community, but he let me know he had a few good contacts if I needed them.

So it didn't surprise me when, one day in those last few weeks of the Assassinations Committee's life, Jim Kelly poked his head into Team Two's doorway and, with an almost imperceptible move of his head, signaled me to join him in the hallway. Turning his back to Blakey's office, he sidled close and, taking an envelope from his inside jacket pocket, quickly slipped it low into my hand, indicating I should make it disappear. I folded it and stuck it in my back pocket.

Jim looked down the hallway as he mumble-whispered. "Got that from a friend," he said. "Can't vouch for it but I can't judge it. It's in your area, maybe you'll recognize some of the names." He started walking away but turned back. "By the way, eyes only, not for the system," he added.

I liked Jim but my first thought was: *What the hell kind of game is this?*

I looked over the document. Considering the road the Committee was on, where it was being steered and the harried chaos imposed on the staff during those final days, any investigation of the information in it was out of the question—no new doors could be opened. As it turned out, the document's principal contention was likely speculative, an assumption, but if the Assassinations Committee were young and had the leadership that would demand the time and resources and, most important, had the determination to conduct a "full and complete investigation," that document would have created dramatic cracks in the intelligence community's walls, maybe even produced a significant breach.

The document was marked "HIGHLY SENSITIVE." It was two pages of single-spaced typing and it contained eleven names, with a paragraph or a few sentences about each one. The list was prefaced with this:

> In September of 1975 [*sic*] an ex-ambassador from Chile named Letilier [*sic*] was assassinated in Washington, D.C. The hit was accomplished by use of a bomb placed in the car in which he was riding.
>
> The press (i.e., Jack Anderson 9/8/77) has announced that it was done by Cubans who were graduates of the Bay of Pigs, 2506 Brigade.
>
> There is a group of current and/or "retired" CIA types who were involved. . . .

Yet, although the document contained that list of names, it provided no evidence or indication of exactly how those individuals were connected to Letelier's murder. Although it said nothing about the Kennedy assassination, I knew there had to be some link because it had been passed to Kelly. It contained sketchy details about who some of the men were and what they were doing, but the presentation of the information smacked of a knowledgeable insider who had overheard a conversation in a bar. It was as if someone who worked for one division of a company had eavesdropped on a group who worked for another division of the company. Factual detail, hearsay and rumor seemed scrambled together. Yet there was enough meat in there to indicate that the writer did, indeed, work in the same company. Certainly, the theme of the document was clear: Here was a group who appeared to be a renegade collection of intelligence operatives for whom assassination was part of the game—whatever the game was or had been.

David Phillips's name was not on the list. In fact, at the time I recognized only a few of the names on it. Since then, a lot more has become known about some of these men and about their relationship with Phillips. Ironically, my knowledge increased long after the Assassinations Committee ended, when I received a call from one of the men on the list.

Kevin Mulcahy called me because he thought the Federal Government had used him and was hanging him out to dry. A husky, dark-haired, 39-year-old Irishman, Mulcahy was an ex-CIA agent who, at that time, was the only witness in a case the Federal Government had brought against two other men on Kelly's list: Edwin Wilson and Frank Terpil. Mulcahy thought the Government was stalling in its prosecution and he feared for his life. Wilson, he said, was a killer, whose current job was arranging to knock off the enemies of Libyan strongman Moammar Khadafy. In response to my direct question, Mulcahy said he knew nothing that would link Wilson to the Kennedy assassination, but Wilson, like David Phillips, was deep inside that CIA clique pulling the strings at the time.

Mulcahy had been born a Company man. His father had worked for the CIA, so did three brothers and a sister. After five years as an Agency communications specialist, Mulcahy quit, announcing he was going to make a bundle in the computer industry. But Mulcahy had a drinking problem and his marriage and his life went to hell. Still, he bounced back, recovered completely and used his energies counseling alcohol and drug abusers at a northern Virginia treatment center. Then, early in 1976, he met Edwin Wilson and was offered a job with Wilson's exporting firm, Consultants International.

To insiders, Wilson was a big-time player in the spook world. He owned a huge estate in Virginia horse country and regularly hosted Washington's top politicians, admirals, generals and key intelligence officers. He had been in the CIA's Special Operations section, which handled covert paramilitary operations around the world. His job was to set up the proprietary companies used to ship supplies for the Agency's secret missions or the coups it supported. Wilson's company shipped incendiary, crowd dispersion and harassment devices to Chile, Brazil and Venezuela, and arms to the Dominican Republic, all areas that came under David Phillips's charge. Wilson also had supplied many of the boats used by Miami exiles for their raids against Cuba. (His case officer at one point was Tom Clines, who then was a top deputy to Ted Shackley at Miami's JM/WAVE station.) Reportedly, Wilson left the CIA when President Nixon, always paranoid about the Agency, ordered a budgetary cutback of its proprietaries. Wilson then went over to a top-secret Navy Intelligence operation called Task Force 157 and basically did the same thing. This job was personally lucrative for Wilson because millions of dollars were involved and the oversight was negligible. At some fuzzy point in time, Wilson supposedly broke his employment ties with the Government and got into business for himself. Yet in the 1980 Reagan campaign, Wilson played a key advisory role, reporting directly to campaign manager William Casey, who would become director of the CIA.

According to the document I got from Jim Kelly, among the products Wilson was shipping to Libya's Khadafy were highly sophisticated assassination devices. No larger than a cigarette box, these were capable of blowing up an entire building and could be set to detonate anywhere from ten seconds to ten days later—or longer. These were developed by ex-CIA bomb expert John Harper, whose wife worked for Wilson. Harper, too, had once worked in Miami for Tom Clines.

Mulcahy told me that when he took the job Wilson gave him the impression he was still operating a CIA proprietary, shipping electronic and computer equipment. Mulcahy spent his early days at Consultants International learning the paperwork labyrinth of the export business. After Wilson started to trust him, Wilson introduced Mulcahy to Frank Terpil, another ex-CIA associate who had also worked for Shackley at JM/WAVE. Eventually, Mulcahy met Shackley himself one weekend at an outing at Wilson's Virginia estate. More than ever, Mulcahy was convinced Wilson was still running proprietaries for the Agency.

Mulcahy then found himself involved in some serious transactions. He learned first of a shipment of machine guns to Zambia. It wasn't so much the guns but the silencers that went with them that had sinister significance. Mulcahy decided to check out Wilson and Terpil with the Bureau of Alcohol, Tobacco and Firearms. BATF told him the men were clean.

Then Wilson and Terpil made Mulcahy the president of what he thought was another proprietary, Inter-Technology Inc., and details of even more sinister deals emerged. Mulcahy learned that the firm of which he was now President had agreed to sell to Khadafy the explosives and delayed-action timers mentioned on the "sensitive" list. I.T.I. had also agreed to set up a training camp to teach Libyans bombing and political assassination techniques and to fill Libya's order for an American-made Redeye missile, which is capable of shooting down a commercial airliner.

Late one Sunday evening in September of 1976, Kevin Mulcahy, drinking again, placed a call to the duty officer at CIA headquarters. "There are problems overseas," Mulcahy reported. He said he had to talk to Ted Shackley, then assistant to the deputy director for clandestine operations. Within the hour, Shackley returned the call. Mulcahy told him of the deals Wilson and Terpil had with Khadafy and then asked him directly: "Is this a CIA operation or not?"

In his call to me, Mulcahy said that Shackley wouldn't give him a straight answer. And as Shackley beat around the bush Mulcahy suddenly got the queasy feeling that he had made a wrong move in calling the clandestine ops boss. Now fearing his life was in danger, Mulcahy went into hiding. Armed with an M-16 rifle, he disappeared into the Shenandoah Valley woods, shifting campsites every evening. A month later he moved to a small town and established a new identity. With his new birth certificate, driver's license, passport and credit cards, he got a job at a health agency as a counselor.

Eventually, Mulcahy went to the FBI with his story. But the Foreign Agents Registration Office of the Justice Department claimed there wasn't enough evidence to prove Wilson and Terpil had violated American laws. When that report crossed the desk of Eugene Propper, a young, aggressive Assistant U.S. Attorney for the D.C. area who had been investigating the Letelier assassination, it gave him pause. He had questioned Wilson earlier and Wilson had emphatically denied any involvement in the sale of detonation devices to Libya. Propper discussed Wilson's apparent lie with Lawrence Barcella, the assistant U.S. Attorney who originally discovered the FBI report and had passed it on to Propper. Despite the Justice Department's Foreign Agents Office's declining to prosecute, Propper and Barcella decided to open an investigation.

As was discovered later, some time prior to the Letelier assassination Wilson had gotten another assignment from Khadafy. The Libyan leader wanted one of his principal enemies, hiding in Cairo, assassinated. Wilson decided to dip into the pool of anti-Castro Cubans in Miami trained as experts in the field by the CIA. He called Rafael "Chi-Chi" Quintero, a veteran of a number of JM/WAVE's sabotage and assassination missions. Wilson didn't mention Libya and gave Quintero the impression it was an Agency job. He talked big money, maybe as high as a million dollars. Quintero called Tom Clines, his old case officer, at the Agency to check out Wilson's request. Clines gave Wilson a ringing endorsement.

Quintero recruited two brothers, Rafael and Raoul Villaverde, who had worked for him in the old days, and all three flew to Geneva to meet Wilson and Terpil and get the details for the hit. They sat down, had a few drinks and Terpil, a burly, rough-edged fellow, got a little soused. He said something about Russian and Chinese terrorists being trained in Libya. That rankled the Cubans, all ardent anti-Communists, and aroused their suspicions. They told Wilson they would go along with the deal but first they had to return to Florida to get their affairs in order. Quintero decided to fly directly to Washington to tell Tom Clines what had happened.

Clines was caught in a bind. He wanted to protect his associate Wilson, but there was no way he could avoid officially reporting Quintero's visit. In a confidential report to the CIA's Inspector General, Clines attempted to fudge as much as possible, taking the liability largely off Wilson and putting it on Terpil.

None of this reached the attention of the newly appointed Director of the CIA, Admiral Stansfield Turner. It wasn't until Turner read about the Justice Department's investigation of Wilson in the *Washington Post* that he called Clines and Shackley into his office and demanded an accounting of their relationship with Wilson. Their explanation didn't satisfy Turner and he reassigned them to what he thought were less sensitive posts. Both Clines and Shackley eventually left the Agency to go to work for one of Edwin Wilson's export companies. Clines later became the first participant in the Iran/Contra scandal to go to jail.

Turner's shake up of the Agency and Shackley's departure as deputy director of clandestine operations came toward the end of the Assassinations Committee investigation.

Because he had headed Miami's JM/WAVE station and was likely more knowledgeable than anyone about the CIA's role with anti-Castro Cubans and, perhaps, even with Organized Crime, I considered Ted Shackley one of the Committee's most valuable potential witnesses, someone who definitely had to testify under oath.* Instead,

---

*Shackley had joined the Agency in 1951 and was promoted to Associate Deputy Director of Operations, the third most powerful position in the CIA, shortly after George Bush was appointed CIA Director by President Ford in 1976. Bush's name only recently popped up in relation to the Kennedy assassination, although it had been connected to earlier CIA operations. (The Agency used his Zapata Off-Shore Oil Company as a front for some of its operations and its oil drilling platforms in the Caribbean as listening posts during anti-Castro actions. The names of George Bush and Zapata Oil also show up, by the way, in the address book I retrieved from George de Mohrenschildt's briefcase after his death.) In FBI files released in response to lawsuits under the Freedom of Information Act, Joseph McBride, writing for *The Nation* in July of 1988, reported a startling discovery: a memo written by FBI Director J. Edgar Hoover on November 29th, 1963, to the director of the State Department's Bureau of Intelligence and Research. The document summarized oral briefings given on the day after the Kennedy assassination to, among others, "Mr. George Bush of the Central Intelligence Agency." *The Nation*'s revelation came four months before the '88 Presidential election and candidate Bush first attempted to shrug it off with a laugh and a denial. Pushed, he had a spokesman tell the media that it "must be another George Bush."

The CIA also initially tried to stonewall, sticking by its policy of neither confirming nor denying anyone's association with the Agency. But also pushed by the press, a few days later the Agency announced that "the record should be clarified" and identified the George Bush mentioned in the Hoover memo as George *William*

Shackley was subjected to only a brief, informal questioning at his CIA office while he was still a deputy chief of clandestine operations.

One summer morning, shortly after he assumed command of the Committee staff, Bob Blakey asked me to join him that afternoon to interview Ted Shackley at the CIA. Blakey was excited because he was angling to get access to the Agency's "Cuban Book," which supposedly was a record of the CIA's association with the anti-Castro groups in Miami. Shackley was to brief us on the book, how it evolved and what it contained. That briefing, said Blakey, would give me the opportunity to ask Shackley a few questions.

I had no files with me and the Committee had very little background from which I could derive meaningful questions. Besides, very little was known about Shackley at the time. He was one of those ghostly spy figures who have played enormously important roles in American history. From Berlin to Miami to Laos and Vietnam, he has been the point man in the Agency's secret wars; of the select inside players in the CIA's Old Boys network, he was among those deepest inside. It would have taken weeks of access to the Agency's files to properly prepare for an interrogation of Shackley.

At the time, the Committee didn't have access to anything. Blakey's plan "to play nice" with the Agency so that he could work out an agreement for "total access" to CIA files was still in the works. That agreement, as detailed earlier, entailed staff members signing the CIA's secrecy oath. That oath, however, was supposed to not only open the files but also the tongues of any CIA agents interviewed. (The Committee would first notify the Agency that it wanted to question an agent or ex-agent, then the Agency would formally release the individual from the CIA's secrecy vows for the duration of the interview.) In other words, the agents were to behave as if Committee staffers were, at least temporarily, members of their secret brotherhood. Hey, would a CIA agent lie to a brother?

Bush, who had left the Agency in 1964 and whose whereabouts were unknown. But when *The Nation*'s McBride found George William Bush, he admitted having worked for the CIA but described himself as having been "a lowly researcher and analyst." He also provided a sworn affidavit which affirmed: "I am not the Mr. George Bush of the Central Intelligence Agency referred to in the memorandum." Later, after the other George Bush had become President, the White House said it wouldn't "give dignity to this matter with any additional comments."

When CIA Director George Bush appointed Ted Shackley to a top Agency slot, some Agency insiders felt there was a bond between them. Their careers had touched at least once: When Bush was Ambassador in Beijing between 1974 and 1976, Shackley was chief of the Far East Division. Under Bush's tenure as CIA Director, Shackley helped develop the concept of "low intensity conflict," the new name for the CIA's covert strategy in Central America. Later, Shackley's relationship to Vice President Bush continued, even though he had been shorn of his official CIA status, when he emerged as an integral player in the Iran/Contra scandal.

At the time of the interview with Shackley, Blakey had not yet worked out the agreement with Admiral Turner, so Shackley wasn't under any compulsion to answer our questions at all—much less truthfully. And Shackley took full advantage of that fact. He was coldly cooperative but not very helpful. A tall, trim man with horn-rimmed glasses, a wide forehead and the pallor of a scholar, Shackley's Teutonic bearing braced an impenetrable wall of restraint. He answered every question without elaboration. He also lied when he thought he had to.

Shackley gave us the Agency's historic line of half truths about the role of the CIA's JM/WAVE station. In its initial phase, he said, its mission was to provide an intelligence assessment of what could be done about "the Cuban problem." Its primary concern, therefore, was organizing its intelligence collection capabilities, such as trying to recruit or place spies into Cuba and debriefing newly arrived exiles. However, said Shackley, JM/WAVE also gave what he called "general assistance" to Cuban exile groups which could infiltrate into Cuba so they could collect information and implant intelligence-gathering communications equipment.

Shackley almost let slip a note of personal bitterness when he spoke of President Kennedy's ignoring the Agency's warnings that Russia was increasing its military presence in Cuba. Kennedy refused to take the Agency's word, saying he needed "hard intelligence." His station knew, Shackley said, that there were missiles in Cuba long before the policymakers would accept that reality. He said Kennedy announced that fact only after receiving a U-2 aerial photograph of the missiles. An edge of cynicism in his tone, Shackley said if he had known what Kennedy meant by "hard intelligence" he would have gotten him a U-2 photograph much earlier.

With the build up of the Russian presence and the tightening of security, Shackley recalled, the JM/WAVE station was forced to support the intelligence gathering groups' infiltration into Cuba and their implantation of communications equipment by paramilitary means. However, Shackley claimed, the station did not support or supervise any anti-Castro operation which had *only* a military mission in going to Cuba.

I blinked in disbelief. Shackley kept a straight face.

Blakey asked Shackley about the Miami station's response to the Kennedy assassination. Shackley said he never handled any follow-up on the Oswald investigation because it was in the hands of the FBI. Besides, he added, the Agency at the time had not penetrated Castro's intelligence service and couldn't pursue the possibility of Castro's involvement.

Given that, Shackley said he couldn't adequately respond to any other questions about the Kennedy assassination because he knew nothing more.

I blinked. Shackley kept a straight face.

What I remember most about that encounter with the CIA's clandestine chief was the aura of absolute command and power that Shackley exuded, despite the fact he was a few rungs from the top. The question of who was really in charge of the Agency came up later, when Blakey reached that working agreement with Director Admiral Turner himself, the titular boss of the CIA. Finally, Committee staffers had complete access to Agency files and personnel. Yet time and again the researchers would come back from Langley to report they were being stonewalled by lower level functionaries. Some of these researchers had become expert at deciphering the hidden keys and references in documents pointing to other relevant documents which weren't being produced as part of the "complete" files on a subject. Where were they? Well, said the Agency's bureaucrats, they may be missing. Or perhaps misfiled. Or perchance they had been routinely destroyed. But, as we later learned when we discovered the CIA memo regarding Oswald's 201 file, information was being deliberately withheld. What we knew at the time was that we were encountering quite a blatant display of ultimate control and the Committee had to deal with it. After all, what the hell difference did it make to the CIA that Admiral Turner had signed an agreement? He'd be gone soon enough. He was an outsider, the temporary leader of an institution which had its own priorities.

Examples abound and one came up in the Edwin Wilson affair. When investigative reporter Peter Maas was researching *Manhunt* [Random House, 1986], a book about tracking down Wilson, he asked Turner what action he had taken against Wilson's associate Tom Clines. Although he lacked hard evidence of Clines's misconduct at the time, Turner said, he was determined at least to have Clines removed from the Washington scene and ordered him assigned to a "small Caribbean nation." Maas asked him which one. Turner said he couldn't tell him, it was classified. The next day, Maas contacted an inside Agency source and told him about the encounter with Turner. "Oh, right," the source said, "it was Jamaica. Except Clines never went." Never went? Maas was shocked. He wrote about it: "Clines had been removed as head of the CIA's Office of Training all right, but he ended up in an equally sensitive spot as the Agency's Pentagon liaison. And Turner still didn't know it. It was a perfect illustration of how the 'Company' could run rings around a director not considered part of the club. . . ."

By the time Kevin Mulcahy called me, he knew something about the depth of the Agency's power. At first, things were looking up. His reports to the FBI had finally brought some action. The Justice Department's Lawrence Barcella had battled the system and produced results. Mulcahy himself had taken a giant step and agreed to appear before a grand jury. And two years later, indictments were handed down against Wilson and Terpil and their munitions supplier, Jerome Brower. (The charges included their deal to ship 40,000 pounds of C-4 *plastique* to Libya. It was the largest illegal shipment of explosives ever known.)

Still, Mulcahy was worried. Only Brower had gone to jail. The CIA was still not cooperating. Terpil had been arrested but his bond had been reduced and he fled to the Middle East. Wilson was still hiding in Europe. Mulcahy didn't know what to do. He said he had heard of my interest in David Phillips and, although he had no hard information, he felt there was some relationship to Wilson and Terpil. He wanted me to know that.

I later read in the newspapers that Edwin Wilson had been seized by officials in Malta and held in custody for ten days. But somehow, before he could be turned over to American authorities for extradition, he managed to flee to London on his revoked passport. A $10,000 payoff to Malta officials was suspected and some thought elements inside the CIA had a hand in Wilson's escape. I never found out what Mulcahy thought. Several months after I last spoke with him he was found dead one cold morning lying outside the door of a motel cabin in rural Virginia. He had been drinking and was suffering from bronchial pneumonia and emphysema, but the coroner said no one of those conditions alone caused his death. It wasn't known what caused his death.

I never did find out what role, if any, David Phillips played in the Wilson-Terpil affair, but Kevin Mulcahy's suspicions gained credibility from a couple of developments after he died. A book titled *The Death Merchant—The Rise and Fall of Edwin P. Wilson,* written by Joseph Goulden, was published by Simon & Schuster while Peter Maas was still working on *Manhunt.* Maas had told me it was Wilson's ability to operate at the highest levels which initially attracted him to doing the book. As he would later write in the prologue, certain questions haunted him: "How deeply did Wilson's corrupting hand reach into the U.S. intelligence community? How much had he compromised it? How could a man like Wilson, who at one point in his cloak-and-dagger career had come within an eyelash of being appointed to an assistant secretaryship of the Army, have operated so brazenly? How could the CIA not have known what he was doing and stopped him?"

That's why Maas was so surprised by Goulden's book when it appeared. Maas thought it strange that Goulden dismissed Wilson as "a fringe player whose low-level agency contract was subject to renewal every couple of years," as someone who "had been recognized early on as a rotten apple and promptly tossed out."

Goulden's perspective of Wilson and players, it turned out, matched the viewpoint of the Old-Boy Agency loyalists. For instance, Goulden handled Ted Shackley very tenderly. Shackley was benignly portrayed as having been suckered by Tom Clines into going into business in the Wilson-backed companies after he left the Agency. (" 'Clines screwed me,' " Shackley was quoted as complaining to "a long-time CIA friend.") And Admiral Turner's dumping Shackley out of his powerful clandestine operations job was shown as an indiscriminate and reckless move by a man ignorant of the Agency's more sophisticated requirements. According to Goulden, Turner further revealed his irresponsibility when, in his mad drive to "reform" the CIA, he dismissed 800 career agents:

> In time the mass firing came to be known within the Agency as "Turner's Halloween Massacre." In the words of one embittered clandestine careerist (a man not touched by Turner; he retired voluntarily three years later), "The Admiral did more damage to the CIA in one afternoon than the Church Committee, the press and the KGB did since its founding. Halloween 'Massacre,' hell—call it the 'Halloween Pearl Harbor.' "

From Goulden's description of this "clandestine careerist," I figured the retirement date was a misdirection and I assumed he was quoting David Phillips. That's an enlightened guess. Joe Goulden was one of David Phillips's closest friends—close enough, in fact, for Phillips to have been his best man at his wedding.

I knew Goulden from my time in Philadelphia. He was one of the best investigative reporters in town and was later made chief of the *Philadelphia Inquirer*'s Washington bureau. He was a man of manifest integrity then, and quit the newspaper on principle over owner Walter Annenberg's heavy-handed interference with its news operation. Goulden went on to write nearly a score of books, most of them successful, including *The Superlawyers*. At some point, Goulden's journalistic objectivity melded with a very conservative ethos and he went to work for Reed Irvine's Accuracy in Media, Inc., whose board was loaded with heavy-duty, wealthy right-wingers, including the ubiquitous Clare Boothe Luce.

While Peter Maas was puzzling over Goulden's portrayal of Wilson and Terpil as low-level rogues, I was wondering if David Phillips, the veteran propagandist and media manipulator, had a role in promoting the divorce of Wilson and Terpil from the tight-spun world of the deepest Agency insiders. Some time later, Frank Terpil seemed to provide a clue to Phillips's interest.

Goulden had depicted Terpil as crude, greedy, a "cheat and petty thief." It did, however, seem strange that a street punk like Terpil could get a full-status officer's job in the Agency, with its known preference for Ivy League graduates. Strange, also, that Terpil should be connected with such old-chap patricians in the blue-blood branch of the Agency as the polysyllable-addicted columnist William F. Buckley, Jr., godfather to one of E. Howard Hunt's children and among David Phillips's most powerful media assets. Terpil's wife was Bill Buckley's secretary.

Then I got a report about Terpil from Jim Hougan, the Washington editor of *Harper's Magazine* and author of *Secret Agenda* [Random House, N.Y., 1984], a book about the CIA's role in the Watergate scandal. Terpil was still a fugitive when Hougan, pursuing a project for National Public Radio (which would become an Emmy Award-winning documentary titled "Confessions of a Dangerous Man"), tape-recorded several lengthy interviews with him in a hotel in Eastern Europe. In one of the interviews, Terpil told Hougan—not in response to a question but simply in passing—that he had known David Phillips for some time. Phillips's name had come up in a conversation that touched on Phillips's group, the Association of Former Intelligence Officers.

Hougan said he asked Terpil how he met Phillips and Terpil said they were introduced in Miami in the early 1960s by a newspaperman named Hal Hendrix, who had a daughter Terpil knew. (Hendrix, you'll recall, was one of Phillips's media resources. Later, as an ITT executive in Chile, he worked with Phillips when the CIA aided the overthrow of Allende.) Although the information wasn't particularly relevant to him, Hougan decided to ask a few questions about Phillips. Well, Terpil said, he actually didn't know Phillips by that name at the time because Phillips was introduced to him as "Bishop"; he didn't remember the first name. Terpil then told Hougan he learned "Mr. Bishop's" real name by checking a CIA security index which he had access to as part of his job. Terpil said he had checked it out simply because he was curious, since "Mr. Bishop" seemed both important and a bit mysterious. Hougan, who had gotten to know Terpil well, told me, "It would have been entirely in character for Terpil to have disregarded 'need-to-know' restrictions and to have checked up on Phillips, or anyone else who attracted his curiosity."

Hougan said he tended to believe Terpil because the subject came up "out of the blue" and wasn't one in which Terpil might think

Hougan had any special interest. Terpil had no reason to lie, Hougan felt. In addition, Terpil had been abroad and in hiding for so long he likely didn't know anything about the Veciana story or the Phillips-Bishop connection or its link to the Kennedy assassination. In fact, Hougan said, when he told Terpil about the significance of his information, Terpil seemed genuinely surprised.

FORTY-TWO

ON THE TRAIL OF THE SHADOW WARRIOR

*T*HE HEADSTONES IN that forlorn and desolate part of the cemetery are slabs set flat on the ground, their weight settling them deep into the earth and letting the parched curls of grass crawl roughly over their edges so that, from a short distance away, they are hidden, covert testimony to the souls who lie buried beneath them. The cemetery itself is hidden, in a remote corner of the small town of Willcox, Arizona, some sixty lonely-road miles east of Tucson. On plot number 89 in that cemetery a modest marker bears a minimum of identification:

DAVID S. MORALES

SFC US ARMY

WORLD WAR II KOREA

1925   1978

It's as if even in his death the CIA has continued its charade of deniability, diminishing the status of one of its highest ranking, most daring, effective and, perhaps, most deadly clandestine agents. Little known outside the inner circle of top operatives, David Sanchez Morales played major roles in the deepest schemes of the Agency's covert activities, from Cuba to Vietnam. Moving undercover or behind the scenes, he was always the action man.

David Morales's name appeared on the "Highly Sensitive" document given to me by Jim Kelly. "He is now 'retired' and living in New Mexico,"* the document said. "He is an alcoholic and possible 'weak link.' " While the name wasn't new to me, I knew little about Morales, except that he was a CIA agent who had worked out of the JM/WAVE station. When I had interviewed Paul Bethel, David Phillips's friend and Agency asset who was the U.S.I.A.'s Press Officer at the American Embassy in Cuba, he mentioned that Morales had also been with the CIA there, in the dirty tricks department. But my general impression was that he was only a minor player, a lower echelon field guy who at one time or other had been one of Phillips's assistants. I couldn't have been more wrong.

Morales came to my attention initially as a result of a vague description—husky, dark bronze skin, Latin-looking but maybe part Mexican. There were a number of reports of Oswald having been in the company of someone who fit that general description. For example:

Oswald's landlord when he lived on Magazine Street in New Orleans, said that Oswald had few visitors, except for one fellow who came by regularly, a dark-skinned Latin-looking man. Eric Rogers, who lived in the front apartment in the same building, and Orestes Peña, the owner of the Habana Bar, both said they had seen Oswald in the company of a fellow who looked like a Latin. In Dallas, there were a number of witnesses who saw a "second" Oswald—when the Warren Commission had put the "real" Oswald somewhere else—with someone described variously as Latin, Cuban, Mexican or Spanish appearing. In addition, Silvia Odio described one of the men who visited her with "Leon Oswald" as possibly being Mexican or part Mexican.

When New Orleans District Attorney Jim Garrison was conducting his investigation, he received an anonymous note from Miami claiming that one of the men involved in the Kennedy assassination was called "Indio." Then, later on in Miami, we heard reports that there was a Latin-appearing fellow involved in anti-Castro activity out of the JM/WAVE station who was sometimes called "El Indio" or "Pancho." So while all the fragments didn't match, the individual pieces did seem to come from the same box.

Finally, another dimension developed when I read David Phillips's "autobiography," *The Night Watch*, and discovered a quick, passing

---

*Although Morales was from Arizona and had always had his home base there, just about everyone I encountered in the course of investigating him claimed Morales had retired to New Mexico. As I learned more about Morales's importance as one of the CIA's deepest-cover operatives, I began to suspect that his New Mexico "address" may be a bit of disinformation, a stone thrown in the path to trip up anyone attempting to follow his trail.

reference to "Indio." Phillips writes of the exultant flight he took back to Washington with a group of his fellow agents involved in the successful CIA-staged Guatemala coup. "Among them," he notes, "were 'Hector,' a handsome para-military officer, and his sidekick "El Indio," a massive American of Mexican and Indian extraction I had seen only briefly during the revolt but was to work with in other operations over the years."

Given that my interest in Phillips's book was more tuned to what he did *not* write about, his seemingly gratuitous references to "Hector" and "El Indio" I took to be a risky but calculated doff of his cap to a couple of men who meant a lot to him. I would later learn that was especially true of "El Indio," who was with him in all his field operations down through the years, including those in Cuba and in the Latin American countries later under his charge. "El Indio" was, of course, David Sanchez Morales.

I remember asking Phillips about Morales. It was during that incredible "informal" session when I watched him smoke three cigarettes at the same time while he waffled and dissembled about the CIA role in the misinformation that came out of Mexico City. At the time so little did we know about the importance of Morales that he wasn't on the list of names I had prepared to run by Phillips. We knew by then that the "El Indio" in Phillips's book was Morales, but we were taken in by the fleeting reference and didn't give Morales any investigative priority. It was only at the end of the session that I remembered to ask the question:

"By the way," I said, "do you know what happened to Dave Morales?"

Phillips took a casual drag on his cigarette. "No, not really," he said. "Last I heard he was down in the Southwest, I don't know where. I think maybe New Mexico. I heard he became a pretty heavy drinker. He may be in pretty bad shape by now."

There was no indication from Phillips that Morales was someone other than an inconsequential figure from his past. I subsequently put David Morales's name down on the list I submitted to Bob Blakey of individuals I thought the Committee should interview before it closed shop. There were a few people on it I thought it was critical to question, but Morales wasn't among them.

Several years ago, in speaking of individuals I thought the Assassinations Committee had neglected or hadn't had enough time to adequately investigate, I mentioned the name of David Morales to Robert Dorff, a successful Palm Springs businessman and someone who has long been an independent researcher into the Kennedy assassination. In thinking about Morales, Dorff remembered a book that had been published more than a dozen years before, written by an ex-Army captain named Bradley Earl Ayers. Titled *The War That Never Was* [Bobbs-Merrill, 1976], it was billed as "An insider's account of CIA covert operations against Cuba." Ayers had been detached from the Army to join JM/WAVE and train Cuban exiles for commando raids and infiltration missions, and his book was a dramatic but very credible account of guerrilla operations at the mangrove level, replete with exciting bullet-dodging missions and even some romantic encounters with exotic Latin señorita freedom fighters. In a way, it was a significant book in that it revealed long-secret details of the CIA's control of the Cuban exiles' activities; but its perspective was from a lower echelon operational level. Moreover, its impact was diminished by Ayers's choosing not to use the true names of the CIA officials who were his bosses and with whom he worked.

The book had been published after I had wrapped up work for Senator Schweiker and before the House Assassinations Committee was organized, and because it dealt with a low level of the Agency's training activity, I had read it hurriedly. (At the time there was only one point which I thought was significant, a reference to a Mob character named John Rosselli.) But now, in answer to my question about Morales, Bob Dorff recalled a few details he thought should be checked out.

Although Ayers had changed the last names of all the key CIA officers with whom he had dealt, he randomly used the true first names for some of them. Assigned to the station's training branch, Ayers had the most contact with the training chief, whom he called "Keith Randall." I knew that was Tom Clines, the top deputy to JM/WAVE Chief Ted Shackley. But Ayres only half-changed Shackley's moniker, calling him "Ted Morely." Now Dorff remembered that Ayers had made a reference to the head of the station's operation branch as "Dave" and had given a rather specific description of the man. Ayers wrote:

> We soon discovered that no one knew what to do with us, and finally we were temporarily assigned to the operations branch. Dave, the big New Mexican Indian who ran it, was the only branch chief who treated us less than respectfully. He ran all the station's activities with a heavy hand and was famous for his temper. We soon learned that no one, save Ted himself, argued with Dave, and to cross him in any way was to invite trouble.

Dorff suggested that the "big New Mexican Indian" could very well be David Morales. But I couldn't agree. Here was a character who, in the records, had never appeared as anything more than a low-level action guy. David Morales running the operations branch? JM/

WAVE was no think tank; it was *all* about operations. If David Morales was head of operations of the largest, best financed and most active CIA station ever run outside of its Langley headquarters, David Morales was a very important person. That was difficult to believe.

Then, in March of 1990, a select group of members of the Cuban American National Foundation gathered in a private room above The Mirabella restaurant on Miami's Calle Ocho. The Foundation, Washington's most powerful lobby, represents the wealthiest and most conservative elements of the exile community. The Foundation is headed by Jorge Mas Canosa, the wealthy Miami businessman who once worked at the CIA's Radio Swan propaganda operation when David Phillips was in charge.**

**David Phillips's Radio Swan served as both a broadcast station into Cuba and a communications link for guerrilla operations. One of Radio Swan's most impressive propagandists was the fiery, fast-talking bantam Jorge Mas Canosa. After the Bay of Pigs debacle in 1961, Mas, like all 2506 Brigade veterans, was offered a chance to receive an officer's commission in the U.S. Army. Most of the Cubans were sent to Fort Knox, Kentucky, or Fort Jackson, South Carolina, but Mas was among a select few sent to Fort Benning, Georgia. There men in civilian suits gave advanced courses in covert operations, including clandestine communications and propaganda. The Agency had chosen the most zealous anti-Castro exiles to become special assets. Mas's closest associates at Fort Benning were two men who would later be ranked among the CIA's most effective and lethal agents: Felix Rodriguez and Luis Posada.

Jorge Mas returned to Miami and, he now claims, survived on petty jobs as a shoe salesman, dishwasher and milkman. Actually, he spent most of his time as one of the most strident members of a CIA-supported exile group called *Representacion Cubana en Exilio*, known by its acronym, *RECE*. (An FBI report written at the time describes how Mas delivered $5,000 to his old buddy, Luis Posada, to blow up a Cuban ship in Mexico's Vera Cruz harbor.)

Soon after Ronald Reagan became President in 1981, he and his clique of rock-hard Cold Warriors decided on a grand strategy of taking the war to the enemy, particularly to the spreading Evil Empire of Godless Communism in Latin America. Chief architect of the strategy was newly appointed CIA Director Bill Casey. To mobilize support for the strategy and neutralize the post-Vietnam public opposition to U.S. military intervention abroad, Casey set up a "public diplomacy" program as cover for a covert domestic propaganda effort. To that end, one of Casey's moves was to establish political and financial power groups that would intimidate and control both the legislature and the public. One of the power groups secretly seeded by Casey's intelligence apparatus was the Miami-based Cuban American National Foundation (CANF), which quickly rose to be the most powerful lobbying force in the country, surpassing the Israeli lobby. Jorge Mas Canosa was handpicked to rule CANF and gather together the wealthiest and most strident right-wing Cubans in Miami.

Mas and CANF would become key backers and financial conduits for the Reagan and Bush Administration's covert arms supply system to the Contras in Nicaragua. ("The road to Havana goes through Managua!" was Mas's fund-raising cry to wealthy Cuban exiles.) An early important cog in the Contra supply system, working out of the Ilopango air base in El Salvador, was Felix Rodriguez, who had remained one of Mas's closest friends. Rodriguez, who has been linked to Vice President Bush's National Security Council, was by then a near-legendary figure in the CIA. He had been involved in the capture and execution of Che Guevara, an operation which also included David Morales.

A select group of the Foundation's members had come to the private room above the restaurant to hear Jorge Mas's distinguished guest reveal the latest intelligence about Castro's involvement in narcotics trafficking. The guest had that inside information because he was once one of the most powerful men in the CIA and such men never lose touch, even though they may retire. But, beyond that, what made Theodore Shackley's appearance that night so special to many of the older exiles in attendance was that, although they had not known him then, not even his name, they had worked for him. Shackley, of course, had been top honcho of the CIA's mammoth JM/WAVE station during that too-brief, glorious heyday of the United States' secret war against Castro.

Among those who slipped in to Shackley's talk that evening was Gordon Winslow, a local archivist specializing in Cuban exile history. Such gatherings gave Winslow the opportunity to chat with and ask questions of the men whose exploits defined Miami's Cuban exile movement. After Shackley finished his formal talk, a cluster of compatriots gathered around him to reminisce about the old days, Winslow among them. He had come loaded with at least one question for Shackley, which I had asked him to pose.

"You were in charge of the JM/WAVE station here back in the early Sixties, weren't you?" Winslow asked innocently.

"Yes, I was," said Shackley.

"By the way," Winslow continued as casually as he could, "do you remember who your chief of staff was?"

Shackley turned to him and, with an expression of pleasant surprise at the memory, said, "Of course! That was Dave Morales. He was my Chief of Operations."

It was an incredible acknowledgment from *the* most authentic source: David Morales *was* Chief of Operations at JM/WAVE. The confirmation completely surprised me. Where had the paper trail been? Was the Committee's request for documents about Morales one of those the Agency dodged simply by waiting for the Committee's demise? Had we not asked the right questions? Did all the agents we interviewed who had worked out of JM/WAVE carefully neglect to mention the name of the man who ran the station's daily operations and was one of the highest ranking officers on the scene? Could it be this was the same David Sanchez Morales who got merely the quickest of mentions in the "revealing" autobiography of a man who would turn out to be one of his closest associates?

Now I had to reassess Ayers's book. Assuming, then, that he really knew what he was writing about, that bit of information about "Dave," especially when coupled with another of his passing revelations, made a combination of some significance. Ayers was writing about his return from a session of training exiles in the hot, mosquito-infested marshes of the Florida Keys. He was looking forward to a bit of rest, starting with a pleasant dinner with a fellow Army officer who had also been temporarily assigned to the CIA. This fellow, whom Ayers called "Wes," was an engineer on an assignment that was separate from Ayers's.

"Wes had been drinking before he got to the house that night," Ayers wrote. "In fact, he confided, he and John Rosselli, the dapper American agent in charge of the continuing attempts to assassinate Fidel Castro, had been on a weekend binge together. They'd become close friends as they worked together, and, with Rosselli a bachelor and Wes without his family in Miami, their drinking friendship was a natural extension of their duty relationship."

Then there is another cursory mention of Rosselli*** later in the book, when Ayers's CIA supervisor, in discussing additional training sites, expressed his concern about various groups' territory overlapping: Ayers quoted him as saying: " 'Besides all my training, Turk has his commandos just up the Key, and Rosselli has his group at Point Mary some of the time.' "

What was John Rosselli, a ranking member of the Organized Crime fraternity, doing with a "group" at the CIA's JM/WAVE station—and, in fact, running an action group that, obviously, came under the supervision of the station's Chief of Operations, David Morales?

Just prior to the publication of Ayers's book, the Church Committee had released its report about the CIA's collaboration with Organized Crime bosses in plans to assassinate Castro, saying that the Agency's representatives had dealt with Rosselli in getting the cooperation of the Mob bosses. The report said that Rosselli was involved in the passing of poison pills, and in one instance, he and William Harvey, the CIA's man in charge of the Cuban Task Force, had transfered a cache of weapons and explosives to the Mob's men in Miami. But the report gave no indication that Rosselli was regularly working on an operational level with the Agency, and certainly not close enough to be involved in the covert activities run out of JM/WAVE.

The fact that David Morales, a key field operative for David

***There is a continuing editorial conflict over the spelling of Rosselli's name. The press and most government reports opt for the one 's' version—except the Senate Intelligence Committee report which went both ways: one 's' in its body text and two in its footnotes. Actually, Rosselli's real name was Filippo Sacco. He took a cover name after he was made a member of Al Capone's crime family, picking the moniker out of an entry in the encyclopedia about a fifteenth-century painter named Cosimo Rosselli.

Phillips, worked closely with John Rosselli at the CIA's JM/WAVE station has a broad web of implications.

Rosselli was an unusual character. A good-looking guy with an easy, beguiling personality, he started as a street hood in Al Capone's Chicago mob. Over the years he transformed himself into a dapper, slick and consummately charming diplomat for Organized Crime, moving among the top family bosses as a broker of mutual interests. He was a "labor relations specialist" for the Mob's interests in Las Vegas and Hollywood. (The story goes that Rosselli, on orders from New York Mafia boss Frank Costello, "suggested" to Harry Cohn, then head of Columbia Pictures, that Frank Sinatra get the Maggio role in *From Here to Eternity*, the part that subsequently saved the crooner's sinking career. Mario Puzo dramatized the incident in *The Godfather*'s horse's-head-in-the-bed scene.)

Rosselli played a vital role in the CIA's Castro assassination plots. According to the Church Committee report, the first plots began before the Bay of Pigs. In a December, 1959, memo to CIA Director Allen Dulles, J.C. King, then Chief of the Western Hemisphere Division, called for Castro's elimination. Dulles obligingly gave the assignment to fellow Yale man Richard Bissell, at the time the Agency's Deputy Director for Plans. (Later, Bissell would be fired along with Dulles after the Bay of Pigs disaster.) Bissell directed Sheffield Edwards, from the Agency's Office of Security, to devise a plan to murder Castro, and Edwards asked his deputy, James O'Connell, to assist him. They, in turn, recruited Robert Maheu, an ex-FBI man who had been on retainer fronting for the Agency in a variety of dirty-tricks operations. Maheu also worked for billionaire Howard Hughes, whose diverse operations were frequently employed by the Agency. Then John Rosselli came into the picture as the link to the top Mob bosses, including Chicago's Sam Giancana and Florida's Santos Trafficante. One interesting point is the Church Committee could never conclude who had originally recruited John Rosselli. The CIA's Edwards testified it was Maheu and Maheu said it was Edwards.

In their biography of John Rosselli [*All American Mafioso*, Doubleday, 1991], Charles Rappleye and Ed Becker trace Rosselli's CIA association to Guatemala, beginning right after the Agency helped overthrow President Jacobo Arbenz in 1954. (Rosselli was reportedly involved in pushing the interests of Standard Fruit, a company allegedly linked to Organized Crime, for a larger cut of the giant United Fruit's hold on the country.) His biographers also claim there was an association between Rosselli and E. Howard Hunt in 1961 when the Dominican Republic dictator Rafael Trujillo was assassinated with weapons supplied by the CIA.

Whatever the history of Rosselli's ties to the CIA, there's every indication he was an enthusiastic player. But as important as it is to understand who John Rosselli was, it may be more important to know how his name first surfaced in relation to the Kennedy assassination.

As noted earlier, Allen Dulles had never told his fellow members on the Warren Commission that the Agency and Organized Crime had plotted to assassinate Fidel Castro. (As the Church Committee would later report, the CIA-Mafia plots took place between 1960 and 1963 and included at least eight attempts.) It wasn't until January, 1967, almost three years after the Warren Report, that Commission Chairman Earl Warren heard about the plots from nationally syndicated columnist Drew Pearson. A Washington lawyer had told Pearson that one of his clients had been involved in U.S. Government efforts to kill Castro and that Castro had decided to retaliate and ordered Kennedy's assassination.

Warren expressed surprise but, obviously averse to stepping back into the bog he helped create, passed the information to the head of the Secret Service who, in turn, quickly passed it over to Hoover's FBI. A month later the FBI decided that "no investigation will be conducted regarding the allegation made . . . to Chief Justice Warren." Why? The FBI supervisor in charge of dealing with the matter later told the Church Committee, "I don't know."

The report of Castro's link to the Kennedy assassination would have gone no further if Jack Anderson, then writing "The Washington Merry-Go-Round" column with Drew Pearson, hadn't juiced it up and pushed it to the public. "President Johnson is sitting on a political H-bomb," as Anderson subtly put it. He wrote that he had learned from "an unconfirmed report that Sen. Robert Kennedy may have approved an assassination plot which then possibly backfired against his late brother." Anderson said that's what led Castro to decide to retaliate: "With characteristic fury, he is reported to have cooked up a counterplot against President Kennedy."

Once Anderson's column hit Washington, it forced an explosion of reactions. Although the bottom line in the initial tip to Pearson and in Anderson's column was that Castro was responsible for Kennedy's murder, the report triggered a greater interest in the CIA's ties to Organized Crime, which eventually occupied the bulk of the Church Committee's time, diverting attention and resources from Senator Schweiker's effforts to focus on the CIA's links to the Kennedy assassination.

It was, as it turned out, John Rosselli who spawned this story. Rosselli had given it to his attorney, Edward P. Morgan, a Washington power broker who was a former FBI colleague of Robert Maheu's. (Interestingly, Maheu's boss Howard Hughes also had a relationship to Morgan. When Hughes decided to move into Las Vegas, he had to play ball with the Mob and Maheu got Morgan to represent Hughes. Rosselli also took part—he got a piece of Morgan's fee.) One thing is for sure: Morgan wouldn't have gone anywhere with Rosselli's Castro-did-it story unless client Rosselli had given him the word. Rosselli gave it to Morgan who was close to Pearson's sidekick, Jack Anderson; Morgan called Anderson who, in turn, set up a meeting with Pearson; Pearson was friendly with Earl Warren. It's clear that Rosselli didn't put the little bird in Morgan's ear to have it sit there. He wanted that sucker to sing to the world.

In fact, Rosselli kept in contact with Jack Anderson through the years and fed him increasingly embroidered editions of the original story. According to one version, the Castro hit team, composed of members of the "Trafficante mob," wasn't just captured and tortured, they were brainwashed and sent back to murder President Kennedy. So now not only was the CIA a boomerang victim of its own plotting, but so was the Mob. All in all, it was a masterful performance.

And, perhaps not so incidentally, when Anderson first broke the report, New Orleans District Attorney Jim Garrison had already begun his own Kennedy assassination investigation and was focusing directly on the CIA. Agency Director Richard Helms, according to his former staff assistant Victor Marchetti, was very concerned that Garrison, despite his wild scatter-gun approach, might blow open some doors the Agency preferred be kept closed. The House Assassinations Committee would later learn that the Agency, in order to keep close track of where Garrison was going, planted several undercover operatives on his staff. Jack Anderson may not have been the Agency's witting messenger, but he did note that his new disclosures indicated that Garrison, in concentrating on the CIA's involvement, was " . . . following the wrong trails."

The Assassinations Committee did some speculating about Rosselli's motivation in pushing the Castro retaliation story, but the Committee was hindered by his inability to testify. In July, 1976, Rosselli had disappeared and in August, the month before the Committee was established, Rosselli surfaced in the shallows off the Intracoastal Waterway in North Miami. He had been smothered to death and shot, then cut open from chest to navel. His legs had been hacked off and stuffed with his torso into a 55-gallon steel drum which was wrapped with heavy chain and moored to a weight in the water. The mooring broke when the gasses from Rosselli's decomposing body forced the drum to float to the surface. It appeared to be an obvious Mob job. But the Dade County coroner discovered something that was quite out of the ordinary for a Mob hit, the possibility that Rosselli had been drugged and immobilized before he was asphyxiated. Other than that, it looked like a Mob hit.

* * *

Clearly, John Rosselli was more than just another CIA asset—and his injecting himself into the Kennedy assassination investigation had some important implications. In both the meticulous media orchestration and the dramatic structure of his Castro-did-it story, I thought I saw the shadow of that master of misinformation, David Atlee Phillips. But what intrigued me most was Rosselli's close links to David Morales.

As noted earlier, in *The War That Never Was,* Brad Ayers had reported that when Rosselli was working in the Keys, handling sniper groups for an assassination mission, Rosselli was directly under the supervision of the JM/WAVE Chief of Operations, David Morales. When I spoke with Ayers to confirm that, he provided a further insight into the association between the two men: "I witnessed a profound sense of camaraderie that transcended the operational situation. Dave was very selective in his relationships but my observations led me to believe that he and Rosselli had a very close relationship."

Meanwhile, in California, researcher Robert Dorff had also been talking with Ayers, who ran a private investigations agency out of Woodbury, Minnesota. Disillusioned when the CIA abandoned the Cuban exiles and shifted its focus to what he considered an immoral war in Vietnam, Ayers had quit the Agency and resigned his Army commission late in 1964. Still a rugged, athletically trim man in his fifties, Ayers calls himself a "cynical idealist." He's had a number of careers in general aviation, real estate development, education and writing. When Bob Dorff sparked his memory about David Morales, Ayers's curiosity as well as his developing interest in the Kennedy assassination led him to want to turn over some old stones.

Coincidentally, one evening not long before he met Dorff, Ayers was in San Diego and was having a drink at the Kona Kai Yacht Club when he spotted a familiar face. It was Bob Wall, the fellow who had been Morales's Assistant Chief of Operations at JM/WAVE. (Ayers remembered Wall as not always having a smooth relationship with Morales, one reason being that Morales was away from the station a lot—usually, says Ayers, on trips to Mexico City, then the Casablanca of international spooks.) During this chance meeting with Wall, it was natural that Morales's name would come up. Wall said the last he heard was that Morales had retired to his home in New Mexico and had subsequently died there.

Ayers decided he wanted to do some checking himself and, with Bob Dorff, began following the trail of the legend of David Morales. Eventually, this led to some significant contacts: One was a Marine officer who had met Morales while attached to the CIA in Vietnam;

the others were among Morales's closest friends, including a family who considered Morales one of their own.

Dorff kept me abreast of the progress he and Ayers were making during the course of their investigation. Initially Dorff was skeptical about some of the sources and information that developed, and he began corroborating as much as possible through documents and records. When so much of it turned out to be valid, he suggested I pursue the trail with him. He thought it might go where the Assassinations Committee had feared to tread and ultimately provide a spotlight that would finally delineate David Atlee Phillips and his alter ego, Maurice Bishop. Dorff was right.

Late in 1992, when I had the opportunity to get to California, Bob Dorff and I took off from Palm Springs and drove up to a small town called Ridgecrest in the rugged country north of Los Angeles. It is a military town, adjacent to the China Lake Naval Weapons Station. There Dorff had been in touch with a Marine officer who will be called "Lt. Colonel Charles Crest."

Shortly after Dorff had rekindled Brad Ayers's interest in his former JM/WAVE associate, Ayers had taken off on a previously planned climbing trip to Mt. Wilson in northern California. There he struck up a friendship with a couple of fellow climbers, a ranking Navy officer and his wife. The officer was then assigned to the Pentagon, and the conversation between the two military men eventually touched on Vietnam and then, inevitably, on the notorious Phoenix Program. Ayers had heard that after JM/WAVE Dave Morales had gotten involved with Phoenix, so he mentioned to his fellow climber that he was looking for a big Mexican-American Indian named Morales. By an incredible coincidence the "Big Indian" was someone the Navy officer had heard about. He said the name had been mentioned by a friend, a field grade Marine officer, who had been in the Phoenix Program in Vietnam. The Marine officer, Lt. Col. Charles Crest, was now working at the China Lake Naval Weapons Station.

Ayers reported that lead to Bob Dorff, who contacted Crest at the Naval Station. They had a series of long telephone conversations and then they met. Impressed with the validity of what he told him, Dorff suggested I question Crest directly. By that time, however, Crest had become exceptionally wary of getting openly involved. That fear resulted from the reactions he got when, at Dorff's suggestion, he contacted a couple of old friends at CIA headquarters and made some inquiries about Morales. There were traces, he was told, that Morales may have died more than one time, perhaps twice in Latin America, before his "official" death. Such a thing, however, is not unusual for intelligence agents who work assassination missions under deep cover and may be the target of retribution operations. But what troubled Crest, and what prompted his request for anonymity, was that after he made his inquiries, he suddenly received calls from two CIA agents he had not heard from in years. Coincidence perhaps, but Crest said he'd rather be careful.

But he did agree to meet with me. Crest is a short muscular man in his early fifties. He was trained by the Marines in counterintelligence and went through the Army's Ranger and parachute training as well as the Navy's underwater demolition course. In 1958, he was detached from the Marines and assigned to the CIA for its covert military operations. He would remain with the Agency for fourteen years. His first posting was to the Belgian Congo, where he taught indigenous insurgents the tactics of guerrilla warfare. In 1960, he went to Vietnam as an "adviser" and remained there until 1972, involved in the roughest, dirtiest assignments, including what he calls "over the fence" clandestine operations into Laos, Cambodia and North Vietnam.

Charles Crest told me he met David Morales in Vietnam. They worked out of what Crest called MAC-VSOG—Military Assistance Command—Vietnam Special Operations Group. He said they didn't work together—Crest worked out of one Corp. area and Morales was in another—but they were both involved in Operation Phoenix.

Later, *New Times* magazine reporter Michael Drosnin wrote about what the CIA did in Operation Phoenix: "[It] oversaw the creation of mercenary terror teams, the founding of a vast and brutal secret police force, the construction of a nationwide network of interrogation centers, and finally devised Phoenix to coordinate and provide a legal cover for the growing campaign of mass murder and political imprisonment." But CIA Director William Colby, who structured the American role in the program, testified in Congressional hearings that Operation Phoenix was not an assassination program—not completely. Phoenix was a secret war waged by hit men. Its purpose was to identify, isolate and eliminate the Viet Cong infrastructure in the South Vietnamese countryside. Counterterrorism tactics were used in the process, with killer squads being sent out at night to raid the homes, kidnap, torture and murder suspected Viet Cong leaders and organizers. Trained assassins from the military and the CIA prepared and led the killer squads, and Crest and Morales were among those experts. The Vietnamese called the program *Phung Hoang*, after an all-seeing, all-powerful mythical bird of prey.

One of the problems with Phoenix was that it relied on the corrupt South Vietnamese National Police to do a lot of the identifying of Viet Cong leaders. Exactly how many innocent people were killed isn't known, nor is the exact total number of those murdered. The figure ranges from twenty thousand to forty-seven thousand people. What is known is that the program cost $1 billion and failed.

I had already found in the records that Morales had been part of Operation Phoenix, working with his former JM/WAVE boss, Ted Shackley. But Crest's report seems credible not only because of his accurate physical description of the Big Indian but, more important, because his perception of the man's character fit almost exactly what Ayers had known about Morales.

"He was a fairly heavy drinker when I met him," Crest recalls. "He was a 'macho' kind of guy, strongly opinionated, an enforcer type. He was a very intimidating person who could be very persuasive if, for instance, he had to recruit two or three guys to make a hit. I got the impression he was always able to control everyone who worked for him. I wouldn't want to cross him."

FORTY-THREE

CONFESSIONS OF A HOME TOWN HERO

DAVID SANCHEZ MORALES WAS a hit man for the CIA. He was a killer. He said it himself. He told Ruben Carbajal he had killed people for the CIA in Vietnam, in Venezuela, in Uruguay and other places. These were not murders in the heat of military combat— although they were done in what he considered the performance of his duty for his country—these were assassinations of individuals or groups selected for annihilation. There are very few people that Morales would have spoken so openly with, but he considered Carbajal closer than a brother.

It was always so, Ruben Carbajal told me. They always trusted each other completely. Like the time when they were teenagers, and were all dressed up and heading for a party and were walking by a group of guys who thought of themselves as pretty tough. "One of them, the biggest guy there, he makes a remark about Mexican-Americans, you know," says Carbajal. "Didi . . . we always called him Didi . . . Didi keeps on walking but, you know me, I stop. The big guy looks down at me and repeats the remark. I turn like I'm gonna go but then I swing around and whack him good in the head. He staggers back and I run like hell. Didi, he doesn't know what the hell's going on and he runs after me. I was always faster than Didi, you know. Jeez, you should've seen us go! No way they was gonna catch us. Trouble was, on the way home we've got to pass these same guys again. This time they see us coming. They take off after us and I'm about to run like hell again. I knew I could get away because I was so fast. I was little but fast. But this time Didi says, 'No, wait!' And he stops. 'What the hell are you doing?!' I yell at him. 'No, wait,' he says. I think he's crazy but I stop, too. Now these guys are on top of us and Didi says to me, 'Get behind me.' The big guy comes right at him and Didi gives him a shot that takes the guy down. Then Didi starts beating the shit out of him. The other guys come at him and Didi beats the shit out of every one of them. And I'm standing there behind him watching it. It was beautiful. I knew I could count on him.''

Ruben—everyone calls him ''Rocky''—Carbajal is telling me this story at the El Molino Restaurant in Phoenix. He is small and wiry, in his mid-sixties, leather tan, a handsome man with a Clark Gable mustache, a full head of wavy gray hair and brown eyes that twinkle with youthful, good-humored lechery at the sight of a shapely female. The El Molino Restaurant has been in his family since the Pima Indians moved to the suburbs. It has seen better times but it is making a comeback. The restaurant is not in the fanciest part of town and from the street it looks like a hideaway neighborhood bar. Painted a bright clay orange with tall shrubbery and a chainlink fence, its main entrance faces the parking lot and is guarded by giant silvery sentries, hollow conquistadors in helmeted suits of spray-painted Spanish armor. Attached to the restaurant is a long addendum of buildings topped with huge, spinning vents where the main work of El Molino takes place: the mass making and marketing of tamales and burritos and other Mexican specialties. It's a good family business but the restaurant is the heart of El Molino. Despite its casual facade—or because of it—it is something of a local institution, a favorite hangout for many of the state's most powerful businessmen and politicians, including Arizona's legendary conservative conscience, Barry Goldwater. El Molino's history is logged with lists of wild parties and political deals. And because it was the place of the Carbajals, it was like a second home to David Sanchez Morales. There remains on the wall today, on either end of the long bar in the restaurant, two carved plaques each bearing a coat of arms: one for the family Carbajal and the other for the family Sanchez.

Dave Morales's father was early out of the picture. ''He didn't know his father,'' Ruben Carbajal told me. ''His mother got remarried and Didi wound up coming to play with me and my brother Paul all the time. My mother raised him like he was one of us. He was always with us.''

The kid grew up a hustler, a happy-go-lucky guy with a million-dollar smile. At Phoenix Union High, the strong, wiry teenager was a four-letter threat—football, baseball, track, basketball. ''I remember he had one of his greatest games against the Tempe Buffaloes that time we beat the shit out of them," recalls Carbajal. Young Didi wasn't the brightest kid in the school but he was among the most popular, elected President of three of the school's most prestigious student clubs. Still, 1944 wasn't a good year to be getting out of high school because a world war was still going on.

"We graduated together and four of us, Didi and two other friends, we all go down to volunteer in the Navy," Carbajal remembers. "I figured I'm the only one who's not gonna pass because I lost so much weight playing football. I was only weighing a hundred and eight pounds after they were done knockin' the shit out of me. But I'm the only one who passes. They say, we'll fatten you up, and they put me in the Seabees. I don't remember what was wrong with the other guys that they didn't pass."

As a result, Morales went on a two-year whirlwind tour of classes at Arizona State College, the University of Southern California and the University of California in Los Angeles. On the side he picked grapes for his brother-in-law, who ran a major orchard outside L.A. "We crossed paths in San Pedro," Carbajal recalls. "I was just getting out of the Seabees and Didi had joined the Army and was heading for paratrooper training."

Before the end of 1946 came, Morales was an enlisted man stationed in Munich. Germany was the action arena for U.S. intelligence at the time as it became increasingly apparent that the focus would have to shift to Russia and the growing Red Menace of Communism. The OSS's Allen Dulles was taking a personal hand in the U.S. Government's adoption of Hitler's old master spy network headed by ex-Nazi General Reinhard Gehlen. Recruitment was hot and heavy and some of the young American agents who were major players in Germany then would one day climb to the top echelons of the Agency, among them Richard Helms, James Angleton, Theodore Shackley and William Harvey. But the records, even the "official" records, of covert intelligence operatives are seldom accurate, so it's difficult to determine exactly when Morales joined the Agency.

"He wasn't in the Army that long, maybe six to eight months," says Carbajal, "before he was working for the Agency. We knew because he used to write to us. He used to write to my mother all the time because he was like family." It's more than likely that Morales was undergoing special training in 1953 when the State Department's Biographic Register shows him as being at the University of Maryland. Later that same year he was listed as a "purchasing agent of a lumber company," but by 1954 his knowledge of plywood had somehow prepared him for a career in diplomacy and he was reported as a "political officer" with the State Department in Caracas. It was in Caracas—where years later Maurice Bishop worked with Antonio

Veciana to plan the assassination attempt on Castro in Chile—that Morales was involved with David Phillips in the CIA's planning of the coup in Guatemala. From 1958 to 1960, Morales worked out of the American Embassy in Havana while Phillips worked undercover in his public relations business. From there, Morales moved with Phillips to take part in the Bay of Pigs operation and, immediately afterwards, to coordinating operations with him at the JM/WAVE station in Miami. Morales popped up in Laos and Vietnam with Ted Shackley for a while, and from there he could be found in most of the CIA's hot spots in Latin America when Phillips headed that division. Morales was the can-do kind of guy Phillips needed.

But Morales always returned to El Molino and the Carbajal family. "Of course, no one was supposed to know what he was doing," Ruben Carbajal recalls, "but we did. Now I'm not saying everything, but in general we knew. And no matter how high he got up in the CIA he would always come back here because he was still one of us. Like when it was my mom and daddy's fiftieth anniversary, he was a big wheel then but he made sure he got here for that party. And don't let that grave marker fool you, he got to a very high rank in the Agency."

Then there was a period when Rocky began seeing his friend Didi more regularly. That's when Carbajal was living in Mexico and working in the "financial consulting" business. What he was really doing, he says, was fronting for Mexican politicians who were not allowed to get involved in commodities investments. Morales was a big help to him, he says, because Morales had access to a lot of information about the economy that other people didn't know. Once Carbajal had a fellow in Panama with a huge load of sulphur and he knew an operation in Colombia that needed sulphur, so he worked out a $600 million deal. Then, afraid that the Panama guy might not be able to come up with such an enormous quantity, Carbajal called Morales and asked him where in the world he could buy some sulphur if the guy came up short. Morales called him back in a few minutes and told him exactly where.

"When I was in Mexico in the early Sixties, Didi would come down to see me a lot," Carbajal recalls. "He was coming down to meet with someone at the American Embassy fairly regularly. But he would never have me meet him there. It would always be somewhere away from the Embassy, usually outside of Mexico City itself."

Years later, Carbajal and attorney Robert Walton, a Harvard Law grad with whom he had become very close, planned to get into their own commodities business, with Morales as a key asset. Morales told Carbajal to bring Walton to Washington because he wanted to meet and evaluate him. They decided to make it a social occasion, with Carbajal bringing his mother and father as well as his wife, and Walton bringing his wife. It was on that first trip, Carbajal says, that he, Walton and Morales, outlasting the others, stayed up until dawn, "just drinkin' and bullshittin' and having a good time." On subsequent trips only he and Walton made, Morales arranged for them to meet some of his Agency associates. At a cocktail party in a large, luxury apartment somewhere in nearby Virginia, among those Carbajal remembers being introduced to were Ed Wilson, Tom Clines and Ted Shackley.

Everyone hit it off so well at that first meeting in Washington, that Morales arranged to fly the whole Carbajal family and the Waltons down to Miami with him, where he also kept an apartment. "I remember when we got to the airport there wasn't enough room on the plane," recalls Rocky, "but Didi pulls out this card, I remember it was a black card, and the stewardesses actually bumped people off that plane so we could get on." Morales showed the group a good time in Miami, and took them around to the old haunts of his anti-Castro comrades, including a visit to Les Violins, the classy Latin show bar where once the Agency spooks, the local soldiers of fortune and the Cubans would huddle at dark tables and plan their next infiltration raids into Cuba. Bob Walton still has his swizzle stick as a souvenir.

Later Morales arranged another trip to Miami for Carbajal to have him make additional contacts who might be helpful in the commodities business. One was Manuel Artime, the CIA's military leader for the Bay of Pigs. Artime was an especially valuable contact since he was then business partners with Nicaragua dictator Anastasio Somoza. Carbajal remembers meeting Artime in E. Howard Hunt's house where, he was told, Artime was living while Hunt was in prison for his Watergate role. (More likely, Artime was simply entertaining there; he actually lived across the street from Hunt.) That Morales should reveal to Carbajal the level of his associations in the Agency illustrates both his own status and his absolute trust in Carbajal. Because of that trust, one of Morales's comrades, Tony Sforza,* also took Carbajal into his confidence.

"Sforza got very close to me because of Didi," Carbajal says. "Didi told him, 'This is my brother, man. He's like a brother.' They both used to tell me some stories. Oh, yeah, they killed people for the

---

*I had not previously mentioned Sforza's name to Carbajal and he didn't know it was familiar to me. It had appeared, along with the names of Morales and Shackley and the others, in that "Highly Sensitive" document I had received in 1978. "This man handled anti-Castro activities on behalf of the CIA," the document noted. "He still runs a Cuban 'blow-up group.' . . . Sforza is a hit man and should be regarded as dangerous." Like Morales a veteran deep-cover agent, Sforza ran an import-export business in Miami after his "retirement" from the CIA. He died within six months of Morales, also from a sudden heart attack.

Agency. Didi told me he knocked a high guy off in Venezuela and then when the Tupamaros got acting up in Uruguay, remember right after they killed that U.S. agent who was training the police down there—what was his name, Mitrano?—they took over this apartment complex or something. Didi told me he went in there and wiped them out. Not that he was a cold-blooded killer. He was one of the most patriotic men I ever knew in my life.''

According to Carbajal, Dave Morales could always hold his liquor.** But in the years prior to his official retirement he apparently took to the juice a bit too much and more frequently let slip the shroud of deceit and cover lies professional covert operatives instinctively cling to, even in most aspects of their private lives. Then what might have been a terrible blunder occurred. It could have happened because he was home among friends, or maybe he had just been down too deep for too long. At any rate, on Saturday night, August 4th, 1973, when the Carbajals threw a special fiesta at El Molino for him—his birthday would be in a few weeks but no one knew where in the world he would be by then—Morales didn't object to having his picture taken by photographer Kevin Scofield of the *Arizona Republic*. And

---

**Morales may have been able to hold his liquor, but he had a history of liquor loosening his tongue. Wayne Smith, a State Department officer in the American Embassy in Havana in 1960 when Morales was stationed there with the CIA, remembers a party he threw at his home for Embassy personnel. "Morales got drunk and remained behind after everyone left," Smith recalls, "but our Cuban bartender was still there and Morales started talking about some of the Agency's secret operations in progress, including something about frog men operating out of our Guantanamo base. I tried to shut him up but he was too bombed to realize the situation. I thought he was being terribly indiscreet."

Smith experienced another of Morales's liquor-induced indiscretions when Smith was stationed in Buenos Aires in 1975. Mickey Kappes, a CIA agent then also working out of the American Embassy there, was very close to Morales. One day, Kappes told Smith that Morales was passing through Buenos Aires and suggested they all have dinner together that evening. Again, Smith recalls, Morales drank heavily and started talking about secret Agency operations in Laos in which he had been involved. "Although we were in a restaurant," Smith says, "luckily there weren't others around, just Americans from the Embassy. But Kappes, who knew him well, told me Dave had a reputation for being indiscreet when he had a few drinks in him."

Wayne Smith, by the way, also knew David Phillips when both were in Havana in 1960. They were in the same little theater group, along with Paul Bethel. Smith didn't know then that Phillips was a covert CIA agent. Antonio Veciana told me that among the Embassy personnel Maurice Bishop had suggested he see to help with visas and papers for relatives was Wayne Smith. Smith recently told me that he didn't see Phillips again until years after both had left Havana, then he ran into him in a State Department hallway. It was during that conversation, Smith says, that he got the impression that Phillips had erroneously assumed that he, Smith, also worked for the CIA. (Smith later became the first head of the U.S. Interests Section in Cuba under President Carter, then resigned over a policy disagreement with the Reagan Administration. He is currently a professor at Johns Hopkins University School of Advanced International Studies.)

so there it was, played large in Sunday's newspaper, a big photo of Morales—white haired now, at nearly 48, and looking more like an aging Caesar Romero than the husky adventurer of his youth—chatting with a local flour mill owner and Ruben's brother Paul. But it was the information in the caption—information obtained by the photographer from Morales himself—that made the prominent newspaper photo a dangerous bleep in the tradecraft of CIA agents:

> Feted by friends at a fiesta Saturday was former American consul to Cuba, David Sanchez Morales, left, who was in that country when Castro took over. . . . In government service for 28 years, Sanchez is now consultant in the office of deputy director for Operations Counterinsurgency and Special Activities in Washington.

Special fiesta or not, it was a slip on Morales's part and the CIA undoubtedly didn't appreciate it.

Ruben Carbajal told me he had the impression that, in those last years, a festering disillusionment and resentment towards the Agency was growing in Morales. Yet even after his "official" retirement in 1974, Morales apparently remained very active. Carbajal remembers talking about it with him: "Well, he told me he had retired, but I said, 'Bullshit! How come every week you've got to fly out of here?' He says, 'Oh, they run into some problems, I have to go up there and take care of them. These people never let go of you.' "

Carbajal remembers all too well the last trip Morales made home from Washington, early in May of 1978. Morales had built a large house outside of Willcox for his wife and the four youngest of his eight children, who were still living at home. The house was a few hours drive from Phoenix, but whenever Morales came back, as soon as he got off the plane he headed for El Molino.

"I was down in Guadalajara on business and he called me long distance, so we tried to arrange flights coming in at the same time. But he beat me by forty, forty-five minutes and when I got here he was sitting outside there with my brothers and the others shooting the breeze and drinking a beer. So we sat down and drank beer a while and I says, 'Man, you don't look up-to-date.' He says, 'I don't know what's wrong with me. Ever since I left Washington I haven't been feeling very comfortable.' I remember him leaning against his truck saying he didn't feel well, but he drove home anyway."

That night Morales had what Carbajal calls "a supposed heart attack." Even today he thinks there is something suspicious about his friend's death. "His brother Robert, who grabbed a plane from Phoenix and flew right there, he told me they were supposed to send an ambulance from that other chickenshit town up there, Benson I think it is, and they had called about nine or nine-thirty but something was wrong with it. Then when it got there the oxygen wasn't working right, none of the equipment was working right. It took about six hours by the time they got him to the hospital over there in Tucson. It all seemed pretty strange to me."

Carbajal went to see Morales early the next morning. "They wouldn't let no one in, they had his room surrounded by sheriff's deputies, but I had a card Didi had given me and I went in to see him. I thought he was dead but he still had all these goddamn tubes sticking in him. There was nothing they could do but pull the plug."

Like his grave marker, Morales's obituary in the *Arizona Range News* didn't come close to reflecting the depth and breadth of his covert role in the history of his country.

> David Sanchez Morales, who moved to Willcox two years ago after retiring from the U.S. Foreign Service, died on May 8, 1978 in Tucson. He was 52.
>
> Mr. Morales maintained an Arizona home while working for the Foreign Service, much of the time as a consular.

He wasn't buried until three days later, because there were a lot of people who had to be notified and some had to fly in from great distances for the funeral. Ruben Carbajal remembers the line of cars that left the Sacred Heart Catholic Church in Willcox and wound its way to the Sunset Cemetery; he says it stretched for more than half a mile. "That whole town was there with their eyes wide open, they couldn't believe what they were seeing. It was the biggest thing they had in Willcox for a while. All the top brass came in from Washington and all over, generals and all. And a lot of guys in civilian clothes with dark glasses. You could tell that Didi was some important person."

There was no autopsy. Morales's wife, Joanne—who had also been working for the government when she met Morales in Germany—requested there not be any. She would later move back to Boston, where they had also kept a home, and pursue her studies in Chinese antiquities. She has reportedly already made a number of trips to China. "I think the Government took good care of her," says Ruben Carbajal.

So David Sanchez Morales—the famous "El Indio," David Atlee Phillips's most valuable action man—died in what is recorded as a natural death. But Didi's old friend Rocky doesn't believe it. He can't get out of his mind what Didi once told him: "He said they are the most ruthless motherfuckers there is and if they want to get somebody, they will. They will do their own people up."

At first, Ruben Carbajal didn't tell me exactly why he felt the way he did, but I would later learn that David Morales told someone else—in Carbajal's presence—why he worried that the Agency would one day do him up.

It was while sitting in the El Molino one night, that Ruben Carbajal told Bob Dorff and me about the times he and Bob Walton had gone to Washington to meet Morales and about the trip on which they met other high-ranking CIA officials. To obtain more details about those meetings, I suggested we talk to Walton. The next morning, a Saturday, Carbajal called him and Walton agreed to drive down from his home in Scottsdale to meet the three of us at the Holiday Inn.

Walton is in his mid-fifties, a pleasant, ruddy-faced fellow with Irish good looks and an easy, straightforward manner. He remembers their first trip to Washington as being in the spring of 1973. "I had had a coronary in November of 1972 and Rocky and I started talking about getting into business shortly after that. When you're from a dry climate like Arizona and you go back there in the summer you're just sweating like a pig. But I don't remember being uncomfortable, so I think it was early in the spring of 1973."

Walton corroborates the reason for the trip and the meeting with Morales: "We felt, or at least Rocky felt, that he could give us an inside track on who were the people who were for real and who were not. That was a big concern of mine because I had already been on one wild goose chase, spent an expensive week in Nassau waiting for a transaction to close and it never did."

Their evening with Morales, Walton remembers, was both very pleasant and, in more than one way, especially memorable. "We all went out for dinner, which was very nice. It was Rocky and his wife, me and my wife and Rocky's mother and father."

Morales, not someone who trusted strangers or even associates easily, obviously was impressed by Walton's character and, although their commodities business never took hold, he later called on Walton to represent him on a few matters back in Phoenix. It was something Morales said at one of those subsequent encounters in Phoenix that makes Walton put what had happened in Washington in a very special perspective.

"Morales was building a big, new house out near Willcox," Walton says. "Actually, it was in a little town called El Frita, which is about half-way between Willcox and the Mexican border. It's a remote area, I've only driven that road once in my life. It's an agricultural area, they grow the famous jalapeños peppers there. I never got to see the house, but he had just finished it and was describing it to me when he mentioned that he put in it the best security system in the United States. And I remember asking him, thinking he was worried about burglars or being robbed, 'What do you need so much security for? You're still thirty miles from the Mexican border.' And he said, 'I'm not worried about those people, I'm worried about my own.' "

That struck Walton as curious. "What do you mean?" he asked.

"I know too much," Morales said, then quickly dropped it.

Remembering that now, Walton views his first meeting with Morales in Washington as being far more significant than he realized. After dinner, the whole party went back to the Dupont Plaza Hotel. It was late and Carbajal's parents and his wife returned to their rooms and Ruben and Morales returned to the Waltons' room with them. "Didi ended up staying all night," Walton recalls. "My wife went to sleep somewhere around two in the morning and Rocky and I and Didi drank and talked from when we got back from dinner—maybe that was about eleven o'clock at night—until about six in the morning."

The drinking got heavy. "We had consumed quite a bit of alcohol," remembers Walton. "At one point, between the three of us we had gone through a fifth of Scotch and we had to reorder. It was a real contest." He pauses and smiles. "Ahh, my younger days, my misspent youth!" And as the night and the drinking go on, defenses come down and candid truths emerge. "You know," says Walton, "you get in a kind of position where you say, 'All right, I told you everything about me, what are you all about?' "

Morales began with his war stories. Walton remembers him talking about the killing in Vietnam and Laos, about being involved in the capture of Che Guevara in Bolivia, of hits in Paraguay and Uruguay and Venezuela. ("He said his wife was [in the country] with him and they had real trouble getting him out of town. They almost bought the farm on that one.")

The drinking and the talking continued. At one point, Morales began probing Walton for a bit of his own background. Walton had gone to Amherst College in Massachusetts and, as part of his developing interest in political science and politics, he had done some volunteer work for Jack Kennedy's Senatorial campaign. Later, at Harvard Law, Walton was head of a student group which invited then-Senator Kennedy to speak at Cambridge.

Walton never got to explain the details of that association. At the first mention of Kennedy's name, he recalls, Morales literally almost hit the ceiling.

"He flew off the bed on that one," says Walton. "I remember he was lying down and he jumped up screaming, 'That no good son of a bitch motherfucker!' He started yelling about what a wimp Kennedy was and talking about how he had worked on the Bay of Pigs and how he had to watch all the men he had recruited and trained get wiped out because of Kennedy."

Walton says Morales's tirade about Kennedy, fueled by righteous anger and high-proof booze, went on for minutes while he stomped around the room. Suddenly he stopped, sat back down on the bed and remained silent for a moment. Then, as if saying it only to himself, he added:

"Well, we took care of that son of a bitch, didn't we?"

I looked at Ruben Carbajal, who had remained silent while Walton was telling me this. Carbajal looked at me and nodded his head. Yes, he was there, it was true. But, in all the long hours we had spent together and all the candid revelations he had provided, it was a remembrance he couldn't bring himself to tell me about his friend Didi.

FORTY-FOUR

THE FINAL CONFIRMATION

WITH THE OFFICIAL EXPIRATION of the Committee that December, I returned to Miami spent and depressed. Blakey had asked me to stay on but I refused. I had no idea what was going to happen to the staff reports that were produced on Antonio Veciana, Silvia Odio and the other areas of anti-Castro activity, and, truthfully, I was so beaten down I didn't care. I kept thinking of what Vincent Salandria had told me more than three years before: "They'll keep you very, very busy and eventually they'll wear you down." I had thought he was crazy. Just before I left, the remnants of the anti-Castro team had given me a farewell gift which, the note attached to it said, would be useful if I ever decided to write about my Committee experiences: It was a well-worn whitewash brush.*

Occasionally, I would get a call from Washington from one of the remaining staffers asking about a detail in my area of the investigation.

---

*Despite the workload and pressure of those last days, the tenacious humor exhibited by many of the staff often alleviated the depression. The hallway bulletin board remained the outlet for many an anonymous staffer venting frustration and/or fantasy. Still, much of the humor was tainted by reality. For instance, I thought this anonymous contribution—titled "Ode to the American People"—clever as it was, reflected both a stifled cry and muzzled effort to get the message out (A preface indicated it should be sung to the melody of "What I Did For Love," from Michael Bennett's *A Chorus Line*):

Kiss two years goodbye, the sweetness, no! the sorrow.
Wish us luck, the same to you,
But we will regret what we could not do, what is hid from view.

One day I got a call from the Committee's Chief Legal Counsel, Jim Wolf. A tall, quick-smiling redhead, Wolf was one of the brighter attorneys on the staff, the guy who once told Blakey, after the Committee had scuttled former Chief Counsel Dick Sprague, that he'd be crazy to take the job. "I told him," said Wolf, "that it was like the owners of the Titanic giving a guy a call and saying, 'Hey, our ship is sinking, we need a new captain.' "

I asked Wolf how the report was progressing. "Oh, not too good," he said. "There's just so much to get done. The morale here is at rock bottom. Hardly anyone talks to anyone else, we just write all day long." He said the pay extension that Blakey had arranged through the House Speaker's office was running out. I asked what happens then. "I guess what we don't finish," Wolf said, "we just leave out."

Through the intervening months I remained in touch with both Antonio Veciana and Silvia Odio. Although I had initially approached them as an official investigator, I had a personal rapport with each of them, which I maintained simply by being honest about what the Committee was doing, especially in terms of themselves. They were both, of course, very interested in what the Committee's final report would say about their testimony.

It was several weeks after the report's release, in July of 1979, before I was able to get a copy of the *Findings and Recommendations* section, its concluding volume. Meanwhile, I had obtained copies of the staff reports I had written in the Veciana and Odio areas of the investigation. Because I felt an obligation to let them both know what my conclusions were after dealing with them for more than three years, I brought them each copies of my reports and promised to eventually get them the final report. Meanwhile, I asked them for their reactions to the staff reports.

I was waiting for their responses when, one evening several days later, the telephone rang. The call was from a friend in Little Havana. His voice was tense. He said Veciana had just been shot. In the head. He was driving home from work and someone ambushed him, fired

---

Said G.R. to us, the guilt is Lee's so prove it.
It's as if he always knew, and we won't forget
What he did to us, what is hid from view.

Gone, truth is ever gone. As we travel on, that's what we'll remember.
Kiss the hill goodbye and give me, please, no byline.
He did what he wished to do. Won't forget, will regret what we could not do,
What was done to us, what is hid from view.

Truth, truth is over wrung. As we travel on, that's what we'll remember.
Kiss it all goodbye and give us not a mention, Bob gets the attention.
So we all are shafted through...Won't forget, will regret
What we did for Lou, what was done to us, and they'll kid you, too.

four shots at him. No, Veciana was not dead, the friend said, but that was all he knew.

I quickly placed a flurry of calls to find out what had happened. Yes, it was true, a reliable source told me, someone had tried to assassinate Veciana. He was in the hospital but he was all right. The hit man had been a bad shot, but a piece of one ricocheting bullet had caught Veciana in the side of the head. Later in the evening I reached one of his daughters who had just returned from the hospital. He was lucky, she said, it was not a serious wound.

Ana Veciana, the oldest daughter, had recently graduated from college and was working as a novice reporter for the *Miami News*. A few days after her father was shot, she wrote a story about it, and it was beautiful. Her family, she said, has come to accept the fact that they must live with danger, but they have refused to live with fear. Fear is the mind killer. Her family, she said, has chosen to live with pride.

"My American friends never understood the politics or the violence that comes with Latin politics," she wrote. "To this day I have not been able to explain, but only to describe, the passion Cubans feel for the freedom that's taken for granted in this country." She was very proud of her father's vociferous anti-Castroism, she said, and has come to accept what she termed "the aberrations from normal life."

"But fear?" she wrote. "Never. The fear we know, if it can be rightly called that, is the fear many others are not fortunate enough to experience.

"I fear that we may have forgotten why we are here.

"I fear that we have grown complacent and smug.

"I fear the satisfaction that comes from having three cars in the driveway and a chicken in every pot, and knowing we can say what we damn well please without valuing that freedom.

"That's what I fear."

Veciana himself called me about a week after the shooting. He was out of the hospital, he was fine and walking about. It was only a slight wound near the left temple. "My wife said if it was higher I might have to wear a toupee," he said, laughing. The reason he called, he said, was because he had read the staff report and he wanted to talk with me and show me some papers.

I drove down to Little Havana the next evening. I did not park my car in front of Veciana's house. He had a small bandage on the side of his head and another one on his right arm. He was pale but appeared in good spirits. He took me back outside to show me the bullet holes in the pick-up truck he was driving when he was shot. He was coming home late, he said, from the marine supply business he and his relatives operate. Normally, he takes different routes home, but this was the one he used the most. He made a left-hand turn into a street not far from his house and saw a brown station wagon parked on the corner facing him. He noticed a lone figure sitting in it, but gave it only a glance and didn't get a good look at the man. Then he heard a loud noise and felt a sharp blow on the side of his head. The front vent window exploded on the second shot. "Then I knew that it was an attempt on my life," Veciana told me quite calmly. The third shot ripped through the door at his ribs, was deflected by the door's interior mechanism, passed in front of his stomach, burned across his right arm and tore out the other side of the truck and into an open field. The fourth shot produced a spiderweb of cracks as it glanced the front windshield.

Veciana showed me the bullet holes with a sense of wonderment. "It's funny I'm still alive, isn't it?" There was a touch of bemusement in his tone, but absolutely no note of fear. On the other hand, I wasn't exactly cool. It was a bit unsettling to be standing there in the eerie shadows of the lone streetlamp looking at the monstrous holes the .45-caliber slugs had made in the truck. The first shot had gone completely through the outside rearview mirror and where it emerged had produced an ugly flower of jagged metal. I suggested to Veciana that we continue our talk inside his house.

I asked Veciana who he thought was trying to kill him. "It was a Castro agent," he said with certainty.

"Have you ever considered," I asked, "that it could be anyone else?"

He looked at me and smiled. "No," he said.

Eventually, our conversation turned to the staff report. Yes, he said, he had read it carefully and that's why he wanted to talk with me. There are certain things in it, he said, that question his credibility. His credibility is very important to him because he is still gathering evidence to overturn his narcotics conviction, even though he had served the sentence.

What bothered him, Veciana said, was the denial by the two individuals in Caracas, Lucilo Peña and Luis Posada, that they were involved with him in the Castro assassination attempt in Chile in 1971. "Sure they were with me," Veciana said. "They are not telling the truth." To prove that to me, he said, he had asked a friend who had just come from Caracas to bring some papers that would verify it and he would give me the name of an individual in Miami who could corroborate it. (Later he did, and the evidence supported him.)

For a few hours we talked in detail about the report and I slowly began to realize that Veciana was not going to bring up the one most important reservation I had expressed about his testimony. In my report, I had written that I doubted his credibility when he told me that David Phillips was not Maurice Bishop. In our discussion now, Veciana didn't contest that point.

In the past, whenever I pointed to evidence which clearly indicated that David Phillips was, indeed, Maurice Bishop, Veciana would simply say, "You know, I have given sworn statements." I would tell him that I understood his position and he would say that he appreciated that. I knew what he meant. I was now absolutely certain I knew the reason that Veciana would not identify David Atlee Phillips as Maurice Bishop. And the attempt on his life—in contrast to his public statements that Castro was behind it—was really a confirmation of what he truly believed. Veciana believed that Bishop was behind his being set up on the drug conspiracy charge. It was Bishop's way of trying to put a halt to Veciana's continuing renegade efforts to assassinate Castro. The Agency was clearly heading into an era of heavier public scrutiny and had decided that all such attempts must end. Bishop severed his relationship with Veciana in July, 1972, two months after CIA agents had been caught breaking into Watergate. When Veciana was arrested in July, 1974, the Rockefeller Commission, the House Pike Committee and the Senate Church Committee were around the corner waiting to pounce on the intelligence agencies. The CIA knew that any new Castro plot, however thin the trace back to it, could backfire and produce disastrous political repercussions, perhaps endangering the Agency's very survival.

When Veciana was released from prison and I showed up at his door, he immediately decided he would use me to build himself a shield against another set up. He decided to reveal just enough to let Bishop and the Agency know that if they continued to play dirty games with him, he would now have a weapon with which to fight back—the threat of Congressional and public exposure. There was no need to take his revelations beyond the existence of a Maurice Bishop. Veciana had nothing more to gain by identifying who Bishop really was—and perhaps a lot to lose, as the attempt on his life no doubt reminded him.

At times, Veciana would admit to me that Bishop *might* be behind his drug charge set up, but then he would revert back to blaming it on Castro. However, he had recently given me a copy of a letter he wrote shortly after he got out of prison. It was to the presiding judge in his case, Dudley Bonsal, in the Southern District of New York, listing why he should be given a new trial. Among Veciana's claims was this admission of his key concern: "I did not testify during the trial for fear that something could happen to my family and because several 'political agencies' of this country wish to keep me quiet."

I think that as a result of my candidly telling him I knew exactly the predicament he was in, we had come to the point of a close but odd relationship, Veciana and I. And that evening as we talked I was moved to take advantage of the camaraderie that had developed between us.

"Tony," I said, "I am not going to put you on the spot, but I would like to ask you just one question and I would like you to be totally honest with me because the answer that you give me is very important to me."

His face got very serious and his dark eyes stared suddenly at me without expression.

"I know that you feel you have a mission in life," I said, "and I want you to know that I respect that and all the things you must do to be faithful to that mission. Believe me, I do not want to interfere with it."

He nodded his head. "I understand," he said softly.

"You know that I believe what you have told me," I went on. "I believe you about everything. Except when you told me that David Phillips is not Maurice Bishop."

His eyes never moved, his expression never changed as I spoke. "Now," I said, "I would like you to tell me this one time very truthfully: Would you have told me if I had found Maurice Bishop?"

A slow smile crossed Veciana's face as he let out his breath. He was happy I had phrased the question so as to not put him in a corner. He put his head down and scratched his forehead, obviously taking time now to think carefully. Then he looked up with that half-smile still on his face.

"Well, you know," he said, "I would like to talk with him first."

That was his answer. I looked at him for a moment, then laughed.

Veciana nodded his head and laughed with me.

FORTY-FIVE

THE ONLY WAY OUT

*D*ECEMBER, 1978, the last official month of the House Assassinations Committee, saw each team racing frantically to complete its report on its special area of investigation. Each of our reports, we were told, would be a chapter in the final report. But when the final report was finally released some seven months later, it was an entirely different entity, having been newly crafted by Chief Counsel Bob Blakey and a few select staffers. Blakey had arranged for himself and his crew to be temporarily attached to the House Speaker's Office in order to remain on the Government payroll. Blakey, therefore, had ultimate control over the structuring of the final product.

There are twelve volumes of accompanying reports, testimony, hearing transcripts and other evidence released along with the final report, but the primary summary, the one titled *Report of the Select Committee on Assassinations—Findings and Recommendations,* is the one that will go down in history, the legacy of the last investigation into the assassination of President John F. Kennedy.

That volume contains 686 pages. Less than two-and-a-quarter pages are devoted to Antonio Veciana and Maurice Bishop.

The name of David Atlee Phillips is not in the report.

The conclusions in that final volume stand in stark contrast to the findings in the staff report I had written before I left Washington. The Committee's report said that although "no evidence was found to discredit Veciana's testimony," and that "there was some evidence to support it," nevertheless, "no definite conclusions could be drawn as to the identity or affiliations" of Maurice Bishop.

The operative word was "definite." There was a huge amount of circumstantial evidence which I felt proved beyond a reasonable doubt that David Atlee Phillips was Maurice Bishop. But that, according to Blakey and the Committee, wasn't a "definite" conclusion. I felt that no other conclusion could be drawn from the evidence, but my arguments for expressing the findings in such terms ran smack up against the tremendous dilemma it would have created for the Committee.

How could the Committee reach such a conclusion without calling for a deeper and more forceful investigation of the Central Intelligence Agency?

And how could it do that without admitting that its investigation of the CIA's possible involvement in the Kennedy assassination was inadequate, that it was bound by the parameters imposed by the Agency?

That's why, in the end, Blakey and the Committee had no choice. In its final report, the Committee was forced to dismiss Veciana's allegations completely.

The Committee found "several reasons to believe that Veciana had been less than candid," and then listed four of those reasons:

> First, Veciana waited more than ten years after the assassination to reveal his story.
> Second, Veciana would not supply proof of the $253,000 payment from Bishop, claiming fear of the Internal Revenue Service.
> Third, Veciana could not point to a single witness to his meetings with Bishop, much less with Oswald.
> Fourth, Veciana did little to help the Committee identify Bishop.

Every one of those reasons is deliberately misleading. Three of them contain blatant distortions of the facts, and one is asinine.

To claim that Veciana "waited" more than ten years implies that he willfully delayed revealing the information. It deliberately ignores the circumstances of his initially telling me the story. He did not approach me, I approached him. He insisted on absolute confidentiality. Until 1973, he had no desire to jeopardize his relationship with Maurice Bishop, who for years had been a loyal and powerful ally. His revelations to me came as a result of his fears and the prison sentence that had given those fears validity. Veciana was trained in the wily art of intelligence and counterintelligence, so when an official representative of an influential U.S. Senator on a powerful Senate committee showed up at his door, he took it as an opportunity to create a defense against the possibility of additional plots against him. Immediately after the Kennedy assassination, when Veciana had the opportunity to reveal his story to a U.S. Customs agent he suspected of being with the CIA, he felt he was being tested, since he himself was trained as an intelligence operative. "That was a very difficult situation," Veciana said. (The Committee never interviewed Cesar Diosdato, the Customs agent, who had been transferred to California. He rebuffed Chief Investigator Cliff Fenton's request for a telephone interview and, when I wanted to subpoena him and do a direct interview, I was denied travel authorization for budgetary reasons.)

Conversely, to claim that Veciana "waited" to reveal his story, also implies that Veciana had ulterior motives and deliberately gave the Committee false information. Now that would have been significant if the Committee had found even a trace of credibility to that statement. It didn't.

As for the $253,000 payment from Bishop, Veciana did, initially, refuse to supply proof of it when asked to do so in his formal hearing before the Congressional members of the Committee. He did claim fear of the Internal Revenue Service. In fact, that's why, before he had agreed to speak with me two years before, he had requested assurances that nothing he told me would be held against him. The Committee refused to grant him immunity from the IRS. When pushed under oath, however, Veciana told the Committee that he would tell me privately what he did with the money and I could then document his claim. The Committee refused that arrangement. Here, the Committee's report ignored two crucial facts: Veciana voluntarily told me about the payment; and he was a professional accountant who could have kept it well hidden if he had wanted to.

For the Committee to implicitly expect that, as a requisite for believing Veciana, there should have been witnesses to his meetings with Bishop, is absurd. That contention alone made it appear that the Committee had acquired absolutely no knowledge of basic intelligence operations during the two years of its existence.

Finally, the claim that Veciana did little to help the Committee identify Bishop, implies a lack of cooperation which is simply not true. In fact, he was ready to testify at a public hearing before the Committee shoved him aside.

In addition to resting on such tortured rationality, the Committee's conclusions are tainted by its inability to dismiss blaring pieces of contradictory evidence. For instance, it noted that the CIA "insisted that it did not at any time assign a case officer to Veciana."

That, the Committee decided, might be tough for the public to swallow without a fine-print footnote, yet it must have wanted to avoid chewing on the CIA. The result was a lumpy evasiveness: "The

Committee found it probable that some agency of the United States assigned a case officer to Veciana, since he was the dominant figure in an extremely active anti-Castro organization. The Committee established that the CIA assigned case officers to Cuban revolutionaries of less importance than Veciana, though it could not draw from that alone an inference of CIA deception of the Committee concerning Veciana. . . ."

In other words, the Committee found the CIA's claim hard to believe, but that didn't mean the Agency was lying. Would the CIA lie to a Congressional committee?

Yet nothing attests more vividly to the incongruity of the Committee's conclusions than the fact that, in the end, it was forced to impeach the testimony of *both* Antonio Veciana and David Phillips. To do that as quietly as possible, it stuck it in a footnote:

> The Committee suspected that Veciana was lying when he denied that the retired CIA officer was Bishop. The Committee recognized that Veciana had an interest in renewing his anti-Castro operations that might have led him to protect the officer from exposure as Bishop so they could work together again. For his part, the retired officer aroused the Committee's suspicion when he told the Committee he did not recognize Veciana as the founder of Alpha 66, especially since the officer had once been deeply involved in Agency anti-Castro operations.

That footnote is the most significant paragraph in all the 686 pages of the House Select Committee on the Assassinations' final report.

The Committee *had to* conclude that both Veciana and Phillips were liars. Any other conclusion would have opened doors that the Committee did not want to open; would have questioned the validity of the Committee's entire relationship with the CIA; would have raised ominous doubts about the worth of the Agency's promise to cooperate with the Committee; would have made suspect the Agency's veracity in responding to questions, in making documents available and in providing access to all its files; and would have challenged the Agency's claim of having had no association with Lee Harvey Oswald and no knowledge of the circumstances of Kennedy's assassination.

Yet the Committee's decision to impeach both Veciana's and Phillips's testimony also impeaches its own conclusions in a key area of evidence.

And that, concurrently, undermines its entire final report.

And the last investigation.

EPILOGUE

LOOKING BEYOND THE CONSPIRACY

*A*FTER THE PUBLIC RELEASE of the Assassinations Committee's final report, a critique was written by Cambridge professor Carl
Oglesby in *Clandestine America*, the Washington newsletter of the
independent Assassination Information Bureau:

> To sum up. This report has serious shortcomings. It pulls its
> punches. It insinuates much about the Mob and JFK's death which it
> then says it doesn't really mean. It is alternately confused and dogmatic
> on the subject of Oswald's motive. It tells us it could not see all the way
> into the heart of CIA or FBI darkness, yet assures us that we are secure.
> Its treatment of the technical evidence in the crucial areas of shot
> sequencing and the medical evidence is shallow and unconvincing.
> Yet still we say that this report, overall, is strongly positive. It has
> moved the Dealey Plaza conspiracy question out of the shadows. It has
> boldly nailed the thesis of conspiracy to the church door of orthodox
> political opinion.

Well, maybe. About the same percentage of Americans disbe-
lieved the Warren Report before the release of the House Assassinations Committee Report as after its release. (Oliver Stone's movie
JFK would change those figures dramatically.) Oglesby's analysis of
the Committee's report is on target, but his conclusion misses the
point.

This was the last investigation and it did not do the job the

American people had asked it to do. I never took a poll of all the Committee's staff members but I know this: There is not one investigator—not one—who served on the Kennedy task force of the Assassinations Committee who honestly feels he took part in an adequate effort, let alone the "full and complete" investigation mandated by Congress. In fact, most of the investigators have bitter memories of the limitations and direction imposed upon them.

But even that's not the point.

This was the *last* investigation. Chief Counsel Bob Blakey himself said it at his very first staff meeting. He is a very meticulous and very conservative lawyer and he demonstrated that his allegiance, first and foremost, is to the standing institutions of government. Again and again, he emphasized the legislative restraints inherent in the nature and scope of a Congressional probe. His vision never rose above that. He never considered a higher mandate. He never considered the Kennedy assassination as a pivotal event in American history or as a possible manifestation of the iniquities within the very institutions he was so bent on protecting. He never considered using his position to demonstrate a loyalty to higher principles. He never considered that the mandate to conduct a "full and complete" investigation came from the American people. He never considered rallying the public to stand with him and demand the complete truth about the assassination.

In fact, in an interview with DIR radio in New York, Blakey revealed the limitations of his perspective.

"What the public wants," he said, "and what the public can get are two different things. . . . The notion that somehow people outside of Washington can come into Washington and do great and noble things in Washington without understanding the place, is just nonsense."

Bob Blakey was fond of telling the staff, whenever anyone would start pushing to investigate an area that threatened to go beyond the limitations he imposed, that we would just have to accept the fact that we were going to leave loose ends. "Life has loose ends," he would say. On such rhetoric were the Committee's compromises structured.

But the final reproach shouldn't fall on Bob Blakey's shoulders. Blakey was the good soldier. He took the Congressmen where they wanted to go. And where the Congressmen wanted to go, as expeditiously as possible, was as far away as possible from the Kennedy assassination. And, no matter which twelve members happened to sit on the Assassinations Committee, it wouldn't have made a difference. Such anxious timidity is pervasive throughout Congress.

With a few exceptions, most of the members of the Committee paid very little attention to the details of the staff's activities. (Off-hand, I think of Connecticut's Christopher Dodd and North Carolina's Richardson Preyer as among the few who did.) Bob Blakey structured the Committee's views of what it was doing and where it was going. Most of its members didn't really care.

I spoke recently with one of my former fellow staffers, who asked not to be identified because he still works in Washington. He was in the clique that helped Blakey put the *final* report together. As they were completed, segments of the report were run by the Congressional Committee members for approval. The staffer was telling me about those last days:

"I remember at the very end I had to go see a bunch of them for some reason and, well, it was almost embarrassing. I had to explain who I was and what I was doing working for them, like some guy off the street. They didn't really care about the subject, they put in their time.

"Yeah, I think they were all sorry they had somehow got involved in the Kennedy assassination. I got the feeling they kind of resented that they were on the fuckin' committee. They didn't really enjoy putting in the time and they were always quick to display a let's-get-it-over-with attitude. And eventually my feeling came to be, why are we doing all this and working so hard when these Congressmen don't give a shit?''

For Congressmen whose priority is political survival—no exception comes to mind here—an investigation into Kennedy's assassination holds absolutely no political profit. It's a no-win game. In fact, most Congressmen see it as a mine field laced with political barbed wire that just might cut a career to shreds—if it doesn't blow it apart. It's just too . . . well, *controversial*. Besides, Jack Kennedy himself was a partisan politician whose political legacy still echoes in many bitter liberal-conservative debates. Then, too, recent revelations about Kennedy's personal penchants and moral character have become highly politicized, and too many Congressmen feel self-consciously uneasy about shining the light of public discussion on these areas. Why bring it all up again? Who needs it?

But even that doesn't really explain why the House Assassinations Committee didn't want to do the job it was mandated to do. When the thick fog of rhetoric is blown away and the muddy waters of debate surrounding the validity of the evidence is drained off, it's absolutely clear where the most penetrating rays of any investigation into the conspiracy to kill President Kennedy had to focus: They had to focus beyond the conspiracy.

Despite the disclaimers and the rhetorical posturing, Kennedy's murder wasn't the real issue at all. In retrospect, perhaps it never was. It's quite obvious that it takes more of a leap of the imagination to accept the hypothesis of Arlen Specter's single-bullet theory and the "evidence" on which it's built—computer-composed charts of bullet trajectories and reams of neutron-activation analyses not withstanding—than it does to simply look at the hardest of facts, such as the bullet holes in the back of Kennedy's jacket and shirt.

It takes an even greater leap into fantasy to believe that Lee Harvey Oswald was a lone nut. Yet, despite all the substantive and overwhelming evidence confirming Oswald's association with the CIA as well as his contacts with a number of Agency assets, the CIA still officially denies that it had any relationship at all with Oswald. Moreover, it fosters and deliberately maintains the issue as a matter of public debate.

Is black white? Of course not, but if we argue about it strongly enough and long enough you might begin having doubts. The ghost of propaganda expert David Atlee Phillips hovers yet.

There are those, such as Vincent Salandria, who contend that studying Kennedy's assassination has to go beyond microanalysis of the evidence because the evidence so early and clearly shouted conspiracy. What's needed now, Salandria says, is what he calls a model of explanation that would fit both the rationale for a blatant conspiracy as well as its aftermath. And Salandria sees as part of that aftermath the domestic turmoil of the Sixties as well as the militarization of foreign policy that produced both the tragedy of Vietnam and, in the decades that followed, the arrogant, worldwide proliferation of illegal covert operations by the intelligence agencies. Salandria believes that for a conspiracy to fit that model of explanation, it must incorporate "forces positioned in the highest echelons of the Federal Government."

Bob Blakey and the members of the Assassinations Committee must have known that the Committee's investigation of the CIA was a charade, mostly a superficial wallowing about in files that only went so far and so deep. And, as in its pursuit of David Phillips's role as Maurice Bishop, the Committee carefully avoided pushing the Agency into a corner by being very selective about who would testify under oath.

In a display of disdain for the American public equal to that exhibited by the Warren Commission, the Committee slips into the body of its final report a paradoxical admission of its failure:

> . . . Finally, taken in their entirety, the items of circumstantial evidence that the committee had selected for investigation as possibly indicative of an intelligence association did not support the allegation that Oswald had an intelligence agency relationship.

This finding, however, must be placed in context, for the institutional characteristics—in terms of the Agency's strict compartmentalization and the complexity of its enormous filing system—that are designed to prevent penetration by foreign powers have the simultaneous effect of making congressional inquiry difficult. For example, CIA personnel testified to the committee that a review of Agency files would not always indicate whether an individual was affiliated with the Agency in any capacity. Nor was there always an independent means of verifying that all materials requested from the Agency had, in fact, been provided.

That admission reflects the Committee's unwillingness to confront a powerful government apparatus and its unwillingness to demand the truth from it—a truth the Committee had the right, by law, and the obligation to know. In avoiding that confrontation, the Congressmen failed in their Constitutional role.

The Committee was simply afraid. Such a confrontation would be too large, too elemental, too risky to all the institutions of government that form the power structure of the Washington establishment. And much too politically risky. So in the end, the House Select Committee on Assassinations, like the Warren Commission before it, produced a report that *looked* comprehensive and complete, but which failed the American people.

It is apparent that the Committee's failure to pursue the new evidence linking the CIA to Lee Harvey Oswald was a monumental dereliction of its duty. To prevent the American people from knowing that, the Committee had to deliberately distort the conclusions in its final report. This is the last investigation's deceptive legacy.

So after all these years and all those spent resources—after the last investigation—what the Kennedy assassination still sorely needs is an investigation guided simply, unswervingly, by the priority of truth.

Why should that be? Because far more is at stake than solving the murder of a President—as important as that is. The aftermath of the assassination has formed our present and, if we allow it to do so, it will shape our future. We are in grave danger of losing our democratic principles to cynicism and a form of enervating pragmatism. But a devotion to realistic and practical goals has never been a requisite to the sustenance of democratic principles. Truth has always been.

After the disdainful treatment she received at the hands of the Assassinations Committee, Silvia Odio, whose testimony stands as the strongest witness to a conspiracy, permitted author Anthony Summers, then working on the BBC documentary about the Kennedy assassination, to film an interview in silhouette. As he relates in

Conspiracy, Summers asked her why she was now prepared to talk, after refusing to for so long.

Odio was silent for a long moment. Then she said: "I guess it is a feeling of frustration after so many years. I feel outraged that we have not discovered the truth for history's sake, for all of us. I think it is because I'm very angry about it all—the forces I cannot understand and the fact that there is nothing I can do against them. That is why I am here."

Bob Blakey and the members of the Assassination Committee never felt what Silvia Odio feels. They never felt the frustration and anger that lives within her, the outrage that our Government still has not told the truth after so many years. I will always remember what she said to me when I told her the Committee had changed its mind about permitting her to tell her story publicly, to the American people. Her words echo in my mind, a soft shroud covering the years of my investigative sojourn through the labyrinth of the Kennedy assassination:

"We lost," she said. "We all lost."

THE LAST NOTE

I HAVEN'T COUNTED, but I'm told that more than 600 books about the assassination of President John F. Kennedy have been published. If you had read every one of them, you would undoubtedly be loaded with a great many more details about the assassination than is provided in this book. You would also be a bit, if not totally, confused, unable to resolve the conflicting degrees of validity various authors have given to the same pieces of evidence or information. That's because most authors simply toss about information acquired from previously published books, adding a bit here, taking out a bit there. So, instead, what I've aimed to do is deal largely with circumstances in which I was personally involved, and with information I *know* to be valid because I took part in developing it or checking its soundness. Of course, such a personal perspective necessarily limits the view of the Kennedy assassination case, including many fascinating areas of investigation. But that, to me, was less vital than providing a clear and, most important, a credible perspective on an historic and important event.

So credibility came first and, with it, the necessity to largely forego ultimate speculations and conclusions. But I realize I can't escape the inevitable. I am eventually always asked the final question: Who killed President Kennedy?

Of course I don't know. I don't know the names of the individuals who held the weapons or synchronized the shooting. But, based on my experiences and knowledge of what I feel is the most valid evidence, I certainly have firm opinions about the character of the conspiracy—and some of the characters in the conspiracy.

And, yes, one of the opinions I've come to is that the issue of conspiracy is not contestable. It never was. Long before the Assassinations Committee received confirmation from the acoustics tests in Dealey Plaza, the evidence of a conspiracy was overwhelming. And, in the narrow perspective of my personal quest for substantiation, I've come to conclude that, for me, two pieces of evidence provide irrefutable verification of conspiracy. One demolishes the single-bullet theory: The locations of the bullet holes in the back of Kennedy's jacket and shirt—hard, tangible, measurable evidence—obliterate the possibility of a bullet emerging from Kennedy's throat and striking Governor Connally. Single-bullet-theory author Arlen Specter conceded that was a worrisome contradiction. The other substantiation came from validating Silvia Odio's report that Oswald, or someone who resembled him (it matters not), appeared at her door in Dallas with two associates, one of whom would link Oswald to the notion of killing the President. That was a deliberate act connecting Oswald to the assassination *before* the assassination. Beyond all the other evidence indicating conspiracy, all the acoustic tests, the autopsy evidence, the bullet trajectory theories and what have you, even beyond all the other evidence of Oswald's associations, the Odio incident absolutely cries conspiracy. In fact, I have no hesitation in declaring the Kennedy assassination a conspiracy based strictly on Silvia Odio's consistently credible testimony and, more important, the fact that our investigation proved it true.

There is also a preponderance of evidence that indicates Lee Harvey Oswald had an association with a U.S. Government agency, perhaps more than one, but undoubtedly with the Central Intelligence Agency. Books have been written dealing with the data indicating Oswald's CIA connections. Some of it simply raises questions, but some of it provides strong indications that Oswald was deep into the intelligence cosmos. (For instance, the word "microdots" was in his notes at a time most Americans weren't even aware of the term.) But, again, I draw on my personal knowledge as the foundation for my opinions—and that includes Alpha 66 leader Antonio Veciana's testimony that he saw intelligence operative "Maurice Bishop" with Oswald in Dallas prior to the assassination.

"Maurice Bishop" was David Atlee Phillips. I state that unequivocally, although Veciana cannot officially identify him publicly as such. In addition to the abundance of evidence detailed in this book which unerringly points to Phillips being Bishop, believe me, I *know* that he was. And Bob Blakey and the House Assassinations Committee knew that he was, although its report did not admit that.

David Atlee Phillips played a key role in the conspiracy to assassinate President Kennedy. I don't embrace the assumption that Phillips's relationship to Oswald may have been extraneous to any conspiratorial role. If there was one most meaningful revelation that emerged from further digging into Phillips's background after the Assassinations Committee probe, it was the fact that David Phillips, the consummate actor, maintained a personal and even familial facade that was in direct contrast to the political realities of his professional life. (His likely prior knowledge of the Letelier assassination, his role in disseminating misinformation afterwards and his association with the Chilean and anti-Castro terrorists who planned and carried out the murder was but a glimpse of his chameleon-like character.)

That Phillips eventually rose to the top echelon of the Agency as Chief of the Western Hemisphere Division is, I think, significant when we talk about "elements" of the CIA being involved in the Kennedy assassination. (Can those who control the ideological soul and operational body of the Agency be considered simply "elements" within it?) Whatever additional factors may have been involved in the motivation to assassinate Kennedy— from his plans to diminish U.S. involvement in Vietnam to his moves toward a permanent détente with the Soviet Union—the triggering impetus, I believe, came with the Cuban missile crisis and Kennedy's "deal" with Khrushchev. The President's promise to abandon efforts to overthrow Castro was a watershed change in U.S. policy toward Cuba. And judging from the furious reaction among the Agency's field operatives who had absorbed and adopted the passions and dedication of their anti-Castro warriors, it was a treasonous act. That fury was palpable in the local radio broadcasts and in the handbills and "war bulletins" flying through Miami's Little Havana. And Kennedy's perfidy was confirmed when the President, realizing his orders were being scorned, forcibly shut down the CIA-sponsored operational bases and, in a few instances, even had recalcitrant anti-Castro Cubans as well as Agency operatives arrested. What more proof did anyone need that Kennedy was, indeed, a "traitor"?

David Atlee Phillips was deeply immersed in this world of all-consuming anti-Castroism. His professional life had been dedicated to it and to battling what he considered the expansionistic tentacles of Communism throughout Latin America. It is no coincidence that the man who emerges as the Maurice Bishop who planned Alpha 66 attempts to sink Russian ships in Havana harbor with the aim of embarrassing Kennedy and sabotaging his negotiations with Khrushchev, was the same man responsible for staging the entire Mexico City scenario designed to link Lee Harvey Oswald to Fidel Castro.*

*Castro recalled his immediate recognition of the consequences of that when he

Nor is Phillips's tight working association with the Agency's most lethal operatives insignificant. His was a cabal of associates whose careers were entwined with the history of CIA assassination plots, top echelon officers that ranged from Richard Helms to E. Howard Hunt and from Ted Shackley to the Agency's Mob liaison William Harvey. And then, of course, there was David Phillips's faithful operative, the CIA's action legend, David Sanchez Morales, whose inebriated admission of involvement in the Kennedy assassination— "*We* took care of that son of a bitch, didn't we?"—closed the circle.

I believe David Phillips's key role was affirmed when he lied under oath. The very fact that he *had* to lie—both about his manipulation of Oswald in Mexico City and his covert operations as Maurice Bishop— was the definitive statement of his guilt.

If there was one point in the House Assassinations Committee investigation which showed without a doubt that the Committee did not want to confront the CIA or open doors that would force it to face facts that it did not want to face, it was this: David Atlee Phillips committed perjury before the Committee. It could have been proven, he would have been convicted. The Chief Counsel and the Committee refused to pursue that option. That would have negated the Committee's final report declaring that it found no evidence the CIA was involved in the Kennedy assassination.

So, again, our Government slapped the American people in the face. We have been slapped in the face over and over again and we still deny it is happening to us. Why?

I am privileged to have access to the round-robin correspondence of a small group of friends who believe that an on-going intellectual exchange on major issues—the Kennedy assassination being a primary one—might foster fresh insights. Among them is Dr. Martin Schotz, a psychiatrist in Brookline, Mass. In one of his recent letters, I thought Dr. Schotz made a particularly incisive observation, relevant to what we're talking about here.

He wrote: "It is so important to understand that one of the primary means of immobilizing the American people politically today is to hold them in a state of confusion in which anything can be believed but nothing can be known, nothing of significance that is.

"And the American people are more than willing to be held in this state because to KNOW the truth—as opposed to only BELIEVE the truth—is to face an awful terror and to be no longer able to evade

---

told his Assassinations Committee visitors: "I said to myself, what would have happened had by any chance that man come to Cuba . . . gone back to the States and then appeared involved in Kennedy's death? That would have been a provocation—a gigantic provocation."

responsibility. It is precisely in moving from belief to knowledge that the citizen moves from irresponsibility to responsibility, from helplessness and hopelessness to action, with the ultimate aim of being empowered and confident in one's rational powers.''

Dr. Schotz is absolutely right. Today most Americans BELIEVE there was a conspiracy to kill President Kennedy, but they don't KNOW it. They don't want to KNOW it—and our Government doesn't want to KNOW it and our elected representatives don't want to KNOW it because KNOWING it would mean having to do something about it. That's an awesome thought.

But perhaps we all might find it easier to come to KNOW it, and to face that awesome thought, if we constantly reminded ourselves that on November 22nd, 1963, a man's life ended in Dallas. *A man's life ended. . . .*

EPILOGUE 2008
by GAETON FONZI

*A*ND STILL IN my mind and in my heart I hear the strong, sweet, soft-edged drawl of Mary Ferrell's voice echoing down through the years from that evening in 1992 in Dallas when she delivered the opening remarks to a gathering of Kennedy assassination researchers. I wrote of her words in the Introduction to the initial publication of *The Last Investigation* but the depth of their relevancy has not diminished.

"As the thirtieth anniversary of the assassination of President John F. Kennedy descends on us," she said, "I am much concerned that we are on the threshold of a failure from which there will be no forgiveness.

"We must win this struggle for truth . . . and do so quickly, lest the assassination of President Kennedy flounder on some remote shoulder of highway, in a century whose history is on the way to the printer."

But Mary wasn't issuing a warning, she was launching a challenge. "Time is our most relentless and uncompromising enemy," she told the gathering, "but history teaches us that significant changes are often accomplished by small numbers of people facing large odds." She spoke of Thomas Paine, John Adams and Thomas Jefferson and our country's early leaders who represented a tiny fraction of the young country's population. "As it was with that tiny fraction," she told the gathering of a few hundred researchers, "I have every confidence that you are representative of millions who share your view . . . . That is what keeps us united in our cause. It is a view, according to the polls, which is held by an overwhelming majority of our fellow citizens—that a conspiracy and government-sponsored cover-up blotted out the rights of our citizens and sanctity of the rule of law."

That's what drove me to write this book. When I joined the House Select Committee on Assassinations the very fact of its formation and the wording of its legal mandate—House Resolution 222—to "conduct a full and complete investigation and study of the circumstances surrounding the assassination and death of President John F. Kennedy" clearly presumed that our Government's initial effort to construct a scenario the American people would embrace was a failure. The Warren Commission Report was, in fact, far more than a failure. Its blatant duplicities and crafty manipulation of evidence soon seeded in the minds of most Americans a depth of suspicion and skepticism toward their Government that bloomed into a distrust and conspiratorial disposition that recent national history seems to regularly fortify.

The House Assassinations Committee had an opportunity which the Warren Commission did not. From its very formation, the Commission's mission was designed not to find and reveal the truth but to avoid or cover it up. Even before it was formed, the Commission's direction was being set by powerful forces within the government. When its 912-page Report was issued, only about 11 percent of it dealt with the alleged facts of the assassination. At the insistence of Commission member Allen Dulles, the former head of the CIA whom Kennedy had fired after the Bay of Pigs failure, most of the Report was devoted to a detailed biography of the designated assailant, Lee Harvey Oswald. And although it dealt with Oswald's anti-Castro/pro-Castro charades and his (or what might have been an imposter's) attempt to get to Cuba, Dulles did not tell the Commission that the CIA itself was involved in Castro assassination attempts.

Considering his close association with Richard Helms, the CIA's Deputy Director of Plans, Dulles more than likely was aware of a significant scenario played out at CIA headquarters beginning only hours after the assassination. An officer named John Whitten, chief of covert operations for Mexico and Central America, received a call from the Mexico City station chief reporting that a CIA surveillance team had photographed Oswald at the Cuban Consulate there. Whitten immediately ordered all photos of Oswald sent to headquarters and then began digging into classified cables indicating the Agency's knowledge of Oswald's anti-Castro *and* pro-Castro activities. As Whitten was developing this information, his boss, Richard Helms, took him off the case. Later, Whitten was shocked to discover that Helms himself had withheld information from him about the CIA's knowledge of Oswald's activities prior to the assassination. Eventually, what the CIA's knowledge or association with Oswald was—or *who* within the Agency knew it or was involved with him—became lost within a jumble of conflicting reports, disinformation and perjured testimony. The so-called photos of Oswald either never surfaced or never existed—a conflicting muddle one might consider a natural characteristic of a discombobulated bureaucracy—unless you're aware that the Agency's surveillance team in Mexico City reported to Helms' top covert operative, David Atlee Phillips, the psych warfare expert who concocted many of the disinformation scenarios which circulated immediately after the assassination.

By the time of the formation of the House Select Committee on Assassinations, any objective and comprehensive evaluation of the issues embedded within any investigative approach to the JFK murder had to conclude that the role of the Government's intelligence apparatus outweighed all others. What primarily gave it that weight was the infinity of questions surrounding Oswald's behavior, so much of which smelled of intelligence or counter-intelligence activity. It didn't take any depth of knowledge to glimpse the possibilities. When Senator Richard Schweiker was a member of the Senate Select Committee on Intelligence, he personally did preliminary research on Oswald's background. That's why he decided to ask Senate Chairman Frank Church to form a Subcommittee on the JFK case. To Schweiker, the link was apparent: "We don't know what happened," Schweiker said, "but we do know that Oswald had intelligence connections. Everywhere you look with him, there are the fingerprints of intelligence."

That the intelligence area should be a priority in any investigative plan was also immediately apparent to the House Committee's first Chief Counsel, Richard Sprague. Although Sprague was forced to resign for what he thought were political factors related to his hiring personnel and his budgetary demands, he later realized that his troubles with the politicians began when he made the CIA his initial investigative target. "I had no problems in Washington until I bucked the CIA," Sprague said.

When former Justice Department attorney and law professor Robert Blakey took over as the Committee's Chief Counsel he immediately established an investigative approach designed to reflect a bureaucratic objectivity. The intelligence community wasn't going to get any special weight in the investigative plan, despite the preponderance of evidence linking Oswald to it. But Blakey knew that working with the CIA would require special attention. Unlike his predecessor Sprague—who refused to sign the CIA's secrecy oath before the Agency would give him access to its files—Blakey saw nothing ludicrous in seeking a "working relationship" with one of the subjects of the Committee's investigation.

Blakey believed he could handle the CIA. He sat down with its top bosses and negotiated and re-negotiated "agreements" that would eventually provide Committee researchers access to all its files. Of course, all the Committee's staffers who wanted access to the files had to first sign the CIA Secrecy Oath.

Blakey always returned from Langley beaming with pride at his skillful handling of the CIA. And on the surface it appeared that Blakey was successful. Even the Agency's liaisons, wing-tipped bureaucrats who handled Committee staff requests for documents, became unusually friendly and smilingly cooperative. And if it were necessary to research documents at CIA's headquarters, Committee staffers were greeted with an organized efficiency. Or so it appeared.

That attitude didn't last long. Yet Blakey continued to maintain his faith in the CIA's professed total cooperation even in the face of his researchers' increasing number of complaints. Despite the unprecedented pact Blakey had made with their top-level bosses, the CIA's operative-level staffers were claiming that more and more requested documents were "unable to be found," or were "missing for some reason," or were "inadvertently" destroyed in routine file purges. Still Blakey refused to be cynical. "Maybe they're telling the truth," he said.

And yet now, a couple of decades later, there is hard evidence that the Agency did lie to Blakey—and to Congress and the American people. And that evidence also reveals the deceit and shocking arrogance with which the Agency handled those who tried to penetrate its serfdom. A defining example that recently came to light:

When Kennedy made a deal to avert a nuclear war stemming from the Cuban Missile Crisis, among his stipulations to Khrushchev was that, in return for removal of the missiles, he would shut down a secret guerilla war the anti-Castro Cubans and the CIA were waging against Castro. Kennedy had quietly supported this secret war and the CIA was providing money and covert advisers to dozens of the groups. Directed by the CIA's "JM/WAVE" station in South Miami, the groups conducted very successful, almost nightly missions into Cuba, destroying both military and civilian targets, burning government buildings, planting bombs in large department stores and committing general acts of terrorism.

But the Missile Crisis was a cathartic awakening for Kennedy. He suddenly realized he had helped bring the world to the brink of nuclear annihilation. His subsequent speeches reflect a more conciliatory approach in dealing with the Soviet Union. And to augment his promise to Khrushchev that the U.S. would not invade Cuba, he ordered the CIA to completely shut down the secret military operations of the anti-Castro Cuban groups.

There are those who believe that in issuing directives to augment his enlightened policy, JFK was signing his own death warrant. Among some of the CIA's own field personnel there appeared pockets of insubordination. A few of the anti-Castro guerilla groups initially ignored his edict against further military operations and one even tried to sink a Russian ship in Havana harbor. To enforce his directive, Kennedy had to call on the U.S. Navy and the Coast Guard to raid a few anti-Castro bases in Miami, the Keys and the Bahamas—bases the CIA itself had helped establish. What more evidence could there be that Kennedy was a "traitor" and maybe, as the leaflets being passed around Little Havana declared, a Communist himself.

In probing this area of their investigation, the Assassinations Committee staffers focused on a small number of anti-Castro Cuban groups that were the most active and militant. The largest was the Student Revolutionary Directorate, called the DRE from its Spanish acronym. What made the DRE more significant than others was that, within hours of the assassination, rumors and reports flew out of the DRE's branch in New Orleans that Lee Harvey Oswald had tried to infiltrate the group. Its leaders, however, claimed they had quickly seen through his guise and later caught him handing out pro-Castro pamphlets to the public. That led to a street brawl which got Oswald arrested briefly by the police and that, in turn, led to his appearance on a local talk radio program defending his Marxist beliefs.

The Warren Commission used that DRE-generated incident to bolster its portrait of Oswald as a pro-Castro fanatic. However, over the years researchers burst that balloon of disinformation, producing evidence that the pamphlets originated with a CIA front and Oswald was likely a willing role player. By the time the Assassinations Committee began probing the DRE, emerging evidence had forced the Agency to retreat from its stance of non-involvement with any anti-Castro Cuban group. It admitted it played an "advisory" role with a few of the groups and, yes, the DRE among them. The Committee researchers immediately requested all documents and records of the Agency's contacts with the DRE. They also asked the Agency to locate and produce the DRE's control officer so that he could answer questions under oath.

Just prior, Chief Counsel Blakey had brought some of his researchers' complaints to the attention of the Agency's main liaison to the Committee, a usually glib lawyer named Scott Breckenridge. Now Breckenridge seemed solicitous and suggested a "new point of contact" for the Committee, an expert the Agency would bring out of retirement to "facilitate" the researchers' requests. His name was George Joannides.

Joannides was a tall, classy-looking guy who wore tailored suits and a dour demeanor around the Committee's offices. It soon became apparent that instead of facilitating document requests he was more and more dancing around, delaying and blocking them. Moreover, Joannides said, he could not find any records indicating the name of the DRE's control officer or documents revealing his operational activities with the group.

Nor did he find any records revealing Oswald's contacts with members of the DRE.

But, Joannides said, he would continue looking for the Agency's DRE files as well as any records which would help him identify and locate the Agency's control officer, the one man who would have the most information about the DRE and its contact with Lee Harvey Oswald.

The tenure of the House Select Committee expired before the CIA ever responded to its DRE document requests. Congressional committees come and go, the CIA is a perpetual institution. The Agency chose to simply "wait out" the Committee's life.

There was no clearer indication that the CIA has evolved into an independent institution, its ultimate priority its own survival. Refusing to comply with dictates issued by elected representatives of the American people reveals its disdain for the basic values of a democratic society. The Assassinations Committee's relationship with the CIA regarding the DRE indicates, in itself, what a renegade institution the Agency had become. Through the lies and deceptions of Joannides, the CIA was able to control and stifle the Committee's efforts to pursue the truth about an important—perhaps pivotally crucial—aspect of President Kennedy's assassination.

The CIA never informed the Committee that Joannides was more than a clerkish agent expert in "facilitating" document requests. When Kennedy was assassinated Joannides was chief of Miami station JM/WAVE's "psychological warfare" branch. He worked with the Agency's legendary psych war guru, David Atlee Phillips.

And it was Phillips who had also been instrumental in helping members of the Student Directorate re-group in Miami after they were forced to flee Havana. Once reorganized and strengthened with zealous exiles anxious to take the fight against Castro to its most effective level, the DRE was deemed by the Agency to be worthy of a high degree of both advisory and monetary support. The control agent the CIA assigned to the DRE soon began handing DRE's leaders a monthly contribution that would reach, in current dollars, $1.5 million a year.

The name of the CIA's control agent assigned to the DRE was George Joannides.

Many of the revelations about Joannides and the CIA's sabotaging the Assassination Committee's investigation were uncovered by *Washington Post* reporter Jeff Morley, who discovered Joannides' personnel file in newly released National Archives documents. Although it was published elsewhere (the weekly *New Times* in Miami ran it prominently), the *Post* never ran his story, the Kennedy assassination being history and the details too esoteric.

Fortunately and to his credit, Chief Counsel Bob Blakey doesn't hold that view. Now a professor at Notre Dame Law, he no longer believes he was right in trusting the CIA. In fact, he now accuses the Agency of "obstruction of justice."

Blakey didn't say he read that first in *The Last Investigation*. But he did.

SELECTED CHRONOLOGY*

07/26/47—Congress establishes the National Security Agency to advise the president on intelligence matters. It also creates the Central Intelligence Agency with a director "subject to no supervision, control, restriction, or prohibition" from the military Joint Chiefs of Staff. The leadership of the new CIA is composed largely of former members of World War II's Office of Strategic Services.

03/10/52—General Fulgencia Batista's military forces take the Columbian army camp in Havana at dawn and depose Carlos Prío from the presidency of Cuba.

11/04/52—Having resigned as supreme commander in Europe, General Dwight D. Eisenhower is elected president of the United States.

07/26/53—Fidel Castro opens his military challenge against Batista by personally leading the charge against the Moncado army barracks in Santiago. It fails and he is captured, but the date goes down in modern Cuban history. At his trial Castro proclaims: "History will absolve me!"

01/14/54—At a meeting of President Eisenhower's National Security Council, it is agreed "that the Director of the Central Intelligence Agency [Allen Dulles], in collaboration with other appropriate departments and agencies, should develop plans, as suggested by the Secretary of State [John Foster Dulles], for certain contingencies in Indochina." Subsequently the CIA

---

*Where specific day dates cannot be authenticated, the first day of the month is used.

421

created the Saigon Military Mission designed to expand its clandestine operations in Vietnam.

06/01/54—To protect the interests of the United Fruit Company, the CIA succeeds in disposing of democratically elected President Jacobo Arbenz in Guatemala. David Atlee Phillips and E. Howard Hunt are Allen Dulles's key operatives in running the Agency's psych warfare and psychological campaigns. One of Phillips's covert operatives is David Sanchez Morales.

07/01/55—Lee Harvey Oswald, fifteen, joins the New Orleans Civil Air Patrol commanded by David Ferrie, an Eastern Airlines pilot and former seminarian who, in 1961, would be twice arrested for "indecent behavior" with juveniles. He would later become an investigator for former FBI agent Guy Banister, with offices at 544 Camp Street.

11/01/55—CIA agent David Sanchez Morales is assigned to work undercover as a State Department political officer at the American embassy in Caracas, Venezuela.

10/26/56—Lee Harvey Oswald reports for duty at the Marine Corps Recruit Depot, San Diego, California.

01/20/57—Eisenhower is sworn in to his second term as president.

09/12/57—Oswald arrives at the U-2 spy airplane base at Atsugi, Japan, and is assigned as a radar operator.

01/01/58—David Atlee Phillips establishes a public relations business in Havana as a front for covert CIA operations.

05/01/58—David Sanchez Morales is assigned to the American embassy in Havana and, according to the embassy's U.S. Information Agency rep, Paul Bethel, is in charge of the CIA's "dirty tricks" section.

11/02/58—At the end of a thirteen-month tour of duty in Japan, Oswald heads back to the U.S. and is assigned to Marine Air Control Squadron Nine in Santa Ana, California.

01/01/59—Military dictator Fulgencio Batista flees Cuba under the pressure of rebel forces of the 26th of July Movement, led by a young attorney named Fidel Castro, sweeping down on Havana.

02/01/59—Nineteen-year-old Marita Lorenz, a captain's daughter, meets Fidel Castro when he welcomes her father's German cruise ship as it anchors in Havana harbor. She later becomes Castro's mistress and then is recruited by Frank Sturgis in a plan to kill Castro with poison pills.

02/25/59—Oswald takes a Marine Corps proficiency examination in the Russian language. He scores well enough to indicate he had to have begun studying while still in Japan, but none of his Marine friends ever saw him learning the language.

03/19/59—Oswald, soon to be discharged from the Marines, applies to the Albert Schweitzer College in Switzerland. He claims a proficiency in Russian.

09/11/59—Oswald is released from the Marine Corps after requesting a hardship discharge on the claim that his mother needs his support.

10/16/59—After leaving New Orleans on September 20, and traveling by way of London, Le Havre, and Helsinki, Oswald arrives in Russia and tells an Intourist guide that he intends to become a Russian citizen.

11/01/59—The "Movimiento de Recuperacion," led by Dr. Manuel Artime, becomes the first anti-Castro action group to organize elements in every province in Cuba.

12/11/59—CIA Director Allen Dulles approves "thorough consideration be given to the elimination of Fidel Castro."

01/18/60—Richard Bissell, Deputy Director for Plans of the CIA and developer of the U-2 spy plane, meets with top-ranking Agency colleagues and announces that CIA boss Allen Dulles has appointed him to organize a "typical Latin political upheaval" in Cuba. It will be based on the "Guatemala model," the CIA's first successful military intervention scheme. Bissell selects E. Howard Hunt and David Atlee Phillips to be among his top field operatives.

03/17/60—President Eisenhower authorizes the CIA to organize, train, and equip Cuban refugees as a guerilla force to overthrow Castro.

05/01/60—Francis Gary Powers's U-2 spy plane is shot down over the U.S.S.R. The incident plays a major role in sabotaging Eisenhower's efforts to begin a peace initiative with Khrushchev. There's speculation that Oswald may have provided the Russians with information enabling it to bring down the U-2.

06/03/60—J. Edgar Hoover sends a memo to the State Department reporting that an imposter may be using Oswald's birth certificate in Russia.

08/01/60—Antonio Veciana, comptroller in Havana's Banco Finaciero, is approached by deep-cover CIA agent "Maurice Bishop" to work with him in anti-Castro activity.

09/24/60—CIA Operational Support Chief James O'Connell meets with asset Robert Maheu, a former FBI and CIA agent working for millionaire Howard Hughes, and Mob representative John Rosselli to discuss involvement of organized crime in attempts to assassinate Castro. Later, O'Connell would be introduced to Mob bosses Sam Giancana and Santos Trafficante who would recruit Miami Cubans for the operation.

10/25/60—U.S. State Department sends a list of defectors to the CIA and requests any information it may have. The name of Lee Harvey Oswald is on the list.

12/09/60—CIA opens a 201-file on Oswald. Agency later tells Warren Commission it was opened as a result of the State Department's request of October 25.

01/01/61—The U.S. embassy in Havana is closed.

01/01/61—Dallas petroleum engineer and CIA asset George de Mohrenschildt arrives in Guatemala with his wife Jeanne. They remain in Guatemala for four months while the CIA is training anti-Castro Cubans there in preparation for the Bay of Pigs invasion.

01/20/61—John F. Kennedy is inaugurated president of the United States.

02/05/61—Oswald writes to Richard Snyder at the U.S. embassy in Moscow and expresses his desire to return home. He adds: "I hope that in recalling the responsibility I have to America that you remember yours in doing everything to help me since I am an American citizen."

02/13/61—The CIA's Technical Services Division records indicate that a box of Castro's favorite cigars treated with a lethal poison were delivered to an unidentified asset. The records do not disclose whether an attempt was made to pass the cigars to Castro.

02/13/61—CIA Support Chief James O'Connell delivers poison pills to Mob liaison John Rosselli who later claims to have given them to a Cuban official close to Castro. The pills are reportedly later returned after the official lost his position.

03/01/61—At President Kennedy's direct order the *Frente,* the umbrella group of anti-Castro organizations organized by the CIA's political liaison E. Howard Hunt, is replaced by a more liberal Cuban Revolutionary Council. It now includes Manolo Ray, whom many consider a democratic socialist. (Silvia Odio's father was one of the key backers of Ray's organization, called *Jure.*) Hunt terms Ray's politics *Fidelissimo sin Fidel* (Fidelism without Fidel), was outraged at the appointment, and (either) resigns or is dismissed from his job as the CIA's political action officer for the Bay of Pigs operation.

04/15/61—The CIA launches the Bay of Pigs invasion. It is over within two days. The Agency-trained forces of Brigade 2506 lose 114 men on the beaches; 1,189 are captured and imprisoned until December 1962 when the U.S. pays a ransom of $53 million worth of food and drugs.

08/23/61—David Phillips is made chief of covert action in Mexico City. He maintains the position until October 1963 when he is promoted to chief of Cuban operations.

09/01/61—In a unilateral move to isolate Cuba from its allies, the United States announces it will stop assistance to any country that assists Cuba.

10/03/61—An assassination attempt against Castro instigated by Maurice Bishop fails and Veciana is forced to flee Cuba. Reynol Gonzalez, one of Veciana's coconspirators, is later arrested hiding on the estate of Amador Odio, a wealthy industrialist and father of Silvia Odio. Gonzales, the elder Odio, and his wife are arrested.

11/01/61—Maurice Bishop contacts Antonio Veciana in Miami and instructs him to establish an anti-Castro organization. The organization is later called Alpha 66.

11/01/61—Presidential Advisor Richard Goodwin and CIA Deputy Edward Lansdale recommend the creation of Operation Mongoose as a coordinated effort to depose Castro's government.

11/16/61—CIA Deputy Director for Plans Richard Bissell directs Cuban Task Force head William Harvey to apply the ZR/RIFLE assassination program to Cuba. Harvey reestablishes the Agency contact with Mob liaison John Rosselli.

11/29/61—President Kennedy fires CIA Director Allen Dulles and his deputy Richard Bissell as a result of the Bay of Pigs debacle; Kennedy appoints an "outsider," John McCone, an industrialist and former chairman of the Atomic Energy Commission, as head of the Agency.

11/30/61—President Kennedy writes memo to Secretary of State Dean Rusk recording his decision to start Operation Mongoose. A presidential advisory group, headed by Robert Kennedy and called Special Group (Augmented), is to control it. The CIA's branch of Operation Mongoose, Task Force W, is headed by William Harvey, boss of the Agency's ZR/RIFLE "Executive Action" section. Miami's JM/WAVE station is the CIA's operational center for Mongoose. Headed by Theodore Shackley, its chief of operations is David Sanchez Morales, David Phillips's close associate. With an official staff of more than three hundred and with fifty-four front corporations, the Agency becomes one of Florida's largest employers.

02/19/62—Richard Helms replaces Richard Bissell as the CIA's deputy director for Plans, in charge of all covert operations.

05/21/62—CIA Technical Services Division gives poison pills to Cuban Ops chief William Harvey to pass to Mob contact John Rosselli who in turn will pass pills on to the same Cuban contact involved in the pre-Bay of Pigs attempt to poison Castro. The Cuban contact would later claim the opportunity to use the pills never came up.

06/13/62—Oswald, with his Russian wife and baby daughter, disembark from the *SS Maasdam* in Hobokon, New Jersey. The CIA claims it took no interest in the returning defector, but the Oswalds are met by Spas T. Raikin, a caseworker with Travelers Aid in New York. Raikin is a member of American Friends of Anti-Bolshevik Nations, a staunch anticommunist group. Late the next day, the Oswalds fly to Fort Worth where they will temporarily stay with his brother Robert. Oswald's mother Marguerite later said he had sent her a letter from Moscow saying he would stop in Washington on the way home. According to *Legend* author Edward J. Epstein, a CIA psychologist code-named Cato interviewed a Russian defector who resembled Oswald at the Roger Smith Hotel in Washington on the evening of June 13.

06/20/62—Oswald is befriended by Peter Paul Gregory, a petroleum engineer teaching Russian language courses at the Fort Worth library. Gregory begins introducing the Oswalds to his friends in the White Russian community in Dallas. Among them is George de Mohrenschildt, who would later say that he first heard of Oswald through J. Walton Moore in late 1961. Moore, of the

CIA's Domestic Contact Service in Dallas, described an ex-Marine working in an electronics factory in Minsk who would soon return to the United States. Moore said the CIA had an "interest" in Oswald.

07/13/62—Oswald obtains a job with Leslie Welding Company in Fort Worth. He assembles doors and windows for $1.25 an hour.

09/10/62—With only Washington's intelligence insiders aware of a brewing Cuban missile crisis, Maurice Bishop directs Alpha 66 leader Antonio Veciana to launch a commando attack on a British ship and two Cuban cargo vessels off the north coast of Cuba. Four days later, the Associated Press reports from San Juan, Puerto Rico, that Veciana declares that Alpha 66 will make five more raids into Cuba in the next sixty days. He claims a war chest of $100,000.

10/07/62—After attending the Van Cliburn piano competition in Fort Worth, George de Mohrenschildt joins his daughter Alexandra and friends from the White Russian community at a gathering at the Oswald apartment. Oswald's mother Marguerite later says she had the impression that de Mohrenschildt had already arranged a job for her son in Dallas.

10/08/62—Under the strategic direction of Maurice Bishop, Antonio Veciana orders commandos of Alpha 66 to attack Soviet merchant ships in Havana harbor.

10/11/62—Oswald is hired by Jaggars-Chiles-Stovall Co., a Dallas photographic firm that has a contract with the U.S. Army Map Service which involves information obtained from U-2 spy flights.

10/28/62—After weeks of tense confrontation that brought the world to the brink of a nuclear holocaust, Russian Premier Khrushchev announces that the U.S.S.R. had decided to dismantle Soviet missiles in Cuba. Kennedy responds by congratulating Khrushchev for "an important contribution to peace." An agreement is reached which includes Kennedy's promise to halt Operation Mongoose raids against Cuba. The confrontation appears to be a cathartic experience for Kennedy. "Our most basic common link is that we all inhabit this small planet," he says in a speech later. "We all breathe the same air, we all cherish our children's futures and we are all mortal."

12/04/62—U.S. Customs officers capture twelve anti-Castro guerillas, mostly American soldiers of fortune trained by the CIA, at a secret training base called No Name Key, north of Key West, as they are about to embark on a raid to Cuba. They are charged with violation of the Neutrality Act. Among those arrested is Gerry Patrick Hemming, founder with Frank Sturgis of the International Anti-Communist Brigade.

01/01/63—Task Force W is replaced by new CIA group called Special Affairs Staff. Desmond FitzGerald replaces William Harvey and continues anti-Castro raids on a smaller scale, despite earlier Kennedy directives to halt all Cuban operations.

02/02/63—The CIA establishes a new Domestic Operations Division under Tracy Barnes, chief of the psychological and paramilitary staff for the

Agency's clandestine branch during the Bay of Pigs, when he worked with David Phillips as propaganda chief. E. Howard Hunt is shifted from chief of the covert action staff in the Western European Division to a deputy position in Barnes's new division. On orders from Deputy Director FitzGerald, Phillips takes over Cuban operations.

02/02/63—George and Jeanne de Mohrenschildt invite the Oswalds to a party at the home of Everett Glover, where Michael Paine, the estranged husband of Ruth Paine, lives; but Paine, who works for Bell Helicopter, isn't present. The Oswalds, however, are introduced to Ruth Paine, who would later invite Marina Oswald and her daughter to live with her when Oswald moved to a rooming house.

03/19/63—At a press conference in Washington arranged by spymaster Maurice Bishop, Alpha 66 leader Antonio Veciana announces that his anti-Castro forces have raided a "Soviet fortress" and ship in a Cuban port east of Havana, causing a dozen Soviet casualties and serious damage. Veciana says his purpose is "to wage psychological warfare against the government of Premier Fidel Castro and the Soviet troops supporting him." *The New York Times* says the Kennedy administration is "embarrassed by the incident."

04/01/63—*The New York Times* reports: "Seventeen heavily armed Cuban exiles planning to attack a Soviet tanker off Cuba were seized yesterday by a British force on a solitary islet in the Bahamas chain. . . . The capture was apparently the first result of an agreement worked out late last week by Washington and London to cooperate in preventing raids by opponents of Premier Fidel Castro . . . [In Miami], Cuban exiles reacted with a mixture of anger, defiance and gloom. . . ." The anti-Castro raiding party was led by Jerry Buchanan, a member of Frank Sturgis's International Anti-Communist Brigade.

04/05/63—The Kennedy administration reveals it is assigning more Navy and Customs planes and boats to police the Florida straits against continuing anti-Castro raids.

04/16/63—Oswald writes V. T. Lee of the Fair Play for Cuba Committee in New York that he had passed out FPCC literature in Dallas and requests that more be sent to him. The FBI steps up its surveillance and mail-intercept program of the FPCC.

04/16/63—Alpha 66 continues to expand, with branches in Miami, New York, Chicago, and Dallas; announces it is now opening a chapter in Los Angeles.

04/19/63—With details of Kennedy's Cuban missile crisis agreement with Khrushchev still emerging, Dr. José Miro Cardona resigns as head of the Cuban Revolutionary Council, originally set up by the U.S. government as a means of controlling the disparate anti-Castro groups. Miro Cardona charges that Kennedy has given Castro "absolute immunity" and accuses him of "liquidating the struggle for Cuba."

04/24/93—Oswald is laid off from Jaggers-Chiles-Stovall and tells his wife he is going to New Orleans to look for work and that she should follow in a few weeks. He temporarily moves in with his aunt and uncle, the Murrets. Charles Murret is a shipyard worker and smalltime bookie who works under the Marcello organized crime family.

05/07/63—After making arrangements through Army Colonel Sam Kail (the contact given to Antonio Veciana by Maurice Bishop when Kail was the military attaché at the American embassy in Havana), George de Mohrenschildt brings his Haitian business partner, Clemard Charles, to a meeting with a CIA staff officer in Washington prior to departing for Haiti. Charles is believed to be a conduit for CIA funds funneled through Haitian dictator François [Duvalier] Duvalier.

05/09/63—Oswald obtains a job at the Reily Coffee Company in New Orleans. The company's owner, William Reily, is a wealthy backer of anti-Castro groups and activities.

05/26/63—Oswald writes V. T. Lee at the New York FPCC: "Now that I live in New Orleans I have been thinking about renting a small office at my own expense for the purpose of forming a FPCC branch here in New Orleans. Could you give me a charter? . . . Also a picture of Fidel, suitable for framing would be a welcome touch."

05/29/63—At Jones Printing Company, next to Reily Coffee, Oswald orders a thousand handbills that read: "HANDS OFF CUBA! Join the Fair Play for Cuba Committee NEW ORLEANS CHARTER MEMBER BRANCH." Some of the handbills are hand stamped with the address 544 Camp Street. That is the office of ex-FBI agent Guy Banister and his investigator David Ferrie, ardent anti-Castro supporters.

06/24/63—Oswald applies for a new passport, receives it the next day.

07/19/63—Oswald is fired from his job at Reily Coffee. Adrian Alba, who manages the parking garage next door, drops in to see him, says Oswald appears in good spirits, tells Alba, "I have found my pot of gold at the end of the rainbow."

07/24/63—A group of anti-Castro Cubans arrives in New Orleans from Miami and joins a training camp off Lake Pontchartrain. Members are from the International Anti-Communist Brigade, established by Frank Sturgis and Gerry Patrick Hemming. The Senate Intelligence Committee Report would later claim that " 'A,' life-long friend of AMLASH [Rolando Cubela]," had helped procure explosives for the camp. "A" is Victor Espinosa Hernandez, who obtained the explosives from Richard Lauchli, cofounder of the paramilitary right-wing Minutemen. During the Garrison investigation, reports were received that Oswald and David Ferrie were seen at this camp.

07/31/63—The FBI seizes more than a ton of dynamite, bomb casing, and napalm material at a home off Lake Pontchartrain but not part of the IAB camp. The home is owned by William McClaney, a well-known Havana gambler and brother of Mike McClaney, former casino owner in Cuba.

08/01/63—Oswald is listed by the House UnAmerican Activities Committee as the secretary of the Fair Play for Cuba chapter in New Orleans.

08/09/63—Oswald is arrested on Canal Street in New Orleans after a confrontation with anti-Castro Cuban exiles, including Carlos Bringuier, a member of the CIA-supported Student Revolutionary Directorate (DRE). Oswald was handing out leaflets for the pro-Castro Fair Play for Cuba Committee. The confrontation seems staged. An FBI agent interviews Oswald in jail, but despite inaugurating a special "Cuban Section" to its Security Index after the Cuban missile crisis, Oswald's name is not added to it.

08/21/63—Oswald appears on New Orleans radio station with Carlos Bringuier. After the show, Oswald goes to a bar to drink beer with talk show host, Bill Stuckey who had been briefed about Oswald by an associate, Ed Butler, head of the Information Council of the Americas, a right-wing propaganda organization.

08/22–
09/17/63—The House Assassinations Committee says there is no corroborated whereabouts for Oswald during this period. However, it was during this time, the Committee concluded, that Oswald was seen with David Ferrie and, likely, Guy Banister at a black voting rights demonstration in Clinton, Louisiana, about 130 miles north of New Orleans.

08/23/63—Silvia Duran begins work as a secretary at the Cuban consulate in Mexico City. Claims she is a socialist sympathizer and had flown to Cuba as government guest in December 1961.

09/01/63—In the last week of August, while officially confined to Dade County by federal authorities for his anti-Castro activities, Antonio Veciana travels to Dallas for a meeting with Maurice Bishop. In the lobby of the Southland Building, Veciana sees Bishop speaking to a young man Veciana later identifies as Lee Harvey Oswald.

09/01/63—William Attwood, special advisor to the U.S.'s United Nations delegation, begins a series of talks with the Cuban ambassador. Robert Kennedy encourages the effort. Attwood reports regularly to the White House and to Adlai Stevenson, U.S. ambassador to the U.N.

09/07/63—CIA case officers meet with AMLASH, a Cuban agent in Castro's inner circle, report AMLASH has an interest in attempting to assassinate Castro, and is awaiting a U.S. plan of action.

09/25/63—According to the Warren Commission, Oswald left New Orleans by bus on his way to Mexico City.

09/27/63—According to the Warren Commission, Oswald arrives in Mexico City at 10:00 A.M., registers at the Hotel Comercio and appears at the Cuban embassy to apply for a visa to Cuba in transit to Russia.

09/27/63—Silvia Odio, a Cuban refugee living in Dallas, reports three men visited her to ask her help in anti-Castro activities. One of the men is introduced to her as "Leon Oswald."

10/01/63—David Phillips, stationed in Mexico City, promoted to chief of Cuban operations, travels to Washington.

10/01/63—*The New York Times* columnist Arthur Krock, in citing a dispatch from Vietnam by reporter Richard Starnes, imbues it with additional significance because of Krock's known close relationship with the Kennedys. Starnes had reported that the CIA twice flatly refused to carry out instructions from Ambassador Henry Cabot Lodge, and in one instance frustrated a plan of action Mr. Lodge brought from Washington because the Agency disagreed with it. Krock also noted this revelation in Starnes's report: "Among the views attributed to United States officials on the scene, including one described as 'a very high American official . . . who has spent much of his life in the service of democracy' . . . are the following: 'The CIA's growth was "likened to a malignancy" which the very high official was not sure even the White House could control . . . any longer. If the United States ever experiences [an attempt at a coup to overthrow the government] it will come from the CIA and not the Pentagon.' The agency 'represents a tremendous power and total unaccountability to anyone.' "

10/01/63—The CIA says that on this day "a reliable and sensitive source in Mexico reported that an American male, who identified himself as Lee Oswald, contacted the Soviet embassy in Mexico City. . . ." It later sends the Warren Commission a photograph of the man who is not Oswald entering the embassy. The CIA says it was simply a "mistake."

10/03/63—According to the Warren Commission, Oswald arrives back in the United States from his trip to Mexico City.

10/04/63—Richard Helms provides the Warren Commission an affidavit claiming that the CIA's photograph of the mystery man misidentified as Oswald was taken on this date—after Oswald had left the city.

10/08/63—David Phillips testified to the Assassinations Committee that on this date he signed off on a cable from Mexico City to CIA headquarters reporting Oswald's visit to the Soviet embassy on October 10. Later, records reveal that Phillips was on leave at the JM/WAVE station in Miami and didn't return to the Mexico City station until October 9.

10/10/63—Oswald appears at the Jobco Employment Agency in Dallas. Lists George de Mohrenschildt as "closest friend."

10/10/63—CIA headquarters sends a teletype to the State Department, FBI, and Navy notifying them of Oswald's October 1 contact with the Soviet embassy.

10/11/63—President Kennedy issues National Security Action Memorandum #263 declaring that the Vietnamese should take over "essential functions now performed by U.S. military personnel . . . by the end of 1965."

10/16/63—Oswald begins job at Texas School Book Depository. He reportedly obtained it through a contact of Ruth Paine, the friend with whom Marina Oswald was living. Paine would later discover and turn over to the FBI much incriminating evidence against Oswald.

10/21/63—During the Cuban missile crisis, after Robert Kennedy tells CIA Director McCone to immediately halt all operations against Cuba, Task Force

W Chief William Harvey sends two raiding parties into Cuba, one headed by Eugenio Martinez, a close associate of E. Howard Hunt and Frank Sturgis and later also involved in the Watergate burglary. Harvey is subsequently yanked off Task Force W by Kennedy and assigned as station chief to Rome.

10/24/63—President Kennedy meets Jean Daniel, a French journalist, who is in transit to Cuba. Kennedy suggests Daniel broach the subject of reestablishing U.S.-Cuba relations with Castro, asks Daniel to report back to him.

10/29/63—CIA senior officer Desmond FitzGerald meets AMLASH, informs him a coup would receive U.S. support, later agrees to provide rifles, telescopic sights and explosives. FitzGerald presents himself as personal representative of Attorney General Robert Kennedy.

11/01/63—South Vietnam president Diem is assassinated by CIA-backed coup.

11/02/63—The Secret Service investigates an alleged plot against the president in Chicago.

11/08/63—Oswald writes to "Dear Mr. Hunt," requests only "information."

11/22/63—President John F. Kennedy is murdered in Dallas at 12:30 P.M. According to the Warren Commission, at 1:45 P.M. police were alerted to a man seen entering the Texas Theater after shooting patrolman Tippit in the Oak Cliff section of Dallas. They surrounded the theater, arrested Lee Harvey Oswald and arrived back at police headquarters by 2:00 P.M. At 7:10 P.M., Oswald was notified he had been formally charged with the murder of Officer Tippit and then, later with the murder of the president.

11/22/63—A CIA case officer representing Desmond FitzGerald meets with AMLASH and provides him poison pen to kill Castro. AMLASH doesn't think it will work and refuses it. As the meeting ends, they are told President Kennedy has been assassinated. Later, FitzGerald orders case officer to omit mention of poison pen in report of his meeting with AMLASH.

11/22/63—CIA sends photos taken in Mexico City of man misidentified as Oswald to Dallas police.

11/22/63—At evening press conference in Dallas police headquarters, Jack Ruby interrupts Chief Curry to identify proper name of Oswald's organization as Fair Play for Cuba Committee.

11/23/63—CIA counterintelligence staff, headed by James Angleton, prepares a memorandum suggesting that Oswald's contacts in Mexico City with Soviet personnel might have sinister implications.

11/23/63—Cuban embassy employee Silvia Duran, who processed a transit visa for an American who identified himself as Lee Harvey Oswald, is arrested by Mexican police on the direction of the CIA.

11/24/63—Lee Harvey Oswald is murdered by Jack Ruby at 11:20 A.M. as Oswald, flanked by Dallas detectives on either side and at his rear, is led from the basement of the Dallas police jail.

11/24/63—The CIA prepares a summary of "relevant" information on Oswald. Agency claims its first information on Oswald came from its Mexico City station on October 9, that Oswald entered Mexico on September 27, "probably by car." It notes Oswald's visits to the Soviet and Cuban embassies but makes no mention of erroneous photo and description of Oswald sent to headquarters on October 10.

11/29/63—President Lyndon Johnson appoints a commission "to ascertain, evaluate, and report on" the facts of the assassination. Chief Justice Earl Warren is asked to head the commission but he refuses. Johnson pushes Warren into accepting the job because, according to Warren biographer Jack H. Pollack, "rumors of the most exaggerated kind were circulating [and] some went so far as attributing the assassination to a faction within the government. . . ." Among those appointed to the commission is former CIA Director Allen Dulles, fired by Kennedy after the Bay of Pigs.

12/09/63—The FBI completes its five-volume report on Kennedy's assassination. Deputy Attorney General Katzenback writes the Warren Commission and recommends that the commission publicly declare that the FBI report concludes Oswald was the lone assassin.

12/31/63—The Fair Play for Cuba Committee disbands.

01/23/64—The CIA designates a subordinate to Chief of Counterintelligence James Angleton as the "point of record" for all matter relating to the Kennedy assassination and the Warren Commission.

02/01/64—Maurice Bishop asks Antonio Veciana to contact his cousin, a Cuban intelligence officer stationed in Mexico City, and offer him a large amount of money if he publicly acknowledges that he had met with Oswald. Veciana attempts but cannot make the contact before his cousin is recalled to Cuba.

02/04/64—Yuri Nosenko, deputy director of the Soviet intelligence service, the KGB, defects to the U.S. He alleges that the KGB took no interest in Oswald because it considered him too unstable. Nosenko is confined and questioned by the CIA for two years before he is declared a legitimate defector.

06/07/64—Interviewed in Dallas prison, Jack Ruby begs Commission Chairman Earl Warren to take him to Washington so he can reveal the truth about the assassination. Warren refuses.

07/01/64—Guy Banister dies of a heart attack.

09/16/64—International Anti-Communist Brigade soldier of fortune Loran Hall allegedly tells FBI agents that it was he, William Seymour, and Lawrence Howard who visited Silvia Odio in Dallas. The Warren Commission uses FBI report in its conclusions to dismiss Odio's assertion that Oswald was among visitors. Later, both Seymour and Howard contradict Hall. Hall eventually tells Assassination Committee he never told FBI of any visit.

09/27/64—The Warren Commission Report is released. It concludes that Lee Harvey Oswald, firing three shots from the sixth floor of the Texas School

Book Depository, killed President Kennedy and wounded Governor Connally. It also concluded that Oswald acted alone, had no coconspirators and "was not an agent of the U.S. government."

10/16/64—Soviet Premiere Khrushchev is overthrown.

11/03/64—Lyndon Johnson is elected president.

01/01/65—After closing down Operation Mongoose and the CIA's JM/WAVE station in Miami, Theodore Shackley and his deputy, Thomas Clines, are sent to Laos to organize opposition to the Pathet Lao guerilla force. Meo hill tribesmen are recruited and conduct a massive extermination program of guerilla sympathizers.

06/01/65—David Sanchez Morales is assigned as a deep-cover operative, working as a public safety officer for the Agency for International Development (AID), in Lima, Peru.

07/05/65—David Phillips is made station chief in Dominican Republic following President Johnson's decision to send the U.S. Marines to bolster the right-wing government's fight against leftist rebels. Serving as CIA adviser to the Dominican Republic's military is Mitchel Livingston WerBell III, an OSS veteran and CIA supplier of sophisticated assassination devices.

03/01/66—CIA contact Rolando Cubela (AMLASH) is arrested in Havana for plotting to assassinate Castro.

06/01/66—President Johnson appoints Richard Helms as director of the CIA.

01/03/67—With the appeal of his death penalty pending and likely to be reviewed in his favor, Jack Ruby dies of cancer as a prisoner in Dallas.

02/17/67—New Orleans newspapers reveal that District Attorney Jim Garrison has been secretly investigating the Kennedy assassination since the previous November.

02/22/67—David Ferrie is found dead in his apartment. Although he left what was described as "a suicide note" to a friend, an autopsy indicated he died of a cerebral hemorrhage. Garrison calls Ferrie "one of history's most important individuals."

03/01/67—Garrison arrests prominent New Orleans businessman and CIA asset Clay Shaw for conspiring to murder President Kennedy.

03/01/67—David Sanchez Morales joins former JM/WAVE station chief Ted Shackley to implement the Phoenix Program in Vietnam. It is a plan devised by future CIA Director William Colby to eliminate the Vietcong infrastructure; it results in the assassination of 40,000 individuals. Morales works under cover of the Agency for International Development's Vientiene area community development administration.

07/23/67—CIA's Desmond FitzGerald, David Phillips former Agency boss, chief of the Cuban task force who personally organized at least three attempts to assassinate Castro, collapses while playing tennis and dies.

08/01/67—CIA Director Richard Helms establishes a new Special Operations Group hidden within the Plans Department's counterintelligence division to monitor the peace movement within the United States.

06/04/68—Robert Kennedy is assassinated in Los Angeles.

08/01/68—Antonio Veciana begins working as a banking consultant in La Paz, Bolivia. He is officially a U.S. government employee salaried by the Agency for International Development. He claims the job was obtained for him by Maurice Bishop to better position him for anti-Castro activities throughout Latin America. The State Department later confirms Veciana's statement that he never signed an application for the job.

11/05/68—Richard M. Nixon, promising to end the Vietnam War, is elected president by the narrowest margin since 1912.

03/01/69—In the Kennedy conspiracy case brought by New Orleans District Attorney Jim Garrison, a jury finds Clay Shaw not guilty.

07/01/69—The CIA station in Santiago, Chile, receives approval from headquarters for a covert program to establish intelligence assets in the Chilean armed services.

09/09/70—Former CIA Director John McCone, a director of International Telephone & Telegraph, tells CIA Director Richard Helms that IT&T is prepared to spend $1 million to prevent socialist Salvadore Allende from becoming president of Chile.

9/15/70—President Nixon orders CIA Director Richard Helms to prevent Allende's accession to office in Chile. The CIA is to play a direct role in organizing a military coup d'etat. Helms puts David Atlee Phillips in charge of this involvement, known as Track II.

11/03/70—Allende is formerly inaugurated President of Chile. Shortly afterwards, a document called "Plan Z," describing a leftist plan to seize power and start a reign of terror is "discovered" by the enemies of Allende. CIA defector Phillip Agee later reveals it was written by a CIA officer under the direction of David Phillips.

04/25/71—Retired Mexico City station chief Winston Scott dies of a heart attack. CIA's Counterintelligence Chief James Angleton arrives from Washington to retrieve Scott's autobiographical manuscript and other files from his personal safe. There remains speculation that Scott kept a photo of Oswald, but Angleton denies it.

06/01/71—E. Howard Hunt joins the Nixon White House as a "consultant," begins planning operations to discredit Senator Edward Kennedy and Daniel Ellsberg and to set up a disinformation scheme to blame President Kennedy for the assassination of Diem. Hunt receives assistance from the CIA's Technical Services Division.

11/31/71—On instructions of Maurice Bishop, Antonio Veciana organizes a Castro assassination attempt in Chile. Bishop does the coordinating with the

Chilean military in setting it up. Veciana says CIA contract agent Luis Posada was also involved in the planning. Later, David Phillips, unaware of Veciana's detailed revelations, would admit to the House Assassinations Committee that Posada worked with him on operations in Chile.

06/17/72—A group of Nixon White House operatives known as The Plumbers are arrested burglarizing the offices of the Democratic National Committee in Washington's Watergate complex. Included are former CIA officer E. Howard Hunt, veteran CIA asset Frank Sturgis, and a legend of JM/WAVE's anti-Castro war, Eugenio Martinez, still on the CIA payroll.

06/23/72—Presidential Assistant W. R. Haldeman, under orders from Nixon, pressures CIA Director Richard Helms to protect the administration from the escalating Watergate scandal. Haldeman quotes Nixon: "Tell them that if it gets out, it's going to make the CIA look bad, it's going to make [E. Howard] Hunt look bad, and it's likely to blow the whole Bay of Pigs, which we think would be very unfortunate for the CIA." Haldeman later concludes that Nixon's mention of the Bay of Pigs was actually a reference to the Kennedy assassination. Helms, obviously understanding the code, explodes in anger when Haldeman mentions it, shouts: "The Bay of Pigs has nothing to do with this!"

11/07/72—Richard Nixon is reelected president in a near-record landslide.

11/20/72—President Nixon fires CIA Director Richard Helms and appoints him ambassador to Iran. Helms feels it is a direct result of his failure to support Nixon during Watergate.

05/01/73—David Atlee Phillips is selected by Director William Colby for chief of the CIA's Western Hemisphere Division, the highest rank not requiring Congressional approval.

06/01/73—Antonio Veciana has a lengthy meeting with Maurice Bishop at the race track in Caracas. Veciana suggests a new plan to assassinate Castro. Bishop says the timing isn't right.

07/01/73—Veciana meets Bishop in the Ramada Inn in Dallas and has a two-day conference with him. Again he presses for a new Castro assassination attempt. Bishop rejects the idea.

07/16/73—Antonio Veciana is arrested and charged with conspiracy to import cocaine. Veciana claims he is innocent. His former business partner in Puerto Rico, previously charged, is the only witness against him. Initially, Veciana says he suspects the arrest was set up by Maurice Bishop, later says it was likely Castro agents.

07/26/73—Maurice Bishop severs his relationship with Antonio Veciana, gives him a $253,000 cash payment for services.

09/11/73—The Chilean military, supported by the CIA's Track II program headed by David Phillips, overthrows the government of Salvadore Allende. Allende is shot during the coup. The military junta massacres tens of thousands of workers and students considered leftists. "There is a strong probability that the CIA station in Chile helped supply the assassination lists," according to ex-agent Phillip Agee.

08/09/74—In the aftermath of Watergate, Nixon resigns and Gerald R. Ford, a former member of the Warren Commission becomes president. Ford nominates Nelson Rockefeller as his vice president.

12/17/74—James Angleton is fired by CIA Director William Colby after Colby was informed by *New York Times* reporter Seymour Hersh that he was going to break a story about two Agency operations—operations CHAOS and HT-LINGUAL—which involve a massive and illegal spying campaign against American citizens. Angleton, the veteran chief of counterintelligence, controlled both programs.

01/04/75—Spurred by media revelations of CIA improprieties, President Ford directs Vice President Rockefeller to establish a "commission on CIA activities within the United States." Ford himself appoints as the Rockefeller Commission's executive director a former assistant counsel of the Warren Commission, David Belin, who had written a book staunchly defending the Warren Report.

01/27/75—After recent allegations of "substantial, even massive wrong-doing within the 'national intelligence system,' " the Senate establishes a select committee headed by Idaho Senator Frank Church. It would conduct a fifteen-month inquiry but, in the end, was forced to acknowledge the limitations imposed on it by the CIA: "Although the Senate inquiry was congressionally ordered and although properly constituted committees under the Constitution have the right of full inquiry, the Central Intelligence Agency . . . [has] limited the Committee's access to the full record."

05/10/75—David Atlee Phillips, shortly after being awarded the Distinguished Intelligence Medal, the CIA's highest honor, announces he is taking early retirement from the CIA to start an association of former intelligence officers and lead a public campaign against the critics of the Agency and the rash of unfavorable revelations issuing from congressional investigations.

05/21/75—CIA Director William Colby testifies before the Senate Intelligence Committee regarding assassination plots. Emerging from the hearing, Chairman Church tells reporters: "It is simply intolerable that any agency of the government of the United States may engage in murder."

06/10/75—The Rockefeller Commission issues a report concluding that the CIA engaged in scores of "plainly unlawful and . . . improper" activities during its twenty-eight-year history, including domestic break-ins, mail openings, testing mind-altering drugs on unsuspecting victims and spying on thousands of Americans. It also concludes that there is "no credible evidence" that the CIA was involved in the assassination of President Kennedy. However, it acknowledges that it had limited its investigation to examination of photographic evidence indicating that E. Howard Hunt and Frank Sturgis might have been among the tramps arrested on the grassy knoll, and to the possibility that someone might have been firing from the grassy knoll. It defends the single-bullet theory, explaining that the violent backward and leftward motion of Kennedy's body was caused by "a seizure-like neuromuscular reaction to major damage inflicted to nerve centers of the brain."

06/19/75—A week before his scheduled appearance before the Church Committee to be questioned about the CIA-Mafia plots, Chicago Mob boss Sam Giancana, preparing a late snack of sausage and escarole on a stove in his basement den, is shot in the back of the head with a .22-caliber pistol. His killer rolls his body over and fires six more shots, one in the mouth and five in a semicircle around his chin.

06/24/75—John Rosselli testifies before the Church Committee and provides the details of his role as a liaison between CIA representatives and Mob bosses Giancana and Trafficante in plans to assassinate Castro. He provides little information about his relationship with the CIA's William Harvey and is not asked about his role at the JM/WAVE station training anti-Castro assassination teams with David Sanchez Morales.

09/08/75—Shocked by revelations that former CIA director Allen Dulles did not tell the Warren Commission that the Agency was conspiring with the Mafia to assassinate Castro, Senate Intelligence Committee member Richard Schweiker conducts a personal preliminary review of the Kennedy assassination and concludes that "the fingerprints of intelligence" were all over Oswald's activities. He convinces Committee Chairman Frank Church to establish a subcommittee to review the role of federal agencies in investigating the Kennedy assassination.

09/21/75—*The Washington Post* reports that "according to reliable sources" former CIA officer E. Howard Hunt "told associates after the Watergate break-in that he was ordered in December 1971 or January 1972, to assassinate syndicated columnist Jack Anderson." Hunt's alleged plan involved the use of a poison obtained from a former CIA physician. *The Post* also reported that Hunt had said that the order came from a "senior official in the Nixon White House," and "was cancelled at the last minute. . . ."

10/23/75—Former U.S. ambassador to Chile Edward Korry reveals to the Church Senate Intelligence Committee his opposition to the CIA's role in overthrowing Allende: "The CIA is amoral. . . . It could operate behind my back, not merely with the president of the United States, but with Chileans. . . . In that sense, the CIA could be an 'invisible' government."

11/02/75—President Ford fires William Colby as CIA director and appoints George Bush to the post.

11/11/75—Senate JFK Subcommittee Chairman Schweiker decides Church Committee staff is focusing investigation on possible Castro involvement in assassination, decides involvement of CIA with anti-Castro groups also needs probing, puts Gaeton Fonzi on staff to pursue leads in Miami's Little Havana.

03/02/76—Anti-Castro leader Antonio Veciana reveals to Schweiker Subcommittee investigator Fonzi that a CIA masterspy named Maurice Bishop was his secret control officer, initiated the founding of Alpha 66, instigated two

Castro assassination plots, and planned anti-Castro raids during the Cuban missile crisis in an attempt to embarrass President Kennedy and provoke Cuban or Russian retaliation that would spark a major U.S. reaction. Veciana also reveals he saw Bishop with Lee Harvey Oswald. After years of sworn denials by the Agency, it is the first evidence that the CIA was directly involved with Oswald.

04/11/76—Senator Richard Schweiker discovers that a police artist's sketch of Maurice Bishop looks very much like a high-ranking retired CIA officer who had testified before the Church Intelligence Committee. His name is David Atlee Phillips.

04/23/76—In a secret session in Washington's old Carroll Arms Hotel, used as an annex for Senate Intelligence Committee staff, Schweiker questions John Rosselli about the revelations he provided Jack Anderson about the Kennedy assassination being a Castro retaliation plan. Rosselli admits it was only his opinion and that he had "no facts" to back it up.

06/23/76—Schweiker releases his JFK Subcommittee report. Limited in its mandate to review intelligence agencies' performance in their investigation of the JFK assassination, the Schweiker Report concludes that both the FBI and the CIA were "deficient and that facts which might have substantially affected the course of the investigation were not provided." Although the committee staff had taken Antonio Veciana's sworn testimony, no mention is made of it or of his control agent Maurice Bishop. Despite release of final report, Schweiker decides to continue JFK investigation with his own senate staff and investigator Fonzi.

06/27/76—Twenty representatives of the most militant exile groups are brought together by Orlando Bosch at a resort in Bonao, Dominican Republic, to form a united coalition called CORU. Within the next several months, CORU claims credit for more than fifty bombings and some of its members are implicated in the Letelier assassination. Among those attending the Bonao meeting is Luis Posada, the CIA agent involved with Antonio Veciana in planning to kill Castro in Chile in 1971.

08/07/76—The body of mobster John Rosselli, the link between the CIA and organized crime leaders involved in Castro assassination plots, is found mutilated and stuffed into a drum floating in Biscayne Bay.

09/17/76—The House of Representatives establishes the Select Committee on Assassinations to investigate the deaths of President Kennedy and Martin Luther King, Jr. It results from joining two resolutions, one submitted by Virginia's Tom Downing and the other from Texan Henry Gonzalez. Despite Downing's scheduled retirement, Speaker-elect Tip O'Neill names him chairman, irking Gonzalez. The new committee, however, will expire at the end of the year and will have to be reconstituted and funded by the new ninety-fifth Congress.

09/18/76—Schweiker investigator Fonzi takes Alpha 66 founder Veciana to a meeting of the Retired Intelligence Officers Association in Reston, Virginia, to confront David Phillips. Fonzi introduces Veciana to Phillips by name. Veciana himself asks Phillips if he is familiar with the name of Veciana. Phillips, once chief of all the Agency's Cuban operations, appears flustered but says no, he never heard of Veciana. He refuses to be questioned further by Fonzi.

09/21/76—Former Chilean foreign and defense minister Orlando Letelier is murdered in Washington with a planted car bomb on orders of the Chilean military junta. Involved are Chilean intelligence agents and anti-Castro Cubans with links to David Phillips. After the assassination, Phillips is involved in disseminating misinformation through his media assets.

10/10/76—Assassinations Committee Chairman Downing appoints Philadelphia First Assistant District Attorney Richard Sprague as chief counsel and staff director. Sprague, who has a national reputation as a homicide prosecutor with a string of sixty-nine out of seventy first-degree convictions, announces he will conduct the Kennedy probe as a murder investigation, a new approach.

11/02/76—Jimmy Carter defeats Ford in presidential election.

11/27/76—David Phillips, among the first witnesses subpoenaed by the Assassinations Committee, is questioned about his role in the CIA supplying the Warren Commission photo of man misidentified as Lee Harvey Oswald about the tape recordings and the transcripts of Oswald's visit to the Russian embassy. Phillips testifies that surveillance cameras were not working when Oswald approached the embassy and that the tape recording had been routinely destroyed. Chief Counsel Sprague asks the CIA for access to its files but the Agency refuses unless Sprague signs a secrecy oath. Sprague says that would be a conflict since the CIA is one of the Committee's targets.

12/21/76—Reviewing Senator Schweiker's files on anti-Castro Cuban connection to the CIA, Bob Tanenbaum, deputy chief counsel of the JFK Assassinations Committee, asks investigator Gaeton Fonzi to join House probe.

01/07/77—William Pawley, millionaire ex-ambassador, backer of the ill-fated Bayo-Pawley raid designed to extricate Russian missile site personnel from Cuba in order to embarrass President Kennedy, kills himself in his Miami Beach home before being questioned by Committee investigator Fonzi.

02/01/77—The House Rules Committee, deviating from its normal procedure of automatically reconstituting standing committees from the previous congressional session, gives the Assassinations Committee funding for only two months and an order to justify its existence during that period. The Committee and Chief Counsel Sprague had been under heavy attack by the major media, notably *The New York Times*, and politicians claiming Sprague is planning to employ hidden tape recorders and lie detectors in the probe. Attacks have increased since Sprague, refusing to use other federal agencies to staff the investigation as the Warren Commission did, said he needed a $6.5 million for the first year of investigation. With Downing's retirement, Texas Democrat Henry Gonzalez assumes chairmanship of the Committee.

02/11/77—Angered by Sprague's refusal to relinquish the power of staff appointments to him, Gonzalez begins a feud with Sprague that culminates in Gonzalez firing Sprague and ordering the Capitol police to evict the chief counsel from his office. Within hours, Gonzalez's dismissal of Sprague is rescinded by the other members of the Committee.

03/01/77—Frustrated at the lack of support from his fellow Committee members, Gonzales resigns as chairman, calls Sprague an "unconscionable scoundrel." Ohio congressman Louis Stokes is appointed the new Committee chairman.

03/01/77—President Carter appoints a Naval Academy classmate, Admiral Stansfield Turner, as CIA director. Turner begins a reorganization of the Agency, fires 820 employees, most in covert operations.

03/16/77—With general congressional support for continuing the Assassinations Committee fading as a result of its internal feuding, Sprague offers to resign if Committee members feel he is a "millstone" that would prevent the Committee's reconstitution. The members refuse his offer.

03/29/77—In Florida, George de Mohrenschildt dies of a shotgun wound to the head hours after receiving a notice from Assassinations Committee investigator Fonzi that he is being sought to testify. That evening in Washington, with the Committee on the verge of losing a House vote for its reconstitution and funding, Chief Counsel Sprague resigns. The next morning, the news of de Mohrenschildt's death and Sprague's resignation produce a victory for the Committee's continuation, although, at $2.5 million a year, with much less funding than Sprague had requested.

05/06/77—Carlos Prío, former president of Cuba linked to the Mob's control of Havana casinos and, involved with Frank Sturgis in anti-Castro activities, kills himself outside his Miami Beach home before he can be questioned by Committee investigator Fonzi.

05/13/77—In an interview with *New York Times* reporter Robert Sam Anson, former Committee Chief Counsel Sprague says he believes his problems with Gonzalez and certain members of Congress about funding was a "smoke screen," that his conflict with the CIA was the underlying source of his troubles. If he had to do it all over again, he said, he would begin by probing "Oswald's ties to the Central Intelligence Agency."

09/18/77—In a public debate with Mark Lane in Los Angeles, David Phillips declares that Oswald "was in no way connected with the CIA" and promises to call for the abolition of the CIA if the Agency is proved guilty of a coverup in the Kennedy assassination.

10/31/77—Richard Helms, director of the CIA who withheld information about the Agency's plotting with the Mafia to kill Castro from the Warren Commission, pleads guilty to lying to the Church Senate Intelligence Committee about the CIA's involvement in overthrowing Allende in Chile.

11/18/77—Cuban exile leader Manuel Artime, a close associate of E. Howard Hunt, dies at the age of forty-five within weeks of being told he has cancer and before he can be questioned by House Committee investigators Fonzi and Gonzales.

06/20/77—G. Robert Blakey, of Cornell Law's Organized Crime Institute, is appointed chief counsel and staff director of the Assassinations Committee.

08/29/77—Staff Director Blakey conducts a Committee staff conference on "investigative techniques and procedures."

10/28/77—Assassinations Committee staff conference signals the beginning of an organized investigation with each team instructed to define the issues in its field. Blakey establishes a working relationship with the CIA for staff to review files, but all notes will be sanitized by the Agency before being released back to the Committee. All contacts with former CIA agents must be cleared through CIA headquarters.

12/04/77—A procedural directive is issued at an Assassinations Committee staff conference. Deputy Chief Counsel Gary Cornwell announces that the time for "foraging" is over, the investigation must now be limited to "linchpin issues," meaning only those to which an answer can be found prior to writing a final report.

01/16/78—A former CIA officer code-named Ron Cross, who worked at the JM/WAVE station with David Phillips, tells Committee investigators Al Gonzales and Gaeton Fonzi that Phillips used the pseudonym of Maurice Bishop. He also recalls Phillips being referred to as "Mr. Bishop" by one of his deputies, a "Doug Gupton." Cross is never called to testify under oath before the Committee. When questioned by Committee staff at CIA headquarters, "Doug Gupton" says he does not remember ever referring to Phillips as "Mr. Bishop." He, too, is never called to testify under oath.

03/02/78—The CIA informs the Assassinations Committee that its office of the Inspector General, its office of the General Counsel, its office of Personnel and the Deputy Directorate of Operations has no record of a Maurice Bishop.

04/25/78—David Phillips testifies under oath before the Assassinations Committee that he never used the name of Maurice Bishop. He also says he was never introduced to Antonio Veciana by name. Committee staff members urge Chief Counsel Blakey to bring perjury charges against Phillips. He declines.

05/07/78—David Sanchez Morales, although officially retired from the CIA, returns from a regular trip to Washington to his home near Phoenix, Arizona. He tells friends he began feeling ill shortly before leaving Washington and that night has sudden heart attack. The ambulance is late in arriving and reportedly has equipment problems. Morales dies the next morning at the Tucson Medical Center. He had told a friend he feared for his life "from his own people" because he "knows too much."

06/12/78—Blakey announces that because of an unforeseen "budget crunch," there will have to be a drastic reduction of Assassinations Committee staff personnel. When the specific cuts are later announced, two-thirds of the Committee's investigative staff are dismissed.

08/01/78—Former CIA Director Richard Helms testifies before the House Select Committee on Assassinations that Oswald "was not an agent of the CIA" and "to the best of my knowledge no contact [by the CIA] was ever made [with Oswald]."

08/17/78—The Assassination Committee takes a deposition from former CIA Director John McCone. He answers affirmatively to two questions: Do you know or did you know Maurice Bishop? Was he an Agency employee? He does not remember with what division of the Agency Bishop was associated.

08/28/78—Questioned by staff researcher Dan Hardway at Assassinations Committee headquarters, David Phillips dissembles regarding his role at the Mexico City CIA station at the time of Oswald's alleged visit. The questioning also reveals that most of the originators of disinformation stories in Mexico City and Miami were Phillips's assets. Unaware of its significance, Phillips also acknowledges his working relationship in Chile with CIA agent Luis Posada, involved with Antonio Veciana in Castro assassination attempt planned by Maurice Bishop.

09/06/78—The Assassinations Committee begins its public hearings. Sixteen days of hearings are scheduled between this date and 12/29. Most of the hearings deal with scientific analysis of the physical evidence and the possibility of organized crime involvement. Many of the hearings are consumed by Chief Counsel Blakey reading narrative of the various areas of the Committee's investigation. Of the more than four dozen witnesses called, only one, former CIA Director Richard Helms, is connected to the intelligence community. (Helms is questioned only about the CIA's treatment of defector Yuri Nosenko and his failure to tell the Warren Commission about Castro assassination plots.)

09/06/78—Governor John Connally and wife Nellie testify for more than three hours on the first day of public hearings. Both repeat their Warren Commission testimony that Connally was hit by the second bullet fired, contradicting the single-bullet theory.

09/11/78—Based on an analysis of a recording from a Dallas motorcycle policeman's radio and tests done in Dealey Plaza, acoustical expert James Barger testifies that there is a 50 percent chance that one shot came from the "grassy knoll" area.

09/18/78—*Time* magazine reports on the Assassinations Committee hearings, concludes that the Committee "added credence to the main finding of the Warren Commission: Lee Harvey Oswald alone killed the president . . ."

10/19/78—The CIA's Office of Legislative Counsel informs the Committee that the information given in a sworn deposition by former Director John McCone is incorrect. Upon being reinterviewed by the Agency, McCone states that he was mistaken in his recollection of knowing a Maurice Bishop.

12/29/78—After further acoustical tests at Dealey Plaza and a reevaluation of Dr. Barger's earlier analysis, two other acoustical consultants, Mark Weiss and Ernest Aschkenasy, testify there is more than a 95 percent probability of a shot having been fired from the "grassy knoll."

03/29/79—The House Assassinations Committee issues its report, concluding that President Kennedy was probably assassinated by Lee Harvey Oswald in a conspiracy with other unknown individuals. Chief Counsel Robert Blakey announces his conclusion that "the Mob did it."

09/21/79—Antonio Veciana is shot in the head by an unknown assailant. He survives. The FBI says it is investigating the assassination attempt "because of a possible connection with agents of a foreign government."

01/24/81—President Reagan names his former campaign chairman, William Casey, as CIA director. Casey, a onetime OSS agent and a board director of David Phillips's Association of Former Intelligence Officers, immediately asks that Congressional restrictions on CIA operations be loosened and the Agency removed entirely from the provisions of the Freedom of Information Act. He later formulates a secret and illegal phase of Project Democracy to control American public opinion to support waging covert wars against communism in Latin America. Casey later becomes chief architect of the Iran-Contra operation.

10/06/86—The CIA's secret Contra arms-supply network begins to unravel when an American cargo plane loaded with arms and ammunition is shot down in Nicaragua. Captured crewman Eugene Hasenfus reveals that a Cuban-American veteran of the Bay of Pigs named "Max Gomez" helped coordinate the supply network from an airbase at Ilopango in El Salvador. "Max Gomez" is CIA veteran Felix Rodriguez, who worked with David Sanchez Morales in the capture of Che Guevara. Hasenfus also reveals that a CIA agent known as "Ramón Medina" is working with Rodrigues at Ilopango. "Medina" turns out to be Luis Posada, who had worked with David Phillips in Chile and was involved with Antonio Veciana in the 1971 Castro assassination attempt there planned by Maurice Bishop.

05/11/87—Former CIA Counterintelligence Chief James Angleton dies of lung cancer.

07/10/88—Retired CIA Chief of Western Hemisphere Division David Atlee Phillips dies after a long bout with cancer. Maurice Bishop is buried with him.

ACKNOWLEDGMENTS

MY WIFE, Marie, knows marathons. She has run five of them, including Boston, in respectable times I'll never likely match. Running a successful marathon is far more than a simple physical feat, it is a lone struggle against mental demons scheming to ambush your will at critical points. Solitary though the ultimate process, it cannot begin, continue or succeed without a support team in place long before the starting gun, from running buddies to help ease some of the hundreds of grueling training miles to cheering friends ready on race day to provide nourishment and encouragement along the way. So it is with writing a book. And I'm both lucky and blessed to have had an exceptional support team to ease my steps. Marie, of course, has been the heart of it, not only with her love and forbearance, but also in her intrepid role as my initial sentinel against factual and grammatical carelessness and literary obfuscation. (Obviously, she hasn't read this note.) I'm fortunate, too, to have friends such as Gordon Winslow, the Miami archivist whose passion for objective research is matched by his generosity in sharing it. I'm grateful for the friendship of Palm Springs businessman Robert Dorff, whose insightful analyses of the issues and his dedication to pursuing the truth about the Kennedy assassination I value. I offer my deepest appreciation also to Irish writer Anthony Summers, an investigative journalist in whose footsteps we all follow but inadequately fill. Bleeker Street's brilliant iconoclast, Alan J. Weberman, the most tenacious of researchers, was generous with both his files and his analytical insights. Mary Ferrell, the Dallas fountainhead for Kennedy researchers, has often been justly recognized for her impressive knowledge of government documents and her unstinting cooperation, but not enough for her beautiful, unconquerable spirit which has been an inspiration to all of us for so long.

Without the initial help of some of my earliest and closest friends and associates, I wouldn't have been able to begin or continue my investigation into the Kennedy assassination. I was more than lucky to have Alan Halpern, the pioneering legend of city magazines, as a friend and supportive editor; Frank King as a valued cohort and astute investigator; and Charles MacNamara, the Mencken of Philadelphia, as my keen-minded editorial comrade. Down through the years, Bernard McCormick, my ex-partner at *Gold Coast Magazine*, retained an enthusiasm for my work that helped me sustain a hope that it would someday make a difference. I'm particularly indebted and grateful for the years of encouragement given by another ex-*Philadelphia Magazine* associate, Nancy Love, now my agent.

In the body of this book I describe how a Philadelphia lawyer named Vincent Salandria initially sparked my interest in the Kennedy case. I'm not sure I should be grateful to Vince for enlightening me about a terrible truth about our government, and I'm not sure I agree with—or even dare to think about—some of the awesome theories he has since developed about the forces behind the assassination, but I am sure I honor and respect him and consider him one of the few truly courageous men I've known in my life.

I still always describe former U.S. Senator Richard Schweiker, whom I had no contact or affiliation with before he hired me, as the only politician I've ever met who I came to respect more after getting to know him. I thank him for the freedom to pursue the leads we developed regardless of where they led. I'm proud to have worked with top quality individuals on his staff, including Dave Newhall, Dave Marston and Troy Gustavson.

Since some would prefer to remain anonymous, I won't name any of the dozens of former House Assassinations Committee staffers who cooperated in helping me reconstruct this inside story. Not one I approached refused. Nevertheless, anonymity isn't an issue when it comes to paying special tribute to my Miami partner, Al Gonzales, a good cop, a good man, a good friend. I relied heavily on the street smarts Al garnered from his tough years as a New York homicide detective, and on his instinctive ability to judge character. He was beside me through much of this story.

Among those most generous with his own experiences and knowledge of that critical period in Miami history when the CIA played the leading role was ex-Army Captain Bradley Earl Ayers, whose own book, *The War That Never Was* [Bobbs Merrill, N.Y.], opened my research door a critical crack. Ayers has yet to tell the rest of the explosive story about his continuing power struggle with the intelligence establishment.

Miami's secret history as the cauldron of anti-Castro activity wasn't easy to penetrate, but I had an excellent guide in Marty Casey, one of the insiders from Nelli Hamilton's boardinghouse crew of soldiers of fortune. Blessed with total recall, the affable, handsome Casey, now a *Soldier of Fortune* magazine writer and irrepressible adventurer, rightfully bears the honor as the unofficial historian of Miami's most tumultuous era. Another player of talent from that period who was most generous with his cooperation was Tom Dunkin, the photographer responsible for much of *Life* magazine's coverage of the CIA's secret war.

The community of JFK assassination researchers, like any group involved in a muddle of conflicting issues, is often rife with controversy and personal friction. Yet I was humbled by the outpouring of cooperation I received from every corner, among them the most respected in the community. Boston author Dick Russell, whose own book, *The Man Who Knew Too Much* [Carroll & Graf, N.Y.], broke new ground, generously shared his research. Attorney Jim Lesar, at the Assassination Archives and Research Center in Washington, D.C., provided invaluable guidance. I'm deeply appreciative also to Washington private investigator Kevin Walsh, one of the research community's truly dedicated pioneers, and to Berkeley's Paul Hoch, among the most respected of analysts. Down through the years, Jerry Policoff, frequent contributor to the *Village Voice* and author of some of the most perceptive magazine articles about the assassination, has regularly alerted me to newly uncovered information and knowledge.

Among those who provided me with critical assistance is Connecticut author and painstaking researcher Peggy Adler Robohm. Another resident of the Nutmeg State, Brenda Brody, graciously let flow both the output from and her analyses of an incredibly comprehensive computerized file system. Scott Malone, a writer who has helped produce award-winning shows for PBS Television's *Frontline* series, was instrumental in sharing the results of his investigative efforts in key areas. My thanks also to Earl Golz, one of the few Dallas reporters who has continued his passionate pursuit of the truth about the Kennedy assassination and, as a result, has uncovered a wealth of significant details down through the years. I'm indebted, too, to Dr. Jerry Rose, publisher of *The Third Decade* research journal at New York State College at Fredonia, for his help and encouragement, and to Bay City, Michigan's G.J. Rowell, publisher of *The Investigator*, another research journal.

Finally, it has been a pleasure working with an editor as competently critical, dedicated and, most important, enthusiastic and supportive as Joan Fucillo. She's responsible for whatever editorial polish and structural flow this book may have picked up in its marathon struggle to the finish line.

Thank you all.

—G.F.

INDEX